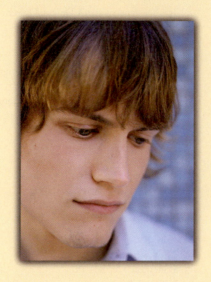
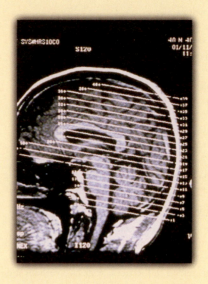

Brain and Behavior

Bob Garrett

California Polytechnic State University
San Luis Obispo

WADSWORTH

™

THOMSON LEARNING

Australia • Canada • Mexico • Singapore • Spain
United Kingdom • United States

WADSWORTH

✦

THOMSON LEARNING™

Executive Editor: Vicki Knight
Development Editor: Penelope Sky
Assistant Editor: Jennifer Wilkinson
Editorial Assistant: Monica Sarmiento
Technology Project Manager: Darin Derstine
Marketing Manager: Lori Grebe
Marketing Assistant: Laurel Anderson
Advertising Project Manager: Brian Chaffee
Project Manager, Editorial Production: Kathryn M. Stewart
Print/Media Buyer: Kristine Waller
Permissions Editor: Joohee Lee

Production Service: Janet Vail
Text Designer: Patrick Devine Design
Photo Researcher: Laura Murray
Copy Editor: Anita Wagner
Illustrator: Accurate Art
Cover Designer: Patrick Devine Design
Cover Image: Getty Images
Cover and Text Printer: Transcontinental Printing/Interglobe
Compositor: New England Typographic Service

Printed in Canada
1 2 3 4 5 6 7   06 05 04 03 02

For more information about our products, contact us at:
Thomson Learning Academic Resource Center
1-800-423-0563
For permission to use material from this text, contact us by:
Phone: 1-800-730-2214   **Fax:** 1-800-730-2215
Web: http://www.thomsonrights.com

Library of Congress Control Number: 2002112141

Student Edition with InfoTrac College Edition:
ISBN 0-534-36582-5
Student Edition without InfoTrac College Edition:
ISBN 0-534-51342-5

Instructor's Edition: ISBN 0-534-51345-X

Wadsworth/Thomson Learning
10 Davis Drive
Belmont, CA 94002-3098
USA

Asia
Thomson Learning
5 Shenton Way #01-01
UIC Building
Singapore 068808

Australia/New Zealand
Thomson Learning
102 Dodds Street
Southbank, Victoria 3006
Australia

Canada
Nelson
1120 Birchmount Road
Toronto, Ontario M1K 5G4
Canada

Europe/Middle East/Africa
Thomson Learning
High Holborn House
50/51 Bedford Row
London WC1R 4LR
United Kingdom

Latin America
Thomson Learning
Seneca, 53
Colonia Polanco
11560 Mexico D.F.
Mexico

Spain/Portugal
Paraninfo
Calle/Magallanes, 25
28015 Madrid, Spain

I owe so much to so many,
but this book is dedicated to those
who matter the most, my family:
Duejean, Geoffrey,
Michael and Heather

A Message from the Author

Growing up in a post-depression, post-world-war home with more love than money has its advantages; one is that I learned the value of an education. And it didn't take long to discover that the real value of education is not in getting a better job but in learning about life and the world and what makes both of them work. That is what led me, after trying one major after another, to discover psychology.

A child of Sputnik and enamored with science, I was especially attracted by the young and promising discipline of biological psychology. And as I pursued that promise I was attracted to  another—sharing my enthusiasm through teaching. For 32 years I taught at DePauw University, where practically every student does two or three internships and the value of research is judged by what students learn from doing it alongside their mentors; similarly, the guiding principle at my current university, Cal Poly at San Luis Obispo, is that students should "learn by doing." I believe in knowledge for its own sake, but I value knowledge that is useful even more. Perhaps that is why I needed to write *Brain and Behavior*; it is my testimonial to the usefulness of scientific knowledge.

Now that the book is done I can look forward to more leisurely ways of spending my time: beach walks and tennis with my wife and hiking the hillsides of our newly-adopted home, tinkering with the car I built, or just pitching horseshoes with our sons. But you can be sure I'll be watching out of the corner of my eye to see whether students are enjoying what I have written, whether they are experiencing the same thrill of discovery I had when I was their age.

Bob Garrett received a bachelor's degree from the University of Texas at Arlington and an MA and PhD from Baylor University. During his tenure as a psychology professor he has also been a department chair, a dean, and the coordinator of faculty development. He has published research in the areas of biofeedback and animal behavior.

TO THE INSTRUCTOR

On the basis of colleagues' comments and my thirty-plus years of experience teaching biopsychology, I decided there is a need for another alternative in textbooks: one suitable for students with no more background than the introductory course, one that leaves out some detail, gives more emphasis to behavior, and speaks directly to the students' interests.

The most obvious difference is the organization. First, the chapter on neurons precedes the discussion of the nervous system. It was difficult deciding to launch into the heady topic of neuronal physiology in the second chapter, but I have found that even an overview of the nervous system is not very meaningful to students who have no idea how neurons work. I did defer to the issue of relative difficulty in reordering audition and vision, though. Vision is a daunting topic, and no one has ever given me a convincing reason for placing it first. Audition is a gentler way to introduce the basic principles and a more intuitive context for concepts like Fourier analysis, which can then be used meaningfully in the vision chapter. Another change in order is that the chapter on motivation and emotion appears earlier than usual, in order to maintain the pace of student interest.

I have also integrated several topics into a behavioral context. For example, the sense of taste is discussed in relation to hunger and feeding, and olfaction with sexual behavior. This results in treatments that are briefer but, I think, more meaningful than standard ones. On the other hand, pain is discussed twice—with the body senses in Chapter 10 and with emotion in Chapter 7, where I make the case that most of what we call pain is a neurally distinct process that may properly be considered an emotion. Then, quoting Hudspeth that the most important aspect of hearing in humans is its role in processing language, I combine those two topics in Chapter 8.

Part Four provides the best opportunity to persuade students of the behavioral relevance of biopsychology. There is enough research now to warrant including intelligence and con-sciousness in a biopsychology text; my goal is to convince students that biopsychology can explain the most distinctively human characteristics. The consciousness chapter in most biopsych texts is usually limited to sleep and split-brain behavior, whereas I venture into the biological bases of consciousness itself.

My hope is that *Brain and Behavior* will invite students to biopsychology, that they will come for the case studies and opening vignettes and the news stories and applications, and that they will stay for the physiology. I hope the course will draw nonmajors as well as majors, that it will change the way students think about behavior, and that they will take it early and carry this way of thinking into their other studies. And, finally, I trust you will find the material accurate and up to date and the explanations clear, and that this book will make your teaching experience easier and even more satisfying than in the past.

For additional assistance, consider the following supplemental materials.

FOR INSTRUCTORS

Available to qualified adopters. Please consult your local sales representative for details.

Test Bank (0-534-51338-7)

Prepared by Brady Phelps, *South Dakota State University* and Debra Spear, *South Dakota State University*

Contains approximately 120 multiple-choice test items for every chapter, including 10 that are marked for the online quiz, and 15 Study Guide items. Each chapter also includes approximately 10 true-or-false and five short-answer questions. Also available in **Examview (0-534-51339-5)**.

Instructor's Manual (0-534-51337-9)

Prepared by Jake Henn, *Grossmont College*

Includes the Resource Integration Guide, chapter outlines, chapter summaries, additional lecture topics and discussion questions, classroom activities, InfoTrac key terms, video resources, and related websites.

Multimedia Manager (0-15-507488-1)

Prepared by Eric Laws, *Longwood University*
This one-stop lecture tool makes it easy to assemble, edit, publish, and present custom lectures for your course, using Microsoft® PowerPoint®. *Multimedia Manager* lets you bring together text-specific lecture outlines, art, video, and animations from the CD-ROM, the Web, and your own resources-for a powerful, personalized, media-enhanced presentation.

FOR STUDENTS

Study Guide (0-534-51336-0)

Prepared by Sheila Steiner, *Jamestown College*
Includes chapter outlines, chapter summaries, approximately five short-answer and 10 fill-in-the-blank quiz items for each main section; a post-test has approximately 40 multiple-choice items covering the entire chapter.

Biological Foundations CD-ROM, free with text!
Featuring animations, video clips, virtual reality animations and interactive exercises, this book-specific CD-ROM provides an engaging multimedia introduction to the basics of biological psychology. Using the CD-ROM will help students master the essential concepts and vocabulary in every chapter of the text. Chapter quizzes with rejoinders and other interactive features let students make the most of their study time.

Supplements are available to qualified adopters. Please consult your local sales representative for details.

TO THE STUDENT

Brain and Behavior grew out of my experience designing a new biopsychology course, one intended to give students a biological perspective on their other courses in psychology rather than to prepare them for the next biopsych course. I needed a textbook that would readily engage the students' interest, with material that was meaningful to them. Though there were several very good texts available, none reached out to students in the way I wanted them to.

I was motivated by the memory of how biopsychology was approached when I was in school. The knowledge was so meager then that only the most tentative links could be drawn between biology and behavior. Fortunately, things are different now, as research breakthroughs plumb the very depths of human experience. These are exceptionally exciting times, comparable in many ways to the renaissance that thrust Europe from the Middle Ages into the modern world. In Chapter 1 I quote Kay Jamison's comparison of neuroscience, which includes biopsychology, to a "romantic, moon-walk sense of exploration." I hope this text will convey that kind of excitement as you read about discoveries that will revolutionize our understanding of what it means to be human.

Each chapter begins with a brief vignette that puts the topic in a real-life context, and the discussion makes liberal use of case studies that illustrate the human side of biopsychology. *In the News* features highlight the fact that neuroscience is one of the hottest newsmakers around, while *Applications* emphasize the practical uses of such knowledge. *Marginal Questions* will help you focus as you read, and *Concept Checks* will assess whether you're getting the major points. When you finish a chapter, *Testing Your Understanding* (also on the CD-ROM) will help you find out how much you've retained, and *For Further Thought* will prompt you to consider the implications of what you have learned. You can continue exploring with the help of sources listed in *For Further Reading* and *On the Web*. Finally, the *Study Guide* will help you prepare for the inevitable exam, with its additional practice test questions and outlines in question form.

More important than all these aids, I think, is that I kept you in mind as I wrote. I tried to stay close to material you would find interesting, and to present it in a way that would hold your interest. I hope you will let me know where I have succeeded and, especially, where I have not (bgarrett@calpoly.edu). I know of no scientific discipline with greater potential to answer the burning questions about ourselves than neuroscience in general and biopsychology in particular. I wish you the satisfaction of discovery and knowledge as you read what I have written *for you*.

Acknowledgments

Along the way I have had a number of mentors, to whom I am forever grateful. A few of them are Wayne Kilgore, who taught the joys of science along with high school chemistry and physics; Garvin McCain, who introduced me to the satisfactions of research; Roger Kirk, my dissertation advisor, who taught me that anything worth doing is worth doing over and over until it's right; and Ellen Roye and Ouilda Piner, who shared their love of language. I learned from these dedicated teachers that *I* was responsible for learning; their contribution was their unique gifts.

At Wadsworth I want to thank Vicki Knight for her patient guidance and her conceptualization of *Brain and Behavior*; Penelope Sky for her good-humored work in moving the manuscript into production, Anita Wagner and Janet Vail for polishing my prose and catching many of my errors, and Jennifer Wilkinson for managing the development of the supplements.

Most of all, though, I want to thank my wife, Duejean, for being more patient than I could ever have asked.

Bob Garrett

The following reviewers gave generously of their time and attention throughout the development of this text, and I greatly appreciate their contributions: Susan Anderson, University of South Alabama; Patrizia Curran, University of Massachusetts—Dartmouth; Lloyd Dawe, Cameron University; Tami Eggleston, McKendree College; James Hunsicker, Southwestern Oklahoma State University; Eric Laws, Longwood College; Margaret Letterman, Eastern Connecticut State University; Doug Matthews, University of Memphis; Grant McLaren, Edinboro University of Pennsylvania; Rob Mowrer, Angelo State University; Anna Napoli, University of Redlands; Robert Patterson, Washington State University; Joseph Porter, Virginia Commonwealth University; Jeffrey Stern, University of Michigan—Dearborn; Aurora Torres, University of Alabama in Huntsville; Michael Woodruff, East Tennessee State University, and Phil Zeigler, Hunter College.

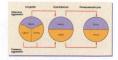

Chapter 12 Biological Bases of Intelligence 338

Chapter 13 Psychological Disorders 364

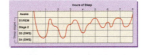

What Is Biopsychology?

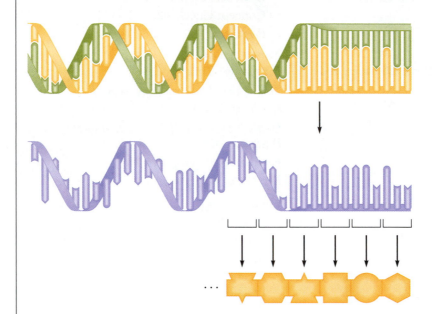

In this chapter you will learn:

- How biopsychology grew out of philosophy and physiology.
- How scientists answer research questions.
- How behavior is inherited and the relationship between heredity and environment.
- Why research in biopsychology creates ethical concerns.

There is a wonderful kind of excitement in modern neuroscience, a romantic, moon-walk sense of exploration and setting out for new frontiers. The science is elegant . . . and the pace of discovery absolutely staggering.

—Kay R. Jamison, *An Unquiet Mind*

Figure 1.1
The original romantic moon-walk
Space exploration and solving the mysteries of the brain offer similar challenges and excitement. Which do you think will have the greater impact on your life?

Neuroscience is a romantic moon-walk? To understand why Kay Jamison chose this analogy, you would need to have watched in astonishment from your back yard one night in October of 1957 as the faint glint of reflected light from Sputnik crossed the North American sky. The American people were stunned and fearful as the Russian space program left them far behind. But as the implications of this technological coup sank in, the U.S. set about constructing its own space program and revamping education in science and technology. Less than four years later, President Kennedy made his startling commitment to put an American astronaut on the moon by the end of the decade. But the real excitement would come on the evening of July 20, 1969, as you sat glued to your television set watching the *Eagle* lander settle down almost effortlessly on the moon and the first human step onto the surface of another world (Figure 1.1). For Kay Jamison and the rest of us involved in solving the mysteries of the brain, there is a very meaningful parallel between the excitement of Neil Armstrong's "giant leap for mankind" and the thrill of exploring the inner space of human thought and emotion.

There is also an inescapable parallel between Kennedy's commitment of the 1960s to space exploration and Congress's declaration thirty years later that the 1990s would be known as the Decade of the Brain. Even the effort required to understand the human brain is comparable to the one it took to put a human on the moon. There were important differences between those two decades, though. President Kennedy acknowledged that no one knew what benefits would arise from space exploration. But as the Decade of the Brain began, we understood that we would not only expand the horizons of human knowledge but advance the treatment of neurological and neuropsychiatric diseases that cost an estimated $400 billion each year (Jones & Mendell, 1999).

Another difference was that the moon landing project was born out of desperation and a sense of failure, while the Decade of the Brain was a celebration of achievements, both past and current. In the last few years we have developed new treatments for depression, identified key genes responsible for the devastation of Alzheimer's disease, discovered agents that block addiction to some drugs, learned ways to hold off the memory impairment associated with old age, and produced a "rough draft" map of the human genes.

The U.S. could not have constructed a space program from scratch in the 1960s; the achievement was built on a long history of scientific research and technological experience. In the same way, the accomplishments of the Decade of the Brain had their roots in a three-hundred-year scientific past, and in twenty-two centuries of thought and inquiry before that. For that reason we will spend a brief time examining those links to our past.

THE ORIGINS OF BIOPSYCHOLOGY

What is biopsychology, and how does it relate to neuroscience?

Neuroscience is the multidisciplinary study of the nervous system and its role in behavior. The term *neuroscience* identifies the subject matter of the investigation rather than the scientist's training. A neuroscientist may be a biologist, physiologist, anatomist, neurologist, chemist, psychologist, or psychiatrist—even a computer scientist or a philosopher. Psychologists who work in the area of neuroscience specialize in biological psychology, or **biopsychology, the branch of psychology that studies the relationships between behavior and the body, particularly the brain.** (Sometimes the term *psychobiology* or *physiological psychology* is used.) For psychologists, "behavior" has a very broad meaning which includes internal events like learning, thinking, and emotion as well as overt behavior. Biological psychologists attempt to answer questions like "What

changes in the brain when a person learns?" "Why does one person develop depression, another becomes anxious, and another is normal?" "What is the physiological explanation for emotions?" "How do we recognize the face of a friend?" and "How does the brain's activity result in consciousness?" Biological psychologists use a variety of research techniques; some of them are described in the appendix, but we will look at the basic principles later in this chapter. Whatever their area of study or their strategy for doing research, biological psychologists try to go beyond the mechanics of how the brain works to focus on the brain's role in behavior.

In the sciences, we are now uniquely privileged to sit side by side with the giants on whose shoulders we stand.
—Gerald Holton

To really appreciate the impressive accomplishments of today's brain researchers it is useful, perhaps even necessary, to understand the thinking and the work of their predecessors. Contemporary scientists stand on the shoulders of their intellectual ancestors, who made heroic advances with far less information at their disposal than is available to today's undergraduate student.

Writers have pointed out that psychology has a brief history, but a long past. What they mean is that thinkers have struggled with the questions of behavior and experience for over two millennia, but psychology arose as a separate discipline fairly recently, when Wilhelm Wundt (Figure 1.2) established the first psychology laboratory in Germany in 1879. Before biological psychology could emerge as a separate subdiscipline, psychologists would have to offer convincing evidence that the physiological approach could answer significant questions in psychology. To do so, they would have to resolve an old philosophical question about the nature of the mind. Because the question forms a thread that helps us trace the development of biological psychology, we will orient our discussion around this issue.

Figure 1.2
Wilhelm Wundt (1832–1920)
Copyright © Archives of the History of American Psychology, University of Akron

Prescientific Psychology and the Mind-Brain Problem

This issue is usually called the mind-body problem, but it is phrased differently here to place the emphasis squarely where it belongs, on the brain. **The *mind-brain problem* deals with the nature of the mind and its relationship to the brain.** There can be no doubt that the brain is essential to our behavior, but does the mind control the brain or is it the other way around? Alternatively, are mind and brain the same thing? How these questions are resolved affects how we ask all the other questions of neuroscience.

The nature of the mind and soul is bodily.

—Lucretius, circa 50 B.C.

At the risk of being provocative, I will say that there is no such thing as mind. Yes, it exists, but only in the sense that, say, weather exists. Weather is a concept we use to include rain, wind, humidity, and related phenomena. We talk as if there is *a weather* when we say things like, "The weather is interfering with my travel plans." But we don't really think that there is a weather. Most, though not all, neuroscientists believe that we should think of the mind in the same way; it is simply the collection of things that the brain does, like thinking, sensing, planning, and feeling. But when we think, sense, plan, and feel, we get the compelling impression that there is *a mind* behind it all, guiding what we do. Most neuroscientists say this is just an illusion, that the sense of mind is nothing more than the awareness of what our brain is doing. Mind, like weather, is also just a concept; it is not a *something*, it does not *do* anything.

This position is known as monism, from the Greek *monos*, meaning "alone" or "single." **Monism is the idea that the mind and the body consist of the same substance.** Idealistic monists believe that everything is nonmaterial mind, but **most monists take the position that the body and mind and everything else are physical; this view is called *materialistic monism*. The idea that the mind and the brain are separate is known as *dualism*.** For most dualists the body is material and the mind is nonmaterial. Most dualists also believe that the mind influences behavior by interacting with the brain.

This question did not originate with modern psychology. The Greek philosophers were debating it in the fifth century B.C. (Murphy, 1949), when Democritus proposed that everything in the world was made up of atoms (*atomos*, meaning "indivisible"), his term for the smallest particle possible. Even the soul, which included the mind, was made up of atoms so it, too, was material. Plato and Aristotle, considered the two greatest intellectuals among the ancient Greeks, continued the argument into the fourth century B.C. Plato was a dualist, while his student Aristotle joined the body and soul in his attempt to explain memory, emotions, and reasoning.

Defending either position was not easy. The dualists had to explain how a nonphysical mind

How do monists and dualists disagree on the mind-brain question?

could influence a physical body, and monists had the task of explaining how the physical brain could account for mental processes like perception and conscious experience. But the mind was not observable, and even the vaguest understanding of nerve functioning was not achieved until the 1800s, so neither side had much ammunition for the fight.

What is a model in science, and how is it useful?

Scientists often resort to the use of models in their work. **A *model* is a proposed mechanism for how something works.** Sometimes a model is in the form of a theory, like the dopamine model of schizophrenia that we will talk about later in this chapter. Other times the model is a simpler organism or system that researchers study in an attempt to understand a more complex one. For example, researchers have used the rat to model everything from learning to Alzheimer's disease in humans, and the computer has often served as a model of cognitive processes.

In the seventeenth century the French philosopher and physiologist René Descartes (Figure 1.3a) used a hydraulic model to explain the brain's activity (Descartes, 1662/1984). Descartes' choice of a hydraulic model was influenced by his observation of the statues in the royal gardens. When a visitor stepped on certain tiles it forced water through tubes to the statues and made them move. Using this model, Descartes then reasoned that the nerves were also hollow tubes. The fluid they carried was not water, but what he called "animal spirits"; these flowed from the brain and inflated the muscles to produce movement. Sensations, memories, and other mental functions were produced as animal spirits flowed through "pores" in the brain. The animal spirits were pumped through the brain by the pineal gland.

Descartes' choice of the pineal gland was based on his belief that it was at a perfect location to serve this function; attached just below the two cerebral hemispheres by its flexible stalk, it appeared capable of bending at different angles to direct the flow of animal spirits into critical areas of the brain (Figure 1.3b). Thus, for Descartes the pineal gland became the "seat of the soul," the place where the mind

Figure 1.3
Descartes (1596–1650) and the hydraulic model
Descartes believed behavior was controlled by animal spirits flowing through nerves.
Source: (a) National Library of Medicine, Bethesda, MD.

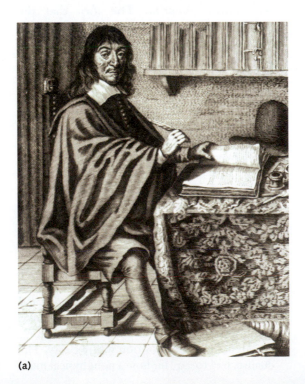

(a)

(b)

interacted with the body. Although Descartes assigned control to the mind, his unusual emphasis on the physical explanation of behavior foreshadowed the physiological approach that would soon follow.

Descartes lacked an understanding of how the brain and body worked, so he relied on a small amount of anatomical knowledge and a great deal of speculation. His hydraulic model represented an important shift in thinking, but it illustrates the fact that a model or a theory can lead us astray. Fortunately, this was the age of the Renaissance, a time not only of artistic expansion and world exploration, but of scientific curiosity. Thinkers began to test their ideas through direct observation and experimental manipulation as the Renaissance gave birth to science. Progress was slow, but two critically important principles would emerge as the early scientists ushered in the future.

Discovering the Brain's Role in Behavior

In the late 1700s the Italian physiologist Luigi Galvani showed that he could make a frog's leg muscle twitch by stimulating the attached nerve with electricity, even after the nerve and muscle had been removed from the frog's body. A century later in Germany, Gustav Fritsch and Eduard Hitzig (1870) produced movement in dogs by electrically stimulating their exposed brains. What these scientists showed was that animal spirits were not responsible for movement; *the principle of operation in nerves was electrical.* But the German physicist and physiologist Hermann von Helmholtz (Figure 1.4) showed that nerves do not behave like wires conducting electricity. He was able to measure the speed of conduction in nerves, and his calculation of about 90 feet per second fell far short of the speed of electricity, which travels at the speed of light (186,000 miles/sec). It was obvious that researchers were dealing with a biological phenomenon, and that the functioning of nerves and of the brain was open to scientific study. Starting from this understanding, Helmholtz's studies of vision and hearing gave "psychologists their first clear idea of what a fully mecha-

Figure 1.4
Hermann von Helmholtz (1821–1895)

Hulton Archive

nistic 'mind' might look like" (Fancher, 1979, p. 41). As you will see in later chapters, his ideas were so insightful that even today we must refer to his theories of vision and hearing before describing the current ones.

The second important principle to come out of this period was *localization,* **the idea that specific areas of the brain are responsible for specific functions.** Intriguing reports had been coming in from brain injury cases as long ago as the early Egyptian civilization, and Fritsch and Hitzig's work with dogs suggested these observations were accurate. But two case studies particularly grabbed the attention of the scientific community in the mid-1800s. In 1861 Phineas Gage, a railroad construction foreman, was injured when a dynamite blast drove an iron rod through his skull and the frontal lobes of his brain. Amazingly, he survived with no

What two discoveries furthered the early understanding of the brain?

impairment of his intelligence, memory, speech, or movement. But he became irresponsible and profane, and unable to abide by social conventions (Damasio, Grabowski, Frank, Galaburda, & Damasio, 1994). Then, in 1861 the French physician Paul Broca (Figure 1.5) performed an autopsy on the brain of a man who had lost the ability to speak after a stroke. The autopsy showed that damage was limited to an area on the left side of his brain now known as Broca's area (Broca, 1861). By the mid-1880s, researchers were convinced about localization, though they would later find that specialization is less absolute than they thought (Murphy, 1949). Nevertheless, showing that language, emotion, motor control, and so on have locations in the brain was an important step toward understanding that behavior and mental processes have a physical basis.

This meant that the mind ceased being *the explanation*, and became *the phenomenon to be explained*. Understand that the nature and role of the mind are still debated in some quarters. But as you explore the rest of this text you will see why most, though certainly not all, brain scientists are material monists: brain research has been able to explain a great deal of behavior without any reference to a nonmaterial mind.

What is the danger of mind-as-explanation?

1

Figure 1.5
Paul Broca
(1825–1880)

Hulton Archive

It was not enough just to sort out issues like the relationship between the brain and the mind, however; success in studying behavior depends on how effectively researchers can answer questions. I mentioned earlier that science distinguished itself from previous inquiry by its methods. Because an understanding of science requires a knowledge of how it obtains information, the research strategies that science uses deserve a brief tour.

CONCEPT CHECK

- *What change in method separated science from philosophy?*
- *What were the important implications of the discoveries that nerve conduction is electrical, and that specific parts of the brain have (more or less) specific functions?*

SCIENCE, RESEARCH, AND THEORY

Science is not distinguished by the knowledge it produces, but by its method of acquiring knowledge. Its primary method is *empiricism,* which means that scientists get their information through observation. Observation is not the casual process it sounds like, though. We could spend the rest of this book talking about how scientists ensure accuracy in their observations, so perhaps you won't begrudge me a few minutes on the topic. Even if you are familiar with these ideas, a brief review will remind you of them as you read the remaining chapters.

Empiricism: How to Answer Scientific Questions

Observation has broad meaning in science. A biological psychologist might observe aggressive behavior in children on the playground to see if there are differences between boys and girls *(naturalistic observation)*, report on a patient who had violent outbursts following a car accident that caused brain injury *(case study)*, use a questionnaire to find out whether some women are more prone to violence during the premenstrual period *(survey)*, or stimulate a part of rats' brains with electricity to see if the brain area controls aggressive behavior *(experiment)*.

The important point is that scientists do not get their information from intuition, or from tradition, or from revelation, or even from logic (alone). Descartes started out with the traditional assumption that there was a soul, and then he located the soul in the pineal gland because it seemed the logical place for the soul to control the brain. Aristotle, using equally good logic, had located the soul in the heart because the heart is so vital to life. (He thought the brain's function was to cool the blood!) **The advantage of observation is that it is** *objective;* **this means that two observers will reach the same conclusion about what is being observed** (though not necessarily about its meaning). At the end of the sixteenth and beginning of the seventeenth centuries pioneers like Galileo and Francis Bacon set the course for science by insisting on observation as its method of inquiry.

The different strategies behavioral researchers use can be broadly categorized as experimental or nonexperimental. **An** *experiment* **is a study in which the researcher manipulates an independent variable; the** *independent variable* **(IV) is some condition that is expected to affect the research participant's behavior.** But the experimenter does not simply watch to see what happens after the independent variable is administered. Research is designed to answer a specific question, so the researcher knows in advance what to look for. The research plan identifies a specific *dependent variable* **(DV), which is the variable used to measure the effect of the independent variable** and to answer the research question. The researcher who wants to know whether general activation of the nervous system will enhance learning might compare the number of words memorized (DV) by individuals given an injection of the stimulant amphetamine (IV) and by control subjects given an injection of an ineffective placebo.

The advantage of the experimental approach is the control it gives the researcher. The experimenter controls the independent variable's intensity and time of application, and eliminates or controls other variables to make sure they do not influence the research participants' behavior. Also, we typically have a control group, which might be matched with the experimental group on several characteristics such as age, sex, and intelligence. In some cases we can get even better control by comparing the subjects with themselves—have them learn a new list on another day without the drug. When we control the independent variable, eliminate other possible variables, and observe the control group under the same conditions except for the IV, we can be reasonably confident that the changes observed are *caused* by the independent variable and not some other variable.

Sometimes we do a study that looks like an experiment but is not. For example, when we compare verbal ability in males and females we cannot assign the sex of the study participants. As a result, we cannot distinguish the effects of sex from the effects of other variables that often differ between males and females, such as rearing practices and educational and social experiences; we say that sex is *confounded* **(mingled or confused)** with these other variables. Because we can observe only that there is an association of verbal ability with the sex of the individuals, this is known as a correlational study.

In a *correlational study* **the researcher does not control an independent variable, but determines whether two variables are related to each other.** The big problem with correlational studies is the inability to draw conclusions about cause and effect. For example, higher verbal ability in females could be due to *being* female (influenced by female hormones, for example) or it could be due to greater emphasis on verbal activities in the rearing of girls. Violent criminals more often have evidence of brain damage than nonviolent criminals. This may mean that brain damage is a cause of criminal violence. On the other hand, it could mean that violent people more

What are the advantages of experimental studies over correlational studies?

Figure 1.6
Experimental versus correlational studies
In an experiment the researcher manipulates the IV and controls other variables or equates them in a control group, so it is likely that any changes in the DV are due to the IV. In a correlational study, we cannot tell whether A influences B, B influences A, or a third variable affects both.

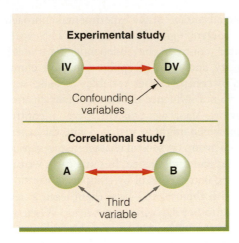

often engage in behaviors that risk brain damage, like fighting, drug use, and contact sports. The correlation between two variables does not help us choose between competing explanations (see Figure 1.6).

So if experimental studies are best, why are correlational studies done at all? Because experiments have their limitations, and correlational studies do provide useful information. A highly controlled experimental situation will interfere with some kinds of behavior; to solve that problem we might resort to naturalistic observation. We can't manipulate sexual behavior in humans, so we use surveys to find out what people do. Knowing that a relationship exists may not reveal the cause, but it tells us to look further. For example, we might observe what happens to the offspring of schizophrenic parents when they are reared by nonrelatives, and do viral and genetic studies of families with schizophrenic members. We need correlational studies, and we equally need to be careful about interpreting their results.

Theory and the Uncertainty of Science

Over and over again in this text you will see statements like "It appears that . . .", "Perhaps . . .", and "The results suggest . . .". You will probably wonder why neuroscientists are so tentative and why so much of the information is stated as theories instead of facts.

What are the characteristics and benefits of theory?

There are two main reasons. The first is the difficulty of the field; as you read through these chapters you will soon see that both human behavior and the nervous system that produces the behavior are very complex.

The second and most important reason is philosophical; it involves the scientist's attitude toward truth. Scientists recognize that knowledge is changing rapidly, and the cherished ideas of today may be discarded tomorrow. Any finding must be verified by additional studies before it can be accepted as fact; often a result fails to hold up to a change in technique or a slightly different sample of subjects. You seldom hear scientists using words like "truth" and "proof," because these terms suggest final answers. Such uncertainty may feel uncomfortable to you, but centuries of experience with people who were certain they had the truth have shown that the alternative can be just as uncomfortable, if not downright scary.

The scientist turns the discomfort of uncertainty into a challenge. One way the researcher has of making sense out of ambiguity is through theory. **A *theory* integrates and interprets diverse observations in an attempt to explain some phenomenon.** For example, schizophrenia researchers noticed that people who overdosed on the drug amphetamine were being misdiagnosed as schizophrenic when they were admitted to emergency rooms with hallucinations and paranoia. They also knew that amphetamine increases activity in brain cells that use the chemical dopamine for transmitting messages. This led several researchers to propose that schizophrenia is due to excess dopamine activity in the brain.

The dopamine theory of schizophrenia, like all good theories, made sense of some of the things researchers had been observing, and it generated new hypotheses. **An *hypothesis* is a statement about the expected relationship between two or more variables.** One hypothesis that came from dopamine theory was that drugs that decrease dopamine activity would improve functioning in schizophrenics. This hypothesis was testable, which is a requirement for a good theory. The hypothesis was confirmed in many cases of schizophrenia, but not in others. Other hypotheses generated by the dopamine theory also met mixed fates. We now realize that the dopamine theory is an incomplete explanation of schizophrenia. However, even a flawed theory inspires further research that will yield more knowledge and additional hypotheses. The idea that behavior is controlled by the mind, on the other hand, is not very testable. But remember that the best theory is still only a theory; theory and empiricism are the basis of science's ability for self-correction and its openness to change and renewal.

We have painted a picture in rather broad strokes about how scientists think and do research. The appendix at the end of this book discusses some of the specific methods biopsychologists and other neuroscientists use to find the answers to their questions. I will refer you to it occasionally as we encounter research studies that include the methods described there, but it would be a good idea to read the entire appendix at one sitting before you go much farther in the text.

✔ CONCEPT CHECK
- *What is the value of empiricism?*
- *A scientist speaking to a group of students says, "I do not expect my research to find the truth." Why?*

NATURE AND NURTURE

The relative importance of heredity and environment, or the *nature versus nurture question,* is one of the most controversial topics in psychology. The arguments are based on emotion and values almost as often as they appeal to evidence and reason. For example, some critics complain that attributing behavior to heredity is just a form of excusing actions for which the person or society should be held accountable. A surprising number of behaviors are turning out to have some degree of hereditary influence, so you will be running into this issue throughout the following chapters. For this reason, it is important that you under-

stand what it means to say that a behavior is hereditary.

The Genetic Code

As you probably know, the gene is the unit of inheritance. The genes are found on the chromosomes, which are located in the nucleus of each cell. Every body cell in a human has 46 chromosomes, arranged in 23 pairs (see Figure 1.7). Each pair is identifiably distinct from every other pair. This is important, because genes for different functions are found on specific chromosomes. The chromosomes are referred to by number, except that the sex chromosomes are designated X or Y. A female has two X chromosomes, while a male has an X and a Y chromosome. Notice that the members of a pair of chromosomes are similar, again with the exception that the Y chromosome is much shorter than the X chromosome.

Unlike the body cells, the male's sperm cells and the female's ova (egg cells) each have 23 chromosomes. When these sex cells are formed by the division of their parent cells, the pairs of chromosomes separate so each daughter cell receives only one chromosome from each pair. When the sperm enters the ovum during fertilization, the chromosomes of the two cells merge to restore the number to 46. **The fertilized egg or** *zygote* then undergoes

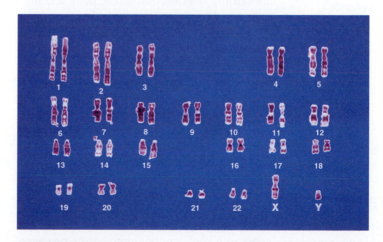

Figure 1.7
A set of human chromosomes
Can you tell whether they came from a male or a female?

rapid cell division and development, on its way to becoming a functioning organism. **For the first eight weeks (in humans) the new organism is referred to as an *embryo,* and from then until birth as a *fetus.***

The mystery of how genes carry their genetic instructions began to yield to researchers in 1953 when James Watson and Francis Crick published a proposed structure for the deoxyribonucleic acid that genes are made of. ***Deoxyribonucleic acid (DNA) is a double-stranded chain of chemical molecules that looks like a ladder that has been twisted around itself;*** this is why DNA is often referred to as the *double helix* (see Figure 1.8). Each rung of the ladder is composed of the bases adenine, thymine, guanine, and cytosine (A, T, G, C), with two bases to each rung. The order in which these bases appear on the ladder forms the code that carries all our genetic information. The four-letter alphabet these bases provide is adequate to spell out the instructions for every structure and function in your body. We only partially understand how genes control the development of the body and its activities, as well as influencing many aspects of behavior. However, we do know that genes exert their influence in a deceptively simple manner: they provide the directions for making proteins. Some of these proteins are used in the construction of the body and others are enzymes; enzymes act as catalysts, modifying chemical reactions in the body. Approximately 99.9% of our genes are identical in different humans; so only one in every thousand genes contributes to the inheritable differences among us.

Because chromosomes are paired, most genes are paired as well; a gene on one chromosome is matched up with one for the same function on the other chromosome. Some characteristics are determined by a single pair of genes; eye color is one example and Huntington's disease, a hereditary disorder in which the brain degenerates, is another. The genes in a pair may be dominant or recessive. For example, the gene for brown eyes is dom-

How are characteristics inherited?

Figure 1.8
A strand of DNA

Why do males more often show characteristics that are caused by recessive genes?

inant over the gene for blue eyes. **A *dominant* gene will produce its effect regardless of which gene it is paired with; a *recessive* gene will have an influence only when it is paired with the same recessive gene on the other chromosome.** Again, we have an exception in the sex chromosomes. Because the Y chromosome is shorter, some genes on the X chromosome are not paired with a gene on the Y chromosome. In this case a recessive gene alone is adequate to produce the characteristic, because it is not opposed by a dominant gene. **A characteristic produced by an unpaired gene on the X chromosome is referred to as *X-linked*.** X linkage explains why, for example, males are red-green color blind eight times as frequently as females.

Dominance and recessiveness are illustrated in Figure 1.9, which shows the results of two different matings of brown-eyed individuals. The figure also illustrates another phenomenon. All four parents have brown eyes, but one of them has two genes for brown eyes and the other three parents have both brown-eye and blue-eye genes. **The parent who has identical genes for eye color is *homozygous* for eye color; each of the others has different genes for eye color and is *heterozygous*.** Although they have the same *phenotype (the characteristic),* their *genotypes (the combinations of genes)* are different. This distinction does not seem important until we look at the offspring. The first couple can produce only brown-eyed children because one parent has only dominant brown-eyed genes to offer. The second couple has one chance in four of producing a blue-eyed child. The heterozygous parents are *carriers* for blue eyes.

Not all inheritance follows this pattern. Some genes blend their effects rather than showing dominance and recessiveness; type AB blood, for example, occurs when a person receives a gene for type A and a gene for type B blood. And **many characteristics are determined by several genes rather than a single gene pair—they are *polygenic*.** Height is polygenic, and many behavioral characteris-

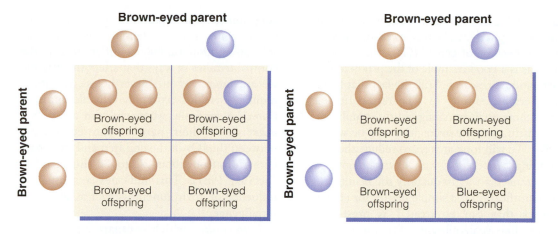

Figure 1.9
Offspring of parents homozygous and heterozygous for brown eyes
The boxes show the possible genotypes and phenotypes that the two matings can produce. Brown circles represent genes for brown eyes, and blue circles represent genes for blue eyes.

tics such as intelligence and psychological disorders are also controlled by multiple genes.

Genes and Behavior

We have known from ancient times that animals could be bred for desirable behavioral characteristics like hunting ability or a mild temperament that made them suitable as pets. Charles Darwin helped establish the idea that behavioral traits can be inherited, but the idea fell into disfavor as an emphasis on learning as the major influence on behavior became increasingly fashionable. But in the 1960s and 1970s the tide of strict environmentalism began to ebb, and the perspective shifted toward a balanced view of the roles of nature and nurture (Plomin, Owen, & McGuffin, 1994). By 1992 the American Psychological Association was able to identify genetics as one of the themes that best represent the present and the future of psychology (Plomin & McClearn, 1993).

Of the behavioral traits that fall under genetic influence, intelligence is the most investigated. Most of the behavioral disorders, including alcoholism and drug addiction, schizophrenia, major mood disorders, and anxiety, are partially hereditary as well (McGue & Bouchard, 1998). The same can be said for some personality characteristics (Bouchard,

1994) and sexual orientation (Bailey & Pillard, 1991; Bailey, Pillard, Neale, & Agyei, 1993).

However, you should exercise caution in thinking about these genetic effects. Genes do not provide a script for behaving intelligently or instructions for homosexual behavior. They control the production of proteins, which in turn affect the development of brain structures, the production of neural transmitters and the receptors that respond to them, and the functioning of the glandular system.

Investigating Heredity

Although the idea that behavior can be inherited is not a recent one, almost all of the methods for doing behavioral genetic research either were introduced or came into maturity in the last three or four decades. Until then, the work was not much more sophisticated than observing that a characteristic runs in families.

Genetic Similarities: The Correlational Approach

People who have similar genes often share a similar environment, so heredity and environment are confounded. In a *family study, which determines the degree of relationship of a characteristic among relatives,* we may discover that intelligent parents usually

What are some of the inheritable behaviors?

have intelligent children. However, as one researcher put it, "Cake recipes run in families, but not because of genes" (Goodwin, 1986, p. 3). This is a good example of the problem with correlational research. Still, the fact that family members are similar in a characteristic tells researchers that pursuing more complicated and costly research strategies could be worthwhile. We will look at ways to reduce the confounding of heredity with environment, but first we need a way to quantify the results.

Quantification is a simple matter for characteristics that can be treated as present or absent, like schizophrenia. We can say, for instance, that the rate of schizophrenia is about 1% in the general population, but increases to around 13% among the offspring of a schizophrenic parent (Gottesman, 1991). For variables that are measured on a numerical scale, like height and IQ (intelligence quotient, a measure of intelligence), we express the relationship with a statistic called correlation. *Correlation* **is a measure that indicates the degree of relationship between two variables on a scale between 0.0 and ±1.0.** The strength of the relationship is indicated by the absolute value—how close the correlation is to either 1.0 or –1.0. A negative value does not mean the relationship is weaker; it means that people who are high on one variable tend to score low on the second variable, and vice versa. As examples, the correlation between the IQs of parents and of their children averages about .42 across studies, and the correlation between brothers and sisters in the same family is about .47 (Bouchard & McGue, 1981). But as I said, these measures confound the effects of heredity and environment.

Adoption studies, **which compare individuals reared in an adoptive home with individuals reared by their biological parents,** eliminate most of the confounding of heredity and environment that occurs in family studies. This kind of study is often called a *natural experiment,* but it lacks the control of a real experiment because we do not manipulate the

How are adoption and twin studies superior to family studies?

adoption variable. Confounding can still occur because, for instance, families that must be split up by adoption may be different from the control families in ways that affect the variable we are interested in. Nevertheless, the technique has yielded extremely valuable information. For example, when children are reared apart from their parents the correlation between the IQs of the children and their parents drops from about .42 to .22 (Bouchard & McGue, 1981). This indicates a substantial influence of environment as well as genes on intelligence.

Twin studies, **which compare a characteristic in twins, provide another way of separating the effects of heredity and environment.** *Fraternal twins* **are produced from two separately fertilized eggs,** while *identical twins* **result from a single egg that splits and develops into two individuals.** For that reason, **fraternal twins are referred to as** *dizygotic (DZ)* **and identical twins as** *monozygotic (MZ).* Fraternal twins share only half of their genes with each other, just like non-twin siblings, but identical twins have the same genes. Because both identical twins and fraternal twins share the same environment, a greater similarity between identical twins in a characteristic is probably due to their greater genetic similarity. (Of course, we have to select fraternal pairs that are of the same sex, because identical twins are the same sex.)

Investigations of schizophrenia and intelligence provide particularly good examples of the value of twin studies. A useful measure for identifying genetic influence in disorders is the *concordance rate,* **the frequency that relatives are alike in a characteristic.** When one fraternal twin is schizophrenic the second twin will also be schizophrenic about 17% of the time; in identical twins the concordance almost triples, to 48% (Gottesman, 1991). (See Figure 1.10.) The correlation between fraternal twins' IQs is about .60, and for identicals it is around .86 (Bouchard & McGue, 1981). Notice that these correlations fall short of a perfect 1.0.

Figure 1.10
The Genain quadruplets at age 4
Identical quadruplets, the sisters all became schizophrenic later in life. The chances of any four unrelated individuals all being schizophrenic is one in 100 million. The name Genain is a nickname derived from the Greek word meaning "dreadful gene."

Even identical twins will rarely have exactly the same IQ, and the identical twin of a schizophrenic will escape schizophrenia about 52% of the time. The nontotal influence of heredity means that environmental effects are also operating.

Genetic Engineering: The Experimental Approach

Although adoption and twin studies reduce confounding, they still share some of the disadvantages of correlational studies. *Genetic engineering* **involves actual manipulation of the organism's genes or their functioning;** studies using this technology qualify as experiments. At present genetic engineering is used mostly with mice, because their genetic makeup is better known than that of any other mammal.

Transgenic mice **are created by inserting a foreign gene into mouse embryos.** The for-

eign gene shows up in only some of the mouse's cells; but after these mice are mated with each other the gene is integrated into all the cells, including the sperm and ova. Another way to determine a gene's effect is to interfere with its function. **In *knockout mice,* a non-functioning mutation is introduced into the isolated gene, and the altered gene is transferred into mouse embryos.** After multiple matings, mice carrying the altered gene on both chromosomes are selected for study.

Antisense RNA **technology temporarily disables a targeted gene or reduces its effectiveness by interfering with the construction of proteins under its control. Protein construction is actually directed by *ribonucleic acid (RNA),* which is a copy the DNA makes of one of its strands** (see Figure 1.11 on page 14). The researcher synthesizes a single-stranded molecule of DNA; the synthesized DNA "docks" with the mouse's RNA and prevents it from participating in protein construction.

Genetic engineering is becoming a therapeutic reality. One pharmaceutical manufacturer is developing antisense drugs for treating a form of cancer, cardiovascular disease, and inflammatory and autoimmune diseases such as rheumatoid arthritis and Crohn's disease (more information is available at http://www.isip.com). And three children have been successfully treated for severe combined immunodeficiency-X1 (SCID-X1) by gene transfer therapy (Cavazzana-Calvo et al., 2000). SCID-X1 is a genetic immune disorder that is fatal unless its victims are kept isolated from the everyday diseases that we take in stride, like the common cold; the isolation required led to the popular term "bubble baby." The infants' doctors used a virus to carry healthy genes into the patients' bone marrow. Within three to four months all three children were able to leave their protective environments and go home to their families, where they were growing and developing normally.

What advantage does genetic engineering have over adoption and twin studies as a research strategy?

Figure 1.11
From DNA to protein
RNA copies a strand of the DNA, then moves out into the cytoplasm where it controls the development of proteins.

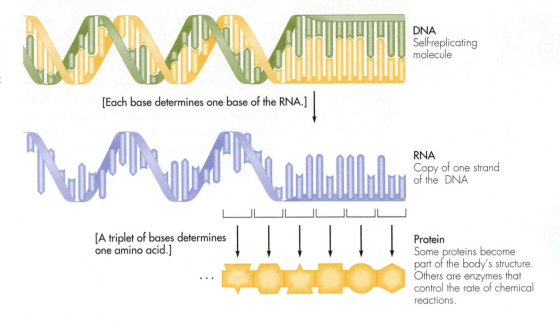

DNA
Self-replicating molecule

[Each base determines one base of the RNA.]

RNA
Copy of one strand of the DNA

[A triplet of bases determines one amino acid.]

Protein
Some proteins become part of the body's structure. Others are enzymes that control the rate of chemical reactions.

What is the Human Genome Project, and how successful has it been?

The Human Genome Project

After geneticists have determined that a behavior is inheritable, the next step is to locate the genes involved. The various techniques for identifying genes boil down to determining whether people who share a particular characteristic also share a particular gene or genes that other people don't have. This task is extremely difficult if the researchers do not know which chromosomes to examine, because the amount of DNA is so great. They often do have clues where to look, though. For instance, sometimes a characteristic typically occurs along with another characteristic; if researchers know the location of the gene that causes this second characteristic, they start their search near that gene. Otherwise, they search the genes of people with the characteristic for strings of DNA bases that they share with each other but not with members of a control group. Obviously, identifying specific genes can be a difficult and time-consuming task; it took 10 years to find the gene responsible for Huntington's disease (Huntington's Disease Collaborative Research Group, 1993).

In behavior the challenge is even greater, partly because multiple genes are involved. However, the gene search received a tremendous boost in 1990 when a consortium of geneticists at 20 laboratories around the world formed the government-financed Human Genome Project.

Landing a person on the moon gave us an extraterrestrial perspective on human life . . . and now the human genome sequence gives us a view of the internal genetic scaffold around which every human life is molded.
—Svante Pääbo

The goal of the *Human Genome Project* **(HGP) was to map the location of all the genes on the human chromosomes, and to determine the base sequences of the genes.** In 1998, a private company named Celera declared that it would sequence the human genome first and patent its results rather than publishing them; this turned the effort into a high-stakes race. Barely two years later, the HGP and Celera made peace in a joint announcement that they had each produced a "working draft" of the human gene map. Both maps were then published simultaneously (International Human Genome Sequencing Consortium, 2001; Venter et al., 2001; see "Genome Milestone: Cracking the Code").

The maps are incomplete in that there are gaps and some of the genes are out of order. Also, it is not even clear yet just how many genes we have. The number appears to be somewhere between 26,000 and 40,000, far fewer than the 100,000 or so that many geneti-

cists were betting on. You might think that geneticists could simply count the genes, but it is difficult to tell where one gene ends and another begins. This problem is complicated by the fact that 98% of the genome consists of long stretches of "junk" DNA that do not code directly for proteins. Even more important than the gaps and the uncertainty about number is that the map does not tell us what the genes do. However, the map will speed the discovery of gene functions; it is a remarkable accomplishment that owes its success to a worldwide team effort and to the development of advanced gene-sequencing techniques.

Genome Milestone: Cracking the Code

IN THE NEWS

Paul Jacobs and Aaron Zitner—In an achievement compared to Lewis and Clark's mapping of the continent, two teams of scientists announced Monday that each has produced a draft version of the human genetic code.

The joint announcement, which came in a transatlantic news conference held by President Clinton and British Prime Minister Tony Blair, followed weeks of secret negotiations between leaders of the rival factions: J. Craig Venter, Celera's president and chief scientific officer, and Francis Collins, leader of the public project. . . .

Clinton, speaking from the East Room of the White House, compared the achievement to the day two centuries ago that Thomas Jefferson met with explorer Meriwether Lewis in the same room to look at the first crude map of the North American continent.

The new genetic maps are of "even greater significance," the president said. "Without a doubt, this is the most important, most wondrous map ever produced by humankind."

Blair, speaking from 10 Downing Street in London, was similarly awe-struck, predicting that the genetic map would bring changes in the first half of the new century as radical as those brought by computer technology in the last half of the century past.

Both leaders, however, expressed concern about the potential for abuse of the new knowledge through genetic discrimination as well as manipulation of human genetics without a clear understanding of the consequences. . . .

"We can see a majority of the genes now, and that's pretty good," said James D. Watson, who won the Nobel Prize as co-discoverer of the structure of DNA. . . .

Cracking the code of the genome—listing all 3 billion in order—won't fully explain how the human organism works nor how the genes interact with one another. That will be work enough to keep scientists busy for another century.
—*Excerpted with permission from the* Los Angeles Times, *June 27, 2000*

Identifying the genes and their functions will improve our understanding of human behavior and psychological as well as medical disorders. We will be able to treat disorders genetically, counsel vulnerable individuals about preventive measures, and determine whether a patient will benefit from a drug or have an adverse reaction, thus eliminating delays in successful treatment.

Do genes lock a person into a particular outcome in life?

Heredity: Destiny or Predisposition?

To many people the idea that several if not most of their behavioral characteristics are hereditary implies that offspring are clones of their parents and their future is engraved in stone by their genes. This is not a popular or a comfortable view, and creates considerable resistance to the concept of behavioral genetics. It also happens to be wrong; a hallmark of genetic influence is, surprisingly, flexibility.

Genes and Individuality

Although family members do tend to be similar to each other, children share only half of their genes with each of their parents or with each other. Besides that, those genes appear in different configurations in different family members. A sex cell receives a random half of the parent's chromosomes; as a result, a parent can produce 2^{23}, or 8 million, different combinations of chromosomes. Add to this the uncertainty of which sperm will unite with which egg, and the number of genetic combinations that can be passed on to offspring rises to 60 or 70 trillion! So, sexual reproduction increases individuality in spite of the inheritability of traits. This variability powers what Darwin (Figure 1.12) called **natural selection, which means that those whose genes endow them with greater speed, intelligence, or health are more likely to survive and transmit their genes to more offspring** (Darwin, 1859).

Gene effects are not necessarily rigid; they can be variable over time and circumstances. Genes are turned on and turned off, upregulated and downregulated, producing more or less of their proteins at different times. If genes

Figure 1.12
Charles Darwin (1809–1882)

were constant there would be no smoothly flowing sequence of developmental changes from conception to adulthood. A large number of genes change their functioning late in life, apparently accounting for many of the changes common to aging (Ly, Lockhart, Lerner, & Schultz, 2000), as well as the onset of diseases like Alzheimer's (Breitner, Folstein, & Murphy, 1986). The functioning of some genes is even controlled by experience, which explains some of the changes in the brain that constitute learning (Bailey, Bartsch, & Kandel, 1996). For the last quarter century, researchers have puzzled over why humans are so different from chimpanzees, our closest relatives, considering that 98% of our DNA sequences are identical (King & Wilson, 1975). Now it appears the answer is that we differ more dramatically in which genes are *expressed* in the brain (Enard et al., 2002).

Genes also have varying degrees of effects; some determine the person's characteristics and others only influence them. A person with the potent form of the Huntington's gene *will* develop the disease, but most behavioral traits depend on many genes; a single gene will account for only a slight increase in intelligence or in the risk for schizophrenia. The idea of risk raises the issue of vulnerability, and returns us to our original question, the relative importance of heredity and environment.

Heredity, Environment, and Vulnerability

To assess the relative contributions of heredity and environment, we need to be able to quantify the two influences. *Heritability* **is the percentage of the variation in a characteristic that can be attributed to heredity.** Heritability can be estimated by comparing the concordance for monozygotic twins with the concordance for dizygotic twins. Heritability estimates are around 50% for intelligence (Plomin, 1990), 60–90% for schizophrenia (Tsuang, Gilbertson, & Faraone, 1991), and 40–50% for personality characteristics and occupational interests

(Plomin et al., 1994). By comparison, the heritability for height is approximately 90% (Plomin, 1990), which makes the values for behavioral characteristics seem modest. On the other hand, heritabilities for behavioral characteristics are higher on average than those for common medical disorders, as Figure 1.13 shows (Plomin et al., 1994).

Since about half of the differences among people in behavioral characteristics is attributable to heredity, then approximately half is due to environmental influences. Surprisingly, relatively little of the environmental influence comes from the family, even for personality characteristics and major psychological disorders (McGue & Bouchard, 1998). Intelligence is the exception, with about 20–30% of the variability due to shared environment, but the percentage drops to near zero in adulthood.

The measures of heritability and environmental effect are not absolute. They are relative, not only to each other but to the circumstances.

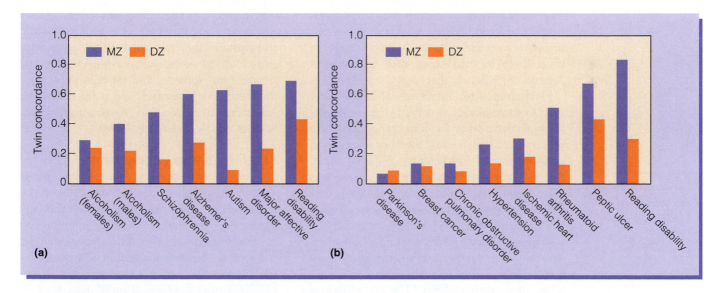

Figure 1.13
Twin studies of behavioral and medical disorders
The concordance of **(a)** behavioral disorders and **(b)** medical disorders in monozygotic and dizygotic twins. Note the greater concordance in identical twins and the (generally) higher concordance for behavioral disorders.

Reprinted with permission from "The Genetic Basis of Complex Human Behavior" by R. Plomin, M.J. Owen and P. McGuffin, *Science*, Volume 264, p. 1734. Copyright © 1994 American Association for the Advancement of Science.

If everyone's environment were identical, the estimated heritability would be 100% because environmental differences would not account for any of the differences observed. For the same reason, environmental influence will appear to be very low if all the individuals come from similar environments. Adoption studies probably underestimate environmental influences somewhat because adopting parents come disproportionately from the middle class (McGue & Bouchard, 1998). An estimate of environmental or hereditary influence tells us the *proportion* of influence, which will vary with the way the subjects are selected.

What do we mean by "genetic disposition"?

Because the influence of genes is only partial, researchers caution us that "We inherit dispositions, not destinies" (Rose, 1995, p. 648). This idea is formalized in the vulnerability model of schizophrenia (Zubin & Spring, 1977). **Vulnerability in this context means that there is some threshold of causes that must be exceeded in order for illness to occur, and environmental challenges may combine with a person's hereditary susceptibility to exceed that threshold.** When multiple genes are involved, heredity may set a broad range in which behavior will occur, with environment determining where in that range the person falls.

Psychologists no longer talk about heredity versus environment, as if the two are competing with each other for importance. Both are required, and they work together to make us what we are. As an earlier psychologist put it, "To ask whether heredity or environment is more important to life is like asking whether fuel or oxygen is more necessary for making a fire" (Woodworth, 1941, p. 1).

What are the main issues in research integrity?

With increasing understanding of genetics, we are now in the position to change our very being. This kind of capability carries with it a tremendous responsibility. The knowledge of our genetic makeup alone raises the question whether it is better for a person to know about a risk that may never materialize. In addition, many worry that the ability to do genetic testing on our unborn children means that some parents will choose to abort a fetus just because

it has genes for a trait they consider undesirable, such as homosexuality. Our ability to plumb the depths of the brain and of the genome is increasing faster than our grasp of either its implications or how to resolve the ethical questions. We will consider some of the ethical issues of genetic research after getting an overview of ethical issues in research.

CONCEPT CHECK

■ *Why is it inappropriate to ask whether heredity or environment is more important for behavior?*
■ *When we say that a person inherits personality characteristic X, what do we really mean?*

RESEARCH ETHICS

As important as research ethics is, the topic usually gets pushed into the background by the excitement of scientific accomplishments and therapeutic promise. To place ethics at the forefront where it belongs, the major scientific and medical organizations have adopted strict guidelines for conducting research, for the treatment of subjects, and for communicating the results of research (see, for example, American Psychological Association, 1992; Society for Neuroscience, 1998).

Plagiarism and Fabrication

The success of research in answering questions and solving problems depends not only on the researchers' skill in designing studies and collecting data but on their accuracy and integrity in communicating results. Unfortunately, research is sometimes intentionally misrepresented; the two cardinal sins of research are plagiarism and the fabrication of data.

Plagiarism is the theft of another's work or ideas. Plagiarism denies individuals the credit they deserve and erodes trust among the research community. The infraction may be as simple as failing to give appropriate credit through citations and references (like those throughout this text) when the other scientist's research or idea is discussed. Occasionally, though, a researcher intentionally assumes credit for another's work. Perhaps the most remarkable example is the case of the Polish medical school professor Andrzej Jendryczko, who included uncredited work of others in 29 of his publications, and republished an entire research article from a foreign journal under his own name (Marshall, 1998). More serious still is the *fabrication, or faking, of results,* because it introduces erroneous information into the body of scientific knowledge. As a result, the pursuit of false leads by others consumes scarce resources and sidetracks researchers from more fruitful lines of research.

More important, fabrication in clinical research can slow therapeutic progress and harm lives. William Simmons appeared well on his way to identifying an undiscovered gene involved in a group of autoimmune diseases when a co-worker caught him "spiking" research laboratory materials with a substance that would shift the experimental results in the hypothesized direction (Malakoff, 2000). Simmons agreed to withdraw four published research papers, he was banned from receiving federal research grants for five years, and at last report his university was considering further disciplinary action that could include financial penalties and the revocation of his doctoral degree.

Although cases like these are rare (Marshall, 2000c), they undermine confidence in scientific and medical research. Increasingly concerned government agencies are taking steps to educate researchers about research ethics (Dalton, 2000), setting aside $1 million of grant money to support studies on research integrity (Marshall, 2000d), and discouraging ties between scientists and the companies whose products they are testing (Agnew, 2000).

Protecting the Welfare of Research Subjects

All the scientific disciplines that use live subjects in their research have adopted stringent codes for the humane treatment of both humans and animals. The specifics of the treatment of human research participants and even the legitimacy of animal research are controversial, however. These are not abstract issues. As a student you are a consumer of the knowledge that human and animal research produce, and you benefit from the medical and psychological advances, so you are more than just a neutral observer.

Research with Humans

In 1953 the psychologist Albert Ax performed a study that was as significant for its ethical implications as for its scientific results. He was attempting to determine whether all emotions result in the same general bodily arousal or each emotion produces a unique pattern of activation. To do so, he measured several physiological variables sensitive to emotional arousal, such as heart rate, breathing rate, and skin temperature, while inducing anger in the individuals at one time and fear at another. To disguise the nature of the study, the researchers said that the experiment was a comparison of people with hypertension (chronic high blood pressure) and people with normal blood pressure.

The "anger" treatment was relatively mild, though annoying: the subject was insulted by the researcher's assistant, who complained at length that the person was not a very good experimental subject. The "fear" situation was very different. During the recordings the subject received a mild electrical shock through the recording electrodes, while sparks jumped from nearby equipment. The experimenter acted alarmed as he explained that there was a dangerous high-voltage short circuit. Apparently the ruse worked. Ax reported that one participant kept pleading, "Please take the wires off. Oh! Please help me" (p. 435). Another said later that she had prayed to be spared, while a man said, "Well, everybody has to go sometime. I thought this might be my time." You will find the results of Ax's study in Chapter 7; in the meantime, the study raises questions about the closely related issues of informed consent and deception.

What are the principal ethical concerns in human research?

Occasionally, research involves some pain, discomfort, or even risk. Before proceeding with a study, a researcher must obtain the participant's informed consent. *Informed consent means voluntary participation after receiving full information about any risks, discomfort, or other adverse effects that might occur.* However, sometimes the nature of a study requires the experimenter to use *deception,* **either failing to tell the participants the exact purpose of the research or what will happen during the study, or actively misinforming them.** Albert Ax's study would have failed if the participants had been fully informed, because it would have altered their behavior. According to the American Psychological Association, deception is acceptable only when the value of the study justifies it, alternative procedures are not available, and the individuals are correctly informed afterward. The APA's guidelines are also clear, that "Psychologists never deceive research participants about significant aspects that would affect their willingness to participate, such as physical risks, discomfort, or unpleasant emotional experiences" (American Psychological Association, 1992, p. 1609). (And some researchers and subjects' rights advocates believe that deception is never justified.) Ax's study could not be done today, but we will see in Chapter 7 that researchers have found interesting alternatives for doing this kind of research.

Research with Animals

What are the opposing views on animal research?

The psychological and medical researcher has perhaps no more important resource than the laboratory animal. As the American Medical Association (1992, p. 11) concluded, "Virtually every advance in medical science in the twentieth century, from antibiotics and vaccines to anti-depressant drugs and organ transplants, has been achieved either directly or indirectly through the use of animals in laboratory experiments." Psychologists have used animals to investigate behavior, aging, pain, stress, and cognitive functions such as learning and perception (Blum, 1994; King, Yarbrough, Anderson, Gordon, & Gould, 1988; Miller,

1985). It may seem that the best subjects for that purpose would be humans, but animals are useful because they live in a controlled environment and have a homogeneous history of experience, as well as a briefer development and life span. In addition, researchers feel it is more ethical to use procedures that are painful or physically or psychologically risky on other animals rather than humans. As a result, U.S. scientists use about 20 million animals a year; 90% of them are rodents, mostly mice and rats, and around 3.5% are primates, mostly monkeys and chimpanzees (U.S. Congress Office of Technology Assessment, 1986).

Every one has heard of the dog suffering under vivisection, who licked the hand of the operator: this man, unless he had a heart of stone, must have felt remorse to the last hour of his life.

—Charles Darwin, *The Descent of Man in Relation to Sex*, 1871

The preference for inflicting discomfort or danger on nonhuman animals rather than humans is based on the assumption that the suffering of animals is more acceptable than suffering in humans. Animal rights activists have called this dual ethical standard *speciesism* (Herzog, 1998), a term chosen to be intentionally similar to *racism*. Some activists work hand-in-hand with researchers to improve conditions for research animals; others have been more aggressive, breaking into labs, destroying equipment and records, and releasing animals. In Europe and Britain activists have attacked researchers, threatened them with death, and forced them to take their work behind high fences (Koenig, 1999; Schiemeir, 1998).

Animal research guidelines provide for humane housing of animals, attention to their health, and minimization of discomfort and stress during research (American Psychological Association, 1992; American Psychological Association, 2001; Public Health Service,

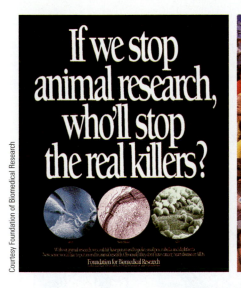

Figure 1.14
Animal research controversy
The poster on the left and the demonstration on the right illustrate the contrasting views of animal research.
Source: (Left) Courtesy of the Foundation for Biomedical Research.

1986). Both the APA and the Society for Neuroscience require review of animal care and research procedures by a local Institutional Animal Care and Use Committee. But critics point out that researchers sometimes do not live up to their professional organizations' standards. The Behavioral Biology Center in Silver Spring, Maryland, was engaged in research that involved severing the sensory nerve in one arm of monkeys to study the reorganization that occurs in the brain. The lab's contributions drew the praise of neuroscientists and led to the design of routines for extensive exercise of an afflicted limb to help people recover from brain injuries. But in 1981 a student summer employee informed police of what he considered to be abuse of the lab's animals, and the police carried out the first raid on a research laboratory in the United States (Orlans, 1993; "A Brighter Day," 1997). The director, Edward Taub, was convicted of animal abuse because of poor postoperative care, but the conviction was overturned because the state lacked jurisdiction over federally supported scientific research. The National Institutes of Health withdrew Taub's funding, and Congress enacted more stringent animal protection laws. In spite of the controversy, Taub received the William James Award from the American Psychological

Society. However, he points out that the award was for work that is no longer permitted, and that animal welfare rules enacted by Congress prevent him from taking measurements in the brain of the one remaining monkey for the length of time that would be needed.

The conflict between animal welfare and research needs is obviously not a simple issue, and is strongly felt on both sides (Figure 1.14). Though psychologists and neuroscientists do not condone mistreatment of research animals, most of them argue that the suffering that does occur is justified by the benefits animal research has produced. The 2000 Nobel Prize in physiology or medicine was shared by three neuroscientists: Arvid Carlsson for his discovery of the role of dopamine as a neurotransmitter in the brain; Paul Greengard, for identifying how dopamine and related neurotransmitters have their effect on neurons; and Eric Kandel, for his work on the molecular changes that occur in the brain during learning. The work of all three prize winners relied heavily on animal research.

It is unlikely that animal research will be banned as the more extreme activists demand, but animal care and use guidelines have been tightened and outside monitoring increased, and states have passed more stringent laws. In addition, researchers have become more sensitive to the welfare of animals, adopting more humane methods of treatment and turning to tissue cultures and computer simulations in place of live animals when possible.

New Technology, New Ethical Concerns

Human research has generated less controversy than the use of animals, largely because scientists are more restrained in their treatment of humans and humans are able to refuse to participate. The balance of concern is shifting, though, particularly in regard to genetic research.

Gene Therapy

What are the problems with gene research and gene therapy?

Gene therapy has enjoyed glowing press reviews because of its potential for correcting humanity's greatest handicaps and deadly diseases. But a distinct chill fell over the research on September 17, 1999, when Jesse Gelsinger, an 18-year-old volunteer, became the first human to die as the direct result of gene research (Lehrman, 1999; Marshall, 2000b). The study was using a deactivated form of adenovirus, which causes the common cold, to transport a gene into the liver in an experimental attempt to correct a genetic liver enzyme deficiency. Gelsinger developed an immune reaction to the adenovirus which resulted in his death.

Penn State University shut down the study, along with all clinical trials of gene therapy (Smaglik, 2000). The Food and Drug Administration (FDA), which was overseeing the study, reprimanded the researchers for not consulting with the FDA when most of the patients developed mild adverse reactions, and for not informing the research participants that two monkeys had died in an earlier study after receiving much larger doses of adenovirus ("US Government Shuts," 2000). The case has slowed gene therapy research across the country, but a positive outcome is that it is expected to lead to stricter supervision of human research (Figure 1.15).

There are additional concerns that gene manipulation could affect the reproductive cells

Figure 1.15
More protection for human subjects
Mounting concerns are leading to more stringent controls on human research.
Source: C. Macilwain, "Self-policing backed for research on humans," *Nature,* Volume 406, p. 7. Copyright © 2000, *Nature.* Reprinted with permission.

and produce effects that would be passed on to succeeding generations. As a result, the American Association for the Advancement of Science (2000) has called for a moratorium on research that might produce inheritable modifications. Even after the technology is deemed safe and reliable, important issues still remain. Some question the ethics of changing the genome of nonconsenting future generations, at least when survival is not at risk. Because it is very expensive, gene therapy is likely to further increase inequalities between the haves and have-nots in our society. And some worry that its application will not be limited to correcting disabilities and disease, but will be used to enhance the beauty, brawn, and intelligence of the offspring of well-to-do parents. The science fiction movie *GATTACA* (whose title is a play on the four letters of the genetic code) depicts a society in which privilege and opportunity are reserved for genetically enhanced "superior" individuals. For some critics of gene manipulation research, the possibility of a GATTACA-like world is frighteningly real (Vogel, 1997). The U.S. Congress wisely set aside 5% of the Human Genome Project budget to fund the study of ethical, legal, and social implications of genetic research (Jeffords & Daschle, 2001).

Using Human Embryos

For almost two decades, Anders Björkland and his colleagues at Lund University in Sweden have been grafting nerve cells into the brains of patients with Parkinson's disease (Lindvall et al., 1990). Patients with Parkinson's disease lose the ability to control their movements and eventually become rigid due to the death of nerve cells that produce dopamine. Dozens of these patients have been treated with nerve cell transplants (Figure 1.16), with reduction of symptoms up to 50% (Barinaga, 2000). So why should work that produces such gratifying results be controversial? Because the trans-

planted nerve cells come from aborted fetuses. Although 90–95% of the transplanted cells die, fetal cells have a greater chance of survival than mature cells. Anti-abortionists say that it is immoral to benefit from abortion, and they have tried to shut down research using tissue from aborted fetuses (Marshall, 2000a).

In any case, doctors will not be treating Parkinson's disease or any other disease by implanting nerve cells from fetuses. It takes six fetuses to produce enough cells to treat one Parkinson's patient, and even if researchers solve the problem of cell die-off there are just not enough fetal cells to be of practical use (Barinaga, 2000). As a result, researchers are turning to cultured stem cells.

Stem cells **are undifferentiated cells that have the potential of becoming any type of cell in the body.** During development before birth, stem cells (Figure 1.17) divide to produce daughter cells that are specialized; the specialized cells form our skin, organs, muscles, bones, blood, and brain. Stem cells also reproduce themselves to maintain a source of replacement cells after birth. Skin and blood cells need the most frequent replacement, but stem cells can also be found in the adult brain where, contrary to a long-held understanding among brain scientists, new nerve cells continue to be produced in some areas (Gage, 2000). Stem cells have the advantage that they can be coaxed into developing into a variety of

What is the promise of stem cells?

Syringe containing fetal neurons or stem cells

Location of Damage

Location of injection

Figure 1.16
Injecting cells into a damaged brain
Although the procedure is promising, it is controversial because of where the cells come from.

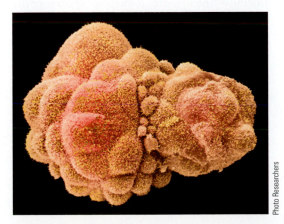

Photo Researchers

Figure 1.17
A stem cell
Because they can develop into any type of cell, stem cells offer tremendous therapeutic possibilities.

New Hope for Stroke Patients

Daniel Q. Haney (AP)—At the annual meeting of the American Association for the Advancement of Science in San Francisco on February 18, 2001, Paul Sanberg of the University of South Florida held out new hope for patients impaired by strokes. He reported that 80% of rats that had suffered strokes recovered within one month after being injected with stem cells, compared to about 20% of untreated rats. An important feature of the study was that the stem cells were injected into the bloodstream instead of directly into the brain, and found their way to the damaged site.

Sanberg plans to try the approach on human patients in a year or two.

Aside from the dramatic results, the study is remarkable for the source of stem cells: umbilical cords. Sanberg noted that four million babies are born every year and 99% of their cord blood is thrown away. He estimates that two umbilical cords would provide enough stem cells to treat one stroke victim, so this source would provide a plentiful and readily available supply of stem cells without the ethical problems associated with fetal stem cells.

different kinds of cells, apparently any cell in the body (Thomson et al., 1998). One hope is that they could be used to grow human organs in the laboratory to supply the unmet need for organ transplants. However, because most stem cells are obtained from aborted embryos their use is controversial.

Because stem cells can develop into nerve cells, it is possible they could be used to repair damaged brains and spinal cords (see "New Hope for Stroke Patients"). Rats have shown improved locomotion after stem cells were injected into their damaged spinal cords (McDonald et al., 1999), and improved movement when stem cells were used to treat brain damage (Ren et al., 2000). Studies suggest that stem cell implants might be just as successful in humans (Aboody et al., 2000; Sasaki et al., 2000); if so, an estimated 128 million people in the United States alone have diseases that are potentially treatable by stem cell therapy (Perry, 2000).

Although stem cells can reproduce in the laboratory, the initial cells are usually obtained from aborted embryos. Most of these are "extra" embryos resulting from fertility treat-

ment and would otherwise be discarded, but anti-abortionists oppose any harvesting of cells from embryos, and federal law prevents the use of government funds to extract cells from embryos (Vogel, 2000b). However, the National Institutes of Health can fund research conducted with stem cells from cell lines that existed before August 2001 (Vogel, 2001).

Just how many of the reported 60 cell lines are research-ready and available to other researchers is uncertain. In the meantime, two lines of research may provide alternatives to embryonic cells. Stem cells from adults can differentiate into a variety of cell types, and their differentiation may be more controllable than it is in embryonic cells (Vogel, 2000a). Also, unfertilized ova from a monkey have been induced to divide without losing half their chromosomes; they yielded stem cells that were then coaxed into developing into muscle cells, heartlike cells, and neurons (Cibelli et al., 2002). If these sources of stem cells turn out to be practical, the ethical issue will have been skirted and the potential for treating neurological disorders may be realized in spite of restraints on the research. As was the case with subjects' rights, the issues are far from simple, and circumstances more than ever require neuroscientists to be as sensitive to human values as they are innovative in the discipline.

Knowledge is power, and with power comes responsibility. For the scientists who study behavior, that responsibility is to the humans and animals that provide the source of our knowledge, and to the people who may be healed or harmed by the new treatments resulting from brain research. When researchers forget the rights of their subjects or ignore the implications of their research, they abuse the power of science.

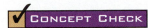

CONCEPT CHECK

- *What are the effects of dishonesty in research?*
- *How do researchers justify their use of animals in research?*
- *What is the major ethical problem with human stem cell research, and how might it be resolved?*

 In Perspective

In the first issue of the journal *Nature Neuroscience*, the editors observed that brain science still has a "frontier" feel to it ("From Neurons to Thoughts," 1998). The excitement Kay Jamison talked about is real and tangible, and the accomplishments are remarkable for such a young discipline. The successes come from many sources: the genius of our intellectual ancestors, the development of new technologies, the adoption of empiricism, and, I believe, a coming to terms with the concept of the mind. Evidence of all these influences will be apparent in the following chapters.

Neuroscience and biopsychology still have a long way to go. For all our successes, we do not fully understand what causes schizophrenia, exactly how the brain is changed by learning, or why some people are more intelligent than others. Near the end of the Decade of the Brain, Torsten Wiesel (whose landmark research in vision you will read about later) scoffed at the idea of dedicating a decade to the brain as "foolish . . . We need at least a century, maybe even a millennium" (quoted in Horgan, 1999, p. 18). As you read the rest of this book, keep in mind that you are on the threshold of that century's journey, that millennium of discovery.

 Summary

The Origins of Biopsychology

- Biopsychology developed out of physiology and philosophy as early psychologists adopted empiricism.
- Most psychologists and neuroscientists treat mind as a product of the brain, believing that mental activity can be explained in terms of the brain's functions.

Science, Research, and Theory

- Of the many research strategies at their disposal, biopsychologists favor the experimental approach because of the control it offers and the ability to determine cause and effect.
- Correlational techniques have value as well, particularly when the researcher lacks control.

continued

- Researchers respect uncertainty but try to reduce it through research and the use of theory.

Nature and Nurture

- We are learning that a number of behaviors are genetically influenced. One does not inherit a behavior itself, but genes influence structure and function in the brain and body in a way that influences behavior.

- Behavior is a product of both genes and our environment. In many cases genes produce a predisposition, and environment further determines the outcome. Separating the influence of heredity and environment is difficult, but twin and adoption studies help clarify the effects.

- With the knowledge of the genome map and the power of genetic engineering, we stand on the threshold of unbelievable opportunity and daunting ethical challenges.

Research Ethics

- A major concern in biopsychology is maintaining the integrity of research; plagiarism and fabrication of data are particularly serious infractions.

- Both the public and the scientific community are increasingly concerned about protecting the welfare of humans and animals in research. The various disciplines have standards for subject welfare, but the need for more monitoring and training is evident.

- An especially difficult ethical issue is the use of embryonic and fetal tissue in research and treatment. Alternatives are being developed which may or may not replace the use of these materials.

 For Further Thought

- Why, in the view of most neuroscientists, is materialistic monism the more productive approach for understanding the functions of the mind? What will be the best test of the correctness of this approach?

- Pay close attention as you read through this text and you will notice that the human studies are more likely than animal studies to be correlational. Why do you think this is so?

- Genetic engineering is mostly a research technique now; what practical uses can you imagine in the future?

- Is it unreasonable coercion to require a student in an Introduction to Psychology course to participate in research? to require a student in a Research Methods course to participate in research exercises during the laboratory sessions as a part of the educational experience? to offer money and a month's housing and meals to a homeless person to participate in a risky drug study?

- Do you think the rights of humans and animals are adequately protected in research? Why or why not? What do you think would be the effect of eliminating the use of animal subjects?

Testing Your Understanding

1. Discuss the relative merits of experimental and correlational research. Include an explanation of why more human studies than animal studies are correlational.

2. Discuss the interaction between heredity and environment in influencing behavior, including the concept of vulnerability.

3. Describe the different types of genetic engineering. How does this differ from the correlational approach of family, twin, and adoption studies as a means of determining whether a characteristic is hereditary?

4. Discuss the conflicts between research needs and animal rights.

Select the one best answer:

1. The idea that mind and brain are both physical is known as:
   a. idealistic monism.
   b. material monism.
   c. idealistic dualism.
   d. material dualism.

2. A model is:
   a. an organism or a system used to understand a more complex one.
   b. an hypothesis about the outcome of a study.
   c. an analogy, not intended to be entirely realistic.
   d. a plan for investigating a phenomenon.

3. Science is most distinguished from other disciplines by:
   a. the topics it studies.
   b. the precision of its work.
   c. the way it acquires knowledge.
   d. its reliance on naturalistic observation.

4. Experiments are considered superior to other research procedures because they:
   a. involve control over the variable of interest.
   b. permit control of variables not of interest.
   c. permit cause and effect conclusions.
   d. all of these.
   e. none of these.

5. A theory:
   a. is the first step in research.
   b. is the final stage of research.
   c. generates further research.
   d. is an opinion widely accepted among researchers.

6. A person with a gene for brown eyes and a gene for blue eyes will be brown-eyed because the gene for brown eyes is:
   a. dominant.   b. recessive.
   c. homozygous.   d. heterozygous.

7. The best way to separate heredity from environmental effects would be to compare the similarity of behavior between:
   a. fraternal and identical twins.
   b. relatives and nonrelatives.
   c. siblings reared together and reared apart.
   d. fraternal and identical twins, half of whom have been adopted out.

8. The most sensitive way to determine whether a particular gene produces a particular behavior would be to:
   a. compare the behavior in identical and fraternal twins.
   b. compare the behavior in people with and without the gene.
   c. use genetic engineering to manipulate the gene and note the behavior change.
   d. find out whether people with the behavior have the gene more often than people without the behavior.

9. The Human Genome Project has:
   a. counted the number of human genes.
   b. made a map of the human genes.
   c. determined the function of each gene.
   d. cloned most of the human genes.

10. The estimated heritability for intelligence will be greatest if the subjects happen to be selected so that their:
   a. genetic differences are great and environmental differences are small.
   b. genetic differences are small and environmental differences are great.
   c. genetic differences and environmental differences are equally great.
   d. genetic differences and environmental differences are equally small.

continued

11. Speciesism refers to the belief that:

    a. humans are better research subjects than animals.
    b. it is more ethical to do risky experiments on lower animals than humans.
    c. humans are the superior species.
    d. all of these.
    e. none of these.

12. The biggest obstacle to using stem cells for research and therapy would be eliminated if researchers could:

    a. get more of them.
    b. get them to differentiate into neurons.
    c. get them to survive longer.
    d. get adult stem cells to work as well as fetal ones.

Answers: 1. **b** 2. **a** 3. **c** 4. **d** 5. **c** 6. **a** 7. **d** 8. **c** 9. **b** 10. **a** 11. **b** 12. **d**

On the Web

1. **Mind and Body** covers the history of the idea from René Descartes to William James. Sections I: 1–5 and II: 1–2 are most pertinent.

   http://serendip.brynmawr.edu/Mind/Table.html

2. You can get updates on the Human Genome Project and news of genetic research breakthroughs from **Functional Genomics** at

   http://www.sciencemag.org/feature/plus/sfg/

   and **Genome Gateway** at

   http://www.nature.com/genomics/

3. *Ethical Principles of Psychologists and Code of Conduct* of the American Psychological Association is at http://www.apa.org/ethics/. A revised version should be available by the time you read this.

4. You can download several articles expressing contrasting opinions on animal research from **Scientific American Archives** at *https://www.sciamarchive.com* Search for February 1997 (or see that issue in library).

   An article describing the **Animal Liberation Front** is available at

   http://www.guardianunlimited.co.uk/Archive/Article/0,4273,3824140,00.html

5. Additional sites:

   Some of the journals publishing neuroscience articles:

   Journal of Neuroscience

   http://www.jneurosci.org/

   Science

   http://www.sciencemag.org/

   Nature

   http://www.nature.com/

   Nature Neuroscience

   http://www.nature.com/neurosci

   Scientific American (nonprofessional; for the general reader)

   http://www.sciam.com

   General information sites:

   Brain Briefings (various topics in neuroscience) at

   http://apu.sfn.org/content/Publications/BrainBriefings/index.html

   Neuroguide (various topics and a search service) at

   http://www.neuroguide.com/

For additional information about the topics covered in this chapter, please look at InfoTrac College Edition, at *http://www.infotrac-college.com/wadsworth*

Try search terms you think up yourself, or use these: *Human Genome Project; natural selection; nature versus nurture; stem cell therapy.*

 ## On the CD-ROM: Exploring Biological Psychology

Video: Offspring of Parents Homozygous and Heterozygous for Brown Eyes

Video: RNA, DNA, and Protein

 ## For Further Reading

"The Emergence of Modern Neuroscience: Some Implications for Neurology and Psychiatry," by W. Maxwell Cowan, Donald H. Harter, and Eric R. Kandel (*Annual Review of Neuroscience*, 2000, 23, 343–391) describes the emergence of neuroscience as a separate discipline in the 1950s and 1960s, then details its most important accomplishments in understanding disorders.

"Neuroscience: Breaking Down Scientific Barriers to the Study of Brain and Mind,"
by E. R. Kandel and Larry Squire (*Science*, 2000, *290*, 111–1120) is a briefer treatment of the recent history of neuroscience, with an emphasis on psychological issues; a time line of events over more than three centuries is included.

Opposing views of several writers on research deception are presented in the *American Psychologist*, July 1997, 746–747, and July 1998, 803–807.

 ## Key Terms

adoption study *12*

antisense RNA *13*

biopsychology *2*

concordance rate *12*

confounded *7*

correlation *12*

correlational study *7*

deception *20*

deoxyribonucleic acid (DNA) *10*

dependent variable *7*

dizygotic (DZ) *12*

dominant *10*

dualism *3*

embryo *10*

empiricism *6*

experiment *7*

fabrication *19*

family study *11*

fetus *10*

fraternal twins *12*

genetic engineering *13*

genotype *10*

heritability *17*

continued

heterozygous *10*

homozygous *10*

Human Genome Project *14*

hypothesis *8*

identical twins *12*

independent variable *7*

informed consent *20*

knockout mice *13*

localization *5*

materialistic monism *3*

mind-brain problem *3*

model *4*

monism *3*

monozygotic (MZ) *12*

natural selection *16*

nature versus nurture *9*

neuroscience *2*

objective *7*

phenotype *10*

plagiarism *18*

polygenic *10*

recessive *10*

ribonucleic acid (RNA) *13*

stem cells *23*

theory *8*

transgenic mice *13*

twin study *12*

vulnerability *18*

X-linked *10*

zygote *9*

one

PART

Neural Foundations of Behavior: The Basic Equipment

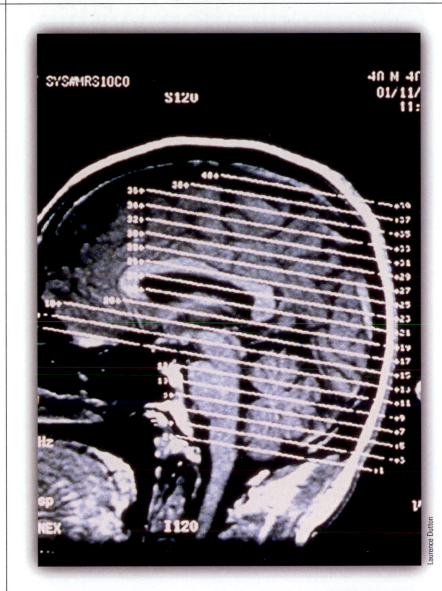

Laurence Dutton

Communication Within the Nervous System

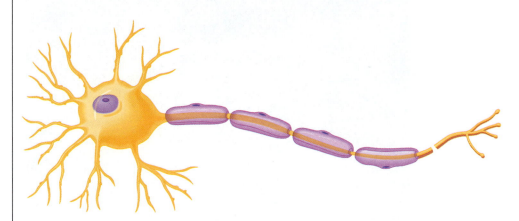

In this chapter you will learn:

- How neurons are specialized to conduct information.

- How glial cells support the activity of neurons.

- How neurons communicate with each other.

- Strategies neurons use to increase their information capacity.

- The functions of some of the major chemical transmitters.

- How computer-simulated neurons are modeling many brain functions

Things were looking good for Jim and his wife. She was pregnant with their first child and they had just purchased and moved into a new home. After the exterminating company treated the house by injecting pesticide under the concrete slab, Jim noticed that the carpet was wet and there was a chemical smell in the air. He dried the carpet with towels and thought no more about it, not realizing that chlordane can be absorbed through the skin. A few days later he developed headaches, fatigue, and numbness. Worse, he had problems with memory, attention, and reasoning. His physician referred him to the toxicology research center of a large university medical school. His intelligence test score was normal, but more specific tests of cognitive ability confirmed the deficiencies he was reporting. Jim and his wife had to move out of their home. At work he had to accept reduced responsibilities because of his difficulties in concentration and adapting to novel situations. The chlordane had not damaged the structure of his brain as you might suspect, but it interfered with the functioning of the individual neurons by impairing a mechanism called the sodium-potassium pump (Zillmer & Spiers, 2001).

THE CELLS THAT MAKE US WHO WE ARE

To understand human behavior and the disorders that affect it, we must understand how the brain works. And to understand how the brain works we must have at least a speaking acquaintance with the cells that carry messages back and forth in the brain and throughout the rest of the body. *Neurons* **are specialized cells that convey sensory information into the brain, carry out the operations involved in thought and feeling and action, and transmit commands out into the body to control muscles and organs.** It is estimated that there are about 100 billion neurons in the human brain (Williams & Herrup, 1988). This means there are more neurons in your brain than stars in our galaxy. But as numerous and as important as they are, neurons make up only 10% of the brain's cells and about half of its volume. The other 90% are *glial cells,* **which provide a variety of supporting services for neurons.**

Neurons

Neurons have the responsibility of producing all the things we do—our movements, our thoughts, our memories, our emotions. It is difficult to believe that anything so simple as a cell can measure up to this task, and the burden is on the neuroscientist to demonstrate that this is true. As you will see, the neuron is deceptively simple in its action but impressively complex in its function.

Basic Structure: The Motor Neuron

Figure 2.1, on the next page, illustrates a typical neuron. I say "typical" guardedly, because there are four major kinds of neurons and variations within those types. This particular type is a *motor neuron,* **which carries commands to the muscles and organs.** It is particularly useful for illustrating the structure and functions that neurons share in common. **The** *soma,* **or cell body, contains the cell's nucleus, most of the cytoplasm, and structures that convert nutrients into energy and eliminate waste materials.** So far, this could be the description of any cell in the body; it is the other structures that enable the neuron to carry out its specialized role. *Dendrites* **are extensions that branch out from the soma to receive information from**

What are the parts of the neuron?

Figure 2.1
Components of a neuron
The illustration is of a motor neuron.

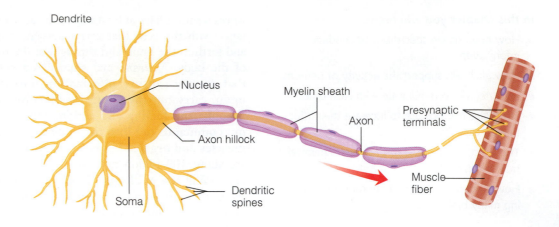

other neurons. Their branching structure allows them to collect information widely. **The *axon* extends like a tail from the cell body and carries information to other locations**, sometimes across great distances. The myelin sheath that is shown wrapped around the axon supports the axon and provides other benefits which we will consider later. **Branches at the end of the axon culminate in swellings called end bulbs or *terminals*. The terminals contain chemical *neurotransmitters*, which the neuron releases to communicate with a muscle or an organ or the next neuron in a chain. The connection between two neurons is called a *synapse*,** a term derived from the Latin word that means "to grasp." In our examples we will talk as if neurons form a simple chain, with one cell sending messages to a single other neuron, and so on; in actuality, a neuron receives input from many neurons and sends its output to many others.

Neurons are usually so small they can be seen only with the aid of a microscope. The soma, the largest part of the neuron, ranges from 0.005 millimeter (mm) to 0.1 mm in diameter in mammals. (In case you are unfamiliar with metric measurements, a millimeter is about the thickness of a dime.) Even the giant neurons of the squid, favored by researchers for their conveniently large size, have cell bodies that are but a millimeter in diameter. Axons, of course, are smaller; in

mammals they range from 0.002 mm to 0.02 mm in diameter. Axons can be anywhere from 0.1 mm to 3 meters in length.

Other Types of Neurons

The second type of neuron is the sensory neuron. ***Sensory neurons*** **carry information from the body and from the outside world into the central nervous system** (the brain and spinal cord). Notice that motor and sensory neurons have the same components; they also work the same way. An obvious difference is the location of the soma (see Figure 2.2a and b). In a motor neuron the axon and the dendrites extend in several directions from the soma, which is why it is called a *multipolar* neuron. The sensory neuron in Figure 2.2a is called a *unipolar* neuron because of the single short stalk that divides into two branches. *Bipolar* neurons have an axon on one side of the soma and a dendritic process on the other (Figure 2.2b); bipolar neurons are also usually sensory. Motor and sensory neurons are specialized for transmission over long distances; their lengths are not shown here in the same scale as the rest of the cell.

Not all neurons can be classified as motor or sensory. ***Interneurons*** **connect one neuron to another in the same part of the central nervous system; they have a short axon or no axon at all** (see Figure 2.2c). In the spinal cord, interneurons bridge between sensory neurons and motor neurons to produce a

How do the major types of neurons differ?

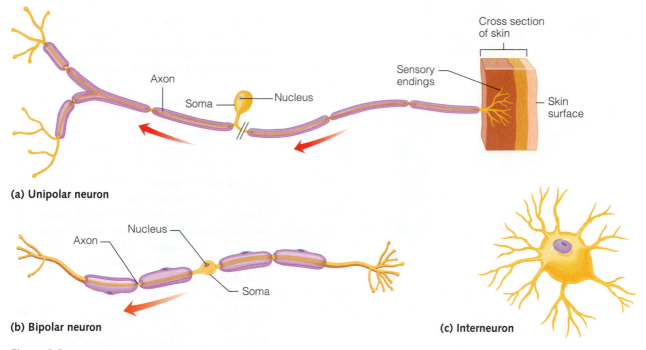

(a) **Unipolar neuron**

(b) **Bipolar neuron**

(c) **Interneuron**

Figure 2.2
Sensory neurons and an interneuron
Compare the location of the soma in relation to the dendrites and axon in these and in the motor neuron.

reflex. In the brain, they connect adjacent neurons to carry out the complex processing the brain is noted for. Considering the major role they play in the central nervous system, it should come as no surprise that interneurons are the most numerous. Finally, *projection neurons* **are similar to interneurons, but they have longer axons and communicate over somewhat longer distances within the central nervous system.**

The different kinds of neurons operate similarly. The big difference among the four types is in their shape that fits them for their specialized tasks. We will examine how neurons work in the next few sections.

The Neural Membrane

The most critical factor for the neuron's ability to communicate is the membrane that encloses the cell. The membrane is exceptionally thin—only about 8 millimicrons (mµ, billionths of a meter) thick, and is made up of lipid (fat) and

protein (see Figure 2.3, on the next page). Each lipid molecule has a "head" end and a "tail" end. The heads of the molecules are water soluble, so they are attracted to water; the tails are water insoluble, and are repelled. The extracellular fluid around the cells and the intracellular fluid inside the cell are similar to seawater. Therefore, as the heads orient toward the fluid and the tails orient away from the fluid, the molecules turn their tails toward each other, and form a double-layer membrane.

The membrane not only holds a cell together, but controls the environment within and around the cell. Some molecules, like water, oxygen, and carbon dioxide, can pass through the membrane freely. Many other substances are barred from entry. Still others are allowed limited passage, through protein channels (shown here in green) that open and close under different circumstances. This selective permeability contributes to the most fundamental characteristic of neurons, *polarization,*

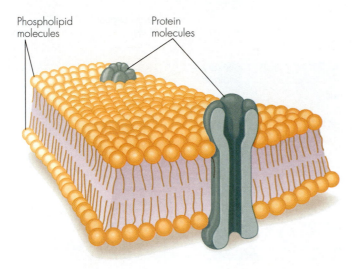

Figure 2.3
Cross section of the cell membrane of a neuron
Notice how the lipid molecules form the membrane by orienting their heads toward the extracellular and intracellular fluids.

which means that there is a difference in electrical charge between the inside and the outside of the cell. A difference in electrical charge is called a *potential*.

The Resting Potential The membrane's potential is due to the unequal distribution of electrical charges on the two sides of the membrane. **The charges come from *ions*, atoms that are charged because they have lost or gained one or more electrons.** Sodium ions (Na^+) and potassium ions (K^+) are positively charged. Chloride ions (Cl^-) are negative, and so are certain proteins and amino acids that make up the organic anions (A^-). The fluid outside the neuron is high in Na^+ and Cl^- ions, and there is more K^+ and A^- on the inside. A voltage can be measured between the inside and the outside of the cell, just like you measure the voltage of a flashlight battery (see Figure 2.4). **The difference in charge between the inside and outside of the**

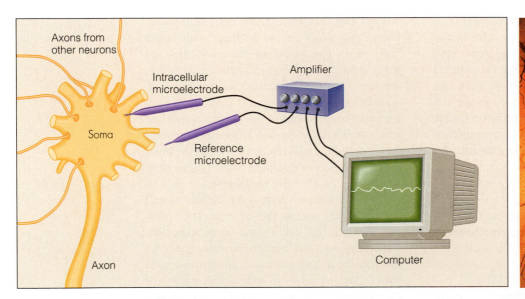

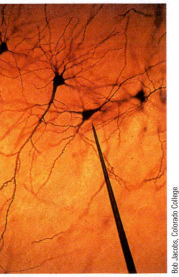

Figure 2.4
Recording potentials in a neuron
Potentials are being recorded in the axon of a neuron, with an electrode inside the cell and one in the fluid outside. On the right is a microscopic view of a microelectrode about to penetrate a neuron.

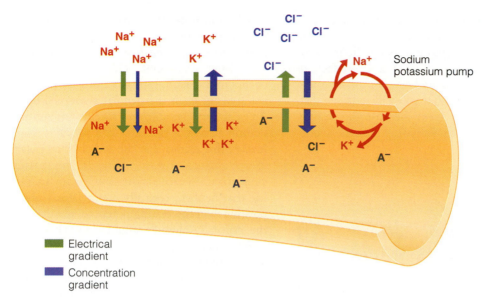

Figure 2.5
Distribution and gradients of ions in a neuron
The arrows indicate the direction of the forces and their widths indicate the relative force.

Sodium potassium pump

■ Electrical gradient

■ Concentration gradient

membrane of a neuron at rest is called the *resting potential.* The voltage varies anywhere from –40 millivolts (mV) to –80 mV in different neurons, but is typically around –70 mV. By arbitrary convention, the membrane voltage is measured with the inside referenced to the outside. Notice that this voltage is quite small—the voltage of each 1.5-V battery in your portable CD player is 25 times greater. No matter; we're moving information and very little power is required.

If you remember from grade-school science that there is a tendency for molecules to diffuse from an area of high concentration to one of low concentration, then you are probably wondering how this imbalance in ion distribution can continue to exist. There are, in fact, two forces that work to balance the location of the ions. **Because of the *concentration gradient,* which is a difference in location of ions between the inside and outside of the neuron, ions move through the membrane to the side where they are less concentrated. Similarly, as a result of the *electrical gradient,* which is a difference in electrical charge between the inside and outside of the neuron, ions are attracted to the side that is oppositely**

charged. However, these balancing forces are opposed by a variety of other influences.

First of all, the organic anions are too large to pass through the membrane, so they are locked inside the neuron (Figure 2.5). The chloride ions are repelled by the organic anions' negative charge, but they are simultaneously attracted inside where they are less concentrated; the forces of the concentration gradient and the electrical gradient cancel each other out. In the case of the potassium ions, the concentration gradient that moves K$^+$ ions outside is slightly greater than the electrical gradient attracting them to the negative interior. Na$^+$ ions are attracted inside by both forces. Ions may cross the membrane only through channels that are selective for particular ions, and the movement most of the time is very slow.

The Na$^+$ ions that make it through the membrane into the neuron and the K$^+$ ions that flow out are returned by the sodium-potassium pump. **The *sodium-potassium pump* consists of large protein molecules that move Na$^+$ ions through the cell membrane to the outside and K$^+$ ions back inside.** Its exchange rate of three sodium ions

What accounts for the resting potential?

How is an action potential different from a graded potential?

for every two potassium ions helps keep the inside of the membrane more negative than the outside. The pump is a metabolic process, which means that it uses energy; in fact, it accounts for an estimated 40% of the neuron's energy expenditure. But you will soon see that this energy is well spent, because the resting potential stores the energy to power the action potential.

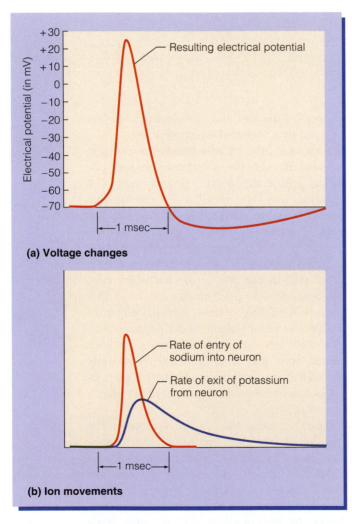

(a) Voltage changes

(b) Ion movements

Figure 2.6
Voltage changes and ion movements during the action potential

The Action Potential **The *action potential* is an abrupt depolarization of the membrane that allows the neuron to communicate over long distances.** The action potential occurs in the axon, typically initiated by a signal arriving from the dendrites and cell body. An excitatory signal from a receptor or another neuron arrives at the axon as a partial *depolarization*; this means that the membrane's polarity is shifted toward zero. If the partial depolarization exceeds the *threshold* for activating that neuron, typically about 10 mV more positive than the resting potential, it will cause the normally closed sodium channels in that area to open.

The potential across the resting neuron membrane is stored energy. Imagine countless sodium ions being held outside the neuron against the combined forces of the concentration gradient and the electrical gradient. Opening the sodium channels allows the Na$^+$ ions in that area to rush into the axon at a rate 500 times greater than normal; they are propelled into the cell's interior so rapidly that the movement is often described as explosive. A small area inside the membrane becomes fully depolarized to zero; the potential even overshoots to around +30 or +40 mV, making the interior at that location temporarily positive. This depolarization is the action potential. Figure 2.6a is a graphic representation of the voltage changes that occur.

Just as abruptly as the neuron "fired," it begins to recover its resting potential. At the peak of the action potential the sodium channels close, so there is no further depolarization. About the same time, the potassium channels begin to open. The positive charge inside the membrane and the force of the concentration gradient combine to move K$^+$ ions out; this outward flow of potassium ions returns the axon to its resting potential. The action potential and recovery require about a millisecond (msec, one-thousandth of a second) or so to complete; the actual duration varies among individual neurons. You can see in Figure 2.6b how the movement of Na$^+$ and K$^+$

ions parallels the voltage changes of the action potential and recovery.

The action potential causes nearby sodium channels to open as well. Thus, a new action potential is triggered right next to the first one. That action potential in turn triggers another farther along, creating a chain reaction of action potentials that move through the axon; thus, a signal flows from one end of the neuron to the other. Nothing physically moves down the axon. Instead, a series of events occurs in succession along the axon's length, much as a line of dominoes stood on end knock each other over when you tip the first one. When the action potential reaches the terminals, they pass the signal on to the next neuron in the chain (or to an organ or muscle). We will talk more about transmission from neuron to neuron later; but for now we need to examine the action potential a bit further.

Although the neuron has returned to its resting potential, a number of extra Na^+ ions remain inside and there is an excess of K^+ ions on the outside. Actually, only the ions in a very thin layer on either side of the membrane have participated in the action potential, so the dislocated ions are able to diffuse into the surrounding fluid. Eventually, though, the ions must be replaced or the neuron cannot continue firing. The sodium-potassium pump takes care of this chore.

The action potential differs in two important ways from the partial depolarization that initiates it. First, the partial depolarization is *graded*, that is, it varies in magnitude with the size of the stimulus that produced it. The action potential is *ungraded*; it operates according to the **all-or-none law, which means that it occurs at full strength or it does not occur at all.** A larger graded potential does not produce a larger action potential; like the fuse of a firecracker, the action potential depends on the energy stored in the neuron. A second difference is that a graded potential is *decremental*, dying out as it goes, while the action potential is *non-decremental*; it travels down the axon without any decrease in

size, propagated anew and at full strength at each successive point along the way.

Because the action potential is all-or-none, its size cannot carry information about the intensity of the initiating stimulus. One way stimulus intensity is represented is in the number of neurons firing, because a more intense stimulus will recruit firing in neurons with higher thresholds. However, there is a way that the individual neuron can encode stimulus strength, as we will see in the discussion of refractory periods.

Refractory Periods

Right after the action potential occurs, the neuron goes through the ***absolute refractory period*, a brief time during which it cannot fire again because the sodium channels cannot reopen.** This delay in responsiveness has two important effects. First, the absolute refractory period limits how frequently the neuron can fire. If a neuron takes a full millisecond to recover to the point it can fire again, then the neuron can fire, at most, a thousand times a second; many neurons have much lower firing rate limits. A second effect of this recovery period is that the action potential will set off new action potentials only in front of it (the side toward the terminals), not on the side where it has just passed. This is critical, because backward-moving potentials would "lock up" the neuron to newly arriving messages.

A second refractory period plays a role in intensity coding in the axon. The potassium channels remain open for a few milliseconds following the absolute refractory period, and the continued exit of K^+ makes the inside of the neuron slightly more negative than usual (see Figure 2.6a and b again). During the ***relative refractory period* the neuron can be fired again, but only by a stronger-than-threshold stimulus.** A stimulus that is greater than threshold will cause the neuron to fire again earlier, and thus more frequently. **The axon encodes stimulus intensity not in the size of its action potential but in its firing rate, an effect called the *rate law*.**

What is the role of the Na^+-K^+ pump following an action potential?

What are the absolute and relative refractory periods?

Targeting Ion Channels

Neuron channel activity is vulnerable to manipulation by external agents, for both good and ill. For example, the *neurotoxins* (neuron poisons) in a number of animal venoms interfere with channel activity to the obvious detriment of the victim. Some snake venoms block Na⁺ channels and others block K⁺ channels (Benoit & Dubois, 1986; Fertuck & Salpeter, 1974). Most scorpion venoms bind to Na⁺ channels and prolong the action potential by enhancing channel opening or delaying channel closing (Catterall, 1984; Chuang, Jaffe, Cribbs, Perez-Reyes, & Swartz, 1998; Pappone & Cahalan, 1987).

Tetrodotoxin (TDT) blocks Na⁺ channels (Kandel & Siegelbaum, 2000a), making it impossible for the neuron to fire; the milder symptoms of TDT poisoning are numbness and weakness, but it can cause paralysis, most importantly in the muscles involved in breathing. This is the most curious example of neuronal poisoning, because TDT is self-administered. TDT is found in puffer fish, a delicacy known in Japan as *fugu* and prized for the tingling sensation it produces in the mouth of the diner. Part of the attraction is also the thrill of the Russian-roulette flirtation with death; a few thousand Japanese gourmands have died from improperly prepared fish dinners.

Fortunately, there is an upside to the effects of neurotoxins: because they influence ion channel activity, they have been a major research tool for identifying ion channels and studying their functioning (Albuquerque, Daly, & Warnick, 1988; Pappone & Cahalan, 1987). Modifying channel activity can also have practical benefits. Most local anesthetics work by attaching to Na⁺ channels; with the channels blocked, little Na⁺ enters the axon and the neuron cannot fire (Ragsdale, McPhee, Scheuer, & Catterall, 1994). General anesthetics open K⁺ channels, allowing K⁺ ions to leak out of the neuron; this increases the polarization of the membrane (makes it more negative) and prevents the neuron from firing (Nicoll & Madison, 1982; Patel et al., 1999).

The channels provide such an important avenue for affecting neurons and nervous system functioning that researchers are experimenting with creating "designer" channels in cells. They are taking advantage of the fact that *Staphylococcus* and *Streptococcus* bacteria produce proteins that bore into cell membranes and form channels that damage or kill the cell. By modifying the protein molecule, it is possible to create channels which can be opened or closed on command, using electrical stimulation, light, enzymes, or chemicals (see the figure). The most obvious use of these customized channels would be as a gateway for delivering drugs directly into cells, particularly neurons or tumor cells (Bayley, 1997).

Laboratory-modified protein molecules creating channels in cell membrane
Custom channels provide controllable access to cells for research or therapeutic purposes.
Source: H. Bayley, "Building doors into cells." Scientific American *(Sept. 1997), pp. 62–67.* Reprinted by permission of Alfred Kamajian.

Glial Cells

The name *glia* is derived from the Greek word for glue, which gives you some idea how the role of glial cells has been viewed in the past. However, glial cells do much more than hold neurons together. One of the glial cells' most important functions is to help increase the speed of communication between neurons.

Survival depends in part on how rapidly messages can move through the nervous system. Conduction speed varies in neurons from 1 meter per second (m/sec) up to 120 m/sec, or about 270 miles per hour. This is much slower than the flow of electricity through a wire, the analogy mistakenly used to describe neural conduction; because conduction speed is so critical to survival, animals have evolved strategies for increasing it. One way is to develop larger axons. Larger axons provide less resistance to the flow of electrical potentials, so impulses are triggered more easily and move down the axon more rapidly. By evolving motor neurons with a diameter of 0.5 mm, the squid has achieved conduction speeds of 30 m/sec, compared to 1 m/sec in the smallest neurons.

However, conduction speed does not increase in direct proportion to axon diameter, but in proportion to the *square root* of the diameter. This makes the speed gain very costly to the organism. To reach our four-times-greater maximum conduction speed of 120 m/sec, our axons would have to be $4^2 = 16$ times larger than the squid axon, or 8 mm in diameter! Obviously, your brain would be larger than you could carry around. In other words, if axon size were the only way to achieve fast conduction speed, you would not exist.

Myelination and Conduction Speed

A better way to increase speed in neurons is employed by vertebrates (animals with backbones), including humans. It is called myelination. **Glial cells produce *myelin*, a fatty tissue that wraps around the axon to insulate it from the surrounding fluid and from other neurons.** Only the axon is covered, not the cell body. Myelin is produced in the brain and spinal cord by *oligodendrocytes* and, in the rest of the nervous system, by *Schwann cells* (see Figure 2.7, on the next page, as well as Figures 2.1 and 2.2).

Myelin does not cover the entire length of the axon in a continuous sheath. Each segment of myelin is about 1 mm long, with a gap of about one or two thousandths of a millimeter between segments. **The gaps in the myelin sheath are called *nodes of Ranvier*** (see Figure 2.7 again, as well as Figures 2.1 and 2.2). Under the myelin there are very few Na^+ channels, so transmission between the nodes is by graded potential (Waxman & Ritchie, 1985). The graded potential triggers an action potential at each node of Ranvier; **action potentials thus jump from node to node in a form of transmission called *saltatory conduction*.** The name is appropriate since it comes from the Latin *saltare*, which means "to dance" or "to jump."

Saltatory conduction is faster than conduction in unmyelinated axons. This is because graded potentials travel down the membrane faster than the membrane can propagate a series of action potentials. Myelination improves further on that speed because the insulating effect of myelin reduces an electrical effect called *capacitance*, which resists the movement of ions during a graded potential. The effect of myelination is the equivalent of increasing the axon diameter by 100 times (Koester & Siegelbaum, 2000). Since graded potentials are faster, you might wonder why neurons rely on action potentials at all; but remember that graded potentials diminish over distance. The action potential at each node of Ranvier renews the graded potential's strength. Speed is not the only benefit of myelination; myelinated neurons use tremendously less energy because there is less work for the sodium-potassium pump to do.

Some diseases, like multiple sclerosis, destroy myelin. As myelin is lost the capacitance rises, reducing the distance that graded potentials can travel before dying out. The individual is worse off than if the neurons had never been myelinated. Due to the reduced number of sodium channels, action potentials may not be generated in the previously myelinated area. Conduction slows or stops in affected neurons.

What are the functions of glial cells?

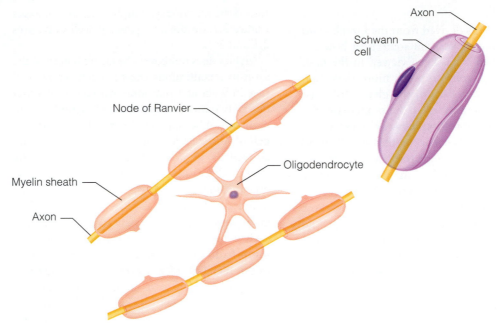

Figure 2.7
Glial cells produce myelin for axons
A single oligodendrocyte provides myelin for multiple segments of the axon, and for multiple neurons. A Schwann cell covers only one segment of an axon.

Other Glial Functions

During fetal development one kind of glial cells forms a scaffold that guides new neurons to their destination. Later on, other glial cells provide physical support for neurons, clean up debris, and absorb leftover neurotransmitter at some synapses. Now we are learning that glia may be intimately involved in neural activity itself. They release neurotransmitters and they have receptors for neurotransmitters. They probably do not transmit information like neurons do, but they respond to activity in neurons and, in turn, probably help regulate activity in the neurons (Bezzi et al., 1998; Kang, Jiang, Goldman, & Nedergaard, 1998; Parpura & Haydon, 2000; Pasti, Volterra, Pozzan, & Carmignoto, 1997). They even appear to be necessary for developing and maintaining connections between neurons at the synapses. Neurons form seven times as many connections in the presence of glial cells, and if glial cells are removed from a culture dish

of neurons the neurons start to lose their synapses (Ullian, Sapperstein, Christopherson, & Barres, 2001).

CONCEPT CHECK

- *How is information conducted in the axon?*
- *How does the all-or-none law limit information transmission?*
- *What benefits do the refractory periods provide?*
- *How does myelin speed up conduction in axons?*

HOW NEURONS COMMUNICATE WITH EACH OTHER

Before the late 1800s, microscopic examination suggested to anatomists that the brain consisted of a continuous web. At that point, however,

2

Camillo Golgi developed a new tissue-staining method that helped them see individual neurons by randomly staining some entire cells without staining others (see the discussion of staining methods in A.1 of the appendix). With this technique the Spanish anatomist Santiago Ramón y Cajal (1937/1989) was able to see that each neuron is a separate cell. **The neurons are not in direct physical contact at the synapse but are separated by a small gap called the synaptic cleft.**

Chemical Transmission at the Synapse

Until the 1920s physiologists assumed that neurons communicated by an electrical current that bridged the gap to the next neuron. The German physiologist Otto Loewi (1953) believed that synaptic transmission was chemical, but he did not know how to test his hypothesis.

I awoke again, at three o'clock, and I remembered what it was. . . . I got up immediately, went to the laboratory, made the experiment . . . and at five o'clock the chemical transmission of the nervous impulse was conclusively proved.

—Otto Loewi

The night before, Loewi had awakened from sleep with the solution to his problem (Loewi, 1953). He wrote his idea down so he would not forget it, but the next morning he could not read his own writing. He recalled that day as the most "desperate of my whole scientific life" (p. 33). But the following night he awoke again with the same idea; taking no chances, he rushed to his laboratory. There he isolated the hearts of two frogs. He stimulated the vagus nerve of one with electricity, which made the heart beat slower. Then he extracted salt solution that he had placed in the heart beforehand and placed it in the second heart. If neu-

rons used a chemical messenger, the chemical might have leaked into the salt solution. The second heart slowed, too, just as Loewi expected (see Figure 2.8). Then he stimulated the accelerator nerve of the first heart, which caused the heart to beat faster. When he transferred salt solution from the first heart to the second, this time it speeded up. So Loewi had demonstrated that transmission at the synapse is chemical, and that there are at least two different chemicals that carry out different functions.

It turned out later that some neurons do communicate electrically, passing ions through channels that connect one neuron to the next, but electrical synapses are found mostly in invertebrates. In addition, some neurons release a gas transmitter. Still, Loewi was essentially correct because most synapses are chemical. By the way, if this example suggests to you that the best way to solve a problem is to "sleep on it," keep in mind that such insight occurs only when people have paid their dues in hard work beforehand!

How does synaptic transmission differ from transmission in the axon?

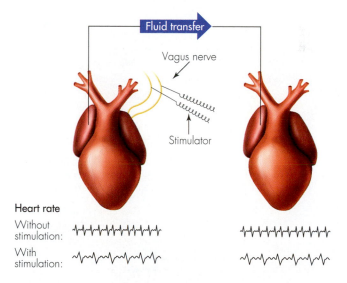

Figure 2.8
Loewi's experiment demonstrating chemical transmission in neurons
Loewi stimulated the first frog heart. When he transferred fluid from it to the second heart, it produced the same effect there as the stimulation did in the first heart.

At chemical synapses, the **neurotransmitter is stored in the terminals in membrane-enclosed containers called** *vesicles;* the term means, appropriately, "little bladder." When the action potential arrives at the terminals it opens channels that allow calcium ions (Ca^{2+}) to enter the terminals from the extracellular fluid. (The $^{2+}$ simply means that the calcium ion has two extra positive charges, compared to one extra positive charge each for sodium and potassium ions, Na^+ and K^+.) The calcium ions cause the vesicles clustered nearest the membrane to fuse with the membrane. The membrane opens there and the transmitter spills out and diffuses across the cleft.

Two terms will be useful to us in the following discussion: **the neuron that is transmitting to another is called the** *presynaptic* **neuron; the receiving neuron is the** *postsynaptic* **neuron.** At the postsynaptic membrane the molecules of neurotransmitter dock in a lock-and-key fashion with specialized chemical receptors that match the molecular shape of the transmitter molecules (Figure 2.9). Activation of these receptors causes ion channels in the membrane to open. The receptors can open the channels directly or by releasing intermediate proteins which open the channels. Opening the channels is what sets off the graded potential that initiates the action potential. We will see in the next section that the effect this has on the postsynaptic neuron depends on which receptors are activated.

The chemical jump across the synapse takes a couple of milliseconds; that is a significant slowing compared to transmission in the axon. In a system that places a premium on speed, inserting these gaps in the neural pathway must add some compensating benefit. As you will see in the following sections, synapses add important complexity to the neuron's simple yes-no response.

Excitation and Inhibition

Opening ion channels has one of two effects: it causes the local membrane potential to shift in a positive direction toward zero, partially depolarizing the membrane, or it shifts the potential farther in the negative direction. **Partial depolarization, or** *hypopolarization,* **is excitatory and facilitates the occurrence of an action potential; increased polarization, or** *hyperpolarization,* **is inhibitory and makes an action potential less likely to occur.** The value of excitation is obvious, but inhibition can communicate just as much information as excitation does. Also, the message becomes more complex if input from one source can partially or completely negate input from another. In addition, inhibition helps prevent runaway excitation; one cause of the uncontrolled neural storms that sweep across the brain during an epileptic seizure is a deficiency in an inhibitory transmitter system (Baulac et al., 2001).

What determines whether the effect on the postsynaptic neuron is facilitating or

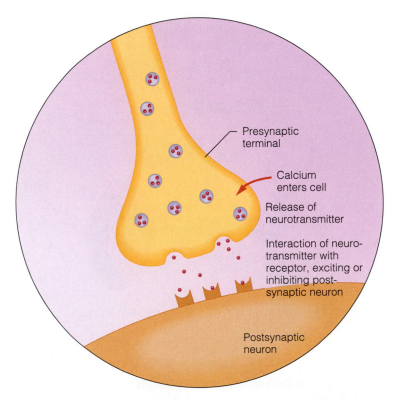

Figure 2.9
A presynaptic terminal releases neurotransmitter at the synapse

Presynaptic terminal

Calcium enters cell

Release of neurotransmitter

Interaction of neurotransmitter with receptor, exciting or inhibiting postsynaptic neuron

Postsynaptic neuron

inhibitory? It depends on which transmitter is released and the type of receptors on the postsynaptic membrane. A particular transmitter can have an excitatory effect at one location in the nervous system and an inhibitory effect at another; however, some transmitters typically produce excitation and others most often produce inhibition. If the receptors open Na$^+$ channels, this produces **hypopolarization of the dendrites and cell body, which is an** *excitatory postsynaptic potential (EPSP)*. Other receptors open potassium channels, chloride channels, or both; as K$^+$ moves out of the cell or Cl$^-$ moves in, it produces a **hyperpolarization of the dendrites and cell body, or an** *inhibitory postsynaptic potential (IPSP)*.

So far we have only a graded potential. The graded potential spreads down the dendrites and across the cell body to the *axon hillock* (where the axon joins the cell body). At the axon, a positive graded potential that reaches threshold will produce an action potential; a negative graded potential makes it harder for the axon to fire. Most neurons fire spontaneously all the time, so EPSPs will increase the rate of firing and IPSPs will decrease the rate of firing (Figure 2.10). So

now we have added another form of complexity at the synapse: the message to the postsynaptic neuron can be *bidirectional*, not just off-on.

You should not assume that excitation of neurons always corresponds to activation of behavior, or that inhibition necessarily suppresses behavior. An EPSP may activate a neuron that has an inhibitory effect on other neurons, and an IPSP may reduce activity in an inhibitory neuron. An example at the behavioral level is the effect of Ritalin. Ritalin and many other medications used to treat hyperactivity in children are in a class of drugs called stimulants, which increase activity in the nervous system. Yet, they calm hyperactive individuals and improve their ability to concentrate and focus attention (Cox, Merkel, Kovatchev, & Seward, 2000; Mattay et al., 1996). They probably have this effect by stimulating frontal areas of the brain where metabolism has been found to be abnormally low (Faigel, Szuajderman, Tishby, Turel, & Pinus, 1995).

Next we will see that the ability to combine the inputs of large numbers of neurons expands the synapse's contribution to complexity even further.

What are the differences between an EPSP and an IPSP?

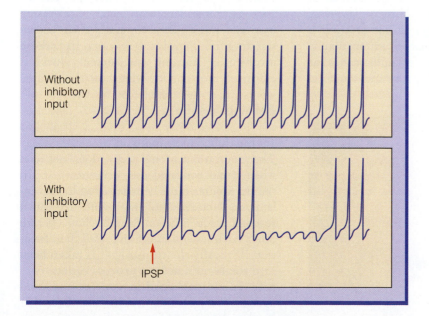

Figure 2.10
Effect of inhibition on spontaneous firing rate
Source: E. R. Kandel & S. A. Siegelbaum, "Synaptic Integration" in E. R. Kandel, J. H. Schwartz, & T. M. Jessell (Eds.), *Principles of Neural Science*, Fourth Edition, p. 207–208. Copyright © 2002 McGraw-Hill. Reprinted by permission.

Without inhibitory input

With inhibitory input

IPSP

Postsynaptic Integration

What are summation and integration?

The output of a single neuron is not enough by itself to cause a postsynaptic neuron to fire, or to prevent it from firing. In fact, an excitatory neuron may depolarize the postsynaptic membrane by as little as 0.2–0.4 mV (Kandel & Siegelbaum, 2000c); remember that it takes an approximately 10-mV depolarization to trigger an action potential. However, a typical neuron receives input from around a thousand other neurons (Figure 2.11); because of the branching of the terminals, this amounts to as many as 10,000 synaptic connections in most parts of the brain, and up to 100,000 in the cerebellum (Kandel & Siegelbaum, 2000a).

Because a single neuron has such a small effect, the postsynaptic neuron must combine potentials from many neurons in order to fire. This requirement is not a burden but a way of ensuring that a neuron is not fired by random activity occurring in a presynaptic neuron. You will also see that it provides a way of enhancing the complexity of the neural message. Graded potentials are combined at the axon hillock in two ways. *Spatial summation combines potentials occurring simultaneously at different locations on the dendrites and cell body.* Summation is not limited to simultaneous potentials, though. *Temporal summation combines potentials arriving a short time apart.* Temporal summation is possible because it takes a few milliseconds for a potential to die out. Spatial and temporal summation occur differently, but they have the same result. Figure 2.12 illustrates the summation of potentials.

As you can see in Figure 2.12, summation can combine EPSPs so that an action potential occurs. Summation of IPSPs drives the membrane's interior even more negative, making it more difficult for incoming EPSPs to trigger an action potential. If both excitatory and inhibitory impulses arrive on the same cell body (which often occurs), they will also summate, but algebraically. The combined effect will equal the difference between the sum of the depolarizations and the sum of the hyperpolarizations. Spatial summation of two excitatory inputs and one inhibitory input is illustrated in Figure 2.13. The effect from temporal summation would be similar.

Each neuron can legitimately be considered a *decision maker* because in combining inputs it makes the determination whether to fire or not to fire. The neuron has also been referred to as an *integrator* because its activity rises above simple summation of signals to the *integration of information*. It is through the interconnections at synapses, with their ability to integrate the excitatory and inhibitory inputs from a thousand neurons, that the nervous system becomes less like a bunch of telephone lines and more like a computer. Our understanding of complex behaviors like those involved in learning and mental illness is enhanced more by knowing how the synapse works than by knowledge of transmission within the neuron.

Terminating Synaptic Activity

The neurotransmitter's story does not end when it has activated the receptors. Usually, the transmitter must be inactivated to prevent it from "locking up" a circuit that must respond frequently, or from leaking over to other synapses and interfering with their function. **Typically the transmitter is taken back into the terminals by a process called *reuptake;* it is repackaged in vesicles and used again.** Acetylcholine (ACh), on the other hand, is deactivated by acetylcholinesterase, an

What happens to the neurotransmitter after it is released?

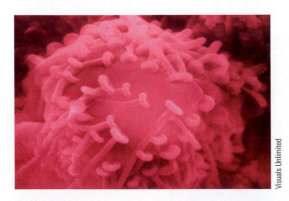

Visuals Unlimited

Figure 2.11
A cell body virtually covered with axon terminals

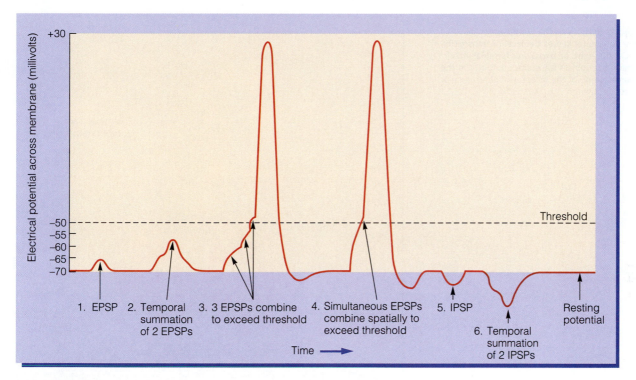

Figure 2.12
Temporal and spatial summation

enzyme that splits the molecule into its components of choline and acetate. Choline is then taken back into the terminals and used to make more acetylcholine. At some synapses, transmitter in the cleft is absorbed by glial cells.

Controlling how much neurotransmitter remains in the synapse is one way to vary behavior, and many drugs capitalize on this mechanism. Cocaine blocks the uptake of dopamine; some antidepressant medications block reuptake of serotonin, norepinephrine, or both; and drugs for treating the muscular disorder myasthenia gravis increase ACh availability by inhibiting the action of acetylcholinesterase.

Synaptic Modulation

The synapses described so far are referred to as *axodendritic* and *axosomatic* synapses, because their targets are dendrites and cell bodies. They are not the only kind of synaptic arrangement; at *axoaxonic* synapses, a third neuron releases transmitter onto the terminals of the presynap-

tic neuron (see Figure 2.14, on the next page). **The result is *presynaptic excitation* or *presynaptic inhibition*, which increases or decreases, respectively, the presynaptic neuron's release of neurotransmitter onto the postsynaptic neuron.** One way an axoaxonic synapse modulates (adjusts) a presynaptic terminal's activity is by regulating the amount of Ca^{2+} entering the terminal.

What are the three ways of modulating synaptic activity?

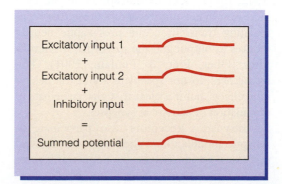

Figure 2.13
Spatial summation of excitatory and inhibitory potentials

Figure 2.14
Modulation adjusts activity at the synapse
On the left, an autoreceptor senses the level of transmitter in the synapse. On the right, an axoaxonic terminal influences the presynaptic terminal's transmitter output. On the postsynaptic neuron, some of the receptors (lighter in color) have become less sensitive.

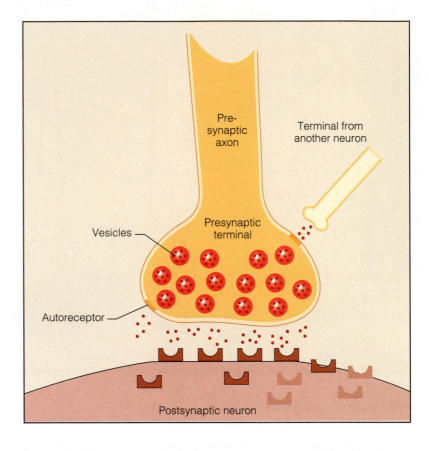

Autoreceptors **on the terminals sense the amount of transmitter in the cleft; if there is excessive transmitter, the presynaptic neuron reduces its output** (see Figure 2.14 again). This brings us to one of the newly discovered ways that glial cells contribute to neural activity (Figure 2.15). In rats that are nursing their young, a type of glial cell that absorbs neurotransmitter withdraws from the synapse. As a result, the amount of transmitter in the cleft increases. When autoreceptors detect the accumulating transmitter, the presynaptic neuron reduces its output and the size of EPSPs diminishes (Oliet, Piet, & Poulain, 2001). The researchers do not speculate about the behavioral effects, but it is clear that glia participate in modulation of activity at synapses.

Postsynaptic receptors also participate in synaptic modulation. When there are unusual increases or decreases in neurotransmitter release, postsynaptic receptors change their sensitivity or even their numbers to compensate. You will see in a later chapter that receptor changes figure prominently in psychological disorders such as schizophrenia.

Neurotransmitters

Table 2.1 (on page 50) lists several transmitters. This is an abbreviated list; there are several other known or suspected transmitters and there are doubtless additional transmitters yet to be discovered. This summary is intended to illustrate the variety in neurotransmitters, and to give you some familiarity with the functions of a few of the major ones. You will encounter most of them again as we discuss various behaviors in later chapters.

The number of different neurotransmitters is one of the ways information complexity is added at the synapse. Having a variety of neu-

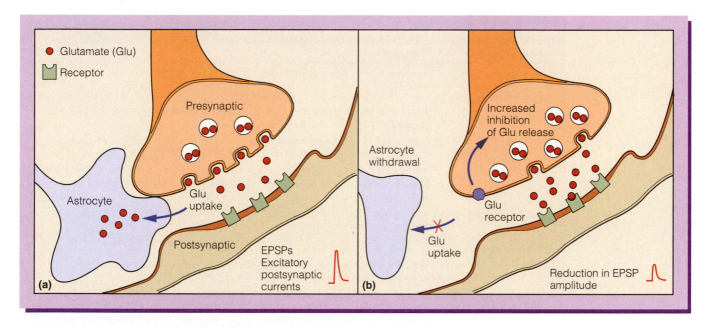

Figure 2.15
Glial cells influence neurotransmitter release
(a) Astrocyte (type of glial cell) absorbs glutamate (Glu), a neurotransmitter. **(b)** Glia withdraw; neurotransmitter accumulates and is detected by autoreceptors, reducing transmitter release and size of EPSP.
Reprinted with permission from "Unwrapping glial cells from the synapse: What lies inside?" by V. Gallo & R. Chittajallu, *Science*, 292, p. 873. Copyright 2001 American Association for the Advancement of Science.

rotransmitters multiplies the effects that can be produced; the fact that there are different subtypes of the receptors adds even more. For example, two types of receptors detect acetylcholine: the nicotinic receptor, so called because it is also activated by nicotine, and the muscarinic receptor, named for the mushroom derivative which can stimulate it. Nicotinic receptors are excitatory; they are found on muscles and, in lesser numbers, in the brain. Muscarinic receptors are more frequent in the brain, where they have an excitatory effect at some locations and an inhibitory one at others. Other transmitters have many more receptor subtypes than acetylcholine does.

For decades neurophysiologists labored under the erroneous belief, known as *Dale's principle,* **that a neuron was capable of releasing only one neurotransmitter.** We learned only fairly recently that many neurons ply their postsynaptic partners with two to four and perhaps even more neurotransmitters. Since then, most researchers have thought that the combination invariably consisted of a single fast-acting "traditional" neurotransmitter and one or more slower-acting neuropeptides that prolong and enhance the effect of the main transmitter (Hökfelt, Johansson, & Goldstein, 1984). Peptides are chains of amino acids (longer chains are called proteins); neuropeptides, of course, are peptides that act as neurotransmitters.

Recent studies have found that some neurons release two fast transmitters (Rekling, Funk, Bayliss, Dong, & Feldman, 2000). Even more surprising, we discovered that the same neuron can release both an excitatory transmitter and an inhibitory transmitter (Duarte, Santos, & Carvalho, 1999; Jo & Schlichter, 1999). It appears that the two types of transmitters are released at *different* terminals (Duarte et al., 1999; Sulzer & Rayport, 2000). This co-release suggests that a neuron can act as a two-way switch (Jo & Schlichter, 1999); one example is in cells in the eye that produce excitation when

What are two additional ways synapses add information complexity?

Table 2.1 Some Representative Neurotransmitters

Neurotransmitter	Functions
Acetylcholine	Transmitter at muscles; in brain, involved in learning, etc.
Monoamines	
Serotonin	Involved in mood, sleep, and arousal, and in aggression, depression, obsessive-compulsive disorder, and alcoholism.
Dopamine	Contributes to movement control and promotes reinforcing effects of abused drugs, food, and sex; involved in schizophrenia and Parkinson's disease.
Norepinephrine	A hormone released during stress. Functions as a neurotransmitter in the brain to increase arousal and attentiveness to events in the environment; involved in depression.
Epinephrine	A stress hormone related to norepinephrine; plays a minor role as a neurotransmitter in the brain.
Amino Acids	
Glutamate	The principal excitatory neurotransmitter in the brain and spinal cord. Vitally involved in learning, and implicated in schizophrenia.
Gamma-aminobutyric acid (GABA)	The predominant inhibitory neurotransmitter. Its receptors respond to alcohol and the class of tranquilizers called benzodiazepines. Deficiency in GABA or receptors is one cause of epilepsy.
Glycine	Inhibitory transmitter in the spinal cord and lower brain. The poison strychnine causes convulsions and death by affecting glycine activity.
Peptides	
Endorphins	Neuromodulators that reduce pain and enhance reinforcement.
Substance P	Transmitter in neurons sensitive to pain.
Neuropeptide Y	Initiates eating and produces metabolic shifts.
Gas	
Nitric oxide	Along with carbon monoxide, one of two known gaseous transmitters. Controls intestinal muscles, dilates blood vessels in the brain, and may participate in learning. Can serve as a retrograde transmitter, allowing the postsynaptic neuron to influence the presynaptic neuron's release of neurotransmitter.

a viewed object moves in one direction and inhibition when movement is in the opposite direction (Duarte et al., 1999).

Computer Models of Neural Processing

Underlying our discussion has been the assumption that behavior can be explained by the functioning of neurons. But we cannot back up that promise as long as we limit ourselves to the example of the single-neuron chain. However, the neural connections involved in learning, perception, reasoning, and so on are discouragingly complex. Some researchers have resorted to modeling behaviors with computers in their attempt to understand neural functioning.

One effort turned into a human-machine competition that eventually resulted in IBM's chess-playing computer *Deep Blue* defeating world champion Garry Kasparov in 1997. The reason humans were able to hold out as long as we did is that humans and computers have different superiorities. The computer is good at *serial processing*, where what you do next depends on what you just did. It can consider billions of possible moves, working through

Agonists and Antagonists in the Real World

Neurotransmitters are not the only substances that affect transmitters. **Many drugs, as well as other compounds, mimic the effect of a neurotransmitter and are called *agonists*. Any substance that reduces the effect of a neurotransmitter is called an *antagonist*.** Practically all of the drugs that have a psychological effect interact with a neurotransmitter system in the brain, and many of them do so by mimicking or blocking the effect of neurotransmitters (Snyder, 1984).

You have already seen that the effect of acetylcholine is duplicated by nicotine and by muscarine at the two kinds of receptors. Opiate drugs like heroin and morphine also act as agonists, stimulating receptors for opiate-like transmitters in the body. Naloxone acts as an antagonist to opiates,

occupying the receptor sites without activating them; consequently, naloxone can be used to counteract an overdose.

The plant toxin curare blocks acetylcholine receptors at the muscle, causing paralysis (Trautmann, 1983). South American Indians in the Amazon River Basin tip their darts with curare to disable their game (see the photo). A synthetic version of curare, *d*-tubocurarine, was used as a muscle relaxant during surgery before safer and more effective drugs were found (Goldberg & Rosenberg, 1987). Ironically, it has even been used in the treatment of tetanus (lockjaw), which is caused by another neurotoxin; a patient receiving this treatment has to be artificially respirated for weeks until recovery occurs, to prevent suffocation.

Amazonian indians tip their darts with the plant neurotoxin curare

each one to determine which is best, in a very short time. Humans are good *parallel processors*, handling separate parts of a problem at the same time and then putting the results together. We are limited to considering tens or possibly hundreds of chess moves in advance, but we can take a "big-picture" approach to quickly select a smaller set of moves to consider more carefully.

In 2001 the largest supercomputer in the world was ASCI White. Housed in 200 cabinets

that fill a room the size of two basketball courts, its 8,000 parallel processors can perform 12.3 trillion operations per second. Still, the human brain with its 100 billion parallel processing neurons is estimated to be a thousand times as powerful ("ASCI White," 2001). Just a year later, ASCI White's power was exceeded by a Japanese computer that was five times faster (Emmen, 2002). If computing power increases by a hundredfold in the next decade as expected, computers could match the brain's power by

How well do artificial neural networks mimic the brain's activity?

2010. While waiting for the power of a brain in a computer, researchers have been programming computers in a different way that may mimic on a small scale the way the brain operates: they are constructing artificial neural networks.

An *artificial neural network* consists of a group of simulated neurons that carry out cognitive-like functions. The "neurons" are usually arranged in layers: an input layer, one or more "hidden" layers where most of the processing occurs, and an output layer (see Figure 2.16). The input layer could be connected to, say, a keyboard, a microphone, or a video camera; the output layer might send its results to a printer or a robot arm or other device. Neurons in each layer are connected with all the neurons of the layer below it; connections can be exciting to some neurons and inhibiting to others, and to differing degrees.

Earlier attempts at computer modeling involved writing very specific programs to tell the computer what to do. The programs reflected how the researcher thought the brain operates. Artificial neural networks *learn* how to perform the task like we do, by doing it. Looking at how the network handles the task may help us understand how the brain works. The researcher "trains" the network by presenting it with a series of inputs (for example, letters of the alphabet in several fonts and handwritings) and giving it the correct output to compare with its own output. Usually a neural network sends feedback to the layers above to adjust the strength or

weight of the connections between the neurons. At first the network's performance is random, but it improves with practice. For example, NETtalk (Sejnowski & Rosenberg, 1987), designed to read and speak English text, initially produced random sounds, which were replaced with babbling and then pseudowords; but after just 10 training trials the speech was intelligible and sounded like a small child's.

An artificial neural network functions like the brain in several ways. Because information is *distributed* throughout the network rather than localized at a particular point, damage has a minimal effect on performance until the damage becomes extensive. Distributed storage does not "use up" the neurons, though, because a neuron can participate in multiple functions; in the case of images, for example, several can be stored "on top of each other" in the network. Different inputs, then, will evoke the separate actions or items of information. This efficiency allows NETtalk to function with only 300 neurons, reminiscent of the tremendous storage capacity of the brain.

Neural networks have been trained to identify precancerous cells in a Pap smear, adjust the mirror of a telescope to correct for atmospheric distortions (Hinton, 1993), and recognize military aircraft and boats by their appearance and sound (Lawrence, 1993). But neural networks are also being used to test the numerous theories about how the brain carries out specific functions. When simulated rats learned to find an "escape platform" hidden just below the surface in a water tank, learning progress matched that of real rats in the original study (Brown & Sharp, 1995). When the platform was deleted from the program, the computer rats would turn and "swim" back in the other direction after passing the location where they previously had found the platform. Other networks learned to recognize curvature of visual objects from gradations in shading (Lehky & Sejnowski, 1990), and simulated the brain's ability to locate objects in space by combining information about the location of an image on the back of the eye with information about eye position (Zipser & Andersen; 1988).

Figure 2.16
A diagrammatic representation of a simple neural network

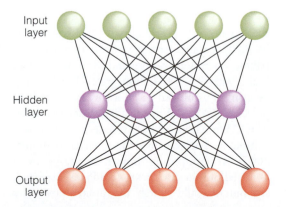

Input layer

Hidden layer

Output layer

These accomplishments make it plausible that neural networks work the same way the brain does, but they do not guarantee it. We will simply have to wait and see how useful artificial neural networks will be in explaining brain functioning. For the time being I find the idea of neural networks a useful way to think about mental processes. The next time you are trying to remember a person's name that is "on the tip of your tongue," imagine your brain activating individual components of a neural network until one produces the name you're looking for. If you visualize the person's face as a reminder, imagine that the name and the image of the face are stored in the same or in related networks, so that activating one memory activates the other. We will talk more about how synaptic connections are formed to create memories when we get to Chapter 11.

 **CONCEPT CHECK**

- *How is information transmitted from neuron to neuron?*
- *It can be said that integration transforms neurons from a "telephone line" to a computer. Explain.*
- *In what ways would neuronal activity be limited if there were no modulation at the synapse?*
- *What is the implication of the fact that Dale's principle is incorrect?*
- *How successful have artificial neural networks been in simulating human brain activity? What does this tell us about whether they work the same way the brain does?*

 In Perspective

It is impossible to understand the brain and impossible to understand behavior without first knowing the capabilities and the limitations of the neuron. Although more complexity is added at the synapse, a simple off-or-on device is the basis for our most sophisticated capabilities and behaviors. However, what happens at the individual neuron is not enough to account for human behavior. Some researchers are using artificial neural networks to understand how the neurons work together to produce thought, memory, emotion, and consciousness. In the next chapter you will learn about some of the functional structures in the brain that are formed by the interconnection of neurons.

 Summary

The Cells That Make Us Who We Are

- There are four major kinds of neurons: motor neurons, sensory neurons, interneurons, and projection neurons. They have the same basic components and function the same way.

- The neural membrane is electrically polarized. This polarity is the resting potential, which is maintained by forces of concentration and electrical gradient, as well as by the sodium-potassium pump.

- This polarization is the basis for the neuron's responsiveness to stimulation in the form of the graded potential and the action potential.

- The neuron is limited in firing rate by the absolute refractory period, and in its ability to represent the strength of the stimulus by the all-or-none law. The neuron's ability to fire during the relative refractory period if the stimulus is more intense provides a way to represent stimulus intensity (the rate law).

continued

- Glial cells provide the myelination that enables neurons to conduct rapidly while remaining small. They also provide several supporting functions for neurons and probably help regulate activity in the neurons.

How Neurons Communicate with Each Other

- Transmission from neuron to neuron is usually chemical, involving neurotransmitters released onto receptors on the postsynaptic dendrites and cell body.

- The neurotransmitter can create an EPSP, which increases the chance the postsynaptic neuron will fire; or it can create an IPSP, which decreases the likelihood of firing.

- Through temporal and spatial summation, the postsynaptic neuron integrates its many excitatory and inhibitory inputs.

- Modulation of synaptic activity is produced by axoaxonic synapses from other neurons, regulation of transmitter output by autoreceptors, and change in the number or sensitivity of postsynaptic receptors.

- Leftover neurotransmitter may be broken down, taken back into the presynaptic terminals, or absorbed by glial cells.

- The human nervous system contains a large number of neurotransmitters, detected by an even greater variety of receptors. A neuron can release combinations of two or more neurotransmitters.

- Several functions of the human brain are being simulated by computers, but whether the brain actually functions like artificial neural networks is not yet clear.

➜ For Further Thought

- What would be the effect if there were no constraints on the free flow of ions across the neuron membrane?

- What effect would it have on neural conduction if the action potential were decremental?

- Sport drinks replenish electrolytes that are lost during exercise. Electrolytes are compounds that dissociate into ions, such as

Na^+ and Cl^+. What implication do you think electrolyte loss might have for the nervous system? Why?

- Imagine what the effect would be if the nervous system used only one neurotransmitter.

- How similar to humans do you think computers are capable of becoming?

➜ Testing Your Understanding

1. Describe the ion movements and voltage changes that make up the neural impulse, from graded potential (at the axon hillock) to recovery.

2. Discuss ways the synapse increases the neuron's capacity for transmitting information.

3. Describe how neural networks function like the brain and what humanlike behaviors they have produced.

Select the one best answer:

1. The inside of the neuron is relatively poor in __ ions and rich in __ ions.
   a. chloride, phosphate
   b. sodium, potassium
   c. potassium, sodium
   d. calcium, sodium

2. The rate law:
   a. explains how the intensity of stimuli is encoded.

b. applies only in the peripheral nervous system, not in the central nervous system.

c. describes transmission in myelinated axons.

d. describes the process of neural integration.

3. Without the sodium-potassium pump, the neuron would become:

a. more sensitive because of accumulation of sodium ions.

b. more sensitive because of accumulation of potassium ions.

c. overfilled with sodium ions and unable to fire.

d. overfilled with potassium ions and unable to fire.

4. There is a limit to how rapidly a neuron can produce action potentials. This is due to:

a. inhibition.

b. facilitation.

c. the absolute refractory period.

d. the relative refractory period.

5. Saltatory conduction results in:

a. less speed and the use of more energy.

b. greater speed with the use of less energy.

c. less speed, but with the use of less energy.

d. greater speed, but with the use of more energy.

6. General anesthetics open K$^+$ channels, allowing K$^+$ ions to leak out of the neuron. This:

a. increases firing in pain-inhibiting centers in the brain.

b. increases firing in the neuron until it is fatigued.

c. hypopolarizes the neuron, preventing firing.

d. hyperpolarizes the neuron, preventing firing.

7. When the action potential arrives at the terminal button, entry of __ ions stimulates release of transmitter.

a. potassium   b. sodium

c. calcium   d. chloride

8. All of the following neurotransmitters are deactivated by reuptake except:

a. acetylcholine.   b. norepinephrine.

c. serotonin.   d. dopamine.

9. An inhibitory neurotransmitter causes the inside of the postsynaptic neuron to become:

a. more positive.   b. more negative.

c. more depolarized.   d. neutral in charge.

10. EPSPs are typically produced by movement of __ ions, whereas IPSPs are typically produced by movement of __ ions.

a. potassium; sodium or chloride

b. potassium; sodium or calcium

c. sodium; calcium or chloride

d. sodium; potassium or chloride

11. Which of the following is *not* an example of modulation?

a. A neuron synapses on the terminals of another and affects its transmitter release.

b. Autoreceptors reduce the amount of transmitter released.

c. A presynaptic neuron inhibits a postsynaptic neuron.

d. Postsynaptic receptors change in numbers or sensitivity.

12. The graph below shows three graded potentials occurring at the same time. Assume that the resting potential is –70 mV, and that each graded potential individually produces a 5-mV change. What is the membrane's voltage after the graded potentials arrive?

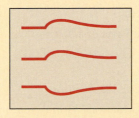

a. –65 mV   b. –70 mV

c. –75 mV   d. +75 mV

continued

13. The presence of synapses in a neuron chain provides the opportunity for:
    a. increases in conduction speed.
    b. modification of neural activity.
    c. two-way communication in a pathway.
    d. regeneration of damaged neurons.

14. Neural networks operate more like the brain than traditional computer programs in that they:

    a. reserve each "neuron" for a single purpose.
    b. operate in a serial fashion.
    c. are already preprogrammed.
    d. learn how to carry out the task themselves.

Answers: 1. **b** 2. **a** 3. **c** 4. **c** 5. **b** 6. **d** 7. **c** 8. **a** 9. **b** 10. **d** 11. **c** 12. **a** 13. **b** 14. **d**

 On the Web

1. **Neuroscience for Kids** (don't be put off by the name!) has a review of the resting and action potentials and an animation of their electrical recording, at

   http://faculty.washington.edu/chudler/ap.html

2. The **Cajal Medical and Scientific Illustration** site has colorful artist's renderings of neurons, synapses, and neuron membranes. You can also listen in on neurons whose action potentials have been amplified and transformed into sounds. Available at

   http://cajal.com/docs/nbuttons.htm

3. **Artificial Brains.com** publicizes work in artificial intelligence with links to a variety of sites. Featured are a lab that is attempting to build a robotic cat with a brain containing 75 million artificial neurons, and another working on a robot expected to reproduce the behaviors of a two-year-old child, at

   http://www.glendhu.com/ai/

    For additional information about the topics covered in this chapter, please look at InfoTrac College Edition, at

   http://www.infotrac-college.com/wadsworth

   Try search terms you think up yourself, or use these: *neurons; neurotransmitters; reuptake; synapses.*

 On the CD-ROM: Exploring Biological Psychology

 The Neuron Structure
   Animation: The Parts of a Neuron
   Virtual Reality: The Structure of the Neuron
   Interactive Puzzle: The Neuron
Conduction of Information Within Neurons
   Animation: The Action Potential
   Animation: Na$^+$ Ions

   Animation: The Resting Potential
   Animation: Postsynaptic Potentials
Communication Between Neurons
   Animation: Cholinergic
   Animation: Release of ACh
   Animation: AChE Inactivates ACh
   Animation: AChE Inhibitors

For Further Reading

"How Neural Networks Learn from Experience," by Geoffrey Hinton. (*Scientific American*, March 1993, 145–151). This brief article explains neural networks and gives examples of their use.

"Debunking the Digital Brain" (*Scientific American*, February 1997). This brief feature article describes the view of Christof Koch at the California Institute of Technology that neurons are much more complicated than we give them credit for, which has implications for computer simulation.

The Computational Brain, by Patricia Churchland and Terrence Sejnowski (Bradford Books, 1994). This treatment of the attempt to model brain functioning with computers is by two of the foremost experts in the field; it is a bit difficult, but lively and well written.

Key Terms

absolute refractory period *39*

action potential *38*

agonist *51*

all-or-none law *39*

antagonist *51*

artificial neural network *52*

autoreceptor *48*

axon *34*

concentration gradient *37*

Dale's principle *49*

dendrites *33*

electrical gradient *37*

excitatory postsynaptic potential (EPSP) *45*

glial cell *33*

hyperpolarization *44*

hypopolarization *44*

inhibitory postsynaptic potential (IPSP) *45*

interneuron *34*

ion *36*

motor neuron *33*

myelin *41*

neuron *33*

neurotoxin *40*

neurotransmitter *34*

nodes of Ranvier *41*

polarization *35*

postsynaptic *44*

potential *36*

presynaptic *44*

presynaptic excitation *47*

presynaptic inhibition *47*

projection neuron *35*

rate law *39*

relative refractory period *39*

resting potential *37*

reuptake *46*

saltatory conduction *41*

sensory neuron *34*

sodium-potassium pump *37*

soma *33*

spatial summation *46*

synapse *34*

synaptic cleft *43*

temporal summation *46*

terminal *34*

vesicle *44*

The Functions of the Nervous System

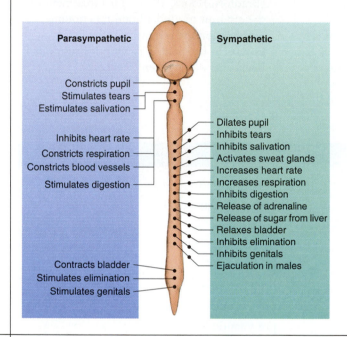

Parasympathetic | Sympathetic

Constricts pupil
Stimulates tears
Estimulates salivation

Inhibits heart rate
Constricts respiration
Constricts blood vessels
Stimulates digestion

Contracts bladder
Stimulates elimination
Stimulates genitals

Dilates pupil
Inhibits tears
Inhibits salivation
Activates sweat glands
Increases heart rate
Increases respiration
Inhibits digestion
Release of adrenaline
Release of sugar from liver
Relaxes bladder
Inhibits elimination
Inhibits genitals
Ejaculation in males

In this chapter you will learn:

- The major structures of the nervous system and some of their functions.

- How the nervous system develops and how it changes with experience.

- The obstacles and strategies for repairing damaged brains and spinal cords.

The brain is wider than the sky,
For, put them side by side,
The one the other will include
With ease, and you beside.

—Emily Dickinson

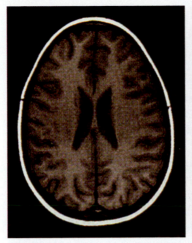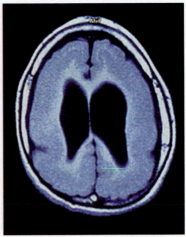

Figure 3.1
Normal brain and a lissencephalic brain
Source: Barinaga, 1996.

Figure 3.1 is the scanned images of the brains of two different people. The brain on the left is normal. Its surface, just inside the perimeter of the skull, has many ridges made up of gray matter, which are interconnected by bands of myelinated axons running between them. The second brain is not normal. During development many of the neurons destined to form the brain's surface made it only halfway from the middle where they were born; the brain is smooth because its outer layer is almost missing. The dark spaces in the middle are greatly enlarged as well, indicating that the amount of brain tissue is deficient. This disorder is *periventricular heterotopia* (Barinaga, 1996; Eksioglu et al., 1996), caused by a mutant gene on the X chromosome. Most afflicted individuals are female; affected males usually die before birth or shortly after, because the mutation is on the X chromosome and unopposed by a gene on the shorter Y chromosome. Usually survivors are *lissencephalic* (smooth-brained), epileptic, and severely retarded.

The woman to whom the smooth-brained scan belongs is so unusual that her scan appeared on the cover of the journal *Neuron*. What is unusual is that she functions nor-mally, in fact, well above average. She is a college graduate, married, and employed in a responsible position. Aside from her strikingly abnormal brain scan, the only indication that anything is wrong is her occasional epileptic seizures. How do we explain why some people escape the consequences of what is usually a devastating developmental error? The answer is that we do not know why. It is one of the mysteries that neuroscientists are attempting to solve in order to understand the brain's remarkable resilience.

You are now well versed in the function of neurons and how they interact with each other. What you need to understand now is how neurons are grouped into the functional components that make up the nervous system. In the next few pages we will review the physical structure of the nervous system so that you will have a road map for more detailed study in later chapters. And we will include an overview of major functions to prepare you for the more detailed treatments to come in later chapters. We will look first at the central nervous system before turning our attention to the peripheral nervous system and additional issues like neural development.

THE CENTRAL NERVOUS SYSTEM (CNS)

The nervous system is divided into two subunits. **The *central nervous system (CNS)* includes the brain and the spinal cord; the *peripheral nervous system (PNS)* is made up of the *cranial nerves* that enter and leave the underside of the brain, and the *spinal nerves* that connect to the sides of the spinal cord at each vertebra.** As we talk about the nervous system, be careful not to confuse the terms *nerve* and *neuron*. **A *neuron* is a single nerve cell; a *nerve* is a bundle of axons running together like a multi-wire cable.** However, the term *nerve* is used only in the PNS; **inside the CNS, bundles of axons are called *tracts*.** Most of the neurons' cell bodies are also clustered together in groups; **a group of cell bodies is called a *nucleus* in the CNS and a *ganglion* in the PNS.**

Figure 3.2 is a photograph of a human brain. It will be easier to visualize the various structures of the brain if you understand that the central nervous system begins as a hollow tube and preserves that shape as it develops (Figure 3.3). The upper end of the tube develops three swellings, which will become the forebrain, midbrain, and hindbrain; the lower part of the tube develops into the spinal cord. The forebrain appears to be perched on top of the lower structures as it enlarges and almost completely engulfs them. By comparing the four drawings in this series you can see that the mature forebrain obscures much of the lower brain from view. We will get a better idea of these hidden structures later when we look at an interior view of the brain.

The Forebrain

The major structures of the forebrain are the two cerebral hemispheres, the thalamus, and the hypothalamus. The outer layer of the hemispheres, the cortex, is where the highest level processing occurs in the brain.

> *. . . one of the key strategies of the nervous system is localization of functions: specific types of information are processed in particular regions.*
>
> —Eric Kandel

Figure 3.2
View of a human brain

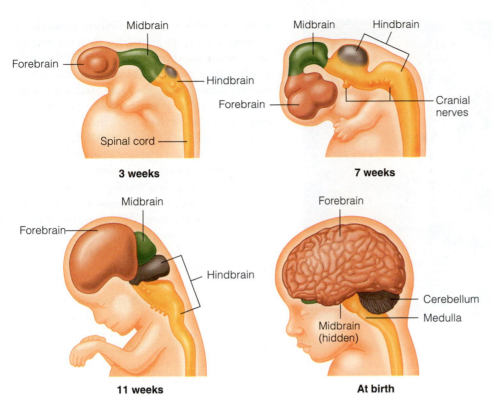

Figure 3.3
The brain develops from a tubular structure

3 weeks

7 weeks

11 weeks

At birth

The Cerebral Hemispheres

The large, wrinkled *cerebral hemispheres* dominate the brain's appearance (Figure 3.4). Not only are they large in relation to the rest of the brain, but they are disproportionately larger than in other primates (Deacon, 1990). **The *longitudinal fissure* that runs the length of the brain separates the two cerebral hemispheres,** which are nearly mirror images of each other in appearance. Often the same area in each hemisphere has identical functions as well, but you will see that this is not always the case. The simplest form of *asymmetry* is that each hemisphere receives most of its sensory input from the *opposite* side of the body (or of the world, in the case of audition and vision), and provides most of the control of the opposite side of the body.

Look again at Figures 3.2 and 3.4. The surface is convoluted by many ridges and grooves that give it a very wrinkled appearance. **Each ridge is** called a *gyrus;* the groove or space between two gyri is called a *sulcus* or, if it is large, a *fissure*. You can see how the gyri are structured in the cross section of a brain in Figure 3.5. **The outer surface is the *cortex* (literally, "bark"), made up mostly of the cell bodies of neurons; because cell bodies are not myelinated, the cortex looks grayish in color, which is why it is referred to as gray matter.** Remember that neural processing occurs where neurons synapse on the cell bodies of other neurons, which indicates why the cortex is so important. The cortex is only 1.5–4 mm thick, but the convolutions increase the amount of cortex by tripling the surface area. The convolutions also provide the axons with easier access to the cell bodies than if the developing cortex thickened instead of wrinkling. The axons come together in the central core of each gyrus, where their myelination gives the area a whitish appearance. Notice how the white matter of each gyrus joins with the white

1

Why is a wrinkled brain better than a smooth one?

Photo Researchers

Figure 3.4
Human brain viewed from above
Showing cerebral hemispheres and longitudinal fissure.

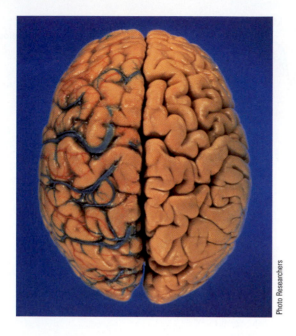

matter of the next gyrus, creating the large bands of axons that serve as communication routes in the brain.

Students often ask whether intelligent people have bigger brains. Bischoff, the leading European anatomist in the nineteenth century, argued that the greater average weight of men's brains was infallible proof of males' intellectual superiority over women. When he died, his brain was removed and added to his extensive

collection as his will had specified; ironically, it weighed only 1,245 grams, less than the average for women of about 1,250 grams ("Proof?", 1942). This example does not mean that there is no relationship between brain size and intelligence. There is a tendency for people with larger brains to be more intelligent (Willerman, Schultz, Rutledge, & Bigler, 1991), but the relationship is highly variable. What this means is that other factors are also important; otherwise, women would be less intelligent than men as Bischoff claimed, but we know from research that this is not the case. When we look at brain size more closely in the chapter on intelligence you will learn that Einstein's brain was even smaller than Bischoff's.

Across species, brain size is more related to body size than to intelligence; the brains of elephants and sperm whales are five or six times larger than ours. It is a brain's complexity, not its size, that determines its intellectual power. Look at the brains in Figure 3.6, then compare them with the human brain in Figure 3.2. You can see two features that distinguish more complex (and phylogenetically higher) brains from less complex ones. One is that the higher brains are more convoluted; the greater number of gyri means more cortex. The other is that the cerebral hemispheres are larger in proportion to the lower parts of the brain. It is no accident that the cerebral hemispheres are perched atop the rest of the brain and the spinal cord. The central nervous system is arranged in a *hierarchy*; as you ascend from the spinal cord through the hindbrain and midbrain to the forebrain, the neural structure becomes more complex and so does the behavior they control.

The Four Lobes

The hemispheres are divided into four lobes, each named after the bone of the skull above it (Figure 3.7). The divisions are somewhat arbitrary, but they are very useful for locating structures and functions, so we will organize our discussion around them. Sometimes we need additional precision in locating structures, so you should get used to seeing the standard

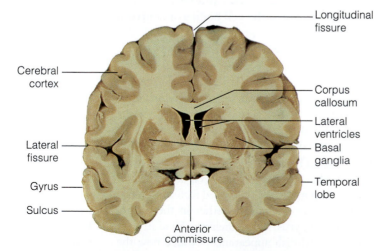

Cerebral cortex

Lateral fissure

Gyrus

Sulcus

Longitudinal fissure

Corpus callosum

Lateral ventricles

Basal ganglia

Temporal lobe

Anterior commissure

Figure 3.5
Section of human brain showing gyri and sulci

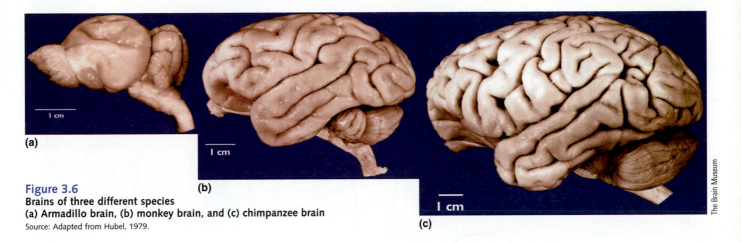

Figure 3.6
Brains of three different species
(a) Armadillo brain, (b) monkey brain, and (c) chimpanzee brain
Source: Adapted from Hubel, 1979.

(a)

(b)

(c)

terms that are used; the most important ones are illustrated in Figure 3.8.

The *frontal lobe* **is the area anterior to (in front of) the** *central sulcus* **and superior to (above) the** *lateral fissure.* A considerable portion of the frontal lobes is involved with the control of movement. **The** *precentral gyrus,* **which extends the length of the central sulcus, is the location of the primary** *motor cortex,* **which controls voluntary (nonreflexive) movement.** The motor area in one hemisphere controls the opposite side of the body, but it also exerts some control over the same side of

the body. The parts of the body are "mapped onto" the motor area of each hemisphere, in the form of a *homunculus,* which means "little man." This means that the cells that control the muscles of the hand are adjacent to the cells controlling the muscles of the arm, which are next to those controlling the shoulder, and so on (see Figure 3.9). The homunculus is distorted in shape, however; the parts of the body that receive fine motor control, like the hands and fingers, have more cortex devoted to their control. The motor area works in concert with the adjacent secondary motor cortex and with

What functions are found in the frontal lobes?

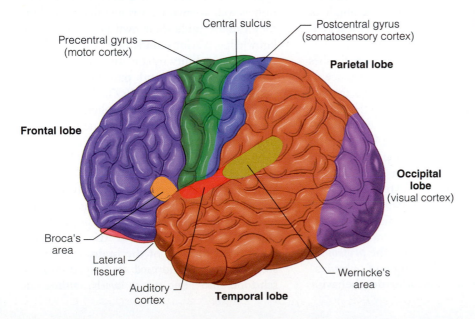

Figure 3.7
Lobes and functional areas on the surface of the hemispheres

Central sulcus

Precentral gyrus (motor cortex)

Postcentral gyrus (somatosensory cortex)

Parietal lobe

Frontal lobe

Occipital lobe (visual cortex)

Broca's area

Lateral fissure

Auditory cortex

Temporal lobe

Wernicke's area

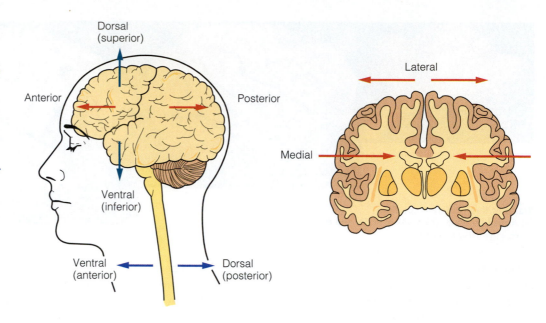

Figure 3.8
Terms used to indicate direction and location in the nervous system
Dorsal means "toward the back," and *ventral* means "toward the stomach." (This terminology was developed with other animals, and becomes more meaningful when you assume the human is on all fours, with the head facing forward.) *Anterior* means "toward the front," and *posterior* means "toward the rear." *Lateral* is "toward the side"; *medial* indicates "toward the middle." *Superior* is a location above another structure, and *inferior* is below another structure.

the *basal ganglia,* **a group of subcortical structures deep in the frontal lobes that smooth movements.** The basal ganglia are also involved in other important behaviors as well as in psychological disorders we will study later, such as obsessive-compulsive behavior.

Looking just in front of the motor area in Figure 3.7, you will see *Broca's area,* **which controls speech and provides grammatical structure to language.** In another example of hemispheric asymmetry, language in most people is located in the left hemisphere.

The more anterior parts of the frontal lobes are functionally complex. The importance of this area to humans is underscored by the fact that it is the single largest region in the human brain, twice as large as in chimpanzees and taking up 29% of the total cortex (Andreasen et al., 1992; Deacon, 1990). The effects of damage vary from patient to patient, depending on just which part is impaired (Mesulam, 1986), but they often strike at the capabilities we consider most human. Schizophrenia and depression, for example, involve dysfunction in the frontal lobes. The cortical area, **the *prefrontal cortex,* is involved in planning and organization, response inhibition, adjusting behavior**

2

in response to rewards and punishments, and some forms of decision making (Bechara, Damasio, Tranel, & Damasio, 1997; Fuster, 1989; Kast, 2001).

People with prefrontal damage often engage in behavior that normal individuals readily recognize will get them into trouble. During clinical interviews they can describe the socially appropriate response to a hypothetical situation as well as anyone; it is just that in real life they cannot guide their own behavior by this knowledge. Various kinds of research indicate that it is the ability to control impulses and to learn from reward and punishment that is impaired (Bechara et al., 1997). If the damage occurs very early in life, the individuals do not learn basic moral and social principles in the first place, so they perform poorly in the interview situation as well as in real life (Anderson, Bechara, Damasio, Tranel, & Damasio, 1999).

In spite of the effects of frontal lobe damage, during the 1940s and 1950s surgeons performed tens of thousands of *lobotomies,* **a surgical procedure that disconnected the prefrontal areas from the rest of the brain.** Initially the surgeries were performed on very disordered schizophrenics, but many overly enthusiastic doctors lobotomized patients with much milder problems. Walter Freeman (Figure 3.10), who did more than his share of the 40,000 lobotomies performed in the United States, exemplified the zeal of some lobotomists (Valenstein, 1986). To train other psychiatrists in the procedure, during a five-week period in 1951 he drove 11,000 miles in his station wagon and performed 111 demonstration lobotomies at 14 hospitals. Whatever calming effects the surgery produced came at a high price; the patients often became emotionally blunted, distractible, and childlike in behavior. In a follow-up study of patient outcomes, 49% were still hospitalized and less than a fourth of the others were living independently (Miller, 1967). Lack of success with lobotomy and the introduction of psychiatric drugs in the 1950s made the surgery a rare therapeutic choice. Now *psychosurgery,* **the use of surgical intervention to treat cognitive and emotional disorders,** is generally held in disfavor, unlike brain surgery to treat problems such as tumors. The accompanying Application describes research with brain-damaged patients, including the study of the most famous case of accidental lobotomy.

The *parietal lobes* **are located above the lateral fissure and between the central sulcus and the occipital lobe. The primary** *somatosensory cortex,* **located on the postcentral gyrus, processes the skin senses (touch, warmth, cold, and pain), and the senses that inform us about body position and movement** (see Figures 3.7 and 3.9 again). Like the motor cortex, the somatosensory cortex is organized as a homunculus, but in this case the size of the parts of the homunculus depends on the sensitivity in that area of the body. The somatosensory area also serves primarily the opposite side of the body.

The parietal lobes also house association areas for the somatosenses and for vision. *Association cortex* **carries out further processing beyond what the primary projection area does, and often combines information from other senses.** Parietal lobe association areas help the person identify objects by touch,

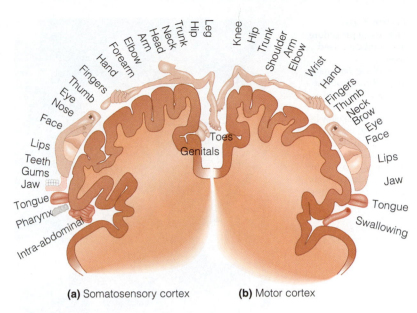

(a) Somatosensory cortex   **(b)** Motor cortex

Figure 3.9
The somatosensory and motor cortex
Adapted from The Cerebral Cortex of Man by W. Penfield & T. Rasmussen. © 1950 Macmillan, © renewed 1978 by Theodore Rasmussen.

determine the location of the limbs, and locate objects in space. Damage to this area may produce *neglect,* **a disorder in which the person ignores objects, people, and activity on the side opposite the damage.** This occurs much more frequently when the damage is in the right parietal lobe. The patient may fail to shave or apply makeup on the left side of the face. In some cases a person whose injury involves paralysis of the left arm or leg will deny anything is wrong, and even claim the affected arm or leg belongs to someone else.

The lateral fissure separates the temporal lobe from the frontal and parietal lobes. **The** *temporal lobes* **contain the auditory cortex, visual and auditory association areas, and an additional language area** (Figure 3.7). **The** *auditory cortex,* **which receives auditory (hearing) information from the ears, lies on the superior (uppermost) gyrus of the temporal lobe,** mostly hidden from view within the lateral fissure. **Just posterior to the auditory cortex is** *Wernicke's area,* **which**

What functions are found in the parietal lobes?

What functions are found in the temporal lobes?

Figure 3.10
Lobotomy procedure and a lobotomized brain
Left: Walter Freeman inserts his instrument between the eyelid and the eyeball, drives it through the skull with a mallet, and moves it back and forth to sever the connections between the prefrontal area and the rest of the brain. Right: A brain showing the gaps (arrows) produced by a lobotomy.
Photo of brain courtesy of Dr. Dana Copeland.

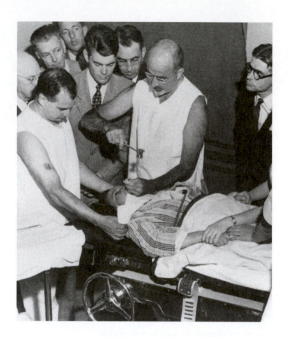

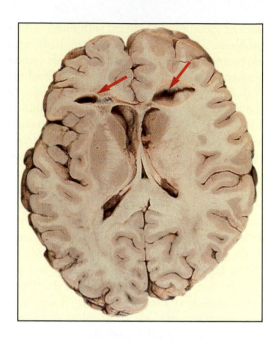

interprets language input arriving from the nearby auditory and visual areas; it also generates spoken language through Broca's area and written language by way of the motor cortex. When Wernicke's area is damaged, the person cannot understand speech or writing; the person can still speak, but the speech is mostly meaningless. Like Broca's area, this structure is found in the left hemisphere in most people.

The *inferior temporal cortex,* in the lower part of the lobe as the name implies, plays a major role in the visual identification of objects. People with damage in this area have difficulty recognizing familiar objects by sight, even though they can give detailed descriptions of the objects. They have no difficulty identifying the same items by touch. They may also fail to recognize the faces of friends and family members, though they can identify people by their voices. The neurologist Oliver Sacks (1990) described a patient who talked to parking meters, thinking they were children. Considering his strange behavior, it seems remarkable that he was unimpaired intellectually. Perhaps as you read about cases like this one

and hear of patients who do things like denying ownership of their paralyzed leg, you will begin to appreciate the fact that human capabilities are somewhat independent of each other, and depend on different parts of the brain.

When the neurosurgeon Wilder Penfield (1955) stimulated patients' temporal lobes, he often elicited what appeared to be memories of visual and auditory experiences. Penfield was doing surgery to remove malfunctioning tissue that was causing epileptic seizures. Before the surgery, Penfield would stimulate the area with a weak electrical current and observe the effect; this allowed him to distinguish healthy tissue and important functional areas from the diseased tissue he wished to remove (see Figure 3.11).

The patients were awake because their verbal report was needed for carrying out this mapping; since brain tissue has no pain receptors, the patient requires only a local anesthetic for the surgery. Stimulation of primary sensory areas provoked only unorganized, meaningless sensations such as tingling, lights, or buzzing sounds. But when Penfield stimulated association areas of the temporal cortex, 25% of the

APPLICATION

Phineas Gage and the Study of Brain Damage

In 1848 Phineas Gage, a 25-year-old railroad construction foreman in Cavendish, Vermont, was tamping explosive powder into a blasting hole when the charge ignited prematurely and drove the 3½-foot-long tamping iron through his left cheek and out the top of his skull. Gage not only regained consciousness immediately and was able to talk and to walk with the aid of his men, but he survived the accident with no impairment of speech, motor abilities, learning, memory, or intelligence. However, his personality was changed dramatically. He became irreverent and profane; and although Gage previously was the most capable man employed by the railroad, he no longer was dependable and had to be dismissed. He wandered about for a dozen years, never able to live fully independently, and he died under the care of his family.

Almost a century and a half later, Hanna Damasio and her colleagues carried out a belated postmortem examination of the skull (Damasio, Grabowski, Frank, Galaburda, & Damasio, 1994). Combining measurements from the skull with a three-dimensional computer rendering of a human brain, they were able to reconstruct the path of the tamping iron through Gage's brain (see the accompanying figure). They concluded that the accident damaged the part of both frontal lobes involved in processing emotion and making rational decisions in personal and social matters. At the time of Gage's accident, physiologists were debating whether different parts of the brain have specific functions or the different parts of the brain are equally competent in carrying out functions. His experience had such an important influence in tipping the balance toward localization of function that in 1998 scientists from around the world gathered in Cavendish to commemorate the 150th anniversary of the event (Vogel, 1998).

It might seem that we would study healthy brains to understand normal function, and study damaged brains to understand malfunction. But observing the brain at work is difficult, and we can often learn a great deal about the normal brain by relating the location of damage to the kind of behavior that is impaired. Brain damage can occur in a variety of ways: gunshot wounds, blows to the head, tumors, infection, toxins, and strokes. The natural experiments provided by brain damage have been extremely valuable to neuroscientists, but they also have major disadvantages: the damage is not confined to a single functional area, and the pattern of damage within an area varies greatly among patients. For these reasons it is necessary to observe large numbers of patients with similar damage (which is not always practical), and try to find some relationship between shared symptoms and common damage sites.

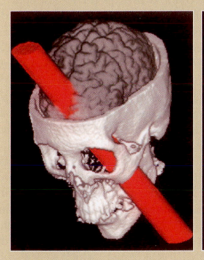 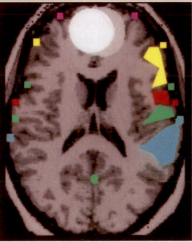

Reconstruction of the damage to Phineas Gage's Brain

Reprinted with permission from Damasio H., Grabowski T., Frank R., Galaburda A.M., Damasio A.R.: The return of Phineas Gage: Clues about the brain from a famous patient. *Science,* 264:1102–1105, 1994. Department of Neurology and Image Analysis Facility, University of Iowa.

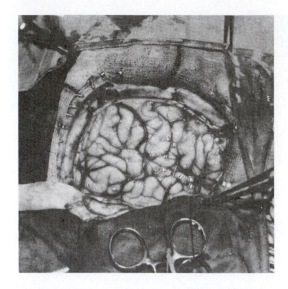

Figure 3.11
Brain of one of Penfield's patients
The numbered tags allowed Penfield to relate areas to patients' responses.
From Wilder Penfield, The Excitable Cortex in Conscious Man, 1958. Courtesy of Dennis Coon and Charles C. Thomas, Publisher, Springfield, Illinois.

What functions do the thalamus and hypothalamus perform?

What functions are found in the occipital lobes?

patients reported hearing music or familiar voices or, occasionally, reliving a familiar event. One time the patient hummed along with the music she was "hearing" and the nurse, recognizing the tune, joined in by supplying the lyrics. (Does this strike you as it does me, like a scene from a Monty Python movie—a sing-along during brain surgery?) People with epileptic activity or brain damage in their temporal lobes sometimes hear familiar tunes as well. The composer Shostakovich reportedly heard music when he tilted his head, shifting the location of a tiny war-time shell fragment in his temporal lobe; he refused to have the sliver removed, saying he used the melodies when composing (Sacks, 1990). Unfortunately, Penfield made no attempt to verify whether the apparent memories were factual or a sort of electrically induced dream; however, we will see in Chapter 11 that part of the temporal lobe has an important role in memory.

Finally, **the *occipital lobes* are the location of the *visual cortex*, which is where visual information is processed.** The primary visual cortex is designated as V1 and occupies the posterior tip of each lobe. Just as the somatosensory and motor areas are organized to represent the shape of the body, the visual cortex contains a map of visual space because adjacent receptors in the back of the eye send neurons to adjacent cells in the visual cortex. Secondary areas V2 through V5 make up the rest of the visual cortex; they detect individual components of a scene, such as color, movement, and form, which are then combined in the association areas.

The Thalamus and Hypothalamus

The *thalamus*, lying just below the lateral ventricles, receives information from all of the sensory systems except olfaction (smell) and relays it to the respective cortical projection areas (Figure 3.12). Many other neurons from the thalamus project more diffusely throughout the cortex and help to arouse the cortex when appropriate. We will see additional functions for the thalamus in later chapters. Actually there are two thalami, a right and a left; they form the walls of the third ventricle.

The *hypothalamus*, a smaller structure just below the thalamus, plays a major role in controlling the internal environment, and in motivated behaviors and emotion (Figure 3.12). It is paired like the thalamus and is also separated by the lower part of the third ventricle. In spite of its size, the hypothalamus contains perhaps the largest concentration of nuclei important to behavior in the entire brain. **It influences the body's hormonal environment by controlling much of the endocrine (internally secreting) gland system through the *pituitary gland*.** In Figure 3.12 the pituitary appears to be hanging down on its stalk just below the hypothalamus. The pituitary is known as the *master gland* because it controls other glands in the body.

Nuclei in the hypothalamus coordinate the expression of a variety of emotional and motivational functions, including sexual activity, feeding and drinking, bodily rhythms, and aggression. The hypothalamus exerts this influence largely through its control of the autonomic nervous system, which we will consider shortly. Though the expression of these

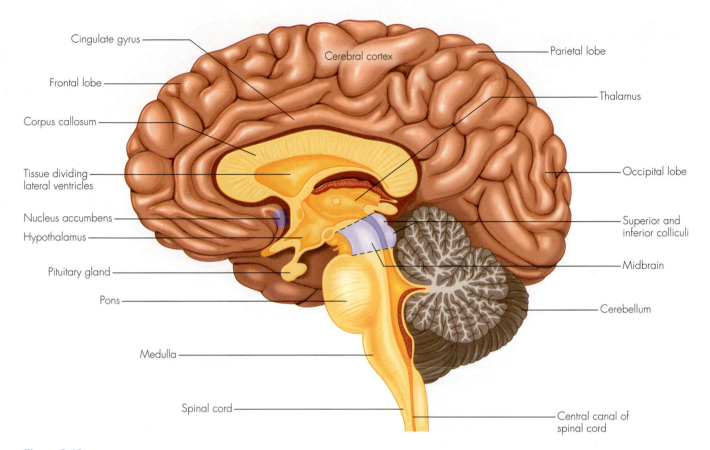

Figure 3.12
View of interior features of the human brain

behaviors is coordinated in the hypothalamus, they often originate in the *limbic system, a group of forebrain structures that have roles in emotion, motivated behavior, and learning* (Figure 3.13). We will look at the limbic system more closely in the chapter on emotion.

Just posterior to the thalamus is the *pineal gland.* You can see in Figure 3.12 why it was Descartes' best candidate for the seat of the soul: a single, unpaired structure, attached by its flexible stalk just below the hemispheres. In reality the pineal gland secretes melatonin, a hormone that induces sleep. It controls seasonal cycles in nonhuman animals and participates with other structures in controlling daily rhythms in humans.

Other Forebrain Structures

The Cerebral Commissures If you were to look inside the longitudinal fissure between the two cerebral hemispheres, you would see that the hemispheres are distinctly separate from each other. A couple of inches below the brain's surface the longitudinal fissure ends where a dense mass of white fibers crosses between the hemispheres. **This is the *corpus callosum*, the largest of the *cerebral commissures*, which carry information between the hemispheres.** The corpus callosum is visible in Figure 3.12; you can see it from another perspective, along with the anterior commissure, by looking back at Figure 3.5. You know that the two hemispheres carry out somewhat different functions, so you can imagine that

Figure 3.13
The structures of the limbic system
The structures encircle the upper brain stem, accounting for the name, which means "ring" or "border."

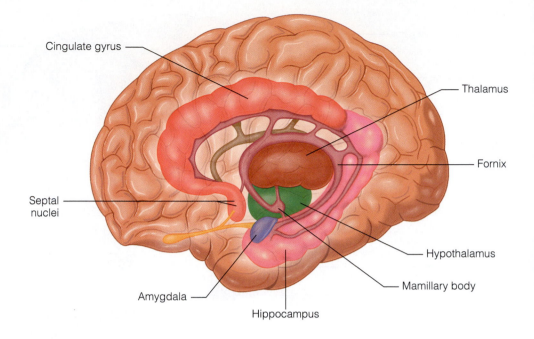

Cingulate gyrus

Thalamus

Fornix

Septal nuclei

Hypothalamus

Mamillary body

Amygdala

Hippocampus

they must communicate with each other constantly in order to integrate their activities. In addition, incoming information is often directed to one hemisphere—for instance, visual information appearing to one side of our field of view goes to the hemisphere on the opposite side. This information is "shared" with the other hemisphere through the commissures; the car that is too close on your left is registered in your right hemisphere, but if you are steering with your right hand it is your left hemisphere that must react.

Occasionally surgeons have to sever the cerebral commissures in epileptic patients whose incapacitating seizures cannot be controlled by drugs. It prevents the out-of-control neural activity in one hemisphere from engulfing the other hemisphere as well. The patient is then able to maintain consciousness during seizures and to lead a more normal life. Individuals who have had this surgery have been very useful for studying differences in the functions of the two hemispheres, because a stimulus can be presented to one hemisphere and the information will not be shared with the other hemisphere. Studies of these patients

have helped establish that the left hemisphere is more specialized for language than the right hemisphere, and that the right hemisphere is better at spatial tasks and recognizing faces (Gazzaniga, 1967; Nebes, 1974).

The Ventricles **During development the hollow interior of the nervous system develops into cavities called *ventricles* in the brain and the central canal in the spinal cord. The ventricles are filled with *cerebrospinal fluid*, which carries material from the blood vessels to the central nervous system, and transports waste materials in the other direction.** The *lateral ventricles* (Figures 3.14 and 3.12) extend forward deeply into the frontal lobes, and in the other direction into the occipital lobes before they curve around into the temporal lobes. Below the lateral ventricles and connected to them, the third ventricle is located between the two thalami and the two halves of the hypothalamus. The fourth ventricle is not in the forebrain, so we will locate it later. Enlarged ventricles are often an indication of a reduction in brain tissue, because the ventricles have expanded to fill the vacated space.

The Midbrain and Hindbrain

The *midbrain* consists of the tectum ("roof") on the dorsal side and the tegmentum on the ventral side (Figure 3.15). Passing between them is the cerebral aqueduct, which connects the third ventricle above with the fourth ventricle below (see Figure 3.14). Notice in Figure 3.15 that the brain takes on a more obvious tubular shape here, reminding us of the central nervous system's origins. You can see why the structures shown here are referred to as the *brain stem*.

The *superior colliculi* and *inferior colliculi* make up the tectum; they participate in visual and auditory functions, respectively. For example, the superior colliculus helps guide eye movements and fixation of gaze, and the inferior colliculus is involved in locating the direction of sounds. The tegmentum contains nuclei involved in the control of movement. One, the *substantia nigra*, is the location of the dopamine-releasing cells that degenerate in Parkinson's disease (Chapters 1, 10).

The hindbrain is composed of the medulla, the pons, and the cerebellum. The *medulla* forms the lower part of the hindbrain; its nuclei are involved with control of essential life processes such as cardiovascular activity and respiration (breathing). The *pons* contains centers related to sleep and arousal, which are part of the reticular formation. The *reticular formation* is a collection of many nuclei running through the middle of the hindbrain and the midbrain. The word *pons* means "bridge" in Latin, which reflects the fact that sensory neurons pass through on their way to the thalamus, and motor neurons pass through between the cortex and the cerebellum.

The cerebellum is the second most distinctive appearing brain structure (Figures 3.12, 3.20). Perched on the back of the brain stem, it is wrinkled and divided down the middle like the cerebral hemispheres—thus its name, which means "little brain." The most obvious function of the *cerebellum* is in refining movements initiated by the motor cortex

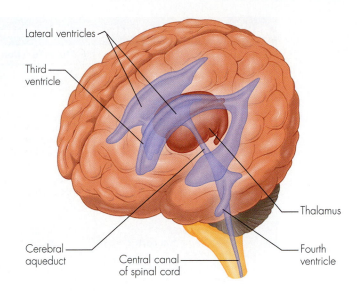

Figure 3.14
The cerebral ventricles

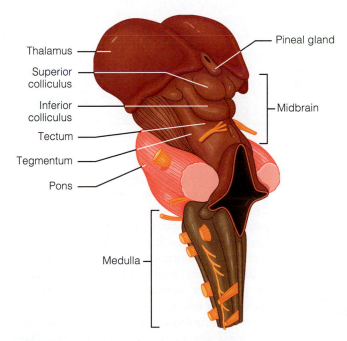

Figure 3.15
The brain stem
(The cerebellum has been removed to reveal the other structures.)

Table 3.1 Major Structures of the Brain and Their Functions	
Structure	**Major Function**
Forebrain	
Frontal lobes	
Motor cortex	Plans and executes voluntary movements
Basal ganglia	Smooths movement generated by motor cortex
Broca's area	Controls speech, adds grammar
Prefrontal cortex	Involved in planning, impulse control
Parietal lobes	
Somatosensory cortex	Projection area for body senses
Association area	Location of body and objects in space
Temporal lobes	
Auditory cortex	Projection area for auditory information
Wernicke's area	Language area involved with meaning
Inferior temporal cortex	Visual identification of objects
Occipital lobes	
Primary visual cortex	Projection area for visual information
Visual association cortex	Processes components of visual information
Corpus callosum	Communication between the hemispheres
Ventricles	Contain cerebrospinal fluid
Thalamus	Relays sensory information to cortex
Hypothalamus	Coordinates emotional and motivational functions
Limbic system	Circuit of structures involved in emotion, motivation, learning
Midbrain	
Superior colliculi	Role in vision, for example eye movements
Inferior colliculi	Role in audition, such as sound location
Pineal gland	Contributes to control of rhythms
Hindbrain	
Medulla	Reflexively controls life processes
Pons	Contains sensory pathways
Reticular formation	Involved with arousal and alertness
Cerebellum	Controls speed, intensity, direction of movements

by controlling their speed, intensity, and direction. A person whose cerebellum is damaged walks with difficulty because the automatic patterning of movement routines has been lost, and has trouble making precise reaching movements. It is not unusual for individuals with cerebellar damage to be arrested by police for drunkenness. The cerebellum also plays a role in motor learning, and recent research implicates it in other cognitive processes and in emotion (Fiez, 1996). With half the brain's neurons in its fist-sized volume, it would be surprising if it did not hold a

What is the alternative to localization and equipotentiality?

number of mysteries waiting to be solved. The cerebellum forms the roof of the fourth ventricle; the pons provides its floor.

We have admittedly covered a large number of structures. It may help to see them and their major functions summarized in Table 3.1.

Localization

Localization of brain function, the idea that specific parts of the brain carry out specific functions, is commonly accepted by researchers (and some humorists, as the quote shows!). I have also been pushing the idea of localization, pointing out that one part of the brain has one function, and another part of the brain has another function, all in the hope of convincing you that it is the brain that is in charge of behavior. Now, a note of caution: it is not unusual for brain theorists to take the principle of localization too far, and we should be on guard lest we make the same mistake. In the nineteenth century, when interest in the brain's role in behavior was really heating up, the German anatomist Franz Gall and his student Spurzheim came up with an extreme and controversial theory of brain localization. **According to *phrenology,* each of 35 different "faculties" of emotion and intellect—like combativeness, inhabitiveness (love of home), calculation, and order—was located in a precise area of the brain** (Spurzheim, 1908). They determined this by feeling bumps on people's skulls and relating any protuberances to the individual's characteristics (Figure 3.16). We now know that bumps on the skull have nothing to do with the size of the brain structures beneath, and that most of the characteristics Gall and Spurzheim identified have no particular meaning at the physiological level. At the other end of the spectrum was *equipotentiality,* **which held that the brain functions as an undifferentiated whole;** according to this view the extent of damage, not the location, is what determines how much function is lost.

I never could keep a promise. . . . It is likely that such a liberal amount of space was given to the organ which enables me to make promises that the organ which should enable me to keep them was crowded out.

—Mark Twain, in *Innocents Abroad*

The truth, as is often the case, lies somewhere between the two extremes. We saw in Chapter 1 that the localization faction, led by investigators like Paul Broca and Fritsch and Hitzig, pretty much won the day; nevertheless,

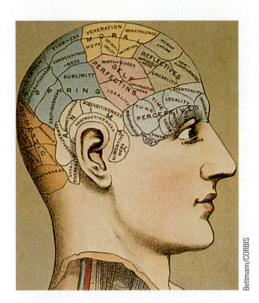

Bettmann/CORBIS

Figure 3.16
A phrenologist's map of the brain
Do any of these functions correspond to those you have been learning about?

any statements about localization must be qualified. Throughout the text as we discuss the functions of particular brain structures I will also emphasize the fact that behavior results from the interaction among many widespread areas of the brain. Though the brain is not equipotential, processes are as much *distributed* as they are localized. In later chapters you will see examples of cooperative relationships among brain areas in language, visual perception, emotional behavior, motor control, and learning. In fact, you will learn that neuroscientists these days less frequently ask where a function is located than how the brain integrates activity from widespread areas into a single experience or behavior. This question is known as the *binding problem,* an issue we will take up in the chapter on vision and again in the discussion of consciousness in the final chapter.

The Spinal Cord

The *spinal cord* is a finger-sized cable of neurons that carries commands from the brain to the muscles and organs, and sensory

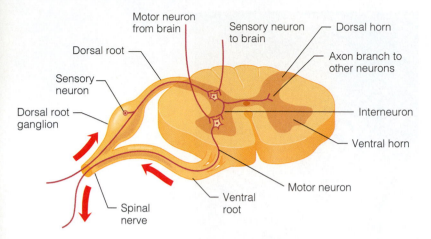

Motor neuron from brain
Sensory neuron to brain — Dorsal horn
Dorsal root
Sensory neuron
Axon branch to other neurons
Dorsal root ganglion
Interneuron
Ventral horn
Motor neuron
Ventral root
Spinal nerve

Figure 3.17
Cross section of spinal cord
A sensory neuron transmits signals (1) into the spinal cord via the dorsal root of the spinal nerve (2) to the dorsal horn, forming a reflex arc with a motor neuron, as well as (3) up to the brain and (4) across the spinal cord to other neurons. A motor neuron from the brain also connects to the motor neuron in the ventral horn and exits the spinal cord through the ventral root. (The spinal nerve and roots on the other side are not shown.)

What is the structure of the spinal cord?

information into the brain. Its role is more complicated than that, though. It controls the rapid reflexive response when you withdraw your hand from a hot stove, and it contains pattern generators that help control routine behaviors such as walking. Notice the appearance of the interior of the spinal cord in Figure 3.17; it is arranged just the opposite of the brain, with the white matter on the outside and the gray matter in the interior. The white exterior is made up of axons—ascending sensory tracts on their way to the brain and descending motor tracts on their way to muscles and organs.

Sensory neurons enter the spinal cord through the *dorsal root* of each spinal nerve. The sensory neurons are unipolar, with their cell bodies located mostly in the dorsal root ganglion; the sensory neuron in Figure 3.17 could be as much as a meter long, with its other end out in a fingertip or a toe. The H-shaped structure in the middle of the spinal

cord is made up mostly of unmyelinated cell bodies. **The cell bodies of motor neurons are located in the *ventral horns,* which is why the ventral horns are enlarged. The axons of the motor neurons pass out of the cord through the *ventral root*.** The dorsal root and the ventral root on the same side of the cord join to form a spinal nerve that exits the spine through an opening in the vertebra.

Most of the motor neurons receive their input from the brain, either from the motor cortex or from nuclei that control the activity of the internal organs. Notice in the illustration, however, that in some cases sensory neurons from the dorsal side connect with motor neurons, either directly or through an interneuron. **This pathway produces a simple, automatic movement in response to a sensory stimulus; this is called a *reflex*.** For example, when you step on a sharp stone with your bare foot, output goes directly out to the muscles of the leg to produce reflexive withdrawal. Many people use the term *reflex* incorrectly to refer to any action a person takes without apparent thought; however, the term is limited to behaviors that are controlled by these direct sensory-motor connections. Reflexes occur in the brain as well as in the spinal cord, and reflexes also affect the internal environment, for example reducing blood pressure when it goes too high.

Protecting the CNS

The brain and spinal cord are delicate organs, vulnerable to damage from blows and jostling, to poisoning by toxins, and to disruption by mislocated or excessive neurotransmitters. Both structures are enclosed in a **protective three-layered membrane called the *meninges.*** The space between the meninges and the CNS is filled with cerebrospinal fluid, which cushions the neural tissue from the trauma of blows and sudden movement. The brain and spinal cord literally float in the cerebrospinal fluid, so the weight of a 1200- to 1400-gram brain is in effect reduced to less than 100 grams.

The tough meninges and the cerebrospinal fluid afford the brain some protection from occasional trauma, but **the *blood-brain barrier* is called on constantly to prevent harmful substances from entering the brain.** In the rest of the body, substances pass rather freely between the bloodstream and the organs they serve. In the brain, the cells that compose the walls of brain capillaries (small blood vessels) overlap each other so tightly that most molecules are too large to get through (Figure 3.18). Substances that can dissolve in fat pass through the wall readily, which accounts for the effectiveness of most drugs. But most substances needed by the brain are water soluble and cannot pass through on their own; they must be actively carried through with the help of specialized transporters. The blood-brain barrier protects the brain against many toxic substances, and from neurotransmitters circulating in the blood such as norepinephrine and glutamate, which increase during stress.

Not all brain areas are protected by the barrier, however. This is particularly true of subventricular organs, brain structures surrounding the ventricles. This absence is not a fault. For example, **toxic substances in the blood enter the *area postrema* and it responds by inducing vomiting**; this empties the stomach, which is the most likely source of the poison.

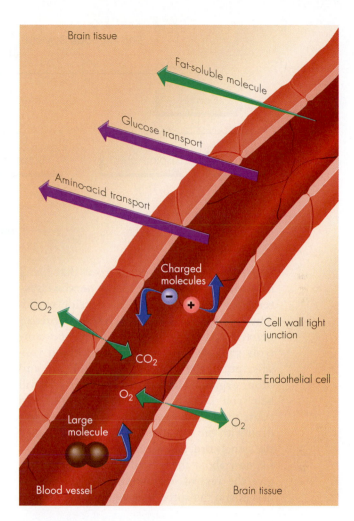

Figure 3.18
The blood-brain barrier

✔ CONCEPT CHECK

- *What is the advantage of the convoluted structure of the cortex?*
- *What has been the fate of psychosurgery, and what clue from past experience did doctors have that lobotomy in particular might have undesirable consequences?*
- *Where do we stand on the localization issue now?*
- *Describe the pathway of a simple reflex, identifying the neurons and the parts of the spinal cord involved.*

THE PERIPHERAL NERVOUS SYSTEM (PNS)

You saw earlier that the peripheral nervous system consists of the 12 pairs of cranial nerves and the 31 pairs of spinal nerves. Alternatively, it can be divided into the somatic nervous system and the autonomic nervous system (ANS). **The *somatic nervous system* includes the motor neurons that operate the skeletal muscles—that is, the ones that move the**

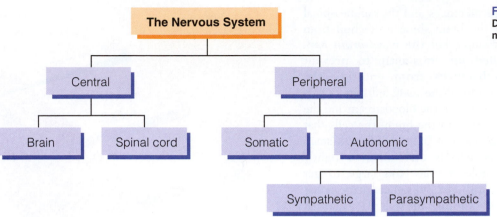

Figure 3.19
**Divisions of the
nervous system**

body—and the sensory neurons that bring information into the central nervous system from the body and the outside world. The *autonomic nervous system* regulates general activity level in the body, and controls smooth muscle (stomach, blood vessels, etc.), the glands, and the heart and other organs. The diagram in Figure 3.19 will help you keep track of these divisions and relate them to the central nervous system. We dealt with the spinal nerves when we discussed the spinal cord, and we have said all we need to for now about the somatic system, so we will give the rest of our attention to the cranial nerves and the autonomic system.

The Cranial Nerves

The cranial nerves enter and exit on the ventral side of the brain (Figure 3.20). While the spinal nerves are concerned exclusively with sensory and motor activities within the body, some of the cranial nerves convey sensory information to the brain from the outside world. Two of these, the olfactory nerves and the optic nerves, have the special status of often being considered part of the brain. This is because of the complexity of the olfactory bulb and of the retina at the back of the eye, and because their receptor cells originate in the brain during development and migrate to their final locations. As a consequence, you will

sometimes see the olfactory and optic nerves referred to as tracts.

Note the optic chiasm where the two optic nerves join and then separate again before entering the brain. This structure provides a useful reference point for locating the rest of the cranial nerves and other structures. At the chiasm the axons from the nasal half of each eye cross to the other side of the brain. This crossing over allows objects in the left visual space to be registered in the right hemisphere and vice versa. Researchers have capitalized on this arrangement to study differences in the capabilities of the two hemispheres (as described in section A.4 of the appendix).

The Autonomic Nervous System (ANS)

The functions of the ANS are primarily motor; its sensory pathways provide internal information for regulating its own operations. The autonomic nervous system is composed of two branches. **The *sympathetic nervous system* activates the body in ways that help it cope with demands, such as emotional stress and physical emergencies.** For instance, it speeds up the heart and respiration, constricts the peripheral blood vessels, increases blood pressure, and activates the sweat glands. **The *parasympathetic nervous system* slows the activity of most organs to conserve energy,**

What are the functions of the autonomic nervous system?

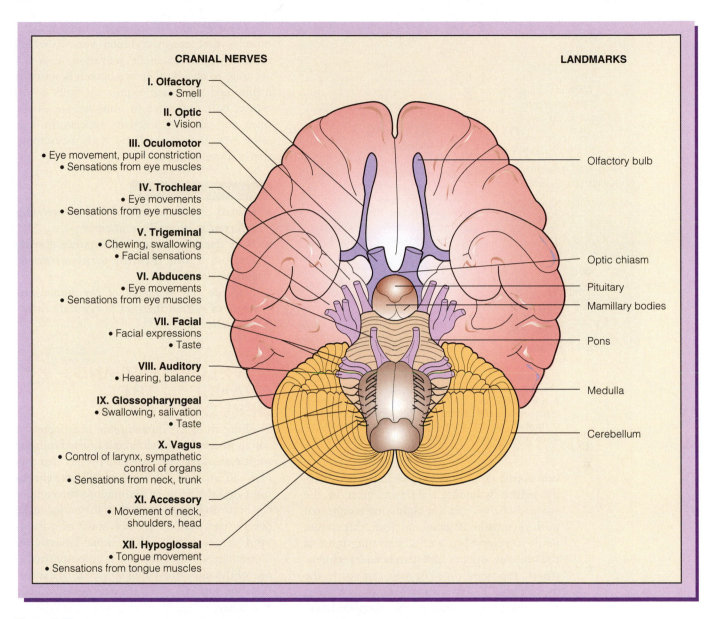

CRANIAL NERVES

I. Olfactory
• Smell

II. Optic
• Vision

III. Oculomotor
• Eye movement, pupil constriction
• Sensations from eye muscles

IV. Trochlear
• Eye movements
• Sensations from eye muscles

V. Trigeminal
• Chewing, swallowing
• Facial sensations

VI. Abducens
• Eye movements
• Sensations from eye muscles

VII. Facial
• Facial expressions
• Taste

VIII. Auditory
• Hearing, balance

IX. Glossopharyngeal
• Swallowing, salivation
• Taste

X. Vagus
• Control of larynx, sympathetic control of organs
• Sensations from neck, trunk

XI. Accessory
• Movement of neck, shoulders, head

XII. Hypoglossal
• Tongue movement
• Sensations from tongue muscles

LANDMARKS

Olfactory bulb

Optic chiasm

Pituitary

Mamillary bodies

Pons

Medulla

Cerebellum

Figure 3.20
Ventral view of the brain showing the cranial nerves and their major functions
Brain landmarks are labeled on the right to help you locate the nerves.

but it also activates digestion to renew energy.

The sympathetic branch arises from the middle (thoracic and lumbar) areas of the spinal cord (see Figure 3.21). **Most sympa-** thetic neurons pass through the *sympathetic ganglion chain* that runs along each side of the spine; there they synapse with postsynaptic neurons that rejoin the spinal nerve and go out to the muscles or glands they serve. (The

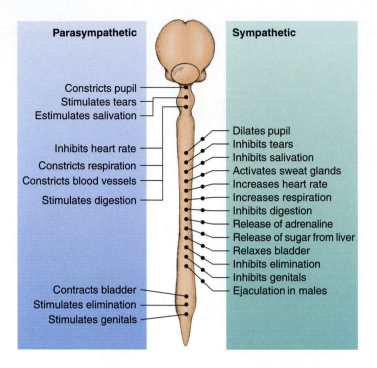

| Parasympathetic | | Sympathetic |

Constricts pupil
Stimulates tears
Estimulates salivation

Inhibits heart rate
Constricts respiration
Constricts blood vessels
Stimulates digestion

Contracts bladder
Stimulates elimination
Stimulates genitals

Dilates pupil
Inhibits tears
Inhibits salivation
Activates sweat glands
Increases heart rate
Increases respiration
Inhibits digestion
Release of adrenaline
Release of sugar from liver
Relaxes bladder
Inhibits elimination
Inhibits genitals
Ejaculation in males

Figure 3.21
The autonomic nervous system
A diagrammatic view of the parasympathetic and sympathetic nerves and their functions. The nerves exit both sides of the brain and spinal cord through the paired cranial and spinal nerves, but are shown on one side for simplicity.

others pass directly to ganglia in the body cavity before synapsing.) Because most of the sympathetic ganglia are highly interconnected in the sympathetic ganglion chain, this system tends to respond as a unit, activating most of the muscles, organs, and glands under its control at the same time. As you can see in the illustration, the parasympathetic branch arises from the extreme ends of the peripheral nervous system—in the cranial nerves and in the spinal nerves at the lower (sacral) end of the spinal cord. The parasympathetic ganglia are not interconnected, but are located on or near the muscles and glands they control; as a result, the components of the parasympathetic system operate more independently than those of the sympathetic system.

Targets are innervated by both branches of the autonomic system, with the exception of

the sweat glands, the adrenal glands, and the muscles that constrict blood vessels, which receive only sympathetic activation. It is not accurate to assume that one branch is active at a time and the other completely shuts down; rather, both are active to some degree all the time, and the body's activity reflects the balance between sympathetic and parasympathetic stimulation.

✔ **CONCEPT CHECK**

- *Which cranial nerves are sometimes referred to as tracts, and why?*
- *Why does the sympathetic system operate more as a unit than the parasympathetic system does?*
- *How do the branches of the autonomic nervous system interact to regulate internal activity?*

DEVELOPMENT AND CHANGE IN THE NERVOUS SYSTEM

Nothing rivals the human brain in complexity, which makes the development of the brain the most remarkable construction project that you or I can imagine. Its hundred billion neurons must find their way to destinations throughout the brain and spinal cord; then they must make precise connections to an average of a thousand target cells each (Tessier-Lavigne & Goodman, 1996). How this is accomplished is one of the most intriguing mysteries of neurology, but a mystery that is being solved a little at a time.

The Stages of Development

You already know that the nervous system begins as a hollow tube that later becomes the brain and the spinal cord. The nervous system begins development when the surface of the embryo invaginates, forming a groove (see Figure 3.22); the edges of this groove curl upward until they meet, turning the groove into a tube. Development of the nervous sys-

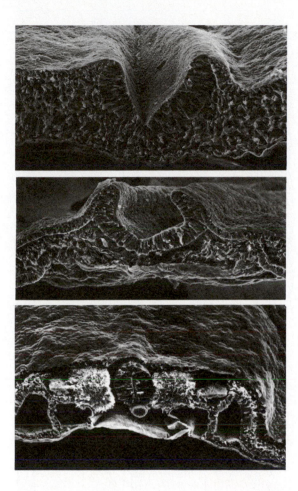

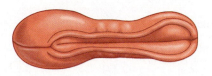

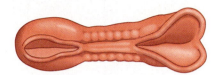

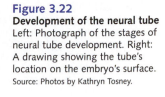

Figure 3.22
Development of the neural tube
Left: Photograph of the stages of neural tube development. Right: A drawing showing the tube's location on the embryo's surface.
Source: Photos by Kathryn Tosney.

tem then proceeds in four distinct stages: cell proliferation, migration, circuit formation, and circuit pruning.

During *proliferation* **the cells that will become neurons divide and multiply at the rate of 250,000 new cells every minute.** Proliferation occurs in the ventricular zone, the area surrounding the hollow tube that will later become the ventricles and the central canal. These newly formed neurons then *migrate* **from the ventricular zone outward to their final location. To do so, the cells climb specialized** *radial glial cells* **that provide a sort of scaffold** (Figure 3.23). The functional role that a neuron will play depends on its location and the time of its "birth"; different structures form during different

stages of fetal development. Prior to birth and for a time afterward the neurons retain considerable functional flexibility, however. In fact, you may remember that fetal tissue can be transplanted into a different part of an adult brain and the transplanted neurons will form synapses and assume the function of their new location.

During *circuit formation*, **the developing neurons send processes to their target cells and form functional connections.** For example, axons of motor neurons grow toward the spinal cord and cells in the retina of the eye send their axons to the thalamus, where they form synapses with other neurons. To find their way, **axons form** *growth cones* **at their tip which sample the environment for**

How do neurons find their correct destination?

Figure 3.23
A neuron migrates along glial scaffolding
At left, immature neurons migrate from the inner layer where they were "born" to their destination between there and the outer layer. Right, a close-up of one of the neurons climbing a radial glial cell scaffold.
Adapted from illustration by Lydia Kibiuk, © 1995.

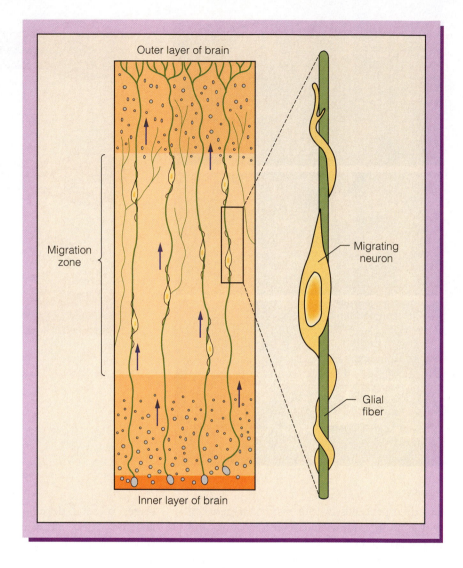

Outer layer of brain

Migration zone

Migrating neuron

Glial fiber

Inner layer of brain

directional cues (Figure 3.24). Chemical and molecular signposts attract or repel the advancing axon, coaxing it along the way (Tessier-Lavigne & Goodman, 1996). By pushing, pulling, and hemming neurons in from the side, the chemical and molecular forces guide the neuron to intermediate stations and past inappropriate targets until they reach their final destinations (see Figure 3.25).

You might wonder why growth doesn't stall when the axon reaches an attractant at an intermediate point. The answer is that the close presence of the attractant triggers genetic up- and downregulation that changes the growth cone's sensitivity to attractant molecules and repellent molecules (Stein & Tessier-Lavigne, 2001). Thus, the axon not only continues but can change directions; for instance, a neuron might be attracted to the midline of the nervous system, cross the corpus callosum to the other side, then turn and travel along the midline to its final location. Special *pioneer neurons* **develop early and forge ahead, "blazing" a trail for later-developing neurons to follow**; if pioneer neurons are destroyed, subsequent neurons do not make the trip. After they are no longer needed, the pioneer neurons die (Klose & Bentley, 1989;

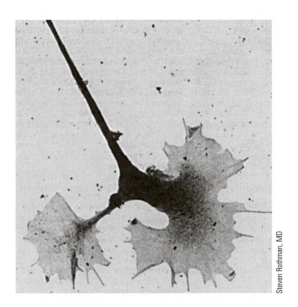

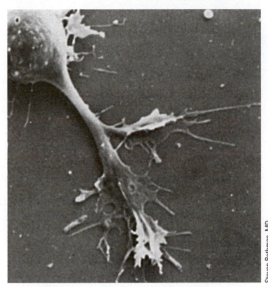

Steven Rothman, MD

Steven Rothman, MD

Figure 3.24
Neurons with growth cones

Kuwada, 1986; McConnell, Ghosh, & Shatz, 1989).

The brain produces extra neurons, apparently as a means of compensating for the errors that occur in reaching targets. This overproduction is not trivial: the monkey's visual cortex contains 35% more neurons at the time of birth than in adulthood, and the number of axons crossing the corpus callosum is four times what it will be later in life (LaMantia & Rakic, 1990; Williams, Ryder, & Rakic, 1987). **The neurons that are unsuccessful in finding a place on a target cell, or that arrive late, die in the first step of *circuit pruning*.** The monkey's corpus callosum alone loses 8 million neurons a day during the first three weeks after birth.

In the second step of circuit pruning, the nervous system refines its organization and continues to correct errors by eliminating large numbers of excessive synapses. For example, in the mature mammal, neurons from the left and right eye project to alternating

What determines which synapses will survive?

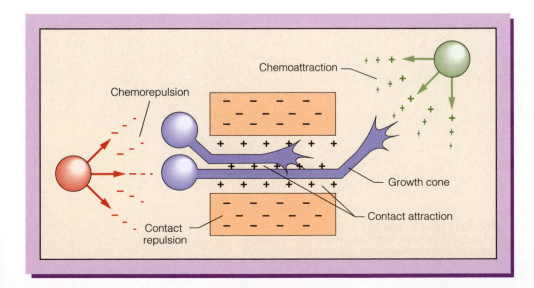

Figure 3.25
Forces that direct axons to their targets
Source: Reprinted with permission from M. Tessier-Lavigne and C.S. Goodman (1996), The molecular biology of axon guidance. *Science,* 274, 1123–1132. Copyright 1996 American Association for the Advancement of Science.

columns of cells in the brain; however, during development the neurons connect to the cells indiscriminately (Kalil, 1989). If the presynaptic neuron and the postsynaptic neuron fire at the same time, their connection is strengthened. This is likely to happen when neighboring presynaptic neurons are active at the same time because, if you remember, a single neuron cannot activate a postsynaptic neuron alone. And if a neuron is firing at the same time as its neighbors, it is a good sign that the neuron has made its connection in the right "neighborhood." It is thought that the postsynaptic neuron sends feedback to the presynaptic terminals in the form of *neurotrophins,* **chemicals that enhance development and survival in neurons.** Later, the *plasticity* **(ability to be modified)** of these synapses decreases. However, the synapses in the cortical association areas are more likely to retain their plasticity, permitting later modification by experience—in other words, learning (Kandel & O'Dell, 1992; Katz & Shatz, 1996; Singer, 1995).

In the visual system, sensory stimulation provides neuronal activation that contributes to this refinement. However, pruning of synapses begins in some parts of the visual system even before birth; so how can this stimulation occur during a time when visual input is impossible? The answer is that waves of spontaneous neural firing sweep across the fetal retina, providing the activation that selects which synapses will survive and which will not (Katz & Shatz, 1996; Meister, Wong, Baylor, & Shatz, 1991). In the first few years of the rhesus monkey's life, 40% of the synapses in the primary visual cortex are eliminated, at the stunning rate of 5,000 per second (Bourgeois & Rakic, 1993). This process of producing synapses that will later be eliminated seems wasteful, but targeting neurons' destinations more precisely would require prohibitively complex chemical and molecular codes.

As impressive as the brain's ability to organize itself during development is, mistakes do occur, and for a variety of reasons. Periventricular heterotopia, described at the beginning of the chapter, is an example of a genetic cause. *Fetal alcohol syndrome (FAS),* **which often produces mental retardation, is caused by the mother's use of alcohol during a critical period of brain development.** FAS brains are often small and malformed, and neurons are dislocated (Figure 3.26). During migration many cortical neurons fail to line up in columns as they normally would because the radial glial cells revert to their more typical glial form prematurely; other neurons continue

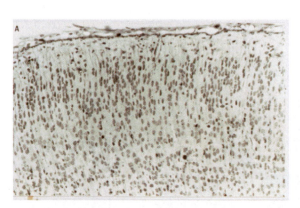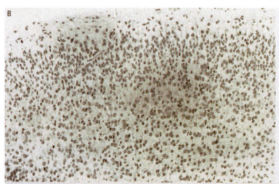

Figure 3.26
Fetal alcohol syndrome in the mouse brain
(a) In the normal brain the neurons (the dark spots) tend to line up vertically. **(b)** In the alcohol-exposed brain the neurons are arranged randomly. Also, a number of the neurons have migrated beyond the rest of the neurons.
Source: Gressens, Lammens, Picard, & Evrard, 1992.

migrating beyond the usual boundary of the cortex (Clarren, Alvord, Sumi, Streissguth, & Smith, 1978; Gressens, Lammens, Picard, & Evrard, 1992; Lewis, 1985). Exposure to ionizing radiation, like that produced by nuclear accidents and atomic blasts, also causes retardation by interfering with neuronal proliferation and migration. The offspring of women who were in the eighth through fifteenth weeks of pregnancy during the bombing of Hiroshima and Nagasaki and during the nuclear meltdown at Chernobyl were most vulnerable, because the rates of proliferation and migration are highest then (Schull, Norton, & Jensh, 1990).

An additional step is required for full maturation of the nervous system, and that is myelination. In the brain it begins with the lower structures, then proceeds to the cerebral hemispheres, moving from occipital lobes to frontal lobes. Myelination starts around the end of the third trimester of fetal development but is not complete until late adolescence or beyond (Sowell, Thompson, Holmes, Jernigan, & Toga, 1999). This slow process has behavioral implications, for instance contributing to the improvement through adolescence on cognitive tasks that require the frontal lobes (Levin et al., 1991). Considering the functions of the prefrontal cortex and the fact that this area is the last to mature (Sowell et al., 1999), it should come as no surprise that parents are baffled by their adolescents' behavior.

How Experience Modifies the Nervous System

Stimulation continues to shape synaptic construction and reconstruction throughout the individual's life. For example, training rats to find their way through a maze or just exposing them to a complex living environment increases the branching of synapses in the cortex (Greenough, 1975). Humans develop more synapses as they age, even while losing neurons (Buell & Coleman, 1979), presumably as the result of experience.

Most of the change resulting from experience in the mature brain involves **reorganization, a shift in connections that changes the func-tion of an area of the brain.** In Braille readers, the space in the brain devoted to the index (reading) finger increases, at the expense of the area corresponding to the other fingers on the same hand (Pascual-Leone & Torres, 1993). Similarly, in string musicians the area in the somatosensory cortex devoted to the fingers on the left (fingering) hand is larger than in other individuals (Elbert, Pantev, Wienbruch, Rockstroh, & Taub, 1995).

These changes can occur rapidly, as we see in a study of individuals born with a condition called *syndactyly*, in which their fingers are attached to each other by a web of skin. Use of the fingers is severely limited, and the fingers are represented by overlapping areas in the somatosensory cortex. Figure 3.27 shows that after surgery the representations of the fingers in the cortex became separate and distinct in just seven days (Mogilner et al., 1993).

The nineteenth-century philosopher and psychologist William James speculated that if a surgeon could switch your optic nerves with your auditory nerves you would then see thunder and hear lightning (James, 1893). James was expressing Johannes Müller's *doctrine of specific nerve energies* from a half-century earlier, that each sensory projection area produces its own unique experience regardless of the kind of stimulation it receives. This is why you "see stars" when your rollerblades shoot out from under you and the back of your head (where the visual cortex is located) hits the pavement.

But even this basic principle of brain operation can fall victim to reorganization during early development. In people blind from birth the visual cortex has nothing to do; as a result, some of the somatosensory pathways take over the area, so the visual cortex is activated by touch. But does the visual cortex still produce a visual experience, or one of touch? To find out, researchers stimulated the visual cortex of blind individuals by applying an electromagnetic field to the scalp over the occipital area (Cohen et al., 1997). In sighted people this disrupts visual performance, but in the blind individuals the procedure distorted their sense of

What kinds of changes occur in the brain due to experience?

Figure 3.27
Changes in somatosensory area following surgery for syndactyly
Left: The hand before (top) and after (bottom) surgery. Center: Images showing brain areas responsive to stimulation of the fingers before and after surgery. Right: Graphic representation of the relative size and location of responsive areas.

Source: From A. Mogilner, et al. (1993). Somatosensory cortical plasticity in adult humans revealed by magnetoencephalography. Proceedings of The National Academy of Science, 90, 3593–3597.

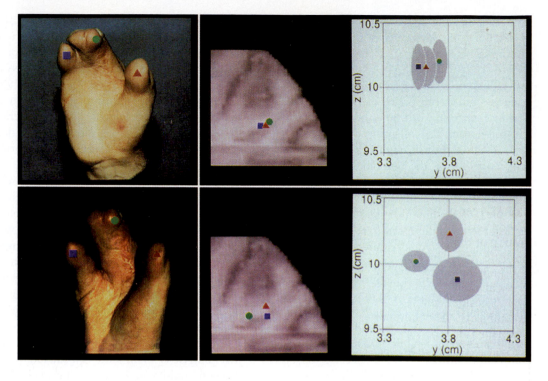

touch and interfered with their ability to identify Braille letters.

Reorganization does not always produce a beneficial outcome. When kittens were reared in an environment with no visual stimulation except horizontal stripes or vertical stripes, they lost their ability to respond to objects in the other orientation. A cat reared, for example, with vertical stripes would play with a rod held vertically, and ignore the rod when it was horizontal. Electrical recording indicated that the cells in the visual cortex that would have responded to other orientations had reorganized their connections in response to the limited stimulation. In Chapter 10 you will see that people who have a limb amputated often experience *phantom pain*, pain that seems to be located in the missing limb. It appears to be caused by sensory neurons from a nearby part of the body growing into the somatosensory area that had served the lost limb (Flor et al., 1995). Doctors and neuroscientists are trying to harness plasticity not only to help brain-damaged people recover but to prevent undesirable effects of reorganization.

What limits central nervous system repair? How might repair be encouraged?

Damage and Recovery in the CNS

In the adult centres the nerve paths are something fixed, ended and immutable. Everything may die, nothing may be regenerated. It is for the science of the future to change, if possible, this harsh decree.

—Santiago Ramon y Cajal, 1928

One reason neuroscientists are interested in the development of the nervous system is because they hope to find clues about how to repair the nervous system when it is damaged by injury, disease, or developmental error. It is difficult to convey the impairment and suffering that results from brain disorders, but Table 3.2 will give you an idea of the staggering financial costs.

Limitations on Recovery

Nervous system repair is no problem for some species, particularly amphibians. For example, when Sperry (1943, 1945) severed the optic

Table 3.2 Annual Costs of Brain Damage and Disorders

Psychiatric disease (schizophrenia, cognitive impairment, etc.)	$136.1 billion
Neurological disorders (dementia, mental retardation, multiple sclerosis, head and spinal cord injuries, stroke, cerebral palsy, epilepsy)	103.7
Alcohol abuse	90.1
Drug abuse	71.2
Total:	$401.1 billion

Source: National Foundation for Brain Research, 1992.

nerves of frogs, the eyes made functional reconnections to the brain even when the disconnected eye was turned upside down or transplanted into the other eye socket. *Regeneration,* **the growth of severed axons,** is limited to the peripheral nervous system in mammals. The disconnected part of a cut axon will die, but the part connected to the cell body will survive and regrow. Myelin provides a guide tube for the sprouting end of a severed neuron to grow through (Freed, de Medinaceli, & Wyatt, 1985), and the extending axon is guided to its destination much as it would be during development (Horner & Gage, 2000). But in the mammalian CNS the neuron encounters a hostile environment.

The axon stump sprouts new growth, but it makes little progress toward its former target. This is partly because the central nervous system in adult mammals no longer produces the chemical and molecular conditions that stimulate and guide neuronal growth. In addition, scar tissue blocks the original pathway, glial cells produce axon growth inhibitors, and immune cells that move into the area may interfere (Chen, Schneider, Martinou, & Tonegawa, 1997; Horner & Gage, 2000; Thallmair et al., 1998).

Another way the nervous system could repair itself is by *neurogenesis,* **the birth of new neurons.** As we saw in Chapter 1, significant numbers of new neurons are known to be produced in only two areas; one is the hippocampus, and the other is near the lateral ventricles, supplying the olfactory bulb (Gage, 2000). Damage to the hippocampus increases the rate of neuron production in rats and gerbils (Bengzon et al., 1997; Liu, Solway, Messing, & Sharp, 1998; Parent et al., 1997), and there is some evidence the mouse

cortex might produce some new neurons when it is damaged (Magavi, Leavitt, & Macklis, 2000). These results foster hope that neurogenesis could be manipulated to bring about self-repair. However, there is no evidence that the new neurons take up the functions of the damaged neurons, and new neurons produced following seizures are known to migrate abnormally and form inappropriate connections (Parent et al., 1997).

This does not mean that there is no recovery of function in the mammalian CNS. There often is, but it has nothing to do with regrowth of severed axons or replacement of damaged neurons.

Compensation

Non-neural improvement comes about as swelling diminishes and glia remove dead neurons (Bach-y-Rita, 1990). **Neural recovery involves** *compensation* **as uninjured tissue takes over functions of lost neurons.** Presynaptic neurons sprout more terminals to form additional synapses with their targets (Fritschy & Grzanna, 1992; Goodman, Bogdasarian, & Horel, 1973) and postsynaptic neurons add more receptors (Bach-y-Rita, 1990). In addition, normally silent collateral synapses from other neurons in the area are unmasked and become active within minutes of the injury (Das & Gilbert, 1995; Gilbert, 1993). These synaptic changes are also similar to those occurring during learning. This would explain why physical therapy can be effective in promoting recovery after brain injury, as illustrated in "Study Offers Hope for Use of Limbs Disabled by Stroke" on the next page.

Sometimes compensation resembles reorganization, but the original function is retained. This

What forms of recovery are possible in the human CNS?

IN THE NEWS

Study Offers Hope for Use of Limbs Disabled by Stroke

Sandra Blakeslee—When a stroke impairs the use of a limb, the victim usually relies on the good limb and allows the affected arm to hang limply or drags the bad leg like so much dead weight. The area of the motor cortex controlling an impaired arm often shrinks by 70 percent; the area controlling the good limb expands, because the patient relies on it. A stroke kills many cells, but not all of them. Now researchers are finding ways to bring those surviving cells back into action.

Using what they call constraint-induced-therapy, researchers immobilized stroke patients' good arms in a splint and sling for 90 percent of their waking hours. The subjects also went to the laboratory for six hours a day, four times a week, where they practiced reaching out, grasping, and moving objects with the partially paralyzed arm. After just two weeks, the patients had regained three-quarters of the normal use of their arms. Brain scans showed that the motor area serving the trained arm almost doubled. Six months later the brain changes appeared to be permanent.

According to Edward Taub, one of the researchers, about 250 patients have been treated with constraint-induced-therapy in laboratories across the country, with excellent results.

—*The* New York Times *on the Web, June 2, 2000. Available at http://www.nytimes.com/library/national/science/health/060200hth-brain-stroke.html*

---

form of compensation is particularly seen in recovery from language impairment *(aphasia)* that results from brain damage or surgery. In most cases this presumably involves nearby areas assuming the role, but there are documented cases where the right hemisphere has taken over language functioning after massive damage to the left hemisphere (Guerreiro, Castro-Caldas, & Martins, 1995). Occasionally an entire diseased hemisphere must be removed for medical reasons. The patients typically do not reach normal levels of performance after the surgery, but they often recover their language and other cognitive skills and motor control to a remarkable degree (Glees, 1980; Ogden, 1989). In these cases malfunction in the removed hemisphere dated back to infancy, so presumably the reorganization began then rather than at the time of surgery in late adolescence or early adulthood.

Recovery from aphasia and periventricular heterotopia challenge our understanding of how the brain works. Hydrocephalus provides another such example. **Hydrocephalus occurs when the circulation of cerebrospinal fluid is blocked and accumulating fluid interferes with the brain's growth, producing severe**
retardation. The condition can be treated if caught in time, by installing a drain that shunts the excess fluid into the bloodstream. However, the occasional individual somehow escapes impairment without this treatment. The British neurologist John Lorber described a 26-year-old hydrocephalic whose cerebral walls were less than 1 millimeter thick, compared to the usual 45 millimeters. Yet he had a superior IQ of 126, had earned an honors degree in mathematics, and was socially normal ("Brain Shrinks," 1983; Lewin, 1980). It is unclear how these individuals can function normally in the face of such enormous brain deficits. What is clear is that somewhere in this remarkable plasticity lies the key to new revelations about brain function.

Possibilities for CNS Repair

Unwilling to accept the limitations on the ability of our central nervous system to repair itself, researchers have been attempting to find ways to enhance the process. In 1995 Christopher Reeve, the movie actor best known for his role as Superman, was paralyzed from the neck down when he was thrown from his horse during a competition (Figure 3.28). If the quote

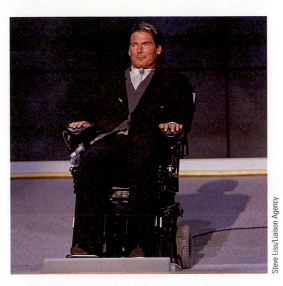

Figure 3.28
Christopher Reeve hopes research will help him walk again

from Ramon y Cajal is correct, then Superman not only cannot fly but will never walk again.

. . . the word impossible is not in the vocabulary of contemporary neuroscience.
—Pasko Rakic

Researchers are developing several strategies for repairing damaged brains and spinal cords. There has been no shortage of possibilities. One line of research involves attempts to replace the lost neurons; you saw in Chapter 1 that grafts of fetal brain tissue or of stem cells are a promising but controversial strategy for repairing dam-

aged nervous systems. This technique has even restored the learning performance of rats whose memory had been impaired by long-term ingestion of alcohol (Arendt et al., 1988).

Other efforts include inserting neuron growth promoters, negating growth inhibitors, providing artificial tubes or other support for axons to follow, and blocking the immune response (Horner & Gage, 2000). The results have been hopeful, with spinal cord–injured rats regaining some normal functioning. Five years after his injury, Christopher Reeve began an experimental therapy that involved rhythmic electrical stimulation of the muscles; for example, stimulation of his leg muscles enable him to pedal an exercise bicycle (McDonald et al., 2002). After three years, he has regained 66% of normal touch sensation and has some movement in his hands and legs. Such improvement more than two years post-injury is unheard of in a patient who had no sensation and no voluntary movement below the injury. Reeve, whose foundation is supporting spinal cord research, sees a day soon when Ramon y Cajal's decree will be lifted and he will walk once again.

 **CONCEPT CHECK**

- *Describe the four steps of nervous system development and the fifth step of maturation.*
- *Give three examples of changes in the brain resulting from experience.*
- *What are the obstacles to recovery from injury in the central nervous system, and the strategies for overcoming them?*

 In Perspective

I could end this chapter by talking about how much we know about the brain and its functions. Or I could tell you how little we know. Either point of view would be correct; it is the classic case of whether the glass is half full or half empty. As I said in Chapter 1, we made remarkable progress during the last decade. We know the functions of most

areas of the brain. We have a good idea how the brain develops and how neurons find their way to their destination and make functional connections. And we're getting closer to understanding how the neurons form complex circuits that carry out the brain's work.

continued

But we do not know just how the brain combines activity going on in widespread areas to bring about an action or a decision or an experience. We don't know what a thought is. And we don't know how to fix a broken brain. But, of course, there is hope, and for good reason. You will see in the following chapters that our knowledge is vast and that we have a solid foundation for making greater advances in the current decade.

 Summary

The Central Nervous System (CNS)

- The central nervous system consists of the brain and spinal cord.

- The central nervous system is arranged in a hierarchy, with physically higher structures carrying out more sophisticated functions.

- The cortex is the location of the most sophisticated functions; the convoluted structure of the cerebral hemispheres provides for the maximum amount of cortex.

- See Table 3.1 for the major structures of the brain and their functions.

- Though localization is an important functional principle in the brain, most functions depend on the interaction of several brain areas.

- The spinal cord contains pathways between the brain and the body below the head, and provides for sensory-motor reflexes.

- The meninges and cerebrospinal fluid protect the brain from trauma; the blood-brain barrier blocks toxins and bloodborne neurotransmitters from entering the brain.

The Peripheral Nervous System (PNS)

- See Figure 3.19 for a summary of the divisions of the nervous system.

- The PNS consists of the cranial and spinal nerves or, alternatively, the somatic and autonomic nervous systems.

- The somatic nervous system consists of the sensory nerves and the nerves controlling the skeletal muscles.

- The sympathetic branch of the autonomic nervous system prepares the body for action; the parasympathetic branch conserves and renews energy.

- Interconnection in the autonomic ganglion chain means that the sympathetic nervous system tends to function as a whole, unlike the parasympathetic branch.

Development and Change in the Nervous System

- Prenatal development of the nervous system involves:

  Proliferation, the multiplication of neurons by division

  Migration, in which neurons travel to their destination

  Circuit formation, the growth of axons to, and connection to, their targets

  Circuit pruning, the elimination of excess and incorrect synapses

- Myelination continues through adolescence or later, with higher brain levels myelinating last.

- Experience can produce changes in brain structure and function.

- Though some recovery of function occurs in the mammalian central nervous system, there is little or no true repair of damage by either neurogenesis or regeneration; enhancing repair is a major research focus.

For Further Thought

- Patients with damage to the right parietal lobe, the temporal lobe, or the prefrontal area may have little or no impairment in their intellectual capabilities, and yet they show deficits in behavior that seem inconsistent with even minimal intellect. Does this modify your ideas about how we govern our behavior?

- Like the heroes in the 1966 science fiction movie *Fantastic Voyage*, you and your crew will enter a small submarine to be shrunk to microscopic size and injected into the carotid artery of an eminent scientist who is in a coma. Your mission is to navigate through the bloodstream to deliver a life-saving drug as directly as possible to the scientist's brain. The drug can be designed to your specifications, and you can decide where in the vascular system you will release it. What are some of the strategies you could consider to ensure that the drug will enter the brain?

- What strategy do you think has the greatest potential for restoring function in brain-damaged patients? Why?

 Testing Your Understanding

1. Describe the specific behaviors you would expect to see in a person with prefrontal cortex damage.

2. Discuss the localization debate, including the alternatives and the evidence.

3. In what ways does the brain show plasticity after birth?

Select the one best answer:

1. Groups of cell bodies in the central nervous system are called:

   a. tracts.   b. ganglia.
   c. nerves.   d. nuclei.

2. The prefrontal cortex is involved in all but which one of the following functions?

   a. responding to rewards
   b. orienting the body in space
   c. making decisions
   d. behaving in socially appropriate ways

3. Because the speech center is usually located in the left hemisphere of the brain, a person with the corpus callosum severed is unable to describe stimuli that are:

   a. seen in the left visual field.
   b. seen in the right visual field.
   c. presented directly in front of him or her.
   d. felt with the right hand.

4. A person with damage to the inferior temporal cortex would most likely experience inability to:

   a. see.
   b. remember previously seen objects.
   c. recognize familiar objects visually.
   d. solve visual problems, such as mazes.

5. Localization means that:

   a. specific functions are found in specific parts of the brain.
   b. the most sophisticated functions are located in the highest parts of the brain.
   c. any part of the brain can take over other functions after damage.
   d. brain functions are located in widespread networks.

6. When police have a drunken driving suspect walk a straight line and touch his nose with his finger, they are assessing the effect of alcohol on the:

   a. motor cortex.   b. corpus callosum.
   c. cerebellum.   d. medulla.

continued

7. Cardiovascular activity and respiration are controlled by the:

   a. pons.   b. medulla.
   c. thalamus.   d. reticular formation.

8. All of the following are involved in producing movement except the:

   a. hippocampus.   b. cerebellum.
   c. frontal lobes.   d. basal ganglia.

9. The reticular formation:

   a. relays sensory signals to the cortex.
   b. controls the autonomic system.
   c. connects parts of the limbic system.
   d. participates in sleep and arousal.

10. If the ventral root of a spinal nerve is severed the person will experience:

    a. loss of sensory input from a part of the body.
    b. loss of motor control of a part of the body.
    c. loss of both sensory input and motor control.
    d. none of these.

11. During a difficult exam your heart races, your mouth is dry, and your hands are icy. In your room after the exam is over, you fall limply into a deep sleep. Activation has shifted from primarily __ to primarily __.

    a. somatic, autonomic
    b. autonomic, somatic
    c. parasympathetic, sympathetic
    d. sympathetic, parasympathetic

12. In the circuit formation stage of nervous system development:

    a. correct connection of each neuron is necessary, since barely enough neurons are produced.
    b. axons grow to their targets and form connections.
    c. neurons continue dividing around a central neuron, and those neurons form a circuit.
    d. neurons that fail to make functional connections die.

13. Fetal alcohol syndrome involves:

    a. loss of myelin.
    b. overproduction of neurons.
    c. errors in neuron migration.
    d. excessive growth of glial cells.

14. The study in which kittens reared with only horizontal or vertical lines were later able to respond only to stimuli at the same orientation is an example of apparent:

    a. compensation.   b. reorientation.
    c. reorganization.   d. regeneration.

15. If a peripheral nerve were transplanted into a severed spinal cord, it would:

    a. fail to grow across the gap.
    b. grow across the gap, but fail to make connections.
    c. grow across the gap and make connections but fail to function.
    d. bridge the gap and replace the function of the lost neurons.

Answers: 1. **d** 2. **b** 3. **a** 4. **c** 5. **a** 6. **c** 7. **b** 8. **a** 9. **d** 10. **b** 11. **d** 12. **b** 13. **c** 14. **c** 15. **a**

On the Web

1. The **Whole Brain Atlas** has images of normal and diseased or damaged brains at

   http://www.med.harvard.edu/AANLIB/home.html

   The **Virtual Hospital** has images of external and internal features of the whole brain and of several components of the brain at

   http://www.vh.org/Providers/Textbooks/BrainAnatomy/TOC.html

2. **The History of Psychosurgery,** from trephining (drilling holes in the skull to let evil spirits out) to lobotomy to more recent experimental attempts, is the subject of this sometimes less than professional but very interesting website. At The Lobotomy Hall of Fame you will learn that sisters of playwright Tennessee Williams and President John Kennedy both had lobotomies.

   http://www.epub.org.br/cm/n02/historia/ psicocirg_i.htm

3. **Brain Briefings** at the Society for Neuroscience site has brief, interesting articles on brain development and other topics at

   http://apu.sfn.org/content/Publications/ BrainBriefings/index.html

   The **Dana Foundation** lists *Brainwork* newsletter articles on brain development at

   http://www.dana.org/brainweb/ brainweb.cfm?CategoryID=11

4. The **National Organization on Fetal Alcohol Syndrome** has information and statistics on the disorder. The opening page has a touchingly childlike crayon drawing done by a 22-year-old with FAS.

   http://www.nofas.org/

5. The **Miami Project to Cure Paralysis** at the University of Miami School of Medicine has summaries of basic and clinical research on central nervous system damage at

   http://www.miami.edu/miami-project/ HOME.HTM

   The **Christopher and Dana Reeve Paralysis Resource Center** carries news and information about spinal cord damage research at

   http://www.crpf.org

 For additional information about the topics covered in this chapter, please look at InfoTrac College Edition, at

http://www.infotrac-college.com/wadsworth

Try search terms you think up yourself, or use these: *cerebellum; fetal alcohol syndrome; neuroplasticity; psychosurgery.*

 On the CD-ROM: Exploring Biological Psychology

Viewing the Brain: Structure and Function
    Sagittal Section: Right Hemisphere 1
    Sagittal Section: Right Hemisphere 2
    Sagittal Section: Right Hemisphere 3
    Virtual Reality: The Brain
    Interactive Puzzle: The Brain
Viewing the Brain: Cerebral Cortex
    Left Hemisphere: Function 1
    Left Hemisphere: Function 2

    Sagittal Plane
    Virtual Reality: The Brain
    Interactive Puzzle: The Cortex
    Animation: The Motor Cortex
    Animation: The Sensory Cortex
    Virtual Reality: Head Planes
    Interactive Puzzle: The Planes
    Video: Brains on Ice

 For Further Reading

The Scientific American Book of the Brain (Lyons Press, 2001). Articles about brain research by renowned researchers, written in the accessible style of *Scientific American*.

The 26 chapters cover brain development, intelligence, memory, emotion, disorders, and consciousness.

continued

The Man Who Mistook His Wife for a Hat and Other Clinical Tales, by Oliver Sacks (Harper Perennial, 1990). This collection of case studies is as entertaining as it is informative as it treats the human side of brain damage and disorder.

Key Terms

anterior *64*

area postrema *75*

association cortex *65*

auditory cortex *65*

autonomic nervous system *76*

basal ganglia *64*

blood-brain barrier *75*

Broca's area *64*

central nervous system (CNS) *60*

central sulcus *63*

cerebellum *71*

cerebral commissures *69*

cerebral hemispheres *61*

cerebrospinal fluid *70*

circuit formation *79*

circuit pruning *81*

compensation *85*

corpus callosum *69*

cortex *61*

cranial nerves *60*

dorsal *64*

dorsal root *74*

equipotentiality *73*

fetal alcohol syndrome (FAS) *82*

fissure *61*

frontal lobe *63*

ganglion *60*

growth cone *79*

gyrus *61*

hydrocephalus *86*

hypothalamus *68*

inferior *64*

inferior colliculi *71*

inferior temporal cortex *66*

lateral *65*

lateral fissure *63*

limbic system *69*

lobotomy *64*

localization *72*

longitudinal fissure *61*

medial *64*

medulla *71*

meninges *74*

midbrain *71*

migrate *79*

motor cortex *63*

neglect *65*

nerve *60*

neurogenesis *85*

neuron *60*

neurotrophins *82*

nucleus *60*

occipital lobe *68*

parasympathetic nervous system *76*

parietal lobe *65*

peripheral nervous system (PNS) *60*

phrenology *73*

pineal gland *69*

pioneer neuron *80*

pituitary gland *68*

plasticity *82*

pons *71*

posterior *64*

precentral gyrus *63*

prefrontal cortex *64*

proliferation *79*

psychosurgery *65*

radial glial cells *79*

reflex *74*

regeneration *85*

reorganization *83*

reticular formation *71*

somatic nervous system *75*

somatosensory cortex *65*

spinal cord *73*

spinal nerves *60*

sulcus *61*

superior *64*

superior colliculi *71*

sympathetic ganglion chain *77*

sympathetic nervous system *76*

temporal lobe *65*

thalamus *68*

tract *60*

ventral *64*

ventral horns *74*

ventral root *74*

ventricle *70*

visual cortex *68*

Wernicke's area *65*

Drugs and Addiction

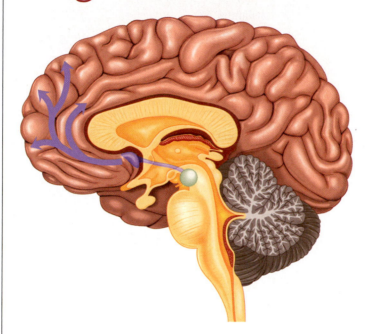

In this chapter you will learn:

- The major classifications of drugs and some of their effects.

- What happens in the brain when it becomes addicted.

- How addiction is treated pharmacologically.

- How inheritance influences addiction.

You illustrious Human Candles . . . who consume your own brilliant selves with the heat and light of your minds . . . I have discovered a horrible, rather brutal method that I recommend only to men of excessive vigor, men with thick black hair and skin covered with liver spots, men with big square hands and with legs shaped like bowling pins.

—Balzac, 1839/1996

Figure 4.1
Honoré de Balzac

Hulton Archive

Honoré de Balzac (Figure 4.1) wrote a phenomenal 45 novels in 20 years. He was aided in his long writing marathons by large amounts of a stimulant drug. The drug's effects pleased him so much that he advocated its use to others. However, he died at the age of 51 in part because of this unrelenting stimulation. What was the powerful drug that contributed both to his success and his untimely death? According to his physician, Balzac died from a heart condition, aggravated by "the use or rather the abuse of coffee, to which he had recourse in order to counteract man's natural propensity to sleep" ("French roast," 1996, p. 28).

There is good reason to consider caffeine an abused drug. Coffee may have milder effects than the other drugs coming out of Colombia, but strength of effect and illegality are not the criteria for classifying a substance as addictive. As you will see, a drug's effect on the brain is the telling feature, and that is our reason for discussing drugs at this particular point: it provides the opportunity to tie together our preceding discussions of brain structures and neural (particularly synaptic) functioning.

PSYCHOACTIVE DRUGS

A *drug* is a substance that on entering the body changes the body or its functioning. Drugs fall into one of two general classes, according to their effect on a transmitter system. As we saw in Chapter 2, an agonist mimics or enhances the effect of a neurotransmitter. It can accomplish this by having the same effect on the receptor as the neurotransmitter, by increasing the transmitter's effect on the receptor, or by blocking the reuptake or the degradation of the transmitter. An antagonist may occupy the receptors without activating them, simultaneously blocking the transmitter from binding to the receptors. Or it may reduce the availability of the neurotransmitter, for example by reducing its production or its release from the presynaptic terminals.

Psychoactive drugs **are those that have psychological effects, such as anxiety relief or hallucinations.** The focus of this chapter is on abused psychoactive drugs, although many of the principles discussed here are applicable more generally. Later, in the chapter on psychological disorders, we will discuss several psychotherapeutic drugs. The effects of abused drugs are extremely varied, but whether they arouse or sedate, expand the consciousness or dull the senses, addictive drugs produce a sense of pleasure in one form or another. They also have several other effects in common; reviewing those effects will give us the language we need for a discussion of how the drugs work.

Most of the abused drugs produce addiction; **addiction is identified by preoccupation with obtaining a drug, compulsive use of the drug, and a high tendency to relapse after quitting.** Many abused drugs also produce withdrawal reactions. *Withdrawal* **is a negative reaction that occurs when drug use is stopped.** Withdrawal symptoms are often the opposite of the effects the drug produces; withdrawal from a drug that produces elation causes depression, and terminating use of a drug that produces sedation results in agitation.

Tolerance also occurs to most abused drugs when they are used regularly; *tolerance* **means that increasing amounts of the drug are required to produce the same results.** Most of the tolerance to psychoactive drugs is due to a compensatory reduction in the number or the sensitivity of the receptors. Tolerance can occur to some of a drug's effects without occurring to others; for example, tolerance may develop to the mood effects of a drug while excitatory or sedating effects are undi-

minished—with obvious threats to the user's health when the dosage is increased. Differential tolerance occurs because a drug affects a variety of transmitters and receptors at several locations in the brain.

Opiates

The *opiates* **are drugs derived from the opium poppy** (see Figure 4.2). Opiates have a variety of effects: they are *analgesic* **(pain relieving)** and *hypnotic* **(sleep inducing),** and they produce a strong *euphoria* **(sense of happiness or ecstasy).** Their downside is their addictive potential. *Opium* has been in use since around 4000 B.C. (Berridge & Edwards, 1981); originally it was eaten, but when explorers carried the American Indians' practice of pipe smoking of tobacco back to their native countries, opium users adopted this technique. *Morphine* was extracted at the beginning of the early 1800s and has been extremely valuable as a treatment for the pain of surgery, battle wounds, and cancer. *Heroin* **was synthesized from morphine** in the late 1800s; at the turn of the century it was marketed by the Bayer Drug Company of Germany as an over-the-counter analgesic until its dangers were recognized. It is now an illegal drug in the U.S. but available for clinical use in Canada and Great Britain (Cherney, 1996). Codeine, another

Do opiates have any legitimate use?

1

Figure 4.2
An opium poppy

ingredient of opium, has been used as a cough suppressant, and dilute solutions of opium (laudanum and paregoric) were once used to treat diarrhea and even administered to children. Opiates have been largely replaced by safer synthetic drugs for pain relief, although morphine continues to be used with cancer patients and is showing promise of safe use with milder pain in a time-release form that virtually eliminates the risk of addiction.

All the opiates are subject to abuse, but heroin is the most notorious, owing to its intense effect: a glowing, orgasm-like sensation that occurs within seconds, followed by drowsy relaxation and contentment. Because heroin is highly soluble in lipids, it passes the blood-brain barrier easily; the rapid effect increases its addictive potential. The major danger of heroin use comes from overdose— either from the attempt to maintain the pleasant effects in the face of increasing tolerance, or because the user unknowingly obtains the drug in a purer form than usual. In a 33-year study of 581 male heroin addicts, 49% were dead at the end of the study, with an average age at death of 46 years (Hser, Hoffman, Grella, & Anglin, 2001). Nearly a fourth of those had died of drug overdoses (mostly from heroin), 19.5% died from homicide, suicide, or accident, and 15% died from chronic liver disease. Half of the survivors who could be interviewed were still using heroin, and the high likelihood of returning to usage even after five years or more of abstinence suggested to the researchers that heroin addiction may be a lifelong condition. In spite of the representation of the horrors of heroin withdrawal in movies, it is best described as similar to a bad case of flu; so apparently fear of withdrawal is not the prime motivator for continued heroin addiction.

Heroin presents a particularly good example of conditioned tolerance. Studies of conditioned tolerance in the lab with humans have used only small doses, for obvious reasons; however, a dosage of heroin that killed 32% of rats injected in the customary environment killed 64% of rats injected in a novel environment (Siegel, Hinson, Krank, & McCully, 1982). There is evidence that a familiar drug-taking environment contributes to tolerance, which would increase the danger of overdose in the addict who takes the same amount of the drug in a new setting (Macrae, Scoles, & Siegel, 1987; Siegel, 1984).

The opiates affect specialized opiate receptors. You might wonder why the brain has receptors for an abused drug. The answer is that the body produces its own ligands for opiate receptors. **A *ligand* is any substance that binds to a receptor.** Opiate drugs are effective because they mimic these *endogenous* ("generated within the body") opiates, known as *endorphins* (Pert & Snyder, 1973). One effect of endorphins is pain relief, as we will see in Chapter 10. Opiates also indirectly affect the release of dopamine, which contributes to their pleasurable effect.

Depressants

Depressants **are drugs that reduce central nervous system activity.** The group includes alcohol, *sedative* (calming) drugs, *anxiolytic* (anxiety-reducing) drugs, and hypnotic drugs. Alcohol, of course, is the most common and also the most abused in this class, so we will start there.

Alcohol

Ethanol, or *alcohol*, is a drug fermented from fruits, grains, and other plant products; it acts at many brain sites to produce euphoria, anxiety reduction, motor incoordination, and cognitive impairment (Koob & Bloom, 1988). It is the oldest of the abused drugs; its origin is unknown, but it was probably discovered when primitive people found that eating naturally fermented fruit had a pleasant effect. (Even elephants sometimes congregate under trees to eat fallen and fermenting fruit until they become intoxicated!) Alcohol has historically played a cultural role in celebrations and ceremonies, provided a means of achieving religious ecstasy and, especially in primitive societies, permitted socially

What are the uses and dangers of depressant drugs?

sanctioned temporary indulgence in hostility and sexual misbehavior. In modern societies controlled group drinking has been replaced by uncontrolled individual abuse.

. . . I had booze, and when I was drinking, I felt warm and pretty and loved— at least for a while.

—Gloria, a recovering alcoholic

2

Alcohol is valued by moderate users as a social lubricant and as a disinhibitor of social constraints, owing largely to its anxiolytic effect. Like many drugs, its effects are complex. At low doses it suppresses normal cortical inhibition, so it acts as a stimulant. As the dosage increases, so does the sedative effect. As a high dose is metabolized to a low blood level it becomes a stimulant again, which is why several drinks in the evening may put you to sleep at bedtime only to awaken you later in the night. Because it interferes with cognitive and motor functioning as well as judgment, a person is legally considered too impaired to drive when the blood alcohol concentration (BAC) reaches 0.08% in Canada and 0.08–

0.10% in different states in the U.S. States that have not adopted the lower standard will begin losing part of their federal highway money in 2004. Higher levels produce unconsciousness, and at a BAC of 0.5% there is risk of death. Alcohol withdrawal involves tremors, anxiety, and mood and sleep disturbances; more severe reactions are known as ***delirium tremens*— hallucinations, delusions, confusion, and, in extreme cases, seizures and possible death**.

A common health risk of chronic alcoholism is cirrhosis of the liver, which in its severest form is fatal. In addition, the vitamin B_1 deficiency that is associated with chronic alcoholism can produce brain damage and Korsakoff's syndrome, which involves severe memory loss along with sensory and motor impairment (Figure 4.3). As you well know, chronic alcoholism is also closely linked with violent crime (see Chapter 7). One reason is that alcohol reduces the anxiety that normally inhibits aggression (Pihl & Peterson, 1993). Considering the health risks, disruption of homes and livelihood, and violence, alcohol is more costly to society than any of the illegal drugs. In view of all the dangers of drinking, it

Figure 4.3
An alcoholic brain and a normal brain
Note that the sulci have deepened and the ventricles have enlarged in the alcoholic brain.

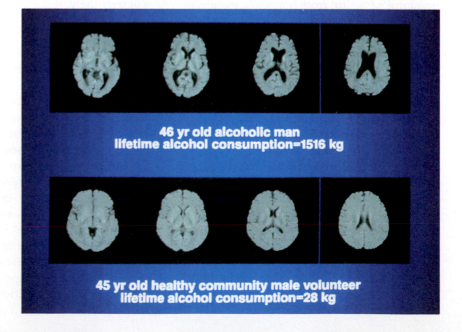

46 yr old alcoholic man
lifetime alcohol consumption=1516 kg

45 yr old healthy community male volunteer
lifetime alcohol consumption=28 kg

seems amazing now that in 1961 a speaker at a symposium of psychiatrists and physicians on drinking expressed the group's consensus that "Alcohol is the safest, most available tranquilizer we have" ("Paean to Nepenthe," 1961, p. 68).

Alcohol inhibits the action of a subtype of glutamate receptor (Hoffman & Tabakoff, 1993; Tsai, Gastfriend, & Coyle, 1995). You may remember from Chapter 2, Table 2.1, that glutamate is the most prevalent excitatory neurotransmitter. There is a compensatory increase in the number of these receptors, and this increase in sensitivity probably accounts for the seizures that sometimes occur during withdrawal. Alcohol also activates the A subtype of receptor for gamma-aminobutyric acid (the GABA$_A$ receptor) (Wan, Berton, Madamba, Francesconi, & Siggins, 1996).

Because of the importance of this receptor, we will give it special attention. It is actually a receptor complex, with at least five kinds of receptor sites (Figure 4.4). One receptor responds to gamma-aminobutyric acid (GABA), the most prevalent inhibitory neurotransmitter. Its activation opens the receptor's chloride channel, and the influx of chloride ions hyperpolarizes the neuron. At other receptors, alcohol, barbiturates, and benzodiazepines increase GABA's binding to its receptor and thus its ability to open the chloride channel.

Alcohol passes easily through the placenta, raising the blood alcohol concentration of a fetus to about the same level as the mother's. You saw in Chapter 3 that prenatal exposure to alcohol can result in fetal alcohol syndrome (FAS) (Figure 4.5), which is the leading cause of mental retardation in the Western world (Abel & Sokol, 1986). Besides being retarded, fetal alcohol syndrome children are irritable and have trouble maintaining attention. Regular alcohol abuse apparently is not required to produce damage. In a recent study, mothers who had FAS children did not drink much more on average than the mothers of normal children but they did report occasional binges of five or more drinks at a time (Streissguth, Barr, Bookstein, Sampson, & Olson, 1999). No safe level of alcohol intake during pregnancy

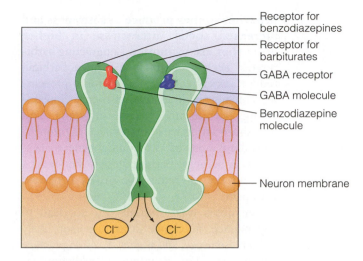

Figure 4.4
The GABA$_A$ receptor complex
The complex has receptors for GABA, barbiturates, benzodiazepines, and alcohol.

has been established, so most authorities recommend total abstention. (Refer to Figure 3.27 for a picture of a mouse brain with FAS.)

What prenatal effects does alcohol have?

Barbiturates and Benzodiazepines

Like alcohol, *barbiturates* in small amounts act selectively on higher cortical centers, especially those involved in inhibiting

Figure 4.5
A child with Fetal Alcohol Syndrome
Besides retardation, FAS is characterized by the facial irregularities you see here.

George Steinmetz

behavior, so they produce talkativeness and increased social interaction; in higher doses they are hypnotics. Long-acting barbiturates, such as barbital and phenobarbital, reduce anxiety and are also useful in preventing convulsions in epileptic patients. Shorter-acting barbiturates relieve insomnia, and ultrashort-acting barbiturates such as thiopental sodium are used as the initial general anesthetic in surgery. Barbiturates do not reduce pain, but they do reduce the anxiety associated with pain.

The doses used clinically do not lead to dependence. Tolerance makes a person likely to increase usage, and higher doses do produce dependence. The symptoms of addiction are similar to those of alcoholism. When the chronic user terminates use abruptly, withdrawal symptoms are more severe than those produced by opiates. Barbiturates are particularly dangerous when they are taken along with alcohol. Overdose or combined use with alcohol depresses the central nervous system and respiratory system, and can produce coma and even death.

Barbiturates, like alcohol, inhibit glutamate activity, though they work through different subtypes of receptors (Hoffman & Tabakoff, 1993). They also enhance activity at $GABA_A$ receptors at their own receptor site, and they are able to open chloride channels whether GABA is present or not (Julien, 2001).

A few decades ago, barbiturates were the drug of choice for treating anxiety and for other applications requiring sedation; their liability is the potential for addiction and for accidental or intentional overdose. They were replaced by *benzodiazepines,* which have effects similar to barbiturates but are safer because they do not open the chloride channel (Julien, 2001). There are several benzodiazepine drugs, the best known of which are Valium (diazepam) and Xanax (alprazolam). They produce their anxiolytic effects in the limbic system, and their sedative, antiseizure, and muscle relaxation effects in other areas, including the cortex and the brain stem.

Though safer than barbiturates, benzodiazepines are also addictive, so they are appropriate only for short-term use. One of the benzodiazepines, Rohypnol *(roofies or rophies)*, has gained notoriety as the date rape drug; it is approved for marketing in Europe but not in the United States.

Stimulants

Stimulants activate the central nervous system to produce arousal, increased alertness, and elevated mood. They include a wide range of drugs, from cocaine to caffeine, which vary in the degree of risk they pose. The greatest danger lies in how they are used.

Cocaine

Cocaine, which is extracted from the South American coca plant, produces euphoria, decreased appetite, increased alertness, and relief from fatigue. It is processed with hydrochloric acid into cocaine hydrochloride, the familiar white powder that is "snorted" (inhaled) or mixed with water and injected. Pure cocaine, or *freebase,* can be extracted from cocaine hydrochloride by chemically removing the hydrochloric acid. When freebase is smoked the cocaine enters the bloodstream and reaches the brain rapidly. A simpler chemical procedure yields *crack,* which is less pure but produces pure cocaine in the vapor when it is smoked. The low cost of crack has spread its use into poor urban communities that could not afford cocaine before.

Cocaine has not always been viewed as a dangerous drug. The coca leaf has been chewed by South American Indians for centuries as a means of enduring hardship and privation. When cocaine was isolated in the late 1800s it was initially used as a local anesthetic and was the only anesthetic available at the time (Julien, 2001). But cocaine soon found its way into over-the-counter medications (Figure 4.6), and until 1906 even Coca-Cola owed much of its refreshment to 60 milligrams of cocaine in every serving (Gold, 1997). Sigmund Freud, the father of psycho-

What neurotransmitter do stimulant drugs have in common?

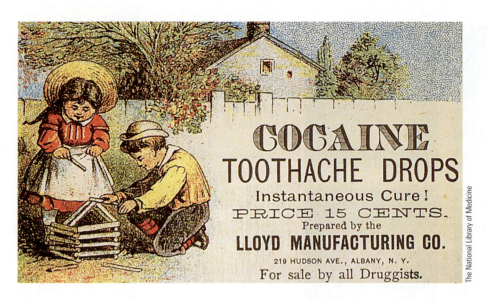

Figure 4.6
Advertisement from around 1900

analysis, championed the use of cocaine, giving it to his fiancé, sisters, friends, and colleagues, and prescribing it to his patients. He even wrote an essay which he called a "song of praise" to cocaine's virtues. He gave up the use of the drug, both personally and professionally, when he realized its dangers (Brecher, 1972).

Cocaine blocks the reuptake of dopamine and serotonin at synapses. Dopamine usually has an inhibitory effect, and cocaine reduces activity in much of the brain as the positron emission tomography (PET) scans in Figure 4.7 show (London et al., 1990). Presumably, cocaine produces euphoria and excitement because dopamine removes the inhibition the cortex usually exerts on lower structures. Reduced cortical activity is typical of drugs that produce euphoria, including benzodiazepines, barbiturates, amphetamines, and morphine (London et al., 1990).

Injection and smoking produce an immediate and intense euphoria, which increases the addictive potential. After the end of a cocaine binge the user crashes into a state of depression, anxiety, and cocaine craving that motivates a cycle of continued use. Withdrawal effects are typically mild, involving anxiety, lack of motivation, boredom, and lack of pleasure. Three decades ago addiction was defined in terms of a drug's ability to produce withdrawal, and because cocaine's withdrawal symptoms are so mild, it was not believed to be addictive (Gawin, 1991). As usage increased in the population we learned that cocaine is one of the most reinforcing and addictive of the abused drugs (Julien, 2001). The intensity of the drug's effect makes treatment very difficult, and no treatment is generally accepted as successful. Complicating rehabilitation is the fact that cocaine addicts typically abuse other drugs and they also have a very high rate of psychological disorders, including depression, anxiety, bipolar disorder, and posttraumatic stress disorder. There have been reports of both successes and failures in attempts to reduce cocaine dependence by treating the accompanying psychological disorders (Julien, 2001).

Cocaine use can cause minor brain damage, and long-term use of high doses produces psychotic-like symptoms. Overdose may result in seizures and death. Cocaine provides a good example of selective tolerance. For example, while increasing amounts of the drug are required to produce the desired psychological effects, the person becomes supersensitive to

3

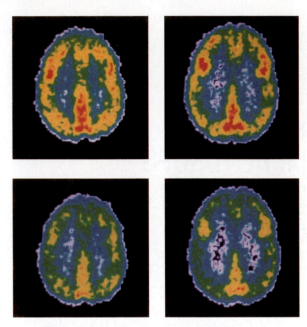

Figure 4.7
A normal brain and a brain on cocaine
The lower two PET scans show greatly decreased activity in the cocaine abuser's brain.
Source: London et al., 1990.

the effect that produces seizures. It is possible that the health risks of cocaine relative to other drugs have been underestimated. In one study rats were allowed to press a lever that caused heroin or cocaine to be injected into their bloodstream; 36% of rats receiving heroin died of self-administered overdose, compared to 90% of rats receiving cocaine (Bozarth & Wise, 1985).

Like alcohol, cocaine passes through the placenta easily, where it interferes with fetal development. It is difficult to separate the effects of alcohol and cocaine on the children's development from the effects of poverty and neglect often seen in the homes. But we do have experimental evidence from animal studies that prenatal exposure to alcohol causes brain damage (Gressens, Lammens, Picard, & Evrard, 1992), and that exposure to cocaine results in abnormal circuit formation among dopamine neurons (Jones et al., 2000). In addition, a Toronto

group was able to control environmental factors by studying 26 cocaine-exposed children who had been adopted. Compared to control children matched for the mother's IQ and socioeconomic status, the cocaine children had lower IQs, poorer language development, and greater distractibility (Nulman et al., 2001).

Amphetamines

Amphetamines **are a group of synthetic drugs that produce euphoria and increase confidence and concentration.** The group includes amphetamine sulfate (marketed as Benzedrine), the three to four times more potent dextroamphetamine sulfate (marketed as Dexedrine), and the still more powerful methamphetamine (known on the street as *speed*, *crank*, and *crystal*). Like cocaine, it can be purified to its freebase form called *ice*, which is smokable. Because it dulls the appetite, reduces fatigue, and increases alertness, amphetamines have shown up in weight-loss drugs and have been used by truck drivers, pilots, and students to postpone sleep. It has been useful in treating ailments like narcolepsy, a disorder of uncontrollable daytime sleepiness.

Amphetamines increase the release of norepinephrine and dopamine. Increased release of dopamine exhausts the store of transmitter in the vesicles, which accounts for the period of depression that follows. The effects of amphetamine injection are so similar to those of cocaine that individuals cannot tell the difference between the two (Cho, 1990).

Heavy use can cause hallucinations and delusions of persecution that are so similar to the symptoms of paranoid schizophrenia that even trained professionals cannot recognize the difference. In laboratory studies, psychotic symptoms develop after one to four days of chronic amphetamine administration. In one study a volunteer on amphetamine was convinced that a "giant oscillator" in the ceiling was controlling his thoughts. Another believed his ex-wife had hired an assassin to kill him, and was perturbed when the doctor would not guard the window while he stood watch at the door (Griffith, Cavanaugh, Held, & Oates, 1972; Snyder, 1972). After an amphetamine psychosis subsides the person may be left with a permanently increased sensitivity to the drug so that using even a small amount years later can revive symptoms (Sato, 1986).

Nicotine

Nicotine **is the primary psychoactive and addictive agent in tobacco.** Tobacco is ingested by smoking, chewing, and inhaling (as snuff, a finely powdered form). Nicotine has an almost unique effect (Schelling, 1992): when tobacco is smoked in short puffs it has a stimulating effect; when inhaled deeply, it has a tranquilizing or depressant effect. In large doses nicotine can cause nausea, vomiting, and headaches; in extremely high doses it is powerful enough to produce convulsions and even death in laboratory animals. The withdrawal reactions are well known because smokers "quit" so often; the most prominent symptoms are nervousness and anxiety, drowsiness, lightheadedness, and headaches. The United Kingdom annually observes a "No Smoking Day" similar to the "Great American Smokeout," in which people voluntarily abstain from smoking for a day; apparently as a result of impairment from withdrawal symptoms, workplace accidents go up by 7% (Waters, Jarvis, & Sutton, 1998).

Because of the 400,000 deaths produced each year by smoking, including 50,000 in non-smokers due to passive inhalation of secondhand smoke, it can reasonably be argued that nicotine is the most important drug of abuse. Heroin and cocaine combined produce no more than 6,000 deaths per year in contrast.

—Charles O'Brien

People who try to give up smoking usually are able to abstain for a while but then relapse; only about 20% of attempts to stop are successful after two years. Before bans on public and workplace smoking, about 80% of male smokers and two-thirds of female smokers smoked at least one cigarette per waking hour (Brecher, 1972). In part because usage is more continuous with tobacco than with other drugs, the health risks are particularly high.

Chronic smokers often experience breathing difficulty, coughing, infections of the bronchial tract, pneumonia, bronchitis (chronic inflammation of the bronchioles of the lungs) and emphysema (reduced elasticity of the lungs). These and other health risks from smoking are not the result of nicotine but of some of the 4,000 other compounds present in tobacco smoke. For example, a metabolite of benzo-[a]pyrene damages a cancer-suppressing gene, resulting in lung cancer (Denissenko, Pao, Tang, & Pfeifer, 1996). Other cancers resulting from smoking occur in the larynx, mouth, esophagus, liver, and pancreas. Smoking can also cause Buerger's disease, constriction of the blood vessels that may lead to gangrene in the lower extremities, requiring progressively higher amputations. Although abstinence almost ensures a halt in the disease's progress, surgeons report that it is not uncommon to find a patient smoking in the hospital bed after a second or third amputation (Brecher, 1972). According to the surgeon general, about 400,000 Americans die each year from smoking-related diseases (Schelling, 1992).

Cigarette package warnings aimed at expectant mothers are not just political propaganda. Effects extend even to behavior; for example, children whose mothers smoked during pregnancy have twice the rate of conduct disorder compared to children of nonsmokers, even after statistical correction for socioeconomic status and impaired child-rearing behaviors (Fergusson, Woodward, & Horwood, 1998). Conduct disorder mainly involves difficulties with impulse control. Another fallout from prenatal smoking is that the number of arrests for nonviolent and violent crimes in males is related to how much the mother smoked during pregnancy (Brennan, Grekin, & Mednick, 1999).

As you saw in Chapter 2, nicotine stimulates nicotinic ACh receptors. In the periphery, it activates muscles and may cause twitching. Centrally, it produces increased alertness and faster response to stimulation. Neurons that release dopamine contain nicotinic receptors, so they are also activated, resulting in a positive mood effect (Svensson, Grenhoff, & Aston-Jones, 1986).

Caffeine

Caffeine, **the active ingredient in coffee, produces arousal, increased alertness, and decreased sleepiness.** It is hardly the drug that amphetamine and cocaine are, but as you saw in Balzac's case it is subject to abuse. It blocks receptors for the neuromodulator adenosine, increasing the release of dopamine and acetylcholine (Silinsky, 1989; Snyder, 1997). Because adenosine appears to have sedative and depressive effects (Julien, 2001), blocking its receptors contributes to arousal. Withdrawal symptoms include headaches, fatigue, anxiety, shakiness, and craving, which last about a week. Withdrawal is not a significant problem, because coffee is in plentiful supply, but heavy drinkers may wake up with a headache just from abstaining overnight. Because 80% of Americans drink coffee, researchers at the Mayo Clinic have recommended intravenous administration of caffeine to patients recovering from surgery to eliminate postoperative withdrawal headaches ("Caffeine prevents," 1996).

Psychedelics

5

How do psychedelic drugs produce their effects?

Psychedelic **drugs are compounds that cause perceptual distortions in the user.** The term comes from the Greek words *psyche* ("mind") and *delos* ("visible"). "Visible mind" refers to the expansion of the senses and the sense of increased insight that users of these drugs report. Although the drugs are often referred to as *hallucinogenic,* they are most noted for producing perceptual distortions: Light, color, and details are intensified, objects may change shape, sounds may evoke visual experiences, and light may produce auditory sensations. Psychedelics may affect the perception of time, as well as self-perception; the body may seem to float or to change shape, size, or identity. These experiences often are accompanied by a sense of ecstasy.

The best-known psychedelic, *lysergic acid diethylamide (LSD),* was popularized in the student peace movement of the 1960s. LSD is structurally similar to serotonin and stimulates serotonin receptors (Jacobs, 1987), possibly disrupting the brain stem's ability to screen out irrelevant stimuli (Julien, 2001). Other serotonin-like psychedelics include *psilocybin* and *psilocin,* both from the mushroom *Psilocybe mexicana.* Eating the mushrooms produces effects similar to those of LSD, but psilocybin and psilocin are only 1/200 as potent (Julien, 2001). *Peyote* is the crown or button on the top of the peyote cactus. It is used for religious purposes by the Native American Church, and this use is protected by the federal government and many states. *Mescaline,* the active ingredient in peyote, also apparently owes its psychedelic properties to stimulation of serotonin receptors (Monte et al., 1997). As you will see later in this chapter and in subsequent chapters, serotonin has a wide variety of psychological functions.

Ecstasy is the street name of a drug developed as a weight-loss compound called *methylenedioxymethamphetamine* (but you can call it MDMA!); it is a popular drug among young people, especially at dance clubs and "raves." Amphetamine-like in structure, it releases serotonin and dopamine. While its sensory distortions are likely due to serotonin, its positive mood effects result from dopamine (Liechti & Vollenweider, 2000). The disturbing news is that, in monkeys at least, it destroys serotonergic neurons (Figure 4.8) (McCann, Lowe, & Ricaurte, 1997).

Phencyclidine (PCP) is an anesthetic that is used by veterinarians but was abandoned for

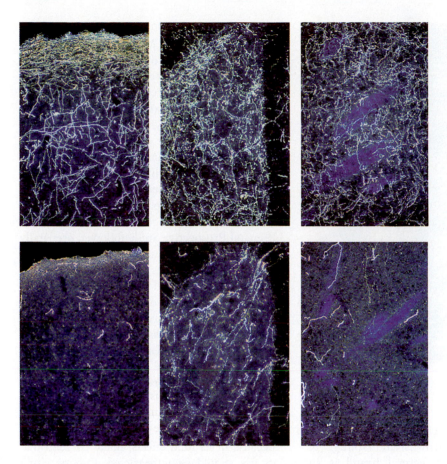

Figure 4.8
Brain damage produced by the drug "Ecstasy"
These brain sections have been stained with a chemical that makes neurons containing serotonin turn white. Photos in the top row are from a normal monkey; those below are from a monkey given MDMA a year earlier.
Source: McCann, Lowe, & Ricaurte, 1997.

human use because it produces schizophrenia-like disorientation and hallucinations (Julien, 2001). It has found recreational popularity as *angel dust.* Monkeys and rats will self-administer PCP, and humans show compulsive use, indicating that PCP is addictive (Carlezon & Wise, 1996; Julien, 2001). PCP increases activity in dopamine pathways, but blocking dopamine activity does not eliminate self-administration in rats; the drug's rewarding properties apparently are partly due to its inhibition of a subtype of glutamate receptors (Carlezon & Wise, 1996; French, 1994).

Scientists became interested in psychedelic drugs at the beginning of the twentieth century because some of the effects resemble psychotic symptoms. This suggested that a chemical imbalance might be the cause of psychosis, so researchers tried to produce "model psychoses" that could be studied in the laboratory. This line of research turned out to be unproductive, but the effects of PCP are renewing researchers' interest (Jentsch & Roth, 1999).

Marijuana

Marijuana **is the dried and crushed leaves and flowers of the Indian hemp plant,** *Cannabis sativa* (Figure 4.9). The hemp plant was heavily cultivated in the U.S. during World War II as a source of material for making rope, and is still found occasionally growing wild along Midwestern roadsides. Marijuana is usually smoked, but can be mixed in food and eaten. The major psychoactive ingredient is *delta-9-tetrahydrocannabinol (THC).* THC is particularly concentrated in the **dried resin from the plant, called** *hashish*.

Figure 4.9
A marijuana branch

6

THC binds with cannabinoid receptors (Matsuda, Lolait, Brownstein, Young, & Bonner, 1990), whose natural ligand is an **endogenous cannabinoid called *anandamide*** (Devane et al., 1992; Tomaso, Beltramo, & Piomelli, 1996). The receptors are found on axon terminals as well as on dendrites, so anandamide apparently modulates neuron excitability both presynaptically and postsynaptically (Ong & Mackie, 1999). Cannabinoid receptors are widely distributed in the brain and spinal cord, which probably accounts for the variety of effects marijuana has on behavior. The pleasurable sensation is likely due to its ability to increase dopamine levels (Tanda, Pontieri, & Di Chiara, 1997). Receptors in the frontal cortex probably account for impaired cognitive functioning and distortions of time sense and sensory perception, receptors in the hippocampus disrupt memory, and those in the basal ganglia and cerebellum impair movement and coordina-

tion (Herkenham, 1992; Howlett et al., 1990; Julien, 2001; Ong & Mackie, 1999). This is a good time to point out that although drugs may reveal a great deal about brain functioning, the pattern of effects they produce is usually atypical; drugs affect wide areas of the brain indiscriminately, whereas normal activation tends to be more discrete and localized.

The effect of marijuana on prenatal development has received little attention, because babies exposed prenatally to marijuana do not show the obvious impairments caused by prenatal cocaine and alcohol. The Ottawa Prenatal Prospective Study followed prenatally exposed children for several years after birth. They had no deficits during the first three years of life compared to control children, but at four years and beyond they showed behavioral problems, decreased performance on visual perception tasks, and deficits in attention, memory, and language comprehension (Fried, 1995). These deficits are consistent with impairment of prefrontal functioning.

Legalization is the major controversy surrounding marijuana (see "Controversy over The Legalization of Marijuana Heats Up"). Because of its mild effects, many contend that its use should be unrestricted. Others, citing reports that it alleviates the nausea of chemotherapy and reduces the severity of the eye disease glaucoma, believe it should be available by a doctor's prescription. The medical claims are controversial, however, because they rely largely on inadequately controlled studies. A few states have legalized the use of marijuana for medical purposes or are considering doing so, which puts these states in conflict with federal laws.

Another controversy concerns whether marijuana is addictive. The importance of this debate is that it requires us to define just what we mean by the term. Marijuana's effects are milder than those of most abused drugs, it is fairly easy to give up, and the negative effects after quitting are usually reported to be minimal. Because addiction has traditionally been equated with a drug's ability to produce withdrawal symptoms, marijuana was considered

What are the two controversies about marijuana?

IN THE NEWS

Controversy over the Legalization of Marijuana Heats Up

The Canadian government is making it possible for certain groups of medical patients to obtain and use marijuana, and for others to grow marijuana for medicinal purposes. There is an increasing attitude of tolerance in parts of the United States as well. In 1996 California and Arizona passed laws permitting medical use of the drug; later, six states and the District of Columbia did the same.

However, the U.S. government will not be following Canada's lead any time soon. In May of 2001, the Supreme Court decided 8–0 that federal law does not allow a "medical necessity" exemption to the ban on marijuana use. Marijuana is listed by Congress as a Schedule 1 drug under the Controlled Substances Act,

which means that it has no currently accepted medical use. Nine months after the decision, federal agents raided three "medical marijuana clubs" in San Francisco, Oakland, and Petaluma, California, arresting four people and fueling the growing dispute between local and federal officials.

—From the following New York Times *articles: "Canadians Lean Toward Easing Marijuana Laws," by Anthony dePalma, June 17, 2001, 1-4. "State Passed the Law, But Never Used It," by Richard Pérez-Peña, April 20, 2001, B-8. "Justices Set Back Use of Marijuana to Treat Sickness," by Linda Greenhouse, May 15, 2001, A-1. "U.S. Raid Sets Off Protests," February 13, 2002, A-27.*

nonaddictive long after cocaine was moved to the list of addictive drugs. Marijuana's compulsive use was attributed to psychological dependence, a concept that was invented to explain the habitual use of drugs like marijuana, nicotine, and caffeine.

Symptoms of anxiety, irritability, and stomach cramps have now been documented during withdrawal from marijuana (Duffy & Milin, 1996; Haney, Ward, Comer, Foltin, & Fischman, 1999). However, there are more important reasons for considering marijuana addictive. For example, monkeys will press a lever to inject THC into their bloodstream in amounts similar to doses in marijuana smoke inhaled by humans (Tanda, Munzar, & Goldberg, 2000). Researchers are reluctant to attribute drug self-administration in animals to psychological dependence and usually consider it evidence of addiction. Earlier we defined addiction in terms of the drug's hold on the individual, without reference to its ability to produce withdrawal symptoms. Next we will examine the reasons for taking this position.

✓ CONCEPT CHECK

- *How does tolerance increase a drug's danger?*
- *Why does alcohol increase the danger of barbiturates?*
- *How are the effects of amphetamine and cocaine at the synapse alike? different?*

ADDICTION

In the past researchers and drug experts assumed that addiction was the result of the user's desire to avoid withdrawal symptoms. There are several important flaws in this withdrawal avoidance hypothesis. One is that it does not explain what motivates the person to use the drug until dependence develops. Second, we know that many addicts go through withdrawal fairly regularly to reset their tolerance level so they can get by with lower and less costly amounts of the drug. Third, it does not explain why many addicts return to a drug after a long period of abstinence and long after withdrawal symptoms have sub-sided. Finally, the addictiveness of a drug is unrelated to the severity of withdrawal symptoms, for example, in the case of crack cocaine and methamphetamine (Leshner, 1997). The concept of psychological dependence is troublesome in itself; if it implies that a drug could produce its effects in a nonphysical way, the idea becomes ludicrous.

The Neural Basis of Addiction

Research indicates that reward and addiction take place in different parts of the brain, and that they are independent of each other. One area that produces withdrawal symptoms is the periaqueductal gray (PAG) in the brain stem (Wise, 1987). Withdrawal symptoms can be produced in rats by giving them regular injections of morphine in the PAG, then terminating the effects quickly with naloxone, a drug that blocks opiate effects by occupying opiate receptors without stimulating them (Bozarth & Wise, 1984). However, the animals would not press a lever to inject morphine into

the PAG, so it does not contribute to addiction. They would press a lever to inject morphine into the ventral tegmental area (see Figure 4.10), and they showed signs of being addicted. However, these rats did not show withdrawal symptoms when they were injected with naloxone. The independence of addiction and withdrawal does not mean that addicts never take drugs to avoid withdrawal symptoms, but that addiction depends on something other than withdrawal symptoms. That something turns out to be reward.

It is as if drugs have hijacked the brain's natural motivational control circuits. . . .
—Alan Leshner

***Reward* refers to the positive effect the drug has on the user.** The major drug reward centers are located in a pathway called the mesolimbic dopamine system (Wise & Rompre, 1989). **The *mesolimbic dopamine system* takes its name from the fact that it**

Figure 4.10
The Mesolimbic Dopamine System
From Clinical Symposia, Vol. 48, No. 1, 1996.

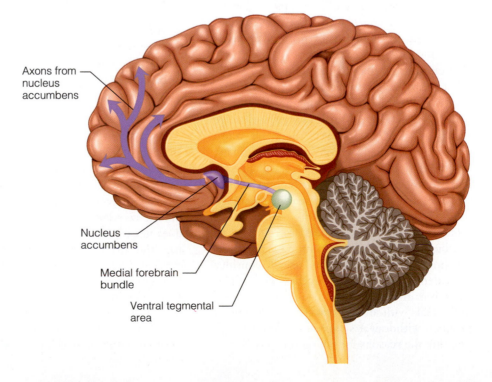

Axons from nucleus accumbens

Nucleus accumbens

Medial forebrain bundle

Ventral tegmental area

begins in the midbrain (mesencephalon) and projects to the limbic system and prefrontal cortex (see Figure 4.10). **Most important of these structures in regard to drug reward effects are the *nucleus accumbens (NAcc)*, the *medial forebrain bundle (MFB)*, and the *ventral tegmental area (VTA)*, which sends neurons to the NAcc.** Rats will learn to press a lever to inject abused drugs into this area (Bozarth & Wise, 1984; Hoebel et al., 1983), and lesioning the NAcc reduces reward effects for many drugs (Kelsey, Carlezon, & Falls, 1989).

Dopamine and Reward

Virtually all the abused drugs increase dopamine (DA) levels in the nucleus accumbens, including opiates, barbiturates, alcohol, THC, PCP, MDMA, nicotine, and even caffeine (Carlezon & Wise, 1996; Chen et al., 1990; Di Chiara & Imperato, 1987; Govoni et al., 1984; Imperato & Di Chiara, 1986; Liechti & Vollenweider, 2000; Pontieri, Tanda, & Di Chiara, 1995; Tanda et al., 1997). In many cases it can be demonstrated that this increase in DA level is the basis for the drug's rewarding effect. For example, a PET scan study of human cocaine abusers showed that a "high" occurs when cocaine has blocked 47% of the dopamine reuptake sites in the area of the NAcc, which increases DA levels in the synapse (Volkow et al., 1997). Further, the intensity of the high depends on what proportion of reuptake sites are occupied.

Interfering with DA activity usually blocks drug reward. In humans, dopamine antagonists reduce the feeling of euphoria from amphetamine use (Gunne, Änggård, & Jönsson, 1972; Jönsson, Änggård, & Gunne, 1971). In rats, drugs that block the reuptake of dopamine at the synapse increase lever pressing to inject amphetamine (Yokel & Wise, 1975). In addition, rats do not seek out a place where they have previously received an abused drug if they are given a drug that blocks dopamine receptors or one that depletes dopamine (Beninger & Hahn, 1983; Schwartz & Marchok; 1974), or if they are genetically engineered to lack a

particular subtype of DA receptor (Maldonado et al., 1997).

Many researchers believe that the mesolimbic dopamine system, and the nucleus accumbens in particular, are part of a general reward system with functions that go beyond its role in drug addiction. As evidence, they point to *electrical stimulation of the brain (ESB), in which animals learn to press a lever to deliver mild electrical stimulation to certain parts of their brain.* Not only will the animals seek the stimulation but they will press at a very high rate, sometimes thousands of times in an hour; they will ignore food and water and tolerate painful shock to engage in this self-stimulation. Sites where ESB is rewarding are scattered throughout much of the brain, but the most sensitive areas are in the medial forebrain bundle (see Figure 4.10 again). The lowest thresholds for effective stimulation are where the density of dopaminergic neurons is greatest (Corbett & Wise, 1980).

There are numerous indications that ESB reward and drug-induced reward involve related mechanisms. Like drugs, ESB increases the release of dopamine in the nucleus accumbens and other locations (Fibiger, LePiane, Jakubovic, & Phillips, 1987; Nakahara, Ozaki, Miura, Miura, & Nagatsu, 1989). And, just as we saw with drug self-administration, dopamine blockers reduce lever pressing for ESB in the lateral hypothalamus (Fouriezos, Hansson, & Wise, 1978). Lesions in the ventral tegmental area, which reduce forebrain DA levels by 94 to 99%, also dramatically reduce lever pressing for ESB (Fibiger et al., 1987).

If you think about it, it is unlikely that a reward system evolved to ensure we would receive pleasure from drugs and electrical stimulation; so we must ask what the normal role of this reward system is. The answer may be that it provides a rewarding effect for the behaviors that are most important to individual and species survival. For example, in male rats the presence of a sexually receptive female increases dopamine release in the nucleus accumbens (Damsma, Pfaus, Wenkstern, &

What is the reward hypothesis of addiction?

What do the similar effects of drugs and ESB suggest?

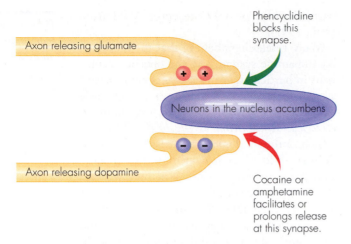

Figure 4.11
Dopamine and glutamate neurons converge on the same neurons in the nucleus accumbens

Phillips, 1992), and eating increases dopamine activity (Fibiger et al., 1987). In one area in which ESB is effective, stimulation by the researcher also produces eating; in another, researcher-administered stimulation initiates sexual activity (Caggiula, 1970). Injections of testosterone (a male hormone) increase the rate of self-stimulation in the posterior hypothalamus in rats, castration decreases it, and testosterone replacement increases it again. (See "Your Brain on Poker.")

However, dopamine cannot account for all reward. The rewarding effect of alcohol,

What alternative role has been suggested for dopamine?

for example, apparently depends partly on opiates (Garbutt, West, Carey, Lohr, & Crews, 1999), and we saw that PCP's effect involves glutamate (Carlezon & Wise, 1996). Because rats will also self-administer PCP into the frontal cortex, the researchers suggested that glutamate-secreting neurons that run from there to the NAcc converge on the same postsynaptic neurons as dopamine neurons, and that either is sufficient to produce reward (Figure 4.11).

Drugs of abuse create a signal in the brain that indicates, falsely, the arrival of a huge fitness benefit.
—Randolph Nesse and Kent Berridge

Some drug researchers question whether dopamine's reward effect is sufficient alone to account for addiction. They point out that addicts often continue taking a drug long after its use has ceased to give pleasure. In rats learning to press a lever for a drug, dopamine release increases early on, but then drops off as the reward becomes predictable (Garris et al., 1999). The fact that DA neurons respond to novel stimuli whether they are rewarding or not suggests that DA serves as a "teaching signal" during learning by adding emphasis to significant stimuli (Young, Joseph, & Gray, 1993; Waeiti, Dickinson, & Schultz, 2001).

Your Brain on Poker

Dr. Hans Breiter and his fellow researchers at Massachusetts General Hospital reported that they may have discovered the basis of the gambler's high. They had 12 men play a simple game of chance while their brain reactions were monitored with functional magnetic resonance imaging (fMRI; see the appendix).

When the men won money, activity increased in their nucleus accumbens. Breiter noted, "Gambling produces a similar pattern of activity to cocaine in the cocaine addict." The full report of the research appeared in the journal *Neuron* (May 2001, pp. 619–639).
—Newsweek, *June 4, 2001, p. 52*

> *. . . the proneness to relapse is based on changes in brain function that continue for months or years after the last use of the drug.*
>
> —Charles O'Brien

The most obvious example of the involvement of learning in addiction is in craving. Stimuli associated with drug use, such as drug paraphernalia, will evoke craving in addicts (Garavan et al., 2000; Grant et al., 1996; Maas et al., 1998). PET scans during the presentation of drug-related stimuli show that activity increases in areas involved in learning and emotion (Figure 4.12). The hippocampus is important in learning, and particularly in learning associations with environmental stimuli like those involved in drug taking. After rats have given up pressing a lever because the drug delivery mechanism has been disconnected, electrical stimulation of the hippocampus is enough to revive the lever pressing (Vorel, Liu, Hayes, Spector, & Gardner, 2001). The researchers believe that the lengthy (30-minute) release of dopamine in the NAcc that follows hippocampal stimulation accounts for this reinstatement. Similarly, some drug researchers believe that changes in the brain due to learning explain why amphetamine still produces an exaggerated reaction years after the last use, and why some addictions can last a lifetime.

Ending Dependence on Drugs

Synanon, the residential community for the treatment of heroin and other addictions, supplied its residents with all their food, clothing, and other necessities including, until 1970, cigarettes—at an annual cost of $200,000 (Brecher, 1972). But then Synanon's founder and head Charles Dederich had a chest X ray that showed a cloudy area in his lungs, and he realized that residents as young as 15 were learning to smoke under his watch. He quit smoking, stopped supplying cigarettes, and banned their use on the premises. Giving up smoking was more difficult for the residents

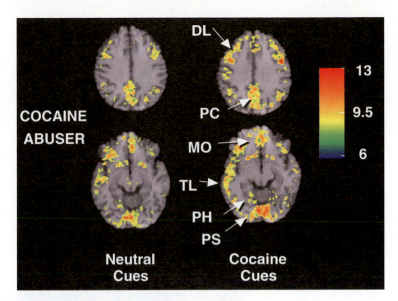

Figure 4.12
The brain of a cocaine abuser during craving
PET scans are shown at two depths in the brain. Notice the increased activity during presentation of cocaine-related stimuli. Frontal areas (DL, MO) and temporal areas (TL, PH) are involved in learning and emotion.
Source: Grant et al., 1996.

than expected. About 100 people left during the first six months rather than do without cigarettes. Some of the residents who quit smoking noticed that they got over withdrawal symptoms from other drugs in less than a week, but the symptoms from smoking hung around for at least six months. As one resident said, it was easier to quit heroin than cigarettes.

Freud had a similarly difficult experience (see Figure 4.13 on page 112). He smoked as many as 20 cigars a day, and commented that his passion for smoking interfered with his work. Though he quit cocaine with apparent ease, each time he gave up smoking he relapsed. He developed cancer of the mouth and jaw, which required 33 surgeries, but he continued smoking. After replacement of his jaw with an artificial one he was in constant pain and sometimes unable to speak, chew, or swallow, but still he smoked. He quit smoking when he died of cancer in 1939 (Brecher, 1972).

The first step in quitting drug use is detoxification. This means giving up the drug and

Figure 4.13
Sigmund Freud and relapse of smoking addiction
Notice that the two legal drugs have relapse rates equal to that of heroin.

Source: (Right) Adapted with permission from "Nicotine becomes Addictive," by R. Kanigel, 1988. Science Illustrated, Oct/Nov, p. 12–14, 19–21. © 1988 Science Illustrated.

Bettmann/CORBIS

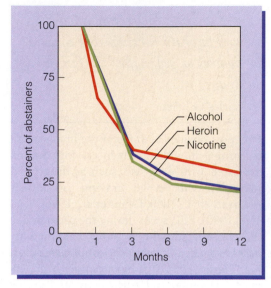

What are the types of pharmacological treatment for addiction?

7

allowing the body to cleanse itself of the drug residues. This is admittedly difficult with nicotine or opiates, but withdrawal from alcohol is potentially life-threatening; medical intervention with benzodiazepines to suppress the withdrawal syndrome may be necessary (O'Brien, 1997). Still, withdrawal is often easier than the subsequent battle against relapse. Psychological intervention may help, but when used alone it produces disappointing rates of recovery. Fortunately, the number of treatment options is increasing; as you will see, they reflect our improving knowledge of how addiction works.

. . . addiction will eventually be seen as analogous to other medical illnesses—as complex constructs of genetic, environmental, and psychosocial factors that require multiple levels of intervention for their treatment and prevention.

—Eric Nestler and George Aghajanian

Pharmacological Treatments

Agonist treatments **replace an addicting drug with another drug that has a similar effect;** this approach is the most common defense against drug craving and relapse. Nicotine gum and nicotine patches provide controlled amounts of the drug without the dangers of smoking, and their use can be systematically reduced over time. Opiate addiction is often treated with **a synthetic opiate called** *methadone.* This treatment is controversial because it substitutes one addiction for another, but methadone is a milder and safer drug and the person does not have to resort to crime to satisfy the habit. As a side note, methadone was developed in World War II Germany as a pain-relieving replacement for morphine, which was not available; it was called *adolphine*, after Adolph Hitler (Bellis, 1981).

Antagonist treatments, **as the name implies, involve drugs that block the effects of the addicting drug.** The potential for this type of treatment is dramatically illustrated in Figure 4.14 (Suzdak et al., 1986). However, antagonist treatment has two disadvantages: the addict must be motivated enough to take the drug regularly; and because the antagonists do not replace the drug effect, addicts do not accept them as readily as they do agonists. An example is ***naltrexone, which is used to treat opiate addictions because of its ability to occupy and block opiate receptors.*** It is also effective in treating alcohol dependency (Garbutt et al., 1999), which suggests that the reward effect of alcohol is partially opiate based.

Rather than blocking drug effects, ***aversive treatments* cause a negative reaction when the person takes the drug. *Antabuse* (disulfiram) prevents the breakdown of one of the by-products of alcohol and makes the person ill**; adding silver nitrate to chewing gum or lozenges makes tobacco taste bad. Compliance is a problem, because the treatment relies on the addict's motivation to take the drug.

Vaccines against drugs might sound far-fetched, but they may soon become a reality. If you were a rat they would be available now to treat your nicotine or cocaine addiction. ***Antidrug vaccines* are synthetic molecules that resemble the drug but have been modified to stimulate the animal's immune system to make antibodies that will break down the drug** (Landry, 1997). Vaccines of this sort reduce the amount of cocaine that reaches the brain by 80% (Carrera et al., 1995) and the amount of nicotine by 65% (Pentel et al., 2000). This treatment avoids the side effects that occur when receptors in the brain are manipulated. Another benefit is that the antibodies are expected to last from weeks to years, which means that therapeutic success will not depend on the addict's decision every morning to take an anti-addiction drug.

Other Treatment Options

Before we leave this topic we need to raise two additional points. One is that diminished serotonin activity has been found across several addictions, as well as a variety of other disor-

Figure 4.14
Effects of a GABA$_A$ receptor blocker
The two rats received the same amount of alcohol, but the one on the right received a drug that blocks the effect of alcohol at the GABA$_A$ receptor.
Source: Photo courtesy of Jules Asher.

ders. As a consequence, drugs that increase serotonin levels have been beneficial in treating alcohol abuse (Pettinati et al., 2000) and smoking (Hall et al., 1998).

Part of the effectiveness of the serotonin-potentiating drugs can be attributed to the fact that serotonin helps regulate activity in the mesolimbic dopamine system (Melichar, Daglish, & Nutt, 2001). This brings us to our second point, that the various neurotransmitter systems are highly interconnected. This provides additional windows of access to the neural mechanism we want to manipulate, and may allow us to choose a more powerful drug or one with fewer side effects. Gamma-aminobutyric acid also modulates dopamine transmission in the mesolimbic system. When alcohol abusers were given a drug that increases inhibitory activity at GABA receptors, it reduced the patients' craving for alcohol (Whitworth et al., 1996). Another drug that enhances GABA inhibition reduced dopamine release in baboons given cocaine (Dewey et al., 1998) and in rats given nicotine (Dewey et al., 1999).

In spite of the promise of pharmacological treatment of addiction, giving a drug to combat a drug is controversial in some segments of society. Some people believe that recovery from addiction should involve the exercise of will and that recovery should not be easy; Antabuse is okay because it causes the backslider to suffer, but methadone is not okay because it continues the pleasures of drug taking (Szalavitz, 2000). The counterargument is that the bottom line in drug treatment is effectiveness. Alcohol dependency alone costs the country an estimated $150 billion a year (Whitworth et al., 1996), but every dollar invested in treatment saves $4 to $12 depending on the drug and the type of treatment (O'Brien, 1997). Pharmacological intervention increases treatment effectiveness dramatically. Methadone combined with counseling produces abstinence rates of 60–80% in heroin addicts, compared to 10–30% for programs that rely on behavioral management alone (Landry, 1997).

Science has yet to defeat the mind/body problem—or those who view psychological problems as failures of will and values.

—Maia Szalavitz

✔ CONCEPT CHECK

- *Why is the term psychological dependence inappropriate? What erroneous idea was it based on?*
- *Where does the reward hypothesis of addiction run into trouble?*
- *What are the strengths and weaknesses of the different types of pharmacological treatment of addiction?*

THE NEURAL AND GENETIC BASES OF ALCOHOLISM

Unfortunately, most of the research on what predisposes a person to addiction has focused on alcoholism to the neglect of other drugs. This is understandable, because there are so many alcoholics, and they are readily accessible to researchers because their drug use is not illegal. Though we would like to have the same kind of information for other drugs, addictions have enough in common that alcoholism research provides us clues for understanding addiction in general.

The EEG as a Diagnostic Tool

The *electroencephalogram (EEG),* a measure of brain activity recorded from electrodes on the scalp, is proving useful in assessing vulnerability to alcoholism. (See section A.3 of the appendix for more information on the EEG.) Male alcoholics produce an excess of high-frequency EEG activity when they are not under the influence of alcohol (Jones & Holmes, 1976), and the sons of alcoholic men show the same characteristic (Gabrielli and Mednick, 1982). Small doses of alcohol increase EEG frequency in nonalcoholics, but the sons of alcoholic men show less EEG responsiveness to alcohol; lowered responsiveness identifies the sons who are most likely to be alcohol dependent 10 years later (Volavka et al., 1996; Wall & Ehlers, 1995).

A brief stimulus produces a fleeting change in the EEG called an *evoked potential* (also described in section A.3 of the appendix). A dip in the potential about 300 msec after the presentation of a stimulus, called the *P300 wave,* occurs when the stimulus is a novel one, like a high tone among several low tones. Differences among people in P300 responsiveness appear to be hereditary (Noble, Berman, Ozkaragoz, & Ritchie, 1994). In alcoholics, even when they are abstaining, the P300 wave is smaller in amplitude and delayed in occurrence (Wall & Ehlers, 1995). This response appears to be a genetic marker (indicator) for alcoholism rather than a result of chronic drinking, because it is also found in children at risk for alcoholism (Hill, 1995; Noble et al., 1994). Figure 4.15 compares P300 waves of children of alcoholics with children of nonalcoholics.

Two Kinds of Alcoholism

Twin and adoption studies indicate that the heritability for alcoholism is around 50–60% (Kendler, Heath, Neale, Kessler, & Eaves, 1992; Kendler, Prescott, Neale, & Pedersen, 1997). People apparently inherit a broad vulnerability to drugs; the proportion of addicts who abuse three or more drugs is around 60–70% (Cadoret, Troughton, O'Gorman, & Heywoood, 1986; Smith et al., 1992). Whether there are also genetic factors that predispose individuals to specific drugs is not clear, because few genetic studies have included more than one drug.

For a long time the role of heredity in alcoholism was a controversial topic, because studies yielded inconsistent results. One reason is that researchers typically treated alcoholism as a unitary disorder; they would study groups such as hospitalized alcoholics and generalize to all alcoholics. An important breakthrough came when Robert Cloninger and his colleagues included all 862 men and 913 women who had been adopted by nonrelatives at an early age (average, 4 months) in Stockholm, Sweden, between 1930 and 1949 (Bohman, 1978).

They concluded that there were two kinds of alcoholism, which had different causes and were associated with different personalities and behaviors (Cloninger, 1987). The characteristics of the two types are summarized in Table 4.1 on page 116. Cloninger cautioned that the two groups should not be considered entirely distinct, because many alcoholics have some characteristics of both groups. Some researchers have proposed additional categories of alcoholism to accommodate these individuals, but their ideas have not gained the same acceptance as Cloninger's.

Type 1 alcoholics typically begin their problem drinking after the age of 25, after a long period of exposure to socially encouraged drinking, such as at lunch with co-workers; I will refer to them as *late-onset alcoholics*. They are able to abstain from drinking for long periods of time, but when they do drink they have difficulty stopping

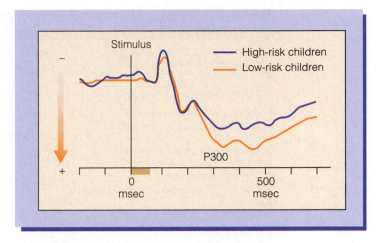

Figure 4.15
Evoked potentials in children at high risk and low risk for alcoholism
Evoked potentials were elicited by high-pitched tones occurring among low-pitched tones. The usual dip of the P300 wave is diminished in the high-risk children.
Source: Reprinted by permission of Elseview Science from S. Y. Hill, D. Muka, S. Steinhauer, and J. Locke, "P300 amplitude decrements in children from families of alcoholic female probands," Biological Psychiatry, 38, 622–632. Copyright 1995 Society of Biological Psychiatry.

(binge drinking), and they experience guilt about their behavior. Their associated personality traits make them cautious and emotionally dependent.

Type 2 alcoholics begin drinking at a young age, so I will call them *early-onset alcoholics*. They drink frequently and feel little guilt about their drinking. They have a tendency toward antisocial behavior, and often get into fights in bars and are arrested for reckless driving. They are typically impulsive and uninhibited, confident, and socially and emotionally detached. In other words, they fit the description of *antisocial personality disorder*. Apparently the personality characteristics appear early; novelty seeking and low harm avoidance in 6- and 10-year-olds predicted drug and alcohol use in adolescence (Mâsse & Tremblay, 1997). Early-onset alcoholics are almost entirely male, and most of the men who are hospitalized for alcoholism fall in this category. Earlier studies had focused mostly on hospitalized alcoholics, which almost excluded late-onset alcoholics and women.

Table 4.1 Distinguishing Characteristics of Two Types of Alcoholism

Characteristic Features	Type of Alcoholism	
	Type 1	Type 2
Alcohol-Related Problems		
Usual age of onset (years)	After 25	Before 25
Spontaneous alcohol-seeking (inability to abstain)	Infrequent	Frequent
Fighting and arrests when drinking	Infrequent	Frequent
Psychological dependence (loss of control)	Frequent	Infrequent
Guilt and fear about alcohol dependence	Frequent	Infrequent
Personality Traits		
Novelty seeking	Low	High
Harm avoidance	High	Low
Reward dependence	High	Low

Source: Cloninger, 1987.

How do hereditary and environmental contributions differ in the two types of alcoholism?

We also now understand why some of the earlier studies had discounted environmental influence on alcoholism. When all of Cloninger's adoptees were considered together, rearing in an alcoholic home did not increase their risk for alcoholism; but the effect of environment was different for the two groups considered separately. Offspring of late-onset alcoholics were likely to become alcoholic themselves only if they were reared in a home where there was alcohol abuse. For offspring of early-onset alcoholics the rearing environment made no difference.

Dopamine and Serotonin Irregularities

What appears to be inherited in alcoholism?

If genetics plays a role in alcoholism just what is it that is inherited? Most research suggests irregularities in transmitter systems. Dopamine not only has a role in the reward effect of alcohol but appears to be one of the factors differentiating alcoholics from nonalcoholics. There are several *alleles, or alternate forms*, of the gene responsible for the development of the D_2 subtype of dopamine receptor. Alcoholics twice as often carry either the A1 allele or the B1 allele (Cloninger, 1991; Noble, 1993;

Smith, et al., 1992; Uhl, Blum, Noble, & Smith, 1993). Also, among the sons of alcoholic fathers those with the A1 allele had greater delays in P300 occurrence than the ones with the A2 allele (Noble et al., 1994). These two alleles are not specific to alcoholism, though; they are also found at a high rate in abusers of other drugs and in multiple-substance abusers.

Autopsies show that individuals with the A1 allele have fewer D_2 receptors than individuals with the A2 allele (Noble, Blum, Ritchie, Montgomery, & Sheridan, 1991). Rats bred for high alcohol consumption also have fewer D_2 receptors. When researchers used adenovirus to deliver the dopamine D_2 receptor gene into these rats' nucleus accumbens, the number of receptors increased by 52% and their alcohol intake dropped 64% (Thanos et al., 2001). Reduced dopamine receptors apparently explains why alcoholics show a paradoxical *reduced* sensitivity to alcohol. They report that even early in their drinking careers not only could they consume large amounts of alcohol, it also had little effect on them. Schuckit (1994) followed male college students for 10 years; the ones who felt less high when drinking and had less motor impairment were twice as likely to be alcoholic a decade later, and four times as likely if they were also the sons of alcoholics.

Presumably, less sensitive individuals are more prone to addiction because they have to consume more alcohol to get high and they fail to experience the negative reactions that limit drinking in other people. This interpretation is supported by the fact that many Asians react to alcohol with intense flushing, nausea, and increased heart rate; as a consequence, they drink less and they less frequently become alcoholic (Reed, 1985; Wall & Ehlers, 1995). The reason is an inheritable deficiency in **the enzyme *aldehyde dehydrogenase (ALDH)*, which normally metabolizes a by-product of alcohol called acetaldehyde into acetate.** The accumulating acetaldehyde in people with deficient ALDH makes them ill when they drink alcohol. Antabuse produces the same effect by inhibiting ALDH. ALDH deficiency is found in only 2% of Japanese alcoholics, compared to 50% of nonalcoholics (Harada, Agarwal, Goedde, Tagaki, & Ishikawa, 1982). A similar genetic deficiency in metabolizing nicotine protects a smaller number of people from nicotine addiction (Pianezza, Sellers, & Tyndale, 1998).

The D_2 gene does not account for all cases of alcoholism. Serotonin (5-hydroxytryptophan, or 5-HT) is involved in drug abuse in general, as well as in mood, sexual behavior, aggression, and the regulation of bodily rhythms and food and water intake. Serotonin functioning, which is genetically influenced in humans (Doria, 1995), is lower than normal in alcoholics (Pihl & Peterson, 1993) and in rats bred for high alcohol consumption (Gongwer, Murphy, McBride, Lumeng, & Li, 1989; Murphy, McBride, Lumeng, & Li, 1987). Alcohol stimulates serotonin pathways (Gongwer et al., 1989; Grant, 1995) and temporarily increases serotonin functioning (Pihl & Peterson, 1993), which elevates mood. Serotonin also activates dopamine pathways and probably enhances dopaminergic reward (Grant, 1995). Drugs that block the 5-HT$_3$ subtype of serotonin receptors reduce some of the subjective effects of alcohol, along with alcohol craving and consumption (Grant, 1995; Johnson & Cowen, 1993). Apparently these drugs interfere with alcohol's rewarding and mood-elevating effects.

Implications of Alcoholism Research

Alcoholism is very similar to other drug addictions, and studying it helps us understand vulnerability to other forms of drug abuse. The study of alcoholism is worthwhile for other reasons as well. It illustrates general principles of behavioral inheritance; for example, alcoholism is not entirely due to genetics or to environmental influences, but results from an interplay of the two. The fact that these two forces operate differently in different types of alcoholism illustrates the fact that no behavior is simple or simply explained. Even after we understand the relative roles of heredity and environment there is further complexity, because we must also understand the mechanisms—the neurotransmitters, receptors, pathways, enzymes, and so on—that mediate the response to alcohol. Finally, we must look beyond simple appeals to willpower in explaining the self-defeating behavior of the alcoholic, just as we must do when we try to understand other kinds of behavior. Our brief look at alcoholism is a good preparation for our inquiries into the physiological systems behind other human behaviors and misbehaviors.

✔ **CONCEPT CHECK**

- *How did the failure to recognize two types of alcoholism create misunderstandings about hereditary and environmental influences and gender distribution in alcoholism?*
- *How can lowered sensitivity to a drug increase the chances of addiction?*
- *What are two kinds of evidence that some people are predisposed to alcoholism from birth?*

In Perspective

The costs of drug abuse include untold suffering, loss of health, productivity, and life, and billions of dollars in expenses for treatment and incarceration. The only upside is that the study of drug abuse reveals the workings of the synapses and brain networks, and helps us recognize that powerful biological forces are molding our behavior. This knowledge in turn helps us understand the behaviors that are the subject of the remaining chapters, including the disorders covered in Chapter 13, and guides research into developing therapeutic drugs.

 Summary

Psychoactive Drugs

- Most abused drugs produce addiction, which is usually accompanied by withdrawal symptoms when drug use is stopped. Tolerance can increase the dangers of drugs because life-threatening effects may not show tolerance.

- The opiates have their own receptors, which are normally stimulated by endorphins. The opiates are particularly addictive and dangerous.

- Depressants reduce activity in the nervous system. Some of them have important uses, but they are highly abused.

- Stimulants increase activity in the nervous system. They encompass the widest range of effects and include nicotine, most notable for its addictiveness and its association with deadly tobacco.

- Psychedelic drugs are interesting for their perceptual/hallucinatory effects, which result from their transmitter-like structures.

- Marijuana is controversial not just in terms of the legalization issue but because it raises questions about what constitutes addiction.

Addiction

- The mesolimbic dopamine system is implicated by several lines of research as a reward center that plays a role in drug addiction, feeding, sex, and other behaviors.

- Dopamine may also contribute to addiction through a role in learning, by emphasizing significant stimuli and/or modifying neural connections.

- Treatment of addiction is very difficult; effective programs combine psychological support with pharmacological strategies, including agonist, antagonist, and aversive treatments and, potentially, drug vaccines.

The Neural and Genetic Bases of Alcoholism

- Research suggests that addiction is partially hereditary and that the inherited vulnerability may not be drug specific.

- Heredity research indicates there are at least two kinds of alcoholism, with different genetic and environmental backgrounds.

- Alcoholics often have dopamine and serotonin irregularities that may account for the susceptibility, and some have a deficiency in evoked potentials that appears to be inherited.

For Further Thought

- Is the legality or illegality of a drug a good indication of its potential for abuse?

- Is it morally right to treat addictions with drug antagonists, aversive drugs, and antidrug vaccines? Is your opinion the same for drug agonists?

- You work for an agency that has the goal of substantially reducing the rate of drug abuse in your state through education, family support, and individualized treatment. Based on your knowledge of addiction, what should the program consist of?

→ Testing Your Understanding

1. Describe the two proposed roles for dopamine in addiction and give two pieces of evidence for each.

2. What are the practical and ethical considerations in using drugs to treat addiction?

3. Sally and Sam are alcoholics. Sally seldom drinks but binges when she does and feels guilty later. Sam drinks regularly and feels no remorse. What other characteristics would you expect to see in them, and what speculations can you make about their environments?

Select the one best answer:

1. In the study of conditioned tolerance:
   a. human subjects failed to show the usual withdrawal symptoms.
   b. human subjects increased their drug intake.
   c. rats were unresponsive to the drug.
   d. rats tolerated the drug less in a novel environment.

2. Withdrawal from alcohol:
   a. can be life-threatening.
   b. is about like a bad case of flu.
   c. is slightly milder than with most drugs.
   d. is usually barely noticeable.

3. The reason alcohol, barbiturates, and benzodiazepines are deadly taken together is that they:
   a. affect the thalamus to produce almost total brain shutdown.
   b. have a cumulative effect on the periaqueductal gray.
   c. affect the same receptor complex.
   d. increase dopamine release to dangerous levels.

4. Psychedelic drugs often produce hallucinations by:
   a. inhibiting serotonin neurons.
   b. stimulating serotonin receptors.
   c. stimulating dopamine receptors.
   d. blocking dopamine reuptake.

5. Marijuana was the subject of disagreement among researchers because some of them:
   a. believed it is more dangerous than alcohol or tobacco.
   b. believed it is highly addictive.
   c. thought it failed to meet the standard test for addictiveness.
   d. overstated its withdrawal effects.

6. Evidence that addiction does not depend on the drug's ability to produce withdrawal symptoms is that:
   a. they don't usually occur together with the same drug.
   b. they are produced in different parts of the brain.
   c. either can be produced without the other in the lab.
   d. a and b.
   e. b and c.

7. When rats trained to press a lever for ESB are given a drug that blocks dopamine receptors, lever pressing:
   a. increases.   b. decreases.
   c. increases briefly   d. remains the same.
      then decreases.

8. The best argument that caffeine is a drug like alcohol and nicotine is that:
   a. it is used compulsively.
   b. quitting produces withdrawal.
   c. it affects the same processes in the brain.
   d. it stimulates dopamine receptors directly.

9. Evidence that dopamine's contribution to addiction may be its effect on learning comes from a study in which:
   a. blocking DA receptors interfered with learning to self-inject cocaine.
   b. hippocampal stimulation released DA and restored learned lever pressing.

continued

c. rats learned to press a lever for injections of DA into the NAcc.

d. rats learned a maze for food reward faster if given a DA uptake blocker.

10. Agonist treatments for drug addiction:

a. mimic the drug's effect.

b. block the drug's effect.

c. make the person sick after taking the drug.

d. reduce anxiety so there is less need for the drug.

11. Critics of treating drug addiction with drugs believe that:

a. getting over addiction should not be easy.

b. it is wrong to give an addict another addictive drug.

c. the drugs are not very effective and delay effective treatment.

d. a and b.

e. b and c.

12. The type of alcoholism in which the individual drinks regularly is associated with:

a. behavioral rigidity.

b. perfectionism.

c. feelings of guilt.

d. antisocial personality disorder.

13. Alcoholics often:

a. have reduced serotonin and dopamine functioning.

b. are more sensitive to the effects of alcohol.

c. are unusually lethargic and use alcohol as a stimulant.

d. have an inherited preference for the taste of alcohol.

Answers: 1. **d** 2. **a** 3. **c** 4. **b** 5. **c** 6. **e** 7. **b** 8. **c** 9. **b** 10. **a** 11. **d** 12. **d** 13. **a**

➤ On the Web

1. The **University of Pennsylvania Health Services** has information on the effects of heroin at

   http://www.uphs.upenn.edu/recovery/ pros/opioids.html

2. The **Alcoholics Anonymous** site has information about AA, testimonials from members, and a quiz for teenagers (or anybody) to help them decide if they have a drinking problem at

   http://www.alcoholics-anonymous.org/

   The **Self-scoring Alcohol Checkup** scores you on alcohol usage at

   http://www.cts.com/crash/habtsmrt/ chkup.html

3. **Cocaine Anonymous** offers news, information, a cocaine problem checklist, and a directory of local groups at

   http://www.ca.org/

The **University of Pennsylvania Health Services** has information on the effects of cocaine, marijuana, and caffeine at

   http://www.uphs.upenn.edu/recovery/ pros/cocaine.html

4. The **University of Pennsylvania Health Services** has information on the effects of nicotine at

   http://www.uphs.upenn.edu/recovery/ pros/nicotine.html

5. The **University of Pennsylvania Health Services** has information on the effects of LSD, PCP, and MDMA at

   http://www.uphs.upenn.edu/recovery/ pros/hallucinogen.html

6. **Marijuana Anonymous** offers a variety of publications for the person who wants to stop using marijuana, or the student who is just interested, at

   http://www.marijuana-anonymous.org/

7. The **Web of Addictions** contains fact sheets, links to a variety of other information sites, contact information for help organizations and other organizations concerned with drug problems, and in-depth reports on special topics, at

   http://www.well.com/user/woa/

8. Additional sites of interest:

   Drugs, Brain, and Behavior is a textbook at

   http://www.rci.rutgers.edu/~lwh/drugs/

   The **National Clearinghouse for Alcohol and Drug Information** has information on drugs and what can be done to prevent abuse; a visitor can choose material appropriate for different audiences including ethnic group, age, gender, and so on, at

   http://www.health.org/

   The **National Institute on Drug Abuse** emphasizes drug abuse prevention. The site includes news, research information, and information on drugs and prevention for parents, teachers, and students at

   http://www.nida.nih.gov/

 For additional information about the topics covered in this chapter, please look at InfoTrac College Edition, at

http://www.infotrac-college.com/wadsworth

Try search terms you think up yourself, or use these: *addiction; electroencephalogram; endorphins; psychoactive drugs.*

On the CD-ROM: Exploring Biological Psychology

Psychoactive Drugs
Animation: Opiate Narcotics
Animation: CNS Depressants

Animation: CNS Stimulants
Animation: Hallucinogenics

For Further Reading

A Primer of Drug Action: A Concise, Nontechnical Guide to the Actions, Uses, and Side Effects of Psychoactive Drugs by Robert M. Julien (Freeman, 2001). Often used as a text in psychopharmacology and upper-level biopsychology courses, this book covers principles of drug action, properties of specific drugs, pharmacotherapy for various disorders, and societal issues. It received good reviews from students on the Amazon book site.

Buzzed: The Straight Facts About the Most Used and Abused Drugs from Alcohol to Ecstasy by Cynthia Kuhn, Scott Swartzwelder, and Wilkie Wilson, Jeremy Foster (contributor), and Leigh Heather Wilson (contributor)

(W. W. Norton, 1998). The book gives technical information about drugs written in a style appropriate for college students (in fact, the two contributors are students). It covers drug characteristics, histories of the drugs, addiction, the workings of the brain, and legal issues.

The Encyclopedia of Psychoactive Substances by Richard Rudgley (St. Martins, 1999). Formatted as a reference book, it devotes just a few pages to each of over 100 drugs, but includes historical information as well as information about changing social attitudes. Coverage ranges from traditional drugs to exotic ones, such as hallucinogenic fish.

→ Key Terms

addiction *96*

agonist treatment *112*

alcohol *97*

aldehyde dehydrogenase (ALDH) *117*

allele *116*

amphetamine *102*

analgesic *96*

anandamide *106*

Antabuse *113*

antagonist treatment *112*

antidrug vaccine *113*

anxiolytic *97*

aversive treatment *113*

barbiturate *99*

benzodiazepine *100*

caffeine *104*

cocaine *100*

delirium tremens *98*

depressant *97*

drug *95*

early-onset alcoholism *115*

electrical stimulation of the brain (ESB) *109*

electroencephalogram (EEG) *114*

endogenous *97*

endorphins *97*

euphoria *96*

evoked potential *114*

hashish *105*

heroin *96*

hypnotic *96*

late-onset alcoholism *115*

ligand *97*

marijuana *105*

medial forebrain bundle (MFB) *109*

mesolimbic dopamine system *108*

methadone *112*

naltrexone *113*

nicotine *103*

nucleus accumbens (NAcc) *109*

opiate *96*

psychedelic *104*

psychoactive drug *96*

reward *108*

sedative *97*

stimulant *100*

tolerance *96*

ventral tegmental area (VTA) *109*

withdrawal *96*

two

PART

Motivation and Emotion:
What Makes Us Go

Nancy R. Cohen

Motivation and Emotion:
What Makes Us Go

CHAPTER

5

Motivation and the Regulation of Internal States

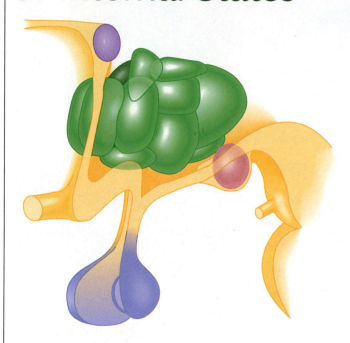

In this chapter you will learn:

- Some of the ways psychologists have viewed motivation.

- How the concepts of drive and homeostasis explain the regulation of internal body states.

- How taste helps us select a safe and nutritious diet.

- How we regulate the amount of food we eat.

- What some of the causes of obesity are.

- What we know about anorexia and bulimia.

I can stuff my face for a long time and I won't feel full.

—Christopher Theros

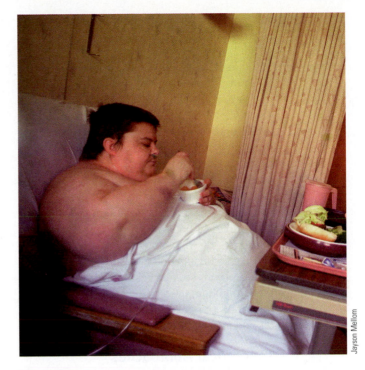

Jayson Mellom

Figure 5.1
Christopher during a hospital stay

When Christopher was born it was obvious there was something wrong (Lyons, 2001). He was a "floppy baby," lying with his arms and legs splayed lifelessly on the bed, and he didn't cry. Doctors thought he might never walk or talk, but he seemed to progress all right until he was in grade school and was diagnosed with Prader-Willi syndrome. The disorder occurs when a small section of the father's chromosome 15 fails to transfer during fertilization. The exact contribution of those genes is not known, but the symptoms are clearly defined, and Christopher had most of them. He stopped growing at 5 feet 3 inches, he had learning difficulties, and he had difficulty with impulse control.

More obviously, Christopher could never seem to recognize when he had eaten enough, so he ate constantly. He even stole his brother's paper-route money to buy midnight snacks at the corner store. At school he would retrieve food from the cafeteria garbage can and wolf it down; his classmates would taunt him by throwing a piece of food in the trash to watch him dive for it. The only way to keep a person like Christopher from literally eating himself to death is to manage his life completely, from locking the kitchen to institutionalization. State law did not permit institutionalization for Chris, because his average IQ did not fit the criteria for inability to manage his affairs. He lived in a series of group homes but was thrown out of each one for rebelliousness and violence, behavior that is characteristic of the disorder. When he died at the age of 28, he weighed 500 pounds (Figure 5.1).

MOTIVATION AND HOMEOSTASIS

When we ask why people (and animals) do what they do, we are asking about their motivation. *Motivation*, **which literally means "to set in motion," refers to the set of factors that initiate, sustain, and direct behaviors.** The need for the concept was prompted by psychologists' inability to explain behavior solely in terms of outside stimuli. Assuming various kinds of motivation, like hunger or achievement need, helped make sense of the individual's responses to stimulus conditions. Keep in mind, though, that *motivation is a concept we have invented and imposed on behavior;* we should not expect to find a "motivation center" in the brain or even a network whose primary function is motivation. The fact that we sometimes cannot distinguish motivation from other aspects of behavior, like emotion, is evidence of how arbitrary the term can be. Still, it is a useful concept for organizing ideas about the sources of behavior. After a brief overview of some of the ways psychologists have approached the problem of motivation, we will take a closer look at temperature regulation, thirst, and hunger as examples before taking up the topics of sexual behavior in the next chapter and emotion and aggression in Chapter 7.

Theoretical Approaches to Motivation

Greeks relied heavily on instinct in their attempts to explain human behavior. **An *instinct* is a complex behavior that is automatic and unlearned, and occurs in all the members of a species.** Migration and maternal behavior are good examples of instinctive behaviors in animals. According to early instinct theorists, humans were guided by instincts, too, waging war because of an aggressive instinct, caring for their young because of a maternal instinct, and so on. At first blush these explanations sound meaningful. But if we say that a person is combative because of an aggressive instinct, we know little more about what makes the person fight than we did before; if we cannot then analyze the supposed aggressive instinct, we have simply dodged the explanation.

The idea of instincts as an explanation of human motivation was popularized in modern times by the psychologist William McDougall (1908). He proposed that human behaviors like reproduction, gregariousness, and parenting are instinctive. It wasn't long until one writer was able to count 10,000 names of instincts in the literature; this led him to suggest, tongue firmly in cheek, that there must also be an "instinct to produce instincts" (Bernard, 1924). Apparently the instinct explanation provided too many theorists an easy way out; the idea of human instincts fell into disrepute. Psychologists today do not deny that there are instincts in animals, but most believe that in human evolution instincts have either dropped out or become weakened. Those who believe some human behaviors are instinctive require any candidate behavior to meet stringent requirements of evidence before it can be declared an instinct. This guards against the temptation to label any behavior that is difficult to explain as an instinct.

Drive theory has fared much better than instinct theory, at least in explaining motivation that involves physical conditions such as hunger, thirst, and body temperature. **According to *drive theory*, the body maintains a condition of *homeostasis*, in which any particular system is in balance or equilibrium** (Hull, 1951). **Any departure from homeostasis, such as depletion of nutrients or a drop in temperature, produces an aroused condition referred to as a *drive*.** The drive impels the human or animal to engage in the appropriate action, to eat or drink or seek warmth. As the body's need is met, the drive and associated arousal subside. This is a temporary state, of course; soon the individual will be hungry or thirsty or cold again, and the cycle will continue. It is also practically impossible for all of our homeostatic systems to be satisfied at the same time; while one system is in a state of equilibrium others will be unstable and initiating internal or behavioral adjustments.

Critics of drive theory point out that it does not explain all kinds of motivation; many motivated behaviors seem to have nothing to do with satisfying tissue needs. For example, a student is motivated by grades, and people work long hours to earn more money than they need for food and shelter. **Incentive theory recognizes that people are motivated by external**

What do homeostasis *and* drive *mean?*

stimuli, not just internal needs (Bolles, 1975); in this respect, money and grades act as *incentives*. Incentives can even be a factor in physiological motivation; consider, for example, the effect of the smell of chocolate chip cookies baking or the sight of a sexually attractive person.

Some people are motivated to jump out of an airplane for the thrill of plummeting toward the earth, hoping to be saved at the last minute by a flimsy parachute; there is no tissue need and no obvious drive involved here. Observations like this have led to the *arousal theory,* which says that people behave in ways that keep them at their preferred level of arousal (Fiske & Maddi, 1961). Different people have different optimum levels of arousal, and some seem to have a need for varied experiences or the thrill of confronting danger (Zuckerman, 1971); this *sensation seeking* finds expression in anything from travel and unconventional dress to skydiving, drug use, and armed robbery.

In the face of challenges to drive theory, psychologists have shifted their emphasis to drives as states of the brain rather than as conditions of the tissues (Stellar & Stellar, 1985). This approach nicely accommodates sexual behavior, which troubled drive theorists because it does not involve a tissue deficit. Even eating behavior is better understood as the result of a brain state. Hunger ordinarily occurs when a lack of nutrients in the body triggers activity in a part of the brain. However, an incentive like the smell of a steak on the grill can also cause hunger, apparently by activating the same brain mechanisms as tissue deficits do. In addition, the person feels satisfied and stops eating long before the nutrients have reached the deficient body cells. Similarly, if the brain is not "satisfied," it little matters how much the person has eaten. In other words, if the information that reserves are excessive fails to reach the brain or to have its usual effect there, the person may, like Christopher, eat to obesity and still feel hungry. In the following pages we will look at the regulation of body temperature, fluid levels, and energy supply from the perspective of drive and homeostasis.

Simple Homeostatic Drives

To sustain life a number of conditions, such as body temperature, fluid levels, and energy reserves, must be held within a fairly narrow range. Accomplishing that requires a *control system*. A mechanical control system that serves as a good analogy is a home heating and cooling system. **Some physiological systems have a set point like the temperature selected on a thermostat.** A departure in the room temperature from the set point is analogous to an organism's drive state. The result is an action, turning on the furnace or the air conditioner. When the room temperature returns to the preset level the system is "satisfied" in the technical sense of the word; homeostasis has been achieved, so the system goes into a quieter state until there is another departure from the set point.

Temperature Regulation

Not only is the regulation of body temperature superficially similar to our thermostat analogy; it is almost as simple. All animals have to maintain internal temperature within certain limits in order to survive, and they operate more effectively within an even narrower range; this is their set point. How they respond to departures from homeostasis is much more variable than with the home heating and cooling system. *Homeothermic* animals like snakes and lizards are unable to regulate their body temperature internally, so they adjust their temperature behaviorally by sunning themselves, finding shade, burrowing in the ground, and so on. *Endothermic* animals, which include mammals and birds, use some of the same strategies along with others that are functionally similar, such as building nests or houses, turning up the thermostat, and wearing clothing. However, endotherms are also able to use their energy reserves to maintain a nearly constant body temperature automatically. In hot weather their temperature regulatory system reduces body heat by causing sweating, reduced metabolism,

How is body temperature regulated?

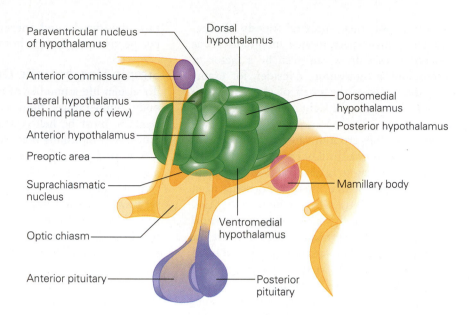

Figure 5.2
Nuclei of the hypothalamus
Source: Adapted from Nieuwenhuys, Voogd, and van Huijzen, 1988.

and dilation of peripheral blood vessels. In cold weather it induces shivering, increased metabolism, and constriction of the peripheral blood vessels. To say that we make these adjustments because we *feel* hot or cold suggests that the responses are intentional behaviors, but that is not the case. So how do these behaviors occur?

In mammals, **the "thermostat" is located in the *preoptic area* of the hypothalamus, which contains separate warmth-sensitive and cold-sensitive cells** (Figure 5.2) (Nakashima, Pierau, Simon, & Hori, 1987). Some of these neurons respond directly to the temperature of the blood flowing through the area; others receive input from temperature receptors in other parts of the body, including the skin. The preoptic area integrates information from these two sources and initiates temperature regulatory responses (Boulant, 1981; Kupferman, Kandel, & Iversen, 2000). Heat-reducing responses such as sweating and panting are produced in the preoptic area, and heat-conserving reactions like shivering are controlled in the posterior hypothalamus. We will be talking about several nuclei in the hypothalamus in this chapter, so you may want to refer to Figure 5.2 often.

How does the body regulate its water reserves?

Thirst

The body is about 70% water, so it seems obvious that maintaining the water balance is critical to life. Water is needed to maintain the cells of the body, to keep the blood flowing through the veins and arteries, and to digest food. You can live for weeks without eating, but only for a few days without water. We constantly lose water through sweating, urination, and defecation. The design of your nose, which could have been just a pair of nostrils on your face, is testimonial to the body's efforts to conserve water. As you breathe you exhale valuable moisture; but as your breath passes through the much cooler nose some of the moisture condenses and is reabsorbed. The next time you get a runny nose on a cold day, you will get some idea how much water the nose recycles.

It is obvious that you drink when your mouth and throat feel dry; but at most a dry mouth and throat determine only *when* you drink, not *how much* you drink. There are two types of thirst, one generated by the water level inside the body's cells and the other reflecting the water content of the blood. Water deprivation affects both kinds of deficit, but the fluid levels in the two compartments can vary independently and so the body manages them separately. *Osmotic thirst occurs when the fluid content decreases inside the cells.* This happens when the individual has not taken in enough water to compensate for food intake, and the blood becomes more concentrated than usual. Eating a salty meal has a greater effect. As a result, water inside the cells is drawn from the cells into the bloodstream by osmotic pressure. *Hypovolemic thirst occurs when the blood volume drops due to a loss of extracellular water.* This can be due to sweating, vomiting, and diarrhea. Of course, another cause is blood loss; that is why you feel thirsty after giving blood.

The reduced water content of cells that contributes to osmotic thirst is detected primarily in areas bordering the third ventricle, particularly in the *organum vasculosum lamina terminalis,* OVLT (see Figure 5.3). Injecting saline (salt) solution into the

bloodstream reduces the water content in cells and causes drinking; but this effect is dramatically reduced when the OVLT is lesioned beforehand (Thrasher & Keil, 1987). The reduced blood volume in hypovolemic thirst is detected by pressure receptors (called *baroreceptors*) in the heart (Fitzsimons & Moore-Gillon, 1980), and signaled to the hypothalamus by the vagus nerve. In addition, lowered blood volume in the kidneys causes the release of the hormone renin, which increases production of the hormone *angiotensin II*. Angiotensin stimulates the *subfornical organ (SFO),* which also borders the third ventricle, to induce drinking (Figure 5.3). Injecting angiotensin into the SFO increases drinking; lesioning the SFO blocks this effect but has no effect on drinking in response to osmotic thirst (Simpson, Epstein, & Camardo, 1978).

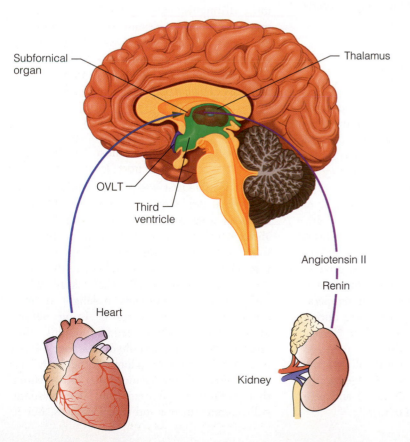

Figure 5.3
Thirst control signals and brain centers

Subfornical organ

Thalamus

OVLT

Third ventricle

Angiotensin II

Renin

Heart

Kidney

Thirst is more complicated than the operation of a furnace or body temperature regulation because there is a significant time lag between drinking and the arrival of water in the tissues. The individual must stop drinking well before tissue need is satisfied. The *satiety* mechanism (satisfaction of appetite) is not well understood, but there is evidence that receptors in the stomach monitor the presence of water (Rolls, Wood, & Rolls, 1980). Also, water infused into the liver reduces drinking, which suggests that either water receptors or pressure receptors are there (Kozlowski & Drzewiecki, 1973). We know more about satiety when it comes to hunger, and will take up the issue again later.

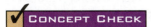

CONCEPT CHECK

- *How do temperature regulation and thirst qualify as homeostatic drives?*
- *What are the different kinds of specialized receptors we have seen so far?*

HUNGER: A COMPLEX DRIVE

Although hunger can be described in terms of drive and homeostasis just like temperature regulation and thirst, the differences almost obscure this similarity. Hunger is more complex in a variety of ways. Eating provides energy for activity, fuel for maintaining body temperature, and materials needed for growth and repair of the tissues. In addition, the set point is so variable that you might think there is none. This is not surprising, because the demands on our resources change with exercise, stress, growth, and so on. A changing set point is not unique to hunger, of course. For example, our temperature set point changes daily, decreasing during our normal sleep time (even if we fly to Europe and are awake during that time). It increases during illness to produce a fever to kill invading bacteria. What is unusual about hunger is that the set point can undergo dramatic and prolonged shifts, for instance in obesity.

Another difference is that the needs in temperature regulation and thirst are unitary, while hunger involves the need for a variety of different and specific kinds of nutrients. Making choices about what foods to eat can be more difficult than knowing when to eat and when to stop eating.

The Role of Taste

Selecting the right foods is no problem for some animals. Some *herbivores* (plant-eating animals) can get all the nutrients they need from a single source; koalas, for instance, eat only eucalyptus leaves, and giant pandas eat nothing but the shoots of the bamboo plant. *Carnivores* (meat eaters) also have it rather easy; they depend on their prey to eat a balanced diet. We are *omnivores;* we are able to get the nutrients we need from a variety of plants and animals. Being able to eat almost anything is liberating but simultaneously a burden; we must distinguish among foods that may be nutritious, non-nutritious, or toxic, and we must vary our diet among several sources to meet all our nutritional requirements. Choosing the right foods and in the right amounts can be a real challenge.

You are what you eat.

—popular adage

It is possible that you plan your diet around nutritional guidelines, but you probably rely more on what you learned at the family table about which foods and what combinations of foods make an "appropriate" meal in your culture. Have you ever wondered where these traditions came from, or why they survive when each new generation seems to delight in defying society's other customs? Long before humans understood the need for vitamins, minerals, proteins, and carbohydrates your ancestors were using a "wisdom of the body" to choose a reasonably balanced diet that ensured their survival and your existence. That wisdom still operates in our individual choices, but it has also been incorporated into cultural food traditions, which usually provide a balanced diet (Rozin, 1976), even when they prescribe unattractive (to us) foods like grub worms or cow's blood. As you will see, the internal forces that guide our selection of a balanced diet are more automatic than the term *choice* usually suggests, but they are also subtle and easily overcome by the allure of modern processed foods that emphasize taste over nutrition.

The simplest form of dietary selection involves distinguishing between foods that are safe and nutritious and those that are either useless or dangerous. This is where the sense of taste comes in. Humans can distinguish five primary tastes: sour, sweet, bitter, salty, and the recently discovered umami (Kurihara & Kashiwayanagi, 1998). These five sensations are called *primaries*; more complex taste sensations are made up of combinations of the primaries.

It is easy to see why we have evolved receptors with these particular sensitivities, because they correspond closely to our dietary needs. We will readily eat foods that are sweet; many nutritious foods, like fruits, have a sweet taste. Of course, food manufacturers have taken advantage of our liking for sweets to enhance that quality in non-nutritious or high-fat foods. We also prefer foods that are a bit salty; salt provides the sodium and chloride ions needed for cellular functioning and for neural transmission. The umami receptor responds to amino acids, including glutamate, a component in meats, cheese, soy products, and the flavor enhancer MSG; little is known about this fifth receptor, but it could be important in our selection of proteins. Just as we are attracted to useful foods by taste, we avoid others. Overly sour foods are likely to be spoiled, and bitter foods are likely to be toxic. You do not have to understand these relationships, much less think about them; they operate quietly, in the neural background.

Taste receptors are located on taste buds, which in turn are found on the surface of papillae; papillae are small bumps on the tongue and elsewhere in the mouth (see Figure 5.4). On

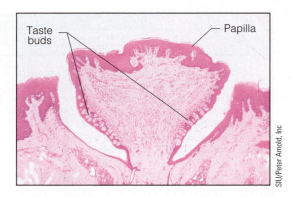

Figure 5.4
A papilla with taste buds, microscopic photo

SIU/Peter Arnold, Inc

their way to the primary gustatory (taste) area of the cortex, taste neurons pass through the nucleus of the solitary tract in the medulla, which we will soon see plays an important role in feeding behavior. Besides providing information about the basic tastes, the taste sense contributes to dietary selection in three additional ways: sensory-specific satiety, learned taste aversion, and learned taste preferences.

Sensory-Specific Satiety: Varying the Choices

One day when I was a youngster a neighbor child joined our family for lunch. At the end of the meal she enjoyed a bowl of my mother's homemade apple cobbler, then another, and another. Halfway through the third serving, she observed in puzzlement that the last serving wasn't nearly as good as the first. Barbara and Edmund Rolls call this experience sensory-specific satiety. *Sensory-specific satiety means that the more of a particular food an individual eats, the less appealing the food becomes.* Humans rate a food less favorably after they have consumed it than before, and they eat more if they are offered a variety of foods instead of a single food (Rolls, Rolls, Rowe, & Sweeney, 1981).

The effect sounds trivial, but it is not; sensory-specific satiety is the brain's way of encouraging you to eat a varied diet, which is necessary for a balanced diet. Back in the 1920s Clara Davis (1928) allowed three newly weaned infants to choose all their meals from a tray of about 20 healthy foods. They usually

In what ways does taste contribute to selection of a proper diet?

Predator Control Through Learned Taste Aversion

Learned taste aversion has been put to practical use in an unlikely context: predator control. As a novel and humane (compared to extermination) means of controlling sheep-killing by wolves and coyotes, Gustavson and colleagues fed captive predators sheep carcasses laced with lithium chloride (see the photo), which made them sick. When they were placed in a pen with sheep, the wolves and coyotes avoided the sheep instead of attacking them. One coyote threw up just from smelling a lamb, and two hesitant wolves were chased away by a lamb that turned on them (Gustavson, Garcia, Hankins, & Rusiniak, 1974; Gustavson, Kelly, Sweeney, & Garcia, 1976). When the researchers placed tainted pieces of bait around a sheep ranch, sheep predation by coyotes dropped 60% compared to previous years.

Janet Haas/Rainbow

One of Gustavson's Coyotes Undergoing Conditioning

selected only two or three foods at one meal and continued choosing the same foods for about a week. Then they would switch to another two or three foods for a similar period. Their self-selected diet was adequate to prevent any deficiencies from developing over a period of six months.

Sensory-specific satiety takes place in the *nucleus of the solitary tract (NST), which is located in the medulla.* Place a little glucose (one of the sugars) on a rat's tongue and it produces a neural response there. But if glucose is injected into the rat's bloodstream first, sugar placed on the tongue has less effect in the NST (Giza, Scott, & Vanderweele, 1992). The brain automatically motivates the rat—or you—to switch to a new flavor and a different nutrient.

Learned Taste Aversion: Avoiding Dangerous Foods

Learned taste aversion, the avoidance of foods associated with illness or poor nutrition, was discovered when researchers were studying bait shyness in rats. Farmers know that if they put out poisoned bait in the barn they will kill a few rats at first but the particular poison will not work for long, thus the term "bait shyness." Rats eat small amounts of a new food; that way, a poison will more likely make them ill instead of killing them and they will avoid that food in the future. Learned aversion is studied in the laboratory by giving rats a specific food and then making them nauseous with a chemical like lithium chloride or with a dose of X-ray radiation. Later they refuse to eat that food.

Learned taste aversion helps wild animals and primitive-living humans avoid dangerous foods; modern-living humans are more likely to experience its effect because they happen to eat a particular food before getting sick for unrelated reasons, for example with stomach flu. In a study of people with strong food aversions, 89% could remember getting sick after eating the food, most often between the ages of 6 and 12 (Garb & Stunkard, 1974). Learned taste aversion appears to be one reason chemotherapy patients lose their appetite. Among children who were given a uniquely flavored ice cream before a chemo session, 79% later refused that flavor compared to 33% of children receiving chemotherapy without the ice cream; the effect was just as strong four months later (Bernstein, 1978).

Learned taste aversion may not be very helpful to modern humans in avoiding dangerous foods, but it may help us avoid non-nutritious ones. When rats are fed a diet deficient in a nutrient, like thiamine (vitamin B), they show an aversion to the food; they eat less of it, and they spill the food from its container in spite of indications they are hungry, like chewing on the wire sides of their cage (Rozin, 1967). Even after recovery from the deficit the rats prefer to go hungry rather than eat the previously deficient food. But aversion to a nutrient-deficient food is just the first step toward selecting a nutritious diet.

Learned Taste Preferences: Selecting Nutritious Foods

Although rats, and presumably humans, can detect salt, sugars, and fat directly by their taste (Beck & Galef, 1989), they must *learn* to select the foods containing other necessary nutrients. This apparently requires the development of **a learned taste preference, which is a preference not for the nutrient itself but for the flavor of a food that contains the nutrient.** In an early study rats fed a diet deficient in one of three vitamins (thiamine, riboflavin, or pyridoxine) later learned to prefer a food enriched with that vitamin and flavored distinctively by adding anise. When the anise was switched to the other food the rats switched their choice as well (Scott & Verney, 1947). Presumably, animals learn to prefer the flavor because the nutrient makes them feel better. A diet-deficient rat enhances its chances of learning which foods are beneficial by eating a single food at a time and spacing its meals so that a nutrient like thiamine has time to produce some improvement (Rozin, 1969). (Notice how similar this is to the sampling behavior of Davis's children.)

How much humans are able to make use of these abilities is unclear; certainly we often choose an unhealthy diet over a healthy one. These bad selections may not be due so much to a lack of *ability* to make good choices as it is to the distraction of tasty, high-calorie foods that are not found in nature. Even rats have trouble selecting the foods that are good for them when the competing foods are flavored with cinnamon or cocoa (Beck & Galef, 1989), and they become obese when they are offered human junk food (Rolls, Rowe, & Turner, 1980). Wisdom of the body is inadequate in the face of the temptation of french fries and ice cream.

Regulating Food Intake

Here we confront a significant inadequacy of our thermostat analogy. To maintain consistent temperature, the thermostat calls on the furnace to cycle on and off frequently. Some species of animals behave like the home furnace and eat almost constantly to provide the steady supply of nutrients the body needs. We do not; we eat a few discrete meals and fast in between. Eating discrete meals leaves us free to do other things with our time, but it requires a complex system for storing nutrient reserves, allocating the reserves during the fasting periods, and monitoring the reserves to determine the timing and size of the next meal.

The Digestive Process

Digestion begins in the mouth, where food is ground fine and mixed with saliva. Saliva provides lubrication and contains an enzyme that starts the breakdown of food. Digestion proceeds in the stomach as food is mixed with the gastric juices hydrochloric acid and pepsin. The partially processed food is then released gradually so the small intestine has time to do its job. (Figure 5.5 shows the organs of the digestive system.)

Figure 5.5
The digestive system

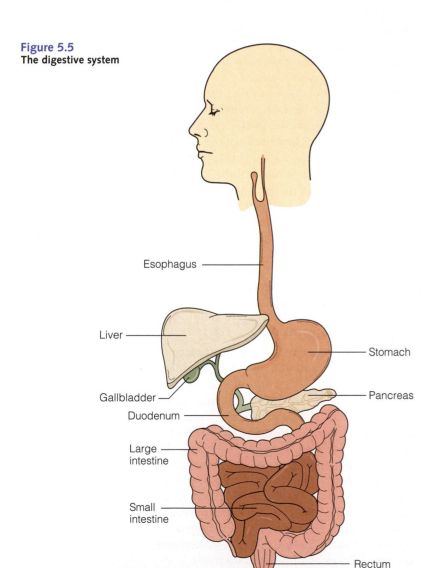

Esophagus

Liver

Stomach

Gallbladder

Pancreas

Duodenum

Large intestine

Small intestine

Rectum

Anal canal

The stomach provides another opportunity for screening toxic or spoiled food that gets past the taste test. If the food irritates the stomach lining sufficiently, the stomach responds by regurgitating the meal. Some toxins don't irritate the stomach, and they make their way into the bloodstream. If so, a part of the brain often takes care of this problem; **the area postrema is one of the places in the brain where the blood-brain barrier is weak, so toxins can activate it to induce vomiting.** The result can be surprisingly forceful; projectile vomiting usually means that you've got hold of something really bad. On the other hand, college students have been known to incorporate this adaptive response into a drinking game called "boot tag," the details of which I will leave to your imagination.

Digestion occurs primarily in the small intestine, particularly **the initial 25 cm of the small intestine called the *duodenum*.** There food is broken down into usable forms. **Carbohydrates are metabolized into simple sugars, particularly *glucose*. Proteins are converted to *amino acids*. Fats are transformed into *fatty acids* and *glycerol*,** either in the intestine or in the liver. The products of digestion are absorbed through the intestinal wall into the blood and **transported to the liver via the *hepatic portal vein*.** Digestion requires the food to be in a semi-liquid mix, and the body can ill afford to give up the fluid; retrieving the excess water is the primary job of the large intestine.

All of this process is under the control of the autonomic nervous system, so digestion is affected by stress or excitement, as you probably well know. If too little or too much acid is secreted into the stomach, you'll take your course exam with an upset stomach. If food moves too slowly through the system, constipation will be the result. Too fast, and there isn't time to remove the excess water, so you may be asking to leave the room in the middle of your exam to go to the bathroom. Because diarrhea causes the body to lose water, you may have to drink more liquids to avoid dehydration. You

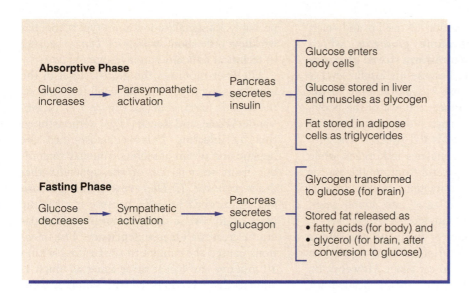

Figure 5.6
Summary of the absorptive and fasting phases

also lose electrolytes, compounds that provide the ions your neurons and other cells need, which is why your doctor may recommend a sport drink as the replacement liquid.

The Absorptive Phase The feeding cycle is divided into two phases, the absorptive phase and the fasting phase; they are summarized in Figure 5.6. **For a few hours following a meal our body lives off the nutrients arriving from the digestive system; this period is called the *absorptive phase.*** The blood level of glucose, our primary source of energy, rises. The brain detects the increased glucose and shifts the autonomic system from predominantly sympathetic activation to predominantly parasympathetic activity. As a result, the pancreas starts secreting ***insulin, a hormone that enables body cells to take up glucose for energy and certain cells to store excess nutrients.*** (Actually, because of conditioning, just the sight and smell of food is enough to trigger insulin secretion, increased salivation, and release of digestive fluids into the stomach. Remember the incentive theory?)

The cells of the body outside the nervous system contain *insulin receptors*, which activate transporters that carry glucose into the cells. The cells of the nervous system have no insulin receptors; their glucose transporters can operate in the absence of insulin, and this gives the brain priority access to glucose. *Diabetes mellitus* results when the pancreas is unable to produce enough insulin or the body's tissues are relatively unresponsive to insulin. The diabetic's blood contains plenty of glucose following a meal, but the cells of the body are unable to make use of it and the diabetic is chronically hungry.

During the absorptive phase the body is also busy storing some of the nutrients as a hedge against the upcoming period of fasting. Some of the **glucose is converted into *glycogen*** and stored in a short-term reservoir in the liver and the muscles. Any remaining glucose is converted into fats and stored in ***adipose tissue, commonly known as fat cells.*** Fats arriving directly from the digestive system are stored there as well. Storage of both glucose and fat is under the control of insulin. After a small proportion of amino acids is used to construct proteins and peptides needed by the body, the rest is converted to fats and also stored.

The Fasting Phase **Eventually the glucose level in the blood drops. Now the body must fall back on its energy stores, which is why this is called the *fasting phase.*** The autonomic system shifts to sympathetic activity. The

What happens during the absorptive and fasting phases?

pancreas ceases secretion of insulin and starts secreting **the hormone *glucagon*, which causes the liver to transform stored glycogen back into glucose.** Because the insulin level is low now, this glucose is available only to the nervous system. To meet the rest of the body's needs, glucagon triggers the breakdown of stored fat into fatty acids and glycerol. The fatty acids are used by the muscles and organs, while the liver converts glycerol to more glucose for the brain. In extreme situations, muscle proteins can be broken down again into amino acids, which are converted into glucose by the liver.

After a few hours of living off the body's stores, the falling level of nutrients signals the brain that it is time to eat again. However, by then you probably have already headed for lunch, cued by the clock rather than a brain center. In the modern, highly structured world, physiological motivations have been so incorporated into social customs that it is difficult to tell where the influence of one leaves off and the other begins. We will turn the power of research to answering the questions "What makes a person eat?" "How does a person know when to stop eating?" and "How does a person regulate weight?" As you will learn, the answers are not simple ones; even what you see here will be an abbreviated treatment. It will help if you refer to the pictorial summary in Figure 5.7 often as you read the following pages.

Signals That Start a Meal

When I ask students in class what being hungry means, the favorite answer is that the stomach feels empty. Your stomach often does feel empty when you are hungry, but we don't eat to satisfy the stomach. The stomach is not even necessary for hunger to occur; people who have their stomach removed because of cancer still report feeling hungry and still eat much like everybody else, though they have to take smaller meals (Ingelfinger, 1944). So what does make us feel hungry?

There are two major signals for hunger; one tells the brain of a low supply of glucose—*glucoprivic hunger*—and the other indicates a deficit in fatty acids, or *lipoprivic hunger*. There

probably is a signal for low amino acids, too, but we know little about *aminoprivic hunger* because of technical difficulties in investigating it.

The liver monitors the glucose level in the blood passing to it from the small intestine via the hepatic portal vein (see Figure 5.7). Novin, VanderWeele, and Rezek (1973) demonstrated this by injecting 2-deoxyglucose into the hepatic portal vein of rabbits. You may remember from section A.1 of the appendix that **2-deoxyglucose (2-DG) resembles glucose** and is absorbed by cells; because it takes the place of glucose in the cells but is not a nutrient, it creates a glucose deficiency. The injections caused the rabbits to start eating within 10 minutes and to eat three times as much as animals that were injected with saline. A compound that blocks metabolism of fatty acids (mercaptoacetate) also increases the amount eaten (Ritter & Taylor, 1990), so the liver monitors fatty acid levels in the blood as well.

Signals of glucose and fatty acid deficits are carried by the vagus nerve to the area postrema and the nucleus of the solitary tract in the medulla. If either of these structures is lesioned, low glucose and fatty acid levels no longer affect feeding. If the vagus nerve is cut, a fat blocker no longer induces eating, and 2-DG has no immediate effect (Ritter & Taylor, 1990). However, the animals do increase their rate of eating three hours after a 2-DG infusion (Novin et al., 1973). This later response is triggered by glucose receptors near the fourth ventricle (Ritter, Slusser, & Stone, 1981). This suggests that the medulla keeps track of nutrient levels in the rest of the body via the vagus nerve, but monitors the brain's supply of glucose directly.

Information about nutrient levels is then relayed to the ***paraventricular nucleus (PVN)* in the hypothalamus. Low levels increase the PVN's release of the neurotransmitter *neuropeptide Y,* a powerful stimulant for eating.** Rats injected with neuropeptide Y in the PVN double their rate of eating and increase their rate of weight gain sixfold (Stanley, Kyrkouli, Lampert, & Leibowitz, 1986). They are so motivated for food they will

What stimuli initiate eating?

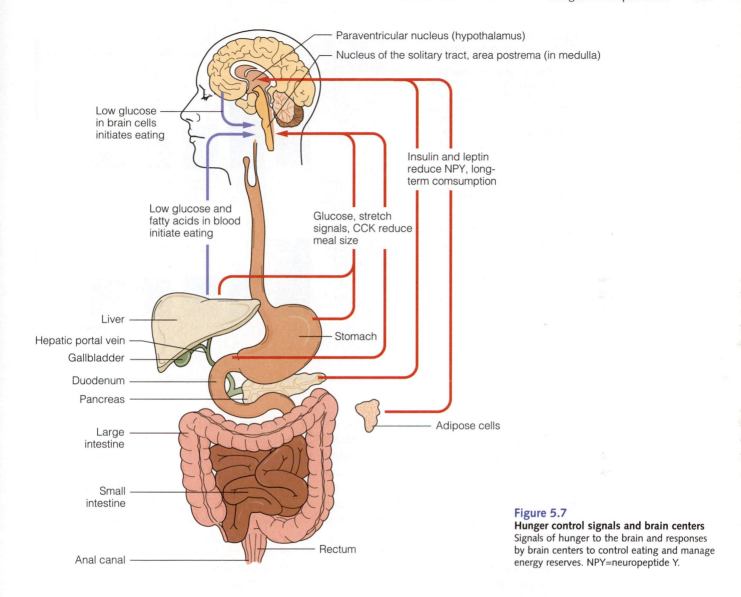

Paraventricular nucleus (hypothalamus)

Nucleus of the solitary tract, area postrema (in medulla)

Low glucose
in brain cells
initiates eating

Insulin and leptin
reduce NPY, long-
term comsumption

Low glucose and
fatty acids in blood
initiate eating

Glucose, stretch
signals, CCK reduce
meal size

Liver

Hepatic portal vein

Gallbladder

Duodenum

Pancreas

Stomach

Large
intestine

Small
intestine

Anal canal

Adipose cells

Rectum

Figure 5.7
Hunger control signals and brain centers
Signals of hunger to the brain and responses
by brain centers to control eating and manage
energy reserves. NPY=neuropeptide Y.

tolerate shock to the tongue in order to drink milk, and will drink milk adulterated with bitter quinine (Flood & Morley, 1991). The fact that their weight gain is three times larger than their increase in food intake suggests that neuropeptide Y conserves energy as well as increasing motivation. During extreme deprivation, neuropeptide Y conserves energy further by reducing body temperature (Billington & Levine, 1992) and suppressing sexual motivation (Clark, Kalra, & Kalra, 1985). If you think about it, sexual activity is a particularly unnecessary luxury during food shortage because it expends energy and produces offspring that compete for the limited resources.

Signals That End a Meal

Just as with drinking, there must be a satiety mechanism that ends a meal well before nutrients reach the tissues. It might seem obvious that we stop eating when we feel "full," and that answer is partly right. Injecting saline into the stomach of a rat will reduce how much food the

What stimuli termi-nate eating?

Figure 5.8
Effect of nutrient concentration on later meal size
In all trials except the baseline, the stomach was preloaded with 5 milliliters (ml) of saline or glucose solution before offering a liquid nutrient solution. The connection between the stomach and small intestine (the *pylorus*) could be closed by inflating a small cuff. **(a)** With the pylorus open the amount eaten diminished as nutrient values increased. **(b)** With the pylorus closed, nutrient value made no difference.

Source: Adapted with permission from R.J. Phillips & T.L. Powley (1996). "Gastric volume rather than nutrient content inhibits food intake." *American Journal of Physiology,* 271, R766–R799.

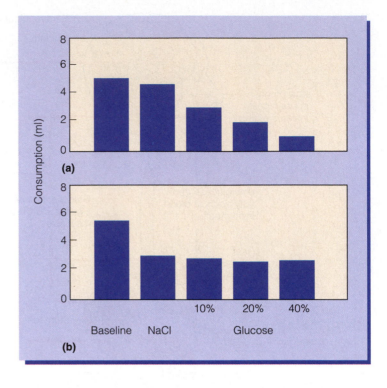

rat will eat later (Phillips & Powley, 1996). To make sure the effect is coming from the stomach the researcher uses a small inflatable cuff to close the connection between the stomach and small intestine. Filling the stomach activates stretch receptors that send a signal by way of the vagus nerve through the structures in the medulla to the paraventricular nucleus (Olson et al., 1993).

A second satiety signal is ***cholecystokinin (CCK), a hormone that is released as food passes into the duodenum.*** Injecting CCK into the bloodstream of obese humans reduces the size of the meals they eat (Pi-Sunyer, Kissileff, Thornton, & Smith, 1982). The signal initiated by CCK travels via the vagus nerve through the medulla to the paraventricular nucleus (Rinaman et al., 1995); cutting the vagus nerve in rats eliminates CCK's satiating effect (Smith, Jerome, & Norgren, 1985).

Animals and humans adjust the amount of food they eat according to the nutritional value of the food. Glucose reaching the small intestine reduces subsequent eating more than

saline does, and in proportion to its concentration (see Figure 5.8) (Phillips & Powley, 1996). The nutrients are detected in the liver (Tordoff & Friedman, 1988), so just as a low level of glucose in the liver initiates eating, a high level of nutrients will stop a meal.

We have been talking about short-term controls that affect meal size, but they are only half of the story. For example, rats injected with cholecystokinin over a period of days will eat smaller meals, but they compensate by eating more often and they do not lose weight (West, Fey, & Woods, 1984). This means there must be additional influences on food intake beyond the levels of readily available nutrients. We turn now to the long-term influences on eating.

Long-Term Controls

Humans and animals regulate body weight or, more precisely, body fat. But how they sense their fat level has not always been clear. In 1952 Hervey surgically joined pairs of rats, so that they shared a very small amount of blood circu-

Figure 5.9
A rat with lesioned ventromedial hypothalamus

lation; animals joined like this are called *parabiotic*. Then Hervey operated on one member of each pair to destroy the *ventromedial hypothalamus*. The surgery increases parasympathetic activity in the vagus nerve and enhances insulin release (Weingarten, Chang, & McDonald, 1985). This creates a kind of persistent absorptive phase in which most incoming nutrients are stored rather than being available for use; as a result, the animal has to overeat to maintain normal energy level. The rat becomes obese, sometimes tripling its weight (see Figure 5.9). Hervey's lesioned rats overate and became obese as expected, but their pairmates began to undereat and lose weight. In fact, in two of the pairs the lean rat starved to death. The message was clear: the obese rat was producing a blood-borne signal which suppressed eating in the other rat, a signal to which the brain-damaged obese rat was insensitive.

What that signal was remained unknown until recently, when researchers discovered that **fat cells secrete a hormone called *leptin*.** The amount of leptin in the blood is proportional to the percentage of body fat, and is about four

times higher in obese than nonobese individuals (Considine et al., 1996). Like cholecystokinin, leptin helps regulate meal size, but it does so in response to the long-term stores of fat rather than the nutrients circulating in the bloodstream. As a person loses weight, decreasing leptin activates neurons that release neuropeptide Y in the paraventricular nucleus; increased leptin during weight gain reduces neuropeptide Y output (Woods, Schwartz, Baskin, & Seeley, 2000). The PVN is very near the ventromedial hypothalamus and probably was damaged by Hervey's surgery, as it often is when researchers destroy the ventromedial hypothalamus.

Insulin levels also are proportional to fat levels (Schwartz & Seeley, 1997); in obese individuals they remain high between meals rather than returning to baseline as they normally would. Like leptin, insulin reduces neuropeptide Y activity in the hypothalamus (Schwartz & Seeley, 1997), probably in the PVN. Why don't high levels of leptin and insulin curtail eating in obese people? Because they have fewer active insulin receptors (Woods & Stricker, 1999), and possibly fewer leptin receptors as well. We will also see shortly that the obese person's set point for weight might be adjusted higher.

What are the signals for controlling body weight?

✔ **CONCEPT CHECK**

- *What is the advantage of the ability to access stored nutrients between meals?*
- *Organizing your knowledge is important. Make a table that summarizes the meal-size and long-term influences on eating, including the signals and the brain structures.*
- *You are about to eat because the glucose and fatty acids in your bloodstream are low. What influence will your level of stored fat have on your meal?*

EATING DISORDERS

Until now we have been considering the ideal situation, the regulation of feeding and weight when all goes well. But in many cases people eat too much, they eat the wrong kinds of foods, or they eat too little. As we will see, these behaviors are not just personal preferences or inconvenient quirks of behavior; too often they are health-threatening disorders.

Obesity

According to the National Health and Nutrition Examination Surveys, the rate of obesity in the U.S. almost doubled over three decades, reaching 22.5% in 1994. Obesity is escalating at such an alarming rate in most countries that the World Health Organization has declared a global epidemic. For the first time in history, the number of people in the world who are overfed and overweight equals the number who are hungry and underweight (Gardner & Halweil, 2000). However, the number of people who are *mal*nourished is almost *double* the number who are *under*nourished, in part because many of the overweight are getting their calories from junk foods that are low in nutritional value.

Obesity increases the risk of a variety of illnesses, including diabetes, heart disease, hypertension, breast and colon cancer, and gallbladder disease (see Figure 5.10). In 1995 the direct medical cost attributable to obesity was estimated at $52 billion in the U.S., with an additional $47 billion in indirect costs such as lost productivity (Wolf & Colditz, 1998). The impact of obesity on health is a controversial topic, but only in terms of what level of overweight is detrimental.

Most research has now adopted the World Health Organization's formula for quantifying leanness and obesity. **The *body mass index (BMI)* is calculated by dividing the person's weight in kilograms by the squared height in meters.** You can check your BMI in Figure 5.11 without having to do the calculation or convert your measurements to metric units. Many authorities consider BMIs of 26 and 27 (shown in yellow in the table) to be moderately risky. There is little doubt that BMIs over 30 are associated with increases in death rate; various studies show increases between 50% and 150% (Wickelgren, 1998).

The Myths of Obesity

Because obesity is dangerous to the person's health as well as the occasion for social and career discrimination, it is important to ask why people become overweight and why obesity rates are rising so dramatically. Although the causes have been difficult to document, most authorities believe that increasing obesity has a simple explanation: people are eating more and richer foods and exercising less (Hill

Figure 5.10
Increased death rate with increased weight

Source: Adapted from "Obesity: Adverse Effect on Health and Longevity," by T. B. VanTallie, 1979, *American Journal of Clinical Nutrition*, 32, 2727. © 1979 American Journal of Clinical Nutrition, American Society for Clinical Nutrition. Reprinted with permission.

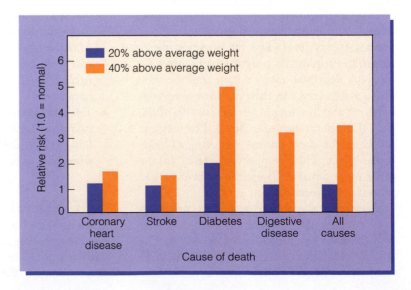

Figure 5.11
Body mass index calculation chart
Source: Reprinted with permission from I. Wickelgren, "Obesity: How big a problem?" *Science,* 280, 1364–1367. Copyright 1998 American Association for the Advancement of Science.

Weight in pounds

Height	100	105	110	115	120	125	130	135	140	145	150	155	160	165	170	175	180	185	190	195	200	205
5'0"	20	21	21	22	23	24	25	26	27	28	29	30	31	32	33	34	35	36	37	38	39	40
5'1"	19	20	21	22	23	24	25	26	26	27	28	29	30	31	32	33	34	36	36	37	38	39
5'2"	18	19	20	21	22	23	24	25	26	27	27	28	29	30	31	32	33	34	35	36	37	37
5'3"	18	19	19	20	21	22	23	24	25	26	27	27	28	29	30	31	32	33	34	35	35	36
5'4"	17	18	19	20	21	21	22	23	24	25	26	27	27	28	29	30	31	32	33	33	34	35
5'5"	17	17	18	19	20	21	22	22	23	24	25	26	27	27	28	29	30	31	32	32	33	34
5'6"	16	17	18	19	19	20	21	22	23	23	24	25	26	27	27	28	29	30	31	31	32	33
5'7"	16	16	17	18	19	20	20	21	22	23	23	24	25	26	27	27	28	29	30	31	31	32
5'8"	15	16	17	17	18	19	20	21	21	22	23	24	24	25	26	27	27	28	29	30	30	31
5'9"	15	16	16	17	18	18	19	20	21	21	22	23	24	24	25	26	27	27	28	29	30	30
5'10"	14	15	16	17	17	18	19	19	20	21	22	22	23	24	24	25	26	27	27	28	29	29
5'11"	14	15	15	16	17	17	18	19	20	20	21	22	22	23	24	24	25	26	26	27	28	28
6'0"	14	14	15	16	16	17	18	18	19	20	20	21	22	22	23	24	24	25	26	26	27	28
6'1"	13	14	15	15	16	16	17	18	19	19	20	20	21	22	22	23	24	24	25	26	26	27
6'2"	13	13	14	15	15	16	17	17	18	19	19	20	21	21	22	22	23	24	24	25	26	26
6'3"	12	13	14	14	15	16	16	17	17	18	19	19	20	21	21	22	22	23	24	24	25	26
6'4"	12	13	13	14	15	15	16	16	17	18	18	19	19	20	21	21	22	22	23	23	24	25

Height in feet and inches

& Peters, 1998; Taubes, 1998). The cause of obesity seems straightforward enough, then: energy in exceeds energy out and the person gains weight. But we would miss the point entirely if we assumed that people get fat just because they cannot resist the temptation to overeat. In spite of popular opinion, research has not found that the obese lack impulse control, are unable to delay gratification, or have a maladaptive eating style (Rodin, Schank, & Striegel-Moore, 1989).

> *. . . most forms of obesity are likely to result not from an overwhelming lust for food or lack of willpower, but from biochemical defects at one or more points in the system responsible for the control of body weight.*
>
> —Michael Schwartz and Randy Seeley

Another popular belief is that obese children learn overindulgence from their family. Obesity does run in families, and body mass index and other measures are moderately related among family members. However, the evidence consistently points to genetic rather than environmental influences as more important (Grilo & Pogue-Geile, 1991); to the extent that environment does play a role it is, surprisingly, from outside the family.

The Contribution of Heredity

Both adoption and twin studies demonstrate the influence of heredity on body weight. Adopted children show a moderate relationship with their biological parents' weights and BMIs, but little or no similarity with their adoptive parents (Grilo & Pogue-Geile, 1991). Among identical twins reared together the correlation for BMI averaged about .74 across 14 studies; for same-sex fraternal twins reared together, the statistic is only about .33 (Grilo

Is obesity due to a lack of willpower?

What is the evidence obesity is hereditary?

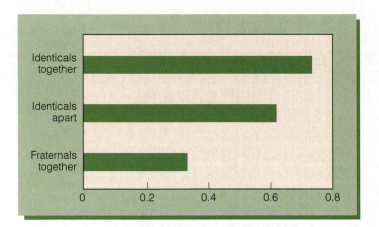

Figure 5.12
Correlations of body mass index among twins
Source: Based on data from Grilo & Pogue-Geile, 1991.

& Pogue-Geile, 1991). Even when identical twins are reared apart, their correlation drops only to .62, still almost double that for fraternals reared together (see Figure 5.12). About 84% of people's differences in BMI can be attributed to heredity (de Castro, 1993).

Weight regulation is complex, involving appetite, satiety, and energy management. It should not be surprising that researchers have come up with a very long list of candidate genes that might be involved in obesity; in fact, 200 different genes have been implicated, and over two dozen have been specifically linked with human obesity (Chagnon, Pérusse, Weisnagel, Rankinen, & Bouchard, 1999; Comuzzie & Allison, 1998). As illustration, I will discuss two genes in some detail.

Thirty years ago it was known that the so-called *obesity gene* **on chromosome 6 and the** *diabetes gene* **on chromosome 4 cause obesity in mice.** Mice that are homozygous for the recessive obesity gene *(ob/ob)* or the recessive diabetes gene *(db/db)* have the same symptoms: overeating, obesity, and susceptibility to diabetes (see Figure 5.13). To find out how the two genes produced these symptoms, D. L. Coleman (1973) used parabiotic pairings of the two kinds of mice and normals (Figure 5.14). When a *db/db*

mouse was paired with a normal mouse, the normal mouse starved to death. The same thing happened to the *ob/ob* mouse when it was paired with the *db/db* mouse. These results suggested that the *db/db* mice were producing a fat signal, but that they were not themselves sensitive to it. The *ob/ob* mouse had no effect on a normal mouse, but its own rate of weight gain slowed. The *ob/ob* mouse apparently was sensitive to a fat signal it did not produce. It was another 20 years before researchers discovered that the fat signal in Hervey's and Coleman's studies was leptin. Following that discovery they were able to test Coleman's hypothesis. Injecting leptin into *ob/ob* mice reduced their weight 30% in just two weeks, while *db/db* mice were not affected by the injections (Halaas et al., 1995).

Although we know very little about other gene effects, we know that heredity influences meal size, meal frequency, energy intake, activity level, metabolic level, and proportion of proteins, fats, and carbohydrates in the diet (Bouchard, 1989; de Castro, 1993). Among these, metabolic level has been investigated most and it is our next topic.

Obesity and Reduced Metabolism

Accounts of dieting are all too often stories of failure; overweight people report slavishly following rigorous diets without appreciable weight loss, or they lose weight and then gain it back within a year's time. One factor in the failures may be dieters' misrepresentation of their efforts, whether intentional or not. One group of diet-resistant obese individuals underreported the amount of food they consumed by 47% and overreported their physical activity by 51% (Lichtman et al., 1992).

But another critical element that can make weight loss difficult is a person's rate of energy expenditure. In the average sedentary adult, about 75% of daily energy expenditure goes into resting or *basal metabolism,* **the energy required to fuel the brain and other organs and to maintain body temperature;** the remainder is spent about equally in physical

How do changes in metabolism defend body weight?

activity and in digesting food (Bogardus et al., 1986).

Differences in basal metabolism may be a key element in explaining differences in weight. When 29 women who claimed they could not lose weight were isolated in a house and monitored closely while they were restricted to a diet of 1,500 kilocalories (a measure of food's energy value), 19 did lose weight, but 10 did not (Miller & Parsonage, 1975). The 10 who failed to lose weight turned out to have a low basal metabolism rate (BMR). Heredity accounts for about 40% of people's differences in BMR (Bouchard, 1989). When identical twins were overfed 1,000 kilocalories a day for three months, the differences in weight gain within pairs of twins were only one-third as great as the differences across pairs (Bouchard et al., 1990).

However, a person's metabolism can shift when the person gains or loses weight. In an unusual *experimental* manipulation, researchers had both obese and never-obese individuals either lose weight or gain weight (Leibel, Rosenbaum, & Hirsch, 1995). Those who lost

Figure 5.13
The mouse on the tight is an *ob/ob* mouse
Source: Zhang et al., 1994. Reprinted by permission of *Nature*, copyright 1994.

weight decreased their total energy expenditures (resting plus nonresting), and the ones who gained weight increased their energy expenditure. This was expected, because energy demands change as weight increases or decreases. However, the energy expenditure

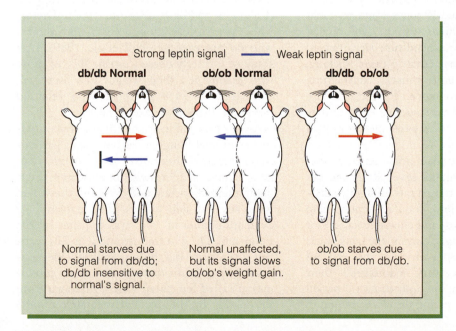

Figure 5.14
Effects of leptin on *ob/ob*, *db/db*, and normal mice
Source: Based on the results of Coleman, 1973.

changes were greater than the weight changes would require, suggesting that the individuals' bodies were "defending" their original weight (see Keesey & Powley, 1986).

So why doesn't this defense of body weight prevent people from becoming obese? One reason is that the body defends less against weight gain than against weight loss (Hill & Peters, 1998). Humans evolved in an environment in which food was sometimes scarce, so it made sense for the body to store excess nutrients during times of plenty and to protect those reserves during famine. That system is adaptive when humans are at the mercy of nature, but a liability when modern agriculture and global transportation provide a constant supply of more food than we need.

A second reason is that people vary tremendously in the strength of their defense response, making some people more vulnerable to becoming overweight than others. When volunteers were overfed 1,000 kilocalories a day, on average only 40% of the excess calories were stored as fat and the remaining 60% were burned off by increased energy expenditure (Levine, Eberhardt, & Jensen, 1999). But some individuals had smaller increases in energy expenditures, and they gained 10 times as much weight as others. Two-thirds of the volunteers' increases in energy expenditure were due to non-exercise physical activity—casual walking, fidgeting, spontaneous muscle contraction, and posture maintenance. Researchers are beginning to think that spontaneous activity may be as important as basal metabolism in resisting obesity.

Prolonged weight gain may actually reset the set point at a higher level. Rolls and her colleagues (1980) fattened rats on highly palatable, high-energy junk food (chocolate chip cookies, potato chips, and cheese crackers) for 90 days. Surprisingly, when the rats were returned to their usual lab chow they did not lose weight. The rats maintained their increased weight for the four-month duration of the study—while eating the same amount of

How can obesity be treated?

food as the control rats! They were defending a new set point. The researchers suggested that the variety of the foods offered, the length of the fattening period, and lack of exercise all contributed to the rats' failure to defend their original weight.

Treating Obesity

There is no greater testimony to the difficulty of losing weight than the lengths to which patients and doctors have gone to bring about weight loss. These include wiring the jaws shut, stapling the stomach or inflating a balloon in the stomach to reduce its capacity, bypassing part of the intestine so less nutrient is absorbed, and surgically removing fat tissue. Often these strategies are ineffective or have undesirable side effects, or patients regain their lost weight once the treatment is ended.

The standard treatment for obesity, of course, is dietary restriction. However, we have seen that the body defends against weight loss, and dieters are usually frustrated. Exercise burns fat, but it takes a great deal of effort to use just a few hundred calories. However, exercise during dieting may increase resting metabolic rate or at least prevent it from dropping (Calles-Escandón & Horton, 1992). Dieters who exercise lose more weight than dieters who do not exercise (Hill et al., 1989). In a study of formerly obese women, 90% of those who maintained their weight loss exercised, compared to 34% of those who relapsed (Kayman, Bruvold, & Stern, 1990).

Another option in the treatment of obesity is medication, although it has not been a particularly attractive alternative. Lack of effectiveness is one problem and, because the drugs manipulate important body systems, they often have adverse side effects. The approval of dexfenfluramine in 1996 was the first by the Food and Drug Administration in 20 years. But just a year later, both it and the older fenfluramine (used in the now-notorious combination called fen-phen) were withdrawn from the market by the manufacturer after reports they caused heart valve leakage (Campfield, Smith, & Burn, 1998). Like the withdrawn drugs, the two currently approved drugs, sibutramine (Meridia) and phentermine, inhibit norepinephrine and serotonin reuptake and act as appetite suppressants.

Serotonin plays an interesting role in weight control. It selectively inhibits carbohydrate appetite (Leibowitz & Alexander, 1998), apparently by reducing neuropeptide Y activity (Dryden, Wang, Frankish, Pickavance, & Williams, 1995). Carbohydrate regulation involves a feedback loop; eating carbohydrates increases serotonin levels, which serves to limit further carbohydrate intake (Leibowitz & Alexander, 1998). Drugs that inhibit serotonin reuptake reduce carbohydrate intake, but only in the group of obese individuals who crave carbohydrates and eat a large proportion of their diet in carbohydrates (Lieberman, Wurtman, & Chew, 1986; Wurtman, Wurtman, Reynolds, Tsay, & Chew, 1987). Serotonin also enhances mood in some people, and people who have trouble maintaining weight loss often say that they use food to make themselves feel better when they are upset (Kayman et al., 1990). A high-carbohydrate meal also improves mood only in carbohydrate cravers; it actually lowers the mood of noncravers and makes them feel fatigued and sleepy (Lieberman et al., 1986). So, serotonin dysregulation may be important in obesity, but only in a subset of people.

New compounds being tested as anti-obesity drugs either reduce appetite or inhibit fat absorption. An obvious strategy would be to enhance leptin activity, and that is one direction research is taking. Two severely obese children (BMIs around 45) were found to be leptin deficient due to a mutation in the gene responsible for leptin (Montague et al., 1997), and one was later treated successfully with leptin therapy (Farooqi et al., 1999). However, we are not sure how frequently leptin deficiency is a factor in human obesity. Nevertheless, leptin treatment has an important advantage that keeps obesity researchers interested: it increases metabolism as well as reducing appetite, so it produces more weight loss in mice than the amount of calorie restriction would predict (Levin et al., 1996).

A newer approach may mark a dramatic breakthrough in obesity treatment (Loftus et al., 2000). Fatty acid synthase (FAS) is needed to form fatty acids. Injecting *ob/ob* mice with a synthetic FAS inhibitor called C75 reduced neuropeptide Y activity in the hypothalamus to lower levels than in mice that had just been fed. As a result, the treated mice reduced their food intake 90% during the first 24 hours, and underwent profound weight loss over 14 days (Figure 5.15). C75 does more than reduce appetite; injected mice lost 45% more weight than mice that were deprived of food, so C75 probably prevents the normal decrease in metabolism that occurs with fasting/dieting.

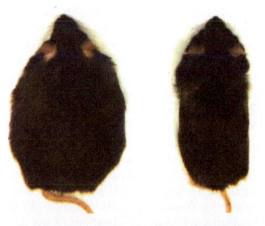

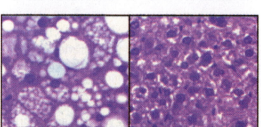

Figure 5.15
Weight loss produced by C75 in *ob/ob* mice
(a) An obese control mouse and a formerly obese mouse treated with C75. **(b)** Microscopic views of fatty tissue in the livers of the mice.
Source: Reprinted with permission from T.M. Loftus, et al., "Reduced food intake and body weight in mice treated with fatty acid synthase." *Science*, 288, p. 2379–2381. Copyright 2000 American Association for the Advancement of Science.

Loss of weight does not cure obesity. Like the drug abusers you read about in Chapter 4, the formerly obese individual typically relapses and gains the weight back within a year of the end of treatment (Bray, 1992). An ideal drug would banish fat without the discomfort of starvation and without side effects, and help the person maintain the weight loss; but such a "magic bullet" is not on the near horizon.

Anorexia and Bulimia

Anorexia nervosa and bulimia nervosa affect about 3% of women over their lifetime (Walsh & Devlin, 1998). Although men are also affected, women patients outnumber them ten to one; this is the most extreme gender discrepancy in medicine and psychiatry (Anderson & Holman, 1997). Because male patients are so rare we will limit our attention to research with females.

Anorexia nervosa **is known as the "starving disease" because the individual restricts food intake to maintain weight at a level so low that it is threatening to health** (Walsh & Devlin, 1998). (See Figure 5.16.) The person may also exercise for hours a day or resort to vomiting to control weight loss. Some anorexic individuals binge on food and then purge by vomiting or using laxatives; they are called *purgers*. *Restrictors* rely only on restriction of food intake to reduce calories. If anorexia continues long enough, it leads to cessation of ovulation, loss of muscle mass, heart damage, reduction in bone density, and even death. The death rate among anorexics is more than double that for female psychiatric patients; half of the deaths are from complications of the disease and another quarter from suicide (Sullivan, 1995).

Bulimia nervosa **also involves weight control, but the behavior is limited to bingeing and purging.** Unlike in anorexics, total calorie intake is reduced in only 19% of bulimic women (Weltzin, Hsu, Pollice, & Kaye, 1991), and most bulimic patients are of normal weight

(Walsh & Devlin, 1998). Both disorders are difficult to treat; although three-quarters of bulimics and a third of anorexics appear to be fully recovered after eight years, a third of these relapse (Herzog et al., 1999).

Environmental and Genetic Contributions

Both anorexics and bulimics are preoccupied with weight and body shape. Because increases in anorexia and bulimia seem to have paralleled an increasing cultural emphasis on thinness and beauty, some researchers have concluded that the cause is social. The male-female difference is consistent with this argument, because women are under more pressure to be slim, while men are encouraged to "bulk up." Cases are more common in Western, industrialized countries, where an impractical level of thinness is promoted by actors, models, and advertisers. Anne Becker of Harvard Medical School has been studying eating habits in the Pacific islands of Fiji since 1988 (Becker, Burwell, Gilman, Herzog, & Hamburg, 2002). Traditionally, a robust, muscled body has been valued for both sexes there. But when satellite television arrived in 1995 the tall, slim actors in shows like *Beverly Hills 90210* became teenage Fiji's new role models. By 1998, 74% of young island girls considered themselves too big or fat, even though they were not more overweight than others; young girls who lived in homes that owned a TV were three times more likely to have an eating problem. Among 17-year-old girls, 11% admitted they had vomited to control weight, compared to just 3% in 1995.

There is little doubt that social pressure contributes to anorexia and bulimia. But the disorders are not unknown in non-Westernized societies, and anorexia has been reported for 300 years, long before the cultural emphasis on thinness. One indication that a sociocultural explanation is an oversimplification is that several studies show a genetic influence. Relatives of patients have a higher than usual incidence of the disorders, and the concordance between identical twins is much higher than between

What are anorexia and bulimia?

3

What is the evidence for social and genetic influences in anorexia and bulimia?

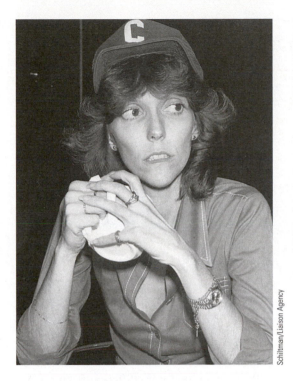

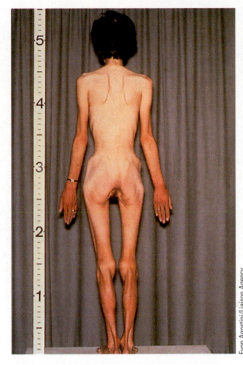

Figure 5.16
Effects of anorexia
Left: Karen Carpenter, a popular singer during the 1980s, soon before her death in 1983 from starvation-induced heart failure. Right: A woman at a late stage of anorexia.

fraternals (44% versus 12.5% for anorexia, 22.9% versus 8.7% for bulimia; Kendler et al., 1991; Kipman, Gorwood, Mouren-Simeoni, & Ad'es, 1999). One gene that appears to contribute to anorexia has been located (Vink et al., 2001), but it accounts for only a small fraction of sufferers.

Anorexic and bulimic patients often share a variety of other disorders with their relatives (Lilenfeld et al., 1998). Because these disorders involve neurotransmitter abnormalities and are partially hereditary, this *comorbidity* is another argument for a biological role in the eating disorders. Major depression is the most frequently reported comorbidity; naturally, researchers have tried to apply what they know about depression to understanding and treating anorexia and bulimia.

See "Born Under a Thin Star" on page 148 for another possible biological contributor to some cases of anorexia.

The Role of Serotonin

Because of the role serotonin has in the control of eating and in obesity, researchers have suspected that anorexics and bulimics have lower than normal serotonin activity. Bulimics do have reduced levels in their cerebrospinal fluid of **the serotonin metabolic by-product *5-hydroxyindoleacetic acid (5-HIAA),* which researchers use as an indicator of serotonin activity**; the reduction persists during symptom-free periods (Weltzin, Fernstrom, & Kaye, 1994). More than a dozen studies have shown that antidepressants, which increase serotonin activity, reduce binge eating (Walsh & Devlin, 1998). Besides depression, bulimics have an increased rate of anxiety, alcoholism and other drug abuse, and impulsive behavior, including stealing and sexual intercourse. All of these characteristics are associated with low serotonin activity (Kendler et al., 1991; Weltzin et al., 1994; Wiederman & Pryor, 1996; also see Chapters 4, 7, and 13).

What role does serotonin appear to have in anorexia and bulimia?

Born Under a Thin Star

Alison Motluk—Being born in the spring or early summer may put a girl at risk for anorexia later in life, according to a researcher in Scotland. John Eagles and his colleagues at the Royal Cornhill Hospital in Aberdeen examined the records of 446 Scottish women who had been diagnosed with anorexia nervosa, and compared them with 5,766 controls. There were 13 percent more anorexics born between March and June, and 30 percent more in June.

The finding suggests that a common winter infection, such as the flu, may predispose an unborn baby to the disorder. This sort of relationship does have a precedent, because schizophrenics are more likely to be born during the first four months of the year, and several studies have linked schizophrenia with influenza or other viruses in the mothers during pregnancy. (The study was published in the *International Journal of Eating Disorders*, vol. 30, p. 167.)
—New Scientist, *August 11, 2001, p. 6*

Antidepressant treatment of anorexia has had mixed results (Kaye, 1997; Walsh & Devlin, 1998). Anorexics appear to have lowered serotonin activity *while they are underweight*, but this could be due to malnutrition (Kaye, Ebert, Gwirtsman, & Weiss, 1984), and there is some question whether their depressive symptoms might have the same origin (Kaye, 1997). Anorexics and their relatives have a higher than usual incidence of perfectionism, rigidity, preoccupation with details, and need for order and cleanliness. These are characteristics of obsessive-compulsive disorder, which we will see in Chapter 13 is associated with *increased* serotonin activity.

The inconsistent treatment effects may be because researchers usually do not distinguish between the two subtypes of anorexics. After weight gain, restrictors have *higher* serotonin activity than normals (Kaye et al., 1984). Symptoms of anorexia in this group are improved by cyproheptadine (trade name Periactin), which *reduces* serotonin (Halmi, Eckert, LaDu, & Cohen, 1986). Kaye (1997) suggests that, just as eating improves mood in some obese people, starvation keeps serotonin low and helps anorexics escape obsessional concerns.

Purging anorexics are different from restrictors in a variety of ways. They tend to be impulsive, socially outgoing, emotionally responsive, and sexually active. These characteristics are typical of people with low serotonin activity, and purging anorexics do not show the same increase in serotonin activity after recovery that restrictors do (Kaye et al., 1984). In addition, cyproheptadine not only does not improve the purgers' symptoms, but impairs treatment (Halmi et al., 1986). So, although both types of anorexics are similar in limiting food intake and losing weight, purgers seem to be more like bulimics in personality and physiology.

✓ CONCEPT CHECK

- *How does defense of body weight contribute to obesity?*
- *How are anorexics and bulimics alike and different? (Don't forget the two types of anorexics.)*

In Perspective

Temperature regulation, thirst, and hunger provide good examples of drive, homeostasis, and physiological motivation in general. Although they are explained best by drive theory, they also illustrate the point that it is ultimately the balance or imbalance in certain brain centers that determines motivated behaviors.

In addition, hunger in particular demonstrates that homeostasis alone does not explain all the facets of motivated behavior. For instance, we saw that the incentives of the sight and smell of food are enough to start the physiological processes involved in the absorptive phase. This suggests that incentives operate through physiological mechanisms and are themselves physiological in nature. We also know that there are important social influences on what and how much people eat, and sensation seeking may explain why some people are gourmands and others enjoy the risks of eating puffer fish (their toxicity was described in Chapter 2 in Application: Targeting Ion Channels).

Most of the factors that determine our eating behavior are in turn influenced by the genes. If it is true that we are what we eat, it is equally true that what we eat (and how much) is the result of who we are. But we will be reminded time and again throughout this text that heredity is not destiny, that we are the products of countless interactions between our genetic propensities and the environment.

Our interest in the motivation of hunger would be mostly theoretical if it were not for the eating disorders, which can have life-threatening consequences. But in spite of their importance, we are unsure about the causes of obesity, anorexia, and bulimia and of what the best treatments are. We do know that, like the motivation of hunger itself, they are complex and have a number of causes.

This chapter has given you an overview of what we mean by motivation. We will broaden that view in the next two chapters by looking at sexuality, emotion, and aggression.

Summary

Motivation and Homeostasis

- Homeostasis and drive theory are key to understanding physiological motivation, but are not adequate alone.

- Temperature regulation involves a simple mechanism for control around a set point.

- Thirst is a bit more complex, compensating for two kinds of deficit.

Hunger: A Complex Drive

- Hunger is a more complex motivation, involving a variety of nutrients and regulation of both short-term and long-term nutrient supplies.

- Taste helps an individual select nutritious foods, avoid dangerous ones, and vary the diet.

- The feeding cycle consists of an absorptive phase, a period of living off nutrients from the last meal, and the fasting phase, when reliance shifts to stored nutrients.

- Eating is initiated when low blood levels of glucose and fatty acids are detected in the liver. The information is sent to the medulla and to the paraventricular nucleus of the hypothalamus, where neuropeptide Y is released to initiate eating.

- Feeding stops when stretch signals from the stomach, increasing glucose levels in the liver, and cholecystokinin released in the duodenum indicate that satiety has occurred.

continued

- How much we eat at a meal is also regulated by the amount of fat we have stored, indicated by leptin and insulin levels.

Eating Disorders

- Obesity is associated with malnutrition and with a variety of illnesses.
- A variety of factors, many of them outside the person's control, contribute to obesity.
- Obesity is partly inheritable, and the environmental influences that exist are not from the family.
- As calorie intake decreases, metabolism decreases to defend against weight loss.

- Obesity is difficult to treat, but drugs that increase serotonin activity, leptin, and the experimental drug C75 are showing promise.
- Anorexia involves restriction of food intake, and sometimes bingeing and purging, to reduce weight. Bulimia is a bingeing disease; weight increase is limited by purging or exercise.
- Social pressure and heredity both appear to be important in anorexia and bulimia.
- Serotonin appears to be low in bulimics, as it is in some obese individuals. It may be low in purging anorexics as well, and high in restricting anorexics.

 For Further Thought

- What hypotheses can you offer for the insatiable hunger of Prader-Willi individuals?
- A group of nuclei in the brain control a particular homeostatic need. What functions must the nuclei carry out?
- Imagine what would happen if we had to adjust the amount and kinds of food we eat under changing conditions by rational decision.

- What do you think would happen if the brain had no way of monitoring stored fat levels?
- What do you think a complete program of obesity treatment would look like?
- Can you propose another way to organize the three subgroups that make up anorexics and bulimics?

 Testing Your Understanding

1. Describe either temperature regulation or thirst in terms of homeostasis, drive, and satisfaction, including the signals and brain structures involved in the process.
2. Describe the absorptive and fasting phases of the feeding cycle; be specific about what nutrients are available, how nutrients are stored, and how they are retrieved from storage.
3. Describe obesity as a problem of metabolism.

Select the one best answer:

1. A problem that makes some question drive theory is that:
   a. an animal remains aroused after the need is satisfied.
   b. some people have stronger drives than others.
   c. not all motivation involves tissue needs.
   d. soon after a drive is satisfied the system goes out of equilibrium again.

2. An animal is said to be in homeostasis when it:

   a. recognizes that it is satisfied.
   b. feels a surge of pleasure from taking a drink.
   c. is in the middle of a high-calorie meal.
   d. is at its set point temperature.

3. Osmotic thirst is due to:

   a. dryness of the mouth and throat.
   b. lack of fluid in the cells.
   c. reduced volume of the blood.
   d. stimulation of pressure receptors.

4. A structure in the medulla that is involved in taste as well as in hunger and eating is the:

   a. nucleus of the solitary tract.
   b. paraventricular nucleus.
   c. area postrema.
   d. subfornical organ.

5. You have trouble with rabbits eating in your garden. Several sprays are available, but they are washed off each day by the sprinklers. The solution with the best combination of kindness, effectiveness, and ease for you would be to:

   a. spray the plants daily with a substance that tastes too bad to eat.
   b. spray the plants occasionally with a substance that makes the rabbits sick.
   c. spray the plants with a poison until all the rabbits are gone.
   d. forget about spraying; run outside and chase the rabbits away.

6. During the absorptive phase:

   a. fat is broken down into glycerol and fatty acids.
   b. insulin levels are low.
   c. glucagon converts glycogen to glucose.
   d. glucose from the stomach is the main energy source.

7. Neurons in the paraventricular nucleus release neuropeptide Y, which:

   a. increases eating.
   b. increases drinking.
   c. breaks down fat.
   d. causes shivering.

8. A long-term signal that influences eating is:

   a. glucose.   b. 2-deoxyglucose.
   b. cholecystokinin.   d. leptin.

9. When we say that the body defends weight during dieting, we mean primarily that:

   a. the person's metabolism decreases.
   b. the person eats less but selects richer foods.
   c. the person eats lower-calorie foods but eats larger servings.
   d. the body releases less neuropeptide Y.

10. Studies comparing the weights of adopted children with their biological parents and their adoptive parents:

    a. show that weight is influenced most by environment.
    b. show that weight is influenced most by heredity.
    c. show that heredity and environment have about equal influence.
    d. have not been in agreement.

11. If a *db/db* mouse is parabiotically attached to a normal mouse, the *db/db* mouse will:

    a. gain weight while the normal loses.
    b. lose weight while the normal gains.
    c. be unaffected while the normal loses.
    d. be unaffected while the normal gains.

12. Serotonin appears to be:

    a. high in anorexics and low in bulimics.
    b. low in anorexics and high in bulimics.
    c. low in bulimics, high in some anorexics, and low in some anorexics.
    d. high in anorexics, high in some bulimics, and low in some bulimics.

Answers: 1. **c** 2. **d** 3. **b** 4. **a** 5. **b** 6. **d** 7. **a** 8. **d** 9. **a** 10. **b** 11. **c** 12. **c**

On the Web

1. A description of **Prader-Willi syndrome** by two researchers is at

   http://www.geneclinics.org/profiles/pws/

   Information about the **Prader-Willi Syndrome Association,** facts about the disorder, journal references, stories of affected families, and other information are available at

   http://www.pwsausa.org

2. You've seen Alcoholics Anonymous's 12-step program applied to every other drug addiction; now it's being used to manage compulsive overeating. **Overeaters Anonymous** has information about its organization and links to local help groups at

   http://www.overeatersanonymous.org/

3. A **search service** devoted to eating disorders is at

   http://www.eating-disorder.com/

The **Center for Eating Disorders** has information, news, and discussion groups at

http://www.eating-disorders.com/

The site **Anorexia Nervosa** has information about the disorder, references to research, and links to other sites at

http://www.mentalhealth.com/dis/p20-et01.html

 For additional information about the topics covered in this chapter, please look at InfoTrac College Edition, at

http://www.infotrac-college.com/wadsworth

Try search terms you think up yourself, or use these: *anorexia nervosa; diabetes; motivation; obesity gene.*

On the CD-ROM: Exploring Biological Psychology

Video: Signals and Brain Centers Involved in Hunger and Control of Energy Reserves

Video: Susan, Anorexia Patient

For Further Reading

The Dieting Maelstrom: Is It Possible and Advisable to Lose Weight? by Kelly Brownell and Judith Rodin (*American Psychologist,* 1994, *49,* 781–791) argues that because there are often biological reasons for being overweight, dieting is sometimes more costly than it is worth.

Caloric Restriction and Aging, by R. Weindruch (*Scientific American,* January 1996, pp. 46–52). A great deal of research has shown that restricting caloric intake in rats and other animals (to as little as 50–70% of the ad lib diet) improves health and extends life. This article summarizes some of that research.

Why We Eat What We Eat: The Psychology of Eating, by Elizabeth D. Capaldi and Elizabeth P. Capaldi (editors; American Psychological Association, 1996). With chapters by 21 researchers, this book explores the determinants of our eating behavior, including cultural, physiological, and genetic. The coverage is thorough, including even the influence of a pregnant woman's food choices on her child's later food preferences.

➡ Key Terms

2-deoxyglucose (2-DG) *136*

5-hydroxyindoleacetic acid (5-HIAA) *147*

absorptive phase *135*

adipose tissue *135*

amino acids *134*

angiotensin II *129*

anorexia nervosa *146*

area postrema *134*

arousal theory *127*

basal metabolism *142*

body mass index (BMI) *140*

bulimia nervosa *146*

cholecystokinin (CCK) *138*

diabetes gene *142*

drive *126*

drive theory *126*

duodenum *134*

fasting phase *135*

fatty acids *134*

glucagon *136*

glucose *134*

glycerol *134*

glycogen *135*

hepatic portal vein *134*

homeostasis *126*

hypovolemic thirst *129*

incentive theory *126*

instinct *126*

insulin *135*

learned taste aversion *132*

learned taste preference *133*

leptin *139*

motivation *125*

neuropeptide Y *136*

nucleus of the solitary tract (NST) *132*

obesity gene *142*

organum vasculosum lamina terminalis (OVLT) *129*

osmotic thirst *129*

paraventricular nucleus (PVN) *136*

preoptic area *128*

sensory-specific satiety *131*

set point *127*

subfornical organ (SFO) *129*

The Biology of Sex and Gender

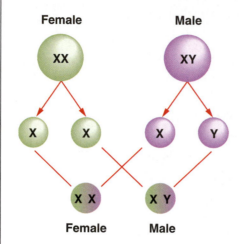

Female   **Male**

XX   XY

X   X   X   Y

X X   X Y

Female   **Male**

In this chapter you will learn:

- Ways sex is similar to and different from other drives.

- How hormones and brain structures control sexual development and behavior.

- Some of the differences between males and females and what causes them.

- How deviations in sexual development affect the body, brain, and behavior.

- How prenatal development may explain heterosexuality and homosexuality.

Fourteen-year-old Jill went to her family physician complaining of a persistent hoarse voice. As is often the case, other concerns surfaced during the course of the examination. At puberty she had failed to develop breasts or to menstruate; instead, her voice deepened and her body became muscular. Once comfortable with her tomboyishness, she was now embarrassed by her appearance and increasingly masculine mannerisms; she withdrew from peers and her school performance began to suffer. But there was an even more significant change at puberty: her clitoris started growing and was 4 centimeters (1½ inches) long when she was examined by the doctor; in addition, her labia (vaginal lips) had partially closed, giving the appearance of a male scrotum. To everyone's surprise, Jill's included, the doctor discovered that she had two undescended testes in her abdomen and no ovaries; further testing showed that her sex chromosomes were XY, which meant that genetically she was a male.

After a psychiatric evaluation Jill's parents and doctors decided that she should be offered the opportunity to change to a male sexual identity. She immediately went home and changed into boy's clothing and got a boy's haircut. The family moved to another neighborhood where they were unknown. At the new high school Jack became an athlete, excelled as a student, was well accepted socially, and began dating girls. Surgeons fin-ished closing the labia and moved the testes into the newly formed scrotum. He developed into a muscular 6-foot-tall male with a deep voice and heavy beard. At the age of 25 he married, and he and his wife reported a mutually satisfactory sexual relationship (Imperato-McGinley, Peterson, Stoller, & Goodwin, 1979).

Humans have a great affinity for dichotomies, dividing their world into blacks and whites with few grays in between. No dichotomy is more significant for human existence than that of male and female: one's sex is often the basis for deciding how the person should behave, what the person is capable of doing, and with whom the person should fall in love. Not only are many of the differences between males and females imposed on them by society, but Jill's experience suggests that typing people as male or female may not be as simple or as appropriate as we think. We will encounter even more puzzling cases later as we take a critical look at the designation of male versus female and the expectations that go with it. In the meantime, we need to continue our discussion of motivation by considering how sex is like and unlike other drives.

SEX AS A FORM OF MOTIVATION

To say that sex is a motivated behavior like hunger may be stating the obvious. But theorists have had difficulty categorizing sex with other physiological drives because it does not fit the pattern of a homeostatic tissue need. If you fail to eat or if you cannot maintain body temperature within reasonable limits, you will die. But no harm will come from forgoing sex; sex ensures the survival of the species, but not of the individual.

There are, however, several similarities with other drives like hunger and thirst. They include arousal and satiation, the involvement of hormones, and control by specific areas in the brain. We will explore these similarities as well as some differences in the following pages.

How is sex like and unlike other drives?

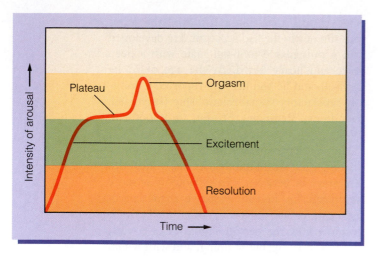

Figure 6.1
Phases of the sexual response cycle
This is a typical response for a male; most females are
capable of multiple orgasms.
Source: Based on Masters & Johnson, 1966.

Arousal and Satiation

The cycle of arousal and satiation is the most
obvious similarity between sexual motivation
and other motivated behaviors. In the 1960s
William Masters and Virginia Johnson conducted groundbreaking research on the human
sexual response. Until then research had been
limited to observing sexual behavior in animals
like rats and monkeys, or interviewing humans
about their sexual activity. Masters and
Johnson (1966) observed 312 men and 382
women and recorded their physiological
responses during 10,000 episodes of sexual
activity in the laboratory. This kind of research
was unheard of at the time; in fact, the
researchers had trouble finding journals that
would publish their work.

Masters and Johnson identified four phases
of sexual response (see Figure 6.1). The *excitement phase* is a period of arousal and preparation
for intercourse. Both sexes experience increased
heart rate, respiration rate, blood pressure, and
muscle tension. The male's penis becomes
engorged with blood and becomes erect. The
female's clitoris becomes erect as well, her vaginal lips swell and open, the vagina lubricates,

her breasts enlarge, and the nipples become
erect.

Hunger is a function mostly of time since
the last meal. Sexual arousal, though, is more
influenced by opportunity and sexual stimuli
such as explicit conversation or the presence of
a sexually attractive person. (In many other
animal species, sexual arousal is a regular event
triggered by a surge in hormones.) Another
difference between sex and other drives is that
we usually are motivated to reduce hunger,
thirst, and temperature deviations, but we seek
sexual arousal. This difference is not unique,
though; for example, we skip lunch to increase
the enjoyment of a gourmet dinner.

During the *plateau phase*, the increase in sexual arousal levels off; arousal is maintained at a
high level for seconds or minutes, though it is
possible to prolong this period. The testes rise
in the scrotum in preparation for ejaculation;
vaginal lubrication increases and the vaginal
entrance tightens on the penis. During *orgasm*,
rhythmic contractions in the penis are accompanied by ejaculation of seminal fluid containing sperm into the vagina. Similar contractions
occur in the vagina. This period lasts just a few
seconds, but involves an intense experience of
pleasure. *Resolution* follows as arousal decreases
and the body returns to its previous state.
Orgasm is similar to the pleasure one feels after
eating or when warmed after a deep chill, but it
is unique in its intensity; the resolution that follows is reminiscent of the period of quiet following return to homeostasis with other drives.

Males have a *refractory phase*, during which
they are unable to become aroused or have
another orgasm for minutes, hours, or even
days, depending on the individual and the circumstances. Females do not experience a
refractory period and are able to have additional orgasms anytime during the resolution
phase. Since we are comparing the sex drive
with other kinds of motivation, the male
refractory period has an interesting parallel
with sensory-specific satiety (see Chapter 5);
it is called the Coolidge effect. According to
a popular but probably apocryphal story,

President Coolidge and his wife were touring a farm when Mrs. Coolidge asked the farmer whether the rooster copulates more than once a day. The farmer answered yes, dozens of times, and Mrs. Coolidge said, "You might point that out to Mr. Coolidge." President Coolidge, so the story goes, then asked the farmer, "Is it a different hen each time?" The answer again was yes. "Tell that to Mrs. Coolidge," the president replied. Whether the story is true or not, the *Coolidge effect—a quicker return to sexual arousal for a male when a new female is introduced*—has been observed in a wide variety of species; we will visit the subject again shortly.

The Role of Testosterone

As important as sex is to humans, it is ironic that so much of what we know about the topic comes from the study of other species. One reason is that research into human sexual behavior was for a long time considered off limits and funding was hard to come by. Another reason is that sexual behavior is more "accessible" in nonhuman animals; rats have sex as often as 20 times a day, and are not a bit embarrassed to perform in front of the experimenter. In addition, we can manipulate their sexual behavior in ways that would be considered unethical with humans. Hormonal control in particular is more often studied in animals because hormones have a clearer role in animal sexual behavior.

Castration, or removal of the gonads (testes or ovaries) is one technique used to study hormonal effects because it removes the major source of sex hormones; castration results in a prompt loss of sexual motivation in nonhuman mammals of both sexes. Humans are less affected by castration than other animals. Of course, we do not castrate humans for research purposes, but many people must have their gonads removed for medical reasons, such as cancer. Sexual interest and functioning decrease in both males and females (Bremer, 1959; Heim, 1981; Sherwin & Gelfand, 1987; Shifren et al., 2000). However, the amount and rapidity of decrease are highly variable among individuals,

probably due to the continued production of sex hormones by the adrenal glands and to individual differences in sensitivity to the hormones.

Castration has been elected by some male criminals in the hope of controlling aggression or sexual predation, sometimes in exchange for shorter prison sentences. Castration is an extreme therapy; drugs that counter the effects of *androgens* (a class of hormones responsible for a number of male characteristics and functions) are a more attractive alternative. Those that block the production of *testosterone,* the major sex hormone in males, have been 80–100% effective in eliminating deviant sexual behavior such as exhibitionism and pedophilia (sexual contact with children), along with sexual fantasies and urges (Rösler & Witztum, 1998; Thibaut, Cordier, & Kuhn, 1996). The effects of castration indicate that testosterone is necessary for male sexual behavior, but the amount of testosterone required appears to be minimal; men with very low testosterone levels can be as sexually active as other men (Raboch & Stárka, 1973).

Frequency of sexual activity does vary with testosterone levels *within* individuals, but it looks like testosterone increases are the *result* of sexual activity rather than the cause. For example, testosterone levels are high in males at the *end* of a period in which intercourse occurred, not before (Dabbs & Mohammed, 1992; Kraemer et al., 1976). A case report (which is anecdotal and does not permit us to draw conclusions) suggests that just the anticipation of sex can increase testosterone level. Knowing that beard growth is related to testosterone level, a researcher working in near isolation on a remote island weighed the daily clippings from his electric razor. He found that the amount of beard growth increased just before planned visits to the mainland and the opportunity for sexual activity (Anonymous, 1970)!

In most species, females are unwilling to engage in sex except during *estrus,* a period when the female is ovulating, sex hormone levels are high, and the animal is said to be in heat. Human females and females of some other

What is the role of testosterone in sexual behavior?

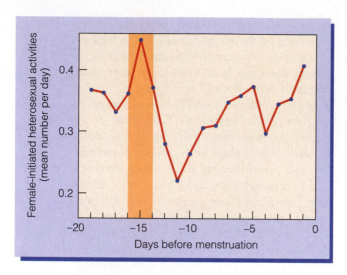

Figure 6.2
Female-initiated activity during the menstrual cycle
What reason(s) can you think of for a decrease following Day-15? for an increase before Day 0?
From D.B. Adams, A.R. Gold, & A.D. Burt (1978). "Rise in female-initiated sexual activity at ovulation and its suppression by oral contraceptives." *New England Journal of Medicine,* 299 (21), 1145–1150, Fig. 2, p. 1147.

What brain structures are involved in sexual behavior?

primate species engage in sex throughout the reproductive cycle. Studies of sexual frequency in women have not shown a clear peak at the time of ovulation. However, initiation of sex is a better gauge of the female's sexual motivation than is her willingness to have sex; women do initiate sexual activity more often during the middle of the menstrual cycle, which is when ovulation occurs (Figure 6.2) (Adams, Gold, & Burt, 1978; Harvey, 1987). The researchers attributed the effect to *estrogen* **(a class of hormones responsible for a number of female characteristics and functions).** Their reasons were that estrogen peaks at midcycle and the women did not increase in sexual activity if they were taking birth control pills, which level out estrogen release over the cycle.

However, testosterone peaks at the same time, and intercourse frequency at midcycle corresponds to the woman's testosterone level (Morris, Udry, Khan-Dawood, & Dawood, 1987). At menopause, when both estrogen and testosterone levels decline, testosterone levels show the most consistent relationship with

intercourse frequency (McCoy & Davidson, 1985). How to interpret these observations is unclear, because testosterone increases in women as a *result* of sexual activity, just as it does in men (Figure 6.3) (Dabbs & Mohammed, 1992). However, studies in which testosterone level was manipulated demonstrate that it contributes to women's sexual behavior. Giving a dose of testosterone to women increases their arousal during an erotic film (Tuiten et al., 2000). More importantly, in women who had their ovaries removed, testosterone treatment increased sexual arousal, sexual fantasies, and intercourse frequency, but estrogen treatment did not (Sherwin & Gelfand, 1987; Shifren et al., 2000).

Brain Structures and Neurotransmitters

Several brain structures that have a role in sexual behavior have been identified in nonhuman animals. This similarity between sex and other drives led motivation researchers to shift their focus from drive as a tissue need to drive as a condition in particular parts of the brain.

Sexual activity, like other drives and behaviors, involves a network of brain structures. This almost seems inevitable, because sexual activity involves reaction to a variety of stimuli, activation of several physiological systems, postural and movement responses, a reward experience, and so on. We do not understand yet how the sexual network operates as a whole, but we do know something about the functioning of several of its components.

The *medial preoptic area (MPOA)* of the hypothalamus is one of the more significant brain structures involved in male and female sexual behavior. (The general preoptic area can be located in Figure 5.2 in the previous chapter.) Stimulation of the MPOA increases copulation (intercourse) in rats of both sexes (Bloch, Butler, & Kohlert, 1996; Bloch, Butler, Kohlert, & Bloch, 1993), and the MPOA is active when they copulate spontaneously (Pfaus, Kleopoulos, Mobbs, Gibbs, & Pfaff, 1993; Shimura & Shimokochi, 1990).

The MPOA appears to be more responsible for performance than for sexual motivation; when it was destroyed in male monkeys they no longer tried to copulate, but instead they would often masturbate in the presence of a female (Slimp, Hart, & Goy, 1978).

A part of the amygdala known as the *medial amygdala* **also contributes to sexual behavior in rats of both sexes.** The medial amygdala is active while they copulate (Pfaus, Kleopoulos, Mobbs, Gibbs, & Pfaff, 1993), and stimulation causes the release of dopamine in the MPOA (Dominguez & Hull, 2001; Matuszewich, Lorrain, & Hull, 2000). The medial amygdala's role apparently is to respond to sexually exciting stimuli, such as the presence of a potential sex partner (de Jonge, Oldenburger, Louwerse, & Van de Poll, 1992).

The *sexually dimorphic nucleus (SDN),* **located in the MPOA, is important in the sexual activity of male rats** (de Jonge et al., 1989). The name comes from the fact that the SDN is five times larger in male rats than in females (see Figure 6.4a and b) (Gorski, Gordon, Shryne, & Southam, 1978). The level of sexual activity in males is related to the size of their SDN, which in turn depends on prenatal ("before birth") exposure to testosterone (Anderson, Fleming, Rhees, & Kinghorn, 1986). Destruction of the SDN reduces male sexual activity (de Jonge et al., 1989).

The *ventromedial nucleus* **of the hypothalamus is important for sexual behavior in female rats** (see Figure 5.2 for location). Activity increases there during copulation (Pfaus et al., 1993), and destruction reduces the female's responsiveness to a male's advances (Pfaff & Sakuma, 1979).

For obvious reasons, we know much less about the brain structures involved in human sexual behavior. We do know that a few brain structures in humans differ in size between males and females. Because their contribution to sexual behavior is not clear but the size differences may also distinguish homosexuals from heterosexuals, I will defer their discussion until we take up the subject of sexual orientation.

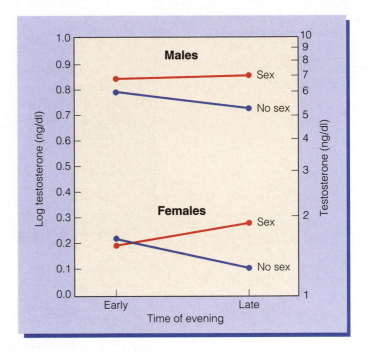

Figure 6.3
Relationship between sexual behavior and salivary testosterone levels in men and women
Reprinted from J.M. Dabbs, Jr. & S. Mohammed (1992). "Male and female salivary testosterone concentrations before and after sexual activity. *Physiology and Behavior,* 52, 195–197, Fig. 1. © 1992 with permission from Elsevier Science.

Several neurotransmitters participate in sexual behavior. In rats, dopamine and serotonin activity increase in the MPOA (Mas, Fumero, & González-Mora, 1995), and injecting a dopamine antagonist into the MPOA reduces sexual behavior (Warner et al., 1991). Drugs that increase dopamine levels in humans, such as those used in treating Parkinson's disease, increase sexual activity, while antidepressants that increase serotonin interfere (Meston & Frolich, 2000). Norepinephrine increases in both men and women during sexual activity (Meston & Frolich, 2000).

We saw in Chapter 4 that sexual activity also increases dopamine in the nucleus accumbens, probably indicating a reward effect. Interestingly, dopamine release there parallels the animal's behavior during the Coolidge effect; it is high during copulation, returns to normal during the period of disinterest in the

Figure 6.4
The sexually dimorphic nuclei of the rat
(a) The SDN is larger in the male than **(b)** the SDN in the female. **(c)** The effects of two masculinizing hormones on the female SDN.
Source: Gorski, 1974.

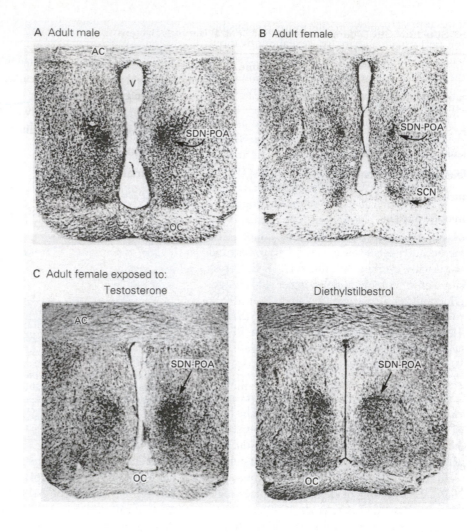

female, then increases again in the presence of a new female and during copulation with her (Fiorino, Coury, & Phillips, 1997) (see Figure 6.5). Dopamine is not the only transmitter involved in sexual reward; injecting men with naloxone reduces their arousal and pleasure during orgasm, indicating that endorphins also participate (Murphy, Checkley, Seckl, & Lightman, 1990).

Sensory Stimuli in Sexual Behavior

Sexual behavior results from an interplay of internal conditions, particularly hormone levels, with external stimuli. Sexual stimuli can be anything from brightly colored plumage or an attractive body shape to particular odors. I mentioned earlier that external stimuli are more important in human sexual behavior than for other drives; now we will explore some of the stimuli that have especially engaged researchers' attention.

The Nose as a Sex Organ

Each human gives off a unique, genetically determined odor (Axel, 1995), and people can distinguish clothing worn by family members from clothing worn by strangers just by smelling them (Porter & Moore, 1981; Schaal

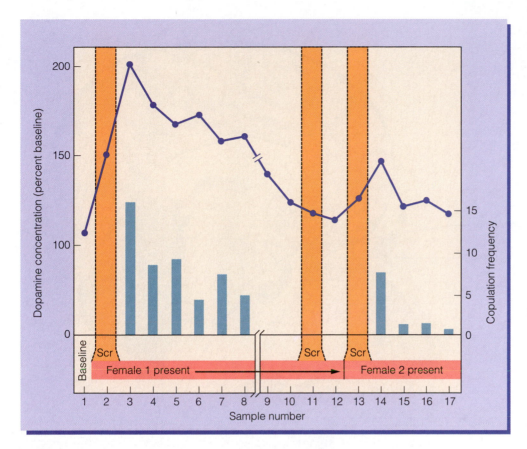

Figure 6.5
Dopamine levels in the nucleus accumbens during the Coolidge effect
Activity was recorded until the male lost interest in Female 1; then Female 2 was presented. During the periods labeled "Scr" the female was separated from the male by a clear screen. Line shows dopamine levels. Bars show the number of intromissions (vaginal penetrations).

From "Dynamic changes in nucleus accumbens dopamine efflux during the Coolidge effect in male rats," by D.F. Fiorino, A. Coury, & A.G. Phillips, p. 4852. Copyright © 1997 Society for Neuroscience. Reprinted with permission.

& Porter, 1991). It is possible that, like other mammals, we use this ability to identify and bond with family members.

There is also some evidence that odor influences mate choice in a way that helps avoid genetic inbreeding. Women rated the odor of men's tee shirts as more pleasant when the man differed from the woman in the *major histocompatibility complex (MHC), a group of genes that contribute to the functioning of the immune system* (Wedekind, Seebeck, Bettens, & Paepke, 1995). Couples similar in MHC are less fertile and have more spontaneous abortions. The women's preference probably influenced their real-life choices; they said that the preferred odors reminded them of current or previous boyfriends.

The actual stimuli may not be the odors themselves. *Pheromones are airborne chemicals released by an animal that have physiological or behavioral effects on another animal of the same species.* Pheromones are involved in the regulation of hormonal cycles and in the attraction and selection of mates in nonhuman animals. Pheromones can be very powerful, as you know if your yard has ever been besieged by all the male cats in the neighborhood when your female cat was "in heat." The female gypsy moth can attract males from as far as two miles away (Hopson, 1979).

To understand the role pheromones play, let's look at the pheromone detection system, which in turn must be understood in the context of the olfactory (smell) system. Olfaction

Figure 6.6
The olfactory and vomeronasal systems

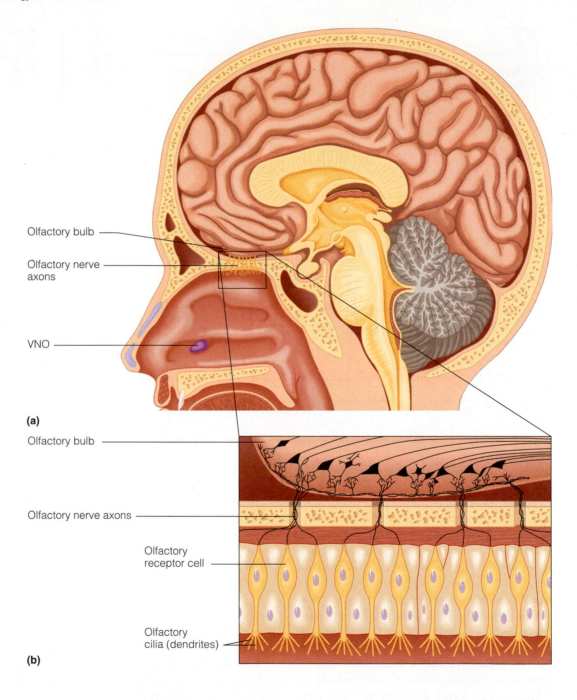

Olfactory bulb

Olfactory nerve axons

VNO

(a)

Olfactory bulb

Olfactory nerve axons

Olfactory receptor cell

Olfactory cilia (dendrites)

(b)

is one of two chemical senses, along with taste. Airborne odorous materials entering the nasal cavity must dissolve in the mucous layer overlying the receptor cells; the odorant then stimulates a receptor cell when it comes in contact with receptor sites on the cell's cilia (see Figure 6.6). Axons from the olfactory receptors pass through openings in the base of the skull to enter the olfactory bulbs, which lie over the nasal cavity. From there, neurons follow the olfactory nerves to the nearby olfactory cortex in the temporal lobes.

Humans can recognize approximately 10,000 odors. But an individual neuron cannot produce the variety of signals required to distinguish among so many different stimuli, and we do not have a different receptor for each odor. Researchers have recently discovered that about 1,000 genes encode an equal number of olfactory receptor types in rats and mice; humans have between 500 and 750 odor receptor genes, although only one-fourth to three-fourths of these appear to be functional (Mombaerts, 1999). Each neuron has a single type of odor receptor; our brain identifies an odor by the combination of neurons that is active.

Pheromones are not detected by the main olfactory system, but by the *vomeronasal organ (VNO), a cluster of receptors also located in the nasal cavity* (Figure 6.6). The two systems are separate, and the VNO's receptors are produced by a different family of genes (Hines, 1997). Not surprisingly, the VNO sends its signals to the medial preoptic area and the ventromedial hypothalamus in animals (Guillamon & Segovia, 1997).

In 1971 Martha McClintock was studying menstrual synchrony among women who live together. She found that the menstrual periods of women in a college dormitory who spent the most time together occurred at about the same time. Suspecting a pheromone-like signal, researchers in follow-up studies dabbed the upper lips (just under the nose) of women each day with pads that had been worn under the arms of other women (Preti, Cutler, Garcia, Huggins, & Lawley, 1986; Stern & McClintock, 1998). Over time, the menstrual cycles of the recipient women became synchronized with the cycles of the donor women. When women were treated with pads from the underarms of males, their menstrual cycles became more regular in length (Cutler et al., 1986); this probably explains why women who engage in weekly sexual activity with men have more regular cycles. The women reported that they smelled nothing but the alcohol used as a solvent on the pads.

Until these studies, most researchers believed that human behavior was not affected by pheromones. One reason was the bias that human behavior is guided by forces within our awareness. More importantly, most researchers thought that humans lack a VNO, at least as adults. However, careful examination revealed the VNO's presence in almost all of 1,000 individuals examined, though in most it was microscopic in size (Garcia-Velasco & Mondragon, 1991). Stimulating the human VNO with puffs of air containing suspected pheromones caused it to give off electrical potentials similar to the ones that olfactory receptors produce (Monti-Bloch, Jennings-White, Dolberg, & Berliner, 1994). The olfactory receptors did not respond to the suspected pheromones, however, and the VNO did not respond to the odors tested. The suspected pheromones also caused autonomic changes that indicated arousal, such as decreases in skin temperature and increases in sweat gland activity. The suspected female pheromones affected men more than they did women and vice versa.

A few studies now suggest that human pheromones may enhance sexual attractiveness. Men were asked to rate the attractiveness of women's photographs and their recorded voices; the men rated the photos and voices as more attractive when they were sniffing inhalers that, unknown to them, contained suspected pheromones called *copulins* from the vaginas of women (Jütte & Grammer, 1998). In another study, men smelled tee shirts that had been slept in for three successive nights by women who were instructed to avoid perfume and scented soap. The tee shirts considered the "sexiest" by the men belonged to the women who had been rated by other judges as the most attractive (Rikowski & Grammer, 1999). The women's ratings of men's odor showed this effect only during the most fertile period of the women's menstrual cycle. The research participants

What is the evidence for pheromones in human sexual behavior?

did not necessarily *like* the odors that they found most attractive; in fact, researchers tell us that the odors are often unpleasant. If pheromones do affect human sexual attractiveness, they apparently do so independently of odor.

But do pheromones influence sexual *behavior* in humans? There is some evidence they do. Male volunteers who used aftershave lotion with a suspected male pheromone reported more frequent sexual intercourse than controls using plain aftershave lotion (Cutler, Friedmann, & McCoy, 1998). The men's masturbation rates did not increase, so the pheromone apparently enhanced the men's sexual attractiveness rather than their motivation. Not everyone is convinced of the existence of human pheromones. Time will tell, but it appears that if pheromones influence human behavior their power is much weaker than in other animals.

Body Symmetry, Fitness, and Fertility

What is considered beautiful varies from one culture to another, but some researchers believe there are a few universally attractive characteristics. These features appear to be related to physical health and to fertility. Body symmetry, for example, has been linked to good health and to superior genetic makeup (Thornhill & Gangestad, 1994); symmetrical mates would be more fertile and better equipped to be good parents, and they would pass on good genes to their offspring. In animals, males that are more symmetrical mate more often than asymmetrical ones, either because they are more attractive to females or because they compete better with other males. In a study in Belize, symmetrical men had more offspring and had fewer life-threatening illnesses (Waynforth, 1998). In a study of U.S. college students, males with more symmetrical body features were rated more attractive, and higher-symmetry males and females had more sexual partners (Thornhill & Gangestad, 1994). In other research, women preferred the odor of tee shirts worn by more symmetrical

men—but only during the part of their menstrual cycle when they would be expected to be ovulating (Gangestad & Thornhill, 1998). Presumably, our attraction to appearance characteristics that are associated with better fitness has a biological basis.

These results do not mean that well-known social influences have no effect on sexual attraction and mating choices. Men and women will continue to be influenced in their choice of sexual partners by personality or hair color or social status. But now we are beginning to see that these social factors do not operate alone, and that we are a bit closer to our animal neighbors than we once believed.

✔ **CONCEPT CHECK**

- *What change in thinking helped researchers see sex as similar to other biological drives?*
- *What role do estrogen and testosterone play in sexual behavior in humans?*
- *In what ways do sensory stimuli influence sexual behavior?*

THE BIOLOGICAL DETERMINATION OF SEX

Now we need to talk about differences between the sexes, and the anomalies (exceptions) that occur. *Sex* **is the term for the biological characteristics that divide humans and other animals into the categories of male and female.** But *gender role* **is simply the set of behaviors society considers appropriate for people of a given biological sex,** and *gender identity* **is the person's subjective feeling of being male or female.** The term sex cannot be used to refer to all three of these concepts, because they are not always consistent with each other. Thus, classifying a person as male or female can sometimes be difficult. You might think that the absolute criterion for identifying a person's sex would be a matter of chromosomes, but you will soon see that it is not that simple.

Chromosomes and Hormones

You may remember from Chapter 1 that when cells divide to produce sex cells, the pairs of chromosomes separate and each sperm or each egg receives only 23 chromosomes. This means that a sex cell has only one of the two sex chromosomes. An egg will always have an X chromosome, but a sperm may have either an X chromosome or a Y chromosome. The procreative function of sexual intercourse is to bring the male's sperm into contact with the female's ovum. When the male ejaculates into the female's vagina, the sperm use their tail-like flagella to swim through the uterus and up the fallopian tubes, where the ovum is descending. As soon as one sperm enters the ovum, the ovum's membrane immediately becomes impenetrable so that only that sperm is allowed to fertilize the egg. The sperm makes its way to the nucleus of the ovum, where the two sets of chromosomes are combined into a full complement of 23 pairs. After fertilization the ovum begins dividing, producing the billions of cells that make up the human fetus. If the sperm that fertilizes the ovum carries an X sex chromosome, the fetus will develop into a female; if the sperm's sex chromosome is Y, the child will be a male (see Figure 6.7).

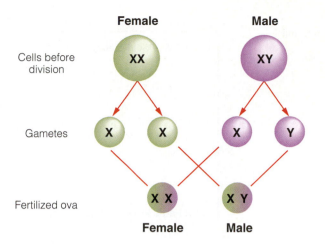

Figure 6.7
X and Y chromosomes in female and male

For the first month, XX and XY fetuses are identical. Later, the primitive **gonads (the primary reproductive organs)** in the XX individual develop into **ovaries, where the ova develop. The *Müllerian ducts* develop into the uterus, fallopian tubes, and the inner vagina,** while the Wolffian ducts that would become the male organs wither and are absorbed (Figure 6.8). The undifferentiated external genitals become a clitoris, the outer segment of the vagina, and the labia, which partially enclose the entrance to the vagina (Figure 6.9).

What makes a person male or female?

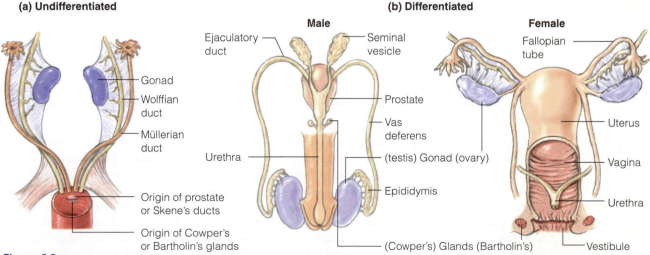

Figure 6.8
Development of male and female internal organs

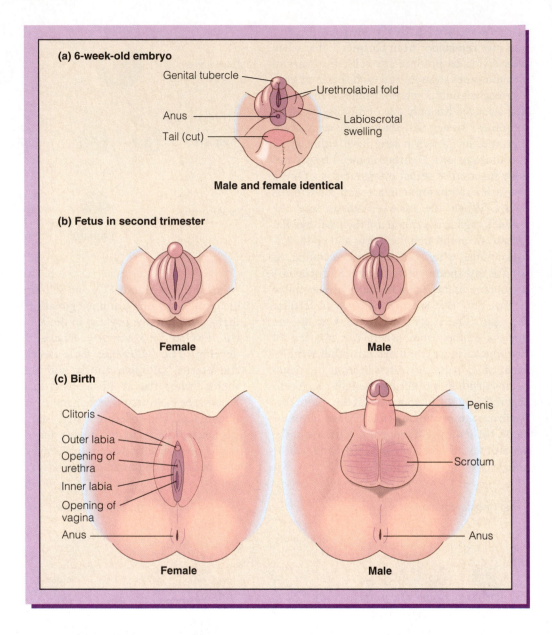

If the fetus receives a Y chromosome from the father, the *SRY* gene on that chromosome causes the primitive gonads to develop into *testes, the organs that will produce sperm.* The testes begin secreting two types of hormones (Haqq et al., 1994). *Müllerian inhibiting hormone defeminizes the fetus by causing the Müllerian ducts to degenerate.* Testosterone, the most prominent member of

the class of hormones called *androgens*, masculinizes the internal organs: **the *Wolffian ducts* develop into the seminal vesicles, which store semen, and the vas deferens, which carry semen from the testes to the penis. A derivative of testosterone, *dihydrotestosterone*, masculinizes the external genitals:** the same structures that produce the clitoris and labia in the female become a penis and a scrotum, into which the testes descend during childhood. There is no corresponding hormonal action in females; only later will the ovaries begin to produce estrogens, and the fetus will develop into a female without the benefit of female hormones as long as testosterone is absent. The testes and ovaries each secrete both male and female hormones, although in differing amounts; the adrenal glands also secrete small amounts of both kinds of hormones.

The hormonal effects we have been discussing are called organizing effects. ***Organizing effects mostly occur prenatally and shortly after birth; they affect structure and are lifelong in nature.*** Organizing effects are not limited to the reproductive organs; they include sex-specific changes in the brains of males and females as well, at least in nonhuman mammals. ***Activating effects* can occur at any time in the individual's life; they may come and go with hormonal fluctuations or be long lasting, but they are reversible.** Some of the changes that occur during puberty are examples of activating effects.

During childhood, differences between boys and girls other than the genitals are relatively minimal. Boys tend to be heavier and stronger, but there is considerable overlap. Boys also are usually more active and more aggressive. Marked differences appear about the time the child enters puberty, usually during the pre-teen years.

At puberty a surge of estrogens from the ovaries and testosterone from the testes complete the process of sexual differentiation that began during prenatal development. Organizing effects include maturation of the genitals and changes in stature. Activating effects include breast development in the girl and muscle increases and beard growth in the boy. In addition, the girl's ovaries begin releasing ova (that is, she *ovulates*) and she starts to menstruate. Boys' testes start producing sperm and ejaculation becomes possible. More important from a behavioral perspective, sexual interest increases dramatically, and in the majority of cases prefer-ence for same-sex company shifts to an attraction to the other sex, along with an interest in sexual intimacy.

Prenatal Hormones and the Brain

Several behaviors and characteristics can be identified as male-typical and others as female-typical. This does not mean that the behaviors are somehow more appropriate for that sex, but simply that they occur more frequently in one sex than the other. These differences are not absolute. For example, consider the stereotypical sexual behavior of rats: the male mounts the female from behind, while the female curves her back and presents her hindquarters in a posture called lordosis. However, females occasionally mount other females, and males will sometimes show lordosis when approached by another male.

The same hormones responsible for the development of gonads and genitals affect behavior as well. If a male rat is castrated shortly after birth or given a chemical that blocks androgens just before birth and for a short time postnatally (after birth), he will regularly accept the sexual advances of other males in adulthood. Similarly, a female rat given testosterone during the critical period will mount other females at a higher rate than usual as an adult (Figure 6.10) (Gorski, 1974). Both typical and atypical sexual behavior apparently result from testosterone's influence on the size and function of several brain structures; in other words, the presence of testosterone masculinizes certain brain structures

What is the effect of "sexualizing" the brain?

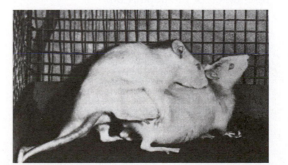

Figure 6.10
A female rat mounting a male
Source: Dörner, 1974.

and its absence results in feminization. This sexualization of the brain is reflected in behavioral differences, affecting not only sexual activity but play behavior, spatial activity, and learning performance (see Collaer & Hines, 1995). Do hormones have a similar influence in humans? In the following pages we will look for evidence.

✔ **CONCEPT CHECK**

- *How is the sex of a fetus determined and what affects prenatal and postnatal sexual development?*
- *What effect do sex hormones have on differentiation of the brain and behavior?*

GENDER-RELATED BEHAVIORAL AND COGNITIVE DIFFERENCES

In his popular book *Men Are from Mars, Women Are from Venus*, John Gray (1992) says that men and women communicate, think, feel, perceive, respond, love, and need differently, as if they are from different planets and speaking different languages. How different are men and women? This question is not easily answered, but it is not for lack of research on the topic. The results of studies are often ambiguous and contradictory. One reason is that different researchers measure the same characteristic in different ways. Also, the research samples are often too small to yield reliable results, and the subjects are usually not selected in a manner that ensures accurate representation of the population.

Some Demonstrated Male-Female Differences

In an effort to overcome some of these problems, Eleanor Maccoby and Carol Jacklin (1974) reviewed over 2,000 studies that included measures of sex differences. They concluded that the evidence firmly supported three differences in cognitive performance and one difference in social behavior: (1) girls have

greater verbal ability than boys; (2) boys excel in visual-spatial ability; (3) boys excel in mathematical ability; and (4) boys are more aggressive than girls. This does not mean that all girls are verbally superior to all boys or that all boys are more aggressive than all girls; there is considerable overlap, with many members of the lower-scoring sex exceeding the average of the other. Additional differences have received some support from research, but we are interested in these four characteristics because Maccoby and Jacklin believe there is a good chance the differences are partially due to biological factors.

Research has mostly supported their conclusions (Daly & Wilson, 1988; Hedges & Nowell, 1995; Hyde, 1986; Voyer, Voyer & Bryden, 1995). However, the cognitive differences have turned out to be rather limited. For example, females excel in verbal fluency and writing, but not in reading comprehension or vocabulary (Eagly, 1995; Hedges & Nowell, 1995). Males' scores exceed females' most on tasks requiring mental rotation of a three-dimensional object and less on other spatial tasks (Hyde, 1996). Although females are better at computation, males do better on tests of broad mathematical ability like those in the Scholastic Assessment Test (SAT) (Hyde, 1996).

Origins of Male-Female Differences

Whether these differences are influenced by biology or are solely the product of experience is controversial. Not only is this an important theoretical issue, but it has practical importance: if the differences are due to experience we might want to rear our children differently. There is good evidence that adults treat boys and girls very differently. When they interact with their own or other children in the laboratory, for example, they encourage more independence in boys while responding more positively to girls' requests for help (Culp, Cook, & Housley, 1983; Fagot, 1978; Frisch, 1977; Smith & Lloyd, 1978).

The best evidence that the three cognitive differences mentioned above are influenced by experience is that they have decreased over the years, presumably as gender roles have changed (Hedges & Nowell, 1995; Hyde, 1986; Hyde, 1996; Voyer et al., 1995). The dramatic variation in murder rate in different countries suggests there is a strong cultural influence on aggression; for example, the rate is 2.4 murders per million people per year in Iceland, 86 in the U.S., and 460 in the Philippines (Daly & Wilson, 1988; Triandis, 1994). However, there is at least as much evidence that these sex differences have some biological basis. Because the difference in mathematical performance in particular has decreased over the years (Hyde, 1996) and no biological basis has been established for the difference that remains, I will limit the discussion to verbal and spatial abilities and aggression.

Levy (1969) hypothesized that women outperform men on some verbal tests because they are able to use both hemispheres of the brain in solving verbal problems, rather than mostly the left hemisphere. This is controversial, but it is consistent with the finding that the posterior part of the corpus callosum (the *splenium*) is larger in females, which would favor more communication between the hemispheres (de Lacoste-Utamsing & Holloway, 1982; Hines & Green, 1991). One study found that verbal ability among women is related to the size of their splenium (Hines, Sloan, Lawrence, Lipcamon, & Chiu, 1988). The size difference between males and females is probably not due to experience, because it is present by the 26th week after conception (de Lacoste, Holloway, & Woodward, 1986). Estrogen probably also contributes to women's verbal superiority; men who take estrogen treatments because they identify sexually as females *(transsexuals)* score higher on a test of verbal learning than similar men who do not take estrogen (Miles, Green, Sanders, & Hines, 1998).

Testosterone, on the other hand, appears to be important for spatial ability. Males who produce low amounts of testosterone during the developmental years are impaired later in spatial ability (Hier & Crowley, 1982); testosterone

replacement in older men improves their spatial functioning (Janowsky, Oviatt, & Orwoll, 1994). Another possible reason for higher spatial ability in males is a gene or genes on the X chromosome. The X chromosome is implicated because it comes exclusively from the mother, and boys' spatial ability is correlated more with their mothers' spatial ability than with their fathers' (Bock & Kolakowski, 1973).

The sex difference in aggression is rather small and situation-specific in the laboratory, but it becomes magnified in real life (Hyde, 1986). For example, men kill 30 times as often as women do (Daly & Wilson, 1988). One study found that boys and girls are punished equally for fighting (Maccoby & Jacklin, 1980), so the difference may not be due to a greater acceptance of male aggression by society. Aggression in males is partly inheritable; genetic effects account for about half of the variance in aggression, and aggression is moderately correlated in identical twins even when they are reared apart (Rushton, Fulker, Neale, Nias, & Eysenck, 1986; Tellegen et al., 1988). Testosterone levels are higher in aggressive males, but it is not clear that the higher testosterone level causes the increased aggression; winning a sports competition can increase testosterone and losing decreases it (Archer, 1991). The source of aggression is a complex subject, and we will deal with it more thoroughly in the next chapter.

The value in studying these differences is not to label one sex as smarter or more aggressive, but to understand what contributes to the characteristics. Keep in mind that aside from physical strength and possibly aggressiveness, the differences are small and do not justify discrimination in society or in the workplace. We are far more alike than we are different; this is a reason to use the term *other sex* instead of *opposite sex*. There are real differences, though, and an understanding of their origins could help us enhance intellectual development or reduce violence. From a scientific perspective, that knowledge also helps us understand how the brain develops, an issue that we will continue to pursue in the next two sections.

What are the origins of male-female differences in verbal and spatial abilities?

 CONCEPT CHECK

■ *What are the arguments for environmental origins and for biological origins of male-female differences in cognitive abilities and behaviors?*

SEXUAL ANOMALIES

John Money (Money & Ehrhardt, 1972) concluded that a child's gender identity is formed in the first few years of life by a combination of rearing practices and genital appearance. Other researchers believe that hormones and chromosomes are better predictors of gender outcomes. We cannot manipulate human development to determine what makes a person male or female, so we look to individuals on whom nature has performed "natural experiments." These lack the control of true experiments, but they can still be informative. Our earlier discussion of the effects of XY and XX chromosomes was the simple version of the sex-determination story; in reality, development sometimes takes an unexpected turn. As you will soon see, the resulting sexual anomalies challenge our definition of what is male and what is female, but they also tell us a great deal about the influence of biology on gender.

Male Pseudohermaphrodites

What are the characteristics of the various pseudohermaphrodites? What are the causes?

1

The Jill who became Jack at the beginning of the chapter is called a male pseudohermaphrodite. A hermaphrodite is a person or animal with the sexual characteristics of both sexes. A very few humans can be referred to as true hermaphrodites because they have both ovarian and testicular tissue, either as separate gonads or combined as ovotestes (Morris, 1953). They are not, however, capable of functioning sexually as both male and female like some simpler animals do. The more common *pseudohermaphrodites* **have ambiguous internal and external organs, but their gonads are consistent with their chromosomes.** Pseudohermaphroditism can result from a variety of causes. The reason for Jill's unusual development was a deficiency in an enzyme (17β-hydroxysteroid) that converts testosterone into dihydrotestosterone, which masculinizes the external genitalia before birth. The large surge of testosterone at puberty enabled her body to partially carry out that process.

A similar anomaly is produced by a deficiency in another enzyme, 5α-reductase; the defect is genetic and is most likely to occur when there is frequent intermarriage among relatives. Of 18 such individuals in the Dominican Republic who were reared unambiguously as girls, all but one made the transition to a male gender identity after puberty, and 15 were living or had lived with women (Imperato-McGinley, Peterson, Gautier, & Sturla, 1979). The men said they realized they were different from girls and began questioning their sex between the ages of 7 and 12. Though their transition argues for the influence of genes and hormones on gender identity, such a conclusion must be tentative because the individuals had a great deal to gain from the switch in a society that puts a high premium on maleness.

Look at the woman in Figure 6.11. She probably does not look unusual to you. She has narrow shoulders and broad hips like other women, and she has large breasts and normal-appearing external genitalia. But she was born with XY chromosomes and two testes. *Androgen insensitivity syndrome (AI)*, **a form of male pseudohermaphroditism, is caused by a mutation of the gene responsible for producing androgen receptors.** Ovary development is suppressed by Müllerian inhibiting hormone but, because the individual is unaffected by androgens, the testes do not descend and the external genitals develop as more or less feminine. There is a vagina, but it ends in a blind pouch. If the genitals are mostly feminine the child is reared as a girl, and at puberty her body is further feminized by estrogen released by the testes and adrenal glands. The condition may not be recognized until menstruation fails to occur at puberty, or when unsuccessful attempts to become pregnant lead to a more complete medical examination. In the absence of testosterone's influence, AI individuals tend to have well-developed breasts and a flawless complexion. Because these characteristics are often combined with long, slender legs, androgen-insensitive males repeatedly turn up among female fashion models (Diamond, 1992).

Female Pseudohermaphrodites

A female fetus may be partially masculinized by excess androgens during fetal development, resulting in a female pseudohermaphrodite. The internal organs are female, because no Müllerian inhibiting hormone is released, but the external genitals are virilized to some extent; that is, they have some degree of masculine appearance. In extreme cases the clitoris is as large as a newborn male's penis and the external labia are partially or completely fused to give the appearance of an empty scrotum. Figure 6.12 shows an example of this more complete masculinization. One cause of female pseudohermaphroditism is *congenital adrenal hyperplasia (CAH)*, **which results from an enzyme defect that causes the individual's adrenal glands to produce large amounts of androgens during fetal development and after birth until the problem is treated.** Hormone levels can be normalized by administering corticosteroids, and the parents may choose reconstructive surgery to reduce the size of the clitoris and eliminate labial fusion, giving the genitals a more feminine appearance. If masculinization is more pronounced, the parents may decide to rear the child as a boy; in that case the surgeons usually finish closing the labia and insert artificial testes in the scrotum to enhance the masculine appearance. We will see shortly that female pseudohermaphroditism can also be produced by exposure to synthetic hormones, as it was in the child in Figure 6.12. (See "Dual-Sex Rodents" on page 172 for a report of environmental pollution that may have produced pseudohermaphrodites among wild rodents.)

Obviously, sex cannot always be neatly divided between male and female. Some experts

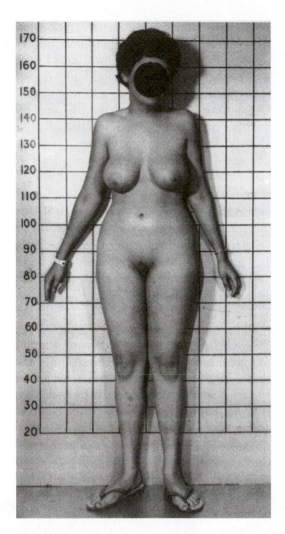

Figure 6.11
An XY male with androgen insensitivity
Source: Money & Ehrhardt, 1972.

believe that two categories are not sufficient to describe the variations in masculinity and femininity. Anne Fausto-Sterling (1993) advocates at least five sexual categories; the ones between male and female are often referred to as *intersexes*. It would be easy to get caught up in the unusual physical characteristics of these individuals and to be distracted from our question: What makes a person male or female? This question is as much about gender behavior as it is about sex.

2

Figure 6.12
Masculinized genitals of a baby girl
During pregnancy the mother took an antimiscarriage drug that had effects similar to testosterone.
Source: Money & Ehrhardt, 1972.

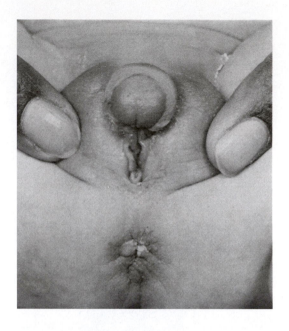

cognitive abilities in humans as well? If so, then we would expect the behavior and abilities of individuals with sexual anomalies, who have experienced an excess or a deficit of androgens during prenatal development, to be at odds with their chromosomal sex.

The evidence accumulated so far strongly suggests that man is no exception with regard to the influence of sex steroids on the developing brain and subsequent behavior . . .

—Anke Ehrhardt and Heino Meyer-Bahlburg

Sex Anomalies and the Brain

As mentioned earlier, reversing the sex hormone balance during prenatal development changes the brain and later behavior in nonhuman animals. Is it possible that masculinization and feminization of the developing brain accounts for sex differences in behavior and

To some extent both gender role behavior and gender identity are affected. CAH women have been described as tomboyish in childhood (Berenbaum & Hines, 1992; Hines, 1982; Money & Ehrhardt, 1972), more oriented to career than marriage (which was atypical at the time), and less satisfied with the female role

IN THE NEWS

Dual-Sex Rodents Examined

Something strange is happening to the rodents at a wildlife refuge near Fresno, California. One-third of the mice and voles trapped there by biologist Gary Santolo were described as pseudohermaphroditic. "They appear to be males from the outside, and lack a vagina, but have a fully developed set of female organs internally." The area had been used as a catch basin for agricultural runoff until an investigation revealed in 1985 that selenium, a byproduct of agricultural runoff, was killing or deforming thousands of birds. The area was closed and biologists have

been monitoring animals there every year. In 1995 just 3% of trapped animals showed intersex characteristics.

It is not clear whether the unusual rodents are the result of the earlier contamination or something entirely new. When asked whether there was any hazard for humans, Santolo said, "That's always a concern whenever we detect something like this in another mammal, but as of now, I don't even want to speculate on that, but it certainly warrants investigation."

—The Fresno Bee, *June 12, 1999*

compared to other women (reviewed in Hines, 1982). Twenty-two percent of a group of surgically corrected CAH women had erotic contact with other women, compared to 10% of female controls (Money, Schwartz, & Lewis, 1984). Androgen-insensitive males are typically feminine in behavior, have a strong childbearing urge, and are decidedly female in their sexual orientation (Hines, 1982; Money et al., 1984; Morris, 1953).

The pattern of cognitive abilities is also what we would expect if gender identity is the result of prenatal effects on the brain. Androgen-insensitive males are like females in that their verbal ability is higher than their spatial performance, and their spatial performance is lower than that of other males (Imperato-McGinley, Pichardo, Gautier, Voyer, & Bryden, 1991; Masica, Money, Ehrhardt, & Lewis, 1969). CAH women, like men, show higher spatial ability than other women (Resnick, Berenbaum, Gottesman, & Bouchard, 1986).

Some critics claim that humans are sexually neutral at birth and that sexual identity and behavior are learned. They attribute the cognitive and behavioral effects we have just seen to feminine or ambiguous rearing in response to the child's genital appearance. (You may be beginning to understand the deficiencies of natural experiments.) However, some of the findings are difficult to explain from an environmental perspective. For example, the AI males performed *more poorly* on spatial tests than their unaffected sisters and female controls (Imperato-McGinley et al., 1991). This result can be explained by a total insensitivity to androgens, but not by "feminine rearing."

Another problem for the environmental position is that behavior is sometimes masculinized even when the genitals are unaffected. During the 1950s and 1960s millions of pregnant women were given synthetic hormones to prevent miscarriage, and some of the hormones masculinized the genitals of a percentage of the female offspring. One of them, *diethylstilbesterol (DES)*, **does not masculinize genitals,** **but does masculinize the sexually dimorphic nucleus in female rats** (see Figure 6.4c), and so it received special interest. If the behavior of women exposed prenatally to DES was masculinized, it could not be because of genital appearance and ambiguous rearing. DES women reported more homosexual contacts and more homosexual fantasies and dreams than did controls. On a self-report scale, 17% scored equally or more homosexual than heterosexual; no women in the control group scored that high (Ehrhardt et al., 1985). Women exposed to a similar hormone that did not masculinize the genitals had higher aggressive responses on a questionnaire than their unexposed sisters (Reinisch, 1981). These results support the hypothesis that gender-specific behaviors and cognitive abilities result from masculinization or feminization of the brain.

Ablatio Penis: A Natural Experiment

The "neutral-at-birth" theorists claim that individuals reared in opposition to their chromosomal sex generally accept their sex of rearing, and that this demonstrates that rearing has more effect on gender role behavior than chromosomes or hormones (studies reviewed in Diamond, 1965). Diamond, who advocates a "sexuality-at-birth" hypothesis, argues that the reason individuals with ambiguous genitals accept their assigned gender is that sex of rearing is usually decided by whether the genital appearance is predominantly masculine or feminine, which in turn reflects the prenatal hormone environment. According to Diamond, there is no case in the literature where an unambiguously male or female individual was successfully reared in opposition to the biological sex. However, he and others (Money, Devore, & Norman, 1986) have described several instances in which individuals assigned as one sex successfully shifted to their chromosomal and gonadal sex in later years, long after Money's window for forming gender identity (the first few years of life) supposedly had closed.

How is the behavior of pseudohermaphrodites different?

. . . gender identity is sufficiently incompletely differentiated at birth as to permit successful assignment of a genetic male as a girl.

—John Money

An extensive search of the literature reveals no case where a male or female without some sort of biological abnormality . . . accepted an imposed gender role opposite to that of his or her phenotype.

—Milton Diamond

In 1967 an 8-month-old boy became the most famous example of resistance to sexual reassignment when the surgeon using electrocautery to perform a circumcision turned the voltage too high and destroyed the boy's penis. At that time it was not possible to fashion a satisfactory replacement. So, after months of consultation and agonizing, Bruce's parents decided to let surgeons transform his genitals to feminine ones. The neutral-at-birth view was widely accepted then, and psychologist John Money counseled the parents that they could expect their son to adopt a female gender identity (Diamond & Sigmundson, 1997). Bruce would be renamed Brenda, and "she" would be reared as a girl. This case study is as good an example of a "natural experiment" as we will find for two reasons: the child was normal before the accident and he happened to have an identical twin who served as a control.

Over the next several years Money (1968; Money & Ehrhardt, 1972) reported that Brenda was growing up feminine, enjoying her dresses and hairdos and choosing to help her mother in the house while her "typical boy" brother played outside. But developmental progress was not nearly as smooth as Money thought (Diamond & Sigmundson, 1997). Brenda was in fact a tomboy who played rough-and-tumble sports and fought, and preferred her brother's toys and trucks over her dolls. She looked feminine but her movements betrayed her, and her classmates called her "caveman." When the girls barred her from the restroom because she often urinated in a standing position, she went to the boys' restroom instead. She had private doubts about her sex beginning in the second grade, and by the age of 11 had decided she was a boy. At age 14 she decided to switch to living as a male. Only then did Brenda's father tell her the story of her sexual transition in infancy. Then, said Brenda, "everything clicked. For the first time things made sense and I understood who and what I was" (p. 300).

Brenda changed her name to David and requested treatment with testosterone, removal of the breasts that had developed under estrogen treatment, and construction of a penis. The child who was isolated and teased as a girl was accepted and popular as a boy, and he attracted girlfriends. At age 25 he married and adopted his wife's three children. Although he is limited in sexual performance, he and his wife engage in sexual play and occasional intercourse.

Ablatio penis ("removed penis") during infancy is rare, and we should be cautious about drawing conclusions from a single case. In another instance in which a boy was reared as a girl, the individual reported no uncertainty about her feminine identity (Bradley, Oliver, Chernick, & Zucker, 1998). The difference may be that gender reassignment was made at 7 months, 10 months earlier than with Bruce/Brenda, and because the mother was less ambivalent about the switch in identity. However, in spite of her commitment to a female gender identity, the individual also reported being a tomboy during childhood, and

Sex at the Olympics

The knowledge sex researchers have accumulated about what makes us male or female is gaining an unlikely relevance—in the field of sports.

In 1966 the International Amateur Athletic Federation (IAAF), which governs track and field competitions, introduced sex tests for female athletes; it was motivated by fears that males were posing as females and competing unfairly in women's events. Testing for sex is a fairly simple procedure; it involves scraping a few cells from the inside of the person's cheek to determine whether the sex chromosomes are XX or XY. The International Olympic Committee (IOC) followed suit in 1968, concerned by rumors that some Eastern European countries were sending men to the women's competitions. Then, when the tennis player Richard Raskin underwent a sex change operation and became Renee Richards (see the photo), organizers of some tennis competitions also instituted chromosome testing to bar Richards from competing with women.

There is only one confirmed case of a man attempting to compete in women's Olympic events: a German athlete in 1936, who was beaten by three women (Grady, 1992). A larger number of athletes have been excluded from competition because they possessed a Y chromosome. How many is uncertain, because the IOC does not publish its findings for reasons of confidentiality, but the number has been estimated at one out of every 500 female competitors (Ferguson-Smith & Ferris, 1991).

As you have probably already concluded, chromosome testing of female athletes is based on an oversimplified view of what determines a person's sex and what constitutes male advantage. Richards, for instance, complained that he was actually at a disadvantage competing against women because he no longer had the benefit of testosterone but still carried a man's frame on the court (Grady, 1992). Androgen-insensitive individuals with XY chromosomes also receive no benefit from testosterone, but still fail the test. In 1985, the Olympic contender Maria Patiño learned for the first time in a car on the way to her event that she had XY chromosomes. She was barred from the competition. Back home in Spain she lost her scholarship, her records and titles, her home in the national athletic residence, her boyfriend, and many of her friends. Three years later she won an appeal before the IOC because, as the geneticist Albert de la Chapelle pointed out in her defense, her chromosomal irregularity conferred no physical advantage (Carlson, 1991).

The IAAF abandoned chromosome verification in 1991 and now relies on physical examinations, which were already required of both male and female athletes. The IOC continued with chromosome tests, with the explanation that physical inspection is unacceptable to many cultures. Some critics argue that a physical examination is a better choice than chromosome testing. It would detect men masquerading as women (if that actually happens), and would bar XX females who have been virilized by androgens and might have a competitive advantage.

Renee Richards
Richards claimed to be at a disadvantage competing against women.

as an adult she chose an occupation that is traditionally masculine. At age 26 her sexual activity was evenly divided between men and women, and her sexual fantasies were predominantly about women.

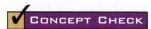

■ *How do the sexual anomalies require you to rethink the meaning of male and female?*

■ *What reasons can you give for thinking that the brains of people with sexual anomalies have been masculinized or feminized contrary to their chromosomal sex?*

SEXUAL ORIENTATION

Sex researchers spend a great deal of time arguing about why people are attracted to members of the other sex. At the same time they are asking why most people are heterosexual. The answer to that question may seem obvious, but the fact that a behavior is nearly universal and widely accepted does not mean that it requires no explanation. People who are attracted to members of their own sex may be able to tell us not only about homosexuality but about the origins of heterosexuality as well.

A word about terminology: **Homosexual men are often referred to as** *gay,* **and homosexual women are often called** *lesbians.* **The term for those who are not exclusively homosexual or heterosexual is** *bisexual.* The large majority of nonheterosexuals are exclusively homosexual, although bisexuality is more common among lesbians than among gays (Pillard & Bailey, 1998). In this chapter the word *homosexual* is used as a general term, and the specific terms are used when needed to designate a particular group. Also, the term *homosexuality* is ordinarily used to refer to *regular* activity or *continuing* preference. As Ellis and Ames (1987) point out, homosexual experiences are fairly common,

especially in adolescence and in the absence of heterosexual opportunities, and these experiences do not make a person homosexual any more than occasional heterosexual activity makes a person heterosexual.

How many people are homosexual is uncertain. In an unusually large survey of 3,432 American men and women, 9% of men and a little over 4% of women said they had had homosexual sex at least once since puberty (Michael, Gagnon, Laumann, & Kolata, 1994). About 2.8% of men and 1.4% of women thought of themselves as homosexual or bisexual. Other studies in the U.S. and abroad suggest that the percentages may be lower (Billy, Tanfer, Grady, & Klepinger, 1993).

Research does not support the belief that gay men are necessarily feminine and lesbians are masculine; only about 44% of gays and 54% of lesbians fit those descriptions (Bell, Weinberg, & Hammersmith, 1981). Even then they usually identify with their biological sex, so you should not confuse sexual orientation with gender identity. Sexual identity reversal is much rarer than homosexuality; estimates range between one and five per thousand people (Collaer & Hines, 1995). Also, individuals with reversed sexual identity are not necessarily homosexual; the sexual orientation of *transsexuals*—**individuals who dress and live as the other sex and often seek surgery to change their sexual appearance**—sometimes is consistent with their biological sex instead of their chosen sex (Dörner, 1988). So gender role, gender identity, and sexual orientation are somewhat independent of each other, and probably have different developmental origins.

It is not clear what causes homosexuality. That means we do not know how to explain heterosexuality either. If there were not evidence for biological influences on sexual orientation, the topic would not appear in this chapter. But social influences are commonly believed to be more important, so we will consider this position first.

The Social Influence Hypothesis

It has been argued that homosexuality arises from parental influences or is caused by early sexual experiences. Bell and his colleagues (1981) expected to confirm these influences when they studied 979 gay and 477 heterosexual men. But they found no support for frequently hypothesized environmental influences, such as seduction by an older male or a dominant mother and a weak father.

Several developmental experiences do seem to differentiate homosexuals from heterosexuals, and these have been considered evidence for a social learning hypothesis (Van Wyk & Geist, 1984). But these experiences—such as spending more time with other-sex playmates in childhood, learning to masturbate by being masturbated by a member of the same sex, and homosexual contact by age 18—can just as easily be interpreted as reflecting an early predisposition to homosexuality. In fact, Bell and associates (1981) concluded that "adult homosexuality . . . [is] just *a continuation of the earlier homosexual feelings and behaviors from which it can be so successfully predicted*" (p. 186; authors' italics). However, they did find more evidence for an influence of learning on bisexuality than on exclusive homosexuality. This suggests that there might be a biological influence that varies in degree, with experience making the final decision in the individuals with weaker predispositions for homosexuality.

The Biological Hypothesis

Seventy percent of homosexuals remember feeling "different" as early as 4 or 5 years of age (Bell et al., 1981; Savin-Williams, 1996). It is difficult to evaluate these reports because yesterday's memories are easily distorted in light of today's circumstances, and because we do not know how frequently heterosexuals felt the same way. However, during development homosexuals do show a high rate of *gender nonconformity*— a tendency to engage in activities usually preferred by the other sex, and an atypical preference for other-sex playmates and companions while growing up (Bell et al., 1981). If we are to entertain a biological hypothesis of sexual orientation, though, we must come up with some reasonable explanation for how it is formed and how it is altered. There are three biological approaches to the question; they are *genetic*, *hormonal*, and *neural*.

Genetic Influence

Genetic studies provide the most documented and most consistent evidence for a biological basis for sexual orientation. Homosexuality is two to seven times higher among the siblings of homosexuals than it is in the population (Bailey & Bell, 1993; Bailey & Benishay, 1993; Hamer, Hu, Magnuson, Hu, & Pattatucci, 1993). Identical twins are more concordant for homosexuality than fraternal twins or non-twin siblings (Figure 6.13) (Bailey & Pillard, 1991; Bailey, Pillard, Neale, & Agyei, 1993; Whitman, Diamond, & Martin, 1993), and heritability estimates range from 31–74%, depending on the statistical assumptions made (Bailey & Pillard, 1991). Because the environment might be somewhat more similar for identical than for fraternal twins, the ideal study would include twins reared apart as well as together; but these individuals are rare and the small number of studies have been based on too few subjects to permit conclusions.

Hamer and associates (1993) found that gay men had more gay relatives on the mother's side of the family than on the father's side. Because the mother contributes only X chromosomes to her sons, Hamer looked there for a gene for homosexuality. To increase the chances of locating a maternally transmitted gene, he confined his search to the 40 pairs of gay brothers who had gay relatives on the mother's side of the family. In 64% of the pairs, the brothers shared the same genetic material at one end of the X chromosome (Figure 6.14); presumably, that material would contain one or more genes for homosexuality. A second study by Hamer's team supported the result (Hu et al., 1995). An investigation by other

What is the evidence for a biological basis for homosexuality?

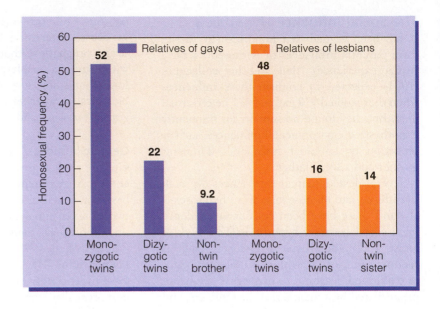

Figure 6.13
Concordance in relatives of homosexuals
Source: Based on data from Bailey & Pillard, 1991, and Bailey, Pillard, Neale, & Agyei, 1993.

researchers failed to find this linkage (Rice, Anderson, Risch, & Ebers, 1999), but Hamer (1999) pointed out that the researchers did not focus on gays with gay maternal relatives.

The issue is not whether heredity influences homosexuality, but whether Hamer has located one of the genes. False alarms are common in genetic research, and only time will tell whether these results will hold up. Even if they do, the gene or genes for homosexuality within that segment of DNA would not alone account for male homosexuality, because over a third of the pairs of gay brothers were discordant for the gene.

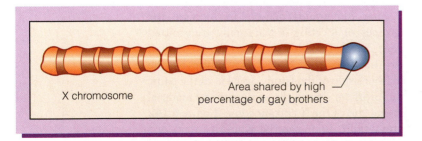

Figure 6.14
Location of a possible gay gene
The genetic material at the end of the X chromosome was the same in a high percentage of gay brothers.

Hormonal Influence

If heredity influences sexual orientation, it must do so through some physiological mechanism. The most obvious possibility is the sex hormones. Studies that have compared hormonal levels in homosexuals and heterosexuals have not supported the commonsense hypothesis that homosexuals have a deficit or an excess of sex hormones (Gartrell, 1982; Meyer-Bahlburg, 1984). Years before, though, doctors tried to reverse male homosexuality by administering testosterone; the treatment did not affect sexual preference, but it frequently did increase the level of homosexual activity (for references, see Kinsey, Pomeroy, Martin, & Gebhard, 1953).

So if there are any hormonal influences in homosexuality, they are likely to have occurred prenatally, and we turn again to animals for clues. Early hormonal manipulation results in same-sex preference later in life in rats, hamsters, ferrets, pigs, and zebra finches (for references, see LeVay, 1996). However, some critics believe this result has little meaning; they claim that homosexual behavior occurs spontaneously in animals only in the absence of members of the other sex and does not represent a shift in sexual orientation.

However, about 10% of male sheep prefer other males as sex partners, and some form pair bonds in which they take turns mounting and copulating anally with each other (Perkins & Fitzgerald, 1992). A few female gulls observed on Santa Barbara Island off the coast of California form "lesbian" pairs. They court each other and the courting ritual occasionally ends in attempted copulation. They take turns sitting on their nest; if some of the eggs hatch because they were fertilized during an "unfaithful" interlude with a male, the two females share parenting like male-female pairs do (Hunt & Hunt, 1977; Hunt, Newman, Warner, Wingfield, & Kaiwi, 1984). The gulls' behavior could be a response to a shortage of males, but it differs from the opportunistic homosexuality usually seen when mates are unavailable, in that the majority stay paired for more than one season.

There is little evidence for prenatal hormone imbalances in homosexual humans, possibly because it is very difficult to determine a human's prenatal hormone environment. The case is stronger for structural and functional differences in the brain—which, in nonhuman animals at least, are influenced by prenatal and early postnatal hormones.

Brain Structures

Studies have identified three brain structures that might differ in size between gay males and heterosexuals. Simon LeVay (1991) found the *third interstitial nucleus of the anterior hypothalamus (INAH 3)* to be half the size in gay men and heterosexual women as in heterosexual men (Figure 6.15; you can locate the anterior hypothalamus in Figure 5.2). In another study, the *suprachiasmatic nucleus (SCN)* was larger in gay men than in heterosexual men and contained almost twice as many cells that secrete the hormone vasopressin (Swaab & Hofman, 1990). Finally, the *anterior commissure* was larger in gay men and heterosexual women than in heterosexual men (see Figure 5.2) (Allen & Gorski, 1992).

The most powerful sex organ is between the ears, not between the legs.

—Milton Diamond

The implication of these differences is unclear. Although INAH 3 is in an area of the brain that is involved in sexual activity in animals, its role in humans is unknown. The SCN regulates the reproductive cycle in female rats and controls daily cycles in rats and humans. (The SCN is not shown in Figure 5.2, but it lies just above the optic chiasm.) When male rats were treated during the prenatal period and for the first few days after birth with a chemical that blocks the effects of testosterone, the number of vasopressin-secreting cells increased in their SCNs (Swaab, Slob, Houtsmuller, Brand, & Zhou, 1995). Given a

Which brain structures are different in male homosexuals?

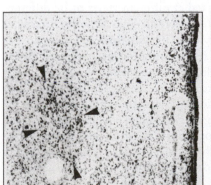 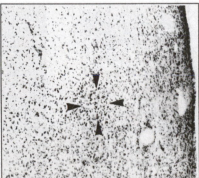

Figure 6.15
INAH 3 in a heterosexual man (left) and a homosexual man (right)

Reprinted with permission from S. LeVay, "A difference in hypothalamic structure between heterosexual and homosexual men." *Science*, 253, 1034–1047. Copyright 1991, American Association for the Advancement of Science.

Figure 6.16
Spatial and verbal performance of heterosexuals and homosexuals
Reprinted from *Brain and Cognition*, Vol 41, N. Neave et al., "Sex differences in cognition: The role of testosterone and sexual orientation," p. 245–262. Copyright © 1999, with permission from Elsevier Science.

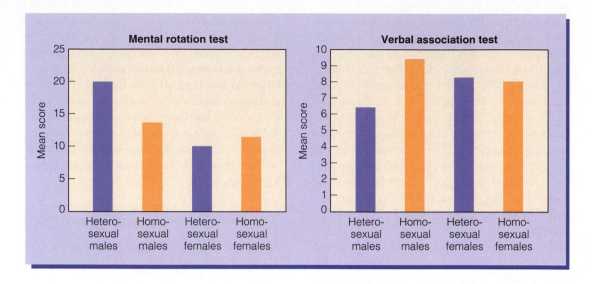

choice between an estrous female and a sexually active male, they spent one-third of their time with the male, with whom they showed lordosis and accepted mounting.

Recall that the anterior commissure is one of the structures connecting the two cerebral hemispheres, and that an enlarged splenium is associated with female superiority in verbal ability. Gay men, like heterosexual women, score lower on spatial tasks and higher on verbal tasks than heterosexual men (Figure 6.16) (McCormick & Witelson, 1991; Neave, Menaged, & Weightman, 1999; Wegesin, 1998).

One more structural difference is worth noting, though it does not differentiate homosexuals from heterosexuals. Earlier you learned that sexual orientation and sexual identity are not necessarily related. Now it appears that transsexuals' gender-shifting may be related to a half-millimeter-diameter structure in the hypothalamus. The bed nucleus of the stria terminalis, which receives input from the amygdala and sends output to the preoptic nucleus, plays a role in the sexual behavior of male rats. **The central subdivision, or *central bed nucleus of the stria terminalis (BSTc)*,** is smaller in women than in men. In a study of

transsexuals the BSTc was smaller in male-to-female transsexuals than in other men, and similar to the size in women; in the one female-to-male transsexual, it was male-sized (Kruijver et al., 2000) (Figure 6.17). However, BSTc size was *not* related to whether the transsexuals were homosexual or heterosexual. Hormonal manipulation at the time of birth affects BST size in rats, so the researchers suggested that the male transsexuals' brains were feminized by a hormone imbalance during prenatal development. How the BSTc might influence gender identity is not clear.

It may seem strange that feminization could alter gender identification without simultaneously affecting sexual preference. However, this result is tenable if different structures are masculinized at different times or by different levels of testosterone. This hypothesis receives credibility from the fact that even masculinization and feminization occur at slightly different developmental periods. As a result, it is possible to produce an animal that shows both male-typical and female-typical behaviors by providing testosterone during the critical period for masculinization and removing it during the critical period for feminization (Collaer & Hines, 1995).

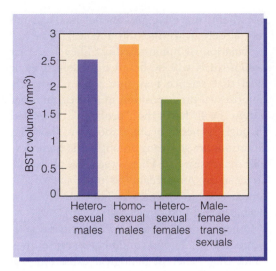

Figure 6.17
Size of the BSTc in transsexuals
Source: Zhou, Hofman, Gooren, & Swaab, 1995. Reprinted by permission of *Nature*, copyright 1995.

But be aware that some of these findings are based on a single study. Even if the differences do turn out to be reliable, they do not provide a clear picture of *how* brain structures contribute to sexual orientation. We are hampered in this research by the difficulties of studying small structures in the living human brain, and by our reliance on brains of deceased homosexuals who are typically older or who had acquired immune deficiency syndrome (AIDS). As imaging techniques improve we will be able to study the brains of younger, healthy, living individuals in whom these confounding factors will be minimized.

The Challenge of Female Homosexuality

Notice that we have been talking almost exclusively about gay men. There is considerably less research on the biological and behavioral characteristics of lesbians, and what there is gives us little to go on. Research does not indicate that lesbians have unusual levels of testosterone or estrogen (Dancey, 1990). With the exception of studies of CAH and DES women there is little evidence that lesbians' brains have been masculinized during prenatal development. Further,

lesbians perform similarly to heterosexual females on verbal and spatial tests (see Figure 6.16 again) (Neave et al., 1999; Wegesin, 1998).

However, the fact that the concordance for homosexuality is about as high for females as it is among males encourages us to continue looking for a biological basis for lesbianism. Two physical characteristics have been found that do distinguish lesbians from heterosexuals, though they seem trivial, at least initially. In women, the index finger tends to be about the same length as the ring finger, but in men the ring finger usually is longer. The index-to-ring-finger ratios of lesbians are indistinguishable from those of heterosexual men (Williams et al., 2000). The second difference involves a peculiar, faint sound given off by the inner ear when it is stimulated, called *click-evoked otoacoustic emissions.* The response is weaker in lesbians and men (both heterosexual and gay) than in heterosexual women (McFadden & Pasanen, 1998). The significance of these two differences is that both of the characteristics are influenced by testosterone levels during prenatal development.

Could prenatal testosterone masculinize these two characteristics along with one or more brain structures to alter female sexual orientation, and leave spatial and verbal abilities unaffected? As with transsexuals, this does seem possible if masculinization of the cognitive abilities occurs at a different developmental time or requires a higher level of testosterone. However, this is pure speculation and it is far too early to be drawing any conclusions; we obviously need more research on sexual orientation in females.

Social Implications of the Biological Model

As is often the case, the research we have been discussing has important social implications. If homosexuality is a choice, as argued by some in the gay community, then federal civil rights legislation does not apply to homosexuals, because protection for minorities depends on the criterion of unalterable or inborn characteristics

What do we know about female homosexuals?

Why is the search for a biological basis of homosexuality a social issue?

Figure 6.18
U.S. congressman Barney Frank and companion Herb Moses
Source: Photo by Burk Uzzle.

(Ernulf, Innala, & Whitam, 1989). If homosexuality is the result of experience, then presumably a homosexual who wanted to avoid the hassle and discrimination could change through psychotherapy, behavior modification, or religious conversion.

As for being gay, I never felt I had much choice . . . I am who I am. I have no idea why.

—Congressman Barney Frank

However, some homosexuals say that they have no choice. When Congressman Barney Frank of Massachusetts (Figure 6.18) was asked if he ever considered whether switching to the straight life was a possibility, he replied, "I wished it was. But it wasn't. I can't imagine that anybody believes that a 13-year-old in 1953 thinks, 'Boy, it would be really great to be a part of this minority that everybody hates and to have a really restricted life'" (Dreifus, 1996, p. 25).

About 75% of homosexuals believe homosexuality is inborn (Leland & Miller, 1998), but some in the gay community think that promoting this view is not in their best interest.

For them, the biological model is associated too closely with the old medical "disease" explanation of homosexuality. They fear that homosexuals will be branded as defective, or even that science may find ways to identify homosexual predisposition in fetuses, and that parents will have the "problem" corrected through genetic manipulation or abortion. Emotions are so strong among some homosexuals that researcher Dick Swaab was physically attacked in Amsterdam by members of the Dutch gay movement who felt threatened by his biological findings (Swaab, 1996).

Other gay and lesbian rights activists welcome the biological findings, because they think that belief in biological causation will increase public acceptance of homosexuality. Researcher Simon LeVay, who is himself gay, supports their view. Between a third and almost one-half of the public believe that homosexuality is something a person is born with (Ellis & Ames, 1987; Ernulf et al., 1989; Leland & Miller, 1998; Schmalz, 1993), and people who believe homosexuality is biologically based have more positive attitudes toward homosexuals than people who believe homosexuality is learned or chosen (Ernulf et al., 1989; Schmalz, 1993). This debate will not be settled any time soon, but most researchers believe that when we understand the origins of homosexuality and heterosexuality they will include a combination of heredity, hormones, neural structures, and experience (LeVay, 1996).

✔ **CONCEPT CHECK**

- *How has the social influence hypothesis fared in explaining homosexuality?*
- *What is the evidence that homosexuality has a biological cause?*
- *Organize your knowledge: make a table of the brain structures that differentiate heterosexual males, heterosexual females, and homosexuals; include how the structures differ between groups and, if known, their functions.*

In Perspective

The fact that sex is not motivated by any tissue deficit caused researchers to look to the brain for its basis. What they found was a model for all drives that focused on the brain, rather than on tissue that lacked nutrients or water or was too cold. This view changed the approach to biological motivation, and it also meant that gender identity and gender-specific behavior and abilities might all be understood from the perspective of the brain.

The fact that a person's sexual appearance, gender identity, and behavior are sometimes in contradiction with each other or with the chromosomes makes sex a somewhat ambiguous category. Research is helping us understand that many differences between the sexes are cultural inventions, and that many differences thought to be a matter of choice have biological origins. As a result, society is slowly coming around to the idea that distinctions should not be made on the basis of a person's sex, sexual appearance, or sexual orientation. These issues are emotional, as are the important questions behind them: Why are we attracted to a particular person? Why do we feel male or female? Why are we attracted to one sex and not the other? The emotion involved often obscures an important point: that the answers keep leading us back to the brain, which is why some have called the brain the primary sex organ.

Summary

Sex as a Form of Motivation

- Although there is no tissue deficit, sex involves arousal and satiation like other drives, as well as hormonal and neural control. Also like the other drives, sex can be thought of as a need of the brain.

- The key elements in human sexual behavior are testosterone, structures in the hypothalamus, and sensory stimuli such as certain physical characteristics and pheromones.

The Biological Determination of Sex

- Differentiation as a male or a female depends on the combination of X and Y chromosomes and the presence or absence of testosterone.

- Testosterone controls the differentiation not only of the genitals and internal sex organs, but of the brain.

Gender-Related Behavioral and Cognitive Differences

- Evidence indicates that girls exceed boys in verbal abilities and boys are more aggressive and score higher in visual-spatial and mathematical abilities.

- With the possible exception of mathematical ability, it appears that these differences are at least partly due to differences in the brain and in hormones.

Sexual Anomalies

- People with sexual anomalies challenge our idea of male and female.

- The cognitive abilities and altered sexual preferences of people with sexual anomalies suggest that the brain is masculinized or feminized before birth.

Sexual Orientation

- The idea that sexual orientation is entirely learned has not fared well.

- Evidence indicates that homosexuality, and thus heterosexuality, is influenced by genes, prenatal hormones, and brain structures.

- The biological view is controversial among homosexuals, but most believe it promotes greater acceptance, and research suggests this is the case.

For Further Thought

- Do you think the cognitive differences between males and females will completely disappear in time? If not, would they in an ideal society? Explain your reasons.
- Some believe parents should have their child's ambiguous genitals corrected early and others think it is better to see what gender identity the child develops. What do you think, and why?
- Do you think neuroscientists have made the case yet for a biological basis for homosexuality? Why or why not?

Testing Your Understanding

1. Compare sex to other biological drives.
2. Describe the processes that make a person male or female (limit your answer to typical development).
3. Discuss sex as a continuum of gradations between male and female rather than a male versus female dichotomy. Give examples to illustrate.
4. Identify any weak points in the evidence for a biological basis for homosexuality (ambiguous results, gaps in information, and so on) and indicate what research needs to be done to correct the weaknesses.

Select the one best answer:

1. The chapter opened with the story of a boy born with female genitals. At puberty he grew a penis, developed muscles, a deep voice, and a beard, and became more masculine in behavior. The changes at puberty were _____ effects.

   a. activating
   b. organizing
   c. activating and organizing
   d. none of these

2. Of the following, the best argument that sex is a drive like hunger and thirst is that:

   a. almost everyone is interested in sex.
   b. sexual motivation is so strong.
   c. sexual behavior involves arousal and satiation.
   d. sexual interest varies from one time to another.

3. There is evidence that pheromones affect _____ in humans.

   a. menstrual cycles
   b. sexual attraction
   c. the vomeronasal organ
   d. a and b
   e. a, b, and c

4. A likely result of the Coolidge effect is that an individual will:

   a. be monogamous.
   b. have more sex partners.
   c. prolong a sexual encounter.
   d. prefer attractive mates.

5. The part of the sexual response cycle that most resembles homeostasis is:

   a. excitement.   b. the plateau phase.
   c. orgasm.   d. resolution.

6. The increase in testosterone on nights that couples have intercourse is an example of:

   a. an organizing effect.
   b. an activating effect.
   c. cause.
   d. effect.

7. The sex difference in the size of the sexually dimorphic nucleus is due to:

   a. experience after birth.
   b. genes.
   c. sex hormone.
   d. both genes and experience.

8. The most prominent structure in the sexual behavior of female rats is the:

    a. MPOA.   b. SDN.
    c. ventromedial   d. medial amygdala.
       nucleus.

9. The chromosomal sex of a fetus is determined:

    a. by the sperm.
    b. by the egg.
    c. by a combination of effects from the two.
    d. in an unpredictable manner.

10. The main point of the discussion of cognitive and behavioral differences between the sexes was to:

    a. illustrate the importance of experience.
    b. make a case for masculinization and feminization of the brain.
    c. make the point that men and women are suited for different roles.
    d. explain why men usually are dominant over women.

11. The term that describes a person with XX chromosomes and masculine genitals is:

    a. homosexual.
    b. male pseudohermaphrodite.
    c. androgen insensitivity syndrome.
    d. female pseudohermaphrodite.

12. The best evidence that the *brains* of people with sexual anomalies have been masculinized or feminized contrary to their chromosomal sex is their:

    a. behavior and cognitive abilities.
    b. genital appearance.

    c. physical appearance
    d. adult hormone levels.

13. Testosterone injections in a gay man would most likely:

    a. have no effect.
    b. increase his sexual activity.
    c. make him temporarily bisexual.
    d. reverse his sexual preference briefly.

14. Evidence that lesbianism is biologically influenced is:

    a. there is a high concordance among identical twins.
    b. lesbians have a couple of distinctive physical features.
    c. a brain structure is larger in lesbians and men than in heterosexual women.
    d. both a and b.
    e. both b and c.

15. The BSTc is probably specific to gender identity, because:

    a. its size differs in transsexuals.
    b. damage causes gender confusion.
    c. stimulation in nonhumans enhances sex-specific behaviors.
    d. several other structures are responsible for homosexuality.

Answers: 1. **c** 2. **c** 3. **e** 4. **b** 5. **d** 6. **d** 7. **c** 8. **c** 9. **a** 10. **b** 11. **d** 12. **a** 13. **b** 14. **d** 15. **a**

 On the Web

1. **Patient Resources** in the form of two booklets on atypical sex differentiation and congenital adrenal hyperplasia that can be ordered, read online, or downloaded are available from the Johns Hopkins University School of Medicine at

    http://www.hopkinsmedicine.org/ pediatricendocrinology/patient.html

continued

2. The **Intersex Society of North America** provides information about intersexuality, ambiguous genitalia, and so on at

   http://www.isna.org/

3. **Answers to Your Questions About Sexual Orientation** are provided in a concise and to-the-point manner by the American Psychological Association at

   http://www.apa.org/pubinfo/answers.html

 For additional information about the topics covered in this chapter, please look at InfoTrac College Edition, at

http://www.infotrac-college.com/wadsworth

Try search terms you think up yourself, or use these: *gender nonconformity; pheromones; suprachiasmatic nucleus; testosterone.*

 On the CD-ROM: Exploring Biological Psychology

 Animation: Menstruation Cycle

Video: Development of Male and Female Internal Organs

 For Further Reading

Why Is Sex Fun? The Evolution of Human Sexuality by Jared Diamond (Basic Books, 1997) takes an evolutionary approach to answer questions like why humans have sex with no intention of procreating, and why the human penis is proportionately larger than in other animals.

The Sexual Brain by Simon LeVay (MIT Press, 1993) is a well-written and technically informative coverage of topics including the evolution of sex, sexual development, and the origins of sexual orientation.

Sexual Differentiation of the Human Brain by S. Marc Breedlove (*Annual Review of Psychology*, 1994, 45, 389–418) is a review of that topic, covering research with both humans and nonhumans.

Sex Differences in the Human Brain by Doreen Kimura (*Scientific American*, September 1992, 119–125) focuses on sex differences in abilities arising from prenatal organization of the brain by hormones.

In *Sexing the Body: Gender Politics and the Construction of Sexuality* by Anne Fausto-Sterling (Basic Books, 1999) and *Intersex in the Age of Ethics* by Alice Domurat Dreger (University Publishing Group, 1999) the authors argue for a more flexible view of sex and gender than our traditional either-or approach, including accepting gradations between male and female and allowing intersexed individuals to make their own gender selection.

As Nature Made Him: The Boy Who Was Raised as a Girl by John Colapinto (HarperCollins, 2000) tells the story of the boy whose penis was damaged during circumcision. Described by reviewers as "riveting," with a touching description of his suffering and of his parents' and brother's support of him.

The Biological Evidence Challenged by William Byne (*Scientific American*, May 1994, 50–55) argues sexual orientation does not have a biological basis.

Key Terms

Emotion and Health

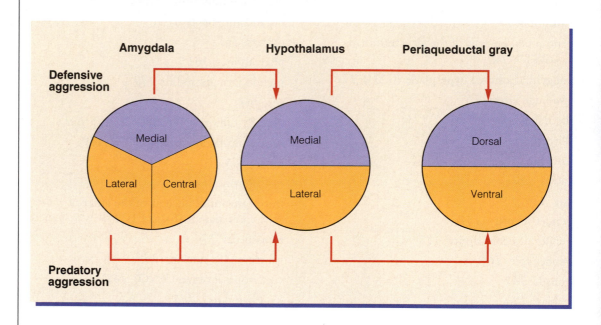

In this chapter you will learn:

- How the brain and the rest of the body participate in emotion.
- How stress affects health and immune functioning.
- Why pain is an emotion as well as a sensation.
- The role of hormones, brain structures, and heredity in aggression.

I had before my eyes the coolest, least emotional, [most] intelligent human being one might imagine, and yet his practical reason was so impaired that it produced . . . a perpetual violation of what would be considered socially appropriate and personally advantageous.

—Antonio Damasio

When Jane was 15 months old she was run over by a vehicle. The injuries seemed minor and she appeared to recover fully within days of the accident. By the age of 3, however, her parents noticed that she was largely unresponsive to verbal or physical punishment. Her behavior became progressively disruptive so that by the age of 14 she had to be placed in the first of several treatment facilities. Her intelligence was normal, but she often failed to complete school assignments. She was verbally and physically abusive to others, she stole from her family and shoplifted frequently, and she engaged in early and risky sexual behavior that resulted in pregnancy at the age of 18. She showed little if any guilt or remorse; empathy was also absent, which made her dangerously insensitive to her infant's needs. Because her behavior put her at physical and financial risk, she became entirely dependent on her family and social agencies for financial support and management of her personal affairs.

Magnetic resonance imaging revealed there was damage to Jane's *prefrontal cortex, which is necessary for making judgments about behavior and its consequences.* People who sustain damage to this area later in life understand moral and social rules but are unable to apply them in their daily lives. However, if the damage occurs early in life it impairs the person's ability to learn from the consequences of their behavior (Anderson, Bechara, Damasio, Tranel, & Damasio, 1999); when presented with hypothetical situations, Jane could not verbalize moral and social principles that others learn readily. In the laboratory, she showed normal skin conductance responses to a loud sound. *Skin conductance response (SCR) is a measure of sweat gland activation and thus sympathetic nervous system activity,* so her reactions suggest that her emotional responsiveness was not impaired. Jane was also tested with the "gambling task." The individual chooses cards from four stacks. Two "risky" stacks contain cards that result in high rewards of play money, along with a few cards that carry a high penalty, for an overall loss; cards in the other two "safe" stacks result in lower rewards and smaller penalties for an overall gain. Normal individuals initially prefer cards from the two risky decks. Then they begin making skin conductance responses as they consider choosing from the risky decks, and eventually shift to choosing from the "safe" decks. People with frontal damage usually do not make the shift, even after they have figured out how the game works. Jane likewise never developed the learned emotional response (the SCR) and did not learn to avoid the risky choices (see Figure 7.1).

My own brain is to me the most unaccountable of machinery—always buzzing, humming, soaring, roaring, diving, and then buried in mud. And why? What's this passion for?

—Virginia Woolf

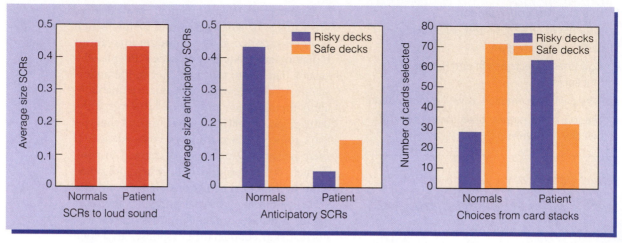

Figure 7.1

Comparison of gambling task behavior in normals and patient with damage to prefrontal cortex

The graphs show that the patient described in the text responded normally to a loud sound (left), but did not produce anticipatory SCRs when considering risky decks (center) and did not learn to avoid the risky decks (right).

Adapted from S.W. Anderson, A. Bechara, H. Damasio, D. Tranel, & A.R. Damasio (1999). "Impairment of social and moral behavior related to early damage in human prefrontal cortex." *Nature Neuroscience*, 2, 1032–1037. Reprinted with permission.

Emotion enriches our lives with its "buzzing, humming, soaring, and roaring." It also motivates our behavior: anger intensifies our defensive behavior, fear accelerates flight, and happiness encourages the behavior that produces it. Emotion adds emphasis to experiences as they are processed in the brain, making them more memorable (Anderson & Phelps, 2001); as a result, we are likely to repeat the behaviors that bring joy and avoid the ones that produce danger or pain. Although Jane's performance on other kinds of learning tasks was normal, because of her injury she was unable to learn from her emotional experiences. According to Antonio Damasio (1994), reason without emotion is inadequate for making the decisions that guide our lives, and in fact make up our lives.

What effect does the autonomic nervous system have during emotions?

EMOTION AND THE NERVOUS SYSTEM

Mention the word *emotion* and you probably think first of what we call "feelings"—the sense of happiness or excitement or fear or sadness. Then you probably think of the facial expressions that go along with these feelings: the curled-up corners of the mouth during a smile, the knit brow and red face of anger. Next you probably visualize the person acting out the emotion by fleeing, striking, embracing, and so on. Emotion is all of these and more; to the neuroscientist especially, emotion means autonomic system activity and activation of brain centers. We will talk about all of these in the following pages, along with some practical implications in the form of aggression and health.

Autonomic and Muscular Involvement in Emotion

To the neuroscientist there is no more obvious emotional response than sympathetic nervous system activation. You may remember from Chapter 3 that the sympathetic system activates the body during arousal; it increases heart rate and respiration rate, increases sweat gland activity, shuts down digestion, and constricts the peripheral blood vessels, which raises the blood pressure and diverts blood to the internal organs and the brain. As you will see in the section on stress, the sympathetic system also stimulates the adrenal glands to release various hormones, particularly *cortisol*.

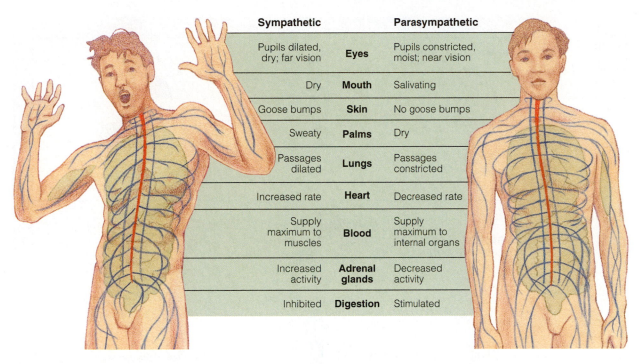

	Sympathetic		Parasympathetic
	Pupils dilated, dry; far vision	**Eyes**	Pupils constricted, moist; near vision
	Dry	**Mouth**	Salivating
	Goose bumps	**Skin**	No goose bumps
	Sweaty	**Palms**	Dry
	Passages dilated	**Lungs**	Passages constricted
	Increased rate	**Heart**	Decreased rate
	Supply maximum to muscles	**Blood**	Supply maximum to internal organs
	Increased activity	**Adrenal glands**	Decreased activity
	Inhibited	**Digestion**	Stimulated

Figure 7.2
Comparison of sympathetic activity during emotional arousal with parasympathetic activity during relaxation

At the end of arousal, the parasympathetic system puts the brakes on most bodily activity with the exception that it activates digestion. In other words, the sympathetic nervous system prepares the body for "fight or flight"; in contrast, the parasympathetic system generally reduces activity and conserves and restores energy (Figure 7.2).

Two Competing Theories

Autonomic arousal during emotion is interesting, but psychologists are just as intrigued by the experience of emotion—the *feelings* of happiness, sadness, anger, and fear. The relationship between emotional experience and the body's responses is controversial. The issue seems like a "no brainer": you see a bear, you become afraid, the sympathetic system kicks into gear, and you flee. It may surprise you that not all emotion theorists agree that this is the true order of events. According to William James (1893) you see a bear, your body reacts,

and then you become afraid. **The idea that physiological arousal is not the result of the emotional experience but precedes and causes feelings is known as the *James-Lange theory*** because the Danish physiologist Carl Lange came up with a similar idea about the same time. That physiological arousal could be the cause of the emotional experience probably sounds strange to you because you have always thought it worked the other way around. James recognized that the idea was counterintuitive, and he predicted that it would be met with "immediate disbelief." But think of the time when you confidently stood up to speak your mind in a meeting and were surprised to find your heart pounding in your chest; only then did you lose your nerve. Or remember when you had to swerve to avoid another car at an intersection; you did not really feel frightened until half a block later, when you were overcome with trembling and weakness.

Figure 7.3
Comparison of the
James-Lange and the
Schachter-Singer
cognitive theories of
emotion

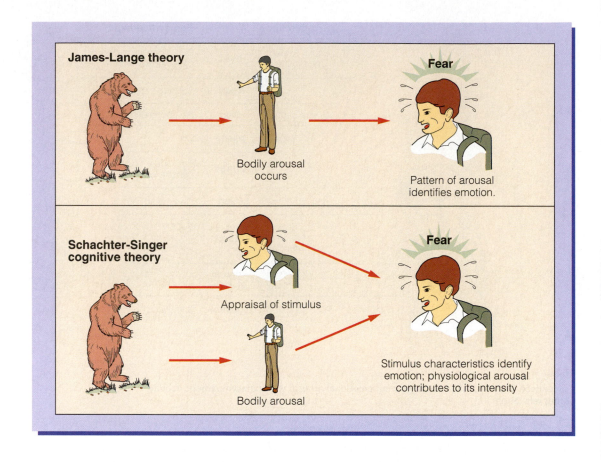

. . . we feel sorry because we cry, angry because we strike, afraid because we tremble . . .

—William James, 1893

How do the James-Lange and cognitive theories disagree?

The James-Lange theory held sway until the 1920s. At that time it was challenged by the physiologist Walter Cannon (1927); Cannon's main argument was that the autonomic nervous system responds the same way during a variety of emotions, so feedback could not account for the variety of our emotional experience. The James-Lange theory lost favor among researchers. In fact, they lost interest in studying emotional experience in general, under the influence of the newly emerging school of *behaviorism*. Behaviorists took the position that only observable behavior was

worthy of study, and that emotional experience was too subjective.

Interest in emotional experience would not be revived until the 1960s; that was when cognitive psychologists decided that a mature science of behavior could no longer ignore internal mental and emotional events. Riding the wave of this cognitive revolution, Stanley Schachter and Jerome Singer (1962) proposed a new way of looking at emotion. **According to their *cognitive theory*, a person relies on a cognitive assessment of the stimulus situation to identify which emotion is being experienced.** In other words, the person sees a bear, becomes aroused, and then labels the emotion as fear because a bear is present. Like Cannon, Schachter and Singer said that emotional experience and arousal are simultaneous, and that physiological arousal is similar for different emotions; physiological arousal merely contributes to the intensity of the emotion. Because of the impact the James-Lange and the cognitive theories have had on thinking about emotion, we will examine the evidence for both of them in some detail. The cognitive theory displaced the James-Lange theory for a time, so we will look at research supporting it first. (See Figure 7.3 for a summary of the two theories.)

Cognitive Aspects of Emotion

It is difficult to determine whether physiological arousal comes first or occurs at the same time as emotional experience. So, most research has focused on an implication of the James-Lange theory: if physiological arousal accounts for all our different emotional experiences, then every emotion must involve a different pattern of arousal. Thus James-Lange theorists attempted to demonstrate unique arousal patterns, while the cognitive camp tried to show that the pattern of arousal is irrelevant. Some of the latter studies have been particularly creative.

Schachter and Singer (1962), for instance, injected volunteers with epinephrine, with the explanation that it was a vitamin which was expected to improve visual performance. Some of the participants were accurately informed that the injection would cause their hearts to race and their hands to tremble, while the others were not given that information. For the next 20 minutes they were asked to wait in a room with another supposed volunteer who was actually a stooge, or accomplice of the experimenters. In the presence of half of the participants the stooge acted euphoric, making and throwing paper airplanes, shooting paper wads with rubber bands, and playing basketball with the wastebasket and wadded-up paper. The other half of the participants were asked to fill out a lengthy and very personal questionnaire; in that case the stooge acted angry, complaining about the questions and finally tearing up the questionnaire and stamping out of the room.

The researchers assumed that the informed individuals would attribute their arousal to the injection, and would not report being emotionally aroused. However, they predicted that the uninformed participants would interpret

eStock Photo

Figure 7.4
The Capilano river bridge
The bridge looks sturdy, but it sways wildly above the gorge as people walk across it.

their epinephrine-induced arousal as euphoria or anger, depending on the stooge's behavior; they would join the stooge in his activities and later report feeling the same emotion that the stooge had displayed. The results mostly supported the predictions.

In a more naturalistic study, Dutton and Aron (1974) had an attractive female researcher interview young men as they crossed a swaying foot bridge suspended 230 feet above a rocky river (Figure 7.4) or 10 minutes after they had crossed. Four times as many men who were interviewed while on the bridge took the woman up on her offer to provide further information about the study, and called the phone number she gave them. According to the researchers, the men on the swaying bridge interpreted their physiological arousal as attraction for the young woman. This interpretation was supported by the fact that men interviewed while crossing the bridge included more sexual content in brief stories they wrote in response to an ambiguous picture than did the men who had crossed the bridge a few minutes earlier.

What evidence is there for each theory?

These studies have been interpreted to mean that an emotional experience does not depend on a particular pattern of arousal, because the same physiological arousal can be interpreted as different emotions. Some researchers have not been able to reproduce the results in their studies, and other explanations of the results are possible (Cotton, 1981), but the theory has had wide influence.

Physical Patterns of Emotional Response

In defense of the James-Lange position, Albert Ax (1953) performed the study described in Chapter 1 as an example of ethically questionable research procedures. You may remember that he used a polygraph to record several physiological measures, including heart rate, blood pressure, muscle tension, skin temperature, and skin conductance, while the research participants were made angry or fearful. **A polygraph is a device for recording several physiological measures at the same time.** (The name is associated with lie detection, but that is only one use of the equipment.) Consistent with the James-Lange theory, the two treatments produced different patterns of autonomic activity. Several other studies have also found distinctive patterns of autonomic activation among emotions, at least the negative ones (reviewed in Levenson, 1992). Anger, fear, and sadness all elevate the heart rate, but anger and fear also involve motor activation; blood pressure increases more in anger and hand temperature decreases more in fear.

A number of studies have examined emotionality in people with spinal cord injuries, on the premise that they would receive much less feedback about bodily arousal and, therefore, would experience less emotion. Several have found decreases in emotionality, which were greater when the break was higher in the spinal cord (Hohmann, 1966), but others have not (Chwalisz, Diener, & Gallagher, 1988). However, the results of these studies may not be as meaningful as they would seem, because the spinal cord–injured patient still gets considerable feedback from internal organs through the vagus nerve. Other cranial nerves also provide feedback from the facial muscles, which are important in producing facial expressions during emotion.

James acknowledged a role for muscular feedback but gave it less importance than the autonomic nervous system; however, it may actually be more important. Researchers are switching their interest to facial expressions as a source of emotional feedback. Facial expressions are a particularly accessible window for observing emotion; but a more important reason for interest is that some facial expressions appear to be innate, or built into the nervous system, and therefore close to the physiological roots of emotion. Part of the evidence for that idea is that facial expressions of emotion are basically the same across cultures (Ekman & Friesen, 1971), and children blind from birth show the same facial expressions of emotion as sighted people (Izard, 1971).

One technique is to have individuals imitate expressions from photographs, and then ask them what emotion they are experiencing. But it is easy to tell what emotional response the researcher is looking for, which might influence the research participant's reports. Other studies have worked around this problem in creative ways. One took advantage of the fact that holding a pen between the teeth produces a sort of smile, while holding the pen between the lips interferes with smiling; you can try this exercise yourself and see if it affects your mood. College students rated *Far Side* cartoons as more amusing when they were holding the pen between their teeth than when it was held between the lips (Strack, Martin, & Stepper, 1988). In another study the researchers gave the subjects detailed instructions on which facial muscles to contract without identifying the emotion expected (Levenson, Ekman, & Friesen, 1990). For example, instructions for producing an angry face consisted of: "(a) Pull your eyebrows down and together. (b) Raise your upper eyelid. (c) Push your lower lip up and press your lips together" (p. 365). Six emotions—happiness, fear, anger, disgust, sadness, and surprise—were posed in this way (see Figure 7.5) while

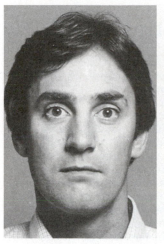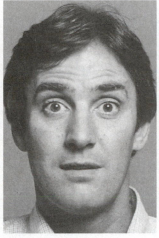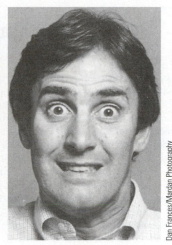

Dan Frances/Mardan Photography

Figure 7.5
Emotional expressions posed using Ekman's instructions

the researchers recorded heart rate, finger temperature, skin conductance, and muscle activity. As predicted by the James-Lange theory, the subjects reported feeling the expected emotion as they produced each of the expressions. Also as predicted, each of the emotions was accompanied by a different pattern of physiological activation.

What We Have Learned

We still have not resolved whether emotional experience depends on feedback from the body or on cognitive assessment of the situation. Apparently the differential patterns of arousal are there as James said, but the facial expression studies are our only evidence that we actually *use* the information to identify our emotions. On the other hand, the fact that we can use external stimuli to identify emotion in ambiguous situations (as cognitive theory research shows) does not mean that we do not typically rely on physiological feedback. At this point I think it makes sense to forgo choosing between the two theories and recognize what we have learned along the way. One point is that emotion can influence behavior without ever coming into awareness. The gambling task used to test Jane provides a good example of this nonconscious aspect of emotion. As normal individuals learn which stacks of cards are more or less risky, they shift their choices to the less

risky decks. Now here is the interesting part: they begin producing a skin conductance response while preparing to select from a risky stack *before* they are able to verbalize that choosing from those stacks is risky (Bechara, Damasio, Damasio, & Lee, 1999).

Another thing we have learned is that the different patterns of physical arousal during emotion may have an adaptive function that is more important than identifying our emotions. As Charles Darwin (1872/1965) pointed out, at the social level our facial expressions and postures communicate our emotional state to others. Internally, increased blood pressure aids the person in responding physically during an angry encounter, and the peripheral constriction of blood vessels that turns your hands into ice during fear reduces bleeding if you are injured.

The Brain and Emotion

Much of what we know about the role of the brain in emotion comes from studies of brain damage, either inflicted on animals by the investigator or in humans by injury, disease, or stroke. Human brain studies give ambiguous results because the damage usually overlaps several areas and it is difficult to be sure which structure is the relevant one. Animal studies give us more control, but are also difficult to interpret; for example, the behavioral results may occur merely because we have interrupted

Camera May Be Able to Spot Liars

Rick Callahan—A heat-sensing camera that can distinguish between people who are lying and people who are telling the truth may be one solution for mass screening of crowds for security.

Scientists from Honeywell Laboratories and Mayo Clinic tested the camera with 20 Army recruit volunteers. Eight of them were randomly assigned to stab a dummy and rob it of $20; another 12 did not participate in the "crime."

Because startling a person with a loud sound causes increased blood flow and flushing around the eyes, the researchers thought the thermal-sensing camera might also detect the emotional arousal caused by lying. When the 20 volunteers denied any knowledge of the crime, the camera correctly identified six out of the eight "guilty" individuals (see the photos);

11 of the 12 "innocent" individuals were also correctly identified.

Polygraph operators who tested the same individuals did no better. A polygraph measures blood pressure, breathing rate, sweating, and other body reactions. It requires a trained professional and considerable time. The thermal camera makes its measurements quickly without the need for a skilled operator. The researchers suggested that the technique might be useful for rapid screening for terrorists as they go through routine questioning at airports. The research was published in the January 3, 2002, issue of the journal *Nature.*

—Excite News, *January 3, 2002; http://apnews.excite.com/article/20020103/ D7GQ52500.html?PG=home&SEC=high2*

Thermal Images of the Face of a "Guilty" Subject
The image on the left was taken before, and the one on the right after, lying in response to the question "Did you steal the $20?" Red, orange, and yellow indicate progressively higher temperatures. White lines indicate the location of the eyes.

Source: Pavlidis, Eberhardt, & Levine, 2002. Reprinted by permission of *Nature,* copyright 2002.

a pathway passing through to another area. Electrical and chemical stimulation techniques can give more precise information than studies of brain damage; but still we are hard pressed to know just what an animal is feeling when it attacks, or flees, or seeks more stimulation. Nevertheless, we have learned a great deal, as the next four sections indicate.

The Limbic System

The most important brain areas in emotion are located in the *limbic system,* **a network of brain structures arranged around the upper brain stem** (Figure 7.6). If you look closely at the shapes of the cingulate gyrus, the parahippocampal gyrus, and the fornix, you will appreciate the fact that there are looping

Figure 7.6
Structures of the limbic system

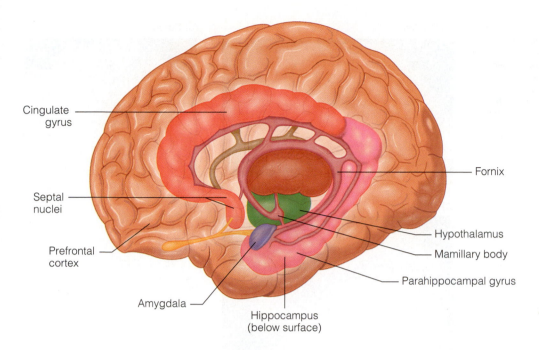

Cingulate gyrus

Septal nuclei

Prefrontal cortex

Amygdala

Hippocampus (below surface)

Fornix

Hypothalamus

Mamillary body

Parahippocampal gyrus

interconnections among the structures. Besides emotion, parts of the limbic system are also involved in learning and memory and in motivated behaviors like sexual activity and aggression.

The functions of the system's components have been investigated mostly in animals because the studies often require stimulation or destruction of the structures. However, in some cases the emotional responses of neurological patients were observed as they received electrical stimulation, either to locate malfunctioning areas prior to surgical removal or, before physicians had the effective drugs that are available now, as an experimental treatment. Robert Heath (1964) implanted electrodes in several locations in the brains of patients in an attempt to treat epilepsy, sleep disorders, or pain that had failed to respond to conventional treatments.

Researchers knew from animal studies that the hypothalamus has primary control over the autonomic system, and is the source of a variety of emotional responses, such as the threatened cat's hissing and bared teeth and claws. Stimulation of the hypothalamus in Heath's patients produced general autonomic discharge and sensations such as a pounding heart and feelings of warmth. Stimulation also evoked feelings of fear, rage, or pleasure, depending on the location of the electrode in the hypothalamus. Septal area stimulation also produced a sense of pleasure, but this time the feeling was accompanied by sexual fantasies and arousal. One patient went from near tears while talking about his father's illness to a broad smile as he described how he planned to take his girlfriend out and seduce her. When asked why he changed the subject, he replied that the thought just came into his head.

We have come a long way in understanding the brain's role in emotion since these early studies. One thing we are learning is that the idea of a single, highly integrated system that controls emotion is an oversimplification. Any particular emotion involves the activation of several structures at all levels of the brain (Damasio et al., 2000); which structures are activated depends on the form of the emotional stimulus as well as the emotion experienced (Lane, Reiman, Ahern, Schwartz, & Davidson,

What are some of the brain structures involved in emotions and what are their functions?

Figure 7.7
Activation of the amygdala while viewing fearful faces
(a–c) Activation in the amygdala (yellow and red area) is seen from different orientations during viewing of pictures of faces depicting fear.
(d) Average amounts of blood flow measured by the PET scan in the amygdala while the individual viewed happy faces and fearful faces.
Source: Morris et al., 1996. Reprinted by permission of *Nature*, copyright 1996.

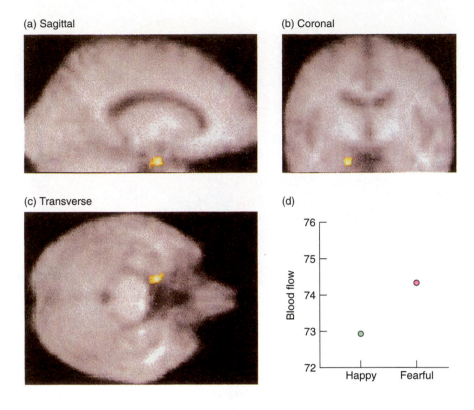

(a) Sagittal

(b) Coronal

(c) Transverse

(d)

1997). The next three topics illustrate some of the progress we have made in understanding the neural control of emotion.

The Amygdala

Of all the structures in the limbic system, **the one most involved in emotion is the *amygdala*, which receives input from all the sense modalities and produces fear and anxiety by targeting a variety of brain structures that produce emotional responses.** It coordinates activity between structures involved in the physiological and facial expression of emotions (hypothalamus, brain stem nuclei, and trigeminal and facial motor nuclei) and cortical areas that are candidates for the location of conscious feelings, especially fear (the prefrontal cortex, cingulate gyrus, and parahippocampal gyrus) (Davis, 1992; Iversen, Kupfermann, & Kandel, 2000). We will see some of the functions of the prefrontal cortex and the cingulate gyrus shortly.

Although the amygdala is involved in other emotions, its major role is in fear and anxiety. *Fear is an emotional reaction to a specific immediate threat; anxiety is an apprehension about a future, and often uncertain, event.* Rats with both amygdalas destroyed will not only approach a sedated cat but climb all over its back and head (Blanchard & Blanchard, 1972). One rat even nibbled on the stuporous cat's ear, provoking an attack; and after the attack ended the rat climbed right back onto the cat.

Like the rats, humans with damage to both amygdalas tend to be unusually trusting of strangers (Adolphs, Tranel, & Damasio, 1998). Stimulating the amygdala produces fear in human subjects (Gloor, Olivier, Quesney, Andermann, & Horowitz, 1982), so this unusual trustfulness is probably the result of reduced fear. Just looking at pictures of fearful faces activates the amygdala (Figure 7.7) (Morris et al., 1996), and amygdala-damaged patients have trouble recognizing fear in other people's facial expressions (Adolphs, Tranel, Damasio, & Damasio, 1995). Not surprisingly, the amygdala is one of the sites where anti-anxiety drugs produce their effect. It contains receptors for benzodiazepines and opiates, and injection of either type of drug directly into the amygdala reduces signs of fear and anxiety in animals (Davis, 1992).

People with amygdala damage on both sides of the brain are able to respond only to the simplest of fear situations; for example, they will startle to a loud sound, but they cannot be conditioned to startle to a visual stimulus that has been paired with a loud sound. They do not recognize that a stimulus or situation may be harmful, nor do they respond emotionally to rewards and punishments, like winning and losing money in a laboratory game (Bechara et al., 1999). These abilities are needed to function successfully in a world that requires us to seek rewards and avoid punishments, and to distinguish the situations in which they occur. For this reason, most people with bilateral amygdala damage have to live in supervised settings (Bechara et al., 1999).

The Prefrontal Cortex

We saw in Chapter 3 that the prefrontal cortex is involved in emotion, and that severing the connections with the rest of the brain blunts emotion and impairs the person's ability to make good behavioral decisions. When we talk about psychological disorders in Chapter 13 you will learn that many people with either depression or schizophrenia have abnormal development or malfunction in the prefrontal area. The role of the prefrontal cortex is not so much in generating emotions as it is in using emotional information for functions like decision making. You will remember that Jane, described at the beginning of this chapter, was unable to anticipate negative consequences of her behavior because her prefrontal area was damaged during infancy. Damage to both amygdalas produces similar deficiencies, because it deprives the prefrontal area of the emotional information needed to make decisions. However, people with damage like Jane's,

in the *ventromedial prefrontal area*, are still able to experience the emotions (see Figure 7.8). Unlike amygdala-damaged patients, they can avoid behaviors that would lead to immediate physical harm to themselves or others; but they are impaired in the ability to anticipate longer-term consequences of their behavior, such as those that would result in financial losses or damage to social relationships (Bechara et al., 1999).

The Right Hemisphere

Just as the left hemisphere is usually dominant for language functions, structures in the right hemisphere play a special role in emotional expression and recognition. People with damage to their right hemisphere are more likely to be impaired emotionally; for instance, they may seem strangely unperturbed by their impairment, even when their arm or leg is paralyzed (Gainotti, Caltagirone, & Zoccolotti, 1993). The right hemisphere is particularly involved in autonomic reactions to emotional stimuli. Slides depicting emotional scenes produce more autonomic response when they are presented to the right hemisphere than the left, using the technique described in section A.4 of the appendix (Spence, Shapiro, & Zaidel, 1996). Much of the emotional suppression in right-hemisphere-damaged patients is due to decreased autonomic response (Gainotti et al., 1993).

Emotional perception is impaired, too; for example, right-hemisphere-damaged patients often have difficulty recognizing emotion in others' facial expressions (Adolphs, Damasio, Tranel, & Damasio, 1996). Perception is impaired only for nonverbal aspects of emotion, though. Patients with right-hemisphere damage can understand the emotion in a verbal description of a situation, such as "Your team's ball went through the hoop with one second left to go in the game," but they have trouble identifying the emotion in descriptions of facial or gestural expressions such as "Tears fell from her eyes" or "He shook his fist" (Blonder, Bowers, & Heilman, 1991). Right-hemisphere-damaged patients have trouble recognizing emotion from the tone of the speaker's voice

How does loss of emotion impair "rational" decision making?

1

Figure 7.8
Location of damage that impairs emotion-based decision making
(a) In one of the patients with amygdala damage, the dark areas in the temporal lobes indicate where the amygdalas were once located.
(b) Location of the lesions in the patients with prefrontal damage. Each color indicates how many patients had damage in that area.
Source: Bechara, Damasio, Damasio, & Lee, 1999. Copyright 1999 by the Society for Neuroscience.

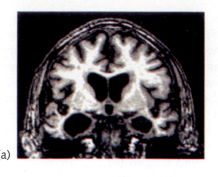
(a)

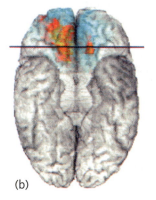
(b)

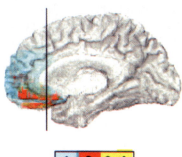

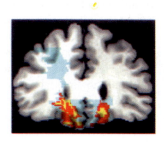

| 1 | 2 | 3–4 |

(Gorelick & Ross, 1987), and their own speech is usually emotionless as well (Heilman, Watson, & Bowers, 1983). When asked to say a neutral sentence like "The boy went to the store" in a happy, sad, or angry tone of voice, they speak instead in a monotone, and often add the designated emotion to the sentence verbally, for example, ". . . and he was sad."

✔ **CONCEPT CHECK**

- *Describe the role of the autonomic nervous system in emotion (including the possible identification of emotions).*
- *Organize your knowledge: list the major parts of the brain described in this section that are involved in emotion, along with their functions.*
- *How are the effects of prefrontal and amygdala damage alike and different?*

STRESS, IMMUNITY, AND HEALTH

Stress is a rather ambiguous term that has two meanings in psychology. *Stress* **is a condition in the environment that makes unusual demands on the organism, such as threat, failure, or bereavement. Stress is also an internal condition, your response to a stressful situation;** you *feel* stressed, and your body reacts in several ways. Whether a situation is stressful to the person is often a matter of individual differences, either in perception of the situation or in physiological reactivity. For some, even the normal events of daily life are stressful, while others thrive on excitement and would feel stressed if they were deprived of regular challenges. In other words, stress in this sense of the term is in the eye of the beholder.

Stress as an Adaptive Response

Ordinarily, the body's response to a stressful situation is positive and adaptive. In Chapter 3 you saw that the stress response includes activation of the sympathetic branch of the autonomic nervous system, which is largely under the control of the hypothalamus. The resulting increases in heart rate, blood flow, and respiration rate help the person deal with the stressful situation. Stress also activates the **hypothalamus-pituitary-adrenal cortex axis (HPA), a group of structures that help the body cope with stress.** The hypothalamus activates the pituitary gland, which in turn releases *adrenocorticotropic hormone (ACTH),* **which stimulates the adrenal glands to release the stress hormones epinephrine, norepinephrine, and cortisol.** The first two hormones increase output from the heart and liberate glucose from the muscles for additional energy. **The hormone *cortisol* also increases energy levels by converting proteins to glucose, increasing fat availability, and increasing metabolism.** Cortisol provides a more sustained release of energy than the sympathetic nervous system does, for coping with prolonged stress. The HPA is illustrated in Figure 7.9.

In pain there is as much wisdom as in pleasure.

—Nietzsche

Brief stress increases activity in the *immune system* **(Herbert et al., 1994), the cells and cell products that kill infected and malig-**

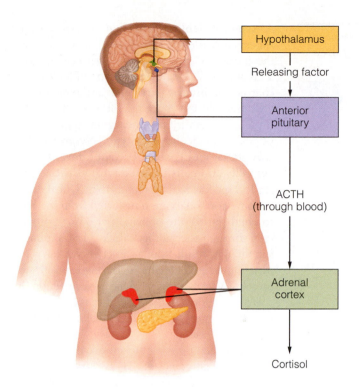

Figure 7.9
The Hypothalamus-Pituitary-Adrenal Cortex Axis

nant cells and protect the body against foreign substances, including bacteria and viruses.** Of course, this is highly adaptive because it helps protect the person from any infections that might result from the threatening situation. The immune response involves two major types of cells, *leukocytes,* **or white blood cells,** and natural killer cells (Table 7.1).

Leukocytes recognize invaders by the unique proteins that every cell has on its surface; these proteins in foreign cells are called *antigens.*

What are the positive effects of stress?

Table 7.1 Major Types of Immune Cells			
Leukocytes			**Natural Killer**
Macrophages	**T Cells**	**B Cells**	**Cells**
Ingest invaders; display antigens, which attract T cells	Multiply and attack invaders	Make antigens, which destroy intruders	Attack cells containing viruses, certain kinds of tumor cells

*What are the nega-
tive effects of stress?*

3

A type of leukocyte called a *macrophage*
ingests intruders (Figure 7.10). Then it displays
the intruder's antigens on its own cell surface.
This attracts *T cells,* **another type of leukocyte
that is specific for particular antigens**; the T
cells multiply and attack the foreign cells. *B cells*
**fight intruders by producing antibodies that
attack a particular cell type.** *Natural killer
cells* **attack and destroy certain kinds of cancer cells and cells infected with viruses**; they
are less specific in their targets than T or B cells.

Some antibodies are transferred from mother
to child during the prenatal period or postnatally through the mother's milk. Most antibodies, though, result from a direct encounter with
invading cells, for example, during exposure to
measles. Vaccinations work because injection of
a weakened form of the disease-causing bacteria
or virus triggers the B cells to make antibodies
for that disease.

The preceding is a description of what happens when all goes well. **In** *autoimmune disorder,* **the immune system goes amok and
attacks the body's own cells.** In the autoimmune disorder multiple sclerosis, for instance,
the immune system destroys myelin in the central nervous system. In the immune deficiency
disease AIDS (acquired immune deficiency
syndrome), on the other hand, T cells fail to
detect invaders and the person dies of an infectious disease.

Figure 7.10
**A macrophage preparing to engulf a
bacterium**

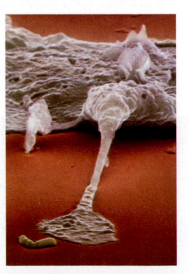

Negative Effects of Stress

We are better equipped to deal with brief stress
than with prolonged stress. Chronic stress can
interfere with memory, increase or decrease
appetite, diminish sexual desire and performance, deplete energy, and cause mood disruptions. Although brief stress enhances immune
activity, prolonged stress compromises the
immune system. After the nuclear accident at
the Three Mile Island electric generating
plant, nearby residents had elevated stress
symptoms and performed less well on tasks
requiring concentration than people who lived
outside the area (Baum, Gatchel, & Schaeffer,
1983). Amid concerns about continued
radioactivity and the long-term effects of the
initial exposure, they had reduced numbers of
B cells, T cells, and natural killer cells as long
as six years after the accident (McKinnon,
Weisse, Reynolds, Bowles, & Baum, 1989).

Disease symptoms were not measured at
Three Mile Island, but other studies have
shown that health is compromised when stress
impairs immune functioning. Healthy individuals were given nasal drops containing common
cold viruses and then were quarantined and
observed for infections. In Figure 7.11 you can
see that their chance of catching a cold
depended on the level of stress they reported on
a questionnaire at the beginning of the study
(Cohen, Tyrrell, & Smith, 1991). In a follow-up
study it turned out that only stresses that had
lasted longer than a month increased the risk of
infection (Cohen et al., 1998). A one-year study
of medical school students showed that their
immune responses were reduced at exam times,
and they reported more infectious illnesses then
than at other times of the year (Glaser et al.,
1987). Women who were recently widowed had
increased cortisol levels and reduced natural
killer cell activity (Irwin, Daniels, Risch, Bloom,
& Weiner, 1988); they deteriorated markedly in
health during the following year compared to
still-married women of comparable age
(Maddison & Viola, 1968).

Decreases in measures of immunity may not
be as much a failure as a switch in the immune
system's priorities. According to the *immunore-*

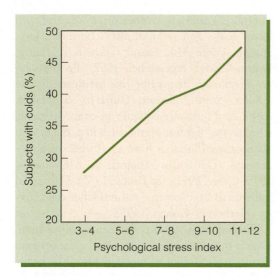

Figure 7.11
Relationship between stress and vulnerability to colds

distribution hypothesis, stress triggers a relocation of immune system cells from the organs to the skin (Braude, Tang-Martinez, & Taylor, 1999). This would be an adaptive response to an external physical threat, but it would leave the internal organs more vulnerable.

The cardiovascular system is particularly vulnerable to stress. Stress increases blood pressure, and high blood pressure, if prolonged, can damage the heart or cause a stroke. Some people are more vulnerable to health effects from stress than others. Researchers subjected children to the cold pressor test, which involves measuring blood pressure while one hand is immersed in ice water; the children were classified as normal reactors or excessive reactors. Forty-five years later, 71% of the excessive reactors had high blood pressure, compared to 19% of the normal reactors (Wood, Sheps, Elveback, & Schirger, 1984).

Extremely high stress can even produce death. A few decades ago this fact was not widely accepted, especially in the scientific and medical communities. In 1942 Walter Cannon reviewed several cases of apparent stress-related death

brought on by fear or by minor injuries. He not only accepted the reports as legitimate but suggested that *voodoo death*, which has been reported to occur within hours of a person being "hexed" by a practitioner of this folk cult, is also due to stress. We now know that fear, loss of a loved one, humiliation, or even extreme joy can result in sudden cardiac death. **In *sudden cardiac death*, stress causes excessive sympathetic activity that sends the heart into fibrillation, contracting so rapidly that it pumps little or no blood.** When one of the largest earthquakes ever recorded in a major North American city struck the Los Angeles area in 1994, the number of deaths from heart attacks increased fivefold (Figure 7.12) (Leor, Poole, & Kloner, 1996).

Extreme stress can also lead to brain damage. Hippocampal volume was reduced in Vietnam combat veterans suffering from posttraumatic stress disorder (Bremner et al., 1995) and in victims of childhood abuse (Bremner et al., 1997), and cortical tissue was reduced in torture victims (Jensen et al., 1982). The abused subjects had short-term memory deficits and some of the torture victims showed slight intellectual impairment. The likely cause of the brain cell loss is increased cortisol level over a long period. When researchers implanted cortisol pellets in monkeys' brains, it caused damage to the hippocampi (Sapolsky, Uno, Rebert, & Finch, 1990). Elderly humans who had elevated cortisol levels over a five-year period had an average 14% decrease in hippocampal volume, along

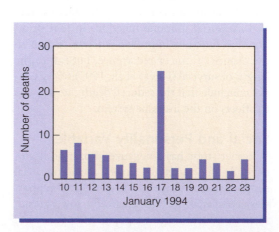

Figure 7.12
Increase in cardiac deaths on the day of an earthquake

with impaired performance on memory tasks (Lupien et al., 1998).

Reducing stress can improve health. Elderly volunteers who were trained in transcendental meditation had a survival rate of 100% after three years, compared to 77.3% for volunteers randomly assigned to receive no training (Alexander, Langer, Newman, Chandler, & Davies, 1989). A group of men infected with the AIDS virus had lower anxiety and higher T-cell counts after 20 hours of relaxation training than a group of similarly infected individuals (Taylor, 1995). Patients with melanoma cancer given training in relaxation and coping skills had a much lower death rate (9%) five to six years later than patients randomly assigned to the untreated control condition (29%) (Fawzy et al., 1993). In three different studies, cancer patients who were provided social support and training in social relations, emotional expression, and pain management lived longer than control patients (Spiegel, 1996). In one, the trained patients survived an average of 36.6 months, compared to 18.9 months for the control patients; at the end of 48 months a third of the trained patients were alive, compared to none of the controls.

As impressive as these results are, there are two major problems. First, there is the possibility that participation in the research motivated the experimental subjects to make lifestyle changes that contributed to their improvement. Second, although evidence suggests that survival might be related to immune functioning (Spiegel, Sephton, Terr, & Stites, 1998), only one of the studies concerned with survival rate also measured immune function. In that study, immune function improvement was related to the chance of cancer recurrence, but not to the length of survival (Fawzy et al., 1993); so we cannot conclude that the reduced death rate was due to effects on the immune system.

Social and Personality Variables

Whether stress has a negative impact on health depends on a variety of factors, including social support, personality, and attitude. Social support was associated with dramatically lower death rates in several different populations (reviewed

In what ways do personality characteristics influence immune functioning?

in House, Landis, & Umberson, 1988), and with lower stress and reduced stress hormone level among Three Mile Island residents (Fleming, Baum, Gisriel, & Gatchel, 1982). People who are hostile are at greater risk for heart disease (Miller, Smith, Turner, Guijarro, & Hallet, 1996), and outcome is better in cancer patients who have a "fighting spirit" than in patients who accept their illness or have an attitude of hopelessness (Derogatis, Abeloff, & Melisaratos, 1979; Greer, 1991; Temoshok, 1987). Depressed individuals have lowered natural killer cell activity (Herbert & Cohen, 1993).

There are two points to keep in mind here. One is that even social influences must operate through physiological mechanisms. The other is that these studies are correlational and do not tell us that a fighting spirit is the cause of cancer survival, or that depression reduces killer cell activity. It is just as possible that the disease influences personality, or that a third variable is responsible for both the personality characteristic and disease susceptibility.

A good example of a third variable's effect is the association between extraversion (an outgoing personality) and immune system activity. People who are low in extraversion tend to have increased natural killer cell activity. However, both low extraversion and immune increases are associated with high levels of the stress hormones norepinephrine and epinephrine (Miller, Cohen, Rabin, Skoner, & Doyle, 1999). The level of stress hormones accounts for more than half of the association between extraversion and immune activity. Thus, a reasonable hypothesis is that stress hormones are responsible for both the low extraversion and enhanced killer cell activity. If so, then low extraversion becomes a "marker" for increased immune activity, rather than the cause. It is possible that other relationships of attitude and emotional state with health will turn out to be due to physiological third variables.

Pain as an Adaptive Emotion

Eighty percent of all visits to physicians are at least partly to seek relief from pain (Gatchel, 1996), and we spend billions each year on nonprescription pain medications. These observations alone qualify pain as a major health problem. A world without pain might sound wonderful, but in spite of the suffering it causes, pain is valuable for its adaptive benefits. It warns us that the coffee is too hot, that our shoe is rubbing a blister, that we should take our skis back to the bunny slope for more practice. **People with *congenital insensitivity to pain* are born unable to sense pain**; they injure themselves repeatedly because they are not motivated to avoid dangerous situations, and they die from untreated conditions like a ruptured appendix. Mild pain tells us to change our posture regularly; a woman with congenital insensitivity to pain suffered damage to her spine because she could not respond to these signals, and resulting complications led to her death (Sternbach, 1968).

Pain is a more terrible lord of mankind than even death itself.

—Albert Schweitzer

Pain is one of the senses, a point we consider in more detail in Chapter 10. Here we focus on the feature that makes pain unique among the senses: it is so intimately involved with emotion that we can say that pain is also an emotion. In fact, when we tell someone about a pain experience we usually are describing an emotional reaction; it is the emotional response that makes pain adaptive.

As Beecher (1956, p. 1609) observed, "the intensity of suffering is largely determined by what the pain means to the patient." In our society, childbirth is considered a painful and debilitating ordeal; in other cultures childbirth is a routine matter, and the woman returns to work in the fields almost immediately. After the landing at the Anzio beachhead in World War II, 68% of the wounded soldiers denied pain and refused morphine; only 17% of civilians with similar "wounds" from surgery accepted their pain so bravely (Beecher, 1956). The soldiers were not simply insensitive to pain, because they complained bitterly about rough treatment or inept blood draws. According to Beecher, who was the surgeon in command at Anzio, the surgery was a major annoyance for the civilians, but the soldiers' wounds meant they had escaped the battlefield alive. Spiritual context can also have a powerful influence on the meaning of pain. Each spring in some remote villages of India a man is suspended by a rope attached to steel hooks in his back; swinging above the cheering crowd, he blesses the children and the crops. Selection for this role is an honor, and the participant seems not only to be free of pain but in a "state of exaltation" (Kosambi, 1967). Figure 7.13 shows an example of culturally sanctioned self-torture.

The pain pathway has rich interconnections with the limbic system, where pain becomes an emotional phenomenon. Besides the somatosensory area, **pain particularly activates the *anterior cingulate cortex (ACC)*, which has many connections to other limbic structures** (Price, 2000; Talbot et al., 1991).

What makes pain an emotional response?

Figure 7.13
Voluntary ritualized torture in religious practice
Cultural values help determine what is painful.

Alain Evrard/Photo Researchers

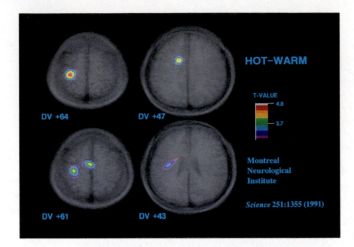

Figure 7.14
PET scan of brain during pain stimulation
The bright area near the midline is the cingulate gyrus;
the one to the left is the somatosensory area. The four
views were taken simultaneously at different depths in
the same brain.
Reprinted with permission from Talbot et al., "Multiple representations of
pain in human cerebral cortex." *Science*, 251, 1355–1358. Copyright
1991 American Association for the Advancement of Science.

The brain scan in Figure 7.14 shows increased activity in the ACC as well as the somatosensory area during painful heat stimulation.

But how do we know that activity in the ACC represents pain emotion? Fortunately it is possible to separate the sensation of pain from its emotional effect. One way is to monitor changes in brain activity while the unpleasantness of pain increases with successive presentations of a painful stimulus. Another involves the use of hypnosis to increase pain unpleasantness without changing the intensity of the stimulus. With both strategies activity increases in the ACC but not in the somatosensory area, suggesting that the ACC's role in pain involves emotion rather than sensation (Price, 2000; Rainville, Duncan, Price, Carrier, & Bushnell, 1997).

If pain continues it also recruits activity in prefrontal areas where, presumably, the pain is evaluated and responses to the painful situation are planned (Price, 2000). The existence of separate structures for processing the emotion of pain may explain the behavior of two groups of people. In pain insensitivity disorders, it is the emotional response that is diminished rather than the sensation of pain; the person can recognize painful stimulation, but simply isn't bothered by it (Melzack, 1973; Price, 2000). The same is true for people who underwent prefrontal lobotomy back when that surgery was used to manage untreatable pain; when questioned, the patients often said they still felt the "little" pain but the "big" pain was gone.

> ☑ **CONCEPT CHECK**
>
> ■ *Describe the positive and negative effects of stress, indicating why the effects become negative.*
> ■ *Discuss the emotional aspects of pain, including the brain structures involved.*

BIOLOGICAL ORIGINS OF AGGRESSION

Both motivation and emotion reach a peak during aggression. Aggression can be adaptive, but it also takes many thousands of lives annually and maims countless others physically and emotionally. The systematic slaughter of thousands of Jews in World War II German concentration camps and the terrorist attack that destroyed the World Trade Center are dramatic examples; but these are rare events, and should not distract attention from the more common thread of daily aggression running throughout human culture.

Researchers agree that there is more than one kind of aggression. They do not agree on what the different kinds are, partly because the forms of aggression differ among species; however, one useful categorization distinguishes offensive, defensive, and predatory aggression. **An unprovoked attack on another person or animal is *offensive aggression*.** Offensive aggression in animals includes competitive aggression between males, territorial aggression, and maternal aggression. ***Defensive aggression* occurs in response to threat and is motivated by fear. *Predatory aggression* is when an animal attacks and kills its prey.** Although aggression is influenced by a person's environment, it should come as no surprise that such a powerful force has hormonal and neural roots.

Hormones

Hormones appear to influence offensive aggression more than the other two types, at least in rats (Albert, Walsh, & Jonik, 1993). In nonprimate animals, aggression is enhanced by testosterone in males and by both testosterone and estrogens in females. **Some women experience mood disruption and occasionally increased aggressiveness just before the menstrual period, an effect known as** *premenstrual syndrome (PMS).* PMS appears to be triggered by estrogens; chemically blocking estrogen activity reduces the symptoms and administering estrogens increases them (Schmidt, Nieman, Danaceau, Adams, & Rubinow, 1998). Some studies have found a relationship between testosterone and violence in male prison inmates. Male prisoners convicted of violent crimes like rape and murder and prisoners rated as tougher by their peers had higher testosterone levels than other prisoners (Figure 7.15) (Dabbs, Carr, Frady, & Riad, 1995; Dabbs, Frady, Carr, & Besch, 1987). Even in women inmates there appears to be a relationship between testosterone level and aggressive dominance while in prison (Dabbs & Hargrove, 1997).

The prison results seem compelling, but the function of testosterone in human aggression is open to question, just as it was in sexual behavior. The studies are correlational, so we must look elsewhere for evidence that testosterone causes aggression. There is no clear evidence that aggression in humans is affected by manipulation of testosterone levels or by disorders that increase or decrease testosterone (Albert et al., 1993). For this reason, critics argue that aggression increases testosterone level, and so far the research is on their side. Not only does testosterone increase after winning a sports event (Archer, 1991; Mazur & Lamb, 1980), but it also goes up after receiving the M.D. degree (Mazur & Lamb, 1980) and even while watching one's team win a sporting event (Bernhardt, Dabbs, Fielden, & Lutter, 1998).

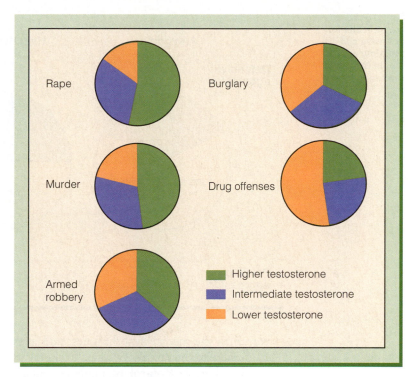

Figure 7.15
Testosterone levels of men convicted of various crimes
The proportion of men with high testosterone levels compared to other prisoners is greater as the violence of the crime increases.
Source: Based on Dabbs, Carr, Frady, & Riad, 1995.

The Brain

Most of the research on the biological basis of aggression has been done with rats and cats. These studies indicate that defensive and predatory aggression are distinct not only behaviorally but neurally (Albert et al., 1993; Siegel, Roeling, Gregg, & Kruk, 1999). The highly emotional nature of defensive aggression is indicated by the cat's familiar arched back, bristling fur, and hissing. Predatory aggression is cold and emotionless, as you realize if you have ever watched a cat stalking and killing its prey.

We know more about the brain structures involved in feline aggression and their connections than in any other animal. The two types of aggression have separate neural pathways, outlined in Figure 7.16. The defensive pathway begins in the medial nucleus of the amygdala,

How are testosterone and estrogen related to aggression?

What brain areas have a role in aggression?

Figure 7.16
Brain circuits for defensive and predatory aggression in the cat
Source: Based on Siegel, Roeling, Gregg, & Kruk, 1999.

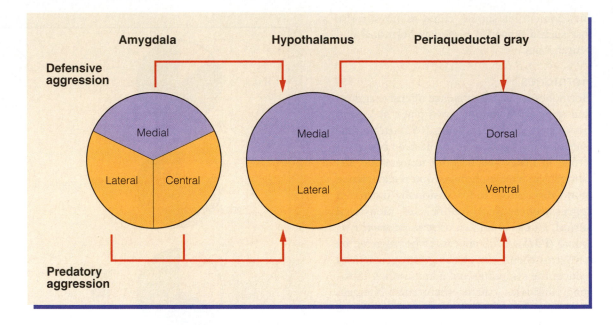

travels to the medial hypothalamus, and goes from there to the dorsal periaqueductal gray in the brain stem. Control of predatory attack flows from the lateral nucleus and central nucleus of the amygdala to the lateral hypothalamus and the ventral periaqueductal gray (Siegel et al., 1999). Of course, threat does not always result in aggression; stimulation of another area in the PAG produces flight (Zhang, Bandler, & Carrive, 1990).

Research on human aggression is understandably constrained, but we have determined that several brain areas are ultimately involved. Tumors can cause aggression if they are in the hypothalamus or the septal region (Albert et al., 1993). Seizure activity in the area of the amygdala increases aggression, and damage to the amygdala reduces it. A PET scan study found higher activity in the right amygdala and the hypothalamus in a group of murderers of both sexes (Raine, Meloy, et al., 1998); surgical lesions in these areas have produced improvement in 70% of patients with uncontrollable aggression (Ramamurthi, 1988).

The prefrontal cortex is critical in restraining aggression, as it is in moderating other behaviors. In the laboratory, males played a game in which they received electric shocks supposedly

delivered by another player, and they had the opportunity to deliver shocks to the fictitious player. The individuals who administered the highest intensity of retaliatory shocks were the ones who also scored the lowest on cognitive tests that are used to detect impaired functioning of the prefrontal cortex (Lau, Pihl, & Peterson, unpublished manuscript cited in Pihl, Peterson, & Lau, 1993).

In real life, brain deficits appear to be a frequent characteristic in murderers (Blake, Pincus, & Buckner, 1995). PET scans revealed decreased activity levels in the prefrontal cortex of male and female murderers (Raine, Meloy, et al., 1998). However, this deficiency was limited to affective murderers, those who had killed in a fit of rage rather than with premeditation. Remember that people with prefrontal damage often have difficulty controlling their impulses, which would explain the connection with affective murder.

Impulsiveness is also a characteristic of people with antisocial personality disorder, a group that makes up an estimated three-quarters of the prison population (Widiger et al., 1996). **People with *antisocial personality disorder (APD)* behave recklessly, violate social norms, commit antisocial acts like fighting,**

stealing, using drugs, and engaging in sexual promiscuity, and show little or no
remorse for their behavior. It is no coincidence that this description reminds us of Jane's
behavior; people with APD are more likely to
have reduced prefrontal gray matter (Raine,
Lencz, Bihrle, LaCasse, & Colletti, 2000).

Serotonin

We have already seen some indication of the
importance of serotonin in motivation. Usually
its role is to suppress motivated behaviors; as a
result, the motivation for food, water, sex, and
drugs of abuse increases when serotonin activity is low (Pihl & Peterson, 1993). Now we will
add aggression to the list.

Inhibition of Aggression

Serotonin inhibits aggression, probably through
its effects in the amygdala, hypothalamus, periaqueductal gray, and prefrontal area (Spoont,
1992; Vergnes, Depaulis, Boehrer, & Kempf,
1988). However, the focus of research has not
been on serotonin's ability to reduce aggression,
but on what happens when serotonin activity is
low. Serotonin activity is usually assessed by
measuring cerebrospinal fluid levels of the serotonin metabolite 5-HIAA. Low serotonin activity is specifically associated with impulsive
aggression; 5-HIAA is lower in impulsive violent offenders than in violent offenders who
planned their crimes (Linnoila et al., 1983).

Figure 7.17 illustrates the link, discussed
in Chapter 4, between violent crime in males
and the mother's smoking during pregnancy
(Brennan, Grekin & Mednick, 1999; Räsänen,
Hakko, Isohanni, Hodgins, & Järvelin, 1999).
That effect probably involves serotonin deficits
as well. When pregnant rats were injected with
nicotine, the offspring showed increased serotonin uptake, which reduces serotonin availability at the synapses (King, Davila-Garcia,
Azmitia, & Strand, 1991). To determine
whether low serotonin can cause aggression in
humans, Moeller and his colleagues (1996) had
males drink an amino-acid mixture that reduces
tryptophan, the precursor for serotonin. Then
the men participated in a computer game in

which one response earned points exchangeable
for money, and a different response subtracted
points from a fictitious competitor. At random
times during the game the player's screen indicated that some of his accumulated points had
been deleted by the fictitious competitor. The
men were more aggressive after drinking the
tryptophan-depleting mixture, deleting more of
the fictitious competitor's points.

Serotonin appears to be involved in the
inhibitory control that the prefrontal cortex
exerts on aggression. Researchers chemically
destroyed serotonin-producing neurons in the
lateral hypothalamus of rats, which depleted
their forebrain serotonin to 25% of its normal
level (Vergnes et al., 1988). Afterward, the rats
were dramatically more aggressive toward
intruder rats. The social restraints on aggression are strong and the penalties are high, so it
makes sense that the increased impulsiveness
of lowered serotonin would increase aggression in humans and animals.

Alcohol and Serotonin

In a study of crime in 14 countries, 62% of violent offenders were using alcohol at the time of
their crime or shortly before (Murdoch, Pihl, &

How does serotonin affect aggression?

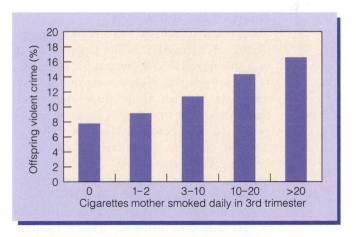

Figure 7.17
Effects of maternal smoking on criminal behavior in sons
As the frequency of smoking increased, so did the risk of
violent crime in the sons.

From "Maternal Smoking During Pregnancy and Adult Male Criminal
Outcomes," by P.A. Brennan, et al., in Archives of General Psychiatry, vol.
56, 215–219, Fig. 1. Copyright © 1999 American Medical Association.
Reprinted with permission.

Does testosterone increase human aggression after all?

Ross, 1990); evidence favors the commonsense interpretation that alcohol *facilitates* aggression rather than simply being associated with it (Bushman & Cooper, 1990). However, alcohol appears to influence aggression only in people who also have low serotonin levels, such as early-onset alcoholics (see Chapter 4). Unlike late-onset alcoholics, they tend to be impulsively aggressive and to have low brain serotonin activity (Buydens-Branchey, Branchey, Noumair, & Lieber, 1989; Virkkunen & Linnoila, 1990, 1997).

The dual influence of low serotonin on alcohol consumption and aggression makes for a deadly combination. After initially increasing serotonin activity, alcohol later depletes it below the original level (Pihl & Peterson, 1993); the alcohol abuser is caught in a vicious cycle as alcohol consumption increases both aggression and the craving for more alcohol. Drugs that inhibit serotonin uptake at the synapse, such as the antidepressant fluoxetine (trade name Prozac), reduce alcohol craving and intake (Naranjo, Poulos, Bremner, & Lanctot, 1994) and they also reduce hostility and aggressiveness (Coccaro & Kavoussi, 1997; Knutson et al., 1998).

Serotonin and Testosterone

Some research findings have reopened the possibility of a causal role for testosterone in human aggression. Higley and his colleagues (1996) suggest that high testosterone and low serotonin interact to produce aggression. Their study of free-ranging male monkeys supported their position. Monkeys with high testosterone were more likely to engage in brief aggression that asserted dominance, such as threats and displacing another monkey from his position. Monkeys with low 5-HIAA levels were impulsive: they more frequently took dangerously long leaps among the treetops, and when they engaged in aggression it was more likely to accelerate into greater violence. The most aggressive monkeys of all had both high testosterone and low 5-HIAA levels. Human data suggest a similar relationship. Violent alcoholic offenders often have both

What roles do heredity and environment play in aggression?

low brain serotonin and high testosterone levels (Virkkunen, Goldman, & Linnoila, 1996; Virkkunen & Linnoila, 1993). If testosterone has any causal influence on human aggression—emphasizing the word *if*—it may well occur only when serotonin's inhibitory effect is reduced.

Heredity and Environment

Like many other behaviors, aggression is genetically influenced. From a review of 24 studies, it was estimated that up to 50% of the variation among people in aggression is genetic in origin (Miles & Carey, 1997). A genetic influence does not necessarily mean that there is a gene for aggression; the influence may be on broader forms of behavior. Crimes against property also appear to be a heritable characteristic (DiLalla & Gottesman, 1991). The common factor in aggression and offenses against property could be lowered impulse control, and the genes that control three subtypes of serotonin receptors have been implicated in the genetic control of impulsive aggression (Virkkunen et al., 1996).

With only half of the variability in aggression accounted for by heredity there is still plenty of room for environmental influence, which has been documented by decades of research. A recent study found that the rate of violent criminality doubled in both men and women who came from homes with inadequate parenting (Hodgins, Kratzer, & McNeil, 2001). Male and female murderers who do not have the prefrontal deficits we saw earlier are more likely to have experienced psychological and social deprivation during childhood (Raine, Stoddard, Bihrle, & Buchsbaum, 1998). Again, as we have seen before and will see repeatedly throughout this text, behavior is the product of genes and environment.

 CONCEPT CHECK

- *What is the evidence that the prefrontal cortex moderates aggression?*
- *How do serotonin, alcohol, and testosterone possibly interact to increase aggression?*

In Perspective

Emotion has been difficult for neuroscientists to get a handle on because so much of emotion is a subjective, private experience. With improved research strategies and new technologies like PET scans, old questions about the role of brain structures are finally yielding. A good example is the ability to separate the emotion of pain from its sensory aspects, at the neural level. On another front, research has confirmed the influence of emotion on health, a topic that was practically relegated to fringe psychology not too long ago.

As we move from the topics of stress and pain to aggression, we complete the triangle of negative emotion. Aggression may have helped to ensure the survival of our evolutionary ancestors, but now it is viewed as one of our greatest burdens. Society needs to ask whether modifying the environment might reduce schoolhouse shootings or crime among the disadvantaged, but it also needs to appreciate the role of hormones, genes, and the brain when judging the accountability of a depressed mother who drowns all her children.

In the meantime, if you find these thoughts about the negative aspects of emotion a bit dismaying, you might want to take a short break while you hold your pen between your teeth. Improving your corner of the world is a good place to start.

Summary

Emotion and the Nervous System

- The autonomic nervous system increases bodily arousal during emotion and decreases it afterward.

- The cognitive theory is that we identify emotions from the stimulus context, and bodily feedback contributes only to the intensity. Studies indicate that in ambiguous situations we interpret arousal as emotion appropriate to the situation, but this does not necessarily mean we typically rely on cognitive feedback.

- The James-Lange theory claims that each emotion involves a different pattern of bodily arousal, and we use the feedback of that arousal to identify the emotion. There is evidence for distinctive patterns, and manipulating facial expressions induces the expected emotions, but evidence that such feedback is necessary is lacking.

- The limbic system is a network of several structures that have functions in emotion. We now know that emotion involves additional structures at all levels of the brain.

- The amygdala has a variety of functions, but its role in fear has received the most attention. Rats and humans with damage to both amygdalas lack fear and often fail to act in their own best interest.

- The prefrontal cortex uses emotion information to make decisions. People with damage there have trouble following moral and social rules, and they have impaired ability to learn from the consequences of their behavior.

- Damage to the right hemisphere particularly blunts emotions and impairs the person's ability to recognize emotion in faces and in voices.

Stress, Immunity, and Health

- Stress is adaptive, mobilizing the body for action and increasing immune system activity.

- Prolonged stress interferes with mental, physical, and emotional functioning, compromises the immune system, and even damages the brain.

- Social support, personality, and attitudes are related to immune functioning and health, including cancer survival. A third factor such as stress hormone level may be the real cause.

continued

- Pain is also an adaptive response; it informs us of danger to the body, and the emotion that accompanies it motivates us to take action.

Biological Origins of Aggression

- Testosterone is involved in male aggression and both testosterone and estrogen in female aggression, though in humans the causal link for testosterone is questionable.
- The amygdala and hypothalamus appear to be the most important brain structures in aggression, both in lower animals and in humans. The prefrontal cortex suppresses aggression, and deficiency there is linked to violent behavior.

- Serotonin inhibits aggressive behavior, and low serotonin level is associated with aggression. Alcohol and lowered serotonin level combine to increase aggression. Low serotonin and high testosterone levels may interact to increase aggression in humans.
- Heredity is estimated to contribute half of the variability in aggression among humans; one genetic link with aggressive behavior involves serotonin receptors. The other half of variation is due to the environment, including inadequate parenting.

 For Further Thought

- Do you think we identify emotions from bodily feedback or from the stimulus situation, or from something else? Why?
- Stress and pain involve considerable suffering, but they are necessary. Explain. What makes the difference between good and bad stress and pain?
- You are an adviser to a government official charged with reducing aggression in the

U.S. From what you have learned in this chapter, what would you recommend?

- In many states attorneys defending a person who pleads "not guilty by reason of insanity" must show that the defendant did not *know* right from wrong— as evidenced, for example, by the defendant's failure to flee or try to conceal the crime. Critique this standard in terms of what you know about controlling behavior.

Testing Your Understanding

1. Discuss the James-Lange and cognitive theories, including evidence for them.
2. Explain the roles of the amygdala and the prefrontal cortex in guiding our everyday decisions and behavior.
3. Describe the role the brain plays in animal and human aggression, including structures and their functions.

Select the one best answer:

1. The James-Lange theory and the cognitive theory disagree on whether:
   a. specific brain centers are involved in specific emotions.
   b. there is any biological involvement in human emotions.
   c. bodily feedback determines which emotion is felt.
   d. individuals can judge their emotions accurately.

2. Some people with brain damage do not seem to learn from the consequences of their behavior and need help managing their lives. Based on the studies in this chapter, you would expect that they would also be lacking in:
   a. sadness.   b. joy.
   c. fear.   d. motivation.

3. A person with partial paralysis seems remarkably undisturbed about the impairment. The paralysis:

   a. probably is on the right side of the body.
   b. probably is on the left side of the body.
   c. probably involves both sides of the body.
   d. is as likely to be on one side as the other.

4. Stress can:

   a. reduce immune system function.
   b. impair health.
   c. mobilize the immune system.
   d. both a and b.
   e. a, b, and c.

5. Long-term exposure to cortisol may affect memory by:

   a. reducing blood flow to the brain.
   b. destroying neurons in the hippocampus.
   c. inhibiting neurons.
   d. redirecting energy resources to the internal organs.

6. AIDS is a deficiency of the:

   a. immune system.   b. autonomic system.
   c. central nervous system.   d. motor system.

7. Indications are that if pain did not have an emotional component we would probably:

   a. be deficient in avoiding harm.
   b. avoid harm effectively, using learning and reasoning.

   c. be more aggressive.
   d. generally lead happier lives.

8. A structure described in the text as involved in both aggression and flight is the:

   a. amygdala.
   b. anterior cingulate cortex.
   c. lateral hypothalamus.
   d. periaqueductal gray.

9. According to research, you would have your best chance of showing that testosterone increases aggression in humans if you injected testosterone into:

   a. males rather than females.
   b. people with prefrontal damage.
   c. people with low serotonin.
   d. people who were being confronted by another person.

10. Based on information in the text, the chance of violent criminal behavior is increased in males if the mother:

    a. took a synthetic estrogen during pregnancy.
    b. smoked during pregnancy.
    c. failed to discipline the child.
    d. was beaten by the father in the son's presence.

Answers: 1. **c** 2. **c** 3. **b** 4. **e** 5. **b** 6. **a** 7. **a** 8. **d** 9. **c** 10. **b**

➡ On the Web

1. **Like Human, Like Machine,** an essay by Brian Aldiss, who wrote the story on which the movie *AI* was based, discusses the obstacles he sees in duplicating human feelings in robots at

   http://www.newscientist.com/hottopics/ai/likehuman.jsp

2. **HealthEmotions Research Institute** at the University of Wisconsin is dedicated to the study of the positive effects of emotions on health. The site describes research and provides a newsletter at

   http://www.healthemotions.org/

3. **Stress Less** features publications for sale, links to other websites on a broad variety of stress topics, and chat rooms organized by stress type at

   http://www.stressless.com/AboutSL/StressLinks.cfm

4. The **National Center for Posttraumatic Stress Disorder** site has information on the topic, including specifics about PTSD resulting from sexual assault, family relationships, automobile accidents, etc., at

   http://www.ncptsd.org/facts/index.html

   continued

Research articles on some topics are also available online.

5. **Type A Behavior: What You Should Know** describes the Type A personality, which research suggests is linked to heart attacks. A 10-item test to see if you fit the description is included at

   http://www.msnbc.com/onair/nbc/night lynews/stress/default.asp

 For additional information about the topics covered in this chapter, please look at InfoTrac College Edition, at

http://www.infotrac-college.com/wadsworth

Try search terms you think up yourself, or use these: *amygdala; limbic system; premenstrual syndrome; T cells.*

 On the CD-ROM: Exploring Biological Psychology

 Multiple Choice Quiz: Facial Expressions of Emotion
Simulation: Stress and Health

Video: Stress and the Brain
Video: Stress and Fat

 For Further Reading

Descartes' Error, by Antonio Damasio (Quill, 2000), covers the various topics of emotion but develops the premise that our rational decision making is largely dependent on input from emotions.

Why Zebras Don't Get Ulcers, by Robert Sapolsky (Freeman, 1998), is a lively discussion of emotion and its effects, including stress, immunity, ulcers, memory, and sex.

 Key Terms

adrenocorticotropic hormone (ACTH) *201*

amygdala *198*

anterior cingulate cortex (ACC) *205*

antisocial personality disorder (APD) *208*

autoimmune disorder *202*

B cell *201*

cognitive theory *192*

congenital insensitivity to pain *205*

cortisol *201*

defensive aggression *206*

hypothalamus-pituitary-adrenal cortex axis (HPA) *201*

immune system *201*

James-Lange theory *191*

leukocytes *201*

limbic system *196*

macrophage *201*

natural killer cells *201*

offensive aggression *206*

polygraph *194*

predatory aggression *206*

prefrontal cortex *189*

premenstrual syndrome (PMS) *207*

skin conductance response (SCR) *189*

stress *200*

sudden cardiac death *203*

T cell *201*

Ryan McVay

Hearing and Language

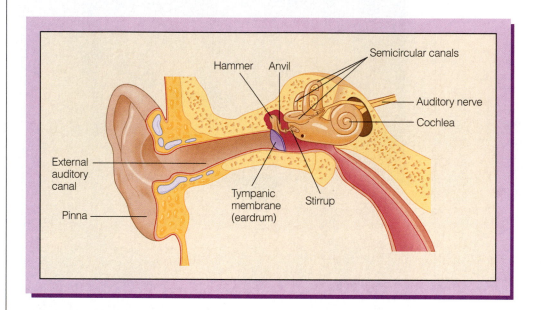

In this chapter you will learn:

- What the auditory mechanism consists of and how it works.
- How the brain processes sounds, from pure tones to speech.
- Which brain structures account for language ability.
- The cause of some of the major language disorders.
- What we know about language abilities in nonhuman animals.

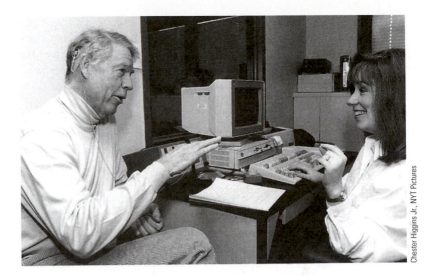

Figure 8.1
Gil McDougald trying out his cochlear implant
The microphone and the transmitter that sends the signal through his skull are visible behind his ear.

To be deaf is a greater affliction than to be blind.
—Helen Keller

Gil McDougald (Figure 8.1) was an infielder for the New York Yankees and played in eight World Series in the 1950s. In 1955 he was hit in the head by a line drive during batting practice. The injury started a slow deterioration of his hearing which eventually left him almost totally deaf. He could hear sounds, but he was unable to understand speech, which isolated him socially from his family and from former teammates like Mickey Mantle and Yogi Berra. After 20 years of deafness and frustration he heard about a procedure that might restore his hearing; it required implanting electrodes from a speech analyzer (a sophisticated kind of hearing aid) next to the auditory nerve, bypassing the damaged parts of his auditory system. Gil had the surgery, and six weeks later he met with the audiologist.

Betsy activated the device, then covered her mouth with a sheet of paper so he couldn't read her lips. She said "Hello," and he replied "Hello." She asked, "Do you hear me?" "Oh yeah!" he said. "Wow! This is exciting." She then asked him to repeat words as she said them. "Cowboy." He answered, "Cowboy." "Outside." He replied, "Outside." Tears welled in Gil's eyes. Across the room his wife Lucille choked out the words, "This is the first time in . . . It's unbelievable." Later, their relatives came to visit the McDougalds. As Lucille put it, "Everyone has come to watch grandpa hear" (Berkow, 1995, p. B8).

Nothing attests to the value of hearing more than the effects of losing it. The person is cut off from much of the discourse that our social lives depend on. There is no music, no song of birds, and no warning from thunder or car horns. When hearing is lost abruptly in later life the effect can be so depressing it eventually leads to suicide.

With the topics of hearing and language we begin the discussion of how we carry on transactions with the world. This communication involves acquiring information through the senses, processing the sensory information, communicating through language, moving about in the world, and acting upon the world. We have already touched on the senses of taste, smell, and pain in the context of hunger, sexual behavior, and emotion. Before we explore additional sensory capabilities we need to establish some basic concepts.

1

How is a stimulus translated into information the brain can use?

First, a sensory system must have a specialized receptor. **A *receptor* is a cell, often a specialized neuron, that is suited by its structure and function to respond to a particular form of energy, such as sound.** A receptor is a form of transducer, which is a term borrowed from engineering just like *stress* and some of our other terms in psychology have been. **A *transducer* is a device that converts energy from one form to another**; a good example is a photoelectric cell, which translates light energy into an electrical signal. In the case of sensory receptors, the conversion is to a neural signal. You will see examples of two kinds of receptors in this and the next chapter, but receptors come in a wide array of forms to carry out their functions.

In order for a receptor to do its job, there must also be an adequate stimulus. **An *adequate stimulus* is the energy form for which the receptor is specialized.** Adequacy of the stimulus is a useful concept because "inadequate" stimuli also produce responses, due to the imperfect specialization of receptors. For example, if you apply pressure to the side of your eyeball (through the lid) you will see a circular dark spot; if you bump your head you will literally see stars, or at least flashes of light.

You will remember from Chapter 3 that, according to Müller's doctrine of specific nerve energies, the neural mechanism rather than the type of stimulus determines the kind of sensory experience you will have. A sensory system will register its peculiar type of experience even if the stimulus is inappropriate, like pressure on the eyeball or electrical stimulation of the auditory cortex. We will see in this and the next two chapters that it is the patterning of the stimulation—that is, the information contained in the stimulus—that makes sensory information meaningful.

Most people consider audition (hearing) and vision the most important senses. As a result, there has been more research on these two senses and we know more about them, so we will give them the most attention.

What is the difference between sensation and perception?

Because audition is a more mechanical sensory mechanism than vision, it is a good place to begin our formal discussion of *sensation*, **the acquisition of sensory information, and** *perception*, **the interpretation of sensory information.**

HEARING

This does not mean that audition is simple. The cochlea, where the auditory stimulus is converted into neural impulses, contains a million moving parts. Our range of sensitivity to intensity, from the softest sound we can hear to the point where sound becomes painful, is a million to one. Our ability to hear low-intensity sounds is limited more by interference from the sound of blood coursing through our veins and arteries than by the auditory mechanism itself. In addition, we are able to hear frequencies ranging from about 20 hertz (Hz, cycles per second) up to about 20,000 Hz, and we can detect a difference in frequencies of only 2 or 3 Hz.

The Stimulus for Hearing

The adequate stimulus for audition is vibration in a conducting medium. Normally the conducting medium is air, but we can also hear under water and we hear sounds conducted through our skull. The air is set to vibrating by the vibration of the sound source—a person's vocal cords, a bell that has been struck, or a stereo speaker. As the air vibrates, it is alternately compressed and decompressed (Figure 8.2). If we graphed these alternating pressure changes, they would look something like the illustrations in Figure 8.3.

The sounds we hear can be classified as either pure tones or complex sounds. We can illustrate that distinction better with graphs than with words alone. If we connected a microphone to an oscilloscope and produced a pure tone (for instance, by striking a tuning fork), we would see a tracing on the face of the oscilloscope that looked like one of the first four graphs in Figure 8.3. The up-and-down

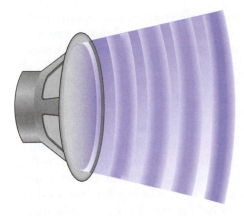

Figure 8.2
Alternating compression and decompression of air by a sound source
The dark areas represent high pressure (a denser concentration of air molecules) and the light areas represent low pressure.

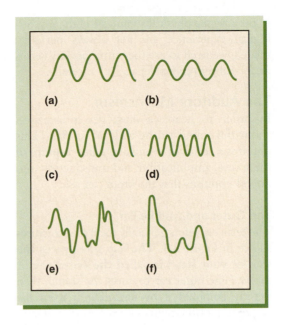

Figure 8.3
Examples of pure and complex sounds
See text for explanation.

squiggles represent increasing and decreasing pressure (transduced by the microphone into increasing and decreasing voltage). Notice that the waveforms of Figure 8.3a–d are a very regular shape, called a sine wave. They are *pure tones:* **each has only one frequency.** Figure 8.3e and f graph *complex sounds:* **each is a mixture of several frequencies.** *Frequency* **refers to the number of cycles or waves of alternating compression and decompression of the vibrating medium that occur in a second.** Figure 8.3a and b have the same frequency, so we would hear these two sounds as having the same, or nearly the same, pitch. Figure 8.3c and d would also sound about the same, but would sound higher in pitch than Figure 8.3a and b. *Pitch* **is our experience of the frequency of a sound.** Although pitch and frequency are related they do not correspond exactly, due to the physical nature of our ears.

Figure 8.3e is a random combination of frequencies and would probably be described by most of us as "noise." Depending on the combination and order of frequencies, a complex sound might seem musical like the last waveform, which was produced by a clarinet (Figure

8.3f). The two waveforms may not look very different to you, but they would certainly sound different. Although what is considered *pleasantly* musical depends on experience and culture (and one's age!), we would recognize even the most foreign music as music.

The sounds represented by Figure 8.3a and c have the same amplitude (the height of the wave), so they would sound about equally loud; Figure 8.3b and d would sound less loud but about equal to each other. *Amplitude* **or** *intensity* **is the term for the physical energy in a sound,** while *loudness* **is the term for our experience of sound energy.** How loud a sound is to the observer depends not just on the intensity but on the frequency of the sound; for example, we are most sensitive to sounds between 2,000 and 4,000 Hz—the range within which most conversation occurs—and equally intense sounds outside this range would seem less loud to us. Again, we make a distinction between the term for the physical characteristic of the sound and the term for our experience of

What is the difference between frequency and pitch? Intensity and loudness?

it. Because the physical stimulus and the psychological experience are not always perfectly related, we need to use the terms *intensity* versus *loudness* and *frequency* versus *pitch* carefully.

The Auditory Mechanism

In order to hear we must get information about the sound to the auditory cortex. This requires a series of events including capture of the sound, amplification, and transduction into neural impulses that the brain can use.

The Outer and Middle Ear

The term *ear* refers generally to all the structures shown in Figure 8.4. **The flap that graces the side of your head is called the outer ear or *pinna*.** The outer ear captures the sound, then slightly amplifies it by funneling it from the larger area of the pinna into the smaller area of the auditory canal. It also selects for sounds in front and to the side of us while blocking sounds coming from behind us. Although dogs and cats can turn their ears toward a sound that is not directly in front of them and some adolescent boys impress their age mates by wriggling their ears, most of us have to turn our heads to orient toward a sound.

The first part of the middle ear, the eardrum or *tympanic membrane*, is a very thin membrane stretched across the end of the auditory canal; its vibration transmits the sound energy to the ossicles. A muscle called the *tensor tympani* can stretch the eardrum tighter or loosen it in order to adjust the sensitivity to changing sound levels. The tympanic membrane is very sensitive. Wilska (1935) ingeniously glued a small rod to the eardrum of a human volunteer (temporarily, of course) and used an electromagnetic coil to vibrate the rod back and forth. He determined that we can hear sounds when the eardrum moves as little as the diameter of a hydrogen atom! The experiment was remarkable for the time and recent studies with more sophisticated equipment have shown that Wilska's measurements were surprisingly accurate (Hudspeth, 1983).

The *ossicles* are tiny bones that transfer vibration from the tympanic membrane to the cochlea; they operate in a lever fashion and produce a further slight amplification of the sound. The *malleus*, *incus*, and *stapes* are named for their shapes, and are better known by their English equivalents *hammer*, *anvil*, and *stirrup*. The ossicles provide a greater amplification by concentrating the energy collected from the larger tympanic membrane onto the much smaller base of the stapes.

Figure 8.4
The outer and inner ear

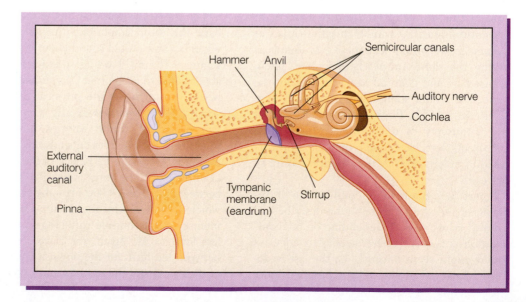

The Inner Ear

The parts of the inner ear are shown in Figure 8.4. The semicircular canals are part of the vestibular organs and not related to hearing; we will cover them in Chapter 10. The snail-shaped structure is the ***cochlea, where the ear's sound-analyzing structures are located.*** You can see from the cochlea's shape where it got its name, which means "land snail" in Latin. Figure 8.5a shows a larger view. It is a tube that is about 35 mm long in humans, and coiled 2½ times. It is subdivided by membranes into three fluid-filled chambers or canals (Figure 8.5b). In this illustration the end of the cochlea has been removed, and you are looking down the three canals from the base end. The stapes (Figure 8.5a) rests on the ***oval window, a thin, flexible membrane on the face of the vestibular canal.*** The *vestibular canal* (scala vestibuli) is the point of entry of sound energy into the cochlea. The vestibular canal is connected with the *tympanic canal* at the far end (the apex) by an opening in the membrane called the *helicotrema*. This opening allows the pressure waves to travel through the cochlear fluid into the tympanic canal more easily. Each time the oval window is pressed inward by the stapes, the ***round window at the base end of the tympanic canal*** bulges outward. Fluid is nearly incompressible, so very little energy could enter the cochlea were it not for the flexibility of the round window.

All this activity in the vestibular and tympanic canals literally bathes the ***cochlear canal, which holds the auditory receptors,*** in

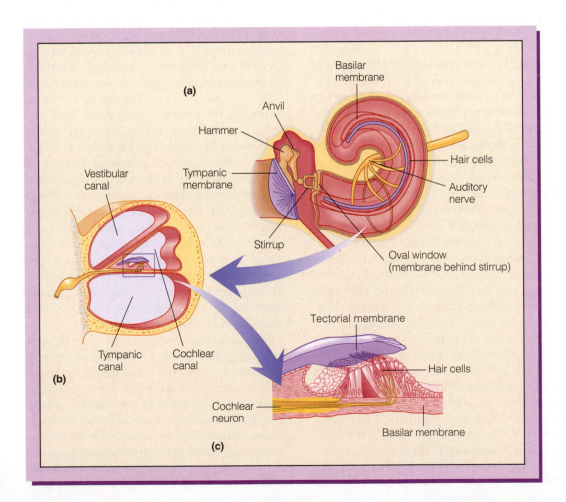

Figure 8.5
The cochlea and the organ of Corti

(a)

Basilar membrane

Anvil

Hammer

Hair cells

Vestibular canal

Tympanic membrane

Auditory nerve

Stirrup

Oval window (membrane behind stirrup)

(b)

Tympanic canal

Cochlear canal

Tectorial membrane

Hair cells

Cochlear neuron

Basilar membrane

(c)

Dr. G. Oran Bredberg/SPL/Photo Researchers

Figure 8.6
Electron microscope view showing the hair cells attached to the tectorial membrane
(The colors are artificial.)

vibration. The vibration passes to the *organ of Corti,* **the sound-analyzing structure that rests on the** *basilar membrane.* **The organ of Corti consists of four rows of specialized cells called hair cells, their supporting cells, and the** *tectorial membrane* **above the hair cells** (Figure 8.5c). To visualize these structures, remember you are looking down a long tube; imagine the four rows of hair cells as picket fences or rows of telephone poles, and the tectorial membrane as a shelf overlying the hair cells and extending the length of the cochlea.

The hair cells are the receptors for auditory stimulation. Vibration of the basilar membrane and the cochlear fluid bends the hair cells, opening potassium channels (not sodium channels, as in neurons) and depolarizing the hair cell membrane. This sets off impulses in the auditory neuron connected to the hair cell. When the hair cell moves back in the opposite direction it relaxes and the potassium channels close. The hair cells are very sensitive; the amount of deflection required to produce a response is equivalent to the Eiffel Tower leaning 10 cm (Hudspeth, 1989).

The human cochlea has about 12,000 *outer hair cells,* **in three rows** (Figure 8.6),

How is the auditory stimulus converted to a neural impulse?

and a single row of 3,400 inner hair cells. **The less numerous** *inner hair cells* **receive 90–95% of the auditory neurons, and apparently provide the majority of information about auditory stimulation** (Dallos & Cheatham, 1976). A strain of mouse lacking inner hair cells due to a mutant gene is unable to hear (Deol & Gluecksohn-Waelsch, 1979). The role of the outer hair cells is uncertain, but we will consider a probable function shortly.

The Auditory Cortex

Neurons from the cochleas form the two auditory nerves (eighth cranial nerves), one of which enters the brain on each side of the brain stem. They pass through brain stem nuclei (see Figure 8.7a) to the inferior colliculi, to the medial geniculate nucleus of the thalamus, and finally to the auditory cortex in each temporal lobe. Neurons from each ear go to both projection areas, but there are more connections to the contralateral (opposite) side than to the ipsilateral (same) side. This means that a sound on your right side is registered primarily, but not exclusively, in the left hemisphere of the brain. Researchers interested in differences in function between the two hemispheres have used an interesting strategy to stimulate one side of the brain. They present an auditory stimulus through headphones to one ear, and present white noise (which contains all frequencies and sounds like radio static) to the other ear to occupy the nontargeted hemisphere. This technique has helped researchers determine that the left hemisphere is dominant for language in most people, and that the right hemisphere is better at other tasks, like identifying melodies.

The auditory cortex is on the superior (upper) gyrus of the temporal lobe of each hemisphere; most of it is hidden inside the lateral fissure, as you can see in Figure 8.7b. The area is *topographically organized,* **which means that neurons from adjacent receptor locations project to adjacent cells in the cortex.** In this case, the projections form a sort of map of the unrolled basilar membrane (Merzenich, Knight, & Roth, 1975), just as we

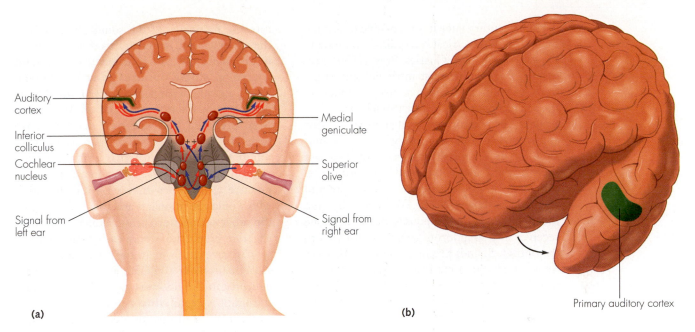

Figure 8.7
The auditory pathway and the auditory cortex

saw in Chapter 3 that the somatosensory cortex contains a map of the body. We will see that this organization is typical in the senses when we study vision in the next chapter.

Frequency Analysis

The sounds that are important to us, such as speech and music, vary greatly in intensity and frequency, and they change intensity and frequency rapidly. It is the task of the cochlea and the auditory cortex to analyze these complex patterns and convert the raw information into a meaningful experience. The neural response to differences in intensity is straightforward: increases in stimulus intensity recruit progressively higher-threshold neurons into firing, so intensity is coded by the number of neurons firing. (You will see shortly why the brain cannot rely on rate of firing, the usual code for stimulus intensity, to determine the intensity of sounds.)

We will concentrate on frequency analysis, which has received the lion's share of attention from researchers. More than 50 years ago Ernest Wever (1949) described 17 versions of the two major theories of frequency analysis, which indicates the difficulty we have had in

figuring out how people experience pitch. We will discuss a few versions that have been important historically. This will introduce you to these two important theories and give you some idea of how theories develop and change in response to emerging evidence.

Frequency Theories

The most obvious explanation of how the auditory system analyzes frequency is the *frequency theory,* **which assumes that the auditory mechanism transmits the actual sound frequencies to the auditory cortex for analysis there.** William Rutherford proposed an early version in 1886; it was called the *telephone theory* **because he believed that individual neurons in the auditory nerve fired at the same frequency as the rate of vibration of the sound source.** The telephone theory was held in favor by many theorists for at least another four decades, but it was fatally flawed from the start. Physiological research at that time had not revealed the basic characteristics of neuronal activity that you are familiar with, but your reading of Chapter 2 should permit you to recognize why the theory was wrong.

How do the frequency and place theories explain frequency analysis?

3

Half a century later it was possible to test the theory with electrical recording equipment. Ernest Wever and Charles Bray (1930) performed one of the most intriguing investigations of auditory frequency analysis found in the scientific literature. They attached an electrode to the auditory nerve of anesthetized cats and recorded from the nerve while they stimulated the cat's ear with various sounds. Because the string-galvanometers used to record neural activity at that time were unable to respond to frequencies above 500 Hz, Wever and Bray ran the amplified neural responses into a telephone receiver in a soundproof room and listened to the output. Sounds produced by a whistle were transmitted with great fidelity. When someone spoke into the cat's ear, the speech was intelligible, and the researchers could even identify the speaker. The auditory nerve was "following," or firing at the same rate as the auditory stimulus. It appeared that the telephone theory was correct, although we know that it could not be.

However, Wever and Bray were not recording from a single neuron, but from all the neurons in contact with the hook-shaped copper electrode they placed around the auditory nerve. Thus they were monitoring the *combined* activity of hundreds of neurons. The explanation of how the nerve was able to duplicate the frequency of the sounds is known as the ***volley theory*, which states that groups of neurons follow the frequency of a sound where a single neuron cannot** (Wever, 1949). Because a single neuron is limited in its firing rate by the refractory period, Wever and Bray proposed that different neurons "take turns" firing; thus a group of neurons is able to follow the frequency whereas a single neuron cannot. The term *volleying* is an analogy to the practice of soldiers with muzzle-loading rifles, who would fire in squads and then reload while the other squads were firing. Volleying is illustrated in Figure 8.8, where each of the neurons synchronizes its firing to the waves of the tone; some neurons fire on each wave but no single neuron can fire on every wave. In this theory the brain is required to combine information from many neurons to determine the frequency. In Wever and Bray's study the auditory nerve was unable to follow frequencies above 5,200 Hz, a figure that subsequent research has shown to be accurate (Rose, Brugge, Anderson, & Hind, 1967). So even with volleying, frequency following can account for only one-fourth of the range of frequencies we hear.

Place Theory

Resonance is the vibration of an object in sympathy with another vibrating object. If you hold a vibrating tuning fork near the strings of a piano, you will notice that the strings begin to vibrate slightly. A high-frequency tuning fork causes the thinner, more tautly stretched strings to vibrate more than the others, and a low-frequency tuning fork causes the thicker, looser strings to vibrate most. In the nineteenth century Hermann von Helmholtz (1863/1948) suggested that the basilar membrane was like a series of piano strings, stretched progressively more loosely with distance down the membrane. This would cause the base end of the membrane to resonate more to high-frequency sounds, the middle portion to moderate frequencies, and the apex to low frequencies. Helmholtz's proposal was a version of ***place theory*, which states that the frequency of a sound is identified by the**

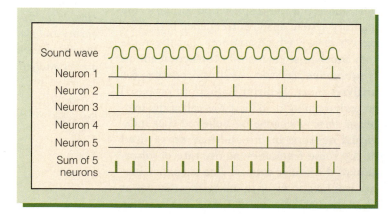

Figure 8.8
Illustration of volleying in neurons
No single neuron can follow the frequency of the sound, but a group of neurons can.

location of maximal vibration on the basilar membrane and which neurons are firing most. Place theory has been the most influential explanation of frequency analysis for a century and a half. It is an example of a theory that has become almost universally accepted but continues to be referred to as a theory.

A century later Georg von Békésy, a communications engineer from Budapest, began a series of innovative experiments that won him the Nobel Prize for physiology in 1961. Békésy constructed mechanical models of the cochlea, and also observed the responses of the basilar membrane in cochleas he removed from deceased subjects as diverse as elephants and humans. When he stimulated these cochleas with a vibrating piston, he could see under the microscope that vibrations peaked at different locations along the basilar membrane; a wave-like peak hovered near the base when the frequency was high and moved toward the apex as Békésy (1951) decreased the frequency. He also learned that the basilar membrane is not like a series of piano strings; its frequency selectivity is due to differences in elasticity, with the membrane near the stapes 100 times stiffer than the apical end (Békésy, 1956).

Figure 8.9 shows how frequency sensitivity is distributed along the membrane's length. Recordings from single auditory neurons have

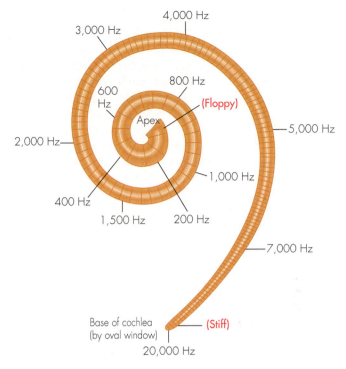

Figure 8.9
Frequency sensitivity on the muman basilar membrane
Notice that the basilar membrane is narrow at the base end of the cochlea and widens toward the apex, the opposite of the cochlea's shape.

confirmed that place information about frequency is carried from the cochlea to the cortex. You can see from the *tuning curves* in Figure 8.10 that each neuron responds most to a

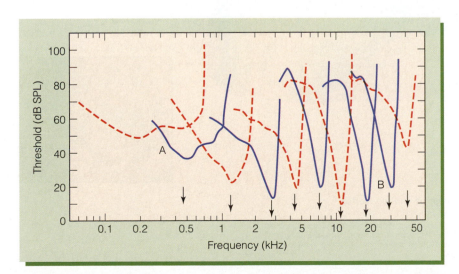

Figure 8.10
Tuning curves of cat auditory nerve fibers
Each curve represents data from a single neuron in the cat auditory cortex; it shows how the intensity of sound required to produce a response increases as the sound's frequency moves away from the neuron's "preferred" frequency. Note that tuning is much sharper at higher frequencies.

Source: A.P. Palmer (1987). "Physiology of the cochlear and cochlear nucleus." In M.P. Haggard and E.F. Evans (eds.), *Hearing*. Edinburgh: Churchill Livingstone, p. 838–855.

narrow range of frequencies (Palmer, 1987). Because the auditory cortex is topographically organized, it also contains a *tonotopic map,* **which means that each successive area responds to successively higher frequencies** (Figure 8.11) Scheich & Zuschratter, 1995).

However, notice in Figure 8.10 that each neuron responds not just to a single frequency but (to a lesser extent) to higher and lower frequencies as well; this is because a particular frequency produces vibrations over a wide area of the membrane. So how can neurons that make such imperfect discriminations inform the brain about the frequency of a sound with the 2- to 3-Hz sensitivity that has been observed? Most likely, the brain compares the rate of firing in neurons from adjacent places on the basilar membrane. In the next chapter we will see evidence of the same kind of comparison of information from color receptors.

Place analysis is the reason we can hear rather clearly through bone conduction. The vibrations enter the cochlea from all sides during bone conduction, rather than through the

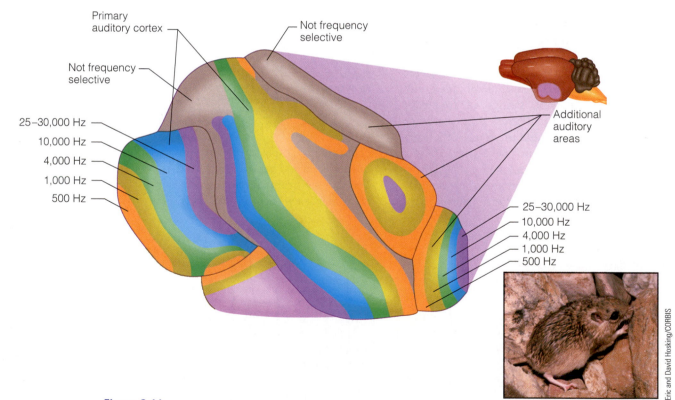

Figure 8.11
Frequency specificity in the gerbil auditory cortex
Each area is a map of the basilar membrane.
Adapted from "Mapping of Stimulus Features and Meaning in Gerbil Auditory Cortex with 2-Deoxyglucose and c-FOS Antibodies" by Scheich & Zuschratter, *Behavioral Brain Research*, vol. 66, p. 195–205. Copyright 1995, with permission from Elsevier Science.

Eric and David Hosking/CORBIS

oval window, but Békésy (1951) demonstrated with his cochleas that this does not disrupt the tonotopic response of the basilar membrane. As he moved his vibrating piston from the base around to the side of the cochlea, or to the apex or anywhere else, the peak of vibration remained in the same location. Thomas Edison was nearly deaf, yet his second most famous invention was the phonograph. He compensated for his impaired hearing by grasping the edge of the phonograph's wooden case between his teeth and listening to the recording through bone conduction. You can still see the bite marks on one of his phonographs in the museum at his winter home and laboratory in Fort Myers, Florida. Figure 8.12 shows another bite-to-listen device.

At low frequencies the whole basilar membrane vibrates about equally, and researchers have been unable to find neurons that are tuned for frequencies lower than 200 Hz (Kiang, 1965). Wever (1949) suggested that individual neurons follow the frequency of sounds up to their firing limit (between 100 and 500 Hz in the auditory system), volleying signals frequency up to 5,000 Hz, and place analysis takes over beyond that point. However, most researchers subscribe to a simpler *frequency-place theory, that frequency following accounts for frequencies up to about 200 Hz and all remaining frequencies are represented by the place of greatest activity*. Whether or not volleying plays any role, it appears that place analysis alone is an inadequate explanation for auditory frequency analysis.

Analyzing Complex Sounds

You may have figured out that we rarely hear a pure tone. The speech, music, and noises that are so meaningful in our everyday life are complex, made up of many frequencies. Forty years before Helmholtz proposed his place theory, the French mathematician Fourier had demonstrated that any complex waveform— sound, electrical, or whatever—can be broken down into two or more component sine waves.

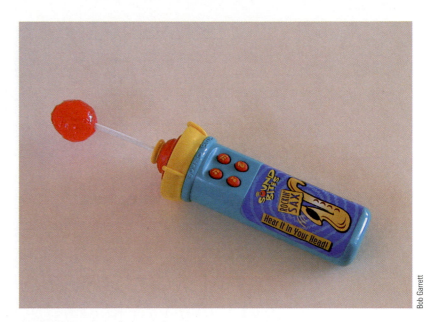

Bob Garrett

Figure 8.12
A musical toy that works by bone conduction
This is a musical lollipop holder. It has no speaker or earplug, but bite down on the lollipop and you literally hear the music in your head, thanks to bone conduction and place analysis. (Yes, it really works . . . but not very well.)

A few years later G. S. Ohm, better known for Ohm's law of electricity, proposed that the ear performs a Fourier analysis of a complex sound and sends information about each of the component frequencies to the cortex (Figure 8.13). Current researchers agree that the basilar membrane acts as the auditory Fourier analyzer, responding simultaneously along its length to the sound's component frequencies.

But actual experience is more complicated than a single complex sound. At a party we hear the music playing loudly and several conversations around us. In spite of the number of complex sounds assaulting our cochleas, we are able to separate the speech of our conversation partner from the other noises in the room. We do more than that: we sample the other sounds regularly enough to enjoy the music and to hear our name brought up in a conversation across the room. **The ability to sort out meaningful auditory messages from a**

How does the auditory system handle complex sounds?

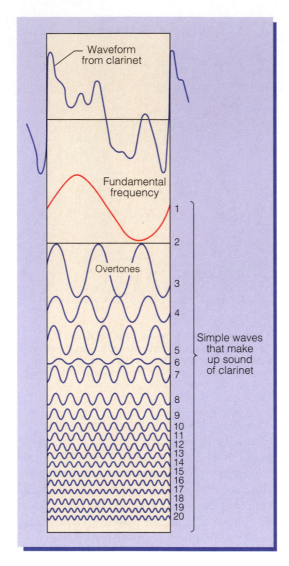

Figure 8.13
Fourier analysis of a clarinet note
The dominant component is a relatively high-amplitude, low-frequency sine wave; the other components are progressively higher frequencies at lower intensities. If we produced sounds at each of these frequencies and amplitudes at the same time, the combined waveform when displayed on an oscilloscope would look like the waveform at the top, and the result would *sound* like the clarinet note.
Source: From T. Miller (1997). How much distraction can you hear? *Stereo Review.*

How does the brain determine the locations of sounds?

what gets through to the brain probably involves efferent stimulation of the inner ear; *efferent* **activity flows from the brain to the periphery.** Electrical stimulation of the descending auditory neurons sends efferent activity to the cochlea and reduces the inner hair cells' response to sound (Brown & Nuttal, 1984; Xiao & Suga, 2002). The odds are that this suppression is accomplished by the outer hair cells. If the outer hair cells are depolarized by an electrical stimulus, they shorten in length; hyperpolarization causes lengthening (Brownell, Bader, Bertrand, & de Ribaupierre, 1985). But what effect does this have?

The outer hair cells' cilia are embedded in the tectorial membrane; Brownell and his colleagues (1985) suggested that shortening and lengthening of the outer hair cells changes the tension between the tectorial membrane and the basilar membrane, and thus adjusts the rigidity of the organ of Corti. Presumably this provides localized sensitivity adjustments that suppress background sounds during attention to a particular sound (Xiao & Suga, 2002). This requires the brain to distinguish auditory objects. **An *auditory object* is the association we form between a sound and its source.** (It is not the source itself.) This is no easy task, because the vibrations from one source are intermingled among the vibrations from others all along the basilar membrane. Yet we do form auditory objects, although how is a mystery. Fortunately, different sound sources are usually in different locations in the environment, so sound localization helps distinguish among auditory objects.

Locating Sounds

The most obvious way to locate a sound is to turn your head until the sound is loudest. This is not very effective because the sound may be gone before the direction is located. Three additional cues permit us to locate sounds quickly and accurately, including those that are too brief to allow turning the head. They are particularly interesting because their detection involves built-in brain circuitry.

complex background of sounds is called the *cocktail party effect.* How do we do it?

No one knows, but the effect involves a form of attention. The mechanism for regulating

4

Cochlear Implants for Artificial Hearing

The device that restored Gil McDougald's hearing is called a cochlear implant. It can be effective when the hair cells are damaged but the auditory nerve is intact, which is the case in about 90% of people with hearing impairment. A microphone picks up the sound and sends it to a shirt pocket–sized speech processor. Then a transmitter behind the ear sends the signal to a receiver that is surgically mounted on the mastoid bone just beneath the skin (see the figure). From there the signal travels through a wire to an electrode threaded through the cochlea. Current models have several channels that send signals representing the different frequencies of a sound to different locations along the length of the electrode. The activation of different neurons by different frequencies mimics the behavior of the basilar membrane and hair cells in an unimpaired individual. In other words, it relies on the principle of place analysis.

The majority of people with implants achieve word recognition rates of 80% and higher (National Institutes of Health, 1995); a 70% recognition rate is sufficient to carry on a telephone conversation. Most others benefit from enhanced lip reading as well as from the alerting signals of sirens and car horns. How well the implant works depends on whether the person learned language before deafness occurred. It also depends on how long the person has been deaf, because over time neurons from other sensory areas intrude into the unused auditory cortex. If a PET scan of the deaf individual's auditory cortex shows elevated activity it means that vision or another sensory function has taken over the auditory cortex, and that a cochlear implant will not improve hearing (Lee et al., 2001).

In children, implantation at an early age and auditory rehabilitation training increases the chances of mainstream classroom placement, even with children who were impaired before learning language. This results in savings of an estimated $30,000 to $200,000 in educational expenses for an individual from kindergarten through 12th grade (Francis, Koch, Wyatt, & Niparko, 1999). On the human side, successful implantation reduces social isolation, loneliness, and depression, and increases self-esteem, independence, and vocational prospects (National Institutes of Health, 1995).

A Cochlear implant device

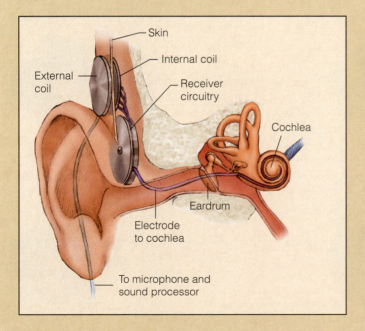

Skin

Internal coil

External coil

Receiver circuitry

Cochlea

Electrode to cochlea

Eardrum

To microphone and sound processor

Figure 8.14
Device used by nineteenth-century sailors to enhance binaural localization cues

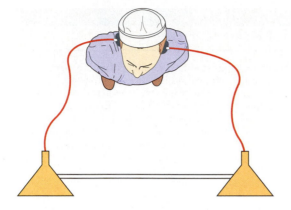

Figure 8.14
Device used by nineteenth-century sailors to enhance binaural localization cues

intensity, and time of arrival. Animals with ears that are very close together (like mice) are at a disadvantage in locating sounds. Grasshoppers and crickets have evolved a compensation for their small head size: their auditory organs are on their legs, as far apart as possible. Nineteenth-century sailors improved their accuracy in locating a foghorn by listening through tubes attached to funnels at the ends of a long rod (Figure 8.14).

Binaural Cues

At low frequencies, a sound arriving from one side of the body will be at a different phase of the wave at each ear, referred to as a *phase difference* (see Figure 8.15). As a result, one eardrum will be pushed in while the other is being pulled out. Some of the auditory neurons in the superior olivary nucleus respond only to phase differences. Above about 1,500 Hz a sound will have begun a new wave by the time it reaches the second ear, so phase difference becomes useless as a cue.

All three of these cues are *binaural,* meaning that they involve the use of both ears; the brain determines the location of the sound based on differences between the sound at the two ears. These cues are useless when a sound source is in the median plane (equidistant from the person's ears), but if the sound is slightly to one side the stimulus will differ between the ears in three ways: phase,

Figure 8.15
Phase difference as a cue for sound localization
At lower frequencies the sound is at a different phase at each ear.

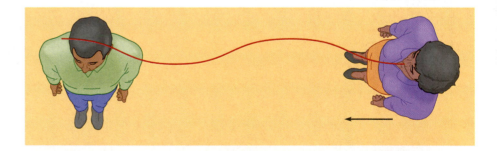

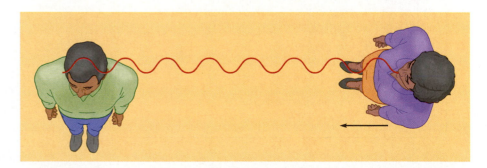

When a sound source is to one side or the other, the head blocks some of the sound energy. The sound shadow this creates produces a ***difference in intensity,*** **so that the near ear receives a slightly more intense sound** (Figure 8.16). Again, some superior olivary neurons respond to differences in intensity at the two ears. Because low frequency sounds tend to bend around obstacles, this cue works best when the sound is above 2,000 or 3,000 Hz.

The final binaural cue for locating sounds is ***difference in time of arrival*** **at the two ears. A sound that is directly to a person's left or right takes about 0.5 millisecond to travel the additional distance to the second ear** (see Figure 8.16 again); humans can detect a difference in time of arrival as small as 10 microseconds (millionths of a second) (Hudspeth, 2000), which means we can locate sounds very near the midline of the head with good accuracy. Such precision requires specialized circuits, which provide a good illustration of automatic processing in the brain in general.

Brain Circuits for Locating Sounds

Of the neural circuits for binaural sound localization, the one for time of arrival has been studied most thoroughly. The circuit has been mapped in the barn owl, which is extremely good at sound localization; in fact, it can locate a mouse in darkness just from the sounds it makes rustling through the grass. The circuit is located in the nucleus laminaris, the avian (bird) counterpart of the mammalian superior olivary nucleus. Electrical recording has revealed the function of its ***coincidence detectors,*** **neurons that fire most when they receive input from both ears at the same time** (Carr & Konishi, 1990). Figure 8.17 is a simplified diagram of a coincidence detector circuit. You can see from the diagram that the leftmost detector would receive simultaneous stimulation when the sound originates on the right side; the delay in arrival of the sound at the left ear is compensated for by the longer

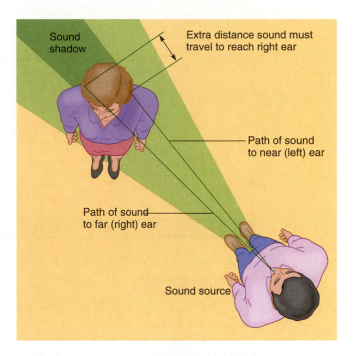

Figure 8.16
Differential intensity and time of arrival as cues for sound localization
The sound is reduced in intensity and arrives later at the distant ear.

pathway from the right ear. The next coincidence detector would fire at its highest rate when the sound is between the right side and the midline; the middle detector would fire at its highest rate when the sound is equidistant from the two ears; and so on.

If this were the end of our discussion of audition it would also be the end of the chapter, and obviously it is not. Beyond the primary auditory cortex are additional areas, as many as nine in some mammals. These secondary auditory areas are involved with the elaboration of particular types of auditory information. For example, some of the cells in the monkey's superior temporal gyrus respond selectively to calls of their own species, and some of those react only to one type of call (Wollberg & Newman, 1972). The most elaborate further processing, of course, involves language, which is our next topic.

Figure 8.17
Diagram of circuit for detecting difference in time of arrival at the two ears
Source: Based on the results of Carr & Konishi, 1990.

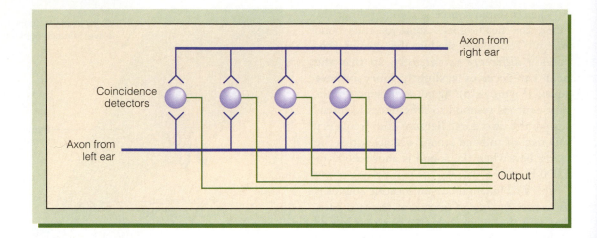

- *Trace an auditory stimulus from the pinna to the auditory neurons.*
- *Explain how, according to place theory, the frequency of sound is coded. Extend this to complex sounds.*
- *Explain how the circuit for detecting difference in time of arrival of sounds at the two ears works.*

LANGUAGE

For humans, the most important aspect of hearing is its role in processing language.

—A. J. Hudspeth

Few would question the importance of language in human behavior. Keep in mind the meaning of the term *language:* it is not limited to speech, but includes the generation and understanding of written, spoken, and gestural communication. Communication through language has important survival value and is inestimably important to human social relationships. A person who cannot speak or write suffers a high degree of isolation; one who cannot comprehend the communications of others is worse off still. These capabilities require learning, but they also depend on specific structures of the brain, and damage to these structures can deprive a person of portions or all of these functions.

The Brain Structures of Language

In 1861 the French physician Paul Broca reported his observations of a patient who for 21 years had been almost unable to speak. Tan, as he was known by the hospital staff because that was one of the few sounds he could make, died shortly after he came under Broca's care. Autopsy revealed that Tan's brain damage was located in the posterior portion of the left frontal lobe. After studying eight other patients, Broca concluded that *aphasia*—**language impairment caused by damage to the brain**—results from damage to the frontal area anterior to the motor cortex now known as Broca's area. Nine years later a German doctor named Carl Wernicke identified a second site where damage produced a different form of aphasia. Located in the posterior portion of the left temporal lobe, this site is known as Wernicke's area. See Figure 8.18 to locate Broca's and Wernicke's areas and the other structures to be discussed here. Most of our understanding of the brain structures involved in language comes from studies of brain-damaged individuals, so this is where we will start.

Broca's Area

Broca's aphasia **is language impairment caused by damage to Broca's area and surrounding cortical and subcortical areas.** The symptoms can best be understood by examining the speech of a stroke patient; as you read this interview you will see why the disorder is also referred to as *expressive aphasia.*

DOCTOR: Why are you in the hospital, Mr. Ford?

MR. FORD: Arm no good. Speech . . . can't say . . . talk, you see.

DOCTOR: What happened to make you lose your speech?

MR. FORD: Head, fall, Jesus Christ, me no good, str, str . . . oh Jesus . . . stroke.

DOCTOR: I see. Could you tell me, Mr. Ford, what you've been doing in the hospital?

MR. FORD: Yes, sure. Me go, er, uh, P.T. nine o'cot, speech . . . two times . . . read . . . wr . . . ripe, er rike, er, write . . . practice . . . getting better. (Gardner, 1975, p. 61)

Mr. Ford's speech is not nearly as impaired as Tan's; he can talk, and you can get a pretty good idea of his meaning, but he shows the classic symptoms associated with damage to Broca's area. First, his speech is *nonfluent;* although well-practiced phrases like "yes, sure" and "oh, Jesus" come out easily, his speech is halting, with many pauses between words. Second, he has trouble finding the right words, a symptom known as *anomia* ("without name"). Often he has *difficulty with articulation;* he mispronounces words, like *rike* for *write.* Finally, notice that his speech is *agrammatic;* it has content words (nouns and verbs) but lacks grammatical, or function, words (articles, adjectives, adverbs, prepositions, and conjunctions). The hardest phrase for a Broca's aphasic to repeat is "No ifs, ands, or buts" (Geschwind, 1972).

Thelma was similarly impaired, but I had some enjoyable conversations with her at the

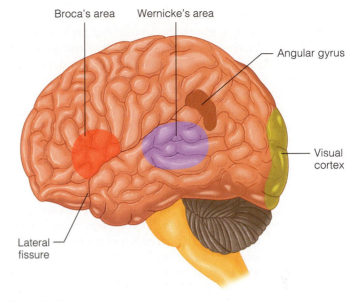

Figure 8.18
Language areas of the cortex

nursing home, mainly because I was willing to piece together her broken speech, and to nod and smile when even that was impossible. She could usually manage only one or two words at a time: she showed me old photos of her parents, pointing and saying "Mother . . . Father." But like Tan, who would occasionally express his frustration with the oath *"sacre nom de Dieu!"* ("holy name of God!"), Thelma would occasionally blurt out something meaningful. Once when she was unable to express herself effectively to an aide she was having a disagreement with, she exclaimed to me, "They can say anything they want to! I know everything. I just can't say."

Broca believed that Broca's aphasia impaired motor instructions for vocalizing words. But Mr. Ford was able to recite the days of the week and the letters of the alphabet, or to sing "Home on the Range," and Thelma would entertain the group at dinner with a song she had composed before she was impaired. So vocalization is not lost, but the ability to translate information into speech patterns is impaired.

What are the differences between Broca's aphasia and Wernicke's aphasia?

5

The problem, then, is "upstream" from speech, so reading and writing are impaired as much as speech is. Comprehension is also as impaired as speech when the meaning depends on grammatical words. For example, the patient can answer questions like "Does a stone float on water?" but not the question "If I say, 'The lion was killed by the tiger,' which animal is dead?" (Gardner, 1975).

Wernicke's Area

In *Wernicke's aphasia* the person has difficulty understanding and producing spoken and written language. This is often called *receptive aphasia*, but that term is misleading because the same problems with understanding language also show up in producing it. For example, the person's speech is fluent but meaningless. A patient asked to describe a picture of two boys stealing cookies behind a woman's back said, "Mother is away here working her work to get her better, but when she's looking the two boys looking in the other part. She's working another time" (Geschwind, 1979). This meaningless speech is called *word salad*, for obvious reasons.

Because the speech of the Wernicke's patient is articulate and has the proper rhythm, it sounds normal to the casual listener. The first time I met a person with Wernicke's aphasia I was knocking on the social worker's door at the nursing home, and I thought it was because my mind was elsewhere that I failed to understand one of the residents when she spoke. But then my "Pardon me" elicited "She's in the frim-fram," and I realized the problem was hers rather than mine. I responded with a pleasantry and she answered, again meaninglessly. That began a long relationship of conversations, in some ways as enjoyable as those with Thelma. The difference was that neither of us ever understood the other; another difference was that it didn't matter, because she seemed strangely unaware that anything was amiss.

What problems have been found in the brains of dyslexics?

Structures Involved in Reading and Writing

Although aphasia affects reading and writing, these functions can be impaired independently of other language abilities. ***Alexia* is the inability to read and *agraphia* is the inability to write.** Presumably they are due to disruption of **pathways in the *angular gyrus* that connect the visual projection area with the auditory and visual association areas in the temporal and parietal lobes** (see Figure 8.18 again). The PET scans in Figure 8.19 show that activity increases in this area during reading.

Reading and writing are also impaired in learning disorders. The most common learning disorders are ***dyslexia,* an impairment of reading;** dysgraphia, difficulty in writing; and dyscalculia, a disability with arithmetic. Because of its importance and the amount of research that has been done, we will focus on dyslexia. Dyslexia can be *acquired*, through damage, but its origin is more often *developmental*. Developmental dyslexia is partially genetic. The child of a dyslexic parent has eight times more risk of being dyslexic than other children. Several gene locations have been identified, and gene linkages for dyslexia have been better replicated than for any other human ability or disability (Grigorenko, 2001; Pennington, 2001). Dyslexia is a complex disorder, with several likely causes, which we will explore briefly.

There are two basic forms of dyslexia. The first involves *visual-perceptual* difficulties. The person often reads words backwards ("now" becomes "won"), confuses mirror-image letters (p and q, b and d), and has trouble fixating on printed words, which seem to move around on the page. These difficulties appear to come from a developmental deficiency in the dyslexic's visual pathway. Dyslexics' brains are slow to respond (as measured by evoked potentials) to low-contrast, rapidly changing visual stimuli (Livingstone, Rosen, Drislane, & Galaburda, 1991). Presumably this makes it difficult for the dyslexic's brain to detect and correct for rapid, unintentional movements of the eye from their fixation. As a result, words seem to jump around and letters reverse themselves. This affects not only reading

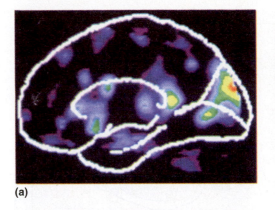

(a)

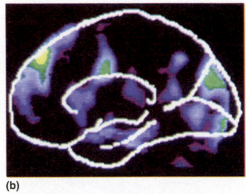

(b)

TWEAL

BOARD

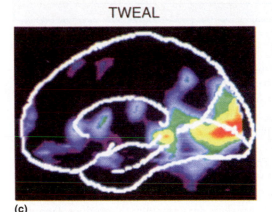

(c)

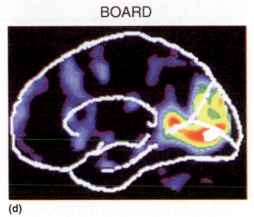

(d)

Figure 8.19
PET scans during reading
Viewing letterlike forms (**a**) and strings of consonants (**b**) did not activate the area between the primary visual cortex and language areas, but reading pronounceable nonwords (**c**) and real words (**d**) did.
Reprinted with permission from S.E. Peterson, P.T. Fox, A.Z. Snyder, and M.E. Raichle, "Activation of extrastriate and frontal cortical areas by visual words and word-like stimuli," *Science*, 249, 1049–1044. Copyright 1990 American Association for the Advancement of Science.

performance but also learning to read in the first place.

Researchers suspected a problem in a major visual route in the brain. The ***magnocellular hypothesis* states that some symptoms of dyslexia result from developmental errors in the magnocellular visual pathway, which is concerned with rapidly moving stimuli and detects eye movements** (Stein, 2001). Comparing the brains of deceased dyslexic and nondyslexic individuals, investigators found that magnocellular system cells were smaller in the thalamus of dyslexics (Galaburda & Livingstone, 1993; Livingstone et al., 1991).

The second type of dyslexia is *phonological* in nature. The phonological dyslexic has trouble distinguishing the variations in frequency and amplitude in speech (Stein, 2001). In reading, the person has difficulty translating letter strings into word sounds, and vice versa. As a result, reading is slow and nonautomatic, spelling is difficult, and the person must rely heavily on visual memory of written words and thus cannot read unfamiliar words.

A group of apparently related defects may account for these symptoms. In a functional MRI study (see section A.3 of the appendix), normal individuals increased their activity in Wernicke's area and the angular gyrus as they read questions that made increasing phonological demands (for example, "*Do T and V rhyme?*" versus "*Do leat and jete rhyme?*") (Shaywitz et al., 1998). Activity level in these areas was low in dyslexic individuals, and did not increase as

Figure 8.20
Brain activation in nonimpaired and dyslexic individuals during reading
Darker shading indicates greater activation. Increased frontal activation in the dyslexic individuals may have been due to greater effort as the difficulty of the tasks increased.

Adapted from S.E. Shaywitz, et al. (1998), "Functional disruption in the organization of the brain for reading in dyslexia," in Proceedings of the National Academy of Sciences, U.S.A., 95, p. 2636–2641, Figure 3 on p. 2639. Copyright 1998 National Academy of Sciences, U.S.A. Used with permission.

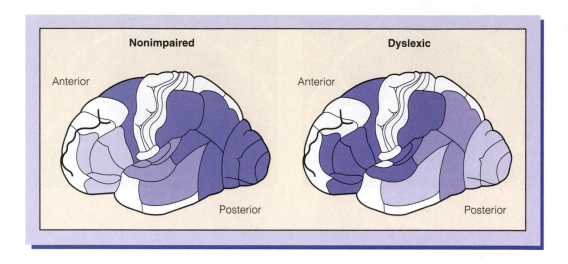

What is the Wernicke-Geschwind model?

phonological difficulty increased (Figure 8.20). The results indicated that their deficit was in translating the written words into auditory form. In most people the ***planum temporale, where Wernicke's area is located,*** is larger in the left hemisphere than in the right. However, in dyslexics it is more frequently equal in size or larger on the right (Humphreys, Kaufman, & Galaburda, 1990; Hynd & Semrud-Clikeman, 1989). In at least some dyslexic brains many of the neurons in the left planum temporale lack the usual orderly arrangement, and some of them have migrated into the outermost layer (Figure 8.21) (Galaburda, 1993; Humphreys et

al., 1990; Kemper, 1984). The strong similarity to the defects in the brain affected by fetal alcohol syndrome that you saw in Chapter 3 suggests that this developmental error occurred prenatally.

The Wernicke-Geschwind Model

Wernicke suggested, and Norman Geschwind elaborated on, a model for how Broca's area and Wernicke's area interact to produce language (Geschwind, 1970; 1972; 1979). The model is illustrated in Figure 8.22 and in the following examples. Answering an orally presented question involves a progression of activity from the

Figure 8.21
Developmental anomalies in dyslexic brain
(a) A normal brain. **(b)** In the dyslexic brain, cells lack the normal layering and arrangement in columns, and some of the cells have migrated into the superficial layer where they would not ordinarily be found.

Courtesy A.M. Galaburda, Harvard Medical School.

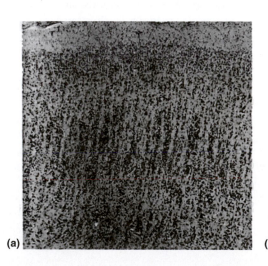

(a)

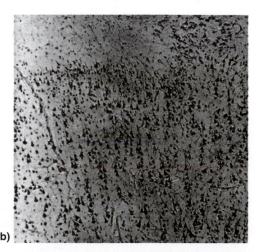

(b)

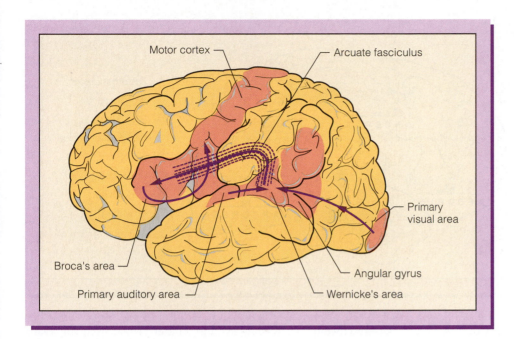

Figure 8.22
The Wernicke-Geschwind model
of language
Adapted from N. Geschwind (1979).
"Specializations of the human brain."
Scientific American, 241 (9), 180–199.

auditory cortex to Wernicke's area, and then to Broca's area. If the response is to be written, Wernicke's area sends output to the angular gyrus, where it elicits a visual pattern. When a person reads aloud, the visual information is translated into the auditory form by the angular gyrus, then passed to Wernicke's area, where a response is formulated and sent to Broca's area. The idea that visual information must be converted to an auditory form for processing arose in part from the fact that language evolved long before writing was invented, and Wernicke's area was believed to operate in an auditory fashion.

This system has long been the primary model for how language operates. It is relatively simple and seems to make sense of the various aphasias. However, there are problems. One is that language functions are not limited to Broca's and Wernicke's areas; damage to the basal ganglia, thalamus, and subcortical white matter also produce aphasia (Hécaen & Angelergues, 1964; Mazzocchi & Vignolo, 1979; Naeser et al., 1982). Broad cortical areas also play an important role, though possibly only because they are storage sites for information. For example, naming objects (using

nouns) produces activity just below the auditory cortex and Wernicke's area (Damasio, Grabowski, Tranel, Hichwa, & Damasio, 1996). Using verbs (describing what is happening in a picture) is impaired by damage to the left premotor cortex, adjacent to the motor cortex. This area is also activated while naming tools, and by imagining hand movements (Martin, Wiggs, Ungerleider, & Haxby, 1996). Apparently when tool names are learned they are stored near the brain structure that would produce the action.

Electrical stimulation studies (Mateer & Cameron, 1989; Ojemann, 1983) and studies of brain damage (Hécaen & Angelergues, 1964) have also shown that the various components of language functioning are scattered throughout all four lobes (see Figure 8.23). This does not mean that there is no specialization of the cortical areas. Damage in a particular lobe can produce a variety of symptoms, but articulation errors are still more likely to result from frontal damage and comprehension problems from damage in the temporal lobes (Hécaen & Angelergues, 1964; Mazzocchi & Vignolo, 1979).

Figure 8.23
Frequency of language deficits resulting from damage in each lobe
The data make clear that the language functions are not restricted to specific areas.
Source: Based on Hécaen & Angelergues, 1964.

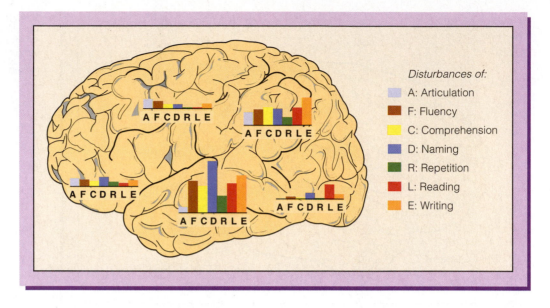

Disturbances of:
A: Articulation
F: Fluency
C: Comprehension
D: Naming
R: Repetition
L: Reading
E: Writing

So it appears that the Wernicke-Geschwind view of a few discrete language areas is too simple. However, the theory is still a good starting point for understanding language. And if it has been misleading, it has also helped researchers organize their thinking about language and has generated volumes of research—which, after all, is how we make scientific sense of our world.

Recovery from Aphasia

There is usually some recovery from acquired aphasia during the first one or two years, more so for Broca's aphasia than for Wernicke's aphasia (Martins & Ferro, 1992). Initial improvement is due to reduction of the swelling that often accompanies brain damage, rather than to any neural reorganization. Just how the remaining recovery occurs is not well understood, but it is a testament to the brain's plasticity.

A woman who suffered a left-hemisphere injury as a child became aphasic, but recovered; then she lost all language capability at age 59 following a right-hemisphere stroke (Guerreiro, Castro-Caldas, & Martins, 1995). This case is often used as an argument that the right hemisphere takes over language functions following massive left-hemisphere injury.

Rasmussen and Milner (1977) used the Wada technique and electrical stimulation to determine the location of language control in patients before removing lesioned tissue that was causing epileptic seizures. (The Wada technique involves anesthetizing one hemisphere at a time by injecting a drug into each carotid artery; when the injection is into the language-dominant hemisphere, language is impaired.) Individuals whose left-hemisphere injury occurred before the age of 5 were more likely to have language control in the right hemisphere, supporting the hypothesis of right-hemisphere compensation. Patients whose left-hemisphere damage occurred later in life more often had left-hemisphere control of language; there was evidence in some cases of left-hemisphere posterior damage that control had shifted into the border of the parietal lobe. Since language functions are scattered widely in the left hemisphere, perhaps the compensation involves enhancing already existing activity rather than establishing new functional areas.

A Language Generating Mechanism?

When Darwin suggested that we have an instinctive tendency to speak (see quote), what he meant was that infants seem very ready to engage in language and can learn it with minimal instruction. Children learn language with such alacrity that by the age of 6 they understand about 13,000 words, and by the time they graduate from high school their working vocabulary is at least 60,000 words (Dronkers, Pinker, & Damasio, 2000). This means that children learn a new word about every 90 waking minutes. The hearing children of deaf parents pick up language just about as fast as children with hearing parents (Lenneberg, 1969), in spite of minimal learning opportunities.

Man has an instinctive tendency to speak, as we see in the babble of our young children.

—Charles Darwin

Noam Chomsky (1980) and later Steven Pinker (1994) interpreted children's readiness to learn language as evidence of a ***language acquisition device, a part of the brain hypothesized to be dedicated to learning and controlling language.*** Not all researchers agree with this idea, but most accept that there are biological reasons why language acquisition is so easy. This ease cuts across forms of language. For example, both hearing and deaf infants of signing parents babble in hand movements (Figure 8.24); the deaf infants' babbling proceeds into signing through the same stages and at about the same pace that children of speaking parents learn vocal language (Petitto, Holowka, Sergio, & Ostry, 2001; Petitto & Marentette, 1991). The researchers suggest that the ease of children's language acquisition is due to a brain-based sensitivity to rhythmic language patterns, a sensitivity that does not depend on the form of the language.

Innate Brain Specializations

Over 90% of right-handed people are left-hemisphere dominant for language. This is also true for two-thirds of left-handers; the remainder are about equally divided between right-

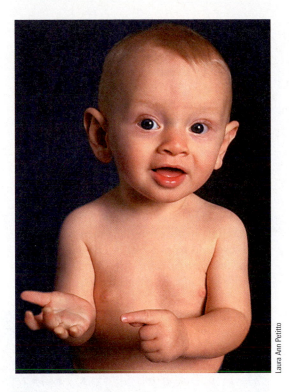

Figure 8.24
Babies of signing parents babble with their hands
Their babbling is unlike the random hand movements of other infants, which they also make at other times. Babbling hand movements are slower and similar in rhythm to their parents' signing, and restricted to the space in front of their bodies.
Source: Petitto, Holowka, Sergio, & Ostry, 2001. By permission of *Nature*, copyright 2001.

Laura Ann Petitto

hemisphere dominant and mixed (Loring et al., 1990; Milner, 1974). In the large majority of autopsied brains, Broca's area is larger (Falzi, Perrone, & Vignolo, 1982), and the lateral fissure (Yeni-Komshian & Benson, 1976) and planum temporale (Geschwind & Levitsky, 1968; Rubens, 1977; Wada, Clarke, & Hamm, 1975) are longer in the left than in the right hemisphere. These differences are not the result of usage. The left planum temporale is already larger by the 29th week of gestation (Wada et al., 1975; Witelson & Pallie, 1973). At the age of 1 week, verbal stimuli produce larger evoked potentials in the left hemisphere, while tones and noise affect the right hemisphere more (Molfese, Freeman, & Palermo, 1975).

Location of Other Languages

Additional evidence for a language acquisition device comes from studies of individuals who communicate with American Sign Language (ASL), which is a separate language with its own grammatical rules. Communicating in ASL activates the same left-hemisphere areas

Is language dominance different in right- and left-handers?

that traditional language does. This is true of deaf as well as hearing signers, so it is not just the result of the brain using pathways already established by a verbal language (Neville et al., 1998). The right hemisphere is also active while processing ASL (Figure 8.25) (Neville et al., 1998), but probably only because it handles visual-spatial information better than the left. Left-hemisphere damage causes lasting impairments in sign language (Hickok, Bellugi, & Klima, 1996; Neville et al., 1998), but right-hemisphere damage has little effect (Hickok et al., 1996; Neville et al., 1998). This suggests that the left-hemisphere language mechanism is predisposed to processing language regardless of its form, a capability that is consistent with the idea of a language acquisition device.

The different languages of multilingual speakers appear to occupy different brain areas, a fact that seems to contradict this hypothesis. For example, epileptic seizures or brain surgery affecting the left temporal lobe sometimes interferes with one language but not another (Gomez-Tortosa, Martin, Gaviria, Charbel, & Auman, 1995; Schwartz, 1994). A colleague who is originally from Lebanon told me an interesting story about his mother. She lives in the U.S., and she was fluent in English until a stroke impaired her English, but not her ability to speak Arabic. Her nearby family members spoke only English, so when they needed to talk with her they had to telephone a relative in another city to translate!

Figure 8.25
Activity in the left and right hemispheres during sign language
Reprinted with permission from H.J. Neville, et al., "Cerebral organizations for language in deaf and hearing subjects: Biological constraints and effects of experience," Proceedings of The National Academy of Sciences, U.S.A., 95, 922–929. Copyright 1998 National Academy of Sciences, U.S.A.

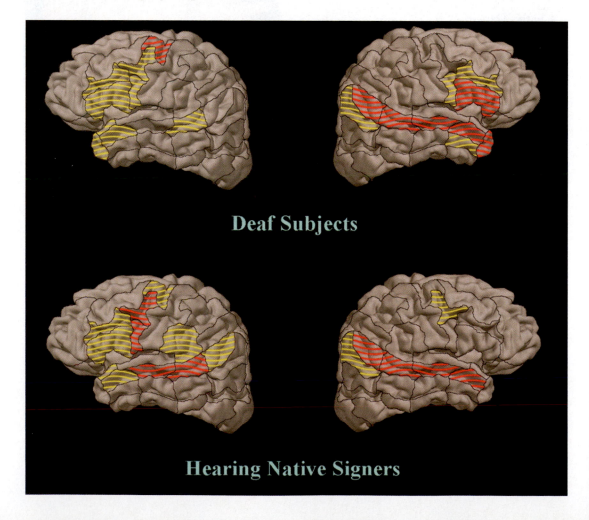

Deaf Subjects

Hearing Native Signers

So are other parts of the brain equivalent when it comes to acquiring new languages? Individuals who learned two languages together from infancy showed activation in the same area while they silently performed tasks in each language (Kim, Relkin, Lee, & Hirsch, 1997). However, in people who learned their second language during adulthood the two languages activated separate areas, with centers as far apart as 4.5 to 9.0 mm in different individuals (Figure 8.26). Nevertheless, the activity for both languages was still located in Broca's area, so in spite of this separation the hypothesis of a single language acquisition device remains intact.

These structures may not have evolved specifically to serve language functions, however. You will see in the next section that some primates show similar enlargements in the left hemisphere, and their possession of language is questionable at best. Another reasonable interpretation of these data is that the structures evolved to handle rapidly changing information and fine discriminations, which language in its various forms requires. Even if these structures have been "borrowed" by language, the concept of a language acquisition device is still meaningful. We will continue to explore this idea in the context of animal language.

Language in Nonhumans

Research has refuted most of humans' claims to uniqueness, including tool use, tool making, and self-recognition. Determining whether humans have exclusive ownership of language has been more difficult. Animal language intrigues us because we want to know whether we have any company "at the top," and because we want to trace the evolutionary roots of language. There are no fossil records of language, so we must look to the behavior of living relatives. Although dolphins, whales, and gorillas have been the subjects of research, the major contender for a copossessor of language has been the chimpanzee. The reason is that we and chimpanzees diverged from common ancestors a relatively recent 8 million years ago, and we still share an estimated 99% of our genes (King & Wilson, 1975).

7

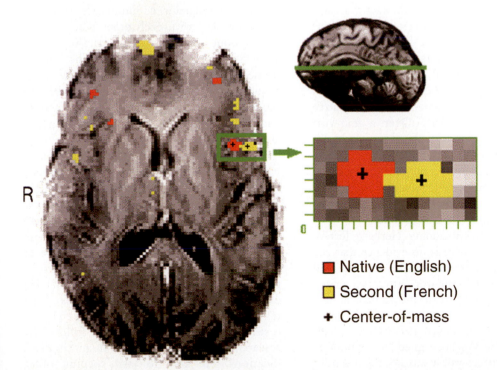

Figure 8.26
Areas activated by different languages in a bilingual subject
The functional MRI image on the left shows where in the brain the activated areas were located. The brain on the right shows the level of the brain from which the "slice" was taken. The image at center right is an enlargement of the area of the brain enclosed in the rectangle. (The left side of the brain is on the right in this image.)

Source: Kim, Relkin, Lee, & Hirsch, 1997. By permission of *Nature*, Copyright 1997.

R

■ Native (English)
□ Second (French)
+ Center-of-mass

A major obstacle has been deciding what we mean by language. Linguists agree that the vocalizations animals use to announce the availability of food or the presence of danger are only signals and have little to do with language. Even the human toddler's request "milk" may initially be just a learned signal to indicate hunger and, like the monkey's alarm call, indicate no language understanding. As you will see in the following discussion, some of the results obtained in language research with animals are equally difficult to interpret.

Chimpanzee Language Research

What skills have chimps achieved in language studies?

Early studies attempted to train chimps to speak. However, after being reared for six years with a human family, the chimpanzee Viki could vocalize only the words "mama," "papa," and "cup" (Hayes & Hayes, 1953; Kellogg, 1968). Researchers have questioned whether chimpanzees have an adequate larynx for forming the sounds (Kellogg, 1968). They also appear to be more visual than auditory, and imitate what they see rather than what they hear (Gardner & Gardner, 1969). Their proficiency with their hands and the fact that they communicate with a number of gestures similar to those used by pre-language children suggested that researchers should try to train chimps in the use of ASL.

Allen and Beatrice Gardner (1969, 1975) attempted to teach a home-reared chimpanzee to communicate in ASL. Over a four-year period, the chimpanzee Washoe learned 132 different signs (Fouts, Fouts, & Schoenfeld, 1984); she was able to identify a number of objects by name; to communicate requests for food, to be tickled (a favorite activity), or to play a game; and to say "sorry" after she bit someone.

However, critics including Herbert Terrace have argued that there is no evidence that any chimpanzee has learned to form a sentence, and that the three- and four-word utterances prized by researchers, like "banana me eat banana," are no more than a running-on of words (Terrace, Petitto, Sanders, & Bever, 1979). Terrace suggests that when Washoe signed "water bird" in the presence of a swan it was not the inventive characterization of "a bird that inhabits water," but the separate identification of the bird and the water it was on. Subsequent researchers have been careful to look for stronger evidence that the use of words represents true language, such as spontaneous requests and statements, use of grammar and proper word order, and use of words in new combinations.

Chimpanzee language research (Figure 8.27) would probably have died were it not for two very fortunate "accidental" outcomes. Roger Fouts took over Washoe and three other chimps that the Gardners had trained in sign language. According to Fouts, the human caretakers used only seven signs with the chimps. However, the chimps taught Washoe's infant adopted son Loulis 47 signs (Fouts et al., 1984). Loulis and the other chimps regularly carried on three-way sign-language conversations, mostly requesting hugs or tickling, signing "smile," and asking to be chased. The majority of all signing was initiated by Loulis, the only untrained chimpanzee.

Duane Rumbaugh and Sue Savage-Rumbaugh use a different approach: chimps learn to press buttons on a panel to communicate with their caretakers and with each other. Each button has a unique symbol on its face and represents a specific word (Figure 8.27b). The chimps trained with this device are able to make requests for food, music, and movies, to request a specific food from another chimp, and so on (Rumbaugh, 1990). The Rumbaughs attempted to teach Mutata, a pygmy chimp, to use the symbol board, but she did not do well (Savage-Rumbaugh, McDonald, Sevcik, Hopkins, & Rubert, 1986; Savage-Rumbaugh, 1987). However, her son Kanzi, who was allowed to play in the training room, began pressing the "chase" symbol to request chase games with the experimenters. Kanzi never received formal training with the board, but by the age of 6 he had mastered 150 symbols. He can request specific food items or ask to be taken to specific locations in the 55-acre research preserve, and he can follow the researchers' requests to take them to those locations. He asks to visit specific other

(a)

Susan Kuklin/Photo Researchers

Enrico Ferorelli

(b)

Figure 8.27
Language research with chimpanzees
(a) A researcher converses with a chimp using American Sign Language. **(b)** Another chimp communicates through the symbol board.

chimps, and makes requests for actions for which he is neither the initiator nor the recipient—for instance, asking a particular person to chase a specific other person. He can also respond to novel sentences; in fact, his language capability is comparable to that of a 2-year-old child (Savage-Rumbaugh et al., 1993). Kanzi's sister Mulika learned to use the symbol board even earlier and progressed faster than he did (Savage-Rumbaugh et al., 1986).

Perhaps these two chimps learned so quickly because their experience with language began in infancy, in a more natural learning environment than formal training. It is also likely that pygmy chimps *(Pan paniscus)* are better suited for the social interactions involved in language research. Unlike the common chimpanzee *(Pan troglodytes)*, they share with humans close male-female relationships, male participation in infant care, frequent eye contact, and—another behavior previously thought to be unique to humans—food sharing between adults of different sexes (Savage-Rumbaugh, 1987; Savage-Rumbaugh et al., 1986).

Even a sampling of studies done with animals other than chimpanzees would take more space than we have here, but one line of research is too interesting to omit. Irene Pepperberg's (1993) African gray parrot, Alex, makes verbal requests like "Tickle me" or

"Wanna go ____ (other location)." This is no great accomplishment, because parrots readily learn to imitate human speech. However, most of Alex's responses are answers to interrogations about concepts—number, color, shape, and size. Not only can Alex identify several objects by name or the material it is made of (wood, plastic, and so on), but he can also tell Pepperberg how many items she is holding, the color of an item, or whether two items differ in shape or color. Alex's vocal responses are rather simple; what is most impressive about his performance is his apparent *understanding* of complex questions, such as "What shape is the green wood?"

Lateralization in Animal Brains

An approach of some researchers has been to determine whether other animals share with us any of the brain organization that is associated with language. The results have been surprising. In the chimpanzee, the lateral fissure is longer and the planum temporale is larger on the left than on the right (Gannon, Holloway, Broadfield, & Braun, 1998; Yeni-Komshian & Benson, 1976). Japanese macaque monkeys respond best to calls of their own species when the recorded calls are presented through headphones to the right ear (and primarily to the left hemisphere) than when they are presented

Do other animals share our brain structures for language?

to the left ear. There is no left-hemisphere advantage for the (nonmeaningful) calls of another monkey species (Petersen, Beecher, Zoloth, Moody, & Stebbins, 1978). Dolphins and the Rumbaughs' chimps Austin and Sherman responded more quickly when symbols or command gestures were presented to their left hemisphere (Hopkins & Morris, 1993; Morrel-Samuels & Herman, 1993). Finally, lesions on the left side of the canary brain render its attempts at song unrecognizable, while birds with right-side lesions continue to sing nearly as well as intact birds (Nottebohm, 1977).

Do we share language ability with animals? The jury is still out. Although the behavior of animals like Loulis, Kanzi, and Alex requires us to rethink our assumptions about human uniqueness, no animal has yet turned in the critical language performance, and so far as we know, no animals in the wild have developed anything resembling a true language. What the animal research does suggest is that we share similar brain structures with other animals, and that these structures may have provided the evolutionary foundation for our development of language (Gannon et al., 1998). Suggesting that language is a product of evolution means, of course, that genes are involved (Figure 8.28). Researchers have recently identified a gene on chromosome 7 that is responsible for a language disorder that involves articulation difficulty, problems identifying basic speech sounds, grammatical difficulty, and trouble understanding sentences (Lai, Fisher, Hurst, Vargha-Khadem, & Monaco, 2001; Pinker, 2001). As geneticists fill in the human and animal genomes it will be interest-

Figure 8.28
Is language genetic?
Reprinted with Special Permission of the North America Syndicate.

ing to see whether this is one of the few gene locations where humans and chimpanzees differ.

✓ **CONCEPT CHECK**

- *In what ways is the Wernicke-Geschwind model correct and incorrect?*
- *What are the different roles of the left and right hemispheres (in most people) in language? (See Chapter 7 for part of the answer.)*
- *What deficiencies do you see in chimp "language"?*

 In Perspective

My guess is that at the beginning of this chapter you would have said that vision is the most important sense. Perhaps now you can appreciate why Helen Keller thought her deafness was a greater handicap than her blindness.

Hearing alerts us to danger, brings us music, and provides for the social interactions that bind humans together. Small wonder that during evolution the body invested such resources in the intricate mechanisms of hearing.

Hearing has important adaptive functions with or without the benefit of language, but from our vantage point as language-endowed humans it is easy to understand Hudspeth's claim that audition's most important role is in processing language. The person who is unable to talk is handicapped; the person who is unable to understand and to express language is nearly helpless. No wonder we put so much research effort into understanding how language works.

One of the most exciting directions language research has taken has involved attempts to communicate with our closest relatives. Whether they possess language capabilities depends on how we define language. It is interesting how the capabilities we consider most characteristic of being human—such as language and consciousness—are the hardest to define. As so often happens, studying our animal relatives, however distant they may be, helps us understand ourselves.

 ## Summary

- Sensation requires a receptor that is specialized for the particular kind of stimulus. Beyond sensation, the brain carries out further analysis, called perception.

Hearing

- The auditory mechanism responds mostly to airborne vibrations, which vary in frequency and intensity.

- Sounds are captured and amplified by the outer and inner ear and transduced into neural impulses by the hair cells on the basilar membrane. The signal is then transmitted through the brain stem and the thalamus to the auditory cortex in each temporal lobe.

- Frequency discrimination depends mostly on the basilar membrane's differential vibration along its length to different frequencies, resulting in neurons from each location carrying frequency-specific information to the brain. At lower frequencies neurons fire at the same rate as the sound's frequency; it is possible that intermediate frequencies are represented by neurons firing in volleys.

- For complex sounds the basilar membrane acts as a Fourier analyzer, breaking the sound down into its component frequencies. When different sounds must be distinguished from each other, efferent activity probably adjusts the sensitivity of the hair cells to emphasize one sound at the expense of others.

- Locating sounds helps us approach or avoid sound sources and to attend to them in spite of competition from other sounds. The brain has specialized circuitry for detecting the binaural cues of differences in phase, intensity, and time of arrival at the two ears.

Language

- Researchers have identified two major language areas in the brain, with Broca's area involved with speech production and grammatical functions, and Wernicke's area with comprehension.

- Damage to either area produces different symptoms of aphasia, and damage to connections with the visual cortex impairs reading and writing. Developmental dyslexia may involve planum temporale abnormalities, reduced activity in Wernicke's area, or deficiencies in the auditory and visual pathways.

- Although damage to the left frontal or temporal lobes is more likely to produce the expected disruptions in language, studies have shown that control of the various components of language is distributed across the four lobes.

- Although some animals have language-like brain structures and have been taught to communicate in simple ways, it is controversial whether they possess true language.

For Further Thought

- Write a modified Wernicke-Geschwind theory of language control, based on later evidence.
- Would you rather give up your hearing or your vision? Why?

- Make the argument that chimps possess language, though at a low level. Then argue the opposite, that their behavior does not rise to the level of language.

 Testing Your Understanding

1. Describe the path that sound information takes from the outer ear to the auditory neurons, telling what happens at each point along the way.

2. State the telephone theory, the volley theory, and the place theory. Indicate a problem with each, and state the theory that is currently most widely accepted.

3. Summarize the Wernicke-Geschwind model of language function. Include structures, the effects of damage, and the steps in reading a word aloud and in repeating a word that is heard.

Select the one best answer:

1. An adequate and an inadequate stimulus, such as light versus pressure on the eyeball, will produce similar experiences because:

   a. they both activate visual receptors and the visual cortex.
   b. the receptors for touch and vision are similar.
   c. touch and vision receptors lie side-by-side in the eye.
   d. our ability to discriminate is poor.

2. Frequency is to pitch as:

   a. loudness is to intensity.
   b. intensity is to loudness.
   c. stimulus is to response.
   d. response is to stimulus.

3. The sequence of sound travel in the inner ear is:

   a. oval window, ossicles, basilar membrane, eardrum.

   b. ossicles, oval window, basilar membrane, eardrum.
   c. eardrum, ossicles, oval window, basilar membrane.
   d. eardrum, ossicles, basilar membrane, oval window.

4. Place analysis depends most on the physical characteristics of the:

   a. hair cells.   b. basilar membrane.
   c. tectorial   d. cochlear canal.
      membrane.

5. The fact that neurons are limited in their rate of firing by the refractory period is most damaging to which theory?

   a. telephone   b. volley
   c. place   d. volley-place

6. The place theory's greatest problem is that:

   a. neurons cannot fire as frequently as the highest frequency sounds.
   b. neurons specific for frequencies above 5,000 Hz have not been found.
   c. the whole basilar membrane vibrates about equally at low frequencies.
   d. volleying does not follow sound frequency above about 5,000 Hz.

7. An auditory neuron's tuning curve tells you:

   a. which frequency it responds to.
   b. which part of the basilar membrane the neuron comes from.
   c. at what rate the neuron can fire.
   d. how much the neuron responds to different frequencies.

8. A cochlear implant works because:

   a. the tympanic membrane is intact.
   b. the hair cells are intact.
   c. it stimulates the auditory cortex directly.
   d. it stimulates auditory neurons.

9. An auditory object is:

   a. a vibrating object in the environment.
   b. a person's perception that a sound source is distinct from others.
   c. the sound source the individual is paying attention to.
   d. none of these.

10. As a binaural sound location cue, difference in intensity works:

    a. poorly at low frequencies.
    b. poorly at medium frequencies.
    c. poorly at high frequencies.
    d. about equally at all frequencies.

11. In the following diagram of coincidence detectors, which cell would respond most if the sound were directly to the person's left?

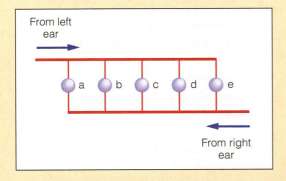

From left ear

a b c d e

From right ear

12. On returning home from the hospital, an elderly neighbor drags one foot when he walks and uses almost exclusively nouns and verbs in his brief sentences. You guess that he has had a mild stroke located in his:

    a. left temporal lobe.
    b. right temporal lobe.
    c. left frontal lobe.
    d. right frontal lobe.

13. A problem in the magnocellular pathway is associated with:

    a. expressive aphasia.
    b. dyscalculia.
    c. agraphia.
    d. dyslexia.

14. Evidence providing some support for a language acquisition device comes from studies showing that ASL activates:

    a. the left hemisphere.
    b. the left and right hemispheres.
    c. both frontal lobes.
    d. the occipital lobe.

15. The most reasonable conclusion regarding language in animals is that:

    a. they can use words or signs, but do not possess language.
    b. they can learn language to the level of a 6-year-old human.
    c. language is "built-in" for humans, but must be learned by animals.
    d. some animals have brain structures similar to human language structures.

Answers: 1. **a** 2. **b** 3. **c** 4. **b** 5. **a** 6. **c** 7. **d** 8. **d** 9. **b** 10. **a** 11. **e** 12. **c** 13. **d** 14. **a** 15. **d**

 On the Web

1. **DEAF-L** is a resource site for information on deafness, including therapies, issues, and deaf humor at

   http://www.zak.co.il/deaf-info/old/home.html

   Brain Briefings' **Hair Cell Regeneration** page describes research aimed at learning how to regenerate hair cells in the human cochlea at

   http://web.sfn.org/content/Publications/BrainBriefings/hair_cell.html

   Hereditary Hearing Loss has recent research and other information on what we know about the 60-plus genes thought to cause hearing loss, at

   http://www.uia.ac.be/dnalab/hhh/

continued

2. **Seeing, Hearing, and Smelling the World,** a site maintained by the Howard Hughes Medical Institute, has several articles on senses, including one on audition, *The Quivering Bundles that Let Us Hear.* Also look for the sidebar *On the Trail of Deafness Genes* at

   http://www.hhmi.org/senses/

3. **The Cochlea** offers several downloadable animations illustrating activity in the cochlea at

   http://www.sissa.it/bp/Cochlea/

4. **Cochlear,** a manufacturer of cochlear implant devices, features implant recipient Heather Whitestone McCallum (Miss America 1995), along with animations showing how the implant works at

   http://www.cochlear.com/About/ MissAmerica.asp

   Brain Briefings' **Restoring Hearing** page has a concise description of cochlear implant therapy at

   http://web.sfn.org/content/Publications/ BrainBriefings/hearing.html

5. The **National Aphasia Association** has information about aphasia and about research on the disorder, as well as resources at

   http://www.aphasia.org/

   Stroke Family has information about recovering speech after a stroke, including free mini-guides, with emphasis on how the family can help at

   http://www.strokefamily.org/

6. **The British Dyslexia Association** provides information on the disorder at

   http://www.bda-dyslexia.org.uk

7. **The Chimpanzee and Human Communication Institute,** operated by Roger and Deborah Fouts, is home to Washoe, Loulis, and three other signing chimps. You can learn about the institute, watch the chimps at play on the chimp cams, and read the chimp biographies at

   http://www.cwu.edu/~cwuchci/main.html

   Machiavellian Monkeys & Shakespearean Apes: The Question of Primate Language is an unusually well-written article on primate language research in the National Zoo's magazine *Zoogoer* at

   http://www.fonz.org/zoogoer/zg1995/ primate_language.htm

   Chimpanzee and Great Ape Language Resources on the Internet has links to information about ape language as well as information on the animals themselves at

   http://www.brown.edu/Departments/ Anthropology/apelang.html

   The Alex Foundation's page **About Our Research** features descriptions of the parrot language research and a video clip at

   http://www.alexfoundation.org/research/ index.html

 For additional information about the topics covered in this chapter, please look at InfoTrac College Edition, at

http://www.infotrac-college.com/wadsworth

Try search terms you think up yourself, or use these: *aphasia; dyslexia; language acquisition; planum temporale.*

 On the CD-ROM: Exploring Biological Psychology

Video: Hearing Loss   *Interactive Puzzle:* The Hearing Process

For Further Reading

The Language Instinct, by Steven Pinker, the director of MIT's Center for Cognitive Neuroscience (Morrow, 1994), concerns the evolution of language. Pinker's expertise and lively writing style garnered one reviewer's evaluation as "An excellent book full of wit and wisdom and sound judgment."

Brain and Language, by Antonio and Hanna Damasio (*Scientific American*, September 1992, 60–67) is a brief and readable introduction by two of the best-known experts.

Sensation and Perception, by E. B. Goldstein (Brooks/Cole, 1999) is a textbook and makes a good reference, including non-physiological aspects not covered here.

 Key Terms

adequate stimulus *218*

agraphia *234*

alexia *234*

amplitude *219*

angular gyrus *234*

aphasia *232*

auditory object *228*

basilar membrane *222*

binaural *230*

Broca's aphasia *233*

cochlea *221*

cochlear canal *221*

cocktail party effect *228*

coincidence detectors *231*

complex sound *219*

difference in intensity *231*

difference in time of arrival *231*

dyslexia *234*

efferent *228*

frequency *219*

frequency theory *223*

frequency-place theory *227*

inner hair cells *222*

intensity *219*

language acquisition device *239*

loudness *219*

magnocellular hypothesis *235*

organ of Corti *222*

ossicles *220*

outer hair cells *222*

oval window *221*

perception *218*

phase difference *231*

pinna *220*

pitch *219*

place theory *224*

planum temporale *236*

pure tone *219*

receptor *218*

round window *221*

sensation *218*

tectorial membrane *222*

telephone theory *223*

tonotopic map *225*

topographical organization *222*

transducer *218*

tympanic membrane *220*

volley theory *224*

Wernicke's aphasia *234*

Vision and Visual Perception

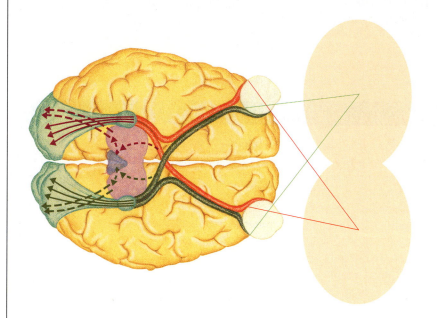

In this chapter you will learn:

- The structure of the eye.

- How the eye begins processing visual information even before it is sent to the brain.

- The major theories of color and form vision.

- How color, form, movement, and spatial location are handled in the brain.

- Some of the visual disorders caused by brain damage and what they tell us about brain function.

Jonathan I. was driving in his car when it was struck on the passenger side by a small truck. In the emergency room he was told he had a concussion. For a few days he was unable to read, saying that the letters looked like Greek, but fortunately this *alexia* soon disappeared. Jonathan was a successful artist who had worked with the renowned Georgia O'Keeffe, and he was eager to return to his work. Driving to his studio he noticed that everything appeared gray and misty, as if he were driving in a fog. When he arrived at his studio he found that even his brilliantly colored paintings had become gray and lifeless.

His whole world changed. People's appearance was repulsive to him, because their skin appeared "rat-colored"; he lost interest in sex with his wife for that reason. Food was unattractive, and he came to prefer black and white foods (coffee, rice, yogurt, black olives). His enjoyment of music was diminished, too; before the accident he experienced *synesthesia*, in which musical tones evoke a sensation of changing colors, and this pleasure disappeared as well. Even his migraine headaches, which had been accompanied by brilliantly colored geometric hallucinations, became "dull." He retained his vivid imagery, but it too was without color.

Over the next two years Jonathan seemed to forget that color once existed, and his sorrow lifted. His wife no longer appeared rat-colored, and they resumed sexual activity. He turned to drawing and sculpting and to paint-ing dancers and race horses rendered in black and white but characterized by movement, vitality, and sensuousness. However, he preferred the colorless world of darkness, and would spend half the night wandering the streets (Sacks & Wasserman, 1987).

Vision enables us to read and to absorb large amounts of complex information. It helps us navigate in the world, build structures, and avoid danger. Color helps distinguish objects from their background, and it enriches our lives with natural beauty and works of art. I suspect that in contrast to Helen Keller's belief that deafness was a greater affliction than blindness, most of you would consider vision the most important of our senses. Apparently researchers share that opinion, because vision has received more research attention than the other senses combined. As a result we understand a great deal about how the brain processes visual information. In addition, studies of vision are providing a valuable model for understanding complex neural processing in general.

LIGHT AND THE VISUAL APPARATUS

From the patterns of stimulation on the retina we perceive the world of objects and this is nothing short of a miracle.
—Richard Gregory

Vision is an impressive capability. There are approximately 126 million light receptors in the human eye, and a complex network of cells connecting them to each other and to the optic nerve. The optic nerve itself boasts a million neurons, compared to 30,000 in the auditory nerve. Our receptors are so sensitive that they can detect a quantum of light, the smallest possible amount of light energy. And that says nothing about what our brain does with the information after the eye receives it. The topics of vision and visual perception form an exciting story, one of high-tech research and conflicting theories and dedicated scientists' lifelong struggles to understand our most amazing sense.

The Visible Spectrum

To understand vision we need to start at the beginning by describing the *adequate stimulus*, as we did with audition. To say that the stimulus for vision is light seems obvious, but the point needs some elaboration. Visible light is a part of the electromagnetic spectrum. The electromagnetic spectrum includes a variety of energy forms, ranging from gamma rays at one extreme of frequency to the radiations of alternating current circuits at the other (Figure 9.1); the portion of the electromagnetic spectrum that we can see is represented by the colored area in the figure, which accounts for just 1/70 of the entire spectrum.

Most of the energies in the spectrum are not useful for producing images; for instance, AM, FM, and television waves pass right through objects. Some of the other energy forms, like X rays and radar, can be used for producing images, but they require powerful energy sources and special equipment for detecting the images. Heat-producing objects give off infrared energy, which some nocturnal animals can use to detect their prey in darkness. Humans can see infrared images only with the aid of specialized equipment, and this capability is very useful to the military and the police for detecting people and heat-producing vehicles

and armament at night. (During the Gulf War, the Iraqi army set up plywood silhouettes of tanks with heaters behind them to distract Allied airplanes.) But infrared images have blurred edges and fuzzy detail. The electromagnetic energy within our detectable range produces well-defined images because it is reflected from objects with minimal distortion. We are adapted to life in the daytime, and we sacrifice the ability to see in darkness in exchange for crisp, colorful images of faces and objects in daylight. In other words, our sensory equipment is specialized for detecting the energy that is most useful to us, just as the night-hunting sidewinder rattlesnake is equipped to detect the infrared radiation emitted by its prey and a bat's ears are specialized for the high-frequency sound waves it bounces off small insects.

Light is a form of oscillating energy and travels in waves just as sounds do. We could specify visible light (and the rest of the electromagnetic spectrum) in terms of frequency, just as we did with sound energy, but the numbers would be extremely large. So, we describe light in terms of its wavelength—the distance the oscillating energy travels before it reverses direction. (We could do the same with sound, but those numbers would be just as inconveniently small.) The unit of measure is the nanometer (nm), which is a billionth of a meter; visible light ranges from about 400 nm to 800 nm. Notice in Figure 9.1 that different wavelengths correspond to different colors of light; for example, when light in the

Figure 9.1
The electromagnetic spectrum
The visible part of the spectrum is the middle (colored) area, which has been expanded to show the color experiences usually associated with the wavelengths. Only 1/70 of the electromagnetic spectrum is visible to humans.

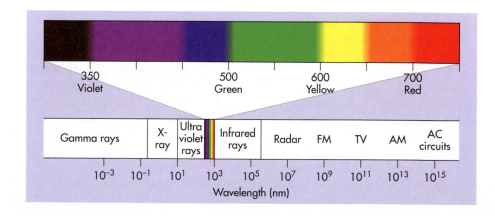

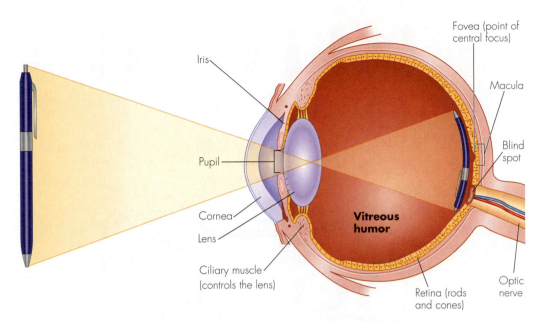

Figure 9.2
The human eye

Iris

Fovea (point of central focus)

Macula

Blind spot

Pupil

Cornea

Lens

Ciliary muscle (controls the lens)

Vitreous humor

Retina (rods and cones)

Optic nerve

range of 500–570 nm strikes the receptors in our eye, we normally report seeing green. Later in the chapter we will qualify this relationship when we examine why wavelength does not always correspond to the color we see.

The Eye and Its Receptors

The eye is a nearly round structure filled with a clear liquid (Figure 9.2). The outer covering is opaque except for the cornea, which is transparent. Behind the *cornea* is the *lens*. Because the lens is a flexible tissue, the muscles attached to it can stretch it out flatter to focus the image of a distant object on the retina, or relax to focus the image of a near object. The lens is partly covered by the *iris*, which is what gives your eye its color. The iris is actually a circular muscle whose opening forms the pupil; it controls the amount of light entering the eye by contracting reflexively in bright light and relaxing in dim light. You can observe this response in yourself by watching in a mirror while you change the level of light in the room.

The *retina*, the light-sensitive structure at the rear of the eye, is made up of light-sensitive receptor cells, and the neural cells that are connected to them. As you can see in Figure 9.3, the receptors are at the very back of

the eye; light must pass through the neural cells to reach the photoreceptors, but this presents no problem because the neural cells are transparent. The photoreceptors are filled with **light-sensitive chemicals called *photopigments*;** when light passes through the photochemical a chemical reaction causes Na^+ channels to close, blocking normal Na^+ influx and *hyperpolarizing* the cell membrane. The photoreceptors spontaneously release neurotransmitter in darkness, which inhibits the activity of the *bipolar cells* and the *ganglion cells* they connect to. (Figure 9.3 shows the relationship of these cells.) When light hyperpolarizes the receptors, neurotransmitter release is *reduced*, the bipolar cell activity is *less* inhibited, and the firing rate in the ganglion cells increases.

The bipolar cells are themselves highly interconnected by horizontal cells. In addition, *amacrine cells* connect across many ganglion cells. This would lead you to suspect that a great deal of processing goes on in the retina itself, which you will soon see is the case. With this complexity, no wonder most vision scientists consider the retina to be part of the brain, and refer to the optic nerve as a tract.

There are two kinds of receptor cells in the retina: rods and cones, which are named for

1

How does the eye detect light?

Figure 9.3
The cells of the retina
From J. E. Dowling and B. B. Boycott, "Organization of the primate retina," in Proceedings of the Royal Society of London, B166, Figure 23 on p. 104. Copyright 1966 by the Royal Society. Used with permission of the publisher and the author.

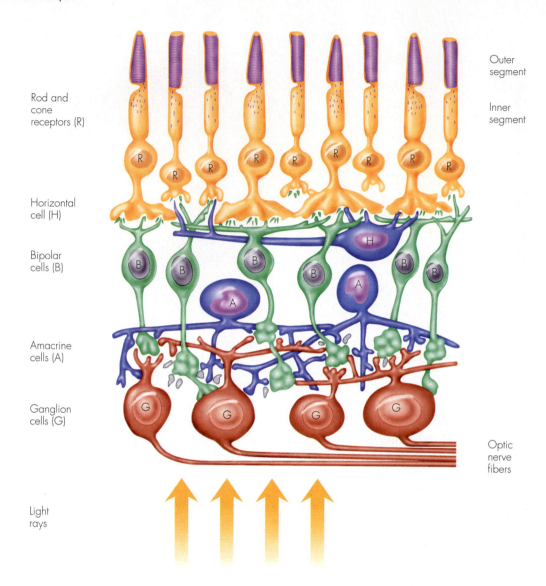

Rod and cone receptors (R)

Outer segment

Inner segment

Horizontal cell (H)

Bipolar cells (B)

Amacrine cells (A)

Ganglion cells (G)

Optic nerve fibers

Light rays

their shapes, as you can see by looking at Figure 9.3 again. The human eye contains about 120 million rods and about 6 million cones. Their photopigments are made up of a protein and a lipid. Light causes the photopigment molecule to break down into its two components; this reaction is what triggers the closing of the Na⁺ channels. The protein and lipid recombine in darkness or reduced light. Although rods and cones function similarly, their chemical contents and their neural connections give them different specializations.

The rod photopigment is called *rhodopsin*; the name refers to its color (from the Latin *rhodon*, "rose"), not to its location in rods. Rhodopsin is more sensitive to light than cone photopigment is. For this reason, rods function better in dim light than cones do; in fact, you rely solely on your rods for vision in dim light. In very bright light the rhodopsin in your eyes stays broken down most of the time, so the rods barely function. The delay in adjusting to a darkened movie theater is due to the time it takes the rhodopsin to resynthesize. ***Iodopsin,*** **the cone photopigment,** requires a high level of light intensity to operate, so your cones are nonfunctional in dim light but function well in daylight. Cone pigment comes in three varieties, which respond differentially to different wavelengths of light; this means that cones can distinguish among different wavelengths, whereas rods differentiate only among different levels of light and dark (which is why you cannot recognize colors in dim light).

Rods and cones also differ in their location and in their amount of neural interconnection. **Cones are most concentrated in the** *fovea,* **a 1.5-mm-wide area in the middle of the retina,** and drop off rapidly with distance from that point. Rods are most concentrated at 20 degrees from the fovea; from that point they decrease in number in both directions and fall to zero in the middle of the fovea. Only one or a few cones are connected to each ganglion cell in the fovea; the number increases with distance from there. Because the fovea's cones share fewer ganglion cells, resolution there is better; thus the fovea has higher *visual acuity,* **or ability to distinguish details.** Many rods share each ganglion cell; this reduces their resolution but enhances their already greater sensitivity to dim light. **The area of the retina from which a ganglion cell (or any other cell in the visual system) receives its input is the cell's** *receptive field.* So, we can say that receptive fields are smaller in the fovea and larger in the periphery.

The axons of the ganglion cells join together and pass out of each eye on the nasal (nose) side to form the two optic nerves (Figure 9.4). Where the nerve exits the eye there are no receptors, so it is referred to as the *blind spot.* The blind spots of the two eyes fall at different points in a visual scene, so you do not notice that any of your visual world is missing; besides, your brain is good at "filling in" missing information, even when a small part of the visual system is damaged. The two optic nerves run to a point just in front of the pituitary, where they join for a short distance at the optic chiasm before traveling to their first synapse in the *lateral geniculate nuclei (LGN)* of the thalamus. Axons from the nasal sides of the eyes cross to the contralateral side at the optic chiasm and go to the occipital lobe (via the LGN) in the opposite hemisphere. Neurons from the other side of the eyes (called the temporal side) do not cross over, but go to the ipsilateral side of the brain.

It seems like splitting the output of each eye between the two hemispheres would cause a major distortion of the image. However, if you look closely at Figure 9.4, you can see that the arrangement actually keeps related information

How does information about an object on the right end up in the left hemisphere?

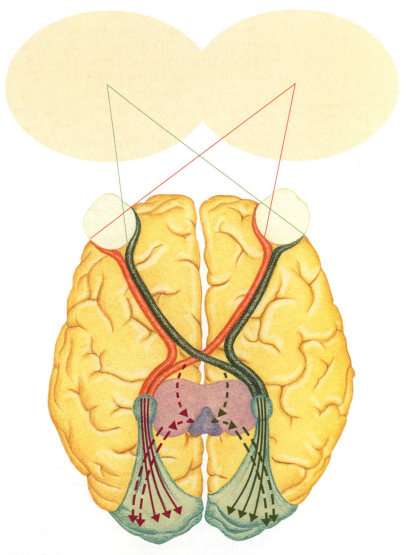

Figure 9.4
Projections from the retinas to the cerebral hemispheres
Notice how an object in one side of the visual field is detected in the opposite sides of the two retinas, and in the opposite visual cortex.

together. Notice that the letter E that appears in the person's left visual field casts an image on the right half of each retina. **The *visual field* is the part of the environment that is being registered on the retina.** The information from the right half of each eye will be transmitted to the right hemisphere. An image in the right visual field will similarly be projected to the left hemisphere. This is why researchers who study differences in functions of the two cerebral hemispheres are able to project a visual stimulus to one hemisphere (see section A.4 of the appendix). They present the stimulus slightly to the left or to the right of the midline, with the exposure too brief for the person to shift the eyes toward the stimulus.

There is a good reason you have two forward-facing eyes, instead of one like the mythical Cyclops, or one on each side of your head like many animals. The approximately 6-centimeter separation of your eyes produces *retinal disparity,* **a discrepancy in the location of an object's image on the two retinas.** Figure 9.5 shows how the image of distant objects in a scene fall toward the nasal side of each retina, and closer objects cast their image in the temporal half. Retinal disparity is detected in the visual cortex, where different neurons fire depending on the amount of lateral displacement and inform the brain about the object's distance. Three-dimensional stereoscopic viewers present each eye with an image photographed at a slightly different angle, to simulate the difference in a scene that each eye sees. The ViewMaster you may have had as a child takes advantage of the brain's retinal disparity processors to produce a striking three-dimensional effect. The popular random-dot stereograms (such as *Magic Eye*) use the same principle to produce a three-dimensional effect from a single picture without a viewer.

As the rest of the story of vision unfolds, you will notice three themes that will help you understand how the visual system works: inhibition, hierarchical processing, and modularity. You will learn that *neural inhibition* is just as

How does retinal disparity help us see 3-D?

2

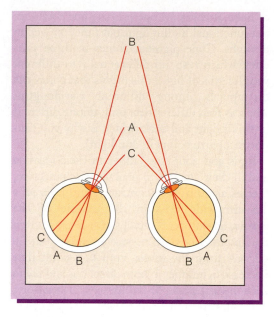

Figure 9.5
Retinal disparity
The image of a focused object (A) falls on the fovea, while the image of a more distant object (B) is displaced to the inside of each retina and the image of a closer object (C) is displaced to the outside. This provides information to the brain for depth perception.

important as excitation; inhibition sharpens information beyond the processing capabilities of a system that depends on excitation alone. *Hierarchical processing* **means that lower levels of the nervous system analyze their information and pass the results on to the next higher level for further analysis.** *Modular processing* **refers to the segregation of the various components of processing into separate locations.** You will find that the visual system carries out its functions in specialized structures, more so than we found for audition or even language.

- *In what ways is human vision adapted for our environment?*
- *How are the rod and cone systems specialized for different tasks?*

COLOR VISION

In Figure 9.1 you saw that there is a correspondence between color and wavelength; this would suggest that color is a property of the light reflected from an object and, therefore, of the object itself. However, wavelength does not always predict color, as Figure 9.6 illustrates. The lines in the upper half of the design reflect the same wavelengths as the ones in the bottom half, but their colors appear different. Just as with the auditory terms *pitch* and *loudness*, the term *color* refers to the observer's experience rather than a characteristic of the object. Thus, it is technically incorrect to say that the light is red or that a book is blue, because *red* and *blue* are experiences that are imposed by the brain. However, in the interest of avoiding vague expressions such as "long-wavelength light" or cumbersome ones such as "light that would ordinarily be perceived by an observer as red," I will be rather casual about this point in future discussions. To understand the experience of color, we must now examine the neural equipment that we use to produce that experience. Our understanding of color vision has been guided over the past two centuries by two competing theories: the trichromatic theory and the opponent-process theory.

Figure 9.6
Independence of wavelength and color
Although the X's are identical, they appear to differ in color, due to the color contrast with their backgrounds.
Source: Josef Albers, courtesy of Yale University Press.

Trichromatic Theory

After observing the effect of passing light through a prism, Newton proposed in 1672 that white light is composed of seven fundamental colors that cannot themselves be resolved into other colors. If there are seven "pure" colors, this suggests that there must be seven receptors and brain pathways for distinguishing color, just as there are five primary tastes. In 1852 Hermann von Helmholtz (whose place theory was discussed in Chapter 8) revived an idea of Thomas Young from a half century earlier. Because any color can be produced by combining different amounts of just three colors of light, Young and Helmholtz recognized that this must be due to the nature of the visual mechanism rather than the nature of light. They proposed a *trichromatic theory, that just three color processes account for all the colors we are able to distinguish.* They chose red, green, and blue as the primary colors because observers cannot resolve these colors into separate components. When you watch television, you see an application of trichromatic color mixing: all the colors you see on the screen are made up of tiny red, green, and blue dots of light.

Opponent Process Theory

The trichromatic theory accounted for some of the observations about color perception very well, but it ran into trouble explaining why yellow also appears to observers to be a

How do we distinguish colors?

APPLICATION

Restoring Lost Vision

Blindness has several causes, so researchers are attacking the problem on several fronts. As you will see, all the examples rely on newer technology that was not available just a few years ago.

Several types of blindness are caused by genetic degeneration of the retina. One promising approach for treatment is stem cell transplantation. When stem cells from the hippocampus of adult rats were injected into rats' diseased retinas, the cells showed signs of maturing into neurons and extended into the optic nerve (Young, Ray, Whiteley, Klassen, & Gage, 2000).

Another type of genetic disorder involves the gene that produces a protein called RPE65, which is needed to create a pigment required for normal vision. Dogs suffer from this disorder, too, so they make good stand-ins for humans. Researchers at the University of Pennsylvania used a virus to insert a good copy of the RPE65 gene into the retinas of three affected dogs (Acland et al., 2001). Afterward, the animals were able to find their way around in a room full of tables and chairs, while untreated animals bumped into the obstacles.

Another approach that sounds as much like science fiction as science involves the use of "bionic" retinas. Three variations are illustrated here. In figure **(a)**, a miniature television camera sends an image through a computer (not shown) to a grid of electrodes on the visual cortex (Dobelle, 2000; Normann, Maynard, Rousche, & Warren, 1999). A problem with this technique is that the brain often rejects implanted electrodes. If the photoreceptors have degenerated but the visual neurons are still intact, retinal implants may be more appropriate. One type of implant being developed substitutes a silicon imaging chip for the TV camera and transmits its signal via radio waves to an electronic chip on the retina [see figure **(b)**] (Chase, 1999). Electrodes in the chip stimulate the ganglion cells and activate the visual cortex more naturally.

Each of these devices produces only about a hundred dots of information, so their ability to transmit information is limited. The third device produces about 3,500 dots and requires no batteries, computer, or wires ("Silicon Chips Implanted," 2001). The Artificial Silicon Retina

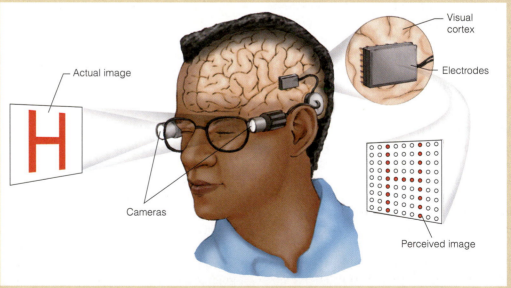

(a)

Three Types of Visual Prosthesis
(a) A miniature video camera sends an image to an array of electrodes in the visual cortex. **(b)** An imaging chip sends its image to an electronic chip in the retina, which stimulates visual neurons. **(c)** A silicon chip detects points of light and stimulates visual neurons.

(ASR) consists of a silicon chip only 2 mm in diameter and 1/1000 in. thick, which is inserted between the diseased retina and the back of the eye [figure **(c)**]. It is made up of an array of what are essentially miniature solar cells, each of which registers a point of light, and uses the light entering the eye as its source of power. The two illustrations show the ASR on a penny for size comparison, and after implantation in the eye. The ASR has been implanted in six patients so far; no information has been published on its effectiveness, but the results indicate that this is a feasible strategy.

3

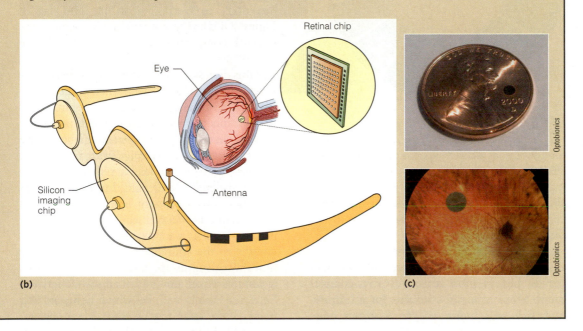

Retinal chip

Eye

Silicon imaging chip

Antenna

Optobionics

Optobionics

(b)

(c)

"pure" color. Ewald Hering (1878) "solved" this problem by adding yellow to the list of physiologically unique colors. But rather than assuming four color receptors, he asserted that there are only two—one for red *and* green and one for blue *and* yellow. ***Opponent process theory* attempts to explain color vision in terms of opposing neural processes.** In Hering's version, the photochemical in the red/green receptor is broken down by red light and regenerates in the presence of green light. The chemical in the second type of receptor is broken down in the presence of yellow light and regenerates in the presence of blue light.

Hering proposed this arrangement to explain the phenomenon of ***complementary colors,* colors that cancel each other out to produce a neutral gray or white.** (Note the spelling of this term; *complementary* means "completing.") In Figure 9.7, the visible spectrum is represented as a circle. This rearrangement of the spectrum makes sense, because violet at one end of the spectrum blends naturally into red at the other end just as easily as the colors adjacent to each other on the spectrum blend into each other. Another reason the color circle makes sense is that any two colors opposite each other on the circle are complementary; mixing equal amounts of light from across the circle results in the sensation of a neutral gray tending toward white, depending on the brightness. An exception to

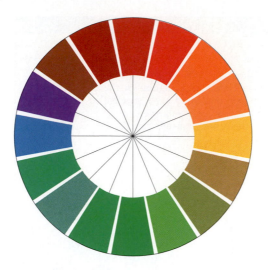

Figure 9.7
The color circle
Colors opposite each other are complementary, that is, equal amounts of light in those colors cancel each other out, producing a neutral gray.

this rule is the combination of red and green; they produce yellow, for reasons you will understand shortly.

Another implication of complementarity is that overstimulation of the eye with one light makes the eye more sensitive to its complement. **Stare at a red stimulus for a minute, and you will begin to see a green edge**

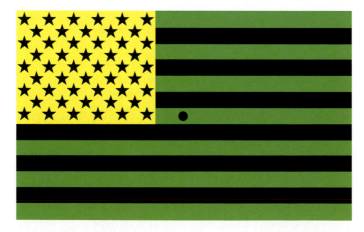

Figure 9.8
Complementary colors and negative color aftereffect
Stare at the flag for about a minute, then look at a white surface (the ceiling or a sheet of paper); you should see a traditional red, white, and blue flag.

around it; then look at a white wall or a sheet of paper and you will see a green version of the original object. This experience is called a *negative color aftereffect*; the butcher decorates the inside of the meat case with parsley or other greenery to make the beef look redder. Negative color aftereffect is what one would expect if the wavelengths were affecting the same receptor in opposed directions, as Hering theorized. The flag in Figure 9.8 is a very good interactive demonstration of complementary colors and negative aftereffects.

If this discussion of color mixing seems inconsistent with what you have learned in the past, it is probably because you learned the principles of color mixing in an art class. The topic of discussion there was *pigment mixing*, whereas we are talking about *mixing light*. An object appears red to us because it reflects primarily long-wavelength (red) light, but it also *absorbs* all other wavelengths of light. The effect of light mixing is *additive*, while pigment mixing is *subtractive*; if we mix lights we add wavelengths to the stimulus, but as we mix paints more wavelengths are absorbed. For example, if you mix equal amounts of all wavelengths of light the result will be white light; mixing paints in the same way produces black because each added pigment absorbs additional wavelengths of light until the result is total absorption and blackness (Figure 9.9).

Now, back to color vision theory. Although Hering's theory did a nice job of explaining complementary colors and the uniqueness of yellow, it received little acceptance. One reason was that researchers had trouble with Hering's assumption of a chemical that would break down in response to one light and regenerate in the presence of another. His theory was, in fact, in error on that point, but developments a hundred years later would bring Hering's thinking back to the forefront.

A Combined Theory

The trichromatic and opponent-process theories appear to be contradictory. Sometimes this means that one position is wrong and the other

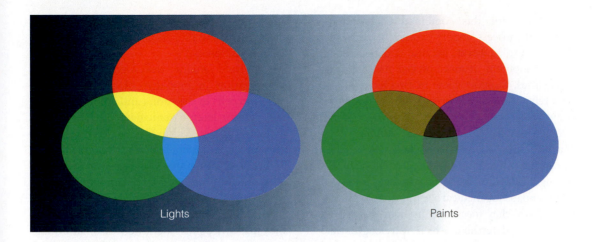

Figure 9.9
Mixing lights Is additive, mixing paints is subtractive
The combination of all three primaries (or all colors) of light produces white; the same combination of pigments produces black, which is the lack of color.

is right, but often it means that each of the competing theories is partially correct, but is just too simple to accommodate all the known facts. Hurvich and Jameson (1957) resolved the conflict with a compromise: they proposed that there are three types of color receptors—red-, green-, and blue-sensitive—which are interconnected in an opponent-process fashion at the ganglion cells.

Figure 9.10 is a simplified version of how Hurvich and Jameson thought this combined color processing strategy might work. Notice that long-wavelength light excites "red" cones and the R-G ganglion cell, to give the sensation of red. Medium-wavelength light excites the "green" cones and inhibits the R-G cell, reducing its firing rate below its spontaneous level and signaling green to the brain. Likewise, short-wavelength light excites "blue" cones and inhibits the Y-B ganglion cell, leading to a sensation of blue. Light midway between the sensitivities of the "red" and "green" cones would stimulate both cone types. The firing rate in the R-G ganglion cell would not change, because equal stimulation and excitation from the two cones would cancel out; however, the cones' connections to the Y-B ganglion cell are both excitatory, so their combined excitation would produce a sensation of yellow. According to this theory, there are three color processes at the receptors and four beyond the ganglion cells.

This scheme does explain very nicely why yellow would appear pure like red, green, and blue. Also, it is easy to understand why certain pairs of colors are complementary. For example, you could have a color that is reddish blue (purple) or greenish yellow (chartreuse) but not a reddish green or a bluish yellow. Negative aftereffects would be explained by overstimulation "fatiguing" a ganglion cell's response in one direction, causing a rebound in the opposite direction and a subtle experience of the opposing color.

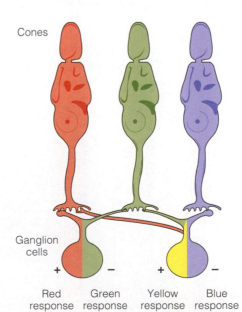

Figure 9.10
Interconnection of three cone types to provide four color responses and complementary colors
The connecting cells between the receptors and ganglion cells are not shown, to keep the illustration simple. + indicates excitation; – indicates inhibition.

Cones

Ganglion cells

+   –   +   –

Red response   Green response   Yellow response   Blue response

Evidence for this combined trichromatic–opponent process theory would be almost a decade away, however, because it depended on the development of more precise measurement capabilities. Support came in two forms. First, researchers produced direct evidence for three color receptors in the retina (Brown & Wald, 1964; Dartnall, Bowmaker, & Mollon, 1983; Marks, Dobelle, & MacNichol, 1964). The researchers shone light of selected wavelengths through individual receptors in eyes removed from humans for medical reasons or shortly after their death; they measured the light that passed through to determine which wavelengths had been lost through absorption. The absorbed wavelengths were the ones the receptor's photochemical was sensitive to. Figure 9.11 shows the results from a study of this type. Note that there are three distinct color response curves, plus a response curve for rods. Notice also that there is no curve that corresponds to yellow, which would indicate the presence of a receptor for yellow. Like the tuning curves for frequency we saw in the previous chapter, these curves are not very sharp; each receptor has a sensitivity peak, but its response range is broad and overlaps with that of its neighbors. The system must *compare activity in all three types of cones* to determine whether you are seeing chartreuse, a weak blue,

or a weak green. (This comparison is an automatic neural process; it does not occur at the level of awareness.)

A second major development was the confirmation in monkeys of color-opponent ganglion cells in the retina and color-opponent cells in the lateral geniculate nucleus of the thalamus (De Valois, 1960; De Valois, Abramov, & Jacobs, 1966; Gouras, 1968). Figure 9.10 illustrates two types of opponent cells, one that is excited by red and inhibited by green (+R-G) and one that is excited by yellow and inhibited by blue (+Y-B); Russell De Valois and his colleagues identified two additional types, blue excitatory/yellow inhibitory (+B-Y) and green excitatory/red inhibitory (+G-R) (De Valois et al., 1966).

A surprise was that some of the color-opponent ganglion cells receive their input from cones that are arranged in two concentric circles (Gouras, 1968; Wiesel & Hubel, 1966). The cones in the center and those in the periphery have color-complementary sensitivities (see Figure 9.12). Of course, the yellow response is provided by the combined output of "red" and "green" cones. Why all this complexity? First, the opposition of cones at the ganglion cells discriminates among wavelengths more efficiently than the separate

Figure 9.11

Relative absorption of light of various wavelengths by visual receptors

Note that each type of cone responds best to wavelengths corresponding to blue, green, and red light, though they respond to other wavelengths as well.

Source: Adapted from "Visual Pigments of Rods and Cones in a Human Retina," by Bowmaker and Darthall, in *Journal of Physiology*, 298, p. 501–511. Copyright 1980, with permission from Elsevier Science.

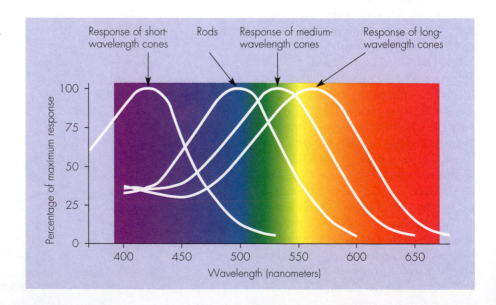

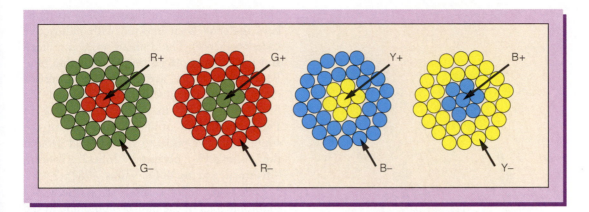

Figure 9.12
Receptive fields of color-opponent ganglion cells
The cones in the center and the cones in the periphery respond to colors that are complementary to each other. The center cones excite the ganglion cell, and the cones in the periphery inhibit it.
Source: Based on the findings of De Valois et al., 1966.

cones could (Goldstein, 1999). Along with this opposition, the concentric-circle receptor fields enhance information about color contrast in objects. This sharpening of information will become clearer when we look at how the retina distinguishes the edge of an object.

A theory is considered successful if it is consistent with the known facts, can explain those facts, and can predict new findings. The combined trichromatic and opponent process color theory meets all three criteria. For example: (1) It is consistent with the observation that all colors can be produced by using red, green, and blue light. (2) It can explain why observers regard red, green, blue, and *yellow* as pure colors. It also explains complementary colors, negative aftereffects, and the impossibility of color experiences like greenish red. (3) It predicted the discovery of three photopigments and of the excitatory/inhibitory neural connections at the ganglion cells.

Color Blindness

Color blindness is an intriguing curiosity; but more than that, it has played an important role in the development of our understanding of color perception by scuttling otherwise successful theories and providing the inspiration for new ones. There are very few completely color-blind people—about one in every 100,000. They usually have an inherited lack of cones; limited to rod vision, they see in shades of gray, they are very light sensitive, and they have poor visual acuity. More typically a person is partially color-blind, due to a defect in one of the cone systems rather than a lack of cones.

There are two major types of color blindness. A person who is red-green color-blind sees these two colors but is unable to distinguish between them. When I was trying to understand a red-green color-blind colleague's experience of color, he explained that green grass appeared to be the same color as peanut butter! I don't know what peanut butter looked like to him, but he assured me that he found grass and trees "very beautiful." People in the second color-blind group do not perceive blue; so their world appears in variations of red and green. Many partially color-blind individuals are unaware they see the world differently from the rest of us. Color vision deficiencies can be detected by having the subject match or sort colored objects, or with a test like the one illustrated in Figure 9.13.

Red-green color-blind individuals show a deficiency in the red end of the spectrum or in the green portion; this suggests that the person is missing either the appropriate cone or photochemical. Acuity is normal in both groups, so there cannot be a lack of cones. Some are unusually sensitive to green light, and the rest are sensitive to red light; this suggests that in one case the normally red-sensitive cones are filled with green-sensitive chemical and, in the other, the normally green-sensitive cones are filled with red-sensitive chemical.

What is it like to be color-blind?

Figure 9.13
A test for color blindness
This is one of the plates from the Ishihara test for color blindness. Most people see the number 74; the person with color deficiency sees the number 21.

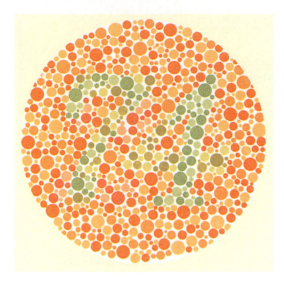

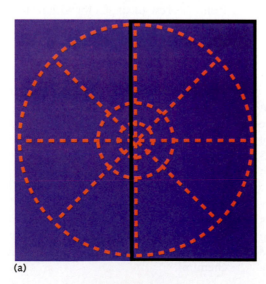

✔ **CONCEPT CHECK**

- *Summarize the three color theories described here.*
- *What causes color blindness?*

FORM VISION

Just as the auditory cortex is organized as a map of the cochlea, the visual cortex contains a map of the retina. Russell De Valois and his colleagues demonstrated this point when they presented the image in Figure 9.14a to monkeys that had been injected with radioactive 2-deoxyglucose. The animals were sacrificed and their brains placed on photographic film. Because the more active neurons absorbed more radioactive glucose, they exposed the film more darkly in the *autoradiograph* in Figure 9.14b; this produced an image of the stimulus that appears to be wrapped around the monkey's occipital lobes (Tootell, Silverman, Switke, & De Valois, 1982).

This result tells us that just as there is a tonotopic map of the basilar membrane in the auditory cortex, we have a *retinotopic map* **in the visual cortex, meaning that adjacent retinal receptors activate adjacent cells in the visual cortex.** However, this does not tell us how we see images; transmitting an object's image to the cortex like a television picture does not amount to perception of the object. Object perception is a two-stage affair, involving (1) *form vision,* **the detection of an object's boundaries and features (such as texture),** and (2) object recognition, which we will discuss later. The story that unfolds here is about more than perception; it provides a model for understanding how the brain processes information in general. It is also a story that begins not in the cortex but in the retina itself.

Figure 9.14
Deoxyglucose autoradiograph showing retinotopic mapping in visual cortex
Monkeys were given radioactive 2-deoxyglucose, then shown the design in **(a)**. They were sacrificed and a section of their visual cortical tissue was placed on photographic film. The exposed film showed a pattern of activation **(b)** that matched the design.

Reprinted with permission from R. B .H. Tootell et al., "Deoxyglucose analysis of retinoptic organization in primate striate cortex." *Science*, 218, 902–904. Copyright 1982 American Association for the Advancement of Science.

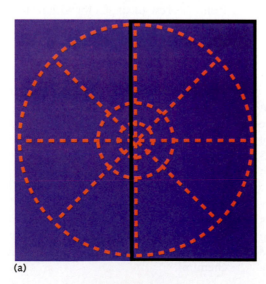

(a)

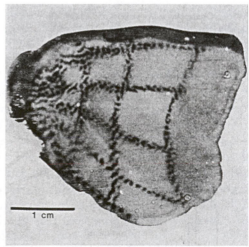

(b)

Contrast Enhancement and Edge Detection

Detecting an object's boundaries is the first step in form vision. It is typical for the nervous system to enhance especially important sensory information; in the case of boundaries, it uses lateral inhibition to exaggerate the contrast in brightness that defines an object's edge. To demonstrate this enhancement for yourself, hold a sheet of paper so an overhead light casts a shadow on another piece of paper on your desk. Notice that the shadow seems to have a slightly darker band at its edge; similarly, the light area appears to have a brighter band along its border (see Figure 9.15). This effect is called the *Mach band illusion* after Ernst Mach, who studied it in the 1880s. An illusion is not simply an error of perception, but an exaggeration of a normal perceptual process.

Deceptions of the senses are the truths of perception.

—Johannes Purkinje

Figure 9.16 will help you understand how your retinas produced the illusion in the demonstration you just did. **In *lateral inhibition*, each neuron's activity inhibits the activity of its neighbors, and in turn its activity is inhibited by them.** The critical point in the illustration is at the middle ganglion cells. Ganglion cell 7 is inhibited more than ganglion cells 1–6; this is because the receptors to its right are receiving intense stimulation and producing high levels of inhibition. The extra inhibition of ganglion cell 7 creates a sensation of a darker band along the shadow's border, as indicated at the bottom of the illustration. Similarly, ganglion cell 8 is inhibited *less* than its neighbors to the right, because the receptors to its left are receiving minimal stimulation and producing little inhibition. As a result, the light area appears brighter at its border with the shadow.

Actually, this description is more appropriate for the eye of the horseshoe crab, where lateral inhibition was originally confirmed by electrical recording (Ratliff & Hartline, 1959). The principle is the same in the mammalian eye,

4

How do we detect objects' boundaries?

Light band

Dark band

Figure 9.15
A demonstration of the mach band illusion
With a reasonably bright light overhead and a bright sheet of white paper on your desk, you should be able to see the illusion: a darker band at the shadow's edge, and a light band at the light edge.
From *Mach Bands: Quantitative Studies on Neural Networks in the Retina,* by F. Ratcliff, 1965. f. 3.25, p. 107. Copyright © 1969 Holden-Day Inc.

Figure 9.16
The neural basis of the mach band illusion
See explanation in text. (For simplicity, cells between the receptors and ganglion cells have been omitted. Also, there would be many more cross connections than shown here.)

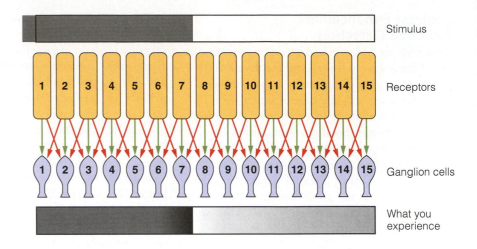

but each ganglion cell's receptive field is made up of several receptors arranged in circles, like the color-coded circular fields we saw earlier (Kuffler, 1953). Light in the center of the field has the opposite effect on the ganglion cell from light in the surround. In *on center* cells, light in the center increases firing, and light in the *off surround* reduces firing below resting levels. Other ganglion cells have an *off center* and an *on surround*. Figure 9.17 illustrates these two types of ganglion cells.

Figure 9.17
Effect of light on center and surround of receptive field
The receptive fields and ganglion cells are shown in cross section. The connecting cells between the receptors and the ganglion cells have been omitted for simplicity.

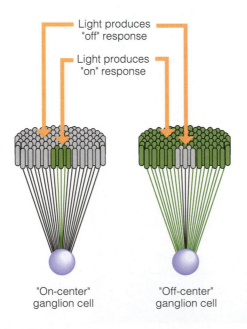

The antagonistic arrangement in these ganglion cells specializes them for detecting light-dark contrast (Hubel, 1982). Look at the three illustrations in Figure 9.18. Light falling across the entire field will have little or no effect on the ganglion cell's firing rate, because the excitation and inhibition cancel each other out (Figure 9.18a). Light that falls only on the *off* surround will suppress firing in the ganglion cell (Figure 9.18b). But the ganglion cell's firing will be at its maximum when the stimulus falls on all of the *on* center and only a part of the *off* surround as in Figure 9.18c. However, the real importance of this light-dark contrast mechanism is yet to come.

Hubel and Wiesel's Theory

Cells in the lateral geniculate nucleus have circular receptive fields just like the ganglion cells from which they receive their input. However, in the cortex the receptive fields of visual neurons are bar shaped. David Hubel and Torsten Wiesel (1959) were probing the visual cortex of anesthetized cats as they projected visual stimuli on a screen in front of the cat. Their electrode was connected to an auditory amplifier so they could listen for indications of active cells. One day they were manipulating a glass slide with a black dot on it in the projector and getting only vague and

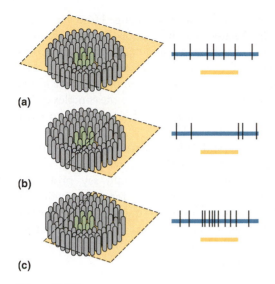

(a)

(b)

(c)

Figure 9.18
Effect of a luminous border on an on-center ganglion cell
The vertical hatchmarks on the solid bar represent neural responses, and the yellow line underneath indicates when the light was on. Notice that maximum activity occurs in the ganglion cell when light falls on all of the center but less than all of the surround.

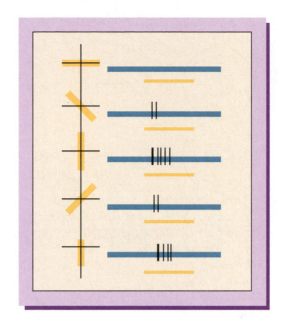

Figure 9.19
Responses to lines at different orientations in a simple cell specialized for vertical lines
The vertical hatchmarks represent neural responses and the yellow line underneath indicates when the stimulus occurred. Notice that the response was greatest when the line was closest to the cell's "preferred" orientation (vertical) and least when the orientation was most discrepant. In the last example the response was diminished because the stimulus failed to cover all of the cell's field (indicated by the stimulus being off-center of the crosshair).
From D. H. Hubel and T. N. Wiesel (1959), "Receptive fields of single neurons in the cat's striate cortex" in *Journal of Physiology*, 148, 574–591, Figure 3. Copyright 1959 by The Physiology Society. Reprinted by permission of the publisher and the author.

How does Hubel and Wiesel's system work?

inconsistent responses . . . when suddenly over the audiomonitor the cell went off like a machine gun. After some fussing and fiddling we found out what was happening. The response had nothing to do with the black dot. As the glass slide was inserted its edge was casting onto the retina a faint but sharp shadow, a straight dark line on a light background. (Hubel, 1982, p. 517)

Hubel and Wiesel then began exploring the receptive fields of these cortical cells by projecting bars of light on the screen. They found that an actively responding cell would decrease its responding if the stimulus was moved to another location or if it was rotated to a slightly different angle. Figure 9.19 shows the changes in response in one cell as the orientation of the stimulus was varied. Hubel and Wiesel called these cortical cells simple cells. **Simple cells respond to a line or an edge that is at a specific orientation and at a specific place on the retina.**

How can we explain the surprising shift in specialization in these cortical cells? Imagine several contrast-detecting circular fields arranged in a straight line (Figure 9.20). Then connect the outputs of their ganglion cells to a *single* cell in the cortex. You now have a mechanism for detecting not just spots of light-dark contrast but a contrasting edge, as in the border of an object that is lighter or darker than its background. Fields with *on* centers would detect a light edge like the one in the figure, and a series of circular fields with *off* centers would detect a dark edge.

In other layers of the cortex, Hubel and Wiesel found ***complex cells,* which continue to respond when a line or edge moves to a different location,** as long as it is not too far from the original site. They explained the complex cell's ability to continue responding essentially the same way they explained the sensitivity of simple cells. They assumed that complex cells receive input from several simple cells that have the same orientation sensitivity, but whose fields are next to each other on the retina. This arrangement is illustrated in Figure 9.21. Notice that as the edge moves horizontally, different simple cells will respond, but the same complex

Figure 9.20
Hubel and Wiesel's explanation for responses of simple cells
When the edge is in this position, the ganglion cell for each of the circular fields increases its firing. The ganglion cells are connected to the same simple cell, which also increases firing, indicating that an edge has been detected. This particular arrangement would be specialized for a vertical light edge.

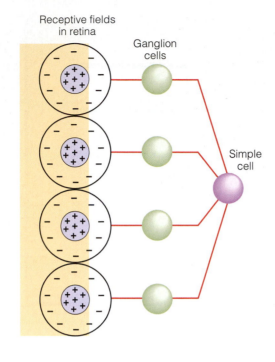

Is spatial frequency theory a better explanation?

cell will continue responding. However, if the edge rotates to a different orientation this complex cell with stop responding, and another complex cell specific for that orientation will take over. Connecting several simple cells to a single complex cell not only enables the complex cell to keep up with an edge as it moves, but to *detect* movement as well.

Hubel and Wiesel shared the Nobel Prize for their work in 1981. However, their model has limitations—some would say problems. For one thing, it accounts for the detection of boundaries, but it is questionable whether edge-detection cells can also handle surface details of the object, such as texture and gradations of shading.

Spatial Frequency Theory
Other researchers have argued that cortical cells are not limited to responding to edges. Think of an edge as an abrupt or high-frequency change in brightness. The more gradual changes across the surface of an object are low-frequency changes. According to De

Figure 9.21
Hubel and wiesel's explanation for responses of complex cells
The complex cell receives input from the simple cells, each of which serves a group of circular fields (as in Figure 9.20). As a result, it continues to respond when the edge moves.

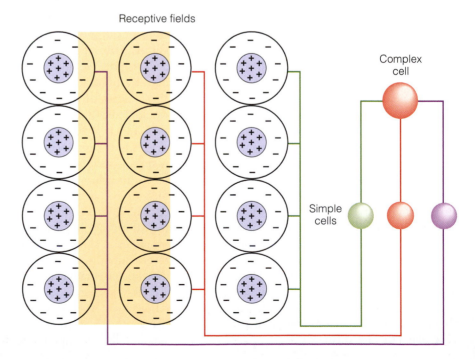

Valois, some complex cells are "tuned" to respond to high frequencies like an edge, while others are tuned to low frequencies, like the slow transition from light to shadow that gives depth to the features of a face (De Valois, Thorell, & Albrecht, 1985). Some cells respond better to "gratings" of alternating light and dark bars—which contain a particular combination of spatial frequencies—than they do to lines and edges. According to *spatial frequency theory,* **visual cortical cells do a Fourier frequency analysis (see Chapter 8) of the luminosity variations in a scene.** According to this view, different visual cortical cells have a variety of sensitivities, not just those required to detect edges (Albrecht, De Valois, & Thorell, 1980; De Valois et al., 1985).

Admittedly, our visual world would be extremely simple and confusing if we were limited to high-frequency information (edges), as you can see in Figure 9.22. The picture in Figure 9.22a was prepared by having a computer average the amount of light over large areas in a photograph; the result was a number of high-frequency transitions, and the image is not very meaningful. In Figure 9.22b, the computer filtered out the high frequencies, producing more gradual changes between light and dark (low frequencies). It seems paradoxical that blurring an image would make it more recognizable, but blurring eliminates the sharp boundaries. You can get the same effect from Figure 9.22a by looking at it from a distance or by squinting your eyes.

Still, some cortical cells do respond better to edges than to gratings (Albrecht et al., 1980; De Valois et al., 1985; von der Heydt, Peterhans, & Dürsteler, 1992). Also, edge-sensitive cells may be more versatile than they appear to be. When Lehky and Sejnowski (1990) trained a neural network (see Chapter 2) to recognize curved visual objects, they later found that some "neurons" in their network had spontaneously developed sensitivity to bars or edges of light—even though the network had never been exposed to such stimuli.

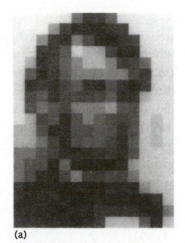 

(a)   (b)

Figure 9.22
Illustration of high and low frequencies in a visual scene
(a) An image limited to abrupt changes in brightness (high spatial frequencies) is not as meaningful as **(b)** one that has both high- and low-frequency information.

Reprinted with permission from L. O. Harmon and B. Julesz, "Masking in visual recognition: Effects of two-dimensional filtered noise." *Science,* 180, 1194–1197. Copyright 1973 American Association for the Advancement of Science.

✓ **CONCEPT CHECK**

- *Explain how the opponent arrangement of a ganglion cell's field enhances brightness contrast.*
- *How do Hubel and Wiesel's theory and the spatial frequency theory differ?*

THE PERCEPTION OF OBJECTS, COLOR, AND MOVEMENT

One of the remarkable characteristics of the visual system is how it dissects an image into its various components and analyzes them in different locations. The separation begins in the retina and increases as visual information flows through all four lobes of the brain, with locations along the way carrying out analyses of color, movement, and other features of the visual scene. Thus, we will see how visual processing is, as mentioned earlier, both hierarchical and modular.

Some neuroscientists reject the modular notion, arguing that any visual function is

Figure 9.23
Color contrast and brightness contrast stimulate different visual systems
(a) Because the image has color contrast it stimulates the parvocellular system and we can see detail; it lacks brightness contrast, so we do not see depth in the picture. **(b)** Depth is apparent in this image because it has brightness contrast and stimulates the magnocellular system.

Reprinted with permission from M. Livingstone and D. Hubel, "Segregation of form, color, movement, and depth: Anatomy, Physiology, and Perception. *Science,* 240, 740–749. Copyright 1988 American Association for the Advancement of Science.

(a)

(b)

instead *distributed,* **meaning it occurs across a relatively wide area of the brain** (Cohen & Tong, 2001). One study found evidence that sensitivity to faces, for example, is scattered over a large area in the temporal lobe (Haxby et al., 2001). Vision may well involve a mix of modular and distributed functioning, rather like the arrangement we saw for language, but this possibility does not contradict the existence of the specialized processing areas we will discuss. For most researchers, the issue is not whether some areas are specialized for a function, but how far to take the idea of modularity. With that caution in mind, we will consider what is known about the pathways and functional locations in the visual system.

The Two Pathways of Visual Analysis

What do the parvocellular and magnocellular systems do?

Visual information follows two routes from the retina through the brain, called the *parvocellular system* and the *magnocellular system* (Livingstone & Hubel, 1988; Schiller & Logothetis, 1990). Parvocellular (P) ganglion cells are located mostly in the fovea. They have circular receptive fields that are small and color opponent, which suits them for **the specialty** of the *parvocellular system,* **the discrimination of fine detail and color.** We first mentioned the magnocellular system in the discussion of dyslexia in Chapter 8. Magnocellular (M) ganglion cells have large circular receptive fields that are brightness opponent and respond only briefly to stimulation. As a result, the *magnocellular system* is **specialized for brightness contrast and movement.**

Figure 9.23 is an interesting demonstration of the specialized nature of these two systems. The bicycle in Figure 9.23a differs from its background in color, but not in brightness, so the image mostly stimulates the P system. The bicycle in Figure 9.23b differs from the background in brightness, but not in color; it mostly stimulates the M system. You can pick out all the details of the first bicycle, because that is one of the P system's capabilities; you get a sense of depth in the second picture, but not the first, because that is a capability of the M system.

We also see evidence of differences in the two systems in our everyday life. The simplest example is that at dusk our sensitivity to light increases but we lose our ability to see color and detail. You cannot read a newspaper under such conditions, or color-coordinate tomorrow's outfit, because the high-resolution, color-sensitive parvocellular system is nearly nonfunctional. The magnocellular system's sensitivity to movement is most obvious in your peripheral vision. Hold your arms outstretched to the side while you look straight ahead, and move your hands slowly forward while wriggling your fingers. When you just notice your fingers moving, stop. Notice that you can barely see your fingers but you are very sensitive to their movement.

The parvocellular and magnocellular pathways travel to the lateral geniculate nucleus and then to the primary visual cortex, which is also known as V1. Although the two systems are highly interconnected, the parvocellular system dominates the *ventral stream* **that flows from the visual cortex into the temporal lobes,** and the magnocellular system dominates the *dorsal stream* **from the visual cortex to the parietal lobes** (Figure 9.24). Because of their specialties, the ventral stream is often referred to as involved with the *what* of visual processing, and the dorsal stream with the *where*. Most of the research on this topic has been done with monkeys, but the two pathways have been confirmed with PET scans in humans (Ungerleider & Haxby, 1994).

Beyond V1 the ventral stream passes through V2 and into V4, which is mostly con-

cerned with color perception. It then projects to the inferior temporal cortex, which is the lower boundary of the temporal lobe; this area shows a remarkable specialization for object recognition, which we will examine shortly.

Magnocellular neurons arrive in V1 in areas that are responsive to orientation, movement, and retinal disparity (Poggio & Poggio, 1984). The dorsal stream then proceeds through V2 to V5 (also known as MT because it is on the middle temporal gyrus in the monkey), which is specialized for the perception of movement and depth. The dorsal stream travels next to the posterior parietal cortex, the area just behind the somatosensory cortex; its role is primarily to locate objects in space, but the behavioral implications of its functions are far more important than that simple statement suggests.

Both streams then proceed into the prefrontal cortex. The prefrontal components apparently manage information from memory that is needed for carrying out the functions that depend on these two pathways (Courtney, Ungerleider, Keil, & Haxby, 1997; Wilson, Ó Scalaidhe, & Goldman-Rakic, 1993). As one example, we will see in Chapter 10 that the prefrontal cortex holds this information in temporary memory during the planning of movements.

What are the functions of the ventral and dorsal streams?

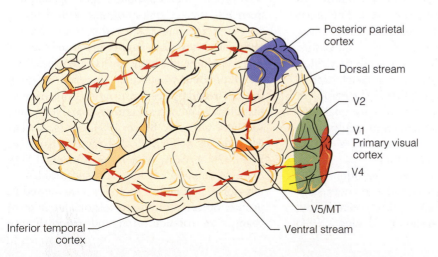

Figure 9.24
The dorsal and ventral streams of visual processing

Posterior parietal cortex

Dorsal stream

V2

V1
Primary visual cortex

V4

V5/MT

Inferior temporal cortex

Ventral stream

Disorders of Visual Perception

Because of the modular nature of the visual system, damage to one of the higher areas can impair one aspect of visual perception while all others remain normal. This kind of deficit is often called an *agnosia*, which means "lack of knowledge." Because the disorders provide a special opportunity for understanding the neural basis of higher-order visual perception, we will orient our discussion of the perception of objects, color, movement, and spatial location around disorders of those abilities.

Object Agnosia

What makes a person unable to identify objects or recognize faces?

Object agnosia **is the impairment of the ability to recognize objects.** In Chapter 3 I described Oliver Sacks's (1990) agnosic patient who patted parking meters on the head, thinking they were children; he was also surprised when carved knobs on furniture failed to return his friendly greeting. Dr. P. was intellectually intact; he continued to perform successfully as a professor of music, and he could carry on lively conversations on many topics. Patients with object agnosia are able to see an object, describe it in detail, and identify it by touch. But they are unable to identify an object by sight or even to recognize an object they have just drawn from memory or copied (Gurd & Marshall, 1992; Zeki, 1992).

Like Dr. P, many object agnosic patients also suffer from *prosopagnosia,* **the inability to visually recognize familiar faces.** The problem is not memory, because they can identify individuals by their speech or mannerisms. Nor is their visual acuity impaired; they often have no difficulty recognizing facial expressions, gender, and age (Tranel, Damasio, & Damasio, 1988). However, they are unable to recognize the faces of friends and family members, or even their own image in a mirror (Benton, 1980; Damasio, 1985).

Prosopagnosics do respond emotionally to photographs of familiar faces they do not recognize, as indicated by EEG evoked potentials and skin conductance response (Bauer, 1984;

Renault, Signoret, Debruille, Breton, & Bolger, 1989; Tranel & Damasio, 1985). This suggests that identification and recognition are separate processes in the brain. This "hidden perception" is not without precedent. Patients blinded by damage to V1 show a surprising capability called *blindsight;* they can locate and track the movement of objects and they can discriminate colors, all the while claiming to be guessing (Zeki, 1992). Blindsight may be due to direct but weak connections from the LGN to visual areas beyond V1 (Crick & Koch, 1992; Hendry & Reid, 2000).

Both object agnosia and prosopagnosia are caused by damage to the inferior temporal cortex (see Figure 9.24 again). It is controversial whether the two are distinct disorders or manifestations of a single disorder. However, the occasional case is reported of a patient with prosopagnosia alone (Benton, 1980), and we will see in the next paragraphs that the cells in the inferior temporal cortex that respond to faces are different from those that respond to objects. Although face-responsive neurons are often intermingled with object-responsive neurons, a part of the fusiform gyrus on the underside of the inferior temporal lobe is so important to face recognition that it is referred to as the *fusiform face area* (see Figure 9.25) (Gauthier, Skudlarski, Gore, & Anderson, 2000; Gauthier, Tarr, Anderson, Skudlarski, & Gore, 1999).

After information about edges, spatial frequencies, texture, and so on has been detected separately, it is put back together in the inferior temporal cortex. Cells have been located there in both monkeys and humans that are specialized for responding to specific categories of visual stimuli, including geometric figures, houses, animals, hands, and faces (Figure 9.26a) (Desimone, Albright, Gross, & Bruce, 1984; Gross, Rocha-Miranda, & Bender, 1972; Kreiman, Koch, & Fried, 2000; Sáry, Vogels, & Orban, 1993). Some of these cells require very specific characteristics of a stimulus, such as a face viewed in profile; others continue to respond in spite of changes in rotation, size, and color (Figure

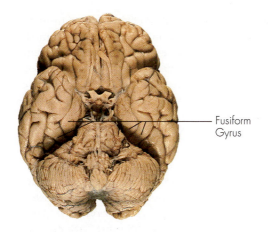

Figure 9.25
View of the underside of a human brain, showing the fusiform gyrus
Source: Courtesy of Dana Copeland.

9.26b) (Miyashita, 1993; Tanaka, 1996; Vogels, 1999). The cells with more complex responsiveness likely receive their input from cells with more specific sensitivities (Tanaka, 1996) like the cells involved in detecting edges.

Some of these capabilities may be "hard wired in" at birth, but experience also determines neural responsiveness (Freedman, Riesenhuber,

Poggio, & Miller, 2001; Kobatake, Tanaka, & Tamori, 1992; Logothetis, Pauls, & Poggio, 1995; Vogels, 1999). To control for familiarity, researchers compared responses to human faces with responses to the heads of fictitious creatures called "greebles" (Gauthier, Tarr, Anderson, Skudlarski, & Gore, 1999). Functional magnetic resonance imaging (fMRI) scans in Figure 9.27a show that pictures of faces activate the fusiform face area (ffa; see section A.3 of the appendix for a description of fMRI). However, greebles did not activate the ffa unless the person had enough familiarity to distinguish individual creatures (Figure 9.27b). Young and Yamane (1992) found further evidence of the effects of experience. They showed monkeys pictures of the faces of lab workers, and neurons in the temporal lobes increased their firing rates according to the monkeys' familiarity with the workers.

Color Agnosia
Jonathan I.'s problem was *color agnosia,* *which is the loss of the ability to perceive colors due to brain damage.* But before we can discuss this disorder we need to revisit the distinction between wavelength and color.

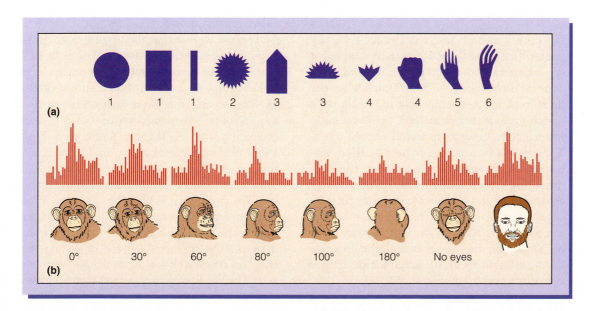

Figure 9.26
Stimuli used to produce responses in "hand-" and "face-" sensitive cells in monkeys
(a) The stimuli are ranked in order of increasing effectiveness. **(b)** The spikes indicate degree of response to the stimulus shown below.

Sources: (a) From Visual properties of neurons in inferotemporal cortex of the macaque by C. G. Gross et al., in *Journal of Neurophysiology*, 35. Reprinted with permission of the publisher. (b) From Stimulus-Selective properties of inferior temporal neurons in the macaque by R. Desimone, et al., p. 2057. in *Journal of Neuroscience*, 4. Copyright © 1984 Society for Neuroscience. Reprinted with permission.

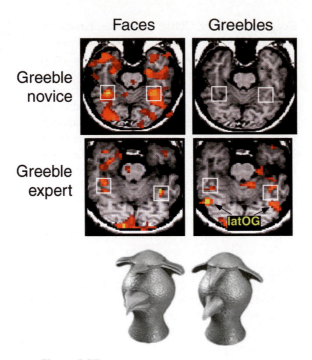

Figure 9.27
Activity in the fusiform face area while viewing faces and "greebles"
Viewing faces activated a part of the fusiform gyrus (indicated by the white squares) both in "greeble novices" and in "greeble experts," who had learned to distinguish individual greebles from each other. Viewing greebles activated the area only in greeble experts.
Source: Gauthier et al., 1999.

Once as I walked past a colleague's slightly open office door I was astonished to see that his face was a distinct green! Opening his door to investigate, I understood why: the light from his desk lamp was reflecting off a bright green brochure he was reading. Immediately his face appeared normal again. **This ability to recognize the so-called natural color of an object in spite of the illuminating wavelength is called *color constancy*.** If it were not for color constancy, objects would seem to change colors as the sun shifted its position through the day or as we went indoors into artificial light. Imagine having to survive by identifying ripe fruit if the colors kept changing.

When I reinterpreted my colleague's skin color it was not because I *understood* that his

How is color coding different from wavelength coding?

face was bathed in green light; it occurred automatically as soon as my eyes took in the whole scene. Monkeys, who do not understand the principles of color vision, apparently have the same experience. When Zeki (1983) illuminated red, white, green, and blue patches with red light, each patch regardless of its color set off firing in V1 cells that preferred long-wavelength (red) light; however, cells in V4 responded only when the patch's natural color matched the cell's color "preference." Zeki concluded that cells in V1 are *wavelength coded*, while cells in V4 are *color coded*. To detect the natural color, a V4 cell must "subtract out" information about the surrounding illumination (Schein & Desimone, 1990). It was my V4 cells that allowed me to see my colleague's face as a normal pink rather than as the green that it was reflecting.

We have no brain scan to tell us where Jonathan I.'s damage was located, but we can do some neurological sleuthing. Like the rest of us he was more sensitive to light in the yellow-green range and some colors appeared as a paler gray than others. Apparently his wavelength discrimination was intact but he was *unaware of color*, which suggests the damage was in area V4.

Movement Agnosia
Movement agnosia **is the inability to perceive movement.** A 43-year-old woman suffered a stroke that damaged the posterior area of her brain. As a result, she could not detect movement, and was aware that an object had moved only when she noticed that it had changed position (Zihl, von Cramon, & Mai, 1983). You might think that would be the same thing as perceiving movement, but she had no sense of the object traveling through the intermediate positions. When she poured coffee she could not perceive the liquid rising in the cup, so she would not stop pouring at the right time and the cup would overflow. When she tried to cross a street a car would seem far away, then suddenly very near. A computerized tomography scan (see section A.3 of the appendix) indicated that the damage was at the bor-

der between the occipital and temporal lobes on both sides. You can see in Figure 9.24 that this is where area V5/MT is located.

Neglect

The posterior parietal cortex combines input from the visual, auditory, and somatosensory areas to help the individual locate objects in space and to orient the body in the environment. Damage impairs abilities such as reaching for objects, but it also often produces *neglect*, **in which the patient ignores visual, touch, and auditory stimulation on the side contralateral to the injury.**

I knew the word "neglect" was a sort of medical term for whatever was wrong but the word bothered me because you only neglect something that is actually there, don't you? If it's not there, how can you neglect it?

—P. P., a neglect patient

The term *neglect* seems particularly appropriate in patients who ignore food on the left side of the plate, shave only the right side of the face, or fail to dress the left side of the body. The manifestations are largely visual. Two patients with this condition, caused by right parietal tumors, were able to report rather accurately whether words and pictures presented simultaneously in the left and right visual fields were the same or different. But they said the task was "silly" because there was no stimulus in the left field to compare (Volpe, Ledoux, & Gazzaniga, 1979). Neglect patients' processing in the left visual field is superior to that of blindsighted individuals, suggesting that their deficit may be in *attention* to the space on one side.

Patients' drawings and paintings help us understand what they are experiencing. When asked to copy drawings, they will neglect one side while completing the other side in detail, like the example in Figure 9.28. Anton

Raderscheidt painted the two portraits in Figure 9.29 two months and nine months after a stroke that damaged his right parietal area. Notice that the first painting has very little detail, and the left half of the image is missing. In the later painting he was using the whole canvas, and the portrait looks more normal; but notice that the left side is still much less developed than the right, with the eyeglasses and face melting into ambiguity (Jung, 1974).

The Problem of Final Integration

Many researchers have wondered where *all* the information about a visual object is brought

What is neglect, and what causes it?

Figure 9.28
Drawings copied by a left-field neglect patient
Source: From F. E. Bloom and A. Lazerson, *Brain, mind and behavior*, 2nd Ed., p. 300. © 1988 W. H. Freeman & Co.

Figure 9.29
Self-portraits demonstrating left visual field neglect
(a) A self-portrait done two months after the artist's stroke, which affected the right parietal area, is incomplete, especially on the left side of the canvas. **(b)** One done nine months after the stroke still shows less attention to detail on the left side.
Source: Jung, 1974. Copyright © Anton Raderscheidt. Photos provided by Ken Roth.

(a)

(b)

back together. Imagine watching a person walking across your field of view; the person is moving, shifting orientation, and changing appearance as the lighting increases and decreases under a canopy of trees. It seems logical that a single center at the end of the visual pathway would combine all the information about shape, color, texture, and movement, constantly updating your perception of this image as the same person. In other words, the result would be a complete and dynamic awareness. Presumably damage to that area would produce symptoms similar to blindsight but that affect all stimuli.

There have been suggestions that our ultimate understanding of an object occurs in a part of the superior temporal gyrus that receives input from both neural streams (Baizer, Ungerleider, & Desimone, 1991), or in the part of the parietal cortex where damage causes neglect (Driver & Mattingly, 1998). But these ideas are highly speculative, and there is no convincing evidence for a master area where all perceptual information comes together to produce awareness (Crick, 1994; Zeki, 1992). It is possible that visual awareness is *distributed* throughout the network of 32 areas of cortex concerned with vision and their 305 interconnecting pathways (Van Essen, Anderson, & Felleman, 1992). We will visit this problem again when we talk about consciousness in the final chapter of the book.

✔ CONCEPT CHECK

- *Organize your knowledge: make a table comparing the characteristics and functions of the parvocellular and magnocellular systems.*
- *Draw a diagram of the brain, add lines showing the two major visual pathways, and label the various areas; for the higher-order processing areas, include their functions.*

In Perspective

Very few subjects in the field of biological psychology can match the interest level that researchers have bestowed on vision. As a result, we know more about the neuroanatomy and functioning of vision than any other neural system. Many challenges remain in the field of vision research, however. A good example is the fact that after four decades of research we have not resolved the relative merits of the two competing explanations of edge and detail detection.

But researchers' fascination with vision goes beyond the problems of vision itself. Our understanding of the networks of neurons and structures in the visual system provides a basis for developing theories to explain other functions as well. Whatever directions future research might take, you can be sure that vision will continue to be one of the most important topics.

 Summary

Light and the Visual Apparatus

- The human eye is adapted to the part of the electromagnetic spectrum that is reflected from objects with minimal distortion.

- The retina contains rods, which are specialized for brightness discrimination, and cones, which are specialized for detail vision and discrimination of colors.

Color Vision

- There are three types of cones, each containing a chemical with peak sensitivity to a different segment of the electromagnetic spectrum.

- Connections of the cones to ganglion cells provide for complementary colors and for the color yellow.

- The most common cause of partial color blindness is the lack of one of the photochemicals.

Form Vision

- Form vision begins with contrast enhancement at edges by ganglion cells with light-opponent circular fields.

- These ganglion cells contribute to cortical mechanisms that detect edges (Hubel and Wiesel's theory), or do a Fourier analysis of a scene (spatial frequency theory).

The Perception of Objects, Color, and Movement

- The components of vision follow two somewhat separate paths through the brain.

- Structures along the way are specialized for different functions, including color, movement, object perception, and face perception.

- We do not know how or where the components of vision are combined to form the percept of a unified object. One suggestion is that this is a distributed function.

 For Further Thought

- Red and green are complementary colors and blue and yellow are complementary, because their receptors have opponent connections to their ganglion cells. How would you explain the fact that bluish green and reddish yellow (orange) are also complementary?

continued

- Considering what you know about the retina, how would you need to direct your gaze to read a book? to find a very faint star?

- Explain why the visual system analyzes an object's edges, texture, and color and then detects the object, instead of the other way around.

Testing Your Understanding

1. Summarize the trichromatic and Hurvich-Jameson theories, indicating what facts about color vision each accounts for.

2. Compare the specialized sensitivities of simple and complex visual cortical cells; describe the interconnections among ganglion cells, simple cells, and complex cells that account for their specializations (according to Hubel and Wiesel).

3. The visual system appears to be hierarchical and modular. What does this mean? (Use examples to illustrate.)

Select the one best answer:

1. The receptive field of a cell in the visual system is the part of the _____ that the cell receives its input from.

    a. external world   b. retina
    c. lateral geniculate d. cortex
       nucleus

2. Stare at a blue object for a while and you will see a yellow afterimage. This is because blue and yellow are:

    a. complementary   b. primary colors.
       colors.
    c. natural colors   d. negative colors

3. If our experience of color were entirely due to the wavelength of light reflected from an object, we would not experience:

    a. complementary   b. primary colors.
       colors.
    c. negative color   d. color constancy.
       after effect.

4. The parvocellular system is specialized for:

    a. fine detail and   b. color and fine
       movement.   detail.

    c. color and   d. movement and
       movement.   brightness contrast.

5. *Retinotopic map* refers to:

    a. a projection of an image on the retina by the lens.
    b. the upside-down projection of an image.
    c. the way the visual neurons connect to the cortex.
    d. the connections among the cells in the retina.

6. Cutting the optic nerve between the right eye and the chiasm would cause a loss of vision in:

    a. the left visual   b. the right visual
       field.   field.
    c. half of each   d. neither field, due
       visual field.   to filling in.

7. People with red-green color blindness:

    a. cannot see either red or green.

    b. see red and green as black.

    c. confuse red and green because they lack either "red" or "green" cones.

    d. confuse red and green because their "red" cones are filled with "green" photopigment, or vice versa.

8. The enhanced apparent brightness of a light edge next to a dark edge is due to the fact that the neurons stimulated by the light edge are inhibited:

    a. less by their   b. more by their
       "dark" neighbors.   "dark" neighbors.
    c. less by their   d. more by their
       "light" neighbors.   "light" neighbors.

9. The ability of complex visual cortical cells to track an edge as it changes position appears to be due to:

   a. input from receptors with similar fields.
   b. input from ganglion cells with similar fields.
   c. input from simple cells with similar fields.
   d. input from other complex cells.

10. According to the spatial frequency theory of visual processing, edges are detected by:

   a. line-detecting cells in the visual cortex.
   b. edge detectors located in the visual cortex.
   c. cells that respond to low spatial frequencies.
   d. cells that respond to high spatial frequencies.

11. The circles represent the receptive field of a ganglion cell; the rectangle represents light. If the receptive field has an off center, in which situation will the ganglion cell's rate of firing be greatest?

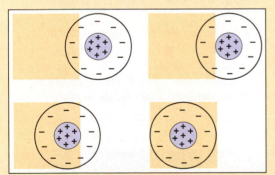

12. Studies of object, color, and movement agnosias indicate that:

   a. the visual system is unstable, and malfunctions with no apparent cause.
   b. components of the visual image are processed separately.
   c. color, object identification, and movement information are integrated in one place.
   d. the functions are processed in one place, but the results are distributed to other parts of the brain.

13. Movement perception is the primary function in visual area:

   a. V1.   b. V2.
   c. V4.   d. V5.

14. A person who has trouble identifying objects visually probably has damage in the:

   a. temporal lobe.   b. parietal lobe.
   c. occipital lobe.   d. frontal lobe.

Answers: 1. **b** 2. **a** 3. **d** 4. **b** 5. **c** 6. **c** 7. **d**
8. **a** 9. **c** 10. **d** 11. **b** 12. **b** 13. **d** 14. **a**

➡ On the Web

1. **Transformations for Perception and Action** answers all your questions about the physiology of vision, from retina to final projection areas, by using interactive animations at

   *http://www.med.uwo.ca/physiology/
   courses/sensesweb/index.htm*

2. **Magic Eye** offers a collection of three-dimensional stereograms and an explanation of how they work at

   http://www.magiceye.com

continued

3. **Optobionics,** the company that makes one of the artificial retinas, has information about the device and about its research at

   http://www.optobionics.com

4. **Sensation and Perception Tutorials** on topics from receptive fields to illusions are available at

   http://psych.hanover.edu/Krantz/ sen_tut.html

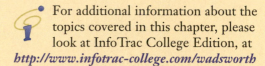 For additional information about the topics covered in this chapter, please look at InfoTrac College Edition, at *http://www.infotrac-college.com/wadsworth*

Try search terms you think up yourself, or use these: *ganglion cells; photopigment; prosopagnosia; visual acuity.*

 On the CD-ROM: Exploring Biological Psychology

Anatomy of the Eye
  Animation: The Retina
  Animation: Inverted Vision

Virtual Reality: The Eye
  Animation: Visual Pathways

 For Further Reading

The Case of the Colorblind Painter, by Oliver Sacks (In Sacks's *An Anthropologist on Mars,* 1995, Vintage Books), is a compelling narrative of the case of Jonathan I.
Visual Object Recognition, by Nikos Logothetis and David Sheinberg (*Annual Review of Neuroscience,* 1996, *19,* 577–621), is a review of research on that topic.

Mind Sights, by R. N. Shepard (Freeman, 1990), is a book of visual tricks and illusions.
The Astonishing Hypothesis, by Francis Crick (Scribner, 1994), is about the scientific search for consciousness; because the search focuses on visual awareness it contains fascinating and readable information about vision.

 Key Terms

color agnosia *273*

color constancy *274*

complementary colors *259*

complex cell *267*

distributed *270*

dorsal stream *271*

form vision *264*

fovea *255*

hierarchical processing *256*

iodopsin *254*

lateral inhibition *265*

magnocellular system *270*

modular processing *256*

movement agnosia *274*

negative color aftereffect *260*

neglect *275*

The Body Senses and Movement

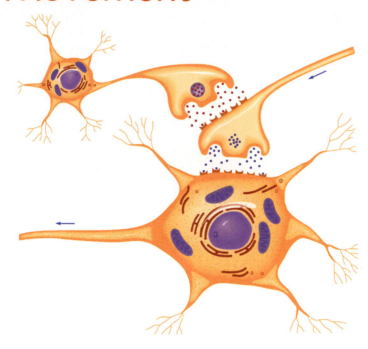

In this chapter you will learn:

- How the brain obtains information about the body and the objects in contact with it.

- What causes pain and ways it can be relieved.

- How several brain structures work together to produce movement.

- What some of the movement disorders are and how they impair movement.

. . . that's what they do with frogs, isn't it? They scoop out the centre, the spinal cord, they pith them. . . . That's what I am, pithed, like a frog. . . .

—Christina, quoted by Oliver Sacks

Christina was a healthy, active woman of 27. One day she began dropping things. Then she had trouble standing or even sitting upright; soon she was bedridden, lying motionless, speaking between shallow breaths in a faint and expressionless voice, and with an equally expressionless face. A spinal tap indicated that she was suffering a neuritis, an inflammation of the nerves. Neurological examination showed that, although she seemed paralyzed, her motor nerves were only slightly affected. She could move, but she could not control her movements or even her posture; if she failed to watch her hands, they wandered aimlessly. She had lost all *proprioception*, the sense that collects information from our muscles and tendons and joints to tell us where our hands are and what movements our feet and legs are making.

The neuritis did not last long, but in the meantime it had damaged her nerves, and the damage was permanent. For a month she was as floppy as a rag doll. But then she began to sit up, with an exaggeratedly erect posture, using only her vision for feedback. After a year of rehabilitation she was able to leave the hospital, to walk and take public transportation and work at home

as a computer programmer, all guided by vision. Christina never recovered from her loss, but she was able to make a remarkable compensation (Sacks, 1990).

In the last two chapters we have discussed audition and vision, sensory systems that provide information about distant objects. Now we turn our attention to the senses that inform us about the objects in direct contact with our bodies and that tell us where our body is in space, where our limbs are in relation to our body, and what is going on inside the body. Christina's case illustrates how important this information is for interacting physically with the world. The most important function of the body senses is to contribute to movement. In fact, the body senses are so intimately involved with our ability to move about in the world and to manipulate it that the movement system is often referred to as the *sensorimotor system*. For that reason we will follow the discussion of the body senses with an exploration of the topic of movement.

THE BODY SENSES

We get our information about the body from the somatosenses, which include the skin senses and proprioception, and from the vestibular sense. Another group of receptors monitor the internal organs; because they operate mostly in the background and participate in behavior less directly than the other senses, we will not take the time to consider them here.

Proprioception

Proprioception (from the Latin *proprius*, "belonging to one's self") is the sense that informs us about the position and movement of our limbs and body. Its sensors report tension and length in muscles and the angle of the limbs at the joints. Proprioception is not as glamorous a sense as vision or audition, or even touch. However, without it we would have a great deal of difficulty, as Christina did, in maintaining posture, moving our limbs, and grasping objects. We will return to this subject later when we discuss the control of movement.

What is proprioception, and why is it important?

The Vestibular Sense

What is the function of the vestibular sense?

In Chapter 8 you saw that the cochlea in the ear is connected to a strange-looking appendage, the vestibular organs. **The *vestibular sense* helps us maintain balance, and it provides information about head position and movement.** The organs are the *utricle*, the *saccule*, and the *semicircular canals* (see Figure 10.1a). The physical arrangement of the semicircular canals makes them especially responsive to rotational movement of the head (and body). At the base of each canal is a gelatinous (jellylike) mass called a cupula, which has a tuft of hair cells protruding into it (Figure 10.1b). During acceleration (increasing rate of movement) the shifting fluid in the canals displaces the cupula, which bends the hair cells. Depending on the direction and angle of rotation, the movement depolarizes the receptor cells and increases the firing rate in the neurons, or hyperpolarizes them, reducing the firing rate.

The utricle and saccule monitor head position in relation to gravity. In Figure 10.1c you can see that the receptors are covered with a gelatinous material embedded with calcium carbonate crystals (called *otoliths*) that add weight. When the head tilts, gravity shifts the gelatinous mass and the hair cells are depolarized or hyperpolarized, depending on the direction of tilt. The hair cell receptors in the utricle are arranged in a horizontal patch, while the saccule's receptors are on its vertical wall; thus, the two organs can detect tilt in any direction. The receptors also respond to acceleration. When we change from a walk to

Figure 10.1
The vestibular organs
(a) The inner ear, showing the cochlea and the vestibular organs. **(b)** Enlarged view of a cupula in a semicircular canal. **(c)** Receptors of the utricle and saccule.

Sources: (a) S. Iurato (1967). Submicroscopic structure of the inner ear. Pergamon Press. (b) Based on M. E. Goldberg & A. J. Hudspeth (2000), "The vestibular system" in E. R. Kandel, J. H. Schwartz, & T. M. Jessell (eds.), *Principles of the Neural Science*, 4th Ed., p. 801–815. © 2000 McGraw-Hill. (c) Based on F. Martini (1988). *Fundamentals of Anatomy and Physiology*, 4th Edition, p. 576. © 1988 Prentice-Hall.

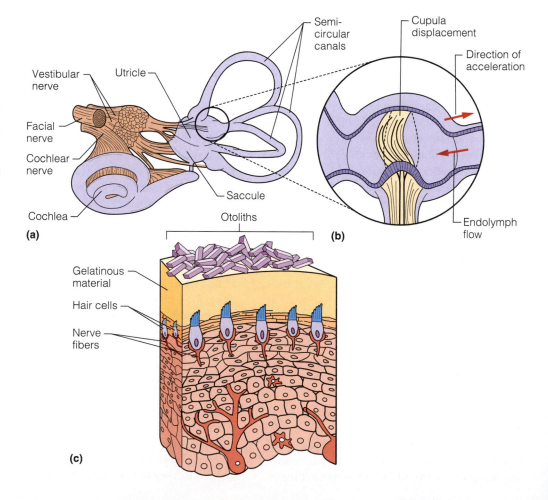

a run, the gelatinous mass lags behind briefly, just as the coffee sloshes out of your cup when you start up from a traffic light. And just as the coffee levels off in your cup when you reach a stable speed, the hair cells return to their normal position and stop responding when your speed stabilizes; otherwise, you would continue to sense the movement throughout a 500-mile-per-hour trip in a jetliner.

You might wonder why a system that operates mostly outside awareness needs to be so elaborate. But consider what would happen without a vestibular system. When Mr. MacGregor walked he tilted 20 degrees to the left because his vestibular sense had been knocked out by disease (Sacks, 1990). His proprioception was working, but it was not enough by itself. Although his friends told him he was in danger of falling over, he was unconvinced anything was wrong until he saw himself on videotape. A retired carpenter, he fashioned a miniature spirit level like carpenters use to determine whether a wall is perfectly vertical, and suspended it in front of his glasses. Using this makeshift device he was able to walk straight and, after a few weeks, checking his tilt became so natural he was no longer aware of it. But the vestibular sense is not just for adjusting the body's position. When we reach for an object we must know the position of our body and the relation of our arm to our body; this information comes from the vestibular sense and proprioception. Proprioception also triggers reflexive eye movements that keep returning our gaze to the scene as we turn our head or as our body bobs up and down when we walk; otherwise, the world would become a meaningless blur.

The Skin Senses

The *skin senses* are touch, warmth, cold, and pain. Although their range is limited to the surface of our body, changes there are often due to external stimulation, so the skin senses inform us both about our body and the world. (We experience these sensations deeper in the body as well, but less often and with less sensitivity.) The skin sense receptors are illustrated in the diagram of a section of skin in Figure 10.2. There are two general types of receptors: free nerve endings

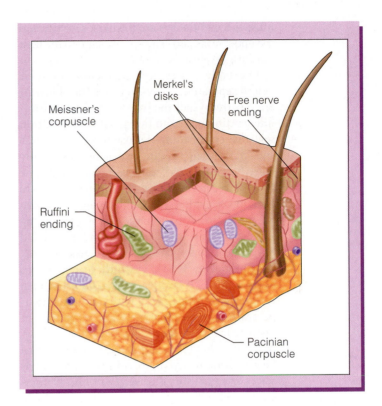

Figure 10.2
Receptors of the skin

and a variety of encapsulated endings. The encapsulated receptors detect touch. Why so many receptors just for touch? Because touch is a complex sense that conveys a great deal of information. In the superficial layers of the skin Meissner's corpuscles respond with a brief burst of impulses, while Merkel's disks give a more sustained response. Located near the surface of the skin, together they detect the texture and fine detail of objects, as well as their movement. They come into play when you explore an object with gentle strokes of your hand or when a blind person reads Braille. Pacinian corpuscles and Ruffini endings are located in the deeper layers, where they detect stretching of the skin and contribute to our perception of the shape of grasped objects (Gardner, Martin, & Jessell, 2000). The unencapsulated free nerve endings detect warmth, cold, and pain. Because the density of the skin receptors varies throughout the body, so does sensitivity—as much as 10-fold in fact. The

Why are there so many kinds of skin receptors?

fingertips and the lips are the most sensitive and the upper arms and calves of the legs are the least sensitive (Weinstein, 1968).

The body senses are remarkable for their neural separation. Their neurons travel in separate pathways all the way to the cortex; carefully cutting nerves in the spinal cord results in selective elimination of sense modalities. Such specificity may seem surprising, especially when warmth, cold, and pain share the same type of receptor. However, the receptors are functionally different. Cold receptors, which are near the skin's surface, have peak firing rates at 25°C; warmth receptors are deeper and have a peak firing rate at 45°C (Gardner et al., 2000; Sinclair, 1981). Warmth receptors *stop firing* at 50°C (Gardner et al., 2000) but pain receptors continue firing with additional temperature increases because pain receptors are distinct from warmth receptors (Han, Zhang, & Craig, 1998). In fact, painful and nonpainful heat activate different areas in the somatosensory cortex (Bushnell et al., 1999). To demonstrate separation of the skin senses yourself, move the point of a lead pencil slowly across your face. You will feel the touch of the pencil pretty continuously, but the lead will feel cold only occasionally—because touch and cold are monitored by different receptors.

The Somatosensory Cortex and the Posterior Parietal Cortex

The body is divided into segments called *dermatomes,* **each served by a spinal nerve,** as Figure 10.3 shows. The divisions are not as distinct as illustrated, because each dermatome overlaps the next by one-third to one-half. This way, if one nerve is injured the area will not lose all sensation. Body sense information enters the spinal cord (via spinal nerves) or the brain (via cranial nerves) and travels to the thalamus. From there **the body sense neurons go to their projection area, the** *somatosensory cortex,* **located in the parietal cortex just behind the central sulcus and the primary motor cortex** (Figure 10.4). As with the auditory system, most of the neurons

How are the body senses and vision similar?

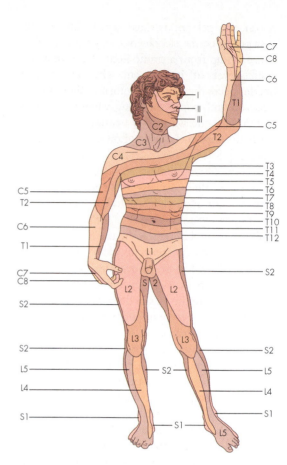

Figure 10.3
Dermatomes of the human body
For sensory purposes, the body is divided into segments called dermatomes, each served by a spinal or cranial nerve. The labels identify the nerve. Letters indicate the part of the spinal cord where the nerve is located (cervical, thoracic, lumbar, sacral, or coccygeal), and the numbers indicate the nerve's position within that section. Areas I, II, and III on the face are innervated by branches of the trigeminal (fifth) cranial nerve.

cross to the other side of the brain, so the touch of an object held in the right hand is registered mostly in the left hemisphere. Because not all neurons cross over, touching the object also stimulates the right somatosensory cortex, though much less.

Sensory systems have a number of organizational and functional similarities; a comparison of the somatosensory cortex with the visual cortex will illustrate this point. First, it contains a map of the body, just as the visual cortex contains a map of the retina; the amount of space given over to different parts of the body corresponds to their sensitivity (Figure 10.5). Second, some cortical cells have fields on the skin with excitatory centers and inhibitory surrounds; this arrangement sharpens the localization of peak excitation, and helps distinguish two points touching the skin (see Figure 10.6) (Mountcastle & Powell, 1959).

Another similarity is that somatosensory processing is hierarchical. **The *primary somatosensory cortex (S-I)* consists of four areas, each of which contains a map of the body and plays a role in processing sensory information from the body.** The thalamus sends its output to two of these subareas, which extract some information and pass the result on to the other two areas, which in turn send their output to the secondary somatosensory cortex.

A fourth similarity with vision is that some S-I neurons are specialized feature detectors, with sensitivities for shape, orientation, direction of movement, surface curvature, or texture (Figure 10.7) (Carlson, 1981; Gardner & Kandel, 2000; Warren, Hämäläinen, & Gardner, 1986). Apparently the S-I neurons combine inputs from neurons with simpler functions, just as complex visual cells integrate the inputs of multiple simple cells (Iwamura, Iriki, & Tanaka, 1994). Some receptors have receptive fields that include multiple fingers; their firing rate depends on how many fingers are touched, so they give some indication of the size of a held object.

The *secondary somatosensory cortex (S-II)* receives input from the left and the right S-I, so it combines information from both sides of the body. S-II neurons are particularly responsive to stimuli that have acquired meaning, for instance, by association with reward (Hsiao, O'Shaughnessy, & Johnson, 1993). S-II connects to the part of the temporal lobe that includes the hippocampus, which is important in learning, so it may serve to determine whether a stimulus is committed to memory (Gardner & Kandel, 2000).

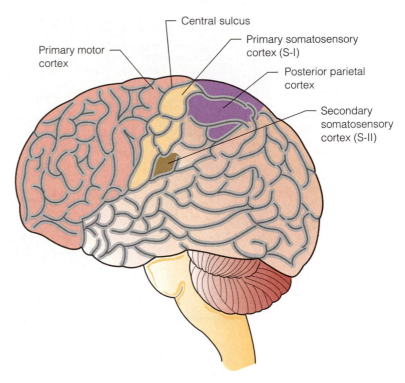

Figure 10.4
The somatosensory and posterior parietal areas

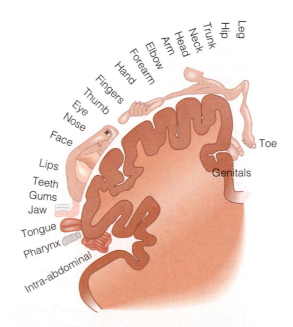

Figure 10.5
The somatosensory cortex

Source: Adapted from *The Cerebral Cortex of Man* by W. Penfield and T. Rasmussen. Copyright © 1950 Macmillan. Copyright renewed 1978 by Theodore Rasmussen.

What cortical areas are involved in the body senses?

Figure 10.6
An opponent receptive field for touch in a monkey

(a) The size and location of the excitatory and inhibitory areas of the receptive field of a single touch neuron in a monkey's somatosensory cortex. (b) The effect on the neuron's activity from stimulating the inhibitory area (8–10 sec) during continuous stimulation of the excitatory area (4–12 sec).

Source: From V. B. Mountcastle and T. P. S. Powell. "Neural Mechanisms Subserving Cutaneous Sensibility, with Special Reference to the Role of Afferent Inhibition in Sensory Perception and Discrimination." *Bulletin of the Johns Hopkins Hospital* 105 (1959), 224, Fig. 14. © The Johns Hopkins University Press. Reprinted with permission of the Johns Hopkins University Press.

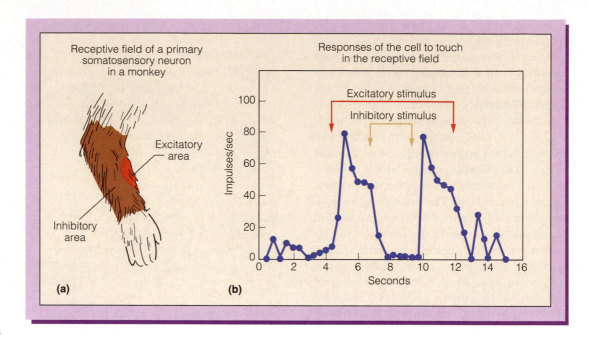

Figure 10.7
Higher-order receptive fields in the monkey somatosensory cortex

(a) The somatosensory cell whose recordings are shown to the right of the hand responds best to a horizontal edge. (b) This cell responds best to movement across the fingertip from (the monkey's) right to left, but not in the opposite direction.

Reprinted from *Journal of Physiology*, Vol. 283, J. Hyvärinen and A. Poranen, "Movement-sensitive cutaneous receptive fields in the hand area of the post-central gyrus in monkeys, p. 523–537, Copyright 1978, with permission from Elsevier Science.

To pick up a forkful of the apple pie on your plate, your brain must not only receive a visual image of the slab of pie, but it must know where your arm and hand are in relation to your body, where your head is oriented in relation to your body, and where your eyes are oriented in relation to your head. That is where the posterior parietal cortex comes in. S-I projects to the posterior parietal cortex as well as to S-II.

As you saw in the previous chapter, the ***posterior parietal cortex (PPC)* is an association area that brings together the body senses,** **vision, and audition** (Colby & Goldberg, 1999; Hyvärinen, 1981; Stricanne, Andersen, & Mazzoni, 1996). See Figure 10.4 again for the location of the PPC in relation to the somatosensory cortex. Here the brain determines the body's orientation in space, the location of the limbs, and the location in space of objects detected by touch, sight, and sound. In other words, it integrates the body with the world. The PPC is composed of several subareas, which are responsive to different sense modalities and make different contri-

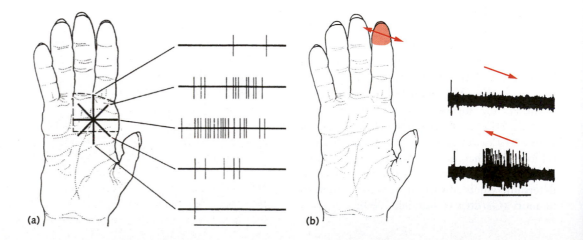

butions to a person's interaction with the world. Some cells combine proprioception and vision to provide information about specific postures, for example the location and positioning of the arm and the hand (Bonda, Petrides, Frey, & Evans, 1995; Graziano, Cooke, & Taylor, 2000; Sakata, Takaoka, Kawarasaki, & Shibutani, 1973). Others contribute to reaching and grasping movements and eye movements toward targets of interest (Batista, Buneo, Snyder, & Andersen, 1999; Colby & Goldberg, 1999). The PPC's function is not solely perceptual, because many of its neurons fire before and during a movement. It does not itself produce movements, but passes its information on to frontal areas that do (Colby & Goldberg, 1999).

The Sensation of Pain

In Chapter 7 we saw how pain functions as an emotion to motivate our behavior. Now we need to put pain in the context of the body senses and see how it works as a sensory mechanism. Don't worry—there are still a few surprises left.

Detecting Pain

Pain begins when certain free nerve endings are stimulated by intense pressure or temperature or by damage to tissue. There are three types of pain receptors. Thermal receptors respond to extreme heat and cold. Mechanical receptors react to intense stimulation like pinching and cutting. Polymodal receptors are activated by thermal and mechanical stimuli and by chemicals released when tissue is injured (Gardner et al., 2000), including bradykinin, histamine, prostaglandins, substance P, and serotonin (Levine, Fields, & Basbaum, 1993). The information travels to the spinal cord over large, myelinated A-delta fibers and small, lightly or unmyelinated C fibers. Because A-delta fibers transmit rapidly, you notice a *sharp pain* almost immediately when you are injured, followed by a longer-lasting *dull pain* later (Basbaum & Jessell, 2000). Sharp pain makes a good danger signal and dull pain hangs around for a longer time to remind you that you have been injured.

In the spinal cord, pain neurons release glutamate and *substance P (SP), a neuropeptide involved in pain signaling* (De Biasi & Rustioni, 1988; Skilling, Smullin, Beitz, & Larson, 1988). In Chapter 2 we saw that neuropeptides enhance the effect of a neurotransmitter at the synapse. In mice lacking SP receptors or the ability to produce SP, moderate and intense pain are impaired but mild pain is unaffected (Cao et al., 1998; De Felipe et al., 1998).

People used aspirin and anesthetics for decades without understanding how they relieved pain; only recently did we discover that local and general anesthetics interfere with the neuron's ion exchange (see Chapter 2), and that aspirin suppresses the synthesis of prostaglandins. But most pain relievers don't work as well as we would like, or they have undesirable side effects; fortunately, in the past few years we have begun to understand the mechanism of pain. One reason pain researchers want to understand how pain works is to find better pain relievers.

Internal Mechanisms of Pain Relief

During a spring break in New Orleans I was touring one of the Civil War-era plantation houses that the area is noted for. In a glass case was an assortment of artifacts that had been found on the plantation grounds. An odd part of the collection was a few lead rifle slugs with what were obviously deep tooth marks on them. When makeshift surgery had to be performed with only a large dose of whiskey for anesthesia, the unfortunate patient would often be given something to bite down on like a piece of leather harness or a relatively soft lead bullet. (You can probably guess what common expression this practice gave rise to.)

As a toddler, whenever you scraped your knee you clenched your teeth and rubbed the area around the wound. And, tribute to your childhood wisdom, it really did help and got you through the pain without the benefit of either a lead bullet or whiskey. You might think that teeth clenching and rubbing simply take attention from the pain. Ronald Melzack and

What causes pain?

Figure 10.8
David Livingstone attacked by a lion
Endorphins allowed Livingstone to endure the pain.
Source: Livingstone, 1858/1971.

Hulton Archive

Patrick Wall (1965) had another idea. In their *gate control theory* they hypothesized that pressure signals arriving in the brain trigger an inhibitory message that travels back down the spinal cord, where it closes a neural "gate" in the pain pathway. They believed this gate mechanism is also involved when emotion increases or decreases pain. One application of gate control theory is *transcutaneous electrical nerve stimulation;* electrical current applied to the skin activates large-diameter neurons, which inhibit activity in pain neurons. Though the gate control theory was not correct in all its details, you will see it surfacing again later.

Two pain questions have been particularly intriguing. One is *why people sometimes suffer no pain in spite of severe injuries.* In the account of his search for the mouth of the Nile river, the explorer and missionary David Livingstone (1858/1971, p. 12) told this story about an attack by a lion (see Figure 10.8):

> Starting, and looking half round, I saw the lion just in the act of springing upon me. I was upon a little height; he caught my shoulder as he sprang, and we both came to the ground below together. Growling horribly close to my ear, he shook me as a terrier dog does a rat. The shock produced a stupor similar to that which seems to be felt by a mouse after the first shake of the cat. It caused a sort of dreaminess, in which there was no sense of pain nor feeling of terror, though quite conscious of all that was happening. It was like what patients partially under the influence of chloroform describe, who see all the operation, but feel not the knife.

David Livingstone's dreamy analgesia is not uncommon during injury; people sometimes are not even aware they are injured until someone calls it to their attention. Solving the mystery of this dramatic pain insensitivity would have to wait until the second question was answered: *why opiate drugs like morphine are such powerful analgesics.* In 1973, Candace Pert and Solomon Snyder asked the question in a new way, by looking for opiate receptors in the nervous system. They placed neural tissue from animals in a bath of naloxone that had been made radioactive. Their reasoning was that if the opiate receptors exist, then naloxone probably blocks opiate effects by binding to those receptors. If so, the naloxone would make the tissue radioactive. The result was just as they expected. But why would the brain have evolved receptors for a drug? The answer had to be that the nervous system manufactures and releases chemicals similar to opiates. Researchers combined the words *endogenous* ("from within") and *morphine* to come up with the name *endorphins* for these chemicals.

How does the brain relieve pain?

Endorphins **function both as neurotrans-mitters and as hormones, and act at opiate receptors in many parts of the nervous system.** Pain is one of the stimuli that release endorphins, but only under certain conditions. Rats were subjected to electric shock that they could terminate by rotating a wheel, while another group was given an equal amount of inescapable shock. Thirty minutes later researchers measured the rats' pain thresholds by timing how long they tolerated a heat lamp on their tail before flicking their tail away. The group given inescapable shock had a much higher tolerance for pain than the escapable shock group (Maier, Drugan, & Grau, 1982). This analgesia is reversible by opiate antagonists such as naloxone. I am sure you can see the benefit of eliminating pain in situations of helplessness like Livingstone's, and preserving pain when it can serve as the motivation to escape. Stress also causes the release of endorphins. For example, endorphin levels are increased in long-distance runners after a strenuous run (Colt, Wardlaw, & Frantz, 1981).

Pain and stress are not the only stimuli that trigger endorphin release. Pain relief produced by acupuncture is in some cases abolished by naloxone, which means that it is opiate based (Watkins & Mayer, 1982). Even the pain relief from a placebo, which doctors once took as evidence that the pain was not "real," is opioid in origin (Basbaum & Fields, 1984). Finally, vaginal stimulation in rats produces analgesia that is reduced by naloxone (Komisaruk & Steinman, 1987). Vaginal self-stimulation reduces sensitivity to pain in women, and presumably is endorphin based as well (Whipple & Komisaruk, 1988). The function of this analgesia is unclear, although it might reduce pain during birth or intercourse.

We do not have a complete understanding of how endorphins relieve pain. One hypothesized mechanism involves a descending pathway from the brain to the spinal cord that is very reminiscent of the one proposed in the gate control theory. **Pain and other stimuli cause the release** **of endorphins in the** *periaqueductal gray* *(PAG),* **a brain-stem structure with a large number of endorphin synapses** (which we first discussed in the chapter on drugs) (Basbaum & Fields, 1984). The endorphins activate PAG neurons. Activity from the PAG passes down to the medulla, and then to the spinal cord. There the descending neurons inhibit the release of substance P. The descending circuit is illustrated in Figure 10.9, and Figure 10.10 shows the inhibitory synapse. Notice that the inhibitory synapse is an example of *presynaptic inhibition,* described in Chapter 2. The accompanying Application describes a practical use of our knowledge of the pain inhibition mechanism.

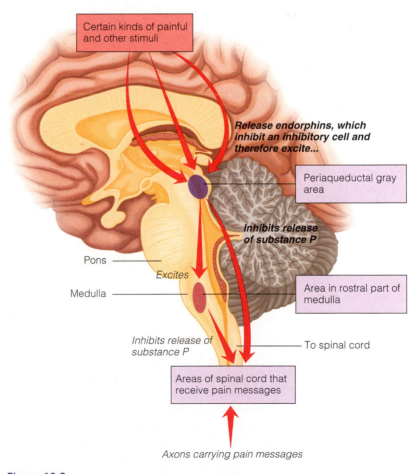

Certain kinds of painful and other stimuli

Release endorphins, which inhibit an inhibitory cell and therefore excite...

Periaqueductal gray area

Inhibits release of substance P

Pons

Excites

Medulla

Area in rostral part of medulla

To spinal cord

Inhibits release of substance P

Areas of spinal cord that receive pain messages

Axons carrying pain messages

Figure 10.9
The descending pain inhibition circuit

Figure 10.10
A pain synapse in the spinal cord
Pain-transmitting neurons release substance
P at their synapses. Neurons from the
descending pain inhibitory pathway release
enkephalin, one of the endorphins, which
inhibits transmission.

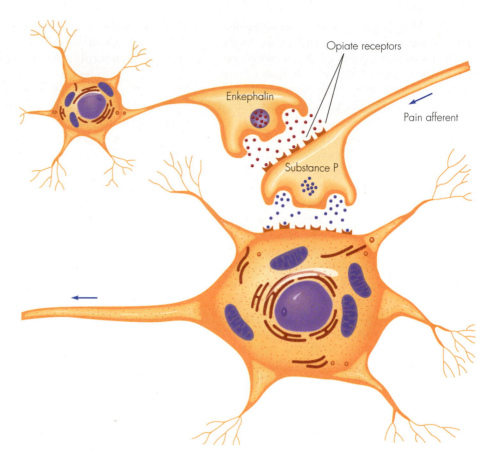

*What causes phan-
tom pain?*

Not all stimulation-induced pain relief comes from endorphins. For example, naloxone does not reduce the analgesic effect of hypnosis (Watkins & Mayer, 1982). Naloxone blocks analgesia produced by acupuncture needles placed at distant points from the pain site, but does not affect the analgesia resulting from needles placed near the site (Watkins & Mayer, 1982). Also, whether pain relief from PAG stimulation is opioid based depends on which part of the PAG is stimulated (Barbaro, 1988). Obviously there are other internal pain-reducing mechanisms, which we know less about. One non-opiate pain relief system depends on substance P, and another involves the neurotransmitter *N*-methyl-D-aspartate (NMDA) (De Felipe et al., 1998). Another non-opioid system responds to nicotine-like drugs which, you may remember, stimulate

acetylcholine receptors. One of these drugs that shows promise as a major pain reliever is ABT-594, which was originally discovered in the skin of Ecuadorian frogs. It equals morphine in pain-relieving effectiveness, but lacks the depressant and addictive effects of opiates (Bannon et al., 1998).

Phantom Pain

If a person's right parietal cortex is damaged, the person may fail to recognize the left arm and leg. So does amputating a person's arm or leg eliminate consciousness of the limb? Most amputees continue to experience the missing limb, not as a memory, but as vividly as if it were real (Melzack, 1992). A phantom leg bends when the person sits down and becomes upright during standing; a phantom arm swings in coordination with the other limbs during walking.

Tapping into the Pain Relief Circuit

Knowledge of the descending pain relief circuit has been put to practical use through electrical stimulation to relieve pain. In one technique, the periaqueductal gray is stimulated directly through implanted electrodes (Barbaro, 1988). Wires from the electrodes run through the neck to a receiver located under the skin, usually on the chest; the patient controls stimulation with an external battery-powered transmitter held directly over the receiver (see the accompanying photo). Typically, a patient uses the stimulator for 15 minutes four times a day. PAG stimulation relieves pain in half or more of pain patients, depending on which pain symptom groups are included in the data analysis. Presumably, the stimulation closes the gate in the spinal cord, although whether it works through endorphin release is unclear from studies.

PAG stimulation has the drawback that it requires brain surgery. Because transcutaneous electrical nerve stimulation uses skin surface electrodes, it avoids the risks of surgery and is more acceptable to patients. TENS electrodes are placed at the pain site or at acupuncture points (Kaye & Brandstater, 2002). Laboratory studies suggest that the stimulation's effect on large nerve fibers reduces activity in pain-conducting C fibers through presynaptic inhibition in the spinal cord's dorsal horns. TENS provides relief in 70-80% of patients, decreasing to 20-30% after a few months of use. TENS is not as effective with some kinds of pain. Low back pain is one example but, fortunately, it does respond to percutaneous electrical nerve stimulation, a variation that uses acupuncture needles to deliver stimulation to deeper tissue.

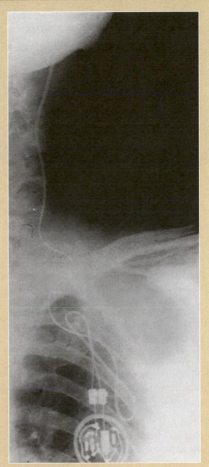

4

X-Ray Showing Implanted PAG Stimulator
Source: Barbaro, 1988.

Seventy percent of amputees experience *phantom pain,* **pain that seems to be located in the missing limb.** Phantom pain is just as real a sensation as the phantom limb, and is a significant problem in postamputation pain management. The classical explanation was that the cut ends of nerves generate impulses that are registered in the part of the brain that once served the missing limb. Surgeons tried to cut off this transmission by cutting pain pathways in the spinal cord and in the thalamus, only to find that relief was temporary at best. Two observations suggested that the phantom originates in the brain: one was that people with a break in the spinal cord high in the upper body sometimes experience phantom legs; the other was the presence of unusually high spontaneous activity in the thalamus in some phantom-limb patients (Melzack, 1992).

Figure 10.11
Location of activity in the hand and face areas in amputees
Squares represent the fingers and the lips are represented by circles. Black symbols are from an amputee with intense phantom pain, white symbols from a pain-free amputee. In the left hemisphere (opposite the intact arm in both patients) activity from the lips and fingers is in adjacent but separate areas. In the right hemisphere, opposite the amputation, activity from the lips has "moved" into the hand area for the patient with intense pain, but not for the other individual.
Reprinted by permission of *Nature,* copyright 1995.

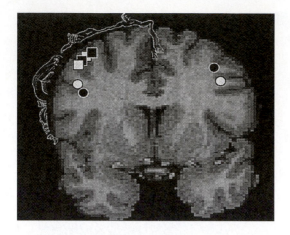

Following the clue that stimulating the face often produces sensations in a phantom arm, a team of researchers in Germany (Flor et al., 1995) used a neuromagnetic imaging technique to map face and hand somatosensory areas in upper-limb amputees. They found that in the hemisphere opposite the amputation, neurons from the face area had invaded the area that normally receives input from the hand (see Figure 10.11). In pain-free amputees the amount of shift averaged 0.43 cm; for those with phantom pain, the shift was 2.05 cm, almost five times as great. Apparently the pain was caused by the intrusion of the "foreign" neurons. We usually think of neural plasticity as adaptive; sometimes it can lead to malfunction and, in this case, truly bizarre results.

✓ **CONCEPT CHECK**

- *What is the contribution of each of the three classes of body senses?*
- *In what ways are the somatosensory cortex and the visual cortex organized similarly?*
- *In what circumstances does the brain reduce pain?*

MOVEMENT

What is the function of antagonistic muscles?

For most psychology students, the subject of movement holds less fascination than other areas of biological psychology. This point of view is inconsistent with the vast amount of brain area devoted to movement, however. It also ignores the fact that only through movements can our intellectual and creative accomplishments achieve reality, or even be communicated to others. It also ignores the historical fact that studies of the control of movement provided one of the earliest windows into the workings of the brain. Our emphasis here will be on what we have learned about the brain's organization and functioning through these studies. Before we launch into that topic we need some understanding of the equipment the brain has to work with.

The Muscles

We have three types of muscles. The ones you are most familiar with are the *skeletal muscles,* **which move the body and limbs**; they are also called *striated* muscles because of their striped appearance. *Smooth muscles* **control the internal organs,** for instance, moving food through the digestive system. *Cardiac muscles* **are the muscles that make up the heart.** Because our focus is on movement, we will concentrate on the skeletal muscles. Anyway, in spite of differences in appearance, the muscles function similarly.

Like other tissues of the body, a muscle is made up of many individual cells, or *muscle fibers* (Figure 10.12). **The muscle cells are controlled by motor neurons that synapse with a muscle cell at the *neuromuscular junction*** (Figure 10.13). The number of cells served by a single axon determines the precision of movement possible. The biceps muscles have about a hundred muscle fibers per axon, but the ratio is around three to one in the eye muscles, which must make very precise movements in tracking objects (Evarts, 1979). Acetylcholine is the neurotransmitter that is released at all skeletal neuromuscular junctions.

Skeletal muscles are anchored to bones by tendons, which are bands of connective tissue. You can see in Figure 10.14 that by pulling against their attachments the muscles are able to operate the limbs like levers to produce

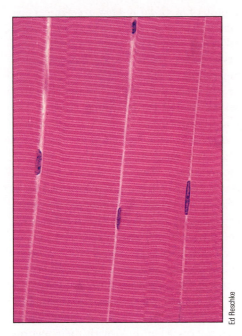

Figure 10.12
Skeletal muscle cells
The horizontal bands are the striations that give skeletal muscles the name *striated*. The dark objects are cell nuclei.

movement. You can also see that limbs are equipped with two *antagonistic muscles,* **muscles that produce opposite movements at a joint.** In this case the biceps muscle flexes the arm, and the triceps extends it. Rather than one muscle relaxing while the other does all the work, movement involves opposing contraction from both muscles. The simultaneous contraction of antagonistic muscles creates a smoother movement, allows precise stopping, and maintains a position with minimal tremor. Standing requires the countering effects of antagonistic muscles in the legs, as well as muscles in the torso. The amount of contraction in a muscle varies from moment to moment, so the balance between two antagonistic muscles is constantly shifting. This requires corrective action. If maintaining the balance between opposed pairs of muscles required conscious, voluntary activity, we would never be able to hold a video camera still enough to get a sharp picture or even to stand

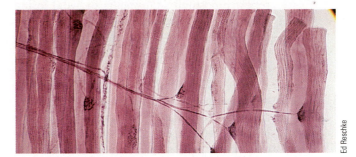

Figure 10.13
Muscle fibers innervated by a motor neuron

without bobbling back and forth. Adjustments this fast have to be controlled by reflexes at the level of the spinal cord.

The Spinal Cord

In Chapter 3 we introduced the idea of the spinal reflex. Everyone is familiar with the reflex that makes you quickly withdraw your hand from a hot stove. When you step on a sharp object, you reflexively withdraw your foot, and simultaneously make a variety of

What do spinal reflexes and central pattern generators do?

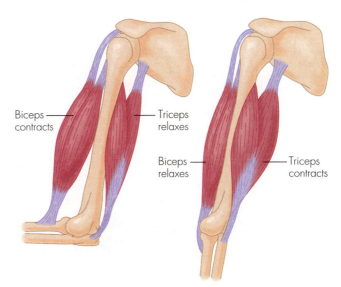

Biceps contracts — Triceps relaxes

Biceps relaxes — Triceps contracts

Figure 10.14
Antagonistic muscles of the upper arm
When the biceps muscle contracts it flexes the arm (left); contracting the triceps muscle extends the arm.
Source: After Starr and Taggart, 1989.

reflexive postural adjustments to avoid losing your balance. The advantage of reflexes is that we can make the appropriate adjustments quickly, without the delay of having to figure out the right action.

The reflex illustrated in Figure 10.15 should also be familiar. Your doctor taps the patellar tendon, which connects the quadriceps muscle to the lower leg bone. This stretches the muscle, which is detected by **muscle stretch receptors called** *muscle spindles* and relayed to the spinal cord. There the sensory neurons synapse on motor neurons, which return to the quadriceps and cause it to contract and extend the lower leg. The function of the stretch reflex is not just to amuse doctors. It enables a muscle to resist very quickly if the muscle is stretched by activity in its antagonistic partner; this helps, for example, to maintain an upright posture. It also allows a muscle to respond quickly to an increased external load, for example when you are holding a book out in front of you and a friend unexpectedly drops another

book on top of it. *Golgi tendon organs,* **receptors that detect tension in a muscle,** trigger a spinal reflex that inhibits the muscle. This prevents muscles from contracting so much that they might be damaged.

More complex patterns of motor behavior are also controlled in the spinal cord. It has been known for some time that cats whose spinal cords have been cut, eliminating control from the brain, will make rhythmic walking movements when they are suspended with their feet touching a treadmill (Grillner, 1985). This behavior depends on *central pattern generators (CPGs),* **neuronal networks that produce a rhythmic pattern of motor activity, such as those involved in walking, swimming, flying, and breathing.** CPGs may be located in the spinal cord or elsewhere. In humans, they are most obvious in infants under the age of 1 year, who also make stepping movements when held with their feet on a treadmill (Lamb & Yang, 2000). CPGs are also present in adults, though less obvious. They can be elicited in individuals with spinal cord injury (Dimitrijevic, Gerasimenko, & Pinter, 1998), which suggests they might be useful in restoring some function after paralysis (Barbeau et al., 1999). Spinal reflexes produce quick, reliable responses, and central pattern generators provide basic routines the brain can call up when needed, freeing the brain for more important matters (see Figure 10.16). But reflexes and CPGs do not constitute a movement system, so we will turn our attention to the contributions the brain makes to movement.

The Brain and Movement

In the motor system we again see a hierarchical organization, progressing from the spinal cord to the brain stem to the forebrain. Brainstem structures modulate (adjust) the activity of spinal cord neurons. The motor cortex modulates activity in both of the lower levels, as well as organizing complex acts and executing precision movements (Ghez & Krakauer, 2000). We will start with the cortex and give it most of our attention.

Figure 10.15
The patellar tendon reflex, an example of a stretch reflex
The hammer stretches the tendon, causing a reflexive contraction of the extensor muscle and a kicking motion.

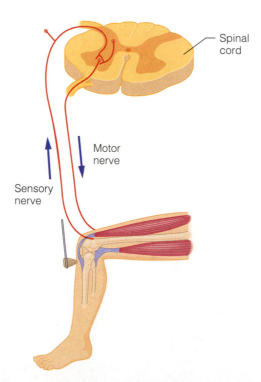

Spinal cord

Motor nerve

Sensory nerve

THE FAR SIDE® BY GARY LARSON

Basic lives

What life would be like without central pattern generators

The motor cortex consists of the primary motor cortex and two major secondary motor areas, the supplementary motor area and the premotor cortex (Figure 10.17). Two additional secondary areas are in the cingulate cortex. Like the primary area, the secondary areas contain a map of the body, with greater amounts of cortex devoted to the parts of the body that produce finer movements (Figure 10.18). The sequence of processing in the motor cortex is just the opposite of what we see in the sensory areas: planning of movement begins in the association areas, and the primary motor cortex is the final cortical motor area.

The Prefrontal Cortex

As an initial step in motor planning, the *prefrontal cortex (PFC)* receives input from the posterior parietal cortex, integrates information about the body with information from the world, then holds the information in memory until the behavior is executed (see Figure 10.17 again). You already know two functions of the PFC that suit it for this role,

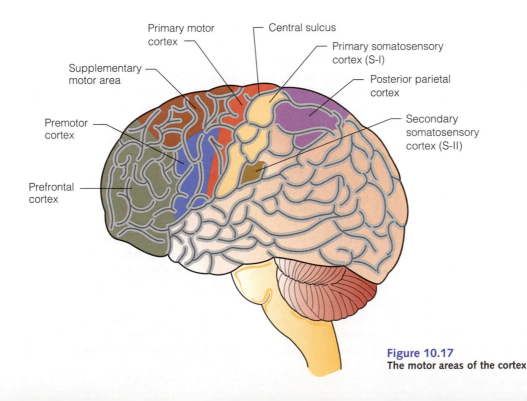

Figure 10.17
The motor areas of the cortex

What is the relationship between the primary motor area and the association areas?

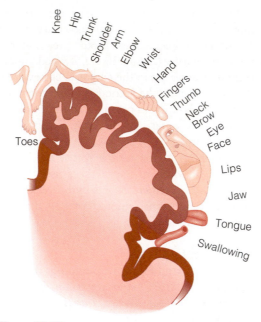

Knee
Hip
Trunk
Shoulder
Arm
Elbow
Wrist
Hand
Fingers
Thumb
Neck
Brow
Eye
Face
Lips
Jaw
Tongue
Swallowing
Toes

Figure 10.18
The primary motor area
The homunculus shows the relative amount of cortex devoted to different parts of the body.
Source: Adapted from *The Cerebral Cortex of Man* by W. Penfield and T. Rasmussen. Copyright © 1950 Macmillan. Copyright renewed 1978 by Theodore Rasmussen.

namely that it plans actions with regard to their consequences, and it receives information about the identity of objects by way of the ventral visual stream, information that is useful in identifying targets of motor activity.

These functions are typically investigated in monkeys while they perform some variation of a *delayed match-to-sample task*. The monkey is presented with a visual stimulus. After a delay of a few seconds in which the stimulus is absent, the monkey is presented two or more stimuli and required to select the original stimulus from among them in order to obtain a reward, such as a sip of juice. The delay period allows the researchers to distinguish between preparatory neural activity and activity related to the actual movement. Recordings show that some PFC cells increase their rate of firing when the first stimulus is presented, and continue to fire during the delay, as if "remembering" the stimulus. When the monkey is cued to make a

choice, activity in additional prefrontal cells begins before activity starts in the premotor areas; this indicates that the prefrontal cortex selects the target of behavior and the appropriate motor response (Goldman-Rakic, Bates, & Chafee, 1992; Hoshi, Shima, & Tanji, 2000; Rainer, Rao, & Miller, 1999).

The Secondary Motor Areas

Using information from both the PFC and the PPC (Krakauer & Ghez, 2000), the *premotor cortex (PM)* **begins programming a movement by combining information needed for the movement.** A good example comes from a study in which monkeys were cued to reach for one of two targets, A or B, in different locations, and to use the left arm on some trials and the right on others. Some premotor neurons increased their firing rate only if target A was cued, and other neurons were selective for target B. Other cells fired selectively depending on which arm was to be used. Still other cells combined the information of the first two kinds of cells; they increased their firing only when a particular target was cued *and* a particular arm was to be used (Hoshi & Tanji, 2000). Some of the cells combine information to provide sensory guidance of movement; two types of cell, for example, contribute to the visual guidance of reaching. One of these responds when a visual stimulus is near a specific part of the body (Figure 10.19a); another shifts the location of its visual receptive field as the monkey moves its hand (Figure 10.19b) (Graziano, Yap, & Gross, 1994).

Sequences of movements, such as those involved in eating or playing the piano, are assembled in the *supplementary motor area (SMA)*. In monkeys trained to produce several different sets of movement sequences, different neurons increase their firing during a delay period depending on which sequence has been cued for performance (Shima & Tanji, 2000; Tanji & Shima, 1994). An important form of movement sequencing is the coordination of movements between the two sides of the body. For example, when a monkey's SMA is dam-

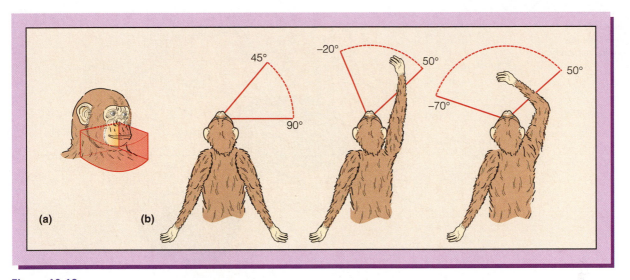

Figure 10.19
Receptive fields of two types of premotor neurons that responded to both visual and body information
(a) The receptive field of a cell that responded when a visual stimulus was in the area outlined near the face. (b) Left, the visual field of the second type of neuron when the arm was out of sight. Middle and right, the visual field as the monkey's arm moved forward and across.
Source: Adapted from Figure 1 in M. S. A. Graziano, G. S. Yap, & C. G. Gross, "Coding of visual space by premotor neurons," in *Science* 266, 1054–1057. Used by permission of the author.

aged in one hemisphere, its hands tend to duplicate each other's actions instead of sharing the task (Brinkman, 1984). Humans with similar damage also have trouble carrying out tasks that require alternation of movements between the two hands (Laplane, Talairach, Meininger, Bancaud, & Orgogozo, 1977).

The Primary Motor Cortex
The *primary motor cortex* is responsible for the execution of voluntary movements; its cells fire most during the movement instead of prior to it (Alexander & Crutcher, 1990; Riehle & Requin, 1989). Individual motor cortex cells are not reserved for a specific movement but contribute their function to a range of related behaviors (Saper, Iverson, & Frackowiak, 2000). It is the task of the primary motor cortex to orchestrate the activity of these cells into a useful movement. Its contributions include the control of a movement's force and direction (Georgopoulos, Taira, & Lukashin, 1993; Maier, Bennett, Hepp-Reymond, & Lemon, 1993). The primary motor cortex receives

input not just from the secondary motor areas but from the somatosensory cortex and the posterior parietal area (Krakauer & Ghez, 2000). Presumably this direct information provides feedback needed for refining movements on the fly.

The Basal Ganglia and Cerebellum
The basal ganglia and cerebellum produce no motor acts themselves. Rather, they modulate the activity of cortical and brain-stem motor systems; in that role, they are necessary for posture and smooth movement (Ghez & Krakauer, 2000). Malfunction in the basal ganglia results in postural abnormalities and involuntary movements in Parkinson's disease and Huntington's disease. Damage to the cerebellum causes loss of coordination and loss of accuracy in limb movements. Alcohol has a similar effect on the cerebellum, so the drunk driver who is pulled over by the police has trouble walking a straight line, standing on one foot with the eyes closed, or touching the nose with the tip of the finger.

What do the basal ganglia and cerebellum add?

Figure 10.20
The basal ganglia
The basal ganglia include the caudate nucleus, putamen, and globus pallidus.

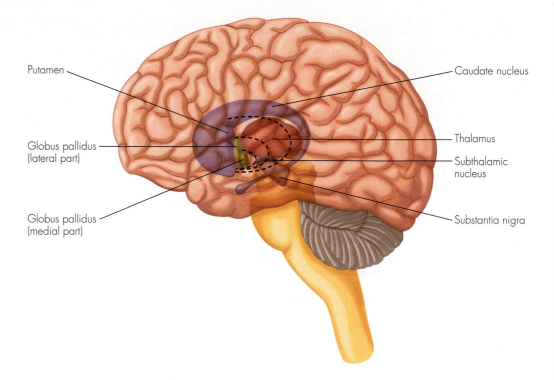

Putamen

Globus pallidus
(lateral part)

Globus pallidus
(medial part)

Caudate nucleus

Thalamus

Subthalamic
nucleus

Substantia nigra

The *basal ganglia*—the caudate nucleus, putamen, and globus pallidus—smooth out movements using information they receive from the primary and secondary motor areas and the somatosensory cortex. (Notice that their name is a misnomer, since the term *ganglia* is ordinarily used only in the peripheral nervous system.) As you can see in Figure 10.20, these structures border the thalamus. They probably accomplish their movement-smoothing function through two antagonistic outputs to the thalamus, one that facilitates movement and another that inhibits it (DeLong, 2000). The basal ganglia also are especially active during complex sequences of movements (Boecker et al., 1998). It appears that they are involved in learning movement sequences so the movements can be performed as a unit (Graybiel, 1998). In fact, impairment of both motor and nonmotor learning is one of the symptoms of Parkinson's disease (Knowlton, Mangels, & Squire, 1996).

The *cerebellum* uses information from the vestibular system to maintain balance, refine movements, and control eye movements that compensate for head movements (Ghez & Thach, 2000). The cerebellum also programs the order of complex movements and controls the timing among them. For example, we begin to shape our hand for grasping while the arm is moving toward the target, but a person with cerebellar damage reaches, pauses, and then shapes the hand. The cerebellum also corrects errors while a movement is in progress. A normal individual touches the nose in what appears to be a single, smooth movement; cerebellar damage results in exaggerated, wavering corrections. Finally, the cerebellum is necessary for learning motor skills (McCormick & Thompson, 1984).

The cerebellum lives up to the meaning of its name, "little brain," by applying its expertise to a variety of tasks. It participates, for example, in nonmotor learning (Canavan, Sprengelmeyer,

Diener, & Hömberg, 1994) and in making time and speed judgments about auditory and visual stimuli (Keele & Ivry, 1990). Also, patients with cerebellar damage have difficulty shifting visual attention to another location in space (whether this involves eye movements or not), taking 800–1,200 msec compared to 100 msec for normal individuals (Townsend et al., 1999). We should think of the cerebellum in terms of its general functions rather than as a motor organ.

Disorders of Movement

You might think that anything as complex as the movement system would be subject to malfunction; if so, you would be correct. Predictably, movement disorders are devastating to their victims. As representatives of these diseases we will consider Parkinson's disease, Huntington's disease, myasthenia gravis, and multiple sclerosis.

Parkinson's Disease

Parkinson's disease (PD) **is characterized by motor tremors, rigidity, loss of balance and coordination, and difficulty in moving, especially in initiating movements** (Olanow & Tatton, 1999; Youdim & Riederer, 1997). Muscle strength is unaffected, but the disease often becomes disabling as it progresses. PD affects about 2% of the population (Polymeropoulos et al., 1997). PD is caused by deterioration of the *substantia nigra,* **the nucleus that sends dopamine-releasing neurons to the** *striatum,* **which is composed of the basal ganglia's caudate nucleus and putamen.**

What causes this degeneration is unclear, but at least some sufferers have a genetic predisposition for the disease, particularly those with an early onset. In about 5–10% of cases, the disease is *familial,* **meaning that it occurs more frequently among relatives of a person with the disease than it does in the population** (Wood, 1998). If a member of a twin pair is diagnosed with Parkinson's disease before the age of 51, the chance of an identical twin also having Parkinson's is six times greater than it is for a fraternal twin (Tanner et al., 1999). The same study found no evidence of a genetic influence in individuals whose symptoms developed later in life.

The search for the responsible genes has yielded the usual blind alleys and contradictory results (Olanow & Tatton, 1999), but recent gene discoveries have removed some of the mystery of familial Parkinson's. Mutations in three genes result in deviant forms of the proteins *parkin, ubiquitin,* and α-*synuclein* (Kitada et al., 1998; Krüger et al., 1998; Leroy et al., 1998; Polymeropoulos et al., 1997). People with these mutations have an accumulation of α-synuclein in the brain, which is one of the pathologies of Parkinson's (Shimura et al., 2001). α-Synuclein is a major component of *Lewy bodies,* **abnormal clumps of protein that form within neurons.** They are found in several brain locations in some Parkinson's patients, as well as in people with a form of Alzheimer's disease, *dementia with Lewy bodies* (see Figure 10.21) (Glasson et al., 2000; Spillantini et al., 1997). Lewy bodies probably contribute to the cognitive deficits and depression that often accompany Parkinson's disease.

In the nonfamilial cases, most of the research points to a variety of toxins, including industrial

What are the causes and effects of the movement disorders?

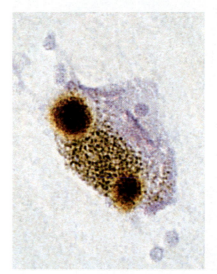

Figure 10.21
Lewy bodies in a brain with Parkinson's disease
A neuron containing two stained Lewy bodies, abnormal clumps of protein.
Reprinted by permission of *Nature,* copyright 1997.

chemicals, carbon monoxide, herbicides, and pesticides (Olanow & Tatton, 1999). The evidence has been mostly correlational, but in one experimental study, administering the pesticide rotenone for several weeks produced tremors in rats (Betarbet et al., 2000). Autopsy showed they had lost dopamine neurons and developed Lewy bodies containing α-synuclein and ubiquitin. There are clues that some Parkinson's sufferers inherit a diminished ability to metabolize toxins (Bandmann, Vaughan, Holmans, Marsden, & Wood, 1997; Smith et al., 1992), so once again we have evidence for the interaction of hereditary and environmental effects.

Interestingly, the risk of PD is reduced as much as 80% in coffee drinkers (Ross et al., 2000). The risk also drops by 50% in smokers (Fratiglioni & Wang, 2000), but of course no benefit of smoking outweighs its dangers. Rat studies indicate that cigarette smoke may prevent the accumulation of neurotoxins (Soto-Otero, Méndez-Alvarez, Sánchez-Sellero, Cruz-Landeira, & López-Rivadulla, 2001), and that caffeine reduces the effect of neurotoxins by blocking adenosine receptors (Chen et al., 2001).

Parkinson's disease is typically treated by administering *levodopa (L-dopa),* **which is the precursor for dopamine**. Dopamine itself will not cross the blood-brain barrier but L-dopa will, and in the brain it is converted to dopamine. Dopamine agonists can also be helpful, and even placebos increase dopamine release (de la Fuente-Fernández et al., 2001). But L-dopa and dopamine agonists cause side effects because they increase dopamine throughout the brain; as more neurons die, more drug is required, increasing the side effects. You saw in Chapter 1 that implanting embryonic neurons or stem cells holds promise for treating neurodegenerative diseases; this technique replaces some of the lost neurons and increases dopamine in the desired area. Transplantation of embryonic tissue for the treatment of PD has gone through its first clinical trial, with a control group and much stricter controls than in previous studies (see Figure 10.22) (Freed et al., 2001). After three years, recipients under the age of 60 had improved 38% and older patients by 14%. These changes are about half that produced by L-dopa, though; in addition, five patients developed severe jerky movements typical of patients who become oversensitive to dopaminergic drugs. The scientific community is eagerly awaiting the outcome of a second clinical trial, which is in progress.

Frustration with other forms of therapy is creating something of a revival in surgical treatments that were largely abandoned when drugs for PD became available (Cosgrove & Eskandar, 1998). *Thalamotomy and pallidotomy,* which involve strategically placed lesions in the thalamus and the globus pallidus, respectively, have provided some improvement for patients who have difficulty using the drugs (Cosgrove & Eskandar, 1998). However, as you might expect, this surgery can produce deficits of its own, so researchers are experimenting with electrical stimulation through implanted electrodes. Patients receiving stimulation to the globus pallidus and the subthalamic nucleus

Figure 10.22

Transplanted embryonic cells in the brain of a Parkinson's patient

Background is a magnetic resonance image of the patient's brain made at the time of surgery. The red lines indicate the paths of the needles used to inject cells into both putamens. The woman's right putamen was removed after a fatal car accident seven months after her surgery and placed in its proper position on the brain scan for the photograph. The dark area along the needle track is due to the staining of cells containing dopamine, and shows the cells beginning to grow out of the area. Copyright 2001 Massachusetts Medical Society.

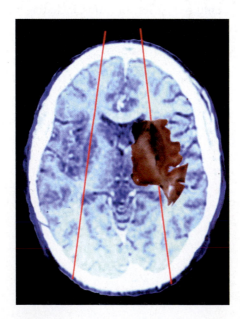

(see Figure 10.20 again) showed improved motor functioning, along with increased metabolism in the premotor cortex and cerebellum (Fukuda et al., 2001; Deep-Brain Stimulation for Parkinson's Disease Study Group, 2001). Electrical stimulation thus holds out the promise of reasonable benefits without the negative effects of drugs or lesioning. However, additional studies will be needed to determine whether the improvements can be maintained over long periods, and whether long-term use will have adverse effects.

Huntington's Disease

Like Parkinson's disease, *Huntington's disease (HD) is a degenerative disorder of the motor system, with critical cell loss in the striatum.* Years before a diagnosis, HD begins with jerky movements that result from impaired error correction (Smith, Brandt, & Shadmehr, 2000). Later, involuntary movements appear, first as fidgeting and then as movements of the limbs and, finally, writhing of the body and facial grimacing. Because these movements sometimes resemble a dance, HD is also called Huntington's chorea, from the Greek word *choreia*, which means "dance." Needless to say, the patient becomes unable to carry out daily activities. Death usually follows within 15 to 30 years after the onset of the disease.

Unlike Parkinson's, HD always involves cognitive and emotional deficits. This includes depression, personality changes, impaired judgment, and difficulty with a variety of cognitive tasks. The motor symptoms are due to the degeneration of neurons in the striatum, while defective or degenerated neurons in the cortex probably account for the psychological symptoms (Figure 10.23) (Martin, 1987; Tabrizi et al., 1999). The loss of neurons probably results from the accumulation of *huntingtin, a protein with unknown function that is produced by the gene of the same name* (DiFiglia et al., 1997).

Huntington's disease results from a mutated form of the gene (Huntington's Disease

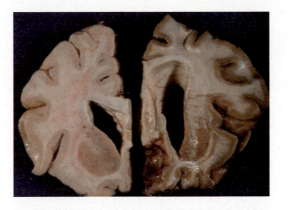

Figure 10.23
Loss of brain tissue in Huntington's disease
Left, a section from a normal brain; right, a section from a person with Huntington's disease. The enlarged lateral ventricle in the diseased brain is due to loss of neurons.
Source: Courtesy of Robert E. Schmidt, Washington University.

Collaborative Research Group, 1993). In normal individuals the *huntingtin* gene has between 10 and 34 repetitions of the bases cytosine, adenine, and guanine (see Chapter 1). The more repeats the person has beyond 37, the earlier in life the person will succumb to the disease (Brinkman, Mezei, Theilmann, Almqvist, & Hayden, 1997). Because the gene is dominant, a person who has a parent with Huntington's has a 50% chance of developing the disease. This is an unusual example of a human disorder resulting from a single gene.

This is a scary thing. . . . There is a test available, but I haven't had the guts to take it yet.
—Shana Martin, at risk for Huntington's disease

Transplant of fetal striatum cells may be an effective treatment for Huntington's disease (Freeman et al., 2000). During the course of a clinical trial of this procedure there was opportunity to examine the brain of one of the patients, who died of unrelated causes. Eighteen months after the surgery, the transplanted cells had grown into the equivalent of 5–10% of normal striatum volume and were extending projections. What is more, these

Figure 10.24
Effect of an acetyl-cholinesterase inhibitor on myasthenia gravis
(a) Patients often have drooping eyelids, as shown here. This patient also could not move his eyes to look to the side.
(b) The same patient one minute after injection of an acetylcholinesterase inhibitor. The eyes are open and able to move freely.
Source: Rowland, Hoefer, & Aranow, 1960.

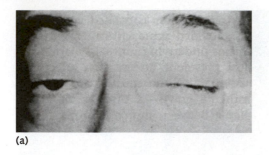

(a)

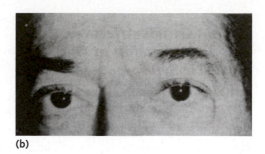

(b)

cells showed no signs of huntingtin aggregates. If this treatment turns out to be successful, its effect may be only to halt progress of the disease; remember that Huntington's involves neuron loss over wide areas of the brain.

Autoimmune Diseases

Myasthenia gravis (MG) is a disorder of muscular weakness caused by reduced numbers or sensitivity of acetylcholine receptors. The muscle weakness can be so extreme that the patient has to be maintained on a respirator. In fact, 25 years ago the mortality rate from MG was about 33%. Now few patients die from the disease, thanks to improved treatment (Rowland, 2000a).

The loss of receptors was demonstrated in an interesting way. The venom of the many-banded Formosan krait, a very poisonous snake from Taiwan, paralyzes prey by binding to the acetylcholine (ACh) receptor. When the venom's active toxin, α-bungarotoxin, is labeled with radioactive iodine and applied to a sample of muscle, it allows researchers to identify and count the ACh receptors. MG patients turned out to have 11–30% as many receptors as normal individuals (Fambrough, Drachman, & Satyamurti, 1973). Drugs that inhibit the action of acetylcholinesterase give temporary relief from the symptoms of MG (Figure 10.24) (Rowland, Hoefer, & Aranow, 1960). Remember that acetylcholinesterase breaks down ACh at the synapse; these inhibitors increase the amount of available neurotransmitter at the neuron-muscle junction.

Myasthenia gravis patients often have tumors of the thymus gland. Doctors noticed that when the thymus was removed *(thymectomy)* the MG symptoms improved (Rowland, 2000a). Because the thymus is the major source of lymphocytes that produce antibodies, this improvement led to research that demonstrated that MG is an autoimmune disease. Although immune system therapy has sometimes been used (Shah & Lisak, 1993), thymectomy has become a standard treatment for myasthenia gravis (Rowland, 2000a). Thymectomy eliminates symptoms com-pletely in almost 80% of patients and results in improvement in another 13–17% (Ashour et al., 1995; Jaretzki et al., 1988).

Multiple sclerosis (MS) is the result of the deterioration of the myelin sheaths (demyelination) in the central nervous system. In Chapter 2 you saw that demyelination causes slowing or elimination of neural impulses. Demyelination thus reduces the speed and strength of movements. Even before that happens, impulses traveling in adjacent neurons, which should arrive simultaneously, become desynchronized because of differential loss of myelin. An early sign of the disorder is impairment of functions that require synchronous bursts of neural activity, like tendon reflexes and vibratory sensation (Rowland, 2000b). As the disease progresses, unmyelinated neurons die, leaving areas of *sclerosis*, or hardened scar tissue (Figure 10.25). As a result, the person experiences muscular weakness, tremor, impaired

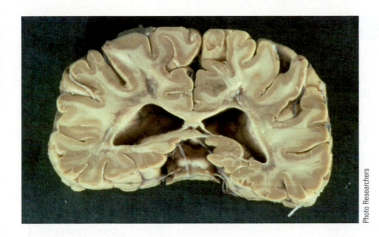

Figure 10.25
The brain of a deceased MS patient
The arrows indicate areas of sclerosis, or hardened scar tissue.

Photo Researchers

coordination, urinary incontinence, and visual problems.

Like myasthenia gravis, multiple sclerosis is an autoimmune disease. Injecting myelin protein into the brains of animals produces symtoms very similar to MS (Wekerle, 1993), and T cells that are reactive to myelin proteins (see Chapter 7) have been found in the blood of MS patients (Allegretta, Nicklas, Sriram, & Albertini, 1990). We do not know what triggers the immune attack on myelin, but one possibility is that the immune system has been sensitized by an earlier viral infection. For example, studies have found antibodies for Epstein-Barr virus in MS patients (Wagner et al., 2000), and MS patients more often had mumps or measles during adolescence (Hernán, Zhang, Lipworth, Olek, & Ascherio, 2001).

✓ **CONCEPT CHECK**

- *Explain how antagonistic muscles and spinal reflexes maintain posture.*
- *What contribution does each of the cortical motor areas make to movement?*
- *What are the genetic and environmental causes of the movement disorders described here?*

In Perspective

Unless we have a disorder, we usually take our body senses and our capability for movement for granted. And yet just standing upright is a remarkable feat. Granted, a mechanical robot could do it easily, but only if it had a rigid body like R2D2's. If the robot had our flexibility of movement and posture, it would have to devote a fair amount of its computer brain to making split-millisecond adjustments to avoid toppling over. Then another chunk of its computer would be required just to locate a visual object in space, to reach out smoothly and quickly for the object, and to shape its hand for grasping, deciding whether to use the whole hand or the finger and thumb and how much pressure to apply, and so on. You get the idea. Better let a human do it, because all that fancy equipment comes standard on the basic model.

Now you see why so much of the brain is concerned with the sensory and motor components of movement. It is a wonder that we have enough left over for the demands of learning, intelligence, and consciousness, but as you will see in the remaining chapters, we do.

Summary

The Body Senses

- The body senses include proprioception, which tells us about the position and movement of our limbs and body; the vestibular sense, which contributes information about head position and movement and helps us maintain balance; and the skin senses, which inform us about the conditions in the periphery of our body.
- The skin senses—touch, warmth, cold, and pain—tell us about conditions at the body surface and about objects in contact with our body.
- The body senses are processed in a series of structures in the parietal lobes, with several similarities to visual processing.
- In their quest to find better ways of relieving pain, researchers have learned how the nervous system detects painful stimulation and found that the body has its own ways of relieving pain.

Movement

- There are three types of muscles; one type is the skeletal muscles, which move the body by tugging against their attachments to bones.
- Spinal reflexes produce quick responses and provide postural adjustments. Central pattern generators provide routines such as rhythmic walking movements.
- Cortical motor areas assess spatial-body information and construct movements by passing information through a succession of brain areas.
- The basal ganglia and cerebellum refine movements produced by the motor cortex.
- A number of diseases attack the motor system at various points of vulnerability. Major causes that have been implicated are heredity, toxins, and autoimmune disorders.

 ## For Further Thought

- Of proprioception, the vestibular sense, pain, and the other skin senses, which do you think you could most afford to give up? Why?
- If pain is beneficial, why does the body have pain relief mechanisms?
- Imagine a robot with a humanlike body. It is programmed to walk, reach, grasp, and so on. It has visual and auditory capabilities, but no body senses. What would its movement be like?
- Judging by the examples given of movement disorders, what are the points of vulnerability in the motor system?

Testing Your Understanding

1. Explain how endorphins relieve pain, describing the receptors and the pathway from the PAG; include how we determine whether pain relief is endorphin based.

2. Walking barefoot, you step on a sharp rock. You reflexively withdraw your foot, plant it firmly on the ground again, and regain your posture. Describe these behaviors in terms of the sensory/pain mechanisms and reflexes involved.

3. Trace the progress of a movement through the parietal and frontal lobes, giving the names of the structures and a general idea of the processing in each.

Select the one best answer:

1. Proprioception gives us information about:
   a. conditions at the surface of our skin.
   b. conditions in the internal organs.
   c. the position and movement of our limbs and body.
   d. balance and head position and movement.

2. The skin senses include:
   a. touch, warmth, and cold.
   b. touch, temperature, and pain.
   c. touch, temperature, movement, and pain.
   d. touch, warmth, cold, and pain.

3. Sharp pain and dull pain are due primarily to:
   a. different kinds of injury.
   b. pain neurons with different characteristics.
   c. the passage of time.
   d. the person's attention to the pain.

4. According to Melzack and Wall, pressing the skin near a wound reduces pain by:
   a. creating inhibition in the pain pathway.
   b. distracting attention from the injury.
   c. releasing endorphins.
   d. releasing histamine into the wound area.

5. Endorphins:
   a. activate the same receptors as opiate drugs.
   b. occupy receptors for pain neurotransmitters.
   c. block reuptake of pain neurotransmitter.
   d. inhibit brain centers that process pain emotion.

6. Research suggests phantom pain is due to:
   a. the patient's stress over the limb loss.
   b. memory of the pain of injury or disease that prompted the amputation.
   c. activity in severed nerve endings in the stump.
   d. neural reorganization in the somatosensory area.

7. Without a posterior parietal cortex we would be most impaired in:
   a. moving.
   b. making smooth movements.
   c. orienting movements to objects in space.
   d. awareness of spontaneously occurring movements.

8. If the nerves providing sensory feedback from the legs were cut, we would:
   a. have to use vision to guide our leg movements.
   b. have trouble standing upright.
   c. lose strength in our legs.
   d. a and b.
   e. b and c.

9. A monkey is presented a stimulus, then must wait a few seconds before it can make the appropriate movement response to the stimulus. Activity in the secondary motor area during the delay suggests that this area:
   a. prepares for the movement.
   b. initiates the movement.
   c. executes the movement.
   d. all of these.

10. Cells in the premotor cortex combine two kinds of information needed for a movement. An example we saw is that:
    a. a touch-sensitive cell responds only if a visual stimulus has occurred just before.
    b. the space a visually sensitive cell responds to depends on the arm's location.
    c. these cells are active during any kind of sensory stimulation.
    d. a cell responds to the sight of an object only after it has been grasped.

continued

11. The primary motor cortex is most involved in:

    a. combining sensory inputs.
    b. planning movements.
    c. preparing movements.
    d. executing movements.

12. The basal ganglia and the cerebellum produce:

    a. no movements.
    b. movements requiring extra force.
    c. reflexive movements.
    d. postural adjustments.

13. Parkinson's disease is characterized most by:

    a. deterioration of the myelin sheath.
    b. dancelike involuntary movements.
    c. deterioration of dopamine-releasing neurons.
    d. immune system attack on acetylcholine receptors.

14. Results of removing the thymus gland suggest that myasthenia gravis is a(n) _____ disease:

    a. genetic
    b. immune
    c. virus-caused
    d. degenerative

Answers: 1. c **2.** d **3.** b **4.** a **5.** a **6.** d **7.** c **8.** d **9.** a **10.** b **11.** d **12.** a **13.** c **14.** b

---

 ## On the Web

1. The **Vestibular Disorders Association** has information about vestibular problems and provides additional resources such as newsletters, books, and videotapes at

   http://www.vestibular.org/

2. The **Pain Foundation** has information for pain patients, testimonials from people suffering pain from an assortment of causes, and links to numerous sites with information about a variety of pain problems at

   http://www.painfoundation.org/

   The **International Association for the Study of Pain** has links to more technical resources on pain, at

   http://www.iasp-pain.org/

   Acupuncture Points of Interest has links to sites supporting a variety of sometimes opposing views on acupuncture at

   http://news.bmn.com/hmsbeagle/116/ reviews/insitu

Site requires free registration.

3. **Probe the Brain,** provided by PBS's *Science Odyssey,* lets you probe the motor cortex with an electrode to verify that there really is a homunculus, at

   http://www.pbs.org/wgbh/aso/tryit/brain/

4. The **Neuromuscular Disease Center** offers information on a variety of neuromuscular disorders, along with recent news items, at

   http://www.neuro.wustl.edu/ neuromuscular/

   The **Michael J. Fox Foundation** has news of this celebrity's work supporting Parkinson's research, and links to other sites with information about the disease, at

   http://www.michaeljfox.org

   The **Huntington's Disease Association Online** offers news and articles on the disease at

   http://www.hda.org.uk/

For additional information about the topics covered in this chapter, please look at InfoTrac College Edition, at *http://www.infotrac-college.com/wadsworth*

Try search terms you think up yourself, or use these: *endorphins; Huntington's disease; phantom limb pain; somatosensory cortex.*

 On the CD-ROM: Exploring Biological Psychology

Animation: The Withdrawal Reflex
Animation: The Crossed Extensor Reflex

Video: The Brain Pacemaker

 For Further Reading

Awakenings, by Oliver Sacks (1999, Vintage Books), describes Dr. Sacks's early use of L-dopa to treat the parkinsonism of sleeping sickness. The movie with Robin Williams was based on this book.

Phantoms in the Brain, by V. S. Ramachandran and Sandra Blakeslee (1998, Quill), called "enthralling" by the *New York Times* and "splendid" by Francis Crick, uses numerous (often strange) cases to explain people's perception of their bodies.

 Key Terms

antagonistic muscles *295*

basal ganglia *300*

cardiac muscles *294*

central pattern generator (CPG) *296*

cerebellum *300*

dermatome *286*

endorphins *291*

familial *301*

gate control theory *290*

Golgi tendon organsx *296*

huntingtin *303*

Huntington's disease (HD) *303*

levodopa (L-dopa) *302*

Lewy bodies *301*

multiple sclerosis (MS) *304*

muscle spindles *296*

myasthenia gravis (MG) *304*

neuromuscular junction *294*

Parkinson's disease (PD) *301*

periaqueductal gray (PAG) *291*

phantom pain *293*

posterior parietal cortex (PPC) *288*

prefrontal cortex (PFC) *297*

premotor cortex (PM) *298*

primary motor cortex *299*

primary somatosensory cortex (S-I) *287*

proprioception *283*

continued

4

PART

Complex Behavior

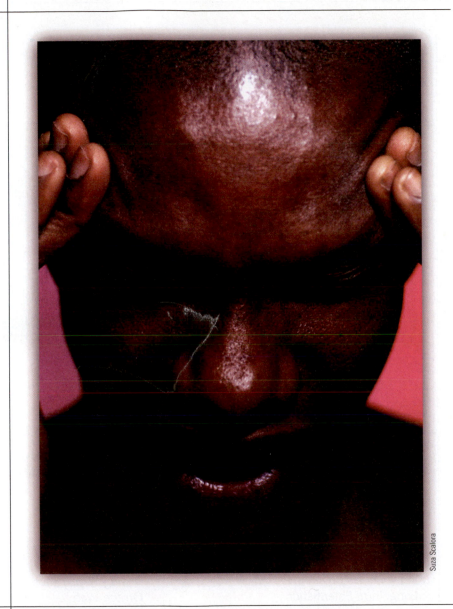

Suza Scalora

Learning and Memory

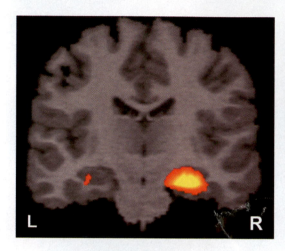
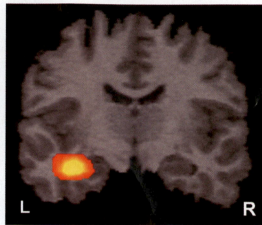

In this chapter you will learn:

- How and where memories are stored in the brain.
- What changes occur in the brain during learning.
- How aging and two major disorders impair learning.

Discovering the physical basis of learning in humans and other mammals is among the greatest remaining challenges facing the neurosciences.

—Brown, Chapman, Kairiss, & Keenan, 1988

At the age of 7, HM's life was forever changed by a seemingly minor incident: he was knocked down by a bicycle and was unconscious for five minutes. Three years later he began to have minor seizures, and his first major seizure occurred on his 16th birthday. Still, HM had a reasonably normal adolescence taken up with high school, science club, hunting, and roller skating, except for a two-year furlough from school because the other boys teased him about his seizures.

After high school he took a job in a factory, but eventually the seizures made it impossible for him to work. He was averaging 10 small seizures a day and one major seizure per week. Because anticonvulsant medications were unable to control the seizures, HM and his family decided on an experimental operation that held some promise. In 1953, when he was 27, a surgeon removed much of both of his temporal lobes where the seizure activity was originating. The surgery worked, for the most part: with the help of medication, the petit mal seizures were mild enough not to be disturbing and major seizures were reduced to about one a year.

HM returned to living with his parents. He helped with household chores, mowed the lawn, and spent his spare time doing difficult crossword puzzles. Later he worked at a rehabilitation center, doing routine tasks like mounting cigarette lighters on cardboard displays. His intelligence was not impaired by the operation; his IQ test performance even went up, probably because he was freed from the interference of seizures.

However, there was one important and unexpected effect of the surgery. Although he can recall personal and public events and remember songs from his earlier life, HM has difficulty learning and retaining new information. He can hold new information in memory for a short while, but if he is distracted or a few minutes pass he can no longer recall the information. After the surgery he could not find his way back to the new home his family had moved to if he was more than two or three blocks away. When he worked at the rehabilitation center, he could not describe the work he did. He does not remember moving into a nursing home in 1980, or even what he ate for his last meal. And although he watches television news every night, he does not know who the President is or remember what Watergate was about (Corkin, 1984; Milner, Corkin, & Teuber, 1968).

In spite of his difficulty in forming new memories, HM has over the years become aware of his condition and is very insightful about it. In his own words:

> Every day is alone in itself, whatever enjoyment I've had, and whatever sorrow I've had. . . . Right now, I'm wondering. Have I done or said anything amiss? You see, at this moment everything looks clear to me, but what happened just before? That's what worries me. It's like waking from a dream; I just don't remember. (Milner, 1970, p. 37)

LEARNING AS THE STORAGE OF MEMORIES

Some one-celled animals learn surprisingly well, for example, to avoid swimming toward a light, where they have received an electric shock before. But if you take a lunch break during your subject's training, by the time you return it

Figure 11.1
Temporal lobe structures involved in amnesia
Above: HM's brain (left) and a normal brain. You can see that the amygdala (A), hippocampus (H), and other structures labeled in the normal brain are partially or completely missing in HM's brain. Below: Structures of the medial temporal lobe (MTL). The frontal lobe is to the right.
Sources: Above: Corkin, Amaral, González, Johnson, & Hyman, 1997. Copyright 1997 by the Society for Neuroscience. Below: adapted with permission from D. L. Schacter and A. D. Wagner, "Remembrance of things past," *Science*, 285, p. 1503–1504. Copyright 1999 American Association for the Advancement of Science.

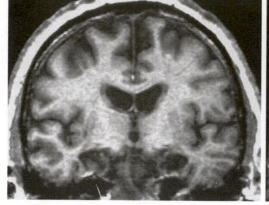

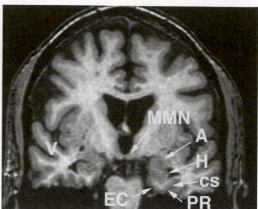

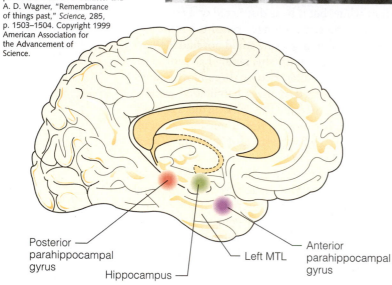

Posterior parahippocampal gyrus

Hippocampus

Left MTL

Anterior parahippocampal gyrus

1

will have forgotten what it learned. Such a temporary form of learning may help an organism avoid an unsafe area long enough for the danger to pass, or to remember from one minute to the next to stay in a place where food is more abundant. But without the ability to make a more or less permanent record, you would not learn a skill, and experience would not shape your personality. We will introduce the topic of learning by examining the problem of storage.

Amnesia: The Failure of Storage or Retrieval

How does studying amnesia help us understand memory?

HM's symptoms are referred to as *anterograde amnesia,* **an impairment in forming new memories.** (*Anterograde* means "moving for-

ward.") This was not HM's only memory deficit; the surgery also caused *retrograde amnesia,* **the inability to remember events prior to impairment.** His retrograde amnesia does not extend back throughout his earlier life; he has memories up to the age of about 16. Although he has some memories after that age, the loss is severe; he does not remember the end of World War II or his own graduation, and when he returned for his 35th high school reunion he recognized none of his classmates. Better memory for earlier events than for recent ones may seem implausible, but it is typical of patients who have brain damage similar to HM's. How far back the retrograde amnesia extends depends on how much damage there is and which specific structures are damaged.

HM's surgery damaged or destroyed the hippocampus, nearby structures that along with the hippocampus make up the *hippocampal formation,* and the amygdala. Figure 11.1 shows the location of these structures; because they are on or near the inside surface of the temporal lobe, they help form what is known as the medial temporal lobe (remember that *medial* means "toward the middle"). Because HM's surgery was so extensive, it is impossible to tell which structures are responsible for the memory functions that were lost. Studies of patients with varying degrees of temporal lobe damage have helped determine which structures are involved in amnesia and, therefore, in memory.

The hippocampus consists of several substructures with different functions. Damage that is limited to the part known as *CA1* in both hippocampi results in moderate anterograde amnesia, and only minimal retrograde amnesia. If the damage includes the rest of the hippocampus, anterograde amnesia is severe. Damage of the entire hippocampal formation results in retrograde amnesia extending back 15 years or more (Reed & Squire, 1998; Rempel-Clower, Zola, Squire, & Amaral, 1996; Zola-Morgan, Squire, & Amaral, 1986). Studies of patients with Korsakoff's syndrome and of a man injured when a roommate accidentally thrust a toy fencing foil up his nostril and into the brain indicate that anterograde amnesia can also be produced by damage to the *medial thalamus* and the *mammillary bodies* (Gabrieli, 1998; Squire, Amaral, Zola-Morgan, Kritchevsky, & Press, 1989).

Mechanisms of Consolidation and Retrieval

HM's memory problems involved both consolidation and retrieval. **Consolidation is the process in which the brain forms a permanent physical representation of a memory. Retrieval is the process of accessing stored memories.** When a rat presses a lever to receive a food pellet or a child is bitten by a dog or you skim through the headings in this chapter, the experience is held in memory at least for a brief time. But just like the phone number that is forgotten when you get a busy signal the first time you dial, an experience does not necessarily become a permanent memory; and if it does, the transition takes time. Until the memory is consolidated, it is fragile. New memories may be disrupted just by engaging in another activity, and even older memories are vulnerable to intense experiences such as emotional trauma or electroconvulsive shock treatment. Researchers divide memory into two stages, short-term memory and long-term memory. There is some evidence that long-term memory consists of an intermediate stage and a second, long-lasting stage (see Figure 11.2) (McGaugh, 2000), but we will not need to make that distinction here.

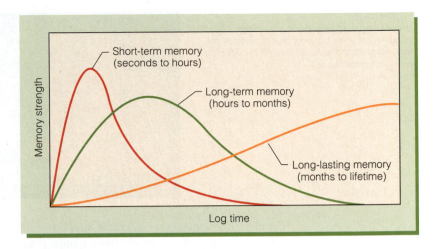

Figure 11.2
Stages of consolidation
Making a memory permanent involves multiple stages and different processes.
Reprinted with permission from J. L. McGaugh, "Memory—A century of consolidation," *Science*, 287, p. 248–251. Copyright 2000 American Association for the Advancement of Science.

Sophisticated research techniques have made it possible to "watch" consolidation as it takes place in the brain. These studies have identified the hippocampal region as playing a lead role in consolidation, which would explain why patients with damage to the medial temporal lobe have trouble learning new material. One group of researchers used EEG evoked potentials to study consolidation as the research participants memorized words (Fernández et al., 1999). You may remember from section A.3 of the appendix that an advantage of EEG is its good time resolution, which allows it to follow rapid changes in neural activity. The researchers were fortunate in having access to epilepsy patients who already had electrodes inserted in their temporal lobes to help locate malfunctioning neural tissue prior to surgery. (The researchers took data only from the temporal lobes that were healthy.) As each stimulus word was presented, it evoked a response in the hippocampus and in the parahippocampal gyrus, a part of the hippocampal formation. Words that evoked larger potentials were the ones the patients remembered when they were tested later. In another

Figure 11.3
Hippocampal activity during learning
(a) Staring at a meaningless object activated the right hippocampal area; (b) reading meaningful words activated the left.
Source: Martin, Wiggs, & Weisberg, 1997.

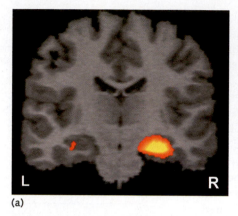 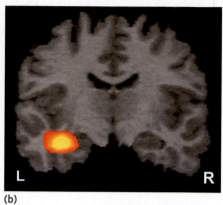

(a)   (b)

study, PET scans showed greater blood flow in the same area as research participants read words that were later remembered (Alkire, Haier, Fallon, & Cahill, 1998). The relationship was so strong that the amount of activity in the hippocampal formation accounted for 80% of the variation in memory success. To some extent, whether the left or right hippocampus is activated most depends on the type of material, as Figure 11.3 shows.

An animal study clearly demonstrates that the hippocampus participates in retrieval as well as consolidation. Rats were repeatedly placed in a water maze, a tank of murky water from which they could escape quickly by learning the location of a platform submerged just under the water's surface (Figure 11.4) (Riedel et al., 1999). At one point they received injections into both

hippocampi of a drug that blocks receptors for the neurotransmitter *glutamate*, temporarily disabling the hippocampi. If the injections were administered during training, the rats did not learn; their swimming performance was haphazard during training and later when the drug had worn off. Even if the drug was given on days 1–5 *following* training, the animals performed poorly during testing 16 days after training. This indicates that (1) consolidation continues for some time following learning, and (2) the drug was not simply affecting motor performance, because there was plenty of time for the drug to wear off between day 5 and day 16. Finally, although animals trained without the injections learned well, if they were then given the drug during testing their recall was impaired, indicating that the hippocampus has a role in retrieval. Researchers have used PET scans to confirm that the hippocampus also retrieves memories in humans (Schacter, Alpert, Savage, Rauch, & Albert, 1996; Squire et al., 1992). Figure 11.5 shows increased activity in the hippocampi during recall of words learned during the experiment.

The involvement of the hippocampus in retrieval seems inconsistent with HM's ability to recall earlier memories. But the memories that hippocampal patients can recall are older ones which concern events that occurred at least two years before their brain damage. Many researchers have concluded that the hippocampal mechanism plays a time-limited role in consolidation and retrieval. According to this view, the hippocampus stores information temporarily in the hippocampal formation;

Figure 11.4
A water maze
The rat learns to escape the water by finding the platform hidden beneath the murky surface.

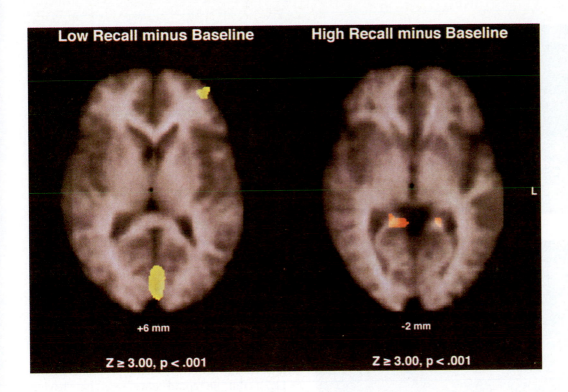

Figure 11.5
Hippocampal activity in the human brain during retrieval
Left: As participants tried to recall visually presented words that had been poorly learned (35% recall rate), the prefrontal and visual areas, but not the hippocampi, were highly activated compared to the baseline condition. Right: However, the successful recall of well-learned words (79% recall rate) activated both hippocampal areas.

Reprinted with permission from D. L. Schacter et al., "Conscious recollection and the human hippocampal formation: Evidence from positron emission tomography." *Proceedings of the National Academy of Sciences, USA*, 93, 321–325. Copyright 1996 National Academy of Sciences, USA.

then, over time, a more permanent memory is consolidated elsewhere in the brain. A study of mice that had learned a spatial discrimination task supported the hypothesis: over 25 days of retention testing, metabolic activity decreased in the hippocampus and increased in cortical areas (Bontempi, Laurent-Demir, Destrade, & Jaffard, 1999). This diminishing role of the hippocampus would explain why recent memories suffer more than older memories after hippocampal damage.

The prefrontal area is also active during learning and retrieval (Schacter et al., 1996; Squire et al., 1992), but its exact role is uncertain. Some think that the prefrontal area directs the search strategy required for retrieval (Buckner & Koutstaal, 1998). Indeed, the prefrontal area is active during effortful attempts at retrieval, whereas the hippocampus is activated during successful retrieval (see Figure 11.5 again) (Schacter et al., 1996). We will look at the role of the frontal area again in the contexts of working memory and Korsakoff's syndrome.

Where Memories Are Stored

The hippocampal area is not the permanent storage site for memories. If it were, patients like HM would not remember anything that happened before their damage occurred. It appears that the hippocampus coordinates interactions among the cortical areas involved in a learning task—for example, between the visual cortex and the motor cortex during and following conditioning of a motor response to a visual stimulus. PET scans performed on human volunteers indicated that the hippocampus associated inputs from the two cortical areas involved, then reactivated the areas during consolidation and again during retrieval (Henke, Weber, Kneifel, Wieser, & Buck, 1999). So we must look elsewhere for the location of memories.

You learned in Chapter 3 that memories for auditory experiences may be located in the auditory association cortex, and in Chapter 8 that languages learned later in life are stored near Broca's area. We also know that naming colors (which requires memory) activates temporal lobe areas near where we perceive color;

Is there a place where memories are stored?

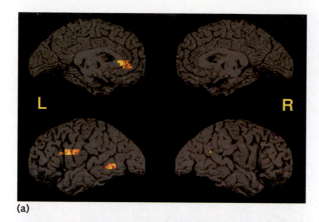

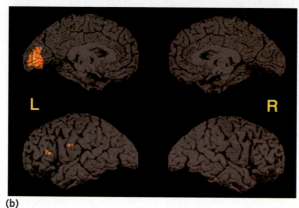

Figure 11.6
Brain areas activated in verbally identifying pictures of tools and animals
(a) Tool naming activates a hand movement area and a temporal area activated by action words. **(b)** The areas activated in naming animals are very different.
Source: Martin, Wiggs, Ungerleider, & Haxby, 1996. Reprinted by permission of *Nature*, copyright 1996.

What are the two kinds of learning?

Figure 11.7
The tower of Hanoi problem
The task is to relocate the rings in order onto another post by moving them one at a time and without ever placing a larger ring over a smaller one.

identifying pictures of tools activates the hand motor area and an area in the left temporal lobe that is also activated by motion and by action words (Figure 11.6) (Martin, Haxby, Lalonde, Wiggs, & Ungerleider, 1995; Martin, Wiggs, Ungerleider, & Haxby, 1996). Thus, memories are not stored in a single area, nor is each memory distributed throughout the brain. Rather, different memories are located in different cortical areas, apparently according to where their information was processed.

Two Kinds of Learning

Learning researchers were in for a revelation when they discovered that HM could still learn some kinds of tasks (Corkin, 1984). One was mirror drawing, in which the individual uses a pencil to trace a path around a pattern, relying solely on a view of the work surface in a mirror. HM improved in mirror-drawing ability over three days of training, and he learned to solve the Tower of Hanoi problem (Figure 11.7). But he could not remember having learned either task, and on each day of practice he denied even having seen the Tower puzzle before (Cohen, Eichenbaum, Deacedo, & Corkin, 1985; Corkin, 1984). What this means, researchers realized, is that there are two categories of memory processing. *Declarative memory* **results in memories of facts, people, and events, which a person can verbalize, or declare.** For example, you can remember being in class today, who was there and what was discussed. *Nondeclarative memory* **involves several kinds of learning that result in nonstatable memories, such as procedural or skills learning, emotional learning, and simple conditioning.** Learning mirror tracing or how to solve the Tower of Hanoi problem are examples of nondeclarative learning; remembering having practiced the tasks involves declarative learning.

The main reason to distinguish between the two types of learning is that they have different origins in the brain; studying them can tell us something about how the brain carries out its tasks. Just as researchers demonstrated the dissociation between declarative and nondeclarative learning in HM and others, McDonald and White (1993) found there is a neural distinction between these learning abilities in rats. They used an apparatus called the radial arm maze, a central platform with several arms radiating from it (Figure 11.8). Rats with damage to both hippocampi could learn the simple conditioning task of going into any lighted arm for food. But if every arm was baited with food, the rats could not remember which arms they had visited and repeatedly returned to arms where the food had already been eaten.

Conversely, rats with damage to the *striatum* could remember which arms they had visited, but could not learn to enter lighted arms. Because Parkinson's disease and Huntington's disease damage the basal ganglia (which include the striatum), people with these disorders have trouble learning to do mirror tracing or to solve the Tower of Hanoi problem (Gabrieli, 1998). Incidentally, the term *declarative* seems inappropriate with rats; researchers have often preferred the term *relational memory*, which implies that the individual must learn relationships among cues, an idea that applies equally well to humans and animals.

You already know that the amygdala is important in emotional behavior, but it also has a significant role in nondeclarative emotional learning. Bechara and her colleagues (1995) studied a patient with damage to both amygdalas and another with damage to both hippocampi. The researchers attempted to condition an emotional response in the patients by sounding a loud boat horn when a blue slide was presented, but not when the slide was another color. Both showed an emotional reaction to the loud noise, indicated by increased skin conductance responses (see Chapter 7). The hippocampal patient showed conditioning; after training, his skin conductance increased whenever the blue slide was presented. But he was unable to tell the researchers which color the loud sound was paired with. The amygdala-damaged patient could tell the experimenters which slide was

©Hank Morgan/Photo Researchers

Figure 11.8
A radial arm maze
The rat learns where to find food in the maze's arms. The arms are often enclosed by walls.

followed by the loud noise, but conditioning to the blue slide was absent. This dissociation between emotional learning and declarative learning may well explain how an emotional experience can have a long-lasting effect on a person's behavior even though the person does not remember the experience.

. . . the person recalls in almost photographic detail the total situation at the moment of shock, the expression of face, the words uttered, the position, garments, pattern of carpet, recalls them years after as though they were the experience of yesterday.
—G. M. Stratton, 1919

The amygdala has an additional function that cuts across learning types. Both positive and negative emotions enhance the memorability of any event; the amygdala strengthens even declarative memories about emotional events, apparently by increasing activity in the hippocampus. Electrical stimulation of the amygdala activates the hippocampus; as a result, it can enhance learning of a non-emotional task, such as a choice maze (McGaugh, Cahill, & Roozendaal, 1996). In humans, memory for both pleasant and aversive emotional material is related to the amount of activity in both amygdalas while viewing the material (Cahill et al., 1996; Hamann, Ely, Grafton, & Kilts, 1999).

Working Memory

Why is working memory important?

The brain stores a tremendous amount of information, but information that is merely stored is useless. It must be available, not just when it is being consciously recalled, but when the brain needs it for carrying out a task. *Working memory provides a temporary "register" for information while it is being used.* This applies, for example, to information like a phone number you have just looked up, which is held in working memory while you dial the number or transfer it into long-term memory. The register also holds information that is retrieved from long-term memory while it is integrated with other information for use in problem solving and decision making. Without working memory we could not do long division, plan a chess move, or even carry on a conversation.

Think of working memory as similar to the RAM in your computer. The RAM holds information temporarily while it is processed before being stored on the hard drive, or later when it is needed for various uses. But we should not take any analogy too far. Working memory has a very limited capacity (with no upgrades available), and information in working memory fades within seconds. So if you dial a new phone number and get a busy signal, you'll probably have to look the number up again. And if you have to remember the area code, too, you'd better write it down in the first place.

A typical laboratory technique for studying working memory is the *delayed match-to-sample task* described in Chapter 10. During the delay, cells are activated in several parts of the brain, apparently helping to maintain the memory of the stimulus. When the stimuli are visual, for instance, certain cells in visual association areas are particularly busy during the delay. Recall from Chapter 9 that the inferior temporal cortex is important in the visual recognition of objects. Some of the IT cells that increase their rate of firing during the delay have a "preferred" color, and increase their rate of firing dramatically if the stimulus is that color (Fuster & Jervey, 1981). Others vary their rate of firing according to the shape of the stimulus presented (Miyashita & Chang, 1988). When monkeys are required to remember the location of the stimulus, activity increases in cells in the parietal lobe (Constantinidis & Steinmetz, 1996).

These findings suggest that the function of working memory is carried out in various parts of the brain. However, the cells in the inferior temporal and parietal areas do not play the major role. If a distracting stimulus is introduced during the delay period, the altered firing abruptly ceases, but the animals are still able to make the correct choice (Constantinidis & Steinmetz, 1996; Miller, Erickson, & Desimone, 1996).

Cells in the prefrontal cortex have several attributes that make them better candidates as working memory specialists. Not only do they increase firing during a delay, but they maintain the increase in spite of a distracting stimulus (Miller et al., 1996). Some respond selectively to the correct stimulus (Di Pellegrino & Wise, 1993; Miller et al., 1996). Others respond to the correct stimulus, but only if it is presented in a particular position in the visual field; they apparently integrate information from cells that respond only to the stimulus with cells that respond to the location (Rao, Rainer, & Miller, 1997). Prefrontal damage impairs humans' ability to remember a stimulus during a delay (D'Esposito & Postle, 1999). All these findings suggest that the prefrontal area plays the major role in working memory.

Although the prefrontal cortex serves as a temporary memory register, its function is apparently more than that of a neural blackboard. In Chapters 3 and 7 you learned that damage to the frontal lobes impairs a person's ability to govern his or her behavior in several ways. Many researchers believe that the primary role of the prefrontal cortex in learning is as a central executive. That is, it manages certain kinds of behavioral strategies and decision making, and coordinates activity in the brain areas involved in the perception and response functions of a task, all the while directing the neural traffic in working memory (Wickelgren, 1997).

✔ **CONCEPT CHECK**

- *What determines the symptoms and the severity of symptoms of amnesia?*
- *Describe the two kinds of learning and the related brain structures.*
- *Working memory contributes to learning and to other functions. How?*

BRAIN CHANGES IN LEARNING

Learning is a form of neural plasticity that changes behavior by remodeling neural connections. Specialized neural mechanisms have evolved to make the most of this capability. We will look at them in the context of long-term potentiation.

Long-Term Potentiation

Remember that in the development of the nervous system (Chapter 3), when presynaptic neurons and postsynaptic neurons fire at the same time their synapse is strengthened. During development this helps determine which neurons will survive. Some of that plasticity is retained in the mature individual and is the foundation of learning. Researchers have long believed that in order to understand learning as a physiological process they would have to figure out what happens at the level of the neuron. Since its discovery three decades ago (Bliss & Lømo, 1973), long-term potentiation has been the best candidate for explaining the neural changes that occur during learning.

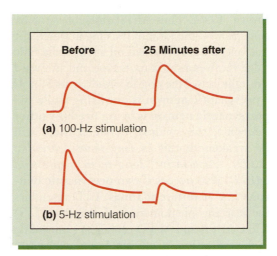

Before **25 Minutes after**

(a) 100-Hz stimulation

(b) 5-Hz stimulation

Figure 11.9
LTP and LTD in the human brain
The graphs show excitatory postsynaptic potentials in response to a test stimulus before and after repeated stimulation. **(a)** 100-Hz stimulation produced long-term potentiation that was evident 25 minutes later. **(b)** 5-Hz stimulation produced long-term depression that blocked potentiation established earlier.
Source: From W. R. Chen, et al., "Long-term modifications of synaptic efficacy in the human inferior and middle temporal cortex," *Proceedings of the National Academy of Sciences,* USA, 93, 321–325. Copyright 1996 National Academy of Sciences, U.S.A.

Long-term potentiation (LTP) is an increase in synaptic strength following repeated stimulation. Before inducing LTP, the researcher excites a group of neurons with a single stimulus and measures the response in the postsynaptic neurons as an index of baseline activity. Then LTP is induced by stimulating the presynaptic neurons with a high frequency of electrical pulses for several seconds. A single stimulus is again applied as a test; this time the postsynaptic neurons produce a larger excitatory postsynaptic potential and, if they fire, a higher rate of action potentials (Figure 11.9a). What is remarkable about LTP is that it can last for anywhere from minutes to a few months. Although LTP has been studied mostly in the hippocampus, it also occurs in several other areas, including visual, auditory, and motor cortex (Aroniadou & Teyler, 1991; Iriki, Pavlides, Keller, & Asanuma, 1989; Weinberger, Javid, & Lepan, 1995). So LTP appears to be a characteristic of much of neural tissue, at least in the areas most likely to be involved in learning.

LTP is complex enough to explain many learning phenomena. For example, **if a synapse is stimulated weakly while another synapse on the same postsynaptic neuron is being stimulated strongly, the "weak" synapse as well as the "strong" synapse will be potentiated; this effect is called** *associative long-term potentiation (ALTP)* (Kelso &

www
2

How do neurons change during learning?

Brown, 1986). Thus ALTP resembles *classical conditioning*—the form of learning in which, for example, a light is turned on at the same time a dog receives a shock to its foot, and afterward the light causes the dog to withdraw its foot. **If a presynaptic neuron is not firing while the postsynaptic neuron is being fired (by other neurons), the synapse between them will be weakened; this is *long-term depression (LTD)*. *Associative long-term depression (ALTD)* also occurs if two presynaptic neurons fire at different times.** LTD resembles the learning phenomenon of *extinction*. LTP, LTD, ALTP, and ALTD can all be summed up in the expression, "Cells that fire together wire together." Remember that we saw similar phenomena during the prenatal development of the nervous system.

Long-term depression can block long-term potentiation that has already occurred (see Figure 11.9b). This was demonstrated with cortical tissue removed from the temporal lobes of epileptic patients, in most cases in the process of exposing a diseased hippocampus underneath (Chen et al., 1996). High-frequency stimulation induced LTP, and low-frequency stimulation resulted in LTD. When low-frequency stimulation was applied to neurons that had previously undergone long-term potentiation, the LTP was eliminated. It has been suggested that the function of LTD is to prevent potentiation from escalating out of control (Sejnowski, 1977). Another possibility is that LTD is the mechanism the brain uses to clear the hippocampal area of old memories, to make room for new information (Stickgold, Hobson, Fosse, & Fosse, 2001).

The long trains of stimulation used to induce LTP are not like any activity that occurs normally in the brain. Researchers later discovered that LTP can be induced more quickly if the inducing stimulation is timed to coincide with theta EEG activity in the hippocampus (Hölscher, Anwyl, & Rowan, 1997). *Theta rhythm* is EEG activity with a frequency range of 3–7 Hz; it typically occurs in the hippocampus when an animal is experiencing a novel situation. Any learning situation is somewhat novel, otherwise there would be nothing to learn. The researchers used a low-tech but effective method for producing theta in their experiment: they pinched the rats' tails. When hippocampal stimulation was timed to coincide with the peaks of theta waves, LTP could be produced by just five pulses of stimulation. Stimulation that coincided with the trough of theta waves reversed LTP that had been induced 30 minutes before. Hölscher and his colleagues believe that the theta rhythm, by responding to novel situations, may emphasize important stimuli for the brain and facilitate LTP and depression.

The theta rhythm appears to be necessary for at least some kinds of memory formation. The double alternation task requires animals to turn the opposite way on alternate trials in a two-choice maze to obtain food; having to remember the previous turn places a demand on working memory. Suppressing hippocampal theta with drugs eliminates rats' ability to perform this task (Givens & Olton, 1990).

Synaptic Changes

As we saw in Chapter 3, plasticity is a hallmark of the nervous system. And nowhere is the value of plasticity more evident than in learning and memory. During LTP, synaptic changes include increased neurotransmitter release, increased receptor sensitivity, and structural changes in the synapse.

Adjusting neurotransmitter release requires some sort of feedback from the postsynaptic neuron. There are probably several messengers, but the one we are most sure of is *nitric oxide (NO)*. When the postsynaptic neuron is activated it releases nitric oxide gas into the synaptic cleft. The NO diffuses across the cleft to the presynaptic neuron, where it induces the neuron to release more neurotransmitter. If the synthesis of NO is blocked chemically, LTP does not occur (Schuman & Madison, 1991). The NO lasts only briefly, but the increase in neurotransmitter release is long term (O'Dell, Hawkins, Kandel, & Arancio, 1991).

In most locations the neurotransmitter involved in LTP is glutamate. There are two

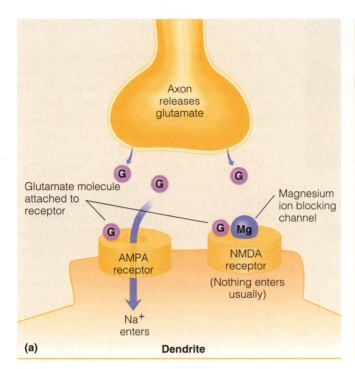 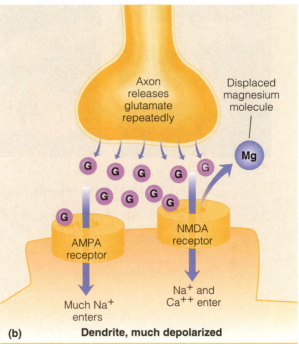

Figure 11.10
Participation of glutamate receptors in LTP
(a) Initially, glutamate activates the AMPA receptors but not the NMDA receptors, which are blocked by magnesium ions.
(b) However, if the activation is strong enough to partially depolarize the postsynaptic membrane, the magnesium ions are
ejected. The NMDA receptor can then be activated, allowing sodium and calcium ions to enter.

types of glutamate receptors. One is the *AMPA receptor* (so called because it also responds to the drug α-amino-3-hydroxy-5-methyl-4-isoazolepropionic acid); the other is the *NMDA receptor* (which also responds to the drug *N*-methyl-D-aspartate). Initially, glutamate activates AMPA receptors but not NMDA receptors, because they are blocked by magnesium ions (Figure 11.10). The first few pulses of stimulation partially depolarize the membrane, which dislodges the magnesium ions. The critical NMDA receptor can then be activated; the resulting influx of sodium and calcium ions increases the depolarization and the likelihood that the neuron will fire. More significantly, the calcium triggers increases in the numbers and sensitivity of AMPA receptors.

A final stage involves alteration of gene activity and the synthesis of proteins (Bailey, Bartsch, & Kandel, 1996; Meberg, Barnes,

McNaughton, & Routtenberg, 1993). These changes are responsible for structural modifications that occur in the dendrites that produce longer-lasting increases in synaptic strength. Within a half hour after LTP, postsynaptic neurons develop increased numbers of *dendritic spines*, **outgrowths from the dendrites that partially bridge the synaptic cleft and make the synapse more sensitive** (see Figure 11.11) (Engert & Bonhoeffer, 1999; Maletic-Savatic, Malinow, & Svoboda, 1999). In addition, existing spines split down the middle and each half enlarges to form two spines (Toni, Buchs, Nikonenko, Bron, & Muller, 1999). Postsynaptic strength is increased further as AMPA receptors move into spines from nearby (Shi et al., 1999).

With all that growth, you might suspect that there would be some increase in the volume of the brain areas involved in LTP. In fact, there

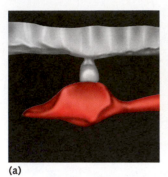 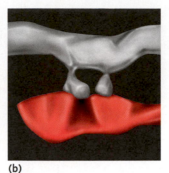

(a) (b)

Figure 11.11
Increase in dendritic spines following long-term potentiation
(a) A single synaptic spine on a dendrite (white) and a presynaptic terminal (red). **(b)** The same spine split into two following LTP.
Reprinted with permission from M. Barinaga, "Learning visualized on the double." *Science*, 286, 1661. Copyright 1999 American Association for the Advancement of Science.

is evidence that this does happen. London taxi drivers, who are noted for their ability to navigate the city's complex streets entirely from memory, spend about two years learning the routes before they can be licensed to operate a cab. Maguire and her colleagues (2000) used magnetic resonance imaging to scan the brains of 16 drivers. The posterior part of their hippocampi, known to be involved in spatial navigation, was larger than in similar-age males. (Overall volume did not change; their anterior hippocampi were smaller.) The difference was greater for cabbies who had been driving for the longest time, which we would expect if the difference were caused by experience.

The Role of LTP in Learning

How important is LTP to learning?

Recent research has supported psychologists' belief that LTP plays a fundamental role in learning. Genetic manipulation was used to decrease the number of NMDA receptors in mice; this reduced LTP in the hippocampus and impaired learning in a water maze (Sakimura et al., 1995). At the other end of the continuum, improving LTP enhances learning. Researchers discovered they could increase LTP with *ampakines*, compounds that increase the time the AMPA receptors are open. Ampakine drugs also enhance maze learning, delayed match-to-sample learning, and condi-

How do the roles of the hippocampus and the cortex differ?

tioning of the fear response (Rogan, Stäubli, & LeDoux, 1997).

It is unlikely that strengthening the synaptic connection between just two neurons constitutes a memory; more likely, memories depend on networks of neurons (Martinez & Derrick, 1996). To refresh your own memory about neural networks, two features make them well suited for storing learned information. One is that a single network can contain many different sets of information. Second, because information is distributed throughout the network it is relatively immune to the effects of damage. You may also remember that both excitation and inhibition are required to form functioning neural networks. With this in mind, long-term potentiation and long-term depression become credible candidates for playing a role in neural network development.

LTP does have one apparent deficiency as an explanation for learning. In the laboratory it has a limited life span, whereas some memories last a lifetime. Either long-term potentiation plays only a temporary role in learning, or the laboratory demonstrations are unrepresentative of real-life LTP. Most studies that have addressed the duration of LTP were conducted in the hippocampus; because the involvement of the hippocampus in learning *is* time-limited, we should expect LTP there to be of brief duration. It is possible that LTP is longer lasting in the cortex (Martinez & Derrick, 1996). There is also some evidence that LTP is stronger if it occurs during a learning experience rather than being electrically induced by the experimenter in a nonbehaving animal (Ahissar et al., 1992).

Consolidation Revisited

A new memory's transition from the hippocampus to the cortex is a lengthy process that depends on the availability of an enzyme called *α-calcium/calmodulin-dependent protein kinase type II (α-CaMKII)*. (An enzyme is a protein that acts as a catalyst, influencing chemical reactions in a cell.) Mice bred to be homozygous for a mutation of the gene responsible for the enzyme (α-CaMKII$^{-/-}$ mice; both copies of the gene are mutations) show no LTP in the hippocampus, and no learning. Apparently mice that are heterozygous for the gene (α-CaMKII$^{+/-}$ mice) produce an intermediate amount of the enzyme; they show LTP in the hippocampus but *not* in the cortex (Frankland, O'Brien, Ohno, Kirkwood, & Silva, 2001). LTP in the cortex probably requires more enzyme than LTP in the hippocampus because the cortex has a lower density of preexisting synapses and must create new ones in order to undergo LTP (Lisman & Morris, 2001). Heterozygous mice show normal learning of a task requiring the hippocampus, but the learning disappears within a few days.

So apparently the hippocampus has the ability to acquire learning "on the fly" while the event is in progress, but the cortex is needed for long-term storage. Many researchers now believe that the hippocampus transfers information to the cortex during times when the hippocampus is less occupied, for example during sleep (Lisman & Morris, 2001; McClelland, McNaughton, & O'Reilly, 1995). In fact, humans improve on a visual discrimination task 2–4 days after training, *without any intervening practice*—but only if they have slept within the first 30 hours after training (Stickgold, James, & Hobson, 2000). During sleep, neurons in the rats' hippocampus and involved cortical areas repeat the pattern of firing sequences that occurred during learning while they were awake (Louie & Wilson, 2001; Skaggs & McNaughton, 1996; Qin, McNaughton, Skaggs, & Barnes, 1997). That replay is synchronized in time with hippocampal theta (Stickgold et al., 2001). Presumably "offline" replay like this provides the cortex the opportunity to undergo long-term potentiation at the more leisurely pace it requires (Lisman & Morris, 2001).

Consolidated memories are rather enduring; you and I have memories that date back to early childhood. But just because memories are long lasting does not mean they are accurate. We have long known that memories get "reconstructed" over time, usually by blending with other memories. They are particularly susceptible to reconstruction at the time of retrieval, when multiple memories may be recalled simultaneously (Schacter, Norman, & Koutstaal, 1998). Reconstruction can be a progressive affair. Evidence suggests that one reason for the "recovery" of *false* childhood memories during therapy may be therapists' repeated attempts to stimulate recall at successive sessions. Laboratory research has shown that people's agreement with memories planted by the experimenter can increase over multiple interviews (Loftus, 1997). A recent study indicates that memories must be *reconsolidated* after each retrieval, and that they are particularly vulnerable for a few hours following retrieval. Mice were conditioned to give a fear response (freezing) to a tone, by pairing the tone with foot shock. Twenty-four hours later, the memory could be disrupted by presenting the tone (to induce retrieval) and injecting both amygdalas with *anisomycin* (Nader, Schafe, & Le Doux, 2000). Anisomycin is an antibiotic that interferes with protein synthesis; it impairs learning if it is given right after conditioning. However, 24 hours after conditioning anisomycin had no effect *unless* the tone was presented at the same time. This implicates retrieval as the reason for vulnerability. Because proteins (like α-CaMKII) play a role in consolidation, we can infer that the memory must be reconsolidated following retrieval. Presumably this gives us the opportunity to refine old memories with new information, but apparently it also makes them susceptible to the introduction of errors.

✓ **CONCEPT CHECK**

- *Make a list of the changes that occur in neurons during learning.*
- *Describe LTP, LTD, ALTP, and ALTD.*
- *Consolidated memory is both stable and vulnerable. Explain.*

DISORDERS OF LEARNING

Learning may be the most complex of human functions. Not surprisingly, it is also one of the most frequently impaired. Learning can be compromised by accidents and violence that damage the structures we have been studying. But more subtle threats to learning ability come from aging and from disorders of the brain, including Alzheimer's disease and Korsakoff's syndrome.

Aging

OLD MAN: *Ah, memory. It's the second thing to go.*

YOUNG MAN: *So what's first?*

OLD MAN: *I forget . . .*

You may or may not find humor in this old joke, but declining memory is hardly a laughing matter to the elderly. The older person might mislay car keys, forget appointments, or leave a pot on the stove for hours. Working memory and the ability to retrieve old memories and to make new memories may all be affected (Fahle & Daum, 1997; Small, Stern, Tang, & Mayeux, 1999). Memory loss is not just inconvenient and embarrassing; it is potentially dangerous, and it is disturbing because it suggests the possibility of brain degeneration.

Until fairly recently, researchers believed that declining memory and cognitive abilities were an inevitable consequence of aging. Although various kinds of cognitive deficits are typical of old age, they are not inevitable. For example, college professors in their 60s perform as well as professors in their 30s on many tests of learning and memory (Shimamura, Berry, Mangels, Rusting, & Jurica, 1995). An active lifestyle in old age has been associated with this "successful aging" (Schaie, 1994), but this fact does not necessarily tell us that staying active will stave off decline. Continued mental alertness may be the reason the person remains active, or health may be responsible for both good memory and a high activity level. However, we do know that rats reared in an enriched environment develop increased dendrites and synapses on cortical neurons (Sirevaag & Greenough, 1987). Also, we will see in the next chapter that cognitive skill

Does the brain age, too?

training produces significant and enduring improvement in the elderly, which suggests that experience can affect the person's cognitive well-being.

For many years researchers believed that deficits in the elderly were caused by a substantial loss of neurons, especially from the cortex and the hippocampus. However, the studies that led to this conclusion were based on flawed methods of estimating cell numbers. More recent investigations have found that the number of hippocampal neurons was not diminished in aged rats, even those with memory deficits, and that neuron loss from cortical areas was relatively minor (see Albert et al., 1999, for a review). In fact, as we saw in Chapter 3, the number of synapses continues to increase with age in humans (Buell & Coleman, 1979).

On the other hand, certain circuits in the hippocampus do lose synapses and NMDA receptors as animals age (Gazzaley, Siegel, Kordower, Mufson, & Morrison, 1996; Geinisman, de Toledo-Morrell, Morrell, Persina, & Rossi, 1992). Probably as a result of these changes, LTP is impaired in aged rats; it develops more slowly and diminishes more rapidly (Barnes & McNaughton, 1985). The rats' memory capabilities parallel their LTP deficits: learning is slower and forgetting is more rapid. There is also a decrease in metabolic activity in the *entorhinal cortex*, the major input and output to the hippocampus (de Leon et al., 2001). In normal elderly individuals, metabolic activity in the entorhinal cortex predicted the amount of cognitive impairment three years later. Another likely cause of learning deficits is myelin loss (Jensen, 1998). Without myelin, neurons conduct more slowly and interfere with each other's activity.

One subcortical area does undergo substantial neuron loss during aging, at least in monkeys. It is the *basal forebrain region* (Smith, Roberts, Gage, & Tuszynski, 1999), whose acetylcholine-secreting neurons communicate with the hippocampus, amygdala, and cortex. It also undergoes substantial cell loss in Alzheimer's disease, which we will discuss

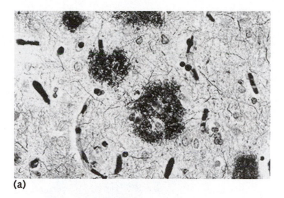

(a)

(b)

Figure 11.12
Neural abnormalities in the brain of an Alzheimer's patient
(a) The round clumps in the photo are plaques. **(b)** The dark twisted features are neurofibrillary tangles.
Source: WebPath, courtesy of Edward C. Klatt, M.D., Department of Pathology, University of Utah, Salt Lake City, Utah, U.S.A.

shortly; the less pronounced degeneration that occurs in normal aging probably contributes to memory deficits as well.

Some of the deficits in the elderly resemble those of patients with frontal lobe damage (Moscovitch & Winocur, 1995). In one study, elderly individuals participated in the "gambling task" described in Chapter 7, choosing playing cards from two "safe" decks and two "risky" decks. Like patients with prefrontal brain damage, 35% of these elderly volunteers never learned to avoid the risky decks, and another 28% were slow in doing so (Tranel & Denburg, in preparation).

Alzheimer's Disease

The loss of memory and other cognitive abilities in the elderly is referred to as *dementia*. **The most common cause of dementia is** *Alzheimer's disease (AD)*, **a disorder characterized by progressive brain deterioration and impaired memory and mental abilities.** Alzheimer's disease was first described by the neuroanatomist and neurologist Alois Alzheimer in the nineteenth century. The earliest and most severe symptom is usually impaired declarative memory. Initially, the person is indistinguishable from a normally aging individual, though the symptoms may start earlier; the person has trouble remembering events from the day before, forgets names, and has trouble finding the right word in a conversation. Later the person repeats questions and tells the same story again during a conversation; as time and disease progress, the person eventually fails to recognize acquain-

tances and even family members. Language, visual-spatial functioning, and reasoning are also affected, and there are often behavioral problems such as aggressiveness and wandering away from home.

Alzheimer's disease is primarily a disorder of aging, although it can strike fairly early in life. It affects 10% of people over 65 years of age, and nearly half of those over 85 (Evans et al., 1989). Zaven Khachaturian, director of the Ronald and Nancy Reagan Research Institute, eloquently described his mother's decline: "The disease quietly loots the brain, nerve cell by nerve cell, like a burglar returning to the same house each night" (Khachaturian, 1997, p. 21).

The Diseased Brain: Plaques and Tangles

There are two notable characteristics of the AD brain, though they are not unique to Alzheimer's. *Plaques* **are clumps of amyloid, a type of protein, that cluster among axon terminals and interfere with neural transmission** (Figure 11.12a). The total number of deposits is only moderately related to the degree of cognitive impairment, but amyloid accumulation appears to initiate additional steps that ultimately lead to cell death (Selkoe, 1997). **Abnormal webs of neurofilaments called** *neurofibrillary tangles* **develop inside neurons and are also associated with the death of brain cells** (Figure 11.12b).

Figure 11.13 shows the brain of a deceased Alzheimer's patient and a normal brain. Notice the decreased size of the gyri and the increased width of the sulci in the AD brain. Internally, enlarged ventricles tell a similar story of severe

3

What causes Alzheimer's disease?

Figure 11.13
Alzheimer's brain (left) and a normal brain
The illustrations show the most obvious differences, the reduced size of gyri and increased size of sulci produced by cell loss in the diseased brain.
Source: Photos courtesy of Dr. Robert D. Terry.

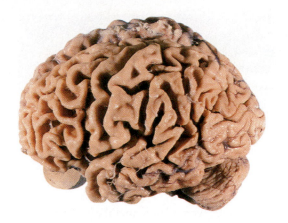
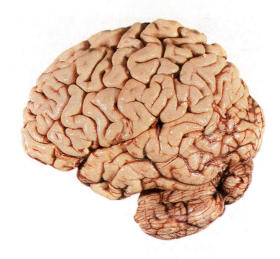

neuron loss. Many of the lesions are located in the temporal lobes; because of their location, they effectively isolate the hippocampus from its inputs and outputs, which partially explains the early memory loss (Hyman, Van Horsen, Damasio, & Barnes, 1984). However, plaques and tangles also attack the frontal lobes, accounting for additional memory problems as well as attention and motor difficulties. The occipital lobes and parietal lobes may be involved as well; disrupted communication between the primary visual area and the visual association areas in the parietal and temporal lobes explains the visual deficits that plague some AD sufferers.

Alzheimer's and Heredity

Heredity is an important factor in Alzheimer's disease. The first clue to a gene location came from a comparison of AD with Down syndrome (Lott, 1982). Down individuals also have plaques and tangles, and they invariably develop AD if they live to the age of 50. Because Down syndrome is caused by an extra chromosome 21, researchers zeroed in on that chromosome; there they found mutations in the *amyloid precursor protein (APP) gene* (Goate et al., 1991). When aged mice were genetically engineered with an APP mutation that increased plaques, both LTP and spatial learning were impaired (Chapman et al., 1999).

Three additional genes that influence AD have been confirmed. All of the genes discovered so far affect amyloid production or its deposit in the brain (Selkoe, 1997).

As you can see in Table 11.1, the genes fall into two classes, those associated with early-onset Alzheimer's disease (often before the age of 60) and one found in patients with late-onset AD. The four genes in the table account for only about half of the cases of AD and environmental causes seem to have little effect on AD, so additional genes must be involved. Analysis of gene expression in the brains of deceased Alzheimer's patients found 31 upregulated genes and 87 downregulated genes in the amygdala and cingulate cortex (Loring, Wen, Lee, Seilhamer, & Somogyi, 2001); if these results are accurate, the causes of the disease will turn out to be even more complex than we have imagined.

Treatment of Alzheimer's Disease

Acetylcholine and neural systems in various parts of the brain that produce acetylcholine are critical for cognitive functions, including attention and learning (Everitt & Robbins, 1997). For example, when normal individuals took an oral dose of an acetylcholine receptor blocker, their performance dropped on a learning task (Newhouse, Potter, Corwin, & Lenox, 1992). Little surprise, then, that acetylcholine-

Table 11.1 Known Genes for Alzheimer's Disease

Gene	Chromosome	Age of Onset	Percentage of Cases
APP	21	45 to 66	<0.1
Presenilin 1	14	28 to 62	1 to 2
Presenilin 2	1	40 to 85	<0.1
ApoE4	19	>60	>50

Sources: Marx, 1998; Selkoe, 1997.

releasing neurons are among the victims of degeneration in Alzheimer's disease. The majority of treatment efforts have focused on restoring cholinergic (acetylcholine-related) functioning. The most successful drugs have been those that inhibit acetylcholinesterase, the enzyme that removes acetylcholine from the synapse following neural activity. Two drugs, *tacrine* and *donepezil*, have received Federal Drug Administration approval, and others that are in the pipeline will likely be available by the time you read this. They provide moderate relief for both memory and behavioral symptoms in mild cases of AD (Krall, Sramek, & Cutler, 1999). But these drugs are little or no help when degeneration is advanced.

Another approach for increasing cholinergic activity was inspired by the discovery that the risk of developing Alzheimer's is almost a third less in smokers (Salib & Hillier, 1997). Of course, doctors are not about to recommend taking up the habit, but transdermal administration of nicotine using a skin patch has produced encouraging improvements in AD patients (Parks et al., 1996). Drug companies are showing an interest in producing synthetic forms of the drug, and you can expect those to appear on the market in the future.

Some promise has been shown by anticholesterol drugs (Yaffe, Barrett-Connor, Lin, & Grady, 2002), nonsteroidal anti-inflammatory drugs (Veld et al., 2001), and even the natural supplement *Ginkgo biloba* (Oken, Storzbach, & Kaye, 1998; Wettstein, 2000). A fourth possibility is estrogen treatment, made more important because three-quarters of the 4 million people in the U.S. with Alzheimer's disease

are women. One reason is that women live longer than men, which increases their vulnerability; the other is that when women reach menopause their estrogen levels decrease, while men continue to produce the same low amount. In rats, the density of dendritic spines in the hippocampus varies with the level of circulating estrogen; removing the female's ovaries impairs learning by decreasing spine density in the hippocampus and cholinergic activity there and in the frontal cortex (Singh, Meyer, Millard, & Simpkins, 1994; Woolley & McEwen, 1993). The incidence of Alzheimer's is reduced by about a third in women who receive estrogen replacement after menopause (Slooter et al., 1999). Whether estrogen treatment could benefit men in the same way is unclear, but genetic risk for Alzheimer's will likely become a factor in a woman's decision whether to take estrogen supplements after reaching menopause.

According to Census Bureau projections, the U.S. population is expected to increase by almost 50% between the years 2000 and 2050. But the elder population will grow much faster; those over the age of 85 are expected to increase sixfold (Bureau of the Census, 2000). This disproportionate increase is due to better nutrition and health care and the aging of the baby boomers. As a result, the Alzheimer's Association (2000) estimates that the number of people with Alzheimer's disease will increase by 350%, to 14.3 million (see Figure 11.14). Treatments that delayed nursing home placement by only one month would save $1 billion a year in health care costs, and a delay of five years would save $50 billion each year.

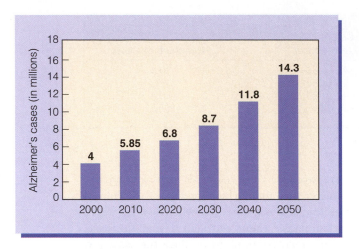

Figure 11.14
Projected numbers of people with Alzheimer's disease
Note that the numbers are in millions.
Reprinted with permission from the Alzheimer's Association.

It is surprising that after so much research only two drugs are currently approved for the treatment of Alzheimer's, and they have only a relatively superficial effect. Recent drug development efforts have turned toward immunization against Alzheimer's, by injecting amyloid-β to produce an immune reaction. In transgenic mice (see Chapter 1) engineered so they accumulate amyloid deposits and have learning deficiencies, immunization reduces plaques and improves learning in a water maze (Janus et al., 2000; Morgan et al., 2000). A similar approach involves vaccination to dissolve plaques, as seen in "Dissolving Plaques and Tangles" below.

Another exciting effort is on the genetic front. But rather than manipulating the genes responsible for the disease, researchers are attempting to reverse atrophy in dying neurons by implanting genes for *nerve growth factor,* which stimulates neuronal growth. In separate studies, untreated aged monkeys had undergone a 43% reduction in the number of basal forebrain region neurons that were secreting acetylcholine (Smith et al., 1999), and a 25% reduction in cholinergic activity in

IN THE NEWS

Dissolving Plaques and Tangles

When the International Conference on Alzheimer's and Related Disorders met for the first time in 1988 there were no presentations on potential Alzheimer drugs. The story was radically different at the conference held in Stockholm, Sweden in 2002.

One exciting possibility is the ability to dissolve amyloid plaques. The plaques are bound together by copper and zinc, metals normally found in the body. Now researchers have learned that the antibiotic *clioquinol* breaks these metal bonds and dissolves the plaques. In aged mice engineered to develop plaques, those given clioquinol had 50% less amyloid deposited in their brains than untreated animals; in mice started on the antibiotic while they were young, 30% developed no detectable plaques at all.

Now Dr. Colin Masters of the University of Melbourne has given the antibiotic to 18

Alzheimer's disease patients. At the end of nine months, their amyloid protein levels were reduced, and they showed some cognitive improvement compared to patients given a placebo. A particularly encouraging result was that the more impaired patients improved the most in cognitive functioning.

Sources:
The 8th International Conference on Alzheimer's and Related Disorders, by Stephen McConnell, http://www.mainealz.org/doc8thConference.htm
An Antibiotic to Treat Alzheimer's?, by Laura Helmuth, *Science* (2000), 290, 1273–1274.
New AD Therapies Focus on Amyloid Theory, by Kylie Taggart, http://www.medicalpost.com/mdlink/english/members/medpost/data/3829/24A.HTM

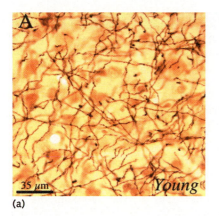

(a)

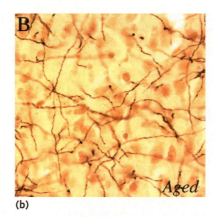

(b)

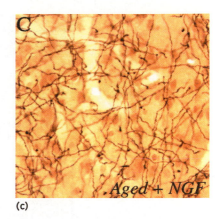

(c)

the cortex (Conner, Darracq, Roberts, & Tuszynski, 2001). After cells containing nerve growth factor were grafted into the basal forebrain region, cholinergic activity was almost completely restored there, and the activity level in the cortex was equal to that of young monkeys (Figure 11.15).

Whatever treatments for Alzheimer's emerge, the trick will be to detect the disease early so treatment can begin before there is substantial cell loss. The changes that lead to Alzheimer's probably begin as much as 10 years before symptoms appear, so there would be a wide window of opportunity for intervention. However, in the past it has been impossible to distinguish the pre-Alzheimer's individual from typically declining elderly people. Now brain imaging techniques may catch Alzheimer's early enough to begin intervention when it might do some good. Earlier I mentioned a study in which reduced activity in the entorhinal cortex predicted the degree of cognitive decline three years later (de Leon et al., 2001). In addition, four individuals who later developed Alzheimer's had a higher rate of atrophy than controls in the general area of the hippocampal formation and in multiple cortical areas; these differences also were distinguishable three or more years before symptoms appeared (Fox et al., 2001).

Korsakoff's Syndrome

Another form of dementia is *Korsakoff's syndrome,* **brain deterioration which is almost always caused by chronic alcoholism.** It is

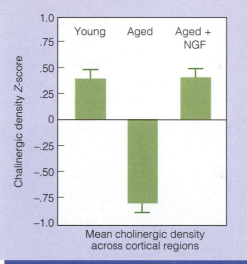

(d)

Figure 11.15
Effect of nerve growth factor on acetylcholine-producing neurons in monkeys
The density of neurons stained with a marker for acetylcholine activity is compared in cortical tissue from **(a)** young and **(b)** aged monkeys. **(c)** Aged monkeys treated with nerve growth factor (NGF) genes show an increase in cholinergic activity. **(d)** Comparison of the relative density of acetylcholine-producing neurons in the three groups.

From J. M. Conner, et al., "Nontropic actions of neurotrophins: Subcortical nerve growth factor gene delivery reverses age-related degeneration of primate cortical cholinergic innervation," *Proceedings of the National Academy of Sciences,* 98, 1941–1946. Copyright 2001 National Academy of Sciences, U.S.A.

not the alcohol itself that causes the problem; rather, the alcoholic consumes large quantities of calories in the form of alcohol and fails to eat an adequate diet. A deficiency in the B vitamin *thiamine* results in damage to brain structures important in learning and memory. The most pronounced symptom is anterograde amnesia, but retrograde amnesia is also severe; procedural memory is intact. The hippocampus and temporal lobes are unaffected; but the mammillary bodies and the medial thalamic area are reduced in size, and structural and functional abnormalities occur in the frontal lobes (Gebhardt, Naeser, & Butters, 1984; Kopelman, 1995; Squire, Amaral, & Press, 1990). Thiamine therapy can relieve the

What are the symptoms of Korsakoff's syndrome?

4

Genetic Interventions for Alzheimer's

On April 5, 2001, a surgical team at the University of California, San Diego, implanted cells that had been augmented with nerve growth factor genes into the brain of a 60-year-old woman who was in the early stages of Alzheimer's disease ("UCSD team performs," 2001). Since that time two others have gone through the surgery ("Risky Alzheimer's surgery," 2002), and five more are to follow. Though the surgery takes 11 hours to complete, the patient is awake throughout, and is able to leave the hospital two days later.

These operations follow the successful use of the procedure with monkeys, and their purpose is to determine the procedure's safety in humans. Barring significant problems in this series, the next step will be clinical trials to assess the effectiveness of the treatment for Alzheimer's. (For detailed information on the surgery and additional photos, see the website mentioned in On the Web item 4 near the end of this chapter.)

Another genetic approach promises to remove the threat of Alzheimer's in some individuals before they are born. A 30-year-old woman who carries the rare but deadly APP gene, (see Table 11.1 again) had 15 of her eggs screened for the gene and four that were free of APP were fertilized with her husband's sperm and implanted in her uterus (Flam, 2002; Verlinsky et al., 2002). The woman will most likely die while the child is still young. Her father died as a result of Alzheimer's at the age of 42, a sister died at 38, and a brother became demented at 35. Without the screening she had a 50-50 chance of passing the gene to her child.

Although it is hard to dispute the woman's concern, ethicists worry that as we learn more about the genetics of disease and the screening procedure becomes more affordable, the result will be unreasonable expectations of perfection in offspring (Flam, 2002). Others fear that the screening will not be limited to protecting offspring from disease but will be used to genetically engineer near-perfect offspring, as in the movie *GATTACA*.

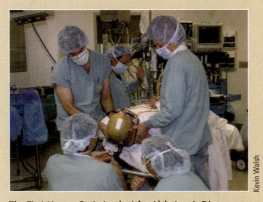
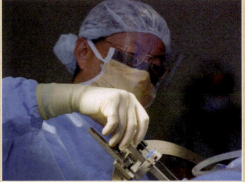

The First Human Brain Implant for Alzheimer's Disease
(a) *The surgical team at the University of California, San Diego, prepares a 60-year-old woman with Alzheimer's disease for surgery to implant cells containing nerve growth factor genes.* **(b)** *Dr. Hoi Sang U inserts a tissue implant into the woman's brain through a small hole in her skull.*
Source: "UCSD team performs first surgery," 2001.

5

symptoms of Korsakoff's syndrome somewhat if the disorder is not too advanced, but the brain damage itself is irreversible.

Some Korsakoff's patients show a particularly interesting characteristic in their behavior, called **confabulation; they fabricate stories and facts to make up for those missing from their memories.** We discuss this more later, but for now refrain from assuming that it involves intentional deception. Non-Korsakoff amnesics also confabulate, and so do normal people occasionally when their memory is vague. However, Korsakoff patients are champions at this kind of "creative remembering," especially during the volatile early period when their symptoms have just heated up.

For some, confabulation becomes a way of life. Mary Francis was a nursing home neighbor of Thelma, the Broca's aphasia patient I described in Chapter 8. She could converse fluently about her distant past as a college and high school English teacher, and recite Shakespeare and poetry that she had written. But, robbed of the memory of more recent years by Korsakoff's disease, she constantly invented explanations for her circumstance. One time she was just "visiting" at the nursing home, and she watched patiently through the glass front doors for her brother who would pick her up shortly for an automobile trip to Florida. Another time she complained she was stranded in a strange place and needed to get back to her "post"; she had in fact been in the Army in World War II, as a speech writer for General Clark. On another occasion she thought she was in prison—perhaps suggested by a memory of actually having been a prisoner of war—and she was querying the nurse about what she had "done wrong."

Confabulation apparently depends on abnormal activity in the frontal lobes, and confabulating patients typically have lesions there (Schnider & Ptak, 1999). A Korsakoff's patient studied by Benson and his colleagues (1996) did poorly on cognitive tests that are sensitive to impairment in frontal lobe functioning, and a brain scan showed that activity levels were reduced in the frontal area as well as in the diencephalon, the lower part of the forebrain that includes the thalamus and hypothalamus. Four months later he had ceased confabulating, although his amnesia remained. Cognitive tests were then normal, as was the scan of the frontal area, with the exception that diencephalic activity remained deficient. Confabulating amnesic patients have more trouble than nonconfabulating amnesics in suppressing irrelevant information they have learned earlier (Schnider & Ptak, 1999). Consequently, Benson and colleagues (1996) suggest that confabulation is due to an inability to distinguish between current reality and earlier memories. We will take up this topic again in the final chapter when we discuss consciousness.

 **CONCEPT CHECK**

- *What changes occur in the brain during aging?*
- *What is the role of plaques and tangles in Alzheimer's disease?*
- *How are Alzheimer's disease and Korsakoff's syndrome similar and different?*

 In Perspective

Learning is a form of neural plasticity. However, that simple statement ignores a variety of complex features that characterize learning. For example, different kinds of learning can be impaired selectively, as we see in patients who can learn and yet have no recollection of having learned. Our exploration of learning has been an abbreviated one, neglecting, for instance, the details of how synaptic changes occur during long-term potentiation and the mechanics of the additional processing that can continue for years after a learning event has occurred.

In spite of all we know about the learning process, we have little ability to enhance it. We know that blueberries can reverse learning deficits in aging rats and that wearing a nicotine patch can improve memory; but we can do little to help the Alzheimer's patient. Curing learning disorders and improving normal learning ability are little more than aspirations today. But there is good reason to think the mysteries will be solved eventually, perhaps with your help.

Summary

Learning as the Storage of Memories

- Brain damage can cause amnesia by impairing the storage of new memories (anterograde) or the retrieval of old memories (retrograde).

- The hippocampus is involved in both consolidation and retrieval. The prefrontal area may play an executive role.

- Memories are stored near the area where they are processed.

- There are at least two kinds of learning: declarative, mediated by the hippocampus, and nondeclarative, which involves the striatum and amygdala.

- Working memory holds new information and information retrieved from storage while it is being used.

Brain Changes in Learning

- Long-term potentiation increases synaptic strength and long-term depression reduces it.

- Changes at the synapse include increases in the number and sensitivity of AMPA receptors, the amount of transmitter released, and the number of dendritic spines.

- LTP is necessary for learning; diminishing it impairs learning and increasing it enhances learning.

- The hippocampus manages new memories, but they are transferred later to the cortex.

Disorders of Learning

- Aging usually involves some impairment of learning and memory, but in the normal brain substantial loss of neurons and synapses is limited to a few areas.

- Alzheimer's disease is a hereditary disorder that impairs learning and other brain functions, largely through the destruction of acetylcholine-producing neurons; plaques and tangles are believed to be the cause of cell death. Treatment usually involves increasing acetylcholine availability, but experimental treatments take other approaches.

- Korsakoff's syndrome is caused by a vitamin B deficiency resulting from alcoholism. Anterograde and retrograde amnesia are results.

For Further Thought

- If you were building an electronic learning and memory system for a robot, what would you change from the human design? Why?

- What are the learning and behavioral implications of impaired working memory?

- What implication does the study in which mice were injected with anisomycin have

for your study conditions as you review material for an exam?

- Which direction of research for the treatment of Alzheimer's do you think holds the greatest promise? Why?

Testing Your Understanding

1. Discuss consolidation, including what it is, when and where it occurs, and its significance in learning and memory.

2. Make the argument that long-term potentiation provides a reasonably good explanation of learning, including some of learning's basic phenomena.

3. Compare Alzheimer's disease and Korsakoff's syndrome in terms of causes, symptoms, and brain areas affected.

Select the one best answer:

1. Anterograde amnesia means that the patient has trouble remembering events:

   a. before the last few minutes.
   b. before the brain damage.
   c. since the brain damage.
   d. since the brain damage and for a few years before.

2. A person or animal born without the ability to consolidate would be unable to:

   a. remember anything.
   b. remember for more than a few minutes.
   c. recall old memories that had been well learned.
   d. recall declarative, as opposed to nondeclarative, memories.

3. The function of the *hippocampal formation* is:

   a. consolidation of new memories.
   b. retrieval of memories.
   c. as a temporary storage location.
   d. a and b.
   e. a, b, and c.

4. If HM's striatum had also been damaged, he would also not remember:

   a. declarative memories of childhood events.
   b. skills learned before his surgery.
   c. skills learned after his surgery.
   d. emotional experiences after his surgery.
   e. all of these.

5. In the course of adding a long column of entries in your checkbook you have to carry a 6 to the next column. If you forget the number in the process, you're having a problem with:

   a. consolidation.
   b. long-term potentiation.
   c. retrieval.
   d. working memory.

6. The researcher sounds a tone, then delivers a puff of air to your eye. After several times, the tone alone causes you to blink. This behavior is probably explained by:

   a. long-term potentiation.
   b. associative long-term potentiation.
   c. long-term depression
   d. associative long-term depression.

7. Long-term potentiation involves:

   a. release of nitric oxide.
   b. increase in cell body size.
   c. increased number of NMDA receptors.
   d. increased sensitivity of NMDA receptors.
   e. all of these.

8. Without long-term potentiation:

   a. long-term memory is impaired.
   b. working memory is impaired.
   c. old memories cannot be retrieved.
   d. no learning occurs.

9. The study in which anisomycin was injected into the amygdalas of mice indicates that:

   a. protein deficiency impairs memory.
   b. memories are particularly vulnerable during recall.
   c. antibiotics can improve memory.
   d. once recalled, a memory takes longer to consolidate.

10. The aged brain is characterized by substantial _____ throughout the cortex.

    a. loss of neurons
    b. loss of synapses.
    c. decreased metabolism
    d. all of these are true.
    e. none of these is true.

11. The symptoms of Alzheimer's disease appear to be caused by:

    a. plaques and tangles.
    b. a few genes.
    c. environmental toxins.
    d. all of these.
    e. none of these.

continued

12. The feature most common between Alzheimer's disease and Korsakoff's syndrome is the:

   a. symptoms.
   b. age of onset.
   c. degree of hereditary involvement.
   d. degree of environmental contribution.

Answers: 1. c 2. b 3. e 4. c 5. d 6. b 7. a 8. d 9. b 10. e 11. a 12. a

---

 ## On the Web

1. **Neuronames,** at the University of Washington, has an interesting view of the hippocampus in a partially dissected human brain at

   *http://rprcsgi.rprc.washington.edu/
   neuronames/interim/hippocampus.html*

2. The professional journal **Learning and Memory** provides free access to published articles from the preceding year and earlier at

   http://www.learnmem.org/

   The **American Psychological Association** is a good source for information on learning and memory and other topics. Many of the articles are brief updates appearing in the *APA Monitor.* Just type a topic name in the search window at

   http://www.apa.org/

3. The **Alzheimer's Association** has information about the disease, help for caregivers, and descriptions of research it is funding at

   http://www.alz.org/

4. The **UCSD School of Medicine News** has photos and a description of the first surgery to implant genetically altered cells in an Alzheimer's patient's brain at

   *http://health.ucsd.edu/news/2001/04_09_
   Tusz.html*

5. The **Family Caregiver Alliance** has a useful factsheet on Korsakoff's syndrome, including characteristics, prevalence, diagnosis, and treatment at

   *http://www.caregiver.org/factsheets/
   wks.html*

 For additional information about the topics covered in this chapter, please look at InfoTrac College Edition, at

http://www.infotrac-college.com/wadsworth

Try search terms you think up yourself, or use these: *Alzheimer's disease; amnesia; long-term depression; working memory.*

 ## On the CD-ROM: Exploring Biological Psychology

Animation: The Withdrawal Reflex
Animation: The Crossed Extensor Reflex

Video: The Brain Pacemaker

 ## For Further Reading

The Machinery of Thought, by Tim Beardsley (*Scientific American*, August 1997), is really about the neural basis of working memory, providing an overview of the research and the researchers.

Also see Martinez and Derrick (1996) in the references for a review of research on long-term potentiation and its role in learning.

Living in the Labyrinth: A Personal Journey Through the Maze of Alzheimer's (1994, Delta Books) is Diana Friel McGowin's personal account of her own slide into Alzheimer's disease.

 Key Terms

The Biological Bases of Intelligence

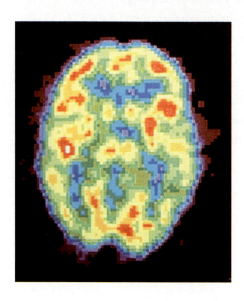
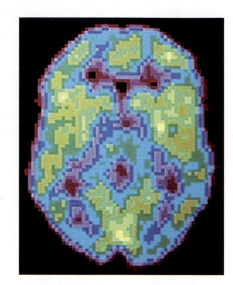

In this chapter you will learn:

- What some problems are in defining and measuring intelligence.

- Some of the neural characteristics that contribute to intelligence.

- The role of heredity and environment.

- How retardation, autism, and aging affect intelligence.

Cambridge theoretical physicist Stephen Hawking may be the most brilliant person living today. Following in Einstein's footsteps, he has developed theories of the origin of the universe that are altering the way scientists think. He lectures around the world, mixing high-powered physics with a keen sense of humor. He has achieved all this despite having Lou Gehrig's disease *(amyotrophic lateral sclerosis, or ALS)*, a degenerative disease that impairs voluntary movement. Confined to a wheelchair and able to make only small movements, he writes and speaks by moving a cursor on the screen of a computer equipped with a voice synthesizer (Figure 12.1).

Figure 12.1
Stephen Hawking
His great intellect is pent up in a body that can communicate only by moving a cursor on a computer screen.

When we consider Hawking, Einstein, or Marilyn vos Savant, who has the highest score ever recorded on an intelligence test (Yam, 1998), we might wonder: What is intelligence and what makes one person more intelligent than another? Is it genes, upbringing, hard work, or luck? And in particular, is the ultra-intelligent brain in some way different?

Because intelligence is so important to our daily lives and our ultimate success, we feel we already know a great deal about it. However, little of the information about intelligence can simply be labeled common sense. This applies not just to the biological bases, but to the definition of intelligence and all the practical issues surrounding its measurement and its implications. We cannot begin to understand our main topic—the biological origins of intelligence—without having some appreciation for what the term itself means.

THE NATURE OF INTELLIGENCE

There are many definitions of intelligence, which is the first clue that we have trouble agreeing what it is. A pretty good definition, in my opinion, is that ***intelligence* is the capacity for learning, reasoning, and understanding** (*Webster's College Dictionary*, 1991). That is what we *think* intelligence is. But as soon as we design and use a test of intelligence, we have defined intelligence as *what that test measures*, or the characteristics associated with high scores on that test.

What Intelligence Tests Measure
The measure typically used for intelligence is the *intelligence quotient (IQ)*. The term originated with the scoring on early intelligence tests designed for use with children. The tests produced a score in the form of a *mental age*, which was divided by the child's chronological age and multiplied by 100. The tests were designed to produce a score of 100 for a child performing at the average for his or her

What do IQ scores mean?

chronological age. The scoring is completely different now, partly because the tests were extended to adults, who do not increase consistently in intellectual performance from year to year. The base score is still 100, a value that was arbitrarily selected and that is artificially preserved by occasional adjustments to compensate for any drift in performance in the population. Most people are near the average, as Figure 12.2 shows, with relatively few people at either of the extremes. For example, only 2% of the population score above 130 points or below 70 points.

The first intelligence test was devised by Alfred Binet in 1905, to identify French school children who needed special instruction. Predicting school performance is what most intelligence tests do best, and intelligence tests have found their greatest use in the school setting. The correlation between IQ scores and school grades typically falls in the range of .40 to .60 (Kline, 1991). However, IQ is also related to job performance, income, socioeconomic level, and negatively to juvenile delinquency (Neisser et al., 1996).

The most dramatic demonstration of the IQ's ability to predict success in everyday life came in a massive study conducted by Lewis Terman (Terman & Oden, 1959). In 1921 he identified 1,500 California children between the ages of 8 and 12 who had IQs above 140, and he and his colleagues followed them for several decades. As they grew up they were taller, stronger, and healthier than other children. (Stephen Hawking is an exception to the principle that intelligent brains are usually found in healthy bodies.) Almost 70% graduated from college, which was 10 times higher than the rate for their age group at that time. As adults they were unusually successful; they produced 92 professional and scholarly books, 38 novels, 2,200 scientific papers, and 235 patents, and earned almost twice as much money per year as the population average.

Terman's conclusions about the relationship between intelligence and success have been questioned because his children were from the higher socioeconomic level, which is associated with better health care and greater educational and career opportunities (Bouchard & Segal, 1985; Locurto, 1990). However, socioeconomic level may not be the important player we have assumed it to be. For example, when tenth graders in the top 1% nationally in mathematical ability were compared with stu-

Figure 12.2
Distribution of IQ scores in the population

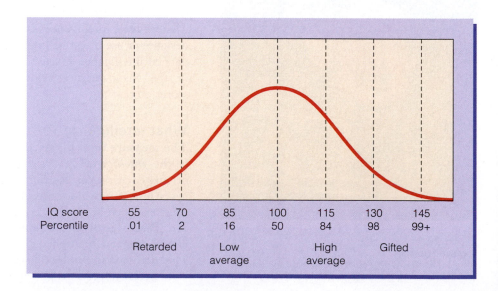

IQ score	55	70	85	100	115	130	145
Percentile	.01	2	16	50	84	98	99+

Retarded   Low average   High average   Gifted

dents in the top 1% in socioeconomic status, the intellectually gifted group was clearly healthier than the socially privileged group (Lubinski & Humphreys, 1992).

Critics believe that scores on traditional intelligence tests are closely related to academic performance and higher socioeconomic levels mostly because the tests were designed to reflect that kind of success. According to these critics, the tests overemphasize verbal ability, education, and Western culture. A few tests are designed to be culture free, like the Raven Progressive Matrices. These tests are mostly nonverbal and the tasks require no experience with a particular culture. They have an obvious advantage for testing people from a very different culture or language background or with impaired understanding of language. Some researchers also believe the Raven gives them a better representation of "pure" intelligence.

Claiming that true intelligence is much more than what the tests measure, these critics often point to instances where practical intelligence or "street smarts" is greater than conventional intelligence. For example, young Brazilian street vendors were adept at performing calculations in their street vending that they were unable to perform in a classroom setting (Carraher, Carraher, & Schliemman, 1985). In another study, expert racetrack gamblers used a highly complex algorithm involving seven variables to predict racetrack odds, but their performance was unrelated to their IQ; in fact, four of them had IQs in the low to mid 80s (Ceci & Liker, 1986). More recently, Robert Sternberg (2000) compared the scores that the presidential candidates George W. Bush, Al Gore, and Bill Bradley made on the verbal section of the Scholastic Assessment Test (SAT) when they applied for college; the SAT has many items similar to those on conventional intelligence tests. Two of the candidates scored above average for college applicants but not markedly so, and one had a score that was *below* average. To Sternberg, their success raises questions about the narrowness of what intelligence tests measure.

Sternberg argues that intelligence does not exist in the sense we usually conceive of it, but is "a cultural invention to account for the fact that some people are able to succeed in their environment better than others" (1988, p. 71). Uncertainty about what intelligence is severely hampers our search for its physiological underpinnings. Perhaps intelligence is, like the mind, just a convenient abstraction we invented to describe a group of processes. If so, we should not expect to find intelligence residing in a single brain location or even in a neatly defined network of brain structures. And to the extent we find processes or structures that are directly involved in intelligence, their performance may not be highly correlated with scores on traditional intelligence tests.

The Structure of Intelligence

One major debate is whether intelligence is a single capability or a collection of several independent abilities. Intelligence theorists tend to fall into one of two groups, *lumpers* or *splitters*. Lumpers claim that intelligence is a single, unitary capability, which is usually called the *general factor*, or simply *g*. General factor theorists admit that there are separate abilities that vary somewhat in strength in an individual, but they place much greater weight on the underlying g factor. They point out that a person who is high in one cognitive skill is usually high in others, so they believe that one score is adequate to describe a person's intellectual ability.

Splitters, on the other hand, hold that intelligence is made up of several mental abilities that are more or less independent of each other. They may agree that there is a general factor, but they give more emphasis to separate abilities and to differences among them in an individual. An accurate description of a person's intelligence would require the scores on all the subtests of these abilities. These theorists point to cases of brain damage in which one capability is impaired without affecting others, and to the *autistic savant*'s exceptional ability in a single area. Splitters disagree with each other, though, on how many abilities there are; a review of intelligence tests identified over 70 different abilities that can be measured by currently available tests (Carroll, 1993).

✔ CONCEPT CHECK

■ *What do IQ scores tell us, and not tell us, about a person's capabilities?*
■ *If intelligence is an "invention," what is the implication for our search for a brain location of intelligence?*
■ *What is the lumper-splitter controversy?*

THE ORIGINS OF INTELLIGENCE

With this background we are now ready to explore the origins of intelligence. On the basis of our introduction we will avoid two popular assumptions—that intelligence tests are the best definition of intelligence and that intelligence is a single capability. Instead, we will also consider performance and achievement as additional indicators of intelligence, and we will first examine the evidence for a biological basis for a general factor and then consider the relationship between brain structures and individual abilities.

How are intelligent brains different?

The Brain and Intelligence

Are there identifiable ways that a more intelligent brain is different from other brains? Anyone asking this question would naturally wonder how Albert Einstein's brain was different from other people's. Fortunately, the famous scientist's brain was preserved, and it has been made available from time to time to neuroscientists (Figure 12.3). In cursory examinations, it has turned out to be remarkably unremarkable. In fact, at 1,230 grams it was almost 200 grams lighter than the control brains (Witelson, Kigar, & Harvey, 1999). The number of neurons did not differ from normal, and studies have disagreed about whether the neurons were more densely packed or the cortex was thinner, perhaps because the samples were taken from different locations (Anderson & Harvey, 1996; Kigar, Witelson, Glezer, & Harvey, 1997). One study found a higher ratio of glial cells to neurons (Diamond, Scheibel, Murphy, & Harvey, 1985), but this was true of only one out of four locations tested. Also, the comparison brains averaged 12 years younger than Einstein's at the time of death, and we know that glial cells continue proliferating throughout life (Hines, 1998). Another study found that each of Einstein's hemispheres was a full centimeter wider than those of control brains, due to larger parietal lobes (Witelson et al., 1999). An enlargement of the parietal lobes is particularly interesting because they are

Figure 12.3
Albert Einstein and his brain
Sources: Historical Pictures Services, Chicago/FPG and Sandra F. Witelson.

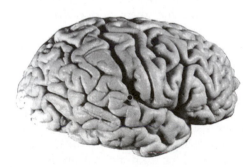

involved in mathematical ability and visual-spatial processing, and Einstein reported that he performed his mathematical thinking not in words but in images. Remember, though, that in Chapter 11 we saw that London cabdrivers have enlarged hippocampi, and no one has suggested that large hippocampi explains why they became cabdrivers. Whether Einstein's large parietal lobes or intense mathematical activity came first is uncertain (assuming they are related).

Words and language . . . do not seem to play any part in my thought processes.

—Albert Einstein

Interestingly, the strongest finding in the examination of Einstein's brain seems to be related to a specific ability rather than to overall intelligence. Another study used PET scans to observe people's brains while they worked

on tasks known to correlate well with measures of the general factor (Duncan et al., 2000). Frontal areas were more active during high-g tasks than during low-g tasks (Figure 12.4); the authors concluded that general intelligence may be located there. Because frontal areas are involved in working memory and executive control of problem solving, it is not surprising that they would contribute to general intelligence. Whether they have the exclusive importance these researchers assign them will be resolved by further investigation. In the meantime, we turn to other promising leads.

Brain Size

Brain size itself does not determine intelligence. Elephants have much larger brains than we do, and not many people think elephants are smarter. What is more important is the ratio of the brain's size to body size; this ratio adjusts for the proportion of the brain needed for managing the body and tells us how much is left over for

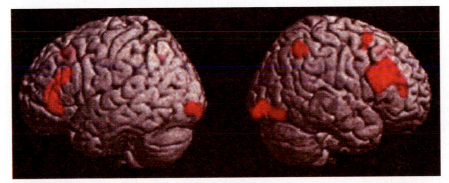

Spatial task

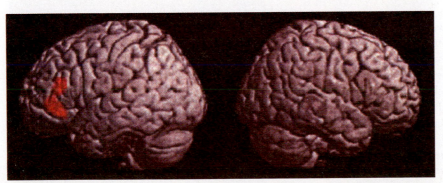

Verbal task

Figure 12.4
PET scans showing activity during tasks requiring general intelligence
The red areas indicate the brain areas that were activated more during the high-g tasks than during low-g tasks. Notice that the spatial task activated left and right frontal areas, while the verbal task activated the left area. Activity in the occipital and parietal areas during the spatial tasks probably reflects sensory and spatial processing.

Reprinted with permission from J. Duncan, "A neural basis for general intelligence." *Science, 289,* 457–460. Copyright 2000 American Association for the Advancement of Science.

intellectual functions. As you might expect, the ratio for humans is one of the highest.

Within a species, though, the answer is a bit different. Magnetic resonance imaging studies have found correlations of IQ and brain size in living humans ranging between .32 and .51 (Egan, Chiswick, Santosh, & Naidu, 1994; Wickett, Vernon, & Lee, 1994; Willerman, Schultz, Rutledge, & Bigler, 1991). Of course, men have larger brains than women, which we have assumed was related to men's greater body size. However, even after adjustment for body size, men's brains average about 118 grams heavier than women's (Ankney, 1992). Presumably, men are no smarter than women; it is actually difficult to tell, because intelligence tests were designed to avoid gender bias. But if men's excess brain matter does not confer additional intelligence, what is its function? There are two credible hypotheses. One is that women's brains are more efficient, because of a greater density of neurons (Witelson, Glezer, & Kigar, 1995) and a higher ratio of gray matter to white matter (Gur et al., 1999). The other hypothesis is that the male's superior spatial intelligence requires greater brain capacity (Falk, Froese, Sade, & Dudek, 1999). But before we go too far in dissecting the issue of brain size, we should keep in mind that Einstein's brain was smaller than the 1,252 grams of the average female brain (Ankney, 1992). So although on average more intelligent brains are also larger brains, other factors must be important in determining intelligence.

Neural Conduction Speed and Processing Speed

Cognitive processes require the person to apprehend, select, and attend to meaningful items from a welter of stimuli arriving at the sensory organs. Then the person must retrieve information from memory, relate the new information to it, and then manipulate the mental representation of the combined information. All of this takes time. In 1883 Francis Galton suggested that higher intelligence depends on greater "mental speed." Because there were no intelligence tests then, he attempted to relate reaction time to measures of intellectual achievement like course grades and occupational status, but he was unsuccessful. However, a number of researchers in the last quarter century have shown that IQ scores do correlate with reaction time (Reed & Jensen, 1992). The relationship is not due to the fact that most intelligence tests emphasize speed, because reaction time and IQ scores are still correlated when the IQ test is given without a time limit (Jensen, 1998).

IQ scores are correlated with *nerve conduction velocity (NCV)*, even more than with reaction time (see Figure 12.5) (McGarry-Roberts, Stelmack, & Campbell, 1992; Vernon & Mori, 1992). People who are more intelligent excel particularly on tasks in which stimuli are presented for an extremely short interval, and on tasks that require choices (Jensen, 1998). These are tasks in which processing speed is important and, presumably, higher NCV contributes to the more intelligent person's superior per-

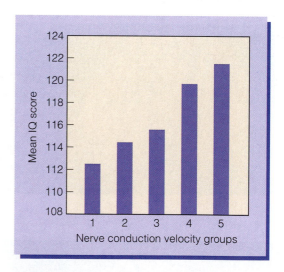

Figure 12.5
Relationship between IQ scores and nerve conduction velocity
The research participants were divided into five groups according to their nerve conduction velocity. Group 1 had the lowest NCV and Group 5 the highest. NCV was calculated by dividing the time between a visual stimulus and the occurrence of the visual evoked potential by the distance between the eyes and the back of the head.
Adapted from *Intelligence*, Vol. 16, T. E. Reed and A. R. Jensen, "Conduction velocity in a brain nerve pathway of normal adults correlates with intelligence level," p. 259–272, Copyright 1992, with permission from Elsevier Science.

formance. We will see in the next section that faster NCV may make its contribution through improved processing efficiency.

Processing Efficiency

One way the brain could achieve greater efficiency is through enhanced myelination of its neurons (Jensen, 1998). Besides improving conduction speed, myelin insulates neurons from each other; this reduces "crosstalk" that would interfere with accurate processing. Humans have a greater proportion of white matter (myelinated processes) to gray matter than other animals, and IQ is related to the degree of myelination among individuals (Willerman, Schultz, Rutledge, & Bigler, 1994). In addition, myelination, speed of information processing, and intelligence all follow a curvilinear time path, increasing from childhood to maturity and then declining in old age.

Some theorists believe that short-term memory is the ultimate limitation on human reasoning and problem-solving ability. In fact, short-term memory is a better predictor of IQ than reaction time is (Miller & Vernon, 1992). Increased NCV may particularly enhance the efficiency of working memory, which is a component of short-term memory (Jensen, 1998; Vernon, 1987). Working memory has a limited capacity, and its contents decay rapidly. A person whose neurons conduct rapidly can complete manipulations and transfer information to long-term memory before decay occurs or short-term storage capacity is exceeded. But if NCV is low, the information is lost and the person must restart the process—rather like the experience of trying to solve a problem when you're not very alert, and having to review the problem over and over.

Further evidence of the role of neural efficiency in intelligence is that individuals higher in IQ use less brain energy. This was indicated by a lower rate of glucose metabolism during a challenging task, playing the computer game *Tetris* (Haier, Siegel, Tang, Abel, & Buchsbaum, 1992). And, as you can see in Figure 12.6, individuals with mild retardation (IQs between 50 and 70) require 20%

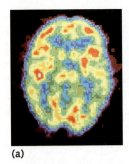 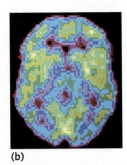

(a)   **(b)**

more neural activity to perform an attention-demanding task than do individuals with IQs of 115 or higher (Haier et al., 1995). You might think the more intelligent brain would be the more active one, but remember we're talking about efficiency.

Specific Abilities and the Brain

Brain size, speed, and efficiency can reasonably be viewed as contributors to general intelligence. Now we will consider evidence for individual components of intelligence. The statistical method called *factor analysis* has been useful in identifying possible components. The procedure involves giving a group of people several tests that measure abilities that might be related to intelligence; the tests may be intelligence tests, or they may measure more limited abilities like verbal skills or reaction time. Then correlations are calculated among all combinations of the tests to locate "clusters" of abilities that are more closely related with each other than with the others. Performance on practically all tests of cognitive ability is somewhat related, which is consistent with the hypothesis of a general factor. However, factor analysis has also identified more specific abilities from the clusters found. Three capabilities have frequently emerged over the past 50 years as major components of intelligence: *linguistic*, *logical-mathematical*, and *spatial* (Jensen, 1998).

Several authors have argued that each of the cognitive abilities depends on a complex network or module in the brain that has evolved to provide that particular function. That is, they believe that the brain is hardwired for functions like language and mathematics

Figure 12.6
Greater efficiency in the more intelligent brain
During an attention-demanding task, PET scans showed 20% more activity (indicated by more reds and yellows) in **(a)** the brain of a retarded individual than in **(b)** the brain of a person with above-average IQ.
Source: Haier et al., 1995.

Are there separate components of intelligence?

(Dehaene, 1997; Pinker, 1994). We have already seen examples of modular functions in earlier chapters. The language (linguistic) module is made up of structures located mainly in the left frontal and temporal lobes. Spatial ability depends on the interaction of somatosensory and visual functions with parietal structures, mostly in the right hemisphere.

Mathematical ability in humans depends on two distinct areas of the brain. One is in the left frontal region and the other is located in both parietal lobes (Dehaene, Spelke, Pinel, Stanescu, & Tsivkin, 1999). When individuals performed precise calculations, activity increased in the frontal language area. This apparently is the storage site of rote arithmetic facts—times tables and arithmetic facts like 4 + 5 = 9. When the research participants only estimated results, activity increased in parts of both parietal lobes. The parietal areas probably employ a visual-spatial representation of quantity, like the "number line" that mathematicians often report using, and finger counting, which is an almost universal stage in learning exact

calculation. (See Figure 12.7.) An EEG study using evoked potentials with 5-year-old children found that they use the same parietal areas as adults when estimating numbers (Temple & Posner, 1998). Studies of brain damage support these conclusions. Individuals with damage to the left frontal language area can arrange numbers in rank order and estimate results, but they cannot perform precise calculations; those with parietal damage are impaired in the opposite direction (Butterworth, 1999; Dehaene & Cohen, 1997). Presumably the frontal and parietal areas cooperate when we perform mathematical tasks.

Neither of these areas is dedicated exclusively to numerical functions. This is consistent with the suggestion in Chapter 8 that the language areas may simply use processing strategies that make them particularly suited to the demands of the task, rather than being dedicated to language processing. However, Wynn (1998) argues that the brain has a specialized mechanism for numbers by pointing to evidence that even infants and lower primates seem to have an inborn ability for estimating quantities. The infants she studied saw two objects placed one at a time behind a screen. They acted surprised—which means that they looked for a longer time—when the screen was removed to reveal three objects or only one object instead of the expected two (Wynn, 1992).

Rhesus monkeys tested in the wild responded the same way to the task (Hauser, MacNeilage, & Ware, 1996). Monkeys can also rank order groups of objects that differ in number by touching their images on a computer monitor in the correct order (Brannon & Terrace, 1998); chimpanzees have learned to do the same with numerals (Kawai & Matsuzawa, 2000). The monkeys continued to perform at the same level of accuracy when the researchers increased the number of items presented, so the monkeys had not simply memorized the stimuli. The researchers were careful to control the spatial size of the groupings, so the monkeys could not distinguish the groups according to the space they covered.

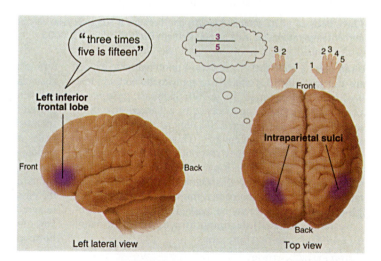

Figure 12.7
Brain locations involved in mathematical calculation
Precise calculation involved left frontal area; estimation was accompanied by activity in both parietal lobes.

Reprinted with permission from B. Butterworth, "A head for figures," *Science* 284, 928–929. Copyright 1999 American Association for the Advancement of Science.

An impartial observer would have to say that there is evidence for characteristics that contribute to an overall intelligence and for somewhat independent capabilities as well. An either-or stance is not justified at this time; it makes sense to continue the two-pronged approach of looking for biological bases for general intellectual ability and for separate capabilities.

Heredity and Environment

We saw in Chapter 1 that intelligence is the most investigated of the genetically influenced behaviors. Our progress in understanding the genetic underpinnings of intelligence hardly matches the amount of effort, however; this is because intelligence is so complex and poorly understood itself, and because many genes are involved. At the same time, environment accounts for half of the differences among us in intelligence, yet the environmental influences have themselves not been clearly identified (Plomin, 1990).

Heritability of Intelligence

Figure 12.8 shows the IQ correlations among relatives, averaged from many studies and several thousand people. You can see that IQ is more similar in people who are more closely related (Bouchard & McGue, 1981). Also, separating family members early in life does not eliminate the correlation; in fact, identical twins reared apart are more similar in IQ than fraternal twins reared together. As you learned in Chapter 1, about half of the variability in IQ is due to heredity (Plomin, 1990). That proportion is not consistent over the life span, however. It increases with age, from 20% in infancy to 40% in childhood, 50% in adolescence, and 60% in adulthood (McClearn et al., 1997). Intuition tells us that environment should progressively overtake genetic effects as a person's experience increases; instead siblings, for instance, become more alike in IQ as they age, in spite of being separated.

Not only do we know that intelligence is partially inheritable, but researchers have documented genetic influence on several of the functions that contribute to it, including working memory, processing speed, and reaction time in making a choice (Ando, Ono, & Wright, 2001; Luciano et al., 2001; Posthuma, de Geus, & Boomsma, 2001). Genetic researchers have located a form of a gene (allele) on chromosome 6 that was twice as frequent among people with IQs above 160 as among those with average IQs (Chorney et al., 1998). The gene accounts for less than 2% of

Which is more important, heredity or environment?

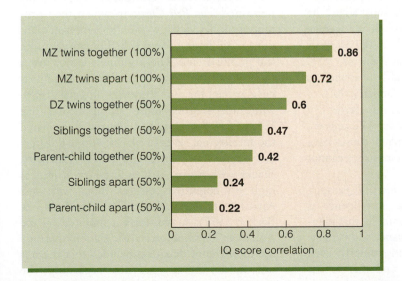

Figure 12.8
Correlations of IQ Scores Among Relatives
Percentages indicate the degree of genetic relatedness. "Together" and "apart" refer to whether related children are raised in the same household.
Source: Data from Bouchard & McGue, 1981.

the variability in IQ, so it represents only a small part of the complement of genes involved in intelligence. In a review of the literature, two researchers compiled a list of over 150 candidate genes that may influence some aspect of cognition (Morley & Montgomery, 2001). Pinning down the rest of the genes responsible for intelligence will not be easy.

The Genetic Controversy

The conclusion that intelligence is highly heritable has not been greeted with unquestioning acceptance. Critics fear that inheritance of intelligence implies that intelligence is inborn and unchangeable (Weinberg, 1989). Nothing could be farther from the truth, however; as Weinberg points out, genes do not fix behavior, but set a range within which the person may vary. By way of illustration, Neisser and colleagues (1996) point out that vocabulary size is highly heritable, but because every word in that vocabulary must be learned, the actual size of the vocabulary depends on experience. Similarly, height is about 90% heritable (Plomin, 1990), yet the average height has increased dramatically over the last few decades, due to improved nutrition. IQ is not immune to these effects. In all the world's countries that collect appropriate data, IQ scores are increasing at the rate of 5 to 25 points in a generation (Flynn, 1987). Test constructors must adjust the test norms occasionally to maintain an average of 100 points. In fact, if people tested 50 years ago were scored under today's norms, 90% would fall below 70 points and be classified as borderline mentally retarded; similarly, 90% of people tested today would score above 130 under the 50-year-old standards (Wickelgren, 1999). Although the environmental causes have not been identified, such rapid increases cannot be due to genetic changes.

Some argue that the correlation of IQ among relatives does not mean that intelligence is inherited. They suggest, for example, that identical twins' similarity in appearance and personality lead others to treat them similarly, even when they are reared apart, and this similar treatment results in similar intellectual development. Although physical features and behavior do affect how others react to a child, there is little evidence that these responses in turn influence intelligence. To test this possibility, researchers compared the IQs of twins who had been either correctly or incorrectly perceived by their parents as fraternal or identical. If similar environmental treatment accounts for IQ similarity then the parents' perception of their twins' classification should be more important than the twins' actual genetic classification. Instead, the studies showed that only the true genetic relationship influenced IQ similarity in the twins, not the parents' perception (Scarr & Carter-Saltzman, 1982).

In another controversy, a debate has raged since the 1930s over whether IQ differences between racial groups are genetically based. Group differences in IQ scores are well documented; what is not clear is whether they are genetic or environmental in origin. The substantial influence of heredity on intelligence does not mean that differences between racial groups are due to genetic differences. However, in 1969 Arthur Jensen argued that environmental and socioeconomic differences are inadequate to account for the 15-point average difference between the IQs of blacks and whites, or those of other racial groups. Two decades later Herrnstein and Murray published *The Bell Curve* in which they promoted similar views; written in layperson's language, the book brought the controversy into the public arena. The argument is not just a theoretical one. Some hereditarian extremists have argued for the inferiority of racial groups while disparaging intervention efforts like Head Start. Scarr and her colleagues compared the intellectual skills of blacks who had different degrees of white and African ancestry. Blacks with more African ancestry scored as high on cognitive tests as those with less African ancestry (Scarr, Pakstis, Katz, & Barker, 1977). A task force appointed by the American Psychological Association to study the intelligence debate concluded that there is not much direct evidence regarding the genetic hypothesis of black-white IQ differences, and what little there is does not support the hypothesis (Neisser et al., 1996).

Environmental Effects

Because we cannot fully understand the genetic basis of intelligence without recognizing its limitations, we will devote more attention than usual to research on the environmental issue. Most intelligence researchers agree that intelligence is the result of the joint contributions of genes and environment. It has been said that intelligence is 100% hereditary and 100% environmental, because both are necessary. However, it has been more difficult than expected to identify just which environmental conditions influence intelligence, other than those that cause brain damage. One of the reasons is that environmental influences are so often hopelessly confounded with genetic effects. For example, family conditions like socioeconomic level and parental education are moderately related to intelligence (Bouchard & Segal, 1985), but these characteristics also reflect the parents' genetic makeup, which they pass on to their children.

Some researchers have attempted to get around this problem by identifying specific environmental influences such as the parents' pressure on the child for achievement. The idea is that this pressure differs among the children in a family because the parents respond to the child's characteristics. Hanson (1975, pp. 478–479) emphasized this point when he reported that in his observational research,

> some children would beg and plead to be read to, while others would resist such efforts by refusing to sit still, making noise, or being generally inattentive. . . . The end result was that the measure of the environment, that is, frequency of times adults read aloud to the child, was very definitely influenced by the child's reaction to it.

However, we could easily argue that the child's acceptance of being read to reflects the child's genetic makeup. The measure suffers from just as much confounding as the ones it was intended to replace.

Another problem besides confounding is that the environmental influences are many and, apparently, weak (Jensen, 1981). In other words, the problem in identifying specific environmental effects appears to be similar to the difficulty in detecting the effect of a single weak gene. One approach that has been tried is to compare identical twins who have undergone different experiences. Surprisingly, none of the variables, including serious illness in infancy, illness in childhood, mother's attention, and birth order, was correlated with scores on the National Merit Scholarship Qualifying Test, which gives results similar to intelligence tests (Loehlin & Nichols, 1976). (For a possible exception, see "New Study Links Breastfeeding with Intelligence" on page 350.)

Results from the Head Start Program, which was designed to provide intervention at an early age, have been mixed (Royce, Darlington, & Murray, 1983). There have been long-term benefits in mathematics, educational attainment, and career accomplishments, which some could argue reflect "true" intelligence better than intelligence tests, but the average increase of 7.42 IQ points compared to controls eventually disappeared. The Abecedarian Project was an experimental preschool program that began at birth and continued support through the eighth grade. It produced IQ gains that were as strong ten years later as those in the Head Start program after two years (Ramey et al., 2000). A new Early Head Start program that begins at birth is being tested at 200 sites (Wickelgren, 1999).

Adoption has the best chance of demonstrating any environmental influences on intelligence, because it alters the entire environment for the child (Scarr and Weinberg, 1976). Adopted children's IQs are more highly correlated with the intelligence of their biological parents than with the intelligence of their adoptive parents (Scarr & Weinberg, 1976; Turkheimer, 1991). However, this does not mean that the children's IQs do not go up or down according to the adoptive environment.

IN THE NEWS

New Study Links Breastfeeding with Intelligence

It has been difficult to pin down just which environmental conditions account for the nongenetic differences among us in intelligence. Now researchers in Copenhagen, Denmark, have evidence that breastfeeding increases intelligence, even in adulthood. Studies in the past had indicated that breastfed babies did better on tests of cognitive skills and in school achievement when in high school. The Copenhagen study included over 3,200 individuals, in two separate samples; their intelligence was assessed with conventional intelligence tests when the individuals were at an average age of 19 and 27 years, respectively.

Those who were breastfed had higher IQs, and the scores increased the longer breastfeeding continued. For example, those breastfed seven to nine months had IQ scores that averaged 6.6 points higher than those who were breastfed for less than one month. The results could not be attributed to the mother's intelligence, because the researchers controlled statistically for the mother's educational level. They also controlled for a number of other possible confounding variables, including the mother's smoking during the third trimester; weight gain, height, and age during pregnancy; and marital status, as well as the infant's birth weight and complications during pregnancy and delivery.

A complete report of the research appeared in 2002 in the *Journal of the American Medical Association, 287,* pp. 2365–2371.

Results of a study in which children were adopted from impoverished homes into middle-class homes speak both to the issue of environmental effects and the question of racial differences (Scarr & Weinberg, 1976). By the age of 6, black children had increased from the 90-point average for black children in the geographic area to 106, eliminating the typical racial discrepancy. The beneficial effects still persisted a decade later (Scarr & Weinberg, 1976; Weinberg, Scarr, & Waldman, 1992). (The authors carefully avoided implying that the adopting homes were "superior," suggesting instead that their environments were "culturally relevant to the tests.")

Does this mean there was no genetic effect at all? No; in fact, the correlation between the children's IQs and their biological parents' educational levels (used in place of IQ scores) actually *increased* over the 10-year follow-up period; correlations *decreased* with their adoptive parents' educational levels (Weinberg et al., 1992). This may be difficult to understand, since the children's IQs had moved into their adoptive parents' range. However, no matter how much children's IQs change, if the *rank order* of their IQs remains about the same—and, thus, about the same as their parents'—then the correlation with their parents' intelligence remains unchanged. What does this matter, if the children's IQs change dramatically in the new environment? Because it tells us that the children's IQs are still tied to their parents' intelligence, as if by an elastic string that can stretch but nevertheless affects *how much* the IQ can change.

✔ CONCEPT CHECK

- *What are the likely neural correlates of general intelligence? of separate components of intelligence?*
- *What are the relative contributions of heredity and environment to intelligence? Why is it so difficult to identify the environmental influences?*

■ *How can adopted children's IQs increase into the range of their adoptive homes and yet be more highly correlated with their parents' intelligence? (Hint: draw a diagram, with made-up IQ scores of children from several families.)*

DISORDERS OF INTELLIGENCE

A listing of the disorders that affect intelligence would be impressively, or depressingly, long. To give you a feel for the problems that can occur in this most revered of our assets, we will look briefly at a few types of retardation, then spend more time on autism in recognition of its half-century-long challenge to neuroscientists' investigative skills. We will finish by adding a few thoughts on aging to what we have already covered in Chapter 11.

Retardation

The criteria for retardation are arbitrary, and are based on judgments about the abilities required to get along in our complex world. In 1994 the American Psychiatric Association set the criteria for retardation as a combination of an IQ below 70 points and difficulty meeting routine needs like self-care. Looking back at Figure 12.2, you can see that 2% of the population falls in this IQ range, and a lower percentage would meet both criteria. Not only is any definition arbitrary, but it is situational and cultural as well; a person considered retarded in our society might fare reasonably well in a simpler environment. The situational nature of retardation is illustrated by the fact that many individuals shed the label as they move from a childhood of academic failure into adulthood and demonstrate their ability to live independent lives.

Retardation is divided into four categories, as shown in Table 12.1. As you can see, by far the majority of the retarded fall in the mild category. Mildly retarded individuals are handicapped in functioning by knowing fewer facts and lacking strategies for solving problems and learning (Campione, Brown, & Ferrara, 1982). And, not surprisingly, they are slower at performing mental operations like retrieving information from memory.

Most cases of mild retardation have no known genetic or physical cause. Most mildly retarded individuals come from families of lower socioeconomic status and have at least one relative who is retarded (Plomin, 1989), so psychologists believe their retardation is due to a combination of environmental and hereditary causes.

About 25% of cases can be clearly attributed to one of the 200-plus physical disorders known to cause retardation (Scott & Carran, 1987). Retardation can be caused by diseases contracted during infancy like meningitis, and by prenatal exposure to viruses such as rubella (measles). As we saw in Chapter 4, maternal alcoholism is now the leading cause of mental retardation; the leading genetic causes are Down syndrome and an X chromosome defect called *fragile X syndrome.* Other causes include phenylketonuria and hydrocephalus.

What causes retardation?

3

Table 12.1 **Categories of Mental Retardation**			
Category	**IQ**	**Percentage**	**Adaptation**
Mild	50–70	85	Educable to sixth grade level; may be self-supporting as adult, with assistance.
Moderate	35–49	10	May achieve education to second-grade level, live outside institution with family, and contribute to support.
Severe	20–34	4	Verbal communication and ability to profit from vocational training are limited.
Profound	Below 20	1	Little or no speech. Requires constant care and supervision.

Figure 12.9
Chris Burke
Some Down syndrome sufferers are more fortunate than others. In spite of the disorder, Chris played a starring role in the television series *Life Goes On.*

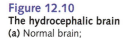

What is autism like?

4

***Down syndrome* is caused by the presence of an extra 21st chromosome, and usually results in individuals with IQs in the 40 to 55 range,** although some are less impaired (for example, see Figure 12.9). Recall that chromosome 21 contains a gene involved in early-onset Alzheimer's disease, the one that produces amyloid precursor protein (Goate et al., 1991; Murrell, Farlow, Ghetti, & Benson, 1991); like Alzheimer's patients, Down syndrome individuals have amyloid deposits in their brains.

***Phenylketonuria* is due to an inherited inability to metabolize the amino acid phenylalanine; the excess phenylalanine interferes with myelination during development.** Newborn infants are routinely tested for phenylalanine in the urine or blood, and retardation can be prevented by avoiding foods containing phenylalanine. The artificial sweetener aspartame is a familiar example of a substance that is high in phenylalanine. Without dietary treatment, the individual is severely or profoundly retarded, with an adult IQ around 20 points.

***Hydrocephalus* occurs when cerebrospinal fluid builds up in the cerebral ventricles; the increased fluid volume crowds out neural tissue, usually causing retardation** (Figure 12.10). As we saw in Chapter 3, hydrocephalus can also be treated if caught early, by installing a valve that allows the excess cerebrospinal fluid to drain from the ventri-cles. Also in that chapter, you learned that some individuals seem not to be harmed by the dramatic loss of cortex; in fact, half of the hydrocephalics whose ventricles fill 95% of the cranium have IQs over 100 (Lewin, 1980).

Autism

***Autism* is a disorder that typically includes compulsive, ritualistic behavior, impaired sociability, and mental retardation** (Frith, 1993; Frith, Morton, & Leslie, 1991). It occurs about once or twice in every 1,000 births, usually showing up between infancy and the fourth year of life (Ciaranello & Ciaranello, 1995). For decades autism was one of the most troubling of cognitive disorders. Lack of evidence for a physical cause implicated poor parenting; this along with the autistic child's social coldness and bizarre rocking, hand flapping, and head banging created an enormous burden of guilt for the parents.

The Autistic Individual

The repetitive behaviors are also characteristics of some retarded children, and about 80% of autistics are retarded; autism accounts for 86% of children with IQs below 20 and 42% of those with IQs of 20 to 49 (Frith, 1993). Whether retarded or not, autistic individuals share a common core of impairment in *communication*, *imagination*, and *socialization* (Frith, 1993). They are mute or delayed in language development,

Figure 12.10
The hydrocephalic brain
(a) Normal brain;
(b) Hydrocephalic brain. Notice the large lateral ventricles and the small amount of cortex around the perimeter in the hydrocephalic brain.

Reprinted with permission from R. Lewin, "Is your brain really necessary?" *Science, 210,* 1232–1234. Copyright 1980 American Association for the Advancement of Science.

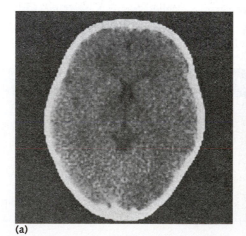

(a)

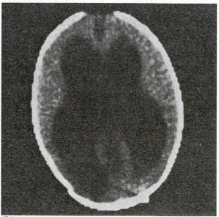

(b)

and they have trouble understanding verbal and nonverbal communication. Their difficulty with imagination shows up in an inability to pretend, or to understand make-believe situations. Their use of language is also very literal and some autistic adults have an obsessive interest in facts. These characteristics make it difficult to socialize with others, which is what sets autistic children apart the most. They usually prefer to be alone and ignore people around them (Figure 12.11). Their interaction with others often is limited to requests for things they want; they otherwise treat people as objects, sometimes even walking or climbing over them. Verbalization is usually limited, and the child often repeats what others say (echolalia).

Some researchers believe that much of the social behavior problem is that the autistic person lacks a *theory of mind,* the ability to impute mental states to oneself and to others; in other words, the autistic person cannot infer what other people are thinking. One autistic man said that people seem to have a special sense that allows them to read other people's thoughts (Rutter, 1983), and an observant autistic youth asked, "People talk to each other with their eyes. What is it that they are saying?" (Frith, 1993). In a study, children watched hand puppet Anne remove a marble from a basket where puppet Sally had placed it, and put it in a box while Sally was out of the room. On Sally's return, children were asked where she would look for the marble. Normal 4-year-olds had no problem with this task, nor did Down syndrome children with a mental age of 5 or 6. But 80% of autistic children with an average mental age of 9 answered that Sally would look in the box (Frith et al., 1991).

In spite of often severe impairments, *autistic savants* have islands of exceptional capabilities (see Figure 12.12). Some can play a tune on the piano after hearing it once, another can

5

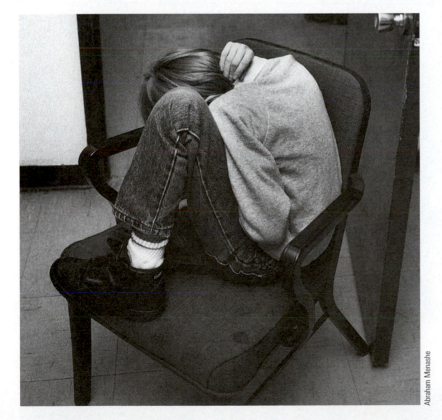

Abraham Menashe

Figure 12.11
An autistic child
Autistic individuals often are distressed by social interaction and prefer to be alone.

memorize whole books, while others take cube roots of large numbers in their heads or calculate the day of the week for any date thousands of years in the past or future. A few "ordinary" individuals can perform similar feats, but the savant's performance is typically faster, more automatic, and without insight into how it is done (Snyder & Mitchell, 1999). The savant's exceptional capability may be limited in scope, however; some who are calendar calculators cannot even add or subtract with accuracy (Sacks, 1990).

The source of the savant's enhanced ability is unknown. Dehaene (1997) suggests it is due to intensely concentrated practice, but more typically the skill appears without either practice or instruction, as in the case of a 3-year-old who began drawing animated and well-proportioned horses in perfect perspective (Selfe, 1977).

Ramachandran and Blakeslee (1998) suggest that a specialized area of the brain becomes enlarged at the expense of others. Allan Snyder and John Mitchell (1999) believe that these are capabilities within us all, and are released when the autistic loses brain centers that control executive or integrative functions. This, they say, gives the savant access to speedy lower levels of processing that are unavailable to us. But, lacking the executive functions, the savants perform poorly on apparently similar tasks that require higher-order processing. The idea gains some credibility from the case of a man impaired in his left temporal and frontal areas by dementia; in spite of limited musical training, he began composing classical music, some of which was publicly performed (Miller, Boone, Cummings, Read, & Mishkin, 2000). (Also see Figure 12.13.) Whatever the

Figure 12.12
Kim Peek, the original Rain Man
Kim was the inspiration for the role of Raymond Babbitt in the movie *Rain Man*. Kim is a true savant; he has memorized 7,600 books as well as every area code, zip code, highway, and television station in the U.S.

Ethan Hill

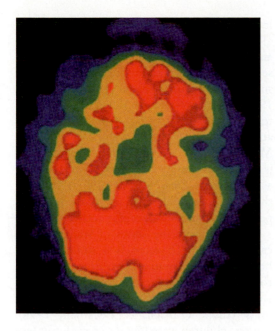

Figure 12.13
Savant-like ability following brain impairment
The scan is from a 64-year-old woman with dementia in the left frontal-temporal area. After the onset of her dementia, she began to do remarkable paintings like the one here.
Sources: Left: Courtesy of B. L. Miller. Right: B. L. Miller et al., "Emergence of artistic talent in frontotemporal dementia," *Neurology*, 51, 978–982. Copyright 1998 by the American Academy of Neurology.

explanation, the phenomenon adds to the argument that intelligence is made up of multiple and somewhat independent modules.

If savants have an island of exceptional ability, autism is an island of impairment in the *high-functioning autistic*. As an infant, Temple Grandin would stiffen and attempt to claw her way out of her affectionate mother's arms (Sacks, 1995). She was slow to develop language and social skills, and she would spend hours dribbling sand through her fingers. A speech therapist unlocked her language capability, starting a slow emergence toward a normal life. Even so, she did not develop decent language skills until the age of 6, and did not engage in pretend play until she was 8.

As an adult Grandin earned a doctorate in animal science; she teaches at Colorado State University and designs humane facilities for cattle, while lecturing all over the world on her area of expertise and on autism. Still, her theory of mind is poorly developed, and she must consciously review what she has learned to decide what others would do in a social situation. She says that she is baffled by relationships that are not centered around her work,

and that she feels like "an anthropologist on Mars."

Brain Anomalies in Autism

Autism was long thought to be purely psychological in origin, because no specific brain defects had been found. The problem was blamed on a lack of maternal bonding or a disastrous experience of rejection that caused the child to retreat into a world of aloneness (Frith, 1993). But no evidence could be found for this kind of influence; autistic children often had exemplary homes, and children with extremely negative experiences did not become autistic. The frequent association with retardation and epilepsy implied that autism was a brain disorder. Later work found subtle but widespread brain anomalies, especially in the brain stem, the cerebellum, and the temporal lobes (Happé & Frith, 1996). The location of the damage is inconsistent, which may only mean that there are various pathways to autism. The evidence is more consistent for defects in neuronal maturation, especially in the limbic system and cerebellum (Ciaranello & Ciaranello, 1995).

6

In the 1960s *thalidomide* was used as a sedative and as a treatment for morning sickness until it became apparent that the drug caused severe birth defects such as absence of limbs. The rate of autism among the offspring was around 4–5%, or about 50 times higher than in the population (Strömland, Nordin, Miller, Åkerström, & Gillberg, 1994). The critical time for exposure to thalidomide to produce autism was during the 20th to 24th days of pregnancy, which is when the neural tube is closing and the brain stem is developing (Rodier, Ingram, Tisdale, Nelson, & Romano, 1996).

Prenatal infection with rubella virus is another cause of autism (Ciaranello & Ciaranello, 1995). It is possible that viral diseases like measles trigger an autoimmune response that interferes with brain development. The vast majority of autistic children with measles and herpes antibodies also had autoantibodies that attack neurons and myelin; none of the nonautistic children with measles and herpes antibodies had brain autoantibodies (Singh, Lin, & Yang, 1998).

Biochemical Anomalies

The biological or biochemical abnormality most consistently found in autistics is elevated serotonin levels (Warren & Singh, 1996). In fact, one of the genes suspected of playing a role in autism is responsible for the mechanism involved in serotonin reuptake (Cook et al., 1997; Tordiman et al., 2001). Risperidone, an antagonist of serotonin receptors, improved several autistic symptoms in adults, but not social behavior or language (McDougle et al., 1998). Antidepressant drugs that enhance serotonin activity also improve symptoms in some autistics (Buchsbaum et al., 2001; Posey & McDougle, 2001). The fact that improvement is brought about by drugs that increase as well as decrease serotonin activity suggests that their therapeutic effect is in producing compensatory changes in receptor activity.

Another promising series of studies implicates oxytocin. *Oxytocin* **is a neuropeptide hormone and neurotransmitter, dubbed the "sociability molecule" because it affects social behavior and bonding in lower animals** (Insel, O'Brien, & Leckman, 1999). Autistic children were found to have lower levels of oxytocin than normal controls, and this difference was pronounced in the autistic children who were diagnosed as aloof (Modahl et al., 1998). Since the various symptoms of autism are somewhat independent of each other, it seems reasonable that they would have different causes. It makes sense that an oxytocin deficit would be involved in the autistic's social aversion, and that a serotonin defect would account for the compulsiveness in autistic behavior.

APPLICATION

Oxytocin as a Treatment for Autism

Eric Hollander of Mount Sinai School of Medicine in New York City believes that a lack of oxytocin activity accounts for the social aloofness of autistics. Autistics often have low levels of oxytocin in their blood, and the social behavior of mice depends on whether their oxytocin systems are functional. In addition, Holland says that the mothers of most of the autistic patients he has seen received the labor-inducing synthetic form of oxytocin, Pitocin, during delivery. He believes the Pitocin crosses the blood-brain barrier and has a negative effect on oxytocin functioning later in life.

So, he is attempting to treat social avoidance symptoms in autistics by replacing oxytocin with injections of Pitocin. In preliminary work, patients became four times as talkative, more energetic, happier, and less anxious. Repetitive behaviors were reduced as well. The problem so far is that the effects occur only while Pitocin is being injected, and Hollander has not come up with a method for continuous delivery.

Sources: *Newsweek*, May 13, 1996, p. 70; *Science*, October 5, 2001, pp. 34–37; http://www.autism-society.org/foundation/Seaver.html

Heredity and Autism

About 2–3% of the siblings of autistic children are also autistic (Folstein & Piven, 1991). This number may seem low, but it is 10–30 times higher than in the general population; it would be even higher, but parents tend to stop having children after the first autistic diagnosis. For the identical twin of an autistic the risk of autism is at least 60%. However, nonautistic relatives frequently have autistic-like cognitive and social abnormalities. When these symptoms are also considered, the concordance for identical twins jumps to 92%, compared to 10% for fraternal pairs (Bailey et al., 1995). **Milder symptoms of a disorder that do not qualify for a diagnosis are referred to as a** *spectrum disorder.* If the correlation increases when the spectrum disorders are considered in relatives along with the primary disorder, it suggests that many genes are involved, and that the symptom severity depends on how many genes the person has inherited.

Autism occurs two to four times more frequently in males than in females (Frith, 1993), which suggests that the genes for autism might be on the X chromosome. Although fragile X syndrome and autism share symptoms of gaze aversion, verbal repetition, hand flapping, and rocking (Reiss & Freund, 1992), research suggests that fragile X syndrome does not cause autism (Hallmayer et al., 1994). Also, about half of the cases of autism appear to involve male-to-male transmission, which would not occur if all the genes are on the X chromosome. There is evidence for a possible gene with small effect on chromosome X (Hallmayer et al., 1996), but other studies (reviewed by Ciaranello & Ciaranello, 1995) found evidence for major-effect genes on other chromosomes. One group of implicated genes is the *major histocompatibility complex* on chromosome 6, which plays a major role in regulating the immune system. This was no surprise, since autistic individuals often have immune deficiencies. Other promising leads point to genes on chromosomes 2, 7, and 16 (Bonora et al., 2002; Buxbaum et al., 2001;

International Molecular Genetic Study of Autism Consortium, 2001).

These findings support our suspicion that autism is caused by a variety of genes, and the combined action of several of them may be required for full-blown autism. The fact that the parents of autistic children often have similar but milder social and cognitive deficits (Folstein & Piven, 1991) was one reason for the suspicion in the early days that the parents had fostered their children's symptoms psychologically. Now we believe that each parent has just enough autism genes to produce a spectrum disorder, but the child receives enough genes from the two parents to become autistic.

Effects of Aging on Intelligence

In the previous chapter we discussed the most widely known cognitive disorder of aging, Alzheimer's disease. Here we will limit our attention to more or less normal declines in cognitive abilities that are associated with aging. Although intelligence and cognitive abilities do typically decline with age, the amount of loss has been overestimated. One reason is that people are often tested on rather meaningless tasks, like learning word lists; older people are not necessarily motivated to perform on this kind of task. When the elderly are tested on the content of meaningful material such as television shows and conversations, the decline is moderate (Kausler, 1985).

Another reason for the overestimation is that early studies were *cross sectional:* people at one age were compared with different people at another age. You have already seen from Flynn's research that more recent generations have an IQ test performance advantage over people from previous generations. When the comparison is done *longitudinally*—by following the same people through the aging process—the amount of loss diminishes (Schaie, 1994). Schaie followed 5,000 adults for 35 years. Perceptual speed dropped from age 25 on, and numeric ability dropped rather sharply after age 60. However, the other capabilities—inductive reasoning, spatial orientation,

How much capability is lost by the elderly?

verbal ability, and verbal memory—increased until middle age before declining gradually to slightly lower than their levels at age 25.

Apparently speed is particularly vulnerable during aging, and its loss turns out to be important. Schaie (1994) found that statistically removing the effects of speed from test scores significantly reduced elderly individuals' performance losses. We saw earlier that working memory is especially important to intellectual capability. A study of people ranging in age from 18 to 82 showed that speed of processing accounted for all but 1% of age-related differences in working memory (Salthouse & Babcock, 1991).

We saw earlier that brain activity is 20% greater in mildly retarded individuals during task performance than in controls, and that reading activates frontal areas in dyslexic brains that are relatively silent in others (Chapter 8). Now studies are showing that gracefully aging older individuals may be hold-ing their own at some expense, neurally speaking (Helmuth, 2002). Tasks that require one hemisphere when performed by young people activate both hemispheres in older brains (Figure 12.14). Researchers are split on whether the older person is calling up multiple strategies in solving a problem or if the aging brain loses its ability to inhibit irrelevant activity. However, the fact that the "extra" activity is highest in some elderly individuals who perform the best suggests that the other hemisphere is compensating for lost efficiency.

Some of the loss in performance is due to nonphysical causes and is reversible. One problem is that oldsters lack opportunity to use their skills. In one study, aged individuals were able to regain part of their lost ability through skills practice and many of them returned to their pre-decline levels; they still had some advantage over controls seven years later (Schaie, 1994). Elderly people also improved in memory test scores when their self-esteem

Figure 12.14
Different levels of activity in young and old brains engaged in cognitive tasks
Young individuals used one hemisphere to carry out tasks; elderly individuals used both.
Source: Courtesy of Roberto Cabeza, Duke University.

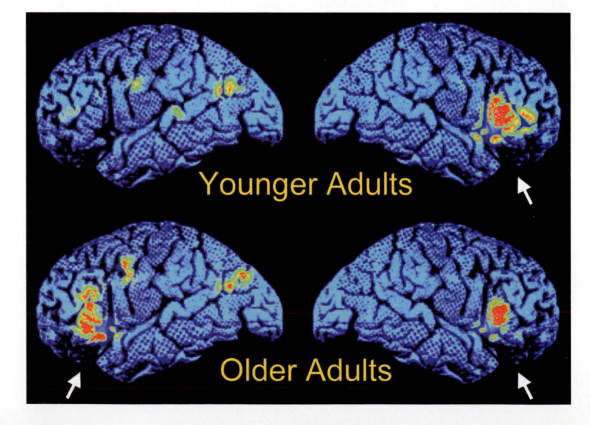

Younger Adults

Older Adults

was bolstered by presenting them with terms that depict old age in positive terms such as *wise*, *learned*, and *insightful* (Levy, 1996).

So losses are smaller than believed, and they differ across people and across skills; we cannot stereotype the older person as a person with diminished abilities. Further, evidence presented here and in the previous chapter suggests that practice, esteem enhancement, and an active lifestyle may slow cognitive decline during aging.

CONCEPT CHECK

- *Make a list of the kinds of retardation described and their causes.*
- *What neural and biochemical differences have been found in autistic brains?*

In Perspective

As important as the measurement of intelligence is in our society in determining our placement in school, our opportunity for continued education, and our employability and promotability, it is remarkable that there is still so much disagreement about what intelligence is. On the other hand, perhaps this disparity is inevitable: when the characteristic under investigation is as socially and emotionally important as intelligence, objectivity has a hard time competing with personal preferences and social biases.

This lack of agreement makes it more difficult to study the brain functions that make up intelligence. Nevertheless, we have identified several features that appear to contribute to greater mental power; brain size, neural conduction speed, processing efficiency, and short-term memory are among these. Although it would be an error to over-localize any function in the brain, we also know that some areas have a special role in important cognitive functions related to intelligence. It remains to be seen whether any particular characteristic of these areas, such as size, explains why some people have a particularly strong talent in one area, such as creative writing or mathematics. Some hope that we will eventually have objective brain measures that will tell us exactly how intelligent a person is or whether a child is autistic.

When we reach that point, perhaps another dream will be realized: the ability to diminish or even reverse some of the defects that rob the retarded, the autistic, and the aged of their capabilities. We may even be able to increase the intelligence of normal individuals. We can only hope that our capacity to make the ethical decisions required keeps pace with our ability to manipulate the human condition.

Summary

The Nature of Intelligence

- Intelligence is usually assessed with tests designed to measure academic ability.

- Some people show strong abilities not tapped by these tests; our understanding of intelligence should be broader than what tests measure.

- Intelligence theorists are divided over their emphasis on a general factor or multiple components of intelligence.

The Origins of Intelligence

- Probable contributors to general intelligence are brain size, neural conduction speed and processing speed, and processing efficiency.

- The involvement of different brain areas in different kinds of tests suggests multiple components of intelligence.

- About half of the variation in intelligence among people is due to heredity. The more

continued

genes relatives share, the more correlated are their IQs. Apparently many genes are involved; there are several leads to specific genes, but little certainty.

- The relative contribution of heredity and environment is controversial, especially when it comes to racial differences in intelligence.

- Although half of the variation in intelligence is due to environment, demonstrating which environmental conditions are important has been difficult. Judging by experience with Head Start and similar programs, any particular influence must be early and intense. Adoption can have dramatic effects if the difference in environments is large.

Disorders of Intelligence

- Retardation has many causes, including disease, fetal alcohol syndrome, Down syndrome, fragile X syndrome, phenylketonuria, and hydrocephalus.

- Down syndrome, caused by a third chromosome 21, produces mild to moderate retardation.

- Retardation due to phenylketonuria, the inability to metabolize phenylalanine, is severe to profound.

- Hydrocephalus can usually be treated to avoid serious impairment, but there are a few hydrocephalic individuals with no apparent deficiencies.

- Autism is partially hereditary, with several gene locations implicated.

- Autism may also be caused by brain damage, for example by agents like the drug thalidomide. The disorder involves abnormalities in several brain areas.

- Autism may also involve anomalies in serotonin and oxytocin functioning.

- Loss of intellectual functioning with age is less than previously believed, and like decreases in learning ability it is not inevitable. Diminished speed of processing appears to be most important.

 For Further Thought

- Environmental influences on intelligence have been hard to identify. Does this mean that we are stuck with our genetic destiny?

- Intelligence is subject to physical disorders and genetic and environmental deviations. Speculate about why intelligence is so vulnerable.

Testing Your Understanding

1. Describe the uncertainties about the measurement of intelligence and how this affects the search for biological bases of intelligence.

2. Discuss the brain characteristics that appear to contribute to general intelligence.

3. Discuss what we know about brain and biochemical differences in autistic individuals.

Select the one best answer:

1. A problem with most intelligence tests is that they:
   a. are not based on theory.
   b. are each based on a different theory.
   c. assess a limited group of abilities.
   d. try to cover too many abilities in one test.

2. Lumpers and splitters disagree on the significance of _____ in intelligence:

   a. heredity.   b. environment.
   c. the g factor.   d. early education.

3. It is likely that _____ is/are important to general intelligence.

   a. size of neurons
   b. processing speed.
   c. processing efficiency.
   d. a, b, and c.
   e. b and c.

4. Research with adults, children, chimpanzees, and monkeys suggest that we are born with:

   a. a specialized mechanism for numbers.
   b. the ability to do the same things as savants.
   c. many times more intellectual capacity than we use.
   d. time-limited abilities that inevitably deteriorate with age.

5. Research suggests that, normally, environmental effect on intelligence:

   a. is almost nonexistent.
   b. is significant, but difficult to identify.
   c. is less important than the effect of heredity.
   d. is more important than the effect of heredity.

6. Some claim the high correlation between identical twins' IQs occurs because they evoke similar treatment from people. This was refuted by a study in which the correlation:

   a. held up when the twins were reared separately.
   b. was unaffected by parents' misidentification of twins as fraternal or identical.
   c. was just as high in mixed-sex as in same-sex identical pairs.
   d. increased as the twins grew older, though they lived apart.

7. The best evidence that racial differences in intelligence are not genetic is that:

   a. the races perform the same on culture-free tests.
   b. no well-done research has shown an IQ difference.
   c. no genes for a racial difference in intelligence have been found.
   d. adoption into a more stimulating environment reduces the difference.

8. Sam has significantly reduced brain tissue, but his IQ is 105; his disorder is most likely:

   a. hydrocephalus.   b. phenylketonuria.
   c. Down syndrome.   d. fragile X syndrome.

9. Most mild retardation is believed to be caused by:

   a. an impoverished environment.
   b. brain damage sustained during birth.
   c. a combination of a large number of genes.
   d. a combination of environmental and hereditary causes.

10. Research with autism spectrum disorders suggests that autism is:

    a. caused by a single gene.
    b. caused by several genes.
    c. caused by heredity alone.
    d. primarily due to environment.

11. Impaired sociability in autistics may involve low levels of:

    a. risperidone.   b. serotonin.
    c. thalidomide.   d. oxytocin.

12. Apparently the most critical effect on intelligence during aging is loss of:

    a. speed.   b. motivation.
    c. neurons.   d. synapses.

Answers: 1. **c** 2. **c** 3. **e** 4. **a** 5. **b** 6. **b** 7. **d** 8. **a** 9. **d** 10. **b** 11. **d** 12. **a**

On the Web

1. **Stephen Hawking's Web Pages** feature a brief biography, information about his professional accomplishments, and downloadable copies of public lectures at

    http://www.hawking.org.uk

2. **The Bell Curve Flattened** is an article published in the online magazine *Slate* presenting objections to ideas about intelligence in *The Bell Curve* at

    http://slate.msn.com/?id=2416

    The Knowns and Unknowns of Intelligence is a summary of the report by an American Psychological Association task force, at

    http://www.apa.org/releases/intell.html

3. The **Association for Retarded Citizens** offers information and resources regarding retardation at

    http://TheArc.org/

    Fragile X Syndrome has numerous links to sites with information about the disorder at

    http://www.genomelink.org/fragile/

4. **Autism,** at the National Institute of Mental Health website, has a wealth of information on the disorder at

    http://www.nimh.nih.gov/publicat/autism.cfm.

Autistic Disorder provides information about autism treatment and research, and links to other sites at

http://www.mentalhealth.com/dis/p20-ch06.html

5. **A Peek Experience** is about Kim Peek, the autistic savant who was the inspiration for the main character in the movie *Rain Man.*

    http://www.bvcriarc.org/kimpeek.html

6. **Center for the Study of Autism** has information about autism and an interview with Temple Grandin, a high-functioning autistic, at

    http://www.autism.org/contents.html#temple

    Temple Grandin's Web Page features her professional work at

    http://www.grandin.com/index.html

 For additional information about the topics covered in this chapter, please look at InfoTrac College Edition, at *http://www.infotrac-college.com/wadsworth*

Try search terms you think up yourself, or use these: *autism; hydrocephalus; intelligence quotient; oxytocin.*

  On the CD-ROM: Exploring Biological Psychology

Video: Child with Autism

 For Further Reading

Frames of Mind, by Ulric Neisser (1983, Basic Books), is a collection of articles on the knowns and unknowns of intelligence. *Thinking in Pictures: And Other Reports from*

My Life with Autism, by Temple Grandin (1996, Doubleday), is Grandin's own account of her journey from severe autism to life as a high-functioning autistic.

Key Terms

autism *352*

autistic savant *353*

Down syndrome *352*

hydrocephalus *352*

intelligence *339*

intelligence quotient (IQ) *339*

oxytocin *356*

phenylketonuria *352*

spectrum disorder *357*

theory of mind *353*

Psychological Disorders

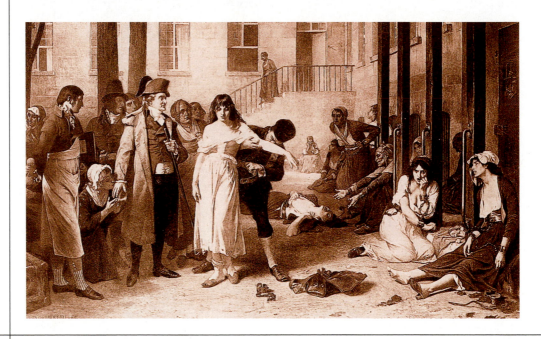

In this chapter you will learn:

- The characteristics and probable causes of schizophrenia.

- How heredity and environment interact to produce disorders.

- What the affective disorders are and their causes.

- The symptoms and causes of the anxiety disorders.

Canst thou not minister to a mind
*   diseas'd*
Pluck from the memory a rooted
*   sorrow*
Raze out the written troubles of
*   the brain*

—Shakespeare, *Macbeth*

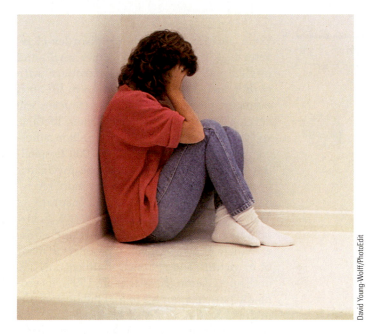

David Young-Wolff/PhotoEdit

Figure 13.1
Psychological disorders impair a person's ability to cope

Lynn Allen left her central coast home in California to drive to her twin sister's home in Capistrano Beach, near Los Angeles. Along the way she had a minor accident, which disabled her vehicle. She called a neighbor and left a message for her husband to come to Long Beach to pick her up after work. He traveled to Long Beach, but the instructions were unclear and she was not where he expected her; he searched through the night but was unable to find his wife. The following afternoon a passerby found her dead in her vehicle on a freeway off-ramp. An autopsy showed that Lynn died from an overdose of prescription antidepressants. The amount of drug in her body was not excessive enough to suggest an intentional overdose. Nevertheless, it was Lynn's depression that killed her. Alone in a disabled car at the side of a potentially dangerous freeway and with darkness approaching, she apparently felt the need for additional medication to cope with the stress. In a sense it is all the more tragic that she would lose her life to a disorder that seemed to be under control.

One reason researchers are interested in psychological disorders is that they are responsible for untold emotional suffering (Figure 13.1) and staggering financial cost. A recent population study indicated that as many as one in five people in the U.S. may experience a psychological disorder, not including drug abuse, during their lifetime (Kessler et al., 1994). So, a major benefit of the research is the development of improved therapeutic techniques. In addition, because the disorders involve malfunctions in neurotransmitter systems and brain structures, studying the disorders helps researchers understand neural functioning. In this chapter we will examine schizophrenia, mood disorders, and anxiety disorders; we will make good use of what you have recently learned about brain structure and neurotransmitter activity as we try to understand what causes these disorders and how they can be treated.

SCHIZOPHRENIA

What is schizo-phrenia, and what causes it?

Schizophrenia **is a disabling disorder characterized by perceptual, emotional, and intellectual deficits, loss of contact with reality, and inability to function in life.** It is estimated that about 3 million Americans will develop schizophrenia during their lifetime, and there are approximately 1¼ million sufferers at any one time. About 100,000 hospitalized patients take up 20% of the psychiatric beds in U.S. hospitals, with many more receiving outpatient care (National Institute of Mental Health, 1986; Roberts, 1990). Schizophrenia is particularly feared because of the extremely bizarre behavior it produces in many of its victims; and although it afflicts only 1% of the population (Kessler et al., 1994), its economic burden amounts to $20 billion annually in the U.S. (Grace, 1991). All social classes are equally vulnerable. Although patients themselves "drift" to lower socioeconomic levels, when they are classified by their parents' socioeconomic class the classes are proportionately represented (Huber, Gross, Schüttler, & Linz, 1980).

Characteristics of the Disorder

The term *schizophrenia* was coined in 1911 by the Swiss psychiatrist Eugen Bleuler (Figure 13.2) from the combination of two Greek words meaning "split mind." Contrary to popular opinion, schizophrenia has nothing to do with multiple personality; the term refers to the distortion of thought and emotion, which are "split off" from reality. The schizophrenic has some combination of hallucinations, delusions, paranoia, disordered thought, inappropriate emotions or lack of emotion, and social withdrawal. Schizophrenics are usually subdivided into diagnostic categories based on these symptoms, such as *paranoid* and *catatonic*. Which symptoms a person has varies with the specific diagnosis, and among individuals within a category. There is not complete agreement on what the true categories of schizophrenia are; European researchers use

Figure 13.2
Eugen Bleuler (1857–1939)
A pioneer in the field, he introduced the term *schizophrenia*.

other classification schemes, and several investigators have proposed additional ones. Researchers have also disagreed about whether to consider related spectrum disorders, such as *schizotypal personality* or *schizoid personality*, as a form of schizophrenia. The definition of the disorder affects conclusions about its frequency and prognosis (outcome), and makes it more difficult to determine which genes contribute to the disorder.

I'm a paranoid schizophrenic and for us life is a living hell. . . . Society is out to kill me. . . . I tried to kill my father. I went insane and thought he ruled the world before me and caused World War Two.

—Ross David Burke in *When the Music's Over: My Journey into Schizophrenia*

Schizophrenia afflicts men and women about equally often. Men usually show the first symptoms during the teens or twenties, while the onset for women usually comes about a decade later (see Figure 13.3). ***Acute**** *symptoms develop suddenly and are usually more responsive to treatment; the prognosis is reasonably good in spite of brief relapses. Symptoms that develop gradually and persist for a long time with poor prognosis are called *chronic*. Movies have overplayed the bizarre features of schizophrenia; many patients are able to function reasonably well, especially if they are fortunate enough to be among those who respond to the antipsychotic drugs. Among patients studied 20 years after their first admission, 22% were fully recovered, another 43% were improved, and the symptoms of the remaining 35% had remained the same or worsened; 56% were fully employed (Huber et al., 1980).

Doctors began to view mental illness as a medical problem in the late 1700s and early 1800s; at that time the mentally ill were literally released from their chains and given treatment (Figure 13.4) (Andreasen, 1984). By the turn of the century it was widely assumed

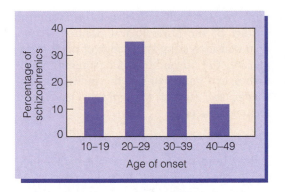

Figure 13.3
Age of risk for schizophrenia
Source: Data from Huber et al., 1980.

that schizophrenia had a physical basis. However, the search for biological causes produced little success. In the 1940s the emphasis shifted to social causes of schizophrenia, especially in America, where Freud's theory of psychoanalysis was in its ascendancy and biologically oriented psychiatrists were in the minority (Andreasen, 1984; Wender, Rosenthal, Kety, Schulsinger, & Welner, 1974). Until the 1960s, research techniques

Figure 13.4
Mental patients freed from their chains

were not up to the task of demonstrating the validity of the physiological position. It was then that increasing knowledge of neurotransmitters, the advent of brain scanning techniques, and improved genetic studies began to change the face of schizophrenia and other mental illnesses.

Heredity

Schizophrenia is familial, with a higher incidence among relatives than in the general population; as Figure 13.5 shows, this shared incidence increases with the genetic closeness of the relationship (Gottesman, McGuffin, & Farmer, 1987; Lenzenweger & Gottesman, 1994; Tsuang, Gilbertson, & Faraone, 1991). Of course, this association is as easily attributed to environmental influence as to heredity; in the 1940s the genetic school and the environmental school argued for their positions from the same data (Wender et al., 1974). However, studies of twins and adoptees provided compelling evidence for a genetic influence.

Twin and Adoption Studies

In Figure 13.5 you can see that the concordance rate for schizophrenia is three times as high in identical twins as in fraternal twins. In other words, identical twins of schizophrenics are three times as likely to be schizophrenic as the fraternal twins of schizophrenics. The heritability for schizophrenia has been estimated at between 60 and 90% (Tsuang et al., 1991). This means that 10–40% of the variability is due to environmental factors.

Information from twin adoption studies gives a more impressive indication of genetic influence; these studies show that adopting out of a schizophrenic home provides little or no protection from schizophrenia. The incidence of schizophrenia *and* schizophrenia-like symptoms was 28% among individuals adopted out of Danish homes in which there was one schizophrenic parent, compared to 10% in matched adoptees from normal homes (Lowing, Mirsky, & Pereira, 1983). Other studies have produced similar findings.

Figure 13.5
Concordances for Schizophrenia among relatives
Source: Data from Lenzenweger & Gottesman, 1994.

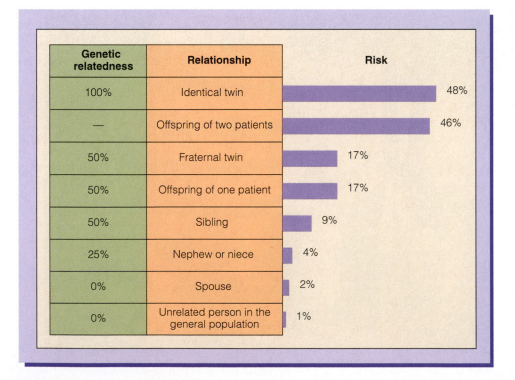

Genetic relatedness	Relationship	Risk
100%	Identical twin	48%
—	Offspring of two patients	46%
50%	Fraternal twin	17%
50%	Offspring of one patient	17%
50%	Sibling	9%
25%	Nephew or niece	4%
0%	Spouse	2%
0%	Unrelated person in the general population	1%

Discordance among identical twins has been used as an argument that schizophrenia is environmentally produced. Gottesman and Bertelsen (1989) examined the offspring of normal identical twins of schizophrenics; their schizophrenia rate was just as high as it was among the offspring of the schizophrenic twins (Figure 13.6). This result would not have occurred unless the normal twins were carrying genes for schizophrenia. It does raise the question, however, whether some environmental factors determine whether the person's schizophrenic genes will remain "silent."

The Search for the Schizophrenia Gene

After a long and discouraging search, researchers are beginning to pin down the locations of genes involved in schizophrenia. So far, locations have been found on chromosomes 1, 6, 8, 10, 13, 18, and 22 (Sawa & Snyder, 2002). Tracking down schizophrenia genes has been difficult, partly because of researchers' inconsistency in including the spectrum disorders in their diagnosis of schizophrenia (Heston, 1970; Lowing, Mirsky, & Pereira, 1983). When identical twins are discordant for schizophrenia, 54% of the nonschizophrenic twins have spectrum disorders,

mostly schizoid personality (Heston, 1970). If the spectrum disorders are due to the same genes, classifying these individuals as normal means that the genes will not appear to distinguish between schizophrenia and normality.

A person's risk of schizophrenia increases with the number of relatives who are schizophrenic and with the degree of the relatives' disability (Heston, 1970; Kendler & Robinette, 1983). This strongly suggests that schizophrenia involves the cumulative effects of multiple genes (Fowles, 1992; Tsuang et al., 1991). The fact that people can have different degrees of genetic risk for schizophrenia brings us to the concept of vulnerability.

The Vulnerability Model

Most researchers agree that both heredity and environment are needed to explain the *etiology* (causes) of schizophrenia (Zubin & Spring, 1977); genes only determine the person's vulnerability for the illness. **According to the *vulnerability model*, some threshold of causal forces must be exceeded in order for the illness to occur; environmental challenges combine with a person's genetic vulnerability to exceed that threshold.** The environmental challenges may be external,

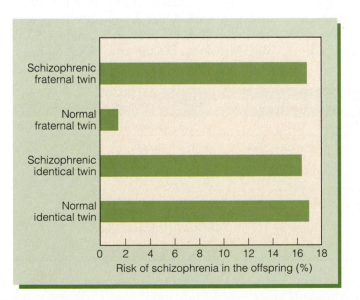

Figure 13.6
Risk of schizophrenia in the offspring of normal and schizophrenic twins
Children of the normal fraternal twin of a schizophrenic do not have an elevated risk. The children of the normal identical twin of a schizophrenic are as likely to become schizophrenic as the children of the schizophrenic identical twin.
Source: Based on data from Gottesman & Bertelsen, 1989.

such as bereavement, job difficulties, or divorce, or they may be internal, such as maturational changes, poor nutrition, infection, or toxic substances. Vulnerability is viewed as a continuum, depending on the number of affected genes inherited. At one extreme, a small percentage of individuals will become schizophrenic under the normal physical and psychological stresses of life; at the other extreme are individuals who will not become schizophrenic under any circumstance or will do so only under the severest stress, such as the trauma of battle (Fowles, 1992).

Two Kinds of Schizophrenia

Researchers disagree not only on what the subtypes of schizophrenia are but on whether schizophrenia represents one disease or many. Whatever the answers to these questions may be, most authorities do agree that the symptoms fall into two major categories: positive and negative. *Positive symptoms* **involve the presence or exaggeration of behaviors, such as delusions, hallucinations, thought disorder, and bizarre behavior.** *Negative symptoms* **are characterized by the absence or insufficiency of normal behaviors, and include lack of affect (emotion), inability to experience pleasure, lack of motivation, poverty of speech, and impaired attention.** Crow (1985) theorized that positive and negative symptoms are due to two different syndromes of schizophrenia, with different causes and different outcomes. His Type I and Type II schizophrenias are described in Table 13.1.

Research has largely supported this distinction. Positive symptoms are more often acute, so they are more likely to respond to antipsychotic drugs than negative symptoms (Fowles, 1992). Negative symptoms tend to be chronic; these patients show poorer adjustment *prior* to the onset of the disease (Andreasen, Flaum, Swayze, Tyrrell, & Arndt, 1990); poorer prognosis after diagnosis (Dollfus et al., 1996); more intellectual and other cognitive deficits, suggestive of a brain disorder (Andreasen et al., 1990); and greater reduction in brain tissue (Fowles, 1992). Because differences in drug responsiveness and presence of structural anomalies may tell us something about what causes schizophrenia, we will examine the *dopamine hypothesis* and the *neurological disorder hypothesis* next.

The Dopamine Hypothesis

Little could be done to treat psychotic patients until the mid-1950s, when a variety of antipsychotic medications arrived on the scene. For the first time in history the size of the hospitalized mental patient population went down. As is often the case in medicine, and more particularly in mental health, these new drugs had not been designed for this purpose—researchers had too little understanding of the disease to do so. Doctors tried chlorpromazine

What neurotransmitters are involved in schizophrenia?

Table 13.1 Positive Versus Negative Schizophrenia

Aspect	Type I (positive)	Type II (negative)
Characteristic symptoms	Delusions, hallucinations, etc.	Poverty of speech, lack of affect, etc.
Response to neuroleptics	Good	Poor
Symptom outcome	Potentially reversible	Irreversible?
Intellectual impairment	Absent	Sometimes present
Suggested pathological process	Increased D2 dopamine receptors	Cell loss in temporal lobe

Source: Crow, 1985.

with a wide variety of mental illnesses because it calmed surgical patients, and it helped with schizophrenics. However, it was not clear *why* chlorpromazine worked because tranquilizers have little or no usefulness in treating schizophrenia.

So investigators tried a counter approach. You will remember from Chapter 4 that chronic amphetamine use causes psychotic behavior indistinguishable from schizophrenia, complete with hallucinations and suspicious delusions. In time, researchers were able to determine that amphetamine produces these symptoms by increasing dopaminergic activity. This discovery eventually led to **the *dopamine hypothesis* that schizophrenia involves excessive dopamine activity in the brain**. Drugs that block dopamine receptors are effective in treating amphetamine psychosis *and* the positive symp-

toms of schizophrenia (Snyder, Bannerjee, Yamamura, & Greenberg, 1974). In fact, the therapeutic effectiveness of most antipsychotic drugs is directly proportional to their ability to block dopamine receptors (Seeman, Lee, Chau-Wong, & Wong, 1976). Figure 13.7 illustrates the results of one study. On the graph you can see that the most potent drug, spiroperidol, requires only a small dosage to block dopamine receptors, and that chlorpromazine, one of the least effective, requires a high dosage.

Does this mean that the blockade of dopamine (DA) receptors accounts for the improvement of schizophrenic symptoms? Not directly. Blockade occurs almost immediately, but symptom improvement usually takes two to four weeks. After a couple of weeks the firing of DA neurons drops below pretreatment levels (Davis, Kahn, Ko, & Davidson,

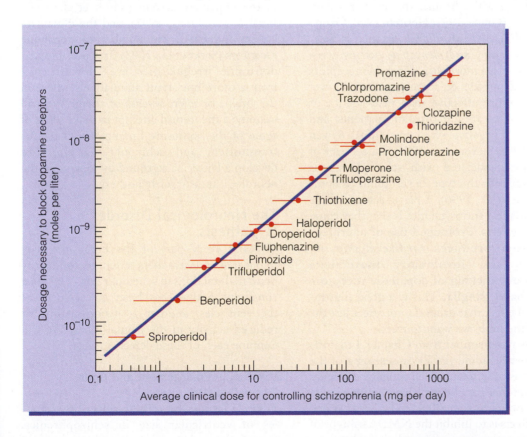

Figure 13.7
Relationship between receptor blocking and clinical effectiveness of neuroleptic drugs
The horizontal axis is the average daily doses prescribed by physicians; the horizontal red lines represent typical ranges of doses. Values on the vertical axis are amounts of the drugs required to block 50% of the dopamine receptors.

Reprinted by permission from Fig 1, p. 718 of P. Seeman, et al., "Antipsychotic drug doses and neuroleptic/dopamine receptors," *Nature*, 261, 717–719. Copyright 1976 Macmillan Publishers, Ltd.

1991). Apparently DA accumulating at the blocked synapse stimulates autoreceptors on the *presynaptic* terminals and decreases DA release. Although most *neuroleptics* (anti-dopamine drugs) reduce firing throughout the DA system, the therapeutic effect appears to be in the parts that project to the prefrontal area and limbic structures; this is the *mesolimbic dopamine system*, which you saw in Figure 4.10 in the drug chapter. We must keep in mind that neuroleptics do not cure schizophrenia, and many patients have to be maintained on the drugs the rest of their lives.

Serotonin and Glutamate

Researchers agree that the dopamine theory is overly simplistic. For one thing, not all schizophrenics show excessive DA activity, and some even appear to have a *dopamine deficiency*, especially those with chronic, treatment-resistant symptoms (Grace, 1991; Heritch, 1990; Okubo et al., 1997). *Atypical antipsychotics* such as *clozapine*, *risperidone*, and *olanzapine* occupy serotonin receptors more than dopamine receptors (Kapur, Zipursky, & Remington, 1999), yet they are more effective than neuroleptics, at least with treatment-resistant patients and those with negative symptoms (Iqbal & van Praag, 1995; Siever et al., 1991). Indeed, one of the genes associated with schizophrenia is responsible for the type 2a serotonin receptor (Williams et al., 1996). A particular advantage of the atypical antipsychotics is that they cause less side effects. **Prolonged use of neuroleptics often produces** *tardive dyskinesia,* **tremors and involuntary movements caused by blocking of dopamine receptors in the basal ganglia.** This is a good illustration of the fact that drugs do not affect just the part of the brain we want to treat.

You may remember from Chapter 4 that the drug phencyclidine (PCP) causes some of the symptoms of schizophrenia; actually, it mimics schizophrenia far better than amphetamine does (Sawa & Snyder, 2002). The fact that one of its effects is to inhibit the NMDA subtype of glutamate receptor suggested that glutamate

What brain defects have been found in schizophrenics?

might be an effective treatment for schizophrenia. It is difficult to administer glutamate to people, but the NMDA receptor can be activated by other natural ligands. One of these, *glycine*, reduced negative symptoms in schizophrenic patients (Javitt, Zylberman, Zukin, Heresco-Levy, & Lindenmayer, 1994). Other studies indicate there may be abnormalities in glutamate receptors in the hippocampus and prefrontal cortex of schizophrenics (Dracheva et al., 2001; Gao et al., 2000). So at this point we can at least say that the **glutamate theory, that reduced glutamate activity is involved in schizophrenia,** holds some promise.

This does not mean that all we have learned about the role of dopamine is incorrect. Both the serotonin and glutamate systems interact with the dopamine system; the serotonin system is one of the forces that modulate activity in the dopamine system (Smith et al., 1997; Iqbal & van Praag, 1995), and the glutamate system influences the number of dopamine receptors (Scott et al., 2002). It is possible that dopamine irregularities are "downstream" from a more important anomaly elsewhere in the brain, or even several of them. We will examine a theoretical attempt to make sense of some of the confusing findings about neurotransmitters and schizophrenia after we develop a better background by looking at the neurological disorder hypothesis.

The Neurological Disorder Hypothesis

Virtually every part of the brain has been implicated in researchers' attempts to identify brain malfunctions in schizophrenia. The most consistent finding has been enlargement of the ventricles; another is hypofrontality, or reduced activity in the frontal lobes. We will examine each of these defects in turn.

Ventricular Enlargement and Brain Tissue Deficits

Figure 13.8 illustrates the results of two studies of ventricular size in schizophrenics. Ventricular enlargement is not a cause of

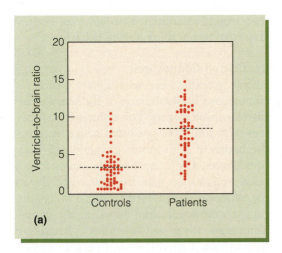

(a)

Figure 13.8
**Ventricle size in normals
and schizophrenics**
(a) Ventricle-to-brain ratios (VBR;
ventricular area divided by brain
area, multiplied by 100) of normal
controls and chronic schizophrenics. Dotted horizontal lines indicate
group means.
(b) Magnetic resonance imaging
scans of identical twins, one normal and one schizophrenic.

Sources: (a) From "Lateral cerebral ventricu-
lar enlargement in chronic schizophrenia,"
by D.R. Weinberger, et al., in *Archives of
General Psychiatry*, vol. 36, 735–739.
Copyright ©1979 American Medical
Association. Reprinted with permission.
(b) Copyright 1990 Massachusetts Medical
Society. All rights reserved.

Ventricles

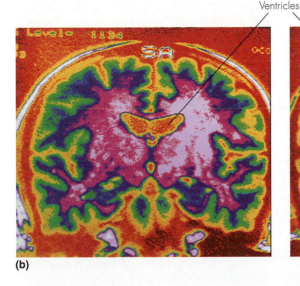
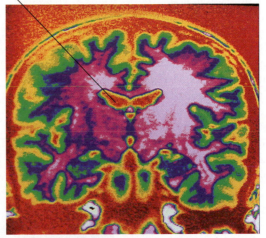

(b)

schizophrenia, but rather a marker or indicator of a deficiency in cerebral tissue—the ventricles expand to take up space normally occupied by brain cells. Several studies have found reduced cortical gray matter, reduced limbic area volume, and enlarged fissures and sulci in the brains of schizophrenics (Breier et al., 1992; Lim et al., 1996; Weinberger, Torrey, Neophytides, & Wyatt, 1979b). The deficiencies are usually subtle—on the order of less than a tablespoonful increase in ventricular volume (Suddath et al., 1989), and a 6-gram decrease in temporal lobe weight (Bogerts, Meertz, & Schönfeld-Bausch, 1985). Ventricular enlargement is not specific to schizophrenia: enlarged ventricles are also associated with old age, dementia (loss of cognitive abilities), Alzheimer's disease, and Huntington's chorea (Weinberger & Wyatt, 1983); even among schizophrenics, most have normal ventricles.

Hypofrontality

To assess frontal cortex functioning, one method we have seen is the gambling task. An alternative is the *Wisconsin Card Sorting Test,* **which requires individuals to change strategies in midstream, first sorting cards using one criterion, then changing to**

another. Many schizophrenics perform poorly on the test, persisting with the previous sorting strategy. Normal individuals show increased activation in the prefrontal area during the test; schizophrenic patients typically do not, in spite of normal activation in other areas (Weinberger, Berman, & Zec, 1986). Figure 13.9 shows a normal brain practically lighting up during the test, in comparison to the schizophrenic brain. This hypofrontality apparently involves dopamine *deficiency* in the frontal area, because administering amphetamine to schizophrenics increases blood flow in the prefrontal cortex and improves performance on the Wisconsin Card Sorting Test (Daniel et al., 1991). Most studies have implicated a particular prefrontal area, the *dorsolateral prefrontal cortex* (DLPFC) (Andreasen et al., 1992). Traumatic injury to the DLPFC causes impairments similar to the symptoms of schizophrenia: flat affect, social withdrawal, reduced intelligence and problem-solving ability, diminished motivation and work capacity, and impaired attention and concentration (Weinberger et al., 1986). Because of the frontal lobes' involvement in planning actions, recognizing the consequences of actions, and managing working memory, it is not surprising that frontal dysfunction would cause major abnormalities in thinking and behavior.

Disordered Connections

Recent attention has emphasized disordered connections between parts of the brain rather than localized lesions. This approach is consistent with findings of reduced white matter in the brains of schizophrenics (Goldman-Rakic & Selemon, 1997). An example comes from a study suggesting that hypofrontality during the Wisconsin Card Sorting Test is due to disrupted communication between the hippocampus and the prefrontal cortex (Weinberger, Berman, Suddath, & Torrey, 1992). Two hypotheses that attempt to explain the cause of hallucinations and delusions further illustrate the potential importance of malfunctioning connections.

Some researchers believe that disrupted connections between the frontal lobes and other brain areas make the schizophrenic unable to recognize the difference between sensory perceptions and internal events (memories and self-generated thoughts and images) (Frith & Dolan, 1996). Scans of schizophrenics' brains show that language areas are active during auditory hallucinations and visual areas are

Figure 13.9
Blood flow in normal and schizophrenic brains during card sorting test
The upper images are of the left and right hemispheres of a normal brain; the schizophrenic brain is below. Lighter colors represent greater blood flow and greater activity. The brains are facing left.
Source: Weinberger et al., 1986.

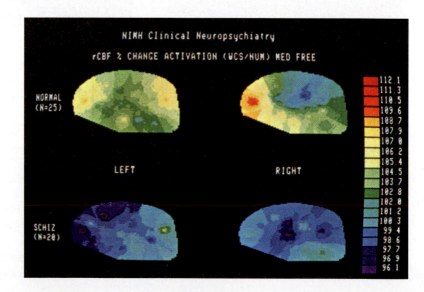

active during visual hallucinations (Figure 13.10) (McGuire, Shah, & Murray, 1993; McGuire et al., 1995; Silbersweig et al., 1995). Because these areas are activated in normal individuals when they are engaged in "inner speech" (talking to oneself) and imagining visual scenes, it appears that the hallucinating schizophrenic is not simply imagining voices and images but misperceiving self-generated thoughts.

Another problem schizophrenics have is an impairment in *auditory gating*. The evoked potential produced by a sound normally diminishes when the sound is repeated several times, but it fails to diminish in many schizophrenics. Outside the laboratory, schizophrenics have trouble suppressing ordinary sounds; traffic noise or a distant conversation not only might not be ignored but may be interpreted by the schizophrenic as threatening or directive (Leonard et al., 1996). Typical neuroleptics do not improve gating but nicotine does, by stimulating nicotinic acetylcholine receptors. Apparently one reason that 70–80% of schizophrenics smoke, versus 30% of the population (de Leon, 1996), is that schizophrenics are self-medicating their disorder. Impaired gating is attributed to reduced inhibition of the auditory pathway by the hippocampus (Leonard et al., 1996).

Causes of the Brain Defects

Many researchers think that prenatal insults are one cause of the brain defects seen in schizophrenia. A clue to their role comes from studies of discordant twins. In spite of sharing the same prenatal environment, twins do not necessarily experience the same prenatal insults (Bracha, Torrey, Gottesman, Bigelow, & Cunniff, 1992). This might explain why schizophrenic identical twins typically have larger ventricles than their healthy twins (Suddath, Christison, Torrey, Casanova, & Weinberger, 1990). Even so, these insults probably produce schizophrenia only in individuals who are already genetically vulnerable (Schulsinger et al., 1984).

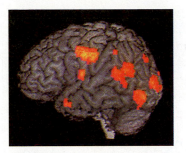

Figure 13.10
Brain activation during visual and auditory hallucinations in a schizophrenic
Reprinted by permission of *Nature*, copyright 1995.

Three prenatal factors are particularly related to the incidence of schizophrenia and the presence of brain defects. They are *birth complications*, *winter birth*, and *viral infection*. **Birth complications include premature or late birth, prolonged labor, umbilical cord around the neck, use of forceps during delivery, and others.** Birth complications are associated with enlarged ventricles later in life (Pearlson et al., 1989). **The *winter birth effect* refers to the fact that more schizophrenics are born during the winter and spring than during any other time of the year.** The effect has been replicated in a large number of studies, some with more than 50,000 schizophrenic patients as subjects (Bradbury & Miller, 1985).

However, cold weather is not the important factor in winter births (Watson, Kucala, Tilleskjor, & Jacobs, 1984). Infants born between January and May would have been in the second trimester of prenatal development in the fall or early winter, when there is a high incidence of infectious diseases. There is good evidence that the mother's exposure to *viral infections* during the fourth through sixth months of pregnancy (second trimester) increases the risk of schizophrenia. Several illnesses have been implicated, but the effect of influenza has been researched most frequently, and a higher incidence of schizophrenic births has been confirmed following influenza outbreaks in several countries. Figure 13.11 shows that the birth rate for schizophrenics was higher during the winter and spring in years of high

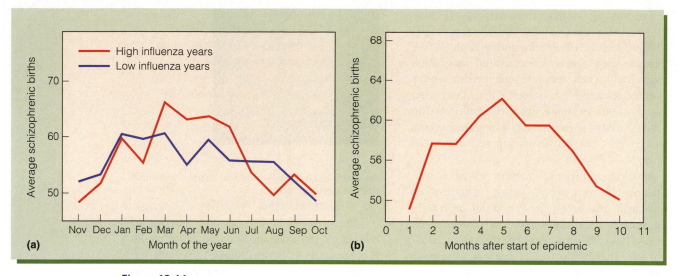

Figure 13.11
Relationship of schizophrenic births to season and influenza epidemics in England and Wales, 1939–1960
(a) Schizophrenic birth rates by month during years of high and low influenza incidence.
(b) Schizophrenic birth rate as a function of time from beginning of epidemic.

Source: From P.C. Sham, et al., "Schizophrenia following pre-natal exposure to influenza epidemics between 1939 and 1960," in *British Journal of Psychiatry*, 160, 461–466. Reprinted with permission of the publisher.

influenza infection, and that the peak birth rate for schizophrenics followed influenza epidemics.

Schizophrenia as a Developmental Disease
The defects in the brains of schizophrenics apparently occur early in life, possibly at the time of birth or before. At the time of diagnosis the brains of schizophrenics show no indication of dying neurons or inflammation, or any other signs of a progressive disease process (Weinberger, 1987). Gray matter deficit and ventricular enlargement have been found at the time of patients' first admission (Degreef et al., 1992), even in teenage patients (Schulz et al., 1983), and ventricular enlargement does not increase with time (Weinberger, 1987). In some schizophrenics' brains it appears that many neurons in the temporal and frontal lobes failed to migrate to the outer areas of the cortex during the second trimester, and are mislocated in the deeper white layers (Akbarian, Bunney, et al., 1993; Akbarian, Viñuela, et al., 1993). The hippocampus and prefrontal cortex of schizophrenics are 30–50% deficient in Reelin, a protein that

functions as a stop factor for migrating neurons (Fatemi, Earle, & McMenomy, 2000; Guidotti et al., 2000). These observations and the association of schizophrenia with birth trauma and prenatal viral infection all argue for early, nonprogressive damage to the brain *or* a disruption of development.

However, the conclusion that the brain defects occur early in life presents a serious problem, because schizophrenia rarely develops before adolescence or young adulthood. The following theory is an attempt to deal with this issue and others that have troubled researchers.

An Integrative Theory
The distinction between positive and negative symptoms has been a useful guiding concept as we examined the literature on schizophrenia, but it implies a misleading separation of patients into two distinct groups. Typically, a patient is hospitalized in a florid (literally, lively) state mostly characterized by positive symptoms, which may give way over time to the more subdued and withdrawn state of neg-

ative symptoms. If it is true that positive symptoms are caused by excess dopaminergic activity and negative symptoms are caused by brain tissue deficits, it is difficult to understand why both kinds of symptoms would be found in the same patient. One theory suggests that frontal lobe dysfunction and dopamine hyperactivity are related rather than independent of each other.

There is evidence that the prefrontal cortex controls a tonic, or continuous, release of dopamine in subcortical areas. Weinberger (1987) suggests that prefrontal dopamine mechanisms manage psychological stress by regulating this subcortical dopamine release. According to the theory, prefrontal cortical dysfunction causes a *decrease* in tonic DA release. The brain compensates by increasing the number of dopamine receptors in the subcortical area, making the neurons more responsive to DA (Davis et al., 1991; Grace, 1991). Adolescence and young adulthood are critical periods because the prefrontal area is undergoing myelination and completing connections with other areas, including temporal limbic areas, and these connections appear to be important in the regulation of subcortical dopaminergic activity (Weinberger & Lipska, 1995). In the person vulnerable to schizophrenia, the connections are improperly carried out, and bad connections can be worse than no connection. The prefrontal area is unable to control subcortical DA release; the response to any stress is a massive, uncontrolled release of DA onto receptors that have already been made supersensitive. As we all know, this period in development is also a time of heightened stress. Previously subtle behavioral abnormalities become more pronounced and positive symptoms appear.

Advancing age brings a normal decrease in dopaminergic activity both in the cortex and subcortically. The decrease in subcortical DA activity results in waning positive symptoms; but decreasing prefrontal DA activity means increasing negative symptoms (Weinberger, 1987). Thus, florid positive symptoms give way to negative symptoms and the withdrawal and apathy of the chronic schizophrenic.

The theory has a reasonable amount of support. The hereditary disease *metachromatic leukodystrophy* impairs the development of connections within the cortex; it often produces a schizophrenia-like illness complete with hallucinations, disordered thinking, and bizarre behavior, but only when the illness appears during adolescence (Weinberger & Lipska, 1995). Similarly, hippocampal lesions in infant rats produce increased reactivity to stress, but not until after puberty. The effect is apparently due to enhanced dopamine activity, because the overreactivity can be eliminated by the antidopaminergic drug *haloperidol* (Lipska, Jaskiw, & Weinberger, 1993). In addition, early brain trauma, temporal lobe epilepsy, and Huntington's disease can cause psychosis, but symptoms often do not appear until adolescence (Weinberger, 1987).

One test of a theory is how well it can explain the known facts. This theory does well on that score. It explains the timing of symptom onset and the progression of symptoms over the course of illness. It also explains why some schizophrenics have dopamine deficits, and why in some patients DA agonists like amphetamine can improve some psychotic symptoms and Wisconsin Card Sorting Test performance (Daniel et al., 1991; Davidson et al., 1990). Weinberger has modified his theory recently, suggesting that the major effect of antipsychotic drugs is in modifying gene expression in the nucleus accumbens in a way that improves neural traffic between prefrontal cortex and temporal limbic sites (Weinberger & Lipska, 1995). Of course, the theory may not be correct, and it does fail to account for the involvement of serotonin or glutamate. This would not be the first time, as Thomas Huxley said, that a beautiful hypothesis was slain by an ugly fact. But this is a good illustration of a theory doing exactly what it should: making sense of diverse research findings in a way that provides a guide for further research.

✔ **CONCEPT CHECK**

- *What is the interplay between heredity and environment in schizophrenia?*
- *Describe the two kinds of schizophrenia.*
- *How are dopamine irregularities and brain deficits proposed to interact?*

AFFECTIVE DISORDERS

What are the affective disorders?

The affective disorders include *depression* and *mania*. Almost all of us occasionally experience *depression, an intense feeling of sadness*; we feel depressed over grades, a bad relationship, or loss of a loved one. While this *reactive* depression can be severe, major depression goes beyond the normal reaction to life's challenges. In *major depression* a person often feels sad to the point of hopelessness for weeks at a time, loses the ability to enjoy life, relationships, and sex, and experiences loss of energy and appetite, slowness of thought, and sleep disturbance; in some cases the person is also agitated or restless. Major depression can occur for no apparent reason, when there is no excessive stress in the person's life. *Mania* involves excess energy and confidence that often lead to grandiose schemes; decreased need for sleep, increased sexual drive, and abuse of drugs are common.

Depression may appear alone as *unipolar depression*, or depression and mania may occur together in bipolar disorder. In *bipolar disorder, the individual alternates between periods of depression and mania*; mania can occur without periods of depression, but this is rare. Bipolar patients often show psychotic symptoms such as delusions, hallucinations, paranoia, or bizarre behavior. Two quotes provide some insight into the disorders from the patients' own perspectives (National Institute of Mental Health, 1986):

> Depression: *I doubt completely my ability to do anything well. It seems as though my mind has slowed down and burned out to the point of being virtually useless . . . [I am] haunt[ed] . . . with the total, the desperate hopelessness of it all. . . . If I can't feel, move, think, or care, then what on earth is the point?*
>
> Mania: *At first when I'm high, it's tremendous . . . ideas are fast . . . like shooting stars you follow until brighter ones appear . . . all shyness disappears, the right words and gestures are suddenly there. . . . Sensuality is pervasive, the desire to seduce and be seduced is irresistible. Your marrow is infused with unbelievable feelings of ease, power, well-being, omnipotence, euphoria . . . you can do anything . . . but, somewhere this changes.*

Women are two to three times more likely than men to suffer from unipolar depression during their lifetime: 5–9% versus 3–4%; bipolar illness occurs in 0.65–0.88% of both sexes (Gershon, Bunney, Leckman, Van Eerdewegh, & DeBauche, 1976; Gold, Goodwin, & Chrousos, 1988). The risk for major depression increases with age in men, whereas women experience their peak risk between the ages of 35 and 45; the period of greatest risk for bipolar disorder is in the early 20s to around the age of 30.

Heredity

As with schizophrenia, there is strong evidence that affective disorders are partially inheritable. Relatives of patients have an increased incidence of affective disorders. When one identical twin has an affective disorder, the probability the other twin will have the illness as well is about 69%, compared to 13% in fraternal twins (Gershon et al., 1976). Lack of complete concordance in identical twins indicates that there is an environmental contribution. However, the concordance rate drops surprisingly little when identical twins are reared apart (Price, 1968), which may mean that the most important environmental influences occur in the prenatal period or shortly after. There is good reason to believe that bipolar and unipolar disorder are genetically independent of each other (Gold et al., 1988; Moldin et al., 1991).

The search for the genes involved in the affective disorders has been less encouraging than the search for the schizophrenic gene, with the studies failing to produce consistent candidates (Moldin et al., 1991). Interest as well as hopefulness have increased recently as researchers have switched to looking for multiple genes instead of a single gene.

The Monoamine Hypothesis of Depression

The first effective treatment for depression was discovered accidentally, and theory again followed practice rather than the other way around. *Iproniazid* was introduced as a treatment for tuberculosis, but it was soon discovered that the drug produced elevation of mood (Crane, 1957) and was an effective antidepressant (Schildkraut, 1965). Iproniazid was later abandoned as an antidepressant because of its side effects, but its ability to increase activity at the monoamine receptors led researchers to the *monoamine hypothesis* that depression involves reduced activity at norepinephrine and serotonin synapses. You will remember that the monoamines include norepinephrine, dopamine, and serotonin. However, because dopamine agonists such as amphetamine produced inconsistent therapeutic results, researchers have limited their interest to norepinephrine and serotonin.

We now know that all the effective antidepressant drugs increase the activity of norepinephrine or serotonin, or both, at the synapses. They do this in different ways. Some block the destruction of excess monoamines in the terminal button (*monoamine oxidase inhibitors*), while others block reuptake at the synapse (*tricyclic antidepressants*). *Second-generation* antidepressants affect a single neurotransmitter; for instance, Prozac (fluoxetine) inhibits reuptake of serotonin. Symptom improvement usually takes weeks, suggesting that receptor changes are involved (see "Brain Waves Forecast Antidepressant Effect").

What is the monoamine hypothesis?

2

Brain Waves Forecast Antidepressant Effect

IN THE NEWS

Up to 40% of depressed patients do not respond to the first medication they try, but they have to wait 6 to 12 weeks to find out. While they wait they continue to suffer and some run the risk of suicide. New research at the Neuropsychiatric Institute at the University of California at Los Angeles promises to cut the period to a couple of days.

Under the direction of Dr. Ian A. Cook, the researchers used a technique called *quantitative EEG* to assess changes in the frontal lobes during treatment with the antidepressant fluoxetine, the antidepressant venlafaxine, or placebo. Thirteen of 25 patients responded to the medication. The patients who improved showed changes in brain wave activity at 48 hours and one week, although their symptoms did not begin to decrease until after four weeks. At the end of eight weeks, patients with the greatest EEG changes also had the most complete response to medication.

Other researchers have shown brain changes following treatment, but according to Cook this is the first study that has found changes that can usefully predict clinical improvement. This technique, once it is simplified enough to be used by physicians, could reduce the patient's trial period with a drug from weeks to days.

—Adapted from a story by Dan Page, UCLA News Bureau (http://newsroom.ucla.edu/Docs/3255.htm). The research report appeared in the journal Neuropsychopharmacology *(2002), 27, pp. 120–131.*

Additional evidence to support the monoamine hypothesis is that serotonin and norepinephrine are involved in behaviors that are disturbed in affective disorders. Serotonin plays a role in mood, activity level, sleep and daily rhythms, feeding behavior, sexual activity, body temperature regulation, and cognitive function (Meltzer, 1990; Siever et al., 1991). Because the noradrenergic system is involved in responsiveness and sensitivity to the environment, reduced norepinephrine activity may be involved in the depressed individual's vegetative symptoms, lack of goal-directed behavior, and lack of responsiveness to environmental change (Siever et al., 1991).

Besides increasing norepinephrine or serotonin activity, most antidepressants also *decrease* the sensitivity of a particular receptor for norepinephrine, the β-noradrenergic receptor (Sulser & Sanders-Bush, 1989). If this seems to contradict the monoamine hypothesis, remember that there are several kinds of norepinephrine receptors. At the same time, it is true that some depressed people are agitated and may experience a painful arousal, which is consistent with increased norepinephrine activity. When we look at brain anomalies later in this chapter we will see further evidence of activation as well as inhibition of brain activity.

A non-nicotine ingredient in tobacco smoke has been found to act as a monoamine oxidase inhibitor. This would explain why smoking is so frequent among depressives and why they have particular difficulty giving up smoking (Fowler et al., 1996). I mention a therapeutic effect of smoking for the second time only to illustrate again how people may self-medicate without being aware they are doing it; if it sounds like the benefits of smoking outweigh the cost to the smoker's health, you should reread the section on nicotine in Chapter 4.

Bipolar Disorder

The mystery of major depression is far from solved, but bipolar disorder is even more puzzling. Bipolar patients vary greatly in their symptoms: the depressive cycle usually lasts longer than mania, but either may predominate. Some patients cycle between depression and mania regularly, whereas others are unpredictable; cycles usually vary from weeks to months in duration, while some patients switch as frequently as every 48 hours (Bunney, Murphy, Goodwin, & Borge, 1972). Stress often precipitates the transition from depression into mania, followed by a more spontaneous change back to depression; the prospect of discharge from the hospital is particularly stressful and often will precipitate the switch into mania. However, as bipolar disorder progresses, manic episodes tend to become independent of life's stresses (Gold et al., 1988).

The neurotransmitter disorder in bipolar illness is not well understood. *Lithium,* **a metal administered in the form of lithium carbonate, is the medication of choice for bipolar illness**; it is most effective during the manic phase, but it also prevents further depressive episodes. Examination of lithium's effects has not led to an explanation of bipolar illness, partly because lithium affects several neurotransmitter systems (Worley, Heller, Snyder, & Baraban, 1988). Lithium most likely stabilizes neurotransmitter and receptor systems to prevent the large swings seen in manic-depressive cycling. The fact that lithium also has some effectiveness as an antidepressant argues for a normalizing effect rather than a specific, directional effect on transmitters or receptors (Gitlin & Altshuler, 1997).

Electroconvulsive Therapy

Electroconvulsive therapy (ECT) **involves applying 70 to 130 volts of electricity to the head of a lightly anesthetized patient, which produces a grand mal seizure, characterized by contractions of the neck and limbs and lasting about a half minute to a minute.** (See Figure 13.12.) Without the seizure activity in the brain that produces the convulsions, the treatment does not work. Within a few minutes the patient is conscious and coherent, though perhaps a bit confused; the patient does not remember the experience.

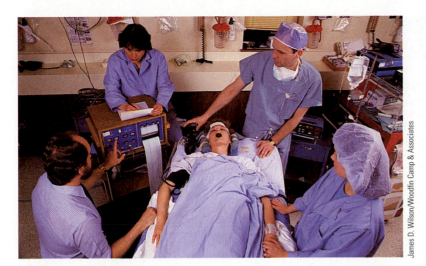

James D. Wilson/Woodfin Camp & Associates

Figure 13.12
A patient being readied for electroconvulsive therapy

About six or eight treatments are usually given over three or four weeks.

Electroconvulsive therapy is the most controversial of the psychiatric therapies. You are probably wondering what would lead doctors to try such a strange form of treatment in the first place. The answer is that they noticed that schizophrenics who also suffered from epilepsy improved after a seizure (Fink, 1984). Although convulsive therapy was effective with schizophrenic patients, when the more easily administered antipsychotic drugs began to arrive on the psychiatric scene in 1953 they replaced electroconvulsive therapy treatment for schizophrenia (Fink, 1978).

Though it is used as a therapy of last resort, ECT is more effective with depression than are antidepressant drugs (Fink, 1984) and as effective as lithium in treating mania (Schou, 1959). In different studies its success rate has varied from 60 to 90% (Fink, 1977). Besides sometimes working when drugs fail, ECT has the advantage of providing more rapid relief, often beginning with the first couple of treatments. This time advantage and greater effectiveness are particularly beneficial for suicidal patients; suicide attempts are 80% lower in patients treated with ECT than in patients treated with antidepressants (Avery & Winokur, 1978). The disadvantage for ECT is that its benefit is often short term, but the patient can usually be maintained on drug therapy once a round of ECT has been completed. In spite of ECT's effectiveness, drugs are the treatment of first resort and are relied on exclusively if they are effective.

ECT produces a large number of changes in the nervous system, and it is unclear which ones account for its therapeutic effects and its superiority over antidepressant drugs. Like the drugs, ECT increases the sensitivity of postsynaptic serotonin receptors (Mann, Arango, & Underwood, 1990), and decreases the sensitivity of β-noradrenergic receptors (Sulser & Sanders-Bush, 1989). A temporary slowing of the EEG, which is correlated with therapeutic effectiveness, suggests that ECT synchronizes neuronal firing over large areas of the brain (Sackeim et al., 1996). ECT also causes brief but dramatic increases in norepinephrine levels (Goffen, 1984). The fact that ECT is effective with depression, mania, and schizophrenia is indicative of how complex its effects are. (For information about a new form of electrical treatment, see the accompanying Application.)

Rhythms and Affective Disorders

Depressed people often have problems with their biological rhythms. The *circadian rhythm*—the one that is a day in length—

What are the roles of daily rhythms and seasons?

APPLICATION

Magnetic Stimulation as a Therapeutic Tool

A pulse of energy from an electromagnetic field (*transcranial magnetic stimulation, TMS*) is often used to disrupt brain activity; this produces a very brief "lesion" a few centimeters under the magnetic coil that allows researchers to determine the function of that area of the brain (see Chapter 3 for an example, and the figure here). Repeated pulses (*rTMS*) can also be used to find out what different parts of the brain do, but the effects of stimulation last longer. At rates of 1–5 Hz, *slow* rTMS depresses brain activity; *rapid* rTMS, at rates above 5 Hz, produce excitation (Hallett, 2000; Helmuth, 2001).

Repeated TMS is finding its way into experimental therapies for a variety of disorders from Parkinson's disease to major depression. In medication-resistant patients, rapid rTMS reduces depression when it is administered over the left prefrontal area daily for a period of two to four weeks (George et al., 1995; Triggs et al., 1999).

Interest in the left prefrontal cortex is consistent with studies that indicate the left hemisphere is more important than the right in depression; however, one study found slow rTMS was effective in the right prefrontal cortex (Klein et al., 1999). Canada's Health Ministry has approved rTMS as a treatment for major depression, and the U.S. Food and Drug Administration is considering the same move (Helmuth, 2001). Some see rTMS as an alternative to ECT, but it remains to be seen just how well it compares to other treatments and how long the benefits can last.

Repetitive TMS may benefit schizophrenic patients as well. Although fewer studies have been done, rTMS over the left temporal area has reduced auditory hallucinations (d'Alfonso et al., 2002) and stimulation aimed at the dorsolateral prefrontal cortex has reduced anxiety and restlessness (Feinsod, Kreinin, Chistyakov, & Klein, 1998).

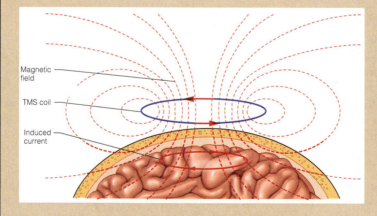

Transcranial Magnetic Stimulation
When the electromagnetic coil is held over the scalp, it induces an electrical current in the brain tissue below.

Reprinted with permission from L. Helmuth, "Boosting brain activity from the outside in." Science, 292, 1284–1286. Copyright 2001 American Association for the Advancement of Science.

Labels on figure: Magnetic field, TMS coil, Induced current

---

tends to be phase advanced in affective disorder patients; this means that the person feels sleepy early in the evening and then wakes up in the early morning hours, regardless of the previous evening's bedtime (Dew et al., 1996). The person also enters REM sleep earlier in the night and spends more time in REM sleep than normal (Kupfer, 1976). **REM, or *rapid eye movement* sleep is the stage of sleep during which**

dreaming occurs; the excess REM sleep is at the expense of the other stages of sleep. (The topic of sleep is covered in the final chapter of this book.) Unipolar depressed patients share this early onset of REM sleep with 70% of their relatives, and depression is three times as frequent in relatives with reduced REM latency compared to relatives without reduced latency (Giles, Biggs, Rush, & Roffwarg, 1988).

Circadian Rhythms and Antidepressant Therapy

Some patients who are unresponsive to medication can get relief from their depression by readjusting their circadian rhythm. They do this by initially following their atypical rhythm—say, by going to bed at 6 P.M. and waking at 2 A.M. Then the person shifts to a normal sleep schedule by delaying sleep a half hour later each night. In some patients this treatment results in a relief from depression that lasts for months (Sack, Nurnberger, Rosenthal, Ashburn, & Wehr, 1985).

Some depressed patients also benefit from a reduction in REM sleep (Wu & Bunney, 1990). This is accomplished by monitoring the person's EEG and waking the person every time the EEG indicates that sleep has moved into the REM stage. Interestingly, most drugs that act as antidepressants also suppress REM sleep (Vogel, Buffenstein, Minter, & Hennessey, 1990). Why reducing REM sleep would alleviate depression is a mystery. But before we assume that this research points to a totally different mechanism for producing depression, we should ask whether REM sleep is somehow linked to what we already know about depression. As it turns out, both serotonin and norepinephrine inhibit REM sleep.

Seasonal Affective Disorder

There is another rhythm that is important in affective disorders; **some people's depression rises and falls with the seasons and is known as *seasonal affective disorder (SAD)*.** Most SAD patients are more depressed during the fall and winter, then improve in the spring and summer. Others are more depressed in the summer and feel better during the winter. Members of either group may experience a mild mania-like activation called hypomania during their "good" season. While depressed, they usually sleep excessively and they often have increased appetites, especially for carbohydrates, and gain weight. The length of day and the amount of natural light appear to be important in winter depression; symptoms improve when the patient travels farther south (or north, if the person lives in the Southern Hemisphere) even for a few days, and some report increased depression during cloudy periods in the summer or when they move to an office with fewer windows. Summer depression appears to be temperature related: traveling to a cooler climate, spending time in an air-conditioned house, and taking several cold showers a day improve the symptoms. About 10% of all cases of affective disorder are seasonal, and 71% of SAD patients are women (Faedda et al., 1993). Although seasonal influences on affective disorder have been known for 2,000 years and documented since the mid-1850s, summer depression has received relatively little attention, so we will restrict our discussion to winter depression.

A treatment for winter depression is ***phototherapy*—having the patient sit in front of high-intensity lights for a couple of hours or more a day** (Figure 13.13). Patients begin to respond after two to four days of treatment with light that approximates sunlight from a window on a clear spring day; they relapse in about the same amount of time following withdrawal of treatment (Rosenthal et al., 1985). Early researchers thought phototherapy worked because early morning and nighttime phototherapy extended the shortened winter day. However, the fact that midday phototherapy is also effective convinced them that the increased amount of light is more important

4

Dan McCoy/Rainbow

Figure 13.13
A woman uses a high-intensity light to treat her seasonal affective disorder

than extending the length of the photoperiod; they support their conclusion with the observation that suicide rate is related to a locale's *amount* of clear sunlight rather than the number of hours of daylight (Wehr et al., 1986). Phototherapy apparently works by resetting the circadian rhythm (Lewy, Sack, Miller, & Hoban, 1987), so it is also helpful with circadian rhythm problems like jet lag, delayed sleep syndrome, and difficulties associated with shift work (Blehar & Rosenthal, 1989).

Lowered serotonin activity is involved in winter depression. Drugs that increase serotonin activity alleviate the depression and reduce carbohydrate craving (O'Rourke, Wurtman, Wurtman, Chebli, & Gleason, 1989). As we saw in Chapter 5, eating carbohydrates increases brain serotonin levels. So, rather than thinking that SAD patients lack willpower when they binge on junk food and gain weight, it might be more accurate to think of them as self-medicating with carbohydrates.

Brain Anomalies in Affective Disorder

What brain irregularities are involved?

The search for structural brain defects has been less rewarding in affective disorder than with schizophrenia. About half the studies of ventricle size and cortical atrophy have found no difference, and differences were small in the studies that did have positive results (Depue & Iacono, 1989). Researchers have more consistently found altered metabolism and blood flow in the brains of affective disorder patients.

Not surprisingly, activity is reduced in the brains of unipolar patients (Sackeim et al., 1990) and bipolar patients when they are depressed (Baxter et al., 1985). Activity is particularly decreased in the *caudate nucleus* and the *dorsolateral prefrontal cortex* in both groups (Baxter et al., 1985; Baxter et al., 1989; Drevets et al., 1992). The lowered activity in the DLPFC led to the suggestion that the onset of depression in adulthood, like schizophrenia, might be due to the late development of the DLPFC (Baxter et al., 1989). See Figure 13.14 for PET scans of these areas.

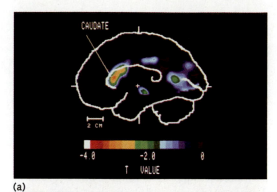

(a)

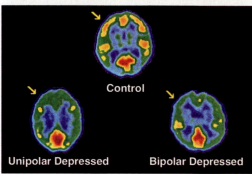

(b)

Figure 13.14
Decreased frontal activity in depression
Blood flow was decreased **(a)** in the caudate nucleus and **(b)** in the dorsolateral prefrontal cortex (where the arrows point). The color scale is reversed in the scan in **(a)**; yellow and red in that image indicate *decreased* activity.
Sources: (a) Drevets et al., copyright 1992 by the Society for Neuroscience; (b) Baxter et al., 1989.

What is surprising *is* that some areas are *more* active in depressed patients. In unipolar depression, blood flow is higher in the amygdala and a frontal area connected to the amygdala called the *ventral prefrontal cortex* (Figure 13.15). The ventral prefrontal area may also be a "depression switch," because activation comes and goes with bouts of depression. The amygdala continues to be active between episodes and returns to normal only after the remission of symptoms; it may indicate the *trait* as opposed to the *state* of depression (Drevets et al., 1992; Drevets & Raichle, 1995).

It is also not surprising that when the bipolar patient begins a manic episode, brain metabolism increases from its depressed level by 4–36% (Figure 13.16) (Baxter et al., 1985).

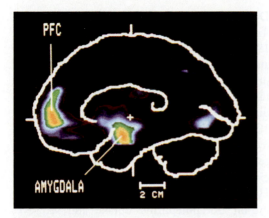

Figure 13.15
Increased activity in the ventral prefrontal cortex and amygdala in depression
Source: Drevets et al., copyright 1992 by the Society for Neuroscience.

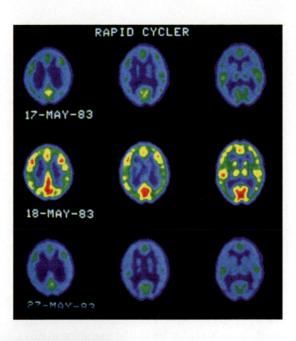

Figure 13.16
Glucose metabolism increase during mania in a rapid-cycling bipolar patient
The three images across the middle are from a scan done during a manic period.
Source: Baxter et al., 1985.

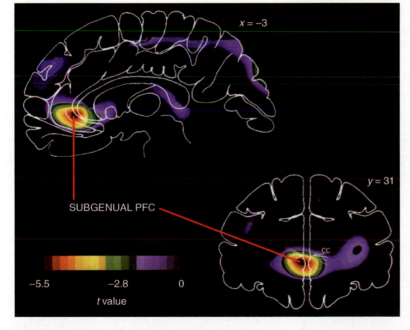

Figure 13.17
The subgenual prefrontal cortex
Activity is decreased during depression (dark areas in the middle of the light areas) but increased during mania.
Reprinted by permission of *Nature*, copyright 1997.

The *subgenual prefrontal cortex* is particularly interesting because it has been suggested as a possible "switch" controlling bipolar cycling (Figure 13.17). Its metabolic activity is reduced during both unipolar and bipolar depression, but increases during manic episodes (Drevets et al., 1997). The structure is in a good position to act as a bipolar switch, because it has extensive connections to emotion centers such as the amygdala and the lateral hypothalamus, and it helps regulate neurotransmitters involved in affective disorders.

Suicide

Suicide is a serious concern in affective disorders; before antidepressant drugs became available an estimated 15–30% of people with major depression committed suicide (Gold et al., 1988). Figure 13.18 compares the suicide rates for three disorders with that of the general population; as you can see, individuals with affective disorders are the most vulnerable. Bipolar patients are most at risk, with a 25–48% attempt rate and a completion rate 7.5 times higher than in unipolars (Gershon & Soares, 1997).

Psychiatric patients who attempt suicide have lower levels of the serotonin metabolite 5-HIAA, which means that their serotonin activity is decreased. When a group of patients at risk for suicide was followed for one year, 20% of those who were below the group median in 5-HIAA level had committed suicide; none of the patients above the median had (Träskman, Åsberg, Bertilsson, & Sjöstrand, 1981). Other studies have confirmed the association between lowered serotonin and suicidality (Mann et al., 1990; Roy,

DeJong, & Linnoila, 1989; Stanley, Stanley, Traskman-Bendz, Mann, & Meyendorff, 1986). Lowered 5-HIAA is found in suicide attempters with a variety of disorders, and probably reflects impulsiveness and aggression rather than the patient's specific psychiatric diagnosis (Mann et al., 1990; Stanley et al., 1986; Träskman et al., 1981). A selective serotonin reuptake inhibitor has shown promise in reducing suicide attempts in nondepressed suicide-prone patients (Verkes et al., 1998). However, antidepressants that selectively inhibit norepinephrine uptake and sedatives such as barbiturates and benzodiazepines may actually increase the risk of suicide. It is believed they do so by increasing drive or by disinhibiting behavior without adequately relieving depression, so the person is able to turn suicidal thoughts into suicidal actions (Feuerstein & Jackisch, 1986).

✔ CONCEPT CHECK

- *State the monoamine hypothesis; what is the evidence for it?*
- *How is affective disorder related to circadian rhythms?*
- *What brain differences are involved in the affective disorders?*

ANXIETY DISORDERS

Anxiety disorders include several illnesses. The major ones—generalized anxiety, phobia, panic disorder, and obsessive-compulsive disorder—have lifetime risks of about 5%, 8–9%, 1.5%, and 2–3%, respectively (Karno, Golding, Sorenson, & Burnam, 1988; Kessler et al., 1994; Robins et al., 1984). Their significance lies less in their prevalence than in the disruptiveness of their symptoms. The panic disorder patient or the phobic patient may be unable to venture out of the house, much less hold down a job; the obsessive-compulsive individual is no better off, tormented by unwanted thoughts and constantly busy with checking and rituals.

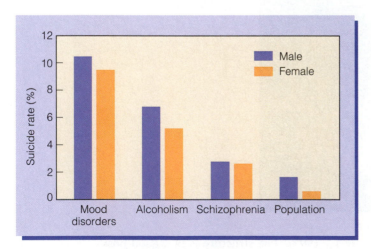

Figure 13.18
Suicide rates for three disorders in men and women
Source: From L. Ciompi, "Catamnestic long-term study on the course of life and aging of schizophrenics," *Schizophrenia Bulletin*, 6, 607–618 (Fig 2, p. 610).

Generalized Anxiety, Panic Disorder, and Phobia

Anxiety is often confused with fear; however, as we saw in Chapter 7, fear is a reaction to real objects or events present in the environment, while anxiety involves anticipation of events or an inappropriate reaction to the environment. A person with generalized anxiety has a feeling of stress and unease most of the time, and overreacts to stressful conditions. In panic disorder the person has a sudden and intense attack of anxiety, with symptoms like rapid breathing, high heart rate, and feelings of impending disaster. A person with a phobia experiences fear or stress when confronted with a particular situation—for instance, crowds, heights, enclosed spaces, open spaces, or specific objects such as dogs or snakes.

Heredity

The anxiety disorders are genetically influenced (Torgersen, 1983; Pauls, Towbin, Leckman, Zahner, & Cohen, 1986). However, although they are all in the same diagnostic category they are not all genetically related. For example, panic disorder and phobia tend to co-occur in relatives, while generalized anxiety is associated with major depression (Kendler et al., 1995). One group of researchers concluded that the environment determines whether the genetically vulnerable person succumbs to depression, generalized anxiety, or both (Kendler, Neale, Kessler, Heath, & Eaves, 1992).

Neurotransmitters

Anxiety appears to involve low activity at serotonin synapses. Anti-anxiety drugs initially suppress serotonin activity, but then they apparently produce a compensatory increase. The idea that a serotonergic increase is involved in anxiety reduction is supported by the fact that some antidepressants also reduce anxiety (Charney, Woods, Krystal, & Heninger, 1990).

However, benzodiazepines are the most frequently used anxiolytic (anti-anxiety) drugs (Costall & Naylor, 1992). You may remember from our earlier discussion of drugs that benzodiazepines increase receptor sensitivity to the inhibitory transmitter GABA. A deficit in benzodiazepine receptors may be one cause of anxiety disorder. Marczynski and Urbancic (1988) injected pregnant cats with a benzodiazepine tranquilizer. When the offspring were 1 year old, they were restless and appeared anxious in novel situations. When their brains were studied later, several areas of the brain had compensated for the tranquilizer by reducing the number of benzodiazepine receptors.

Brain Structures

A number of brain structures are activated in anxiety, including the *amygdala* and the *locus coeruleus*. Both structures participate in more specific emotions like fear, but the locus coeruleus may be particularly important, because drugs which decrease its action are anxiolytic and drugs which increase its action increase anxiety (Charney et al., 1990). Panic disorder patients have increased activity in the whole brain, even during symptom-free periods; activity in the *parahippocampal gyrus*, which is connected to the amygdala and the hippocampus, is lower on the left side than on the right (Reiman et al., 1986).

Obsessive-Compulsive Disorder

Obsessive-compulsive disorder (OCD) consists of two behaviors that occur in the same person, obsessions and compulsions. An obsession is a recurring thought; a person may be annoyed by a tune that mentally replays over and over, or by troubling thoughts such as wishing harm to another person. Normal people have similar thoughts, but for the obsessive individual the experience is extreme and feels completely out of control. Just as the obsessive is a slave to thoughts, the compulsive individual is a slave to actions. He or she is compelled to engage in ritualistic behavior (such as touching a door frame three

What causes anxiety disorders?

What causes obsessive-compulsive disorder?

times before passing through the door), or endless bathing and hand washing, or checking to see if appliances are turned off and the door is locked (Rapoport, 1991). One psychiatrist had a patient who tired of returning home to check whether she had turned her appliances off, and solved the problem by taking her coffee maker and iron to work with her (Begley & Biddle, 1996). The playwright David Sedaris (1998) wrote that his short walk home from school during childhood took a full hour because of his compulsion to stop every few feet and press his nose to the hood of a particular car, lick a certain mailbox, or touch a specific leaf that demanded his attention. Once home, he had to make the rounds of several rooms, kissing, touching, and rearranging various objects before he could enter his own room. About a fourth of OCD patients have a family member with OCD, suggesting a genetic involvement; boys are afflicted more often than girls, but the ratio levels off in adulthood (Swedo, Rapoport, Leonard, Lenane, & Cheslow, 1989).

Brain Anomalies

PET studies show that OCD patients have increased activity in the *orbital frontal cortex* and in a part of the basal ganglia, the *caudate nuclei* (Figure 13.19); this excess activity decreases following successful drug treatment and even behavior therapy (Baxter et al., 1987; Schwartz et al., 1996; Swedo, Schapiro, et al., 1989). Apparently disruption of a circuit involving those two structures and the cingulate gyrus results in a loss of impulse control (Insel, 1992).

OCD occurs with a number of diseases that damage the basal ganglia (Leonard et al., 1992) which, you will remember, are involved in motor activity; it has also been reported in cases of head injury (McKeon, McGuffin, & Robinson, 1984). The most famous obsessive-compulsive individual was the multimillionaire Howard Hughes (Fowler, 1986). Some signs of disorder during childhood and his mother's obsessive concern with germs suggest either genetic vulnerability or environmental influence. However, symptoms of OCD did not begin until after a series of airplane crashes and automobile accidents that left him virtually unrecognizable (Figure 13.20). When a business associate died, Hughes gave explicit instructions that flowers for the funeral were to be delivered by an independent messenger who would not have any contact with the florist or with Hughes' office—even to the point of sending a bill—to prevent "backflow" of germs (Barlett & Steele, 1979). Assistants were required to handle his papers with gloves—sometimes several pairs—and he in turn handled them only by grasping them with a tissue. He instructed his assistants not to touch him, talk directly to him, or even look at

Figure 13.19
Brain structures involved in obsessive-compulsive disorder
(a) The caudate nucleus (a part of the basal ganglia) and the orbital gyrus; (b) the caudate nucleus before and after behavior therapy.
Sources: (a) Baxter et al., 1987; (b) Schwartz et al., 1996.

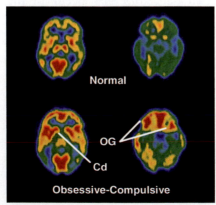

(a)

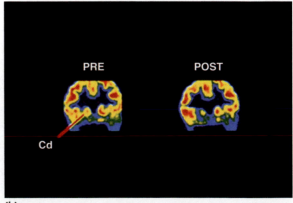

(b)

Figure 13.20
Howard Hughes before head injuries
Source: Fowler, 1986.

him; his defense for this behavior was that everybody carries germs and he wanted to avoid germs (Fowler, 1986).

Serotonin

Researchers believe that OCD patients are high in serotonergic activity. This was suggested by the fact that obsessive-compulsives are inhibited in action and feel guilty about aggressive impulses; sociopaths, on the other hand, feel no guilt after committing impulsive crimes and they have lowered serotonin activity. But the only drugs that consistently improve OCD symptoms are antidepressants that inhibit serotonin reuptake (Insel, Zohar, Benkelfat, & Murphy, 1990). So, if OCD patients do have high serotonergic activity, then reuptake inhibitors must work by causing a compensatory reduction in activity; there is some evidence that treatment does decrease the sensitivity of serotonin receptors (Insel et al., 1990).

Related Disorders

The symptoms of OCD, particularly washing and "grooming" rituals and preoccupation with cleanliness, suggest to some researchers that it is a disorder of "excessive grooming" (Leonard, Lenane, Swedo, Rettew, & Rapoport, 1991; Rapoport, 1991). Dogs and cats sometimes groom their fur to the point of producing bald spots and ulcers, in a disorder known as *acral lick syndrome*. Some chimpanzees and monkeys engage in excessive self-grooming and hair pulling, and 10% of birds in captivity compulsively pull out their feathers, occasionally to the point that the bird is denuded and at risk for infection and hypothermia. Clomipramine, an antidepressant used to treat OCD, is effective in reducing all these behaviors (Grindlinger & Ramsay, 1991; Hartman, 1995; Rapoport, 1991).

If you think the excessive grooming idea sounds far-fetched, consider the human behaviors of nail biting and obsessive hair pulling, in which the person pulls hairs out one by one until there are visible bald spots or even complete baldness of the head, eyebrows, and eyelashes. There are several similarities between hair pulling and OCD: both behaviors appear to be hereditary, and hair pullers have a high frequency of relatives with OCD; both symptoms also respond to serotonin reuptake inhibitors (Leonard et al., 1991; Swedo et al., 1991).

Another disorder associated with OCD is *Tourette's syndrome*, whose victims suffer from a variety of motor and phonic (sound) tics. They twitch and grimace, throw punches at the air, cough, grunt, bark, swear, blurt out racial slurs or sexual remarks, insult passersby, echo what others say, and mimic people's facial expressions and gestures. Both OCD and Tourette's sufferers can manage their symptoms for short periods of time; for instance, Touretters are usually symptom free while driving a car, having sex, or performing surgery (yes, some of them are surgeons!). But neither OCD nor Tourette's is a simple matter of will: children often suppress compulsive rituals at school and "let go" at home, or suppress tics

What causes the bizarre behavior of Tourette's?

during the day then tic during their sleep. The neurologist Oliver Sacks (1990) described a woman on the streets of New York who was imitating other people's expressions and gestures as she passed them on the street.

> Suddenly, desperately, the old woman turned aside, into an alley-way which led off the main street. And there, with all the appearances of a woman violently sick, she expelled . . . all the gestures, the postures, the expressions, the demeanours, the entire behavioural repertoires, of the past forty or fifty people she had passed. (p. 123)

Symptoms begin between the ages of 2 and 15 years and usually progress from simple to more complex tics, with increasing compulsive or ritualistic qualities. About one person in 2,000 is afflicted, with males outnumbering females three to one (Price, Kidd, Cohen, Pauls, & Leckman, 1985). Tourette's syndrome is genetically influenced, with a concordance rate of 53% for monozygotic twins and 8% for dizygotic twins (Price et al., 1985). Touretters have a high incidence of family members with OCD; the co-incidence has been estimated by various researchers to be between 55 and 74% and appears to increase with age to as much as 80 or 90% (Pauls et al., 1986). Some researchers believe that OCD and Tourette's are due to the same gene, and are different expressions of the same disease (Leonard et al., 1992).

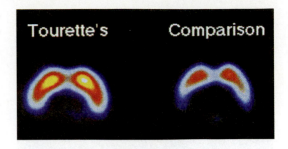

Figure 13.21
Increased dopamine activity in the caudate nuclei in Tourette's syndrome
Source: Malison et al., 1995.

Tourette's disorder, like OCD, involves increased activity in the *basal ganglia*. However, the most frequently prescribed drug for Tourette's is the antidopaminergic drug haloperidol. One of the effects of dopamine is motor activation. Using a specialized PET scanning technique with Tourette's sufferers, Malison and his colleagues (1995) were able to show increased dopamine activity in a part of the basal ganglia, the *caudate nuclei* (Figure 13.21).

- *What neurotransmitter deviations are involved in anxiety disorders?*
- *What are the brain differences in the anxiety disorders?*
- *Describe OCD and the related disorders.*

In Perspective

The last three decades have seen enormous progress in research, and we now know a great deal about the physiological causes of disorders. We owe these breakthroughs to advances in imaging techniques and genetics research technology, and to our greatly improved understanding of the physiology of synapses, not to mention the persistence of dedicated

researchers. The result is that we can now explain at the biological level many disorders that previously were considered to be purely "psychological" in origin or that were only suspected of having an organic basis.

In spite of these great research advances, we cannot reliably distinguish the schizophrenic brain from a normal one or diagnose depression or an anxiety disorder from a blood test. We may be able to some day, but in the meantime we rely for diagnosis on the behavior of the individuals. We know, at least to some extent, the physiological components of mental illness, but we do not understand the unique combination that determines who will become disordered and who will not. As long as that is true our treatments will remain a pale hope rather than a bright promise.

We have been repeatedly reminded that genetic vulnerability is not the same thing as destiny. In most cases, the genes produce an illness only with the cooperation of the environment. The message is that improving the physical and psychological welfare of the population can go a long way toward preventing mental illness or reducing its severity.

Just before the dawning of this new age of research one frustrated schizophrenia researcher concluded, "Almost everything remains to be done" (Heston, 1970, p. 254). Since then our knowledge of both the brain and its participation in the symptoms of mental illness has increased dramatically, but as you can see much of our understanding remains tentative. The pace is quickening, and I am sure the first decade of the new millennium will see even more impressive advances than the past.

 ## Summary

Schizophrenia

- Schizophrenia is characterized by some mix of symptoms such as hallucinations, delusions, thought disorder, and withdrawal.

- Twin and adoption studies indicate that heritability is 60–90%, and several possible gene locations have been found. Genes apparently produce a particular level of vulnerability.

- Schizophrenia is usually divided into positive and negative symptoms, possibly distinguished by excess dopamine activity versus brain deficits.

- Although there is evidence for the dopamine hypothesis, it is an incomplete explanation. Additional hypotheses involve serotonin, glutamate, and brain irregularities.

- The brain irregularities include ventricular enlargement (due to tissue deficits), hypofrontality, and impaired connections; these apparently arise from prenatal insults and irregular prenatal development, in interaction with genetic vulnerability.

Affective Disorders

- The affective disorders include depression and bipolar disorder, an alternation between mania and depression.

- The affective disorders are also highly heritable.

- The most prominent explanation of affective disorders is the monoamine hypothesis.

- Bipolar disorder is less understood than unipolar depression.

- ECT is a controversial, last-resort therapy which has value when medications fail and as a temporary suicide preventative.

- People with affective disorders often have disruptions in their circadian rhythm. Others respond to seasonal changes with winter depression.

- A number of brain anomalies distinguish depressed people from bipolar patients and both from normal people.

- Depression and low serotonin levels are associated with suicide risk.

continued

Anxiety Disorders

- The anxiety disorders are partially hereditary. There are apparent genetic links between generalized anxiety and depression, and between panic disorder and phobia.
- Anxiety apparently involves low serotonin activity, while OCD patients have high serotonin activity.
- The amygdala and locus coeruleus are active during anxiety; OCD involves activity in the orbital frontal cortex and the caudate nuclei.
- OCD and related disorders, including Tourette's, appear related to grooming behaviors.

 For Further Thought

- Now that we are nearing the end of the text, summarize what you know about the interaction of heredity and environment. Give examples from different chapters, and include the concept of vulnerability.
- Give an overall view of what produces deviant behavior (going back to earlier chapters as well as this one). What effect does this have on your ideas about responsibility for one's behavior?
- Behavior appears vulnerable to a number of disturbances, due to problems ranging from genetic disorders to addictions to psychological disorders. Consider the different ways complexity of the brain contributes to this vulnerability.

 Testing Your Understanding

1. Explain the integrative theory of schizophrenia discussed here. What are its deficiencies?
2. Describe the monoamine hypothesis of depression; include the evidence for it and a description of the effects of the drugs and ECT used to treat depression.
3. Describe the similarities and associations between OCD and the related "grooming" behaviors and Tourette's.

Select the one best answer:

1. If you were diagnosed with schizophrenia, you should prefer ___ symptoms:

   a. positive   b. negative

   c. chronic   d. bipolar

2. The fact that schizophrenia involves multiple genes helps explain:

   a. vulnerability to winter viruses.

   b. the onset late in life.

   c. positive symptoms.

   d. different degrees of vulnerability.

3. Most drugs used to treat schizophrenia owe their effectiveness to their:

   a. interference with reuptake of dopamine.

   b. blockage of dopamine receptors.

   c. stimulation of glutamate receptors.

   d. inhibition of glutamate receptors.

4. Schizophrenia apparently involves:

   a. tissue deficits.   b. frontal misfunction.

   c. disrupted   d. a and b.
   connections.

   e. a, b, and c.

5. One hypothesis about the timing of the onset of schizophrenia is that:

   a. the individual is vulnerable to the effect of viruses then.

   b. dopamine levels decrease with age.

c. the frontal lobes are undergoing maturation.

d. it takes several years for the neural tissue to deteriorate.

6. The monoamine hypothesis states that depression results from:

a. reduced activity in norepinephrine and serotonin synapses.

b. increased activity in norepinephrine and serotonin synapses.

c. reduced activity in norepinephrine, serotonin, and dopamine synapses.

d. increased activity in norepinephrine, serotonin, and dopamine synapses.

7. ECT appears to relieve depression by:

a. producing amnesia for depressing memories.

b. the same mechanisms as antidepressant drugs.

c. conditioning the person through punishment.

d. increasing EEG frequency.

8. A frontal area hypothesized to switch between depression and mania is the:

a. dorsolateral prefrontal cortex.

c. ventral prefrontal cortex.

b. caudate nucleus.

d. subgenual prefrontal cortex.

9. Studies indicate that risk for suicide is related to:

a. low norepinephrine and serotonin.

b. high norepinephrine and serotonin.

c. low serotonin.

d. low norepinephrine.

10. Generalized anxiety is associated genetically with:

a. panic disorder.   b. phobia.

c. depression.   d. all of these.

e. none of these.

11. OCD can be caused by:

a. genes.

b. diseases and head injury.

c. example of a family member

d. a and b.

e. a, b, and c.

12. OCD and Tourette's both involve compulsive rituals, probably because they involve:

a. increased dopamine.

b. increased activity in the basal ganglia.

c. a stressful home life

d. all of these.

Answers: 1. **a** 2. **d** 3. **b** 4. **e** 5. **c** 6. **a** 7. **b** 8. **d** 9. **c** 10. **c** 11. **d** 12. **b**

On the Web

1. **Schizophrenia.com** provides basic information about schizophrenia along with in-depth information for professionals at

http://www.schizophrenia.com/

The website **Schizophrenia** has a variety of resources on the disorder, including diagnosis, drugs, clinical research, and case studies, at

http://www.mhsource.com/schizophrenia/index.html

The Experience of Schizophrenia is the home page of Ian Chovil, who describes his ongoing experience with schizophrenia at

http://www.chovil.com/

2. The **New York University School of Medicine** has an online screening questionnaire for depression at

http://www.med.nyu.edu/Psych/screens/depres.html

continued

3. The **Depression and Bipolar Support Alliance** organization's site has information, resources, links, and a self-screening questionnaire for bipolar disorder at

   http://www.ndmda.org/

4. The **Society for Light Treatment and Biological Rhythms** has information about the use of phototherapy for SAD (and a variety of other disorders) at

   http://www.sltbr.org/

5. **Mental Health: A Report of the Surgeon General** is the source for the surgeon general's report which concludes

that mental health is an issue that must be addressed by the nation, at

http://www.surgeongeneral.gov/library/ mentalhealth/index.html

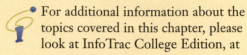 For additional information about the topics covered in this chapter, please look at InfoTrac College Edition, at

http://www.infotrac-college.com/wadsworth

Try search terms you think up yourself, or use these: *schizophrenia; Wisconsin Card Sorting Test; bipolar disorder; circadian rhythms.*

 On the CD-ROM: Exploring Biological Psychology

Schizophrenia
  Video: Common Symptoms of
    Schizophrenia
  Video: Etta 1
  Video: Etta 2
Major Depressive Disorder
  Video: Barbara 1
  Video: Barbara 2

Bipolar Disorder
  Video: Mary 1
  Video: Mary 2
  Video: Mary 3
Video: Sources of Phobias

 For Further Reading

When the Music's Over: My Journey into Schizophrenia, by Ross Burke (1995, Plume/Penguin), is the author's account of his battle with schizophrenia, published by his therapist after he ended the battle with suicide.

An Unquiet Mind, by Kay Jamison (1995, Knopf), tells the story of her continuing battle with bipolar disorder, which rendered her "ravingly psychotic" three months into her first semester as a psychology professor.

With the aid of lithium, she has become an authority on mood disorders. (Kay Jamison is the writer quoted in the introduction to Chapter 1.)

Abnormal Psychology: An Integrative Approach, by David Barlow and Mark Durand (2002, Wadsworth), is an introductory text that covers many of the topics of this chapter in greater detail.

→ Key Terms

Sleep and Consciousness

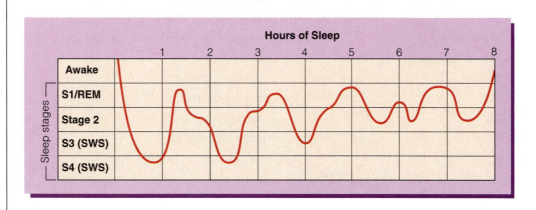

In this chapter you will learn:

- About the rhythm of sleep and waking and its neural controls.
- About a shorter rhythm throughout the day, and its possible functions during sleep.
- Some of the neural processes that contribute to consciousness.
- Some of the biological origins of the sense of self.

Studying the brain without studying consciousness would be like studying the stomach without studying digestion.

—John R. Searle

Kenneth Parks got up from the couch where he had been sleeping and drove 14 miles to his in-laws' home. There he struggled with his father-in-law before stabbing his mother-in-law repeatedly, killing her. He then drove to the police station, where he told the police he thought he had "killed some people." In court his defense was that he was sleepwalking. Based on the testimony of sleep experts and the lack of motive—Ken had an affectionate relationship with his in-laws—the jury acquitted him of murder (Broughton et al., 1994).

Did Ken's actions contradict his claim that he was sleepwalking? Or was he really asleep and therefore not responsible? This case raises the question of what we mean by *consciousness*. Many psychologists and especially neuroscientists avoid the topic because they think consciousness is inaccessible to research. This has not always been so; consciousness was a major concern of the fledgling discipline of psychology near the end of the nineteenth century. But the researchers' technique of *introspection* was *subjective*: the observations were open only

to the individuals doing the introspecting, who often disagreed with each other. This failing encouraged the development of *behaviorism*, which was based on the principle that psychology should study only relationships between external stimuli and observable responses.

Behaviorism was a necessary means of cleansing psychology of its subjective methodology, but its purge discarded the subject matter along with the methodology. The interests of psychologists would not shift back to include internal experience until the emergence of *cognitive psychology* in the 1950s and '60s.

Many cognitive psychologists were finding it difficult to understand psychological functions like learning and perception without taking account of various aspects of consciousness like learning and perception. Still, few of them tackled the subject of consciousness itself. The problem seemed too big, there was no clear definition of consciousness, and the bias that consciousness was a problem for philosophers still lingered. Gradually, some of them began to ally themselves with philosophers, biologists, and computer experts to develop new research strategies for exploring this last frontier of psychology. The greatest inroads have been made in the study of sleep, largely because sleep is readily observable. Also, because sleep is open to study by objective techniques, it has not had the stigma among researchers that characterizes other aspects of consciousness. We will begin the last leg of our journey with the topic of sleep and dreaming.

SLEEP AND DREAMING

Each night we slip into a mysterious state that is neither entirely conscious nor unconscious. Sleep has intrigued humans throughout history: metaphysically, dreaming suggested to our forebears that the soul took leave of the body at night to wander the world; practically, sleep is a period of enforced nonproductivity and vulnerability to predators and enemies.

In spite of thousands of research studies, we are still unclear on the most basic question—

what the function of sleep is. The most obvious explanation is that sleep is *restorative*. Support for this idea comes from the observation that species with higher metabolic rates typically spend more time in sleep (Zepelin & Rechtschaffen, 1974). A less obvious explanation is the *adaptive* hypothesis; according to this view, the amount of sleep an animal engages in depends on the availability of food and on safety considerations (Webb, 1974). Elephants, for instance, which must graze for many hours to meet their food needs, sleep briefly. Animals with low vulnerability to predators, like the lion, and those that find safety by hiding, like bats and burrowing animals, sleep much of the time. Vulnerable animals that are too large to burrow or hide, like horses and cattle, sleep very little (see Figure 14.1). In a study of 39 species, the combined factors of body size and danger accounted for 80% of the variability in sleep time (Allison & Cicchetti, 1976).

Early to bed and early to rise, makes a man healthy, wealthy, and wise.

—Benjamin Franklin

Whatever the function of sleep may be, its importance becomes apparent when we look at the effects of sleep deprivation. These effects are nowhere more evident than in shift work. Shift workers sleep less than day workers, and as a result their work performance suffers (Tepas & Carvalhais, 1990). Also, they typically fail to shift their sleep-wake cycle adequately, because their sleep is disturbed during the day and they conform to the rest of the world's schedule on weekends. With their work and sleep schedules at odds with their biological rhythm, sleep intrudes into their work and daytime arousal interferes with their sleep.

In long-term sleep deprivation studies impairment follows a rhythmic cycle—performance declines during the night, then shows some recovery during the daytime (Horne, 1988). The persistence of this rhythm represents a safety hazard of gigantic proportions when people try to function at night. The largest number of single-vehicle traffic accidents attributed to "falling asleep at the wheel" occur around 2 A.M. (Mitler et al., 1988), and the number of work errors peaks at the same time (Broughton, 1975). In addition, the Three Mile Island nuclear plant accident took place at 4 A.M., the Chernobyl nuclear plant

Figure 14.1
Time spent in daily sleep for different animals
Observations support the hypothesis that sleep is an adaptive response to feeding and safety needs.

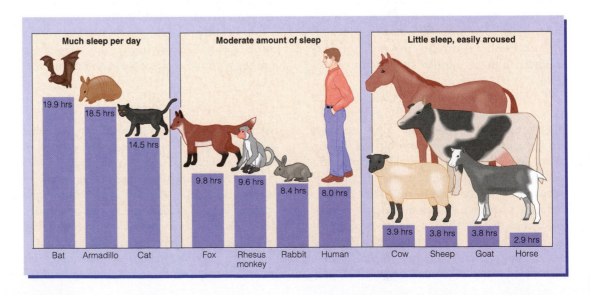

Much sleep per day			Moderate amount of sleep				Little sleep, easily aroused			
19.9 hrs	18.5 hrs	14.5 hrs	9.8 hrs	9.6 hrs	8.4 hrs	8.0 hrs	3.9 hrs	3.8 hrs	3.8 hrs	2.9 hrs
Bat	Armadillo	Cat	Fox	Rhesus monkey	Rabbit	Human	Cow	Sheep	Goat	Horse

meltdown began at 1:23 A.M., and the Bhopal, India, chemical plant leakage that poisoned more than 2,000 people began shortly after midnight (Mapes, 1990; Mitler et al., 1988).

Travel across time zones also disrupts sleep and impairs performance, particularly when you travel eastward. It is difficult to quantify the effects of *jet lag*, but three researchers have attempted to do so in a novel way by comparing the performance of baseball teams. When East Coast and West Coast teams played at home, their percentage of wins was nearly identical—50% and 49%, respectively. When they traveled across the continent but had time to adjust to the new time zone, they showed a typical visitor's disadvantage, winning 45.9% of their games. Teams traveling west without time to adjust won about the same, 43.8% of their games, while teams traveling east won only 37.1% (Recht, Lew, & Schwartz, 1995). The quality of sleep is better when you extend the day's length by traveling west, rather than shorten it as you do when you travel east. One way of looking at this effect is that it is easier to stay awake past your bedtime than it is to go to sleep when you are not sleepy. We will examine a more specific explanation when we consider circadian rhythms.

Circadian Rhythms

We saw in Chapter 13 that a *circadian rhythm* is a rhythm that is about a day in length; the term *circadian* comes from the Latin *circa*, meaning "approximately," and *dia*, meaning "day." We work, sleep, and eat on a cycle of about 24 hours, in synchrony with the solar day. We sleep once every 24 hours, and body temperature, alertness, urine production, steroid secretion, and a variety of other activities decrease during our normal sleep period and increase during our normal waking period, even when we reverse our sleep-wake schedule temporarily. **The main biological clock that controls these rhythms in mammals is the *suprachiasmatic nucleus (SCN)* of the hypothalamus.** Lesioning the SCN in rats abolishes the normal 24-hour rhythms of sleep, activity, body temperature,

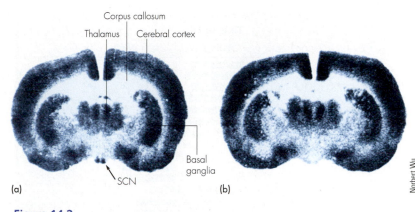

Figure 14.2
The suprachiasmatic nucleus
The nuclei, indicated by the arrows, took up more radioactive 2-deoxy-glucose in the scan on the left because the rat was injected during the day; the rat on the right was injected at night.
Source: Reprinted with permission from W. J. Schwartz and H. Gainer, "Suprachiasmatic nucleus: Use of ^{14}C-labeled deoxyglucose uptake as a functional marker." *Science, 197*, 1089–1091. Copyright 1977 American Association for the Advancement of Science.

drinking, and steroid secretion (Abe, Kroning, Greer, & Critchlow, 1979; Stephan & Nunez, 1977). The SCN is what is known as a *pacemaker*, because it keeps time and regulates the activity of other cells. We know that the rhythm arises in the SCN, because rhythmic activity continues in isolated SCN cells (Earnest, Liang, Ratcliff, & Cassone, 1999; Inouye & Kawamura, 1979). Lesioned animals do not stop sleeping; but instead of following the usual day-night cycle, they sleep in naps scattered throughout the 24-hour period. So the SCN controls timing of sleep, but sleep itself is controlled by other brain structures we will discuss later. Feeding is not affected, which suggests that the brain has other clocks besides the SCN. The SCN is shown in Figure 14.2 and again in Figure 14.8.

The SCN is *entrained* to the solar day by cues called *zeitgebers* ("time-givers"). If humans are kept in isolation from all time cues in an underground bunker or a cave, they usually lose their synchrony with the day-night cycle; in many studies, zeitgeber-deprived individuals "drifted" to a day that was about 25 hours long (see Figure 14.3) (Aschoff, 1984). For a long time, researchers believed that alarm clocks and the activity of others were the most

Why is the circadian rhythm important?

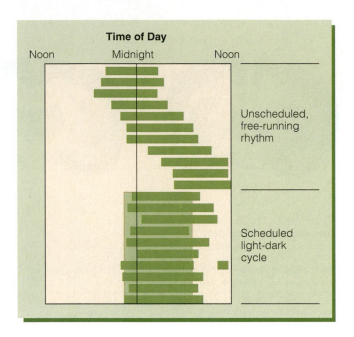

Figure 14.3
Sleep and wake periods during isolation from time cues
Each dark bar indicates the timing and length of sleep during a day. During the unscheduled period (without time cues) the subject's activity assumed a 25-hour rhythm and began to advance around the clock. When light-dark periods were scheduled, he resumed a normal sleep and activity rhythm.
From *Introduction to Psychology* 9th ed. by Dennis Coon, Wadsworth. Based on data from Czeisler et al. (1981).

important influences that entrain our activity to the 24-hour day; but research points more convincingly to light as the primary zeitgeber. During the four-month darkness of the Antarctic winter, sleep times and physiological measures of four Greenpeace volunteers free-ran on a roughly 25-hour interval, even though the volunteers had access to time information and social contact with each other (Kennaway & van Dorp, 1991).

The difference in light intensity between the light and dark periods is important for entraining the day-night cycle. One group of night workers worked under bright lights and slept in complete darkness during the day (*light discrepant*); a second group worked under normal light and slept in the typical semidarkness of the day sleeper (*similar light*). The light-

discrepant workers improved in performance and alertness compared to the similar-light workers. Their physiological measures also synchronized with the new sleep-wake cycle; for example, in the similar-light workers body temperature continued to drop to its low value around 3:30 A.M., but shifted to 3:00 P.M. in the light-discrepant group (Czeisler et al., 1990).

Isolation studies convinced researchers that our internal clock operates on a 25-hour cycle. According to them, it is this "slow-running" clock that makes phase delays (going to sleep later) easier than phase advances (going to sleep earlier). So adjustment after westward travel is easier than after traveling east, and workers who rotate shifts sleep better and produce more if the rotation is to later shifts rather than to earlier ones (Czeisler, Moore-Ede, & Coleman, 1982). Some people are unable even under normal circumstances to synchronize with a 24-hour day; like a clock that runs too slowly, their physical and cognitive functioning moves in and out of phase with the rest of the world, resulting in insomnia and impaired functioning. The greater ease of phase delay than phase advance led to an insomnia treatment that was completely counterintuitive: patients with a 5- to 15-year history of sleep-onset insomnia were required to stay up three hours later each night than the night before; after five or six days of this routine they were going to bed at their desired bedtime. On average, their sleep onset time advanced from 4:50 A.M. to 12:20 A.M., and their average waking time shifted from 1:00 P.M. to 7:55 A.M. All five patients were able to give up the sleeping pills they had become dependent on, and improvement was long lasting (Czeisler et al., 1981).

Why the internal clock would operate on a 25-hour cycle is unclear, especially since animals kept in isolation typically run on a 24-hour cycle (Czeisler et al., 1999). Some believe it has something to do with the 24.8-hour lunar cycle, which influences the tides and some biological systems (Bünning, 1973; Miles, Raynal, & Wilson, 1977), but Czeisler and his colleagues (1999) suggest that the 25-hour cycle in isolation studies is no more than an artifact of allowing the individuals to control the room lighting. Bright light late in the day causes the cycle to lengthen. Czeisler kept the light at a level that was too low to influence the circadian rhythm while people lived on a 28-hour sleep-wake schedule. Under that condition, their body temperature cycle averaged 24.18 hours, which led Czeisler to believe that the *biological* rhythm is approximately 24 hours. However, body temperature tends not to follow the sleep-wake cycle when the sleep-wake cycle is lengthened (Aschoff, 1969); so we will have to await further research to know whether Czeisler's results raise serious questions about the length of the sleep-wake cycle.

The SCN regulates the pineal gland's secretion of *melatonin,* **a hormone that induces sleepiness.** Melatonin is often used to combat jet lag and to treat insomnia in shift workers and in the blind (Arendt, Skene, Middleton, Lockley, & Deacon, 1997). Light resets the biological clock by suppressing melatonin secretion (Boivin, Duffy, Kronauer, & Czeisler,

1996). Most totally blind individuals are not entrained to the 24-hour day and suffer from insomnia in spite of regular schedules of sleep, work, and social contact. These individuals do not experience a decrease in melatonin production when exposed to light; however, totally blind people *without* insomnia do show melatonin suppression, even though they are unaware of the light (Czeisler et al., 1995). Recent studies explain how blind individuals are able to entrain to the light-dark cycle. Light information reaches the SCN by way of a direct connection from the retinas called the *retinohypothalamic pathway.* The normal photoreceptors are not involved, because mice lacking rods and cones still show entrainment to light and cycle normally (Freedman et al., 1999; Lucas, Freedman, Muñoz, Garcia-Fernández, & Foster, 1999). Instead, the retinohypothalamic neurons come from specialized ganglion cells containing the photopigment *melanopsin,* which was recently found in the retina. The melanopsin is located in widely branching dendrites, which makes these ganglion cells well suited for detecting

In Space, No One Gets to Sleep

IN THE NEWS

James Randerson—A few years after Jerry Linenger's five-month stay on the Russian space station, Timothy Monk of the University of Pittsburgh Medical Center has looked at the astronaut's sleep data. The analysis focused on sleep quality, body temperature, and performance on psychological tests. Linenger was very careful about keeping to a regular sleep-wake schedule, but that turned out to be difficult. Mir was aging badly and the mission was fraught with problems; to conserve energy the lights were dimmed. This meant that the brightest light was from the sun streaming in the station's windows; so there

should have been no problem, because this enhanced the normal circadian cues, right? Trouble was, Mir was orbiting Earth every 90 minutes, so light and dark alternated 16 times a day.

After 90 days the astronaut's sleep quality deteriorated rapidly, Monk reported. At four months, Linenger said, "I lost it." It was worse for the two Russian cosmonauts, who were less meticulous about their sleep schedule. "They'd nod off and float right past you," he recalled.

—*"This Week" section in* New Scientist, *December 1, 2001, p. 16*

overall light levels (Figure 14.4) (Berson, Dunn, & Takao, 2002; Hannibal, Hindersson, Knudsen, Georg, & Fahrenkrug, 2002; Hattar, Liao, Takao, Berson, & Yau, 2002).

But synchronizing the rhythm does not account for the rhythm itself. The clock consists of a few genes and their protein products (Clayton, Kyriacou, & Reppert, 2001; Shearman et al., 2000). The genes fall into two groups; one is turned on while the other is turned off. When the genes are on, their particular protein products build up. Eventually the accumulating proteins turn their genes off, and the other set of genes is turned on. This feedback loop provides the approximately 24- or 25-hour cycle which then must be reset each day by light. The clock does not always operate properly, as we saw in the previous chapter with some depressed patients. Similarly, people with *familial advanced sleep phase syndrome* are

What rhythms occur throughout the day and night?

"larks" as opposed to "owls"; their circadian rhythm is advanced by approximately 4 hours, so they go to bed around 7:30 P.M. and wake up about 4:30 A.M. The disorder has been traced to a mutation in one of the genes of the SCN clock (Toh et al., 2001).

Rhythms During Waking and Sleeping

Riding on the day-long wave of the circadian rhythm are several *ultradian rhythms, rhythms that are shorter than a day in length*. Hormone production, urinary output, alertness, and other functions follow regular cycles throughout the day. For example, the dip in alertness and performance in the wee hours of the morning is mirrored by another in the early afternoon that cannot be accounted for by postlunch sleepiness, because it occurs in people who skip lunch (Broughton, 1975). Incidentally, this dip coincides with the time of siesta in many cultures, and a rest period in nonhuman primates. The *basic rest and activity cycle* is a rhythm that is about 90–100 minutes long. When people wrote down what they were thinking every five minutes for 10 hours the content showed they were daydreaming on a 90-minute cycle; electroencephalogram recordings verified that these were periods of decreased brain activity (Kripke & Sonnenschein, 1973).

The common view of sleep is that it is a cessation of activity that occurs when the body and brain become fatigued. Sleep, however, is an active process. This is true in two respects. First, you will soon see that sleep is a very busy time; a great deal of activity goes on in the brain. Second, sleep is not like a car running out of gas, but is turned on by brain structures and later turned off by other structures.

The most important measure of sleep activity is the electroencephalogram, or EEG. When a person is awake, the EEG is a mix of *alpha* and *beta* waves. Alpha is activity whose voltage fluctuates at a frequency of 8–12 Hz and moderate amplitude; *beta* has a frequency of 13–30 Hz and a lower amplitude. Beta waves, which are associated with arousal and

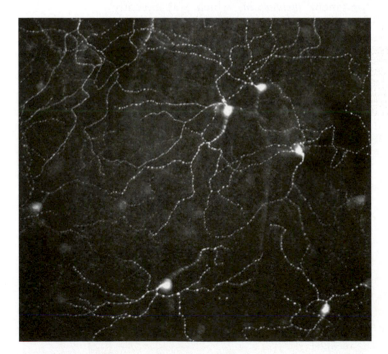

Figure 14.4
Retinal ganglion cells containing melanopsin
The cells were labeled with a fluorescent substance that reacts to melanopsin. Notice the widespread dendrites, which contain melanopsin.
Source: Hannibal et al., 2002. Copyright 2002 by the Society for Neuroscience.

alertness, are progressively replaced by alpha as the person relaxes. It may seem strange that the amplitude of the EEG is lower during arousal. Remember that the EEG is the sum of the electrical activity of all the neurons between the two recording electrodes. When a person is cognitively aroused, neurons under the electrodes are mostly desynchronized in their firing as they carry out their separate tasks; with the neurons firing at different times, the EEG has a high frequency, but the amplitude is rather low. As the person relaxes, the neurons have less processing to do, and fall into a pattern of synchronized firing. The rate is low, but the cumulative amplitude of the neurons firing at the same time is high.

As the person slips into the light first stage of sleep, the EEG shifts to *theta* waves, with a frequency of 4–7 Hz (see Figure 14.5). About 10 minutes later Stage 2 begins, indicated by *sleep spindles* and *K complexes*. Sleep spindles are brief bursts of 12- to 14-Hz waves; K complexes are sharp, large waves that occur about once a minute. **Stages 3 and 4 are known as *slow wave sleep (SWS)* and are characterized by large, slow delta waves at a frequency of**

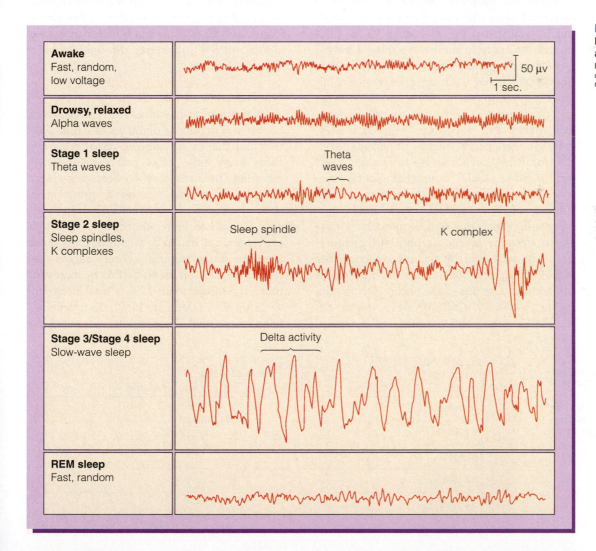

Figure 14.5
Electroencephalogram and the stages of sleep
From P. Hauri, "Current concepts: The sleep disorders." Copyright 1982 by Upjohn.

Awake Fast, random, low voltage	
Drowsy, relaxed Alpha waves	
Stage 1 sleep Theta waves	Theta waves
Stage 2 sleep Sleep spindles, K complexes	Sleep spindle K complex
Stage 3/Stage 4 sleep Slow-wave sleep	Delta activity
REM sleep Fast, random	

50 μv
1 sec.

1–3 Hz. The person moves around in bed during this period, turning over and changing positions. Sleepwalking, bed-wetting, and night terrors, disturbances that are common in children, occur during SWS, too. Night terrors are not nightmares, but involve screaming and apparent terror that are forgotten in the morning; they are not a sign of a disorder unless they continue beyond childhood. After Stage 4 the sleeper moves rather quickly back through the stages in reverse order. But rather than returning to Stage 1, the sleeper enters REM sleep.

REM, or rapid eye movement, sleep **is so called because the eyes dart back and forth horizontally during this stage.** The EEG returns to a pattern similar to a relaxed waking state, but the person does not wake up; in fact, the sleeper is not easily aroused by noise, but does respond to meaningful sounds such as the sleeper's name. You can see why some researchers call this stage *paradoxical sleep*, because *paradoxical* means "contradictory." During REM sleep respiration rate and heart rate increase. Males experience genital erection, and vaginal secretion increases in females. In spite of these signs of arousal, the body is very still, in fact, in a state of muscular paralysis or *atonia*. If people sleeping in the laboratory are awakened by the researcher during REM sleep, about 80% of the time they report dreaming. Dreams also occur during **the other,** *non-REM (NREM)* **sleep stages,** but they are less frequent, less vivid, and less hallu-

cinatory. Even people who say they do not dream report dreaming when they are awakened from REM sleep; their dreams are less frequent, though, and they often describe their experience as "thinking" (Lewis, Goodenough, Shapiro, & Sleser, 1966). Apparently "non-dreamers" just fail to remember dreams in the morning; in fact, we ordinarily remember a dream only if we wake up before the short-term memory of the dream has faded (Koulack & Goodenough, 1976). A complete cycle through the stages of sleep—like the day-dreaming cycle—takes about 90 minutes to complete. The night's sleep is a series of repetitions of this ultradian rhythm, although the length of REM sleep periods increases and the amount of SWS decreases through the night (Figure 14.6).

The Functions of REM Sleep

To find out what functions REM sleep serves, researchers deprived volunteers of REM sleep; they did this by waking the research participants every time EEG and eye movement recordings indicated they were entering a REM period. When this was done, the subjects showed a "push" for more REM sleep. They went into REM more frequently as the study progressed and had to be awakened more often; then, on uninterrupted recovery nights they tended to make up the lost REM by increasing their REM from about 20% of total sleep time to 25 or 30% (Dement, 1960). To psychoanalytically oriented theorists, these results were

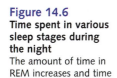

What are the functions of REM and slow wave sleep?

Figure 14.6
Time spent in various sleep stages during the night
The amount of time in REM increases and time in deeper sleep decreases.

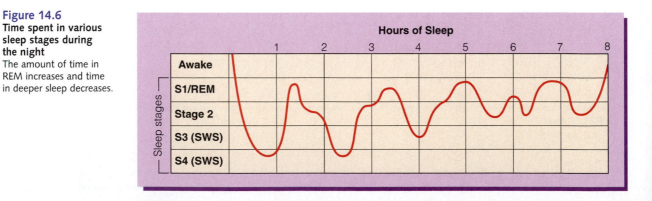

evidence of a psychological need for dreaming. You are probably familiar with the theory that dreams reveal the contents of the unconscious, not through their manifest content—the story the person tells on awakening—but through symbolic representations (Freud, 1900).

Most neuroscientists, on the other hand, believe that dreaming is merely the by-product of spontaneous neural activity in the brain. **According to the** *activation-synthesis hypothesis,* **during REM sleep the forebrain integrates neural activity generated by the brain stem with information stored in memory** (Hobson & McCarley, 1977); in other words, the brain engages in a sort of confabulation, using information from memory to impose meaning on nonsensical random input. This explanation does not imply that dream content is always insignificant; there is evidence that daytime events and concerns do influence the content of a person's dreams (Webb & Cartwright, 1978). But neuroscientists consider dreams to be the least important aspect of REM sleep, and note that after a century of intense effort, there is no agreed-upon method of dream interpretation (Crick & Mitchison, 1995).

Instead, neuroscientists argue that the pervasiveness of REM sleep among mammals and birds demands that any explanation for the function of REM sleep be a biological one. There are several proposals as to what biological needs might be met during REM sleep, but the number of hypotheses indicates that we are still unsure about REM sleep's function. One hypothesis is that REM sleep promotes neural development during childhood. REM sleep does seem to be especially important during childhood. Infant sleep starts with REM rather than NREM, and the proportion of sleep devoted to REM is around 50% during infancy and decreases through childhood until it reaches an adult level of around 20% in adolescence (Roffwarg, Muzio, & Dement, 1966). According to this hypothesis, excitation that spreads through the brain from the pons during REM sleep encourages differentiation, maturation, and myelination in higher brain centers, similar to the way spontaneous waves of excitation sweep across the retina during development to help organize its structure (Chapter 3). There is some evidence from studies of the immature visual systems of newborn cats that REM sleep, and particularly these waves from the pons, regulate the rate of neural development (Shaffery, Roffwarg, Speciale, & Marks, 1999).

Another hypothesis, that REM sleep is involved in learning, has considerable support. The amount of REM increases during the next sleep period after a session of learning, and REM sleep deprivation after learning reduces retention (see review in Dujardin, Guerrien, & Leconte, 1990; Karni, Tanne, Rubenstein, Askenasy, & Sagi, 1994; Smith, 1995). Early studies were equivocal in their support for a relationship between REM sleep and learning in humans, though. Apparently the reason was the same one we encountered in research on the role of the hippocampus in learning: animal studies used learning tasks that require nondeclarative memory (see Chapter 11); human studies usually involved declarative memory. REM sleep enhances memory for nondeclarative tasks, but apparently has no effect on declarative learning (Karni et al., 1994; Smith, 1995).

It is not clear just what happens in REM sleep that aids learning, but studies suggest that the amount of REM sleep is directly related to learning. For example, whether REM sleep increases and how much it increases depends on how well the subject learned (Hennevin, Hars, Maho, & Bloch, 1995). Also, if training occurs over several days REM increases daily and reaches its peak in the 24-hour period before the peak in correct performance (Dujardin et al., 1990; Smith, 1996).

As we saw in Chapter 11, some researchers believe that REM enhances consolidation. Although critics think the research can be interpreted in other ways (Siegel, 2001), several studies do support this hypothesis. For example, "cueing" rats during REM sleep with the stimulus that had signaled shock in an avoidance task improved their performance the next day compared to controls; presenting the stimulus during slow wave sleep did not (Hennevin et al., 1995). Reticular formation activity, which increases during REM sleep, may be the key to REM-period enhancement of learning. Learning performance is enhanced in rats by electrical stimulation of the reticular formation during REM sleep, but not during NREM sleep (Hennevin et al., 1995).

In Chapter 11 we saw that consolidation seems to be strengthened by the replay during REM sleep of the hippocampal activity that occurred during daytime learning. That replay is synchronized with theta-frequency (3–7 Hz) activity occurring simultaneously in the hippocampus (Stickgold, Hobson, Fosse, & Fosse, 2001). After four to seven days of synchrony, the time period over which memories become independent of the hippocampus, the replay shifts to *out-of-phase*, with the peaks of one wave coinciding with the troughs of the other. This may indicate a shift from long-term potentiation and memory consolidation to long-term depression and memory erasure in the hippocampus (Stickgold et al., 2001).

The idea of memory deletion is consistent with Crick and Mitchison's (1995) *reverse learning hypothesis.* They suggest that neural networks involved in memory must have a way to purge themselves occasionally of erroneous connections, and that activity during REM sleep provides the opportunity to do this. Researchers studying computer neural networks found that when they added a reverse learning process it improved their networks' performance (Hopfield, Feinstein, & Palmer, 1983). According to Crick and Mitchison, reverse learning makes more efficient use of our brain, allowing us to get by with a much smaller brain; they point out that the only mammals so far found not to engage in REM sleep—the *Echidna* (a nocturnal burrower in Australia) and two species of dolphin—have unusually large brains for their body size.

The Functions of Slow Wave Sleep

Slow wave sleep increases following exercise; after athletes competed in a 92-kilometer race SWS was elevated for four consecutive nights (Shapiro, Bortz, Mitchell, Bartel, & Jooste, 1981). Apparently the effect is due to overheating rather than fatigue. When people ran on treadmills their body temperature increased; that night, SWS sleep increased, at the expense of REM sleep. However, when they ran while being sprayed with water their body temperature increased less than half as much and there was no change in SWS (Horne & Moore, 1985).

Horne (1988) believes that SWS is more related to the increase in the temperature of the brain than the increase in body temperature; heating only the head and face with a hair dryer was sufficient to increase slow wave sleep later (Horne & Harley, 1989). According to Horne (1992), slow wave sleep promotes cerebral recovery, especially in the prefrontal cortex. Slow wave sleep may also restore processes involved in cognitive functioning. Bonnet and Arand (1996) gave people either caffeine or a placebo before a 3.5-hour nap. The caffeine group had reduced SWS during the nap; although they felt more vigorous and no sleepier than the placebo group, they performed less well on arithmetic and vigilance tasks during a subsequent 41-hour work period. In another study, volunteers who engaged in a day of stimulating but nonstrenuous activities, including viewing a movie and visiting a museum, an amusement park, and a zoo, had increased SWS that night (Horne & Minard, 1985).

There is some evidence SWS plays a role in consolidation of declarative memory. Humans deprived of SWS had impaired memory for a list of words they had learned beforehand, but not for their learning of mirror tracing, a nondeclarative task (Plihal & Born, 1997). Other research suggests that consolidation is a multistep process requiring both REM and SWS. Overnight improvement on a visual discrimination task in humans was correlated with the percentage of SWS sleep during the first quarter of the night *and* the percentage of REM sleep in the last quarter of the night (see Figure 14.7) (Stickgold, Whidbee, Schirmer, Patel, & Hobson, 2000). These measures together accounted for 80% of the differences in learning among the research participants.

Brain Structures and Sleep

We have seen one of the ways sleep can be regarded as an active process: a great deal of activity goes on in the brain during sleep. For the second aspect of this active process we turn to the brain structures involved in turning sleep on and off. There is no single sleep center or waking center; as usual, the behaviors are controlled by a widespread network of structures. However, the ***basal forebrain area,*** **located just anterior to the hypothalamus, contains both sleep-related and waking-related cells and is critically important in both processes.** Brain structures involved in sleep are illustrated in Figure 14.8.

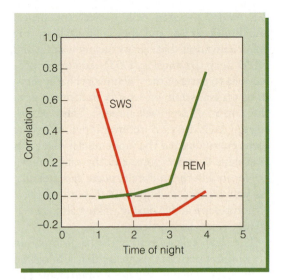

Figure 14.7
Correlation of SWS and REM sleep with overnight task improvement
For overnight improvement on a visual discrimination task, SWS was important during the first quarter of the night; REM sleep was important during the fourth quarter.

Adapted with permission from Stickgold et al., "Sleep, learning, and dreams: Off-line memory reprocessing." *Science,* 294, 1052–1057. Copyright 2001, American Association for the Advancement of Science.

What brain structures are responsible for sleep and waking?

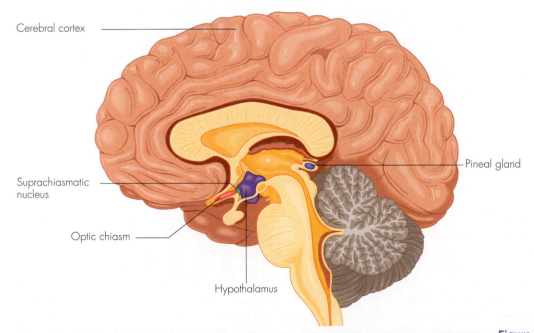

Figure 14.8
The major brain structures involved in sleep

The waking-related cells project to cortical and limbic areas, and they help regulate the EEG activation that occurs during waking and REM sleep (Szymusiak, 1995). Additional projections to parts of the thalamus probably facilitate transmission of sensory information to the cortex during wakefulness. The waking-related cells in turn receive input from the locus coeruleus and the raphe nuclei; the locus coeruleus is in the pons, and the raphe nuclei are located in the midbrain, pons, and medulla. As you can see in Figure 14.9, both of these structures are active during waking and are relatively quiet during sleep.

The sleep-related cells in the basal forebrain area inhibit activating systems that are located in the hypothalamus and in the brain stem. The sleep cells receive their input from the nearby *preoptic area* and *anterior hypothalamus*, known collectively as the *POAH*. Cells in the POAH area are involved in several functions, including regulation of body temperature. Warming the POAH activates sleep-related cells and inhibits waking-related cells in the basal forebrain, and enhances slow wave EEG (Alam, Szymusiak, & McGinty, 1995; Sherin, Shiromani, McCarley, & Saper, 1996; Szymusiak, 1995). The POAH no doubt accounts for the sleepiness you feel in an overheated room or when you have a fever. The preoptic area has receptors for *adenosine*, a neuromodulator that accumulates in the brain during wakefulness (Ticho & Radulovacki, 1991). Caffeine inhibits the effects of adenosine, and the preoptic area is one of the places in the brain where coffee and other caffeinated drinks help keep you awake.

The pons is involved in several aspects of sleep. One is the **PGO waves seen in REM sleep. The name refers to the path of travel that waves of excitation take from the pons through the lateral geniculate nucleus of the thalamus to the occipital area.** PGO waves are as characteristic of REM sleep as rapid eye movements are (Figure 14.10). They begin about 80 seconds before the start of a REM period and apparently trigger the EEG desynchrony of REM sleep (Mansari, Sakai, & Jouvet, 1989; Steriade, Paré, Bouhassira, Deschênes, & Oakson, 1989). The pons also sends impulses downward to the *magnocellular nucleus* in the medulla, to bring about the atonia that accompanies REM sleep. When Shouse and Siegel (1992) lesioned this nucleus in cats, the cats were no longer paralyzed during REM sleep; in fact, their movements during REM sleep often woke them up. The opposite effect occurs in humans suffering from the sleep disorder called *cataplexy*. Cataplexy is a common symptom of **narcolepsy, a disorder in which individuals fall asleep suddenly during the daytime and go directly into REM sleep. In *cataplexy*,** the person has a sudden experi-

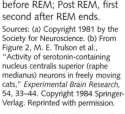

Figure 14.9
Firing rates in arousal centers during waking and sleep
(a) Activity in the locus coeruleus; **(b)** activity in the raphe nuclei. AW, alert waking; QW, quiet waking; DRO, drowsy; SWS, slow wave sleep; Pre REM, 60 seconds before REM; Post REM, first second after REM ends.
Sources: (a) Copyright 1981 by the Society for Neuroscience. (b) From Figure 2, M. E. Trulson et al., "Activity of serotonin-containing nucleus centralis superior (raphe medianus) neurons in freely moving cats," *Experimental Brain Research*, 54, 33–44. Copyright 1984 Springer-Verlag. Reprinted with permission.

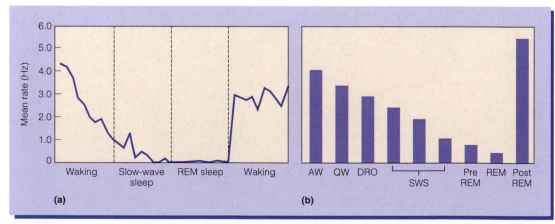

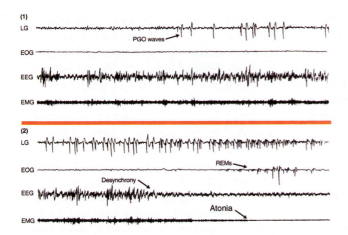

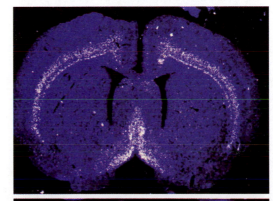

Figure 14.10
PGO waves, EEG desynchrony, and muscle atonia
The records are of electrical activity in the lateral geniculate nucleus (LG), eye movements (EOG, electrooculogram), electroencephalogram (EEG), and muscle tension (EMG, electromyogram). Notice how PGO waves signal the beginning of EEG desynchrony, rapid eye movements, and atonia several seconds later.
Source: Copyright 1989 by the Society for Neuroscience.

ence of one component of REM sleep—atonia—and falls to the floor paralyzed but fully awake. The pons also contains adenosine receptors, and is another site for the effect of your morning cup of coffee (Rainnie, Grunze, McCarley, & Greene, 1994).

Research on narcolepsy is leading to a better understanding of the sleep-wake cycle. The neuropeptide *orexin*, which is also called *hypocretin* because it is secreted by neurons from the hypothalamus, increases eating. (See Figure 14.11.) To study this effect, medical researchers created knockout mice in which the genes for the neuropeptide were disabled. Then they used infrared cameras to monitor the eating behavior of the mice at night, when the rodents are most active (Chemelli et al., 1999). What they saw was more interesting than eating. Occasionally the mice would suddenly collapse, often while walking around or grooming; the mice were narcoleptic! Most narcoleptic humans (those with cataplexy) have low or undetectable levels of orexin/hypocretin, due to a loss of orexin neurons in the hypothalamus (Higuchi et al., 2002; Kanbayashi et al., 2002). But the implications are broader than sleep dysfunction: infusing the neuropeptide into the basal forebrain area of sleeping rats produces rapid waking (España, Baldo, Kelley, & Berridge, 2001). The orexin/hypocretin system is only a part of the brain's control

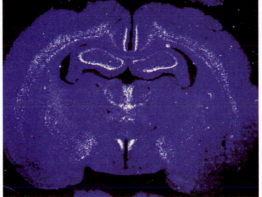

Figure 14.11
Locations of hypocretin/orexin receptors in the rat brain
The receptors appear in white. Notice how widespread they are.
Reprinted by permission of *Nature,* copyright 2001.

of waking (Saper, Chou, & Scammell, 2001); otherwise, narcoleptics would be constantly sleepy, if not asleep.

Sleep as a Form of Consciousness

When you are asleep, are you unconscious?

At the beginning of this discussion I said that sleep is neither entirely conscious nor unconscious. Francis Crick (1994), who shared a Nobel Prize for the discovery of DNA's structure in 1953 before turning to neuroscience and the study of consciousness, believes that we are in a state of diminished consciousness during REM sleep and that we are unconscious during NREM sleep. Certainly there are some elements of consciousness in the dream state. This particularly appears to be true in people who are *lucid dreamers.* You have probably had the occasional experience of realizing during a bad dream that it is not actually real and will end soon. That kind of experience is common for lucid dreamers—they are often aware during a dream that they are dreaming. People can increase their awareness during dreaming through practice, and they have been trained in the laboratory to the point that they can signal to the researcher when they are dreaming by pressing a handheld switch (Salamy, 1970). They can even learn to *control* the content of their dreams; they may decide before sleeping what they will dream about, or they may interact with characters in their dream (Gackenbach & Bosveld, 1989). This ability tells us that the sleeping person is not necessarily as detached from reality as we have thought.

People can also be very active physically during sleep. Even though the sleeper is usually paralyzed during REM, people with *REM sleep behavior disorder* (also known as REM without atonia) kick their bed partner, throw punches, and leap out of bed. A 67-year-old man had tied himself to his bed with a rope at night for six years because he had a habit of leaping out of bed and landing on furniture or against the wall. One night he was awakened by his wife's yelling because he was choking her; he was dreaming that he was wrestling a deer to the ground and was trying to break its neck

(Schenck, Milner, Hurwitz, Bundlie, & Mahowald, 1989). Sleepwalkers have driven cars, wandered the streets, and brandished weapons (Schenck et al., 1989), and have even strangled, stabbed, and beaten people to death. Jurors do not always believe a defense of sleepwalking, but in the case of Ken Parks, described in the opening vignette, they found the evidence convincing. He was sleep deprived due to stress over gambling debts and the loss of his job for embezzling, there was a personal and family history of sleepwalking, sleep talking, and bed-wetting, and he produced a high level of slow wave sleep during sleep monitoring (Broughton et al., 1994).

So it is not clear that the transition from consciousness to nonconsciousness occurs between REM and NREM. The idea of a dividing line is blurred even further by reports that surgical patients can sometimes remember the surgical staff's conversations while they were anesthetized, and they show some memory later for verbal material presented at the time of surgery (Andrade, 1995; Bonebakker et al., 1996). Whether you draw the line of consciousness between waking and sleeping or between REM and NREM sleep or between sleep and coma depends more on your definition of consciousness than on any clear-cut distinctions between these conditions (but see the accompanying Application). Perhaps it is better to think of sleep as a different state of consciousness along a continuum of consciousness. We can then concentrate on what the differences between waking and sleeping tell us about consciousness rather than worrying about classifications.

✔ CONCEPT CHECK

- *Describe the circadian and ultradian rhythms discussed here.*
- *What, according to research, are the functions of REM and slow wave sleep?*
- *Make a table showing the brain structures involved in sleep and waking, with their functions.*

APPLICATION

Determining Consciousness When It Counts

About 25,000 Americans are in a vegetative state as the result of illness or injury. Unlike comatose patients, they have daily cycles of wakefulness. Their eyes open and they may laugh, swear, or move their limbs, but they are unresponsive to their environments and their brain activity is reduced by half (Boyce, 2000). A subgroup has brain activity that is closer to 75%, although they are indistinguishable behaviorally from the others. Are they conscious or unconscious? This question is worth asking even if it doesn't have a yes-or-no answer. The patients with more brain activity have a better chance of recovering and, in the meantime, knowing their status will determine whether relatives and hospital staff attempt to find ways to communicate with them.

Hidden responsiveness in "locked-in" patients may predict their eventual outcome (Menon et al., 1998). After an illness a 26-year-old woman had to be tube fed and she required a tracheotomy to breathe; she showed sleep-wake cycles but no responsiveness. However, a PET scan showed that activity in her fusiform gyrus distinguished between photographs of familiar faces and pictures of jumbled faces. Eight months after the illness began she was showing clear recognition of faces and using short sentences, such as "Don't like physiotherapy." A second patient appeared to be blind, so the researchers used auditory stimulation with her. Her language area distinguished between meaningful words and other sounds; like the first patient, she also regained some awareness (Boyce, 2000). A third patient showed no response to either faces or words, and did not recover.

THE NEURAL BASES OF CONSCIOUSNESS

One is always a long way from solving a problem until one actually has the answer.

—Stephen Hawking

What do we mean when we use the term *consciousness*? Few researchers try to define the term; Crick (1994) believes that at our current level of understanding any definition we might come up with would be misleading and overly restrictive. However, I think most researchers would be comfortable with the following assertions about consciousness: The person is aware, at least to some extent; as a part of awareness, the person holds some things in attention while others recede into the background; and the person also has a sense of self. Consciousness varies in level, with coma and deep anesthesia on one extreme, alert wakefulness on the other, and sleep in between. There are also altered states of consciousness, including hypnosis, trances, and meditative states. Consciousness is a phenomenon of the brain, but almost all researchers agree that there is no "consciousness center." Consciousness appears to result from the interaction of widely distributed brain structures; which ones are active probably depends on the task the person is engaged in. Partly because consciousness appears to be distributed and partly because the problem is so overwhelming, researchers have resorted to looking for structures responsible for the components of consciousness. We will consider two of them here, *awareness* and *attention*.

Awareness

Awareness may be just as highly distributed as consciousness. A good illustration is a study that involved learning a discrimination between a tone that predicted an upcoming visual stimulus and a tone that did not (McIntosh, Rajah, & Lobaugh, 1999). Research participants who became aware of the association between the tone and the visual stimulus responded to the two tones with different levels of blood flow in the left prefrontal cortex (measured by PET scan). In addition, left prefrontal activity became coordinated with activity in other areas, including the right prefrontal cortex, auditory association areas, visual cortex, and the cerebellum. The researchers concluded that awareness involves the integration of activity in distributed regions.

They also suggested that the prefrontal cortex might be the key player in producing awareness. Others have suggested the hippocampus for that role, because of its involvement in declarative learning, which by definition involves awareness (Clark & Squire, 1998). Others claim that the parietal lobes' ability to locate objects in space is necessary for combining the features of an object; as evidence, they describe a patient with damage to both parietal lobes who often attributed one object's color or direction of movement to another object (Bernstein & Robertson, 1998; Treisman & Gelade, 1980). However, most researchers have turned to the thalamus, which appears to play a vital role in consciousness in general and awareness in particular.

Thalamic activity is profoundly depressed when a person is unconscious or deeply anesthetized (Tononi & Edelman, 1998), and lesions of the thalamus, particularly the *intralaminar nuclei*, cause a loss of consciousness (Smythies, 1997). In a celebrated case which led to new medical and legal treatment guidelines, Karen Ann Quinlan survived for 10 years in a vegetative state after a drug overdose. Although she showed signs of arousal, such as sleep-wake cycles and eye-opening to auditory stimuli, she did not respond in any meaningful way to her environment. Autopsy showed that the severest damage to her brain was in the thalamus, which suggested that the thalamus is critical for cognition and awareness but not for arousal (Kinney, Korein, Panigrahy, Dikkes, & Goode, 1994).

How does the brain solve the binding problem?

Many consciousness researchers also focus their attention on the visual system; we know that system well, and they believe that object awareness could provide a model for how the brain combines all the separate pieces of information into a perception of the complete object. **Researchers refer to the question of how the brain combines all the information about an object into a unitary whole as the *binding problem*.** Francis Crick (1994) hypothesized that the thalamus coordinates simultaneous firing of neurons in all the brain areas involved. Early studies found that during visual stimulation 50 to 70% of neurons in the visual area of cats fire in synchrony at an average of 40 Hz (Engel, König, Kreiter, & Singer, 1991; Engel, Kreiter, König, & Singer, 1991). For an illustration of 40-Hz synchrony see Figure 14.12.

A study with humans has shown that feedback from the area that detects movement (V5) to the primary visual area (V1) is necessary for awareness of movement to occur (Pascual-Leone & Walsh, 2001). This makes it all the more interesting that one of the cat studies found synchrony between these two areas (Engel, Kreiter, et al., 1991). (You may want to review Figure 9.24 for the location of V1 and V5.) More recent studies have used surface EEG recording to confirm firing synchrony in humans. In one of these studies, synchrony increased between the parietal-occipital area

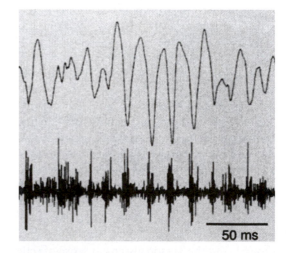

Figure 14.12
40-Hertz oscillations in neurons
Top: Recording of the combined activity of all neurons in the vicinity of the electrode. **Bottom:** Activity recorded at the same time from two neurons adjacent to the electrode. Note that the two neurons are firing in synchrony with all the others in the area.
Courtesy of Wolf Singer, Max-Planck-Institut für Hirnforschung.

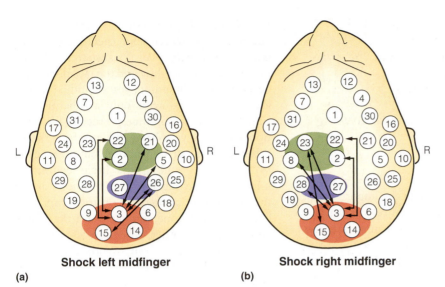

Shock left midfinger

(a)

Shock right midfinger

(b)

Figure 14.13
Synchronized activity among areas involved in learning
After a light was paired several times with shock to the middle finger, the light alone produced synchronized firing between the visual cortex and the somatosensory cortex where the fingers are represented. The lines indicate the locations of pairs of electrodes between which synchrony was observed. **(a)** Synchrony occurred in the right hemisphere when shock had been applied to the left hand, and **(b)** in the left hemisphere when shock had been applied to the right hand.
Adapted from Miltner et al., 1999. Reprinted by permission of *Nature*, copyright 1999.

and the frontal-temporal area at the moment the participants became aware of a face in an ambiguous figure (Rodriguez et al., 1999). In another, activity became synchronized between the visual cortex and the finger area of the somatosensory cortex when researchers presented a light that had previously been paired with finger shock (see Figure 14.13) (Miltner, Braun, Arnold, Witte, & Taub, 1999).

Awareness is obviously important to human functioning, but it is not necessary for all the important things the brain does. You have already seen in previous chapters that prosopagnosics are aroused by familiar faces that they do not otherwise recognize, that people with blindsight locate objects they deny seeing, and that patients with hippocampal damage improve over time on tasks that they deny having performed before. In a series of laboratory studies, research participants were able to learn and use a pattern for predicting the location of a target on a computer screen, but not one of them was able to state what the pattern was—even when offered a reward of $100 for doing so. In another series of studies, people learned to associate a particular facial feature with a particular personality characteristic, without being aware they had done so; in fact, when questioned they did not believe that

such a relationship existed (reviewed in Lewicki, Hill, & Czyzewska, 1992). We like to believe that our behavior is rational and guided by conscious decisions; perhaps we invent logical-sounding explanations for our behavior when we are not aware of its true origins.

Attention

Attention **is the brain's means of allocating its limited resources.** I doubt I need to tell you how important attention is. When you are paying attention to a fascinating book, you may not notice all the hubbub around you. Some stimuli "grab" your attention, though; for example, someone's voice calling your name stands out above all the din. What is attended to is easily remembered, and what escapes attention may be lost forever. The practical importance of attention was demonstrated in a study of automobile accidents among cellular phone users (Redelmeier & Tibshirani, 1997). Among 699 drivers who had cell phones in their cars and who had been involved in accidents, the risk of a collision was four times higher when the person was talking on the cell phone. This was not because the driver had one hand off the wheel, since the risk was just as high when the driver used a speaker phone; clearly, the problem was attention.

Neural scientists are thus beginning to address aspects of the fundamental question of consciousness by focusing on a specific, testable problem: What neural mechanisms are responsible for focusing visual attention?

—Eric R. Kandel

Although you are aware of the importance of attention, you probably do not realize just how powerful it is. An interesting demonstration is the *Cheshire cat* effect, named after the cat in *Alice in Wonderland* who would fade from sight until only his smile remained. Have a friend stand in front of you while you hold a mirror in your left hand so that it blocks your right eye's view of your friend's face but not the left eye's (Figure 14.14). Then hold your right hand so you can see it in the mirror. (This works best if you and your friend stand in the corner of a room with blank walls on two sides.) Your hand and your friend's face will appear to be in the same position, but your friend's face, or part of

it, will disappear. If you hold your hand steady you will begin to see your friend's face again, perhaps through your "transparent" hand; move your hand slightly and the face disappears again. By experimenting, you should be able to leave your friend with only a Cheshire cat smile. Your brain continues to receive information from both your hand and your friend's face throughout the demonstration; but because the two eyes are sending the brain conflicting information, telling it that two objects are in the same location, *binocular rivalry* occurs. The brain attends to one stimulus for a time, then switches to the other. Attention also switches when your hand or your friend's head moves and demands attention.

Attention is not just a concept; it is a physiological process, and changes in attention are accompanied by changes in neural activity. For example, during binocular rivalry activity shifts from one group of neurons in the visual cortex to another, even though the stimulus inputs do not change (Leopold & Logothetis, 1996). Activity shifts from one cortical area to another when individuals are instructed to notice different aspects of visual objects. PET scans showed that activity increased in visual area V4 when they focused on the object's color, shifted to the inferior temporal cortex when they attended to its shape, and changed to area V5 during attention to its movement (Chawla, Rees, & Friston, 1999; Corbetta, Miezin, Dobmeyer, Shulman, & Petersen, 1990). We know the shifts were due to attention, because activation increased in V4 during color attention even when the stimuli were uncolored, and in V5 during movement attention when the stimuli were stationary (Chawla et al., 1999).

So our experience of attention is a reflection of changes in brain activity. However, notice that we have not identified "attention centers." Attention and other aspects of consciousness may not be distinct functions as much as they are specific applications of other functions. For example, attention and awareness both involve synchronous firing (Fries, Reynolds, Rorie, & Desimone, 2001). In addition attention often, if

What is the neural basis of attention?

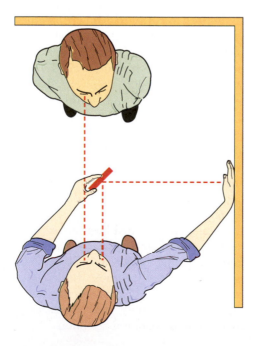

Figure 14.14
Setup for demonstrating the cheshire cat effect
Your view will alternate between your hand and the left side of your friend's face.

not always, requires working memory (Kastner & Ungerleider, 2000); loading up working memory with a string of random numbers impairs a person's ability to screen out distracting stimuli during an attention-demanding task (de Fockert, Rees, Frith, & Lavie, 2001). However, one structure may have a special role. **Several studies suggest that the *pulvinar*, a cluster of nuclei in the thalamus, shifts attention among stimuli** (Robinson & Petersen, 1992); for instance, PET scans show that the pulvinar is more active in humans when they attempt to identify objects among distractors than when no distractors are present.

✔ CONCEPT CHECK

■ *What is the binding problem? Describe a proposed solution.*
■ *What four changes in the brain accompany shifts of attention?*

THE SENSE OF SELF

Consciousness is usually studied in relation to external reality (for example, object recognition); this is in keeping with psychology's preference during much of its history for studying phenomena that are "out there" where we can observe them objectively. But an important aspect of consciousness is what we call the self; the sense of self includes an identity—what we refer to as "I"—and the sense of *agency*, the recognition that the actions we initiate affect external events. Consideration of self-awareness adds the dimension of "who" to the "what" and "where" that we explored in studying visual awareness.

Possibly nothing seems more real to us than this self. The self seems so real most likely because we have lived with it almost all our lives; it emerges so early in life that lack of language ability is the major obstacle to studying its development. Researchers have a cleverly simple way of getting around this reporting problem in preverbal children. They put a spot of rouge on a child's nose or forehead and place the child in front of a mirror. Infants younger than about 15 months reach out and touch the child in the mirror or kiss it or hit it. Older children begin to understand that the image in the mirror is not another child; we know this because they begin to use the mirror to examine the mysterious rouge spot on their face (Lewis & Brooks-Gunn, 1979). Chimpanzees are also able, after a time, to recognize themselves in the mirror; they examine the rouge spot, and they use the mirror to investigate parts of their body they have never seen before, like their teeth and their behinds (Figure 14.15). So do orangutans and porpoises, but not monkeys (Gallup, 1983; Reiss & Marino, 2001). Monkeys learn how a mirror works, because they turn to face a person whose reflection they see in the mirror. But after 17 years of

Figure 14.15
One of Gallup's chimps demonstrates concept of self
Source: Gallup & Povinelli, 1998. Photos courtesy of Cognitive Evolution Group, University of Louisiana at Lafayette.

continuous exposure to a mirror in their cage, Gallup's monkeys still treated their reflections like an intruder (Gallup & Povinelli, 1998).

Some Origins of the Self

A few investigators have searched the brain for neural bases of the self. They have found, for example, that damage to the right frontal-temporal cortex may produce a detachment from the self (Wheeler, Stuss, & Tulving, 1997), and that perceiving oneself as the cause of an action activates a different part of the brain compared to attributing the action to someone else (Farrer & Frith, 2002). We do not find a brain location for the self but, rather, scattered bits and pieces. This is because the self, like the mind, is the sum of many functions. But however scattered its parts, we will examine two of them: body image and memory.

Body Image

Where does our sense of self come from?

We can see evidence of the importance of body image in our cultural obsessions with weight, body build, and beauty. But the significance of body image goes deeper than that, as we see in people whose body image is disrupted, like Christina in Chapter 10. The person is almost paralyzed at first, not because of any motor dysfunction but rather because there is no feedback to guide movements. The ability to sit up, to stand, and to walk, when it does return, depends entirely on vision. But even more remarkable than the impairment or the heroism of people like Christina is how devastating the loss can be emotionally. Watching a home movie of herself before the illness, she exclaimed,

> Yes, of course, that's me! But I can't identify with that graceful girl any more! She's gone, I can't remember her, I can't even imagine her. It's like something's been scooped right out of me, right at the centre. (Sacks, 1990, p. 51)

Amputation has a similar effect on the person's body image, and the sense of self can be impaired as well. S. Weir Mitchell, a Civil War physician who saw numerous amputees, presented some of his observations in the fictionalized account *The Case of George*

Dedlow (Mitchell, 1866). Mitchell's hero, who has lost both arms and both legs in battle, says,

> I found to my horror that at times I was less conscious of myself, of my own existence, than used to be the case. . . . I felt like asking someone constantly if I were really George Dedlow or not. (p. 8)

We have only recently realized the importance of body image to the self, partly through studies of patients with *phantom limbs*. You learned earlier that many amputees experience phantom limb pain; a larger majority, probably around 80%, experience a nonpainful but more bizarre illusion that the hand or arm or leg is still there (see Figure 14.16). For some, the phantom limb seems to be stuck in a particular position. One man's phantom arm was bent behind him; he was unable to sleep on his back because of this illusion. Another's amputated arm seemed to be elevated to the side; when he walked through a

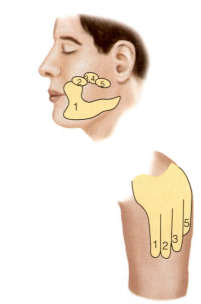

Figure 14.16
Maps of a patient's phantom hand
Touching the arm above the stump produced sensations of the missing hand. The same thing happened on the face, confirming what we saw in Chapter 10, that neurons from the face have invaded the hand area in the somatosensory cortex.

Source: Figure 2.2 from *Phantoms in the Brain* by V. S. Ramachandran, M. D., Ph.D., and Sandra Blakeslee. Copyright 1998 by V. S. Ramachandran and Sandra Blakeslee. Reprinted by permission of HarperCollins Publishers Inc., William Morrow.

doorway he had to turn sideways (Melzack, 1992). Some amputees feel that the imaginary limb is still under voluntary control. One man, when asked to reach with his nonexistent arm and grasp a cup on the table, felt he was doing so; though he knew it was all an illusion, he grimaced in pain when the researcher moved the cup away, saying that it felt like the cup had been ripped from his fingers (Shreeve, 1993). Researchers once thought that phantoms occurred only after a person developed a *learned* body image, but we now know that phantoms can occur in young children and even in people born with a missing limb. Because the body image is part of the equipment we are born with, it becomes an important part of the self—even when it conflicts with reality.

Memory

Without long-term memory it is doubtful there can be a self, because there is no past and no sense of who the person is. In the words of memory researcher James McGaugh, memory "is what makes us us" (Wilson, 1998). Loss of short-term memory is not as disruptive; patients like HM (described in Chapter 11) have a lifetime of information about their past and about themselves as a background for interpreting current experience, even if they do not remember events that have occurred since their brain damage. However, for Korsakoff's and Alzheimer's patients, memory loss extends back several years before the onset of illness, as well as after the onset. You might think that a patient with an extreme loss of memory would simply withdraw into unresponsiveness. To some extent that is true. Oliver Sacks's patient Jimmie had lost 40 years of memories to Korsakoff's disease; restless, unable to say whether he was miserable or happy, he reported that he had not felt alive for a very long time (Sacks, 1990).

Mary Francis, whom you met in Chapter 11, took another approach, explaining her situation with one false scenario after another. Another confabulator was Mr. Thompson, Sacks's Korsakoff patient. One day he strode up to the hospital's front desk, introduced himself as the Reverend William Thompson, ordered a cab, and took a day's liberty from the hospital. On his return the staff had a chance to talk to the cabdriver, who said he had never had so fascinating a passenger, who told amazing stories of personal adventures. "He seemed to have been everywhere, done everything, met everyone. I could hardly believe so much was possible in a single life." According to Sacks, Mr. Thompson had to "make himself (and his world) up every moment," by turning everyone on the ward into characters in his make-believe world, and weaving story after story as he attempted to create both a past and a present for himself (Sacks, 1990, p. 110).

Many amnesics do not confabulate, so amnesia alone does not explain confabulation. In those who do, their stories can usually be traced back to fragments of actual experiences. This is consistent with the hypothesis introduced in Chapter 11, that confabulation is a failure to suppress irrelevant memories due to damage in the frontal area (Benson et al., 1996; Schnider & Ptak, 1999). Lack of suppression may explain the content of confabulations, but researcher Tim Shallice (1999) does not believe it accounts for the consistency of the stories over time, much less the richness with which the confabulator weaves the memory fragments into a meaningful story. The confabulations of Mr. Thompson and Mary Francis appear to be highly motivated behaviors, suggesting the importance of real or imagined memories to the person's identity. As the movie director Luis Buñuel said as he waited for his own amnesia to advance,

> . . . memory is what makes our lives. Life without memory is no life at all. . . . Our memory is our coherence, our reason, our feeling, even our action. Without it, we are nothing. (quoted in Sacks, 1990, p. 23)

Disorders of Self

Chapter 3 describes a surgical procedure that separates the two cerebral hemispheres by cutting the corpus callosum and the anterior commissure. This surgery is used to prevent severe epileptic seizures from crossing the commissures and engulfing the other side of the brain. Psychologists are interested in these patients because they provide a unique opportunity to study the differing roles of the two hemispheres. Studies of split-brain patients also raise important questions about consciousness and the self. Because severing the commissures deprives the hemispheres of the opportunity to share information, some researchers say that the surgery divides the normally unitary consciousness into two, and others go so far as to say that there are actually two selves.

The Split Brain and the Self

What do the disorders tell us?

If we look at the behavior of split-brain patients, it is easy to see how some people would conclude that one person has been split into two selves. Gazzaniga (1970) described a patient who would sometimes find his hands behaving in direct conflict with each other, for instance, one pulling up his pants while the other tried to remove them. Once he shook his wife violently with his left hand (controlled by the more emotional right hemisphere), while his right hand tried to restrain the left. Another time, he and Gazzaniga were playing horseshoes in the patient's backyard when the man wandered over and picked up an axe with his left hand; Gazzaniga "discreetly left the scene—not wanting to be the victim of the test case of which half-brain does society punish or execute" (p. 107).

Over a period of time these patients' separated hemispheres begin to cooperate rather than compete with each other. The person appears normal, and only close observation in the laboratory during tasks that emphasize the differences in the hemispheres' capabilities will reveal that anything is wrong. If the person is asked to use the right hand to form a specified design with colored blocks, performance is poor because the left hemisphere is not very good at spatial tasks; sometimes the left hand, controlled by the more spatially capable right hemisphere, joins in to set the misplaced blocks aright, and has to be restrained by the experimenter.

Different researchers interpret these studies in different ways. At one extreme are those who believe that the major or language-dominant hemisphere is the arbiter of consciousness, and that the minor hemisphere functions as an unconscious automaton. At the other extreme are the researchers who believe that each hemisphere is capable of consciousness, and that severing the corpus callosum divides consciousness into two selves. Sixty years of research have prompted most theorists into positions somewhere along the continuum between those extremes.

Gazzaniga, for instance, points to the right hemisphere's differing abilities, such as the inability to form inferences, as evidence that the right hemisphere has only primitive consciousness (Gazzaniga, Ivry, & Mangun, 1998). He says the left hemisphere not only has language and inferential capability, but contains a module that he calls the "brain interpreter." **The role of the *brain interpreter* is to integrate all the cognitive processes going on simultaneously in other modules of the brain.** Gazzaniga was led to this notion by observing the patient PS performing one of the research tasks. Presented a snow scene in the left visual field and a picture of a chicken's foot in the right, he was to point to a picture that was related to what he had just seen. With the right hand he pointed to the picture of a chicken, and with the left he selected a picture of a shovel (see Figure 14.17). When asked to explain his choices he (his left hemisphere) said that the chicken went with the foot, and the shovel was needed to clean out the chicken shed. Unaware of what the right hemisphere had seen, the left hemisphere gave a reasonable but inaccurate explanation for the choice. The right hemisphere is capable of responding to simple written commands; if the command "Walk" is presented to the right hemisphere, the person will get up and start to walk away. When asked where he or she is going, the patient will say something like, "I'm going to get a Coke." According to Gazzaniga, these confabulations are examples of the brain interpreter making sense of its inputs, even though it lacks complete information.

Figure 14.17
Split-brain patient PS engaged in the task described in the text
His verbal explanation of his right hand's selection was accurate, but his explanation of his left hand's choice was purely confabulation. Source: Gazzaniga, 2002. Based on an Illustration by John W. Karpelou, BioMedical Illustrations.

Perhaps researchers who view the right hemisphere's consciousness as primitive are confusing consciousness with the ability to verbalize the contents of consciousness. It may be premature to assign different levels of consciousness to the two hemispheres. However, the behavior of split-brain subjects makes us aware of the need to avoid simple conceptions of consciousness.

Dissociative Identity Disorder

The case of Eve White illustrates another disorder of self. Eve went to a psychiatrist because of headaches and blackouts—periods of time she could not account for. During one interview she closed her eyes, and when she opened them again she was no longer shy and reserved, but animated and talkative. She denied that Eve's husband and daughter were her family; she knew them, she said, and did not like them. Over the course of therapy she—referred to as Eve Black—explained Eve White's blackouts; she

would take over and spend a night on the town dancing and drinking with strange men. The puritanical Eve White would have to deal with the hangover, explain a closetful of expensive clothes she didn't remember buying, and sometimes fend off an amorous stranger she found herself with in a bar. These "possessions" dated back to childhood, when a puzzled and protesting Eve White would be punished for Eve Black's mischief, such as biting the toes of the twin sisters who had usurped her parents' attention (Lancaster, 1958; Thigpen & Cleckley, 1957). Eve, whose real name is Chris Sizemore, went on to develop 22 different personalities before she was able to integrate them into a single self (Figure 14.18) (Sizemore, 1989).

Her experience is more or less typical of the unusual problem called **_dissociative identity disorder (DID)_, formerly known as multiple personality, which involves shifts in consciousness and behavior that appear to be distinct personalities or selves.** The causes of DID are not understood, but around 90 to 95% of patients report childhood physical and/or sexual abuse (Lowenstein & Putnam, 1990; Ross et al., 1990). In Sizemore's case the emotional trauma came from several sources: her sense of parental rejection, fear of a scaly monster her mother invented to frighten her into being "good," and the horror of witnessing the grisly death of a sawmill worker who was cut in two by a giant saw (Lancaster, 1958). Most therapists

Figure 14.18
Chris Sizemore
The story of her struggle with multiple personalities was the basis for the movie *The Three Faces of Eve*.

believe that the individual creates alternate personalities ("alters") as a defense against persistent emotional stress; the alters provide escape and, often, the opportunity to engage in prohibited forms of behavior (Fike, 1990; Ross et al., 1990).

Although the disorder had been reported occasionally since the middle 1600s (Bliss, 1980), it was the account of Sizemore's case in the book and movie *The Three Faces of Eve* that brought DID to the attention of clinicians and the public. As you can imagine, DID has been very controversial. The main reason for this controversy is the great increase in the number of reported cases; the total number of reports jumped from 500 in 1979 to 5,000 in 1985 (Braun, 1985). Some therapists believe that DID was underdiagnosed earlier, because therapists failed to recognize it among the other psychological disorders that often accompany DID (Fike, 1990; Lowenstein & Putnam, 1990; Putnam, 1991). But critics are convinced that the alternate personalities are created intentionally by the patient. The motivation, they say, is that a diagnosis of DID provides the patient a ready explanation for bizarre and troubling behavior or, in some cases, a defense for criminal behavior; overzealous therapists may intentionally or unintentionally lead patients to "discover" these alternate personalities (Spanos, 1994). There probably are many bogus cases, but extensive documentation by therapists and inclusion of DID in the *Diagnostic and Statistical Manual of Mental Disorders* (American Psychiatric Association, 1994) lend credibility to the diagnosis.

The earlier term, multiple personality disorder, inappropriately suggests that there are multiple selves or people living in one person's body. It is very difficult to read a typical DID case study without getting the feeling that the individual is more like an apartment house than a single person, especially when two of the personalities carry on a conversation among themselves and the therapist; in fact, many therapists talk about their patients as if there are multiple selves. Of course, if the self is just a concept, you can see how this characterization of the DID patient is misleading. However, if we throw out the "multiple person" interpretation the symptoms of multiple identity still remain, and several characteristics of DID beg explanation of any theorist who believes that all human behavior has a physiological basis.

There is relatively little physiological information for the neuroscientist to go on, but what does exist is intriguing. Therapists often report that alters differ from each other in handedness, reaction to medications, immune system responsiveness, allergies, and physical symptoms (Hall, O'Grady, & Calandra, 1994; Lowenstein & Putnam, 1990; Putnam, Zahn, & Post, 1990). Laboratory studies have found differences among the alters in several physiological measures, including heart rate, respiration, skin conductance, EEG, and cerebral blood flow. Even if these physical differences are due to changes in arousal and muscle tension, as some researchers suggest (Miller & Triggiano, 1992; Putnam et al., 1990), they still represent an interesting physiological mechanism that is worthy of explanation.

Bower (1994) attempts to explain the amnesia of DID as an example of *state-dependent learning*. In state-dependent learning, material learned in one state is difficult to recall in the other state; the altered states can be induced in the laboratory by alcohol and other drugs, and even by different moods. Bower's hypothesis is that abuse or other stresses create an altered state in which separate memories and adaptive strategies develop to the point that they form a distinct personality.

A learning explanation of DID does have some support at the neural level. Donald Condie and Guochuan Tsai studied a 33-year-old DID patient who as a child had been abused verbally, physically, and sexually for years by her alcoholic mother (Tsai, Condie, Wu, & Chang, 1997). Not surprisingly, the woman's hippocampus was half the normal size. The researchers asked the woman to switch personalities, which she was able to do voluntarily, while undergoing a functional magnetic resonance imaging scan. Activity in her right hippocampus and part of the temporal lobe increased and decreased as she switched back and forth (see Figure 14.19). Imagining a new personality required as much effort, but it did not have the same effect. The researchers blame the woman's malfunctioning hippocampus for the dissociation between memories formed during her tormented childhood.

Perhaps research on neural networks will help us understand how a person can develop a whole constellation of separate memories and personality characteristics. We should consider dissociative identity disorder not just a challenge but an added opportunity for studying neural functioning and, specifically, cognitive processes like learning.

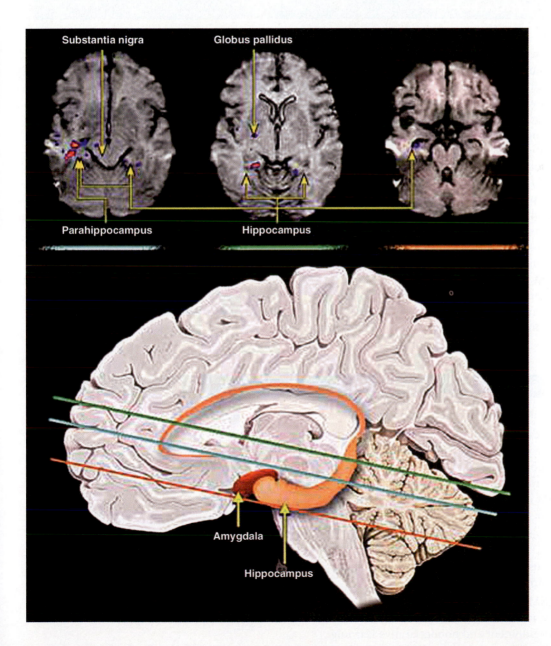

Figure 14.19
Hippocampal activity during switch between multiple personalities
The scans, taken at different brain levels, show activity in the hippocampus during the switch between personalities. The lower illustration shows the location of the scans above.
Source: Tsai et al., 1999.

CONCEPT CHECK

- *What roles do body image and memory play in the sense of self?*
- *What controversy about consciousness have the split-brain studies produced?*

- *What physical differences have been found between alternate personalities in DID patients?*

In Perspective

Time was when the topic of sleep was totally mysterious, and dreaming was the province of poets and shamans (witch doctors). Now sleep and dreaming are both yielding to the scrutiny of neuroscience. Although we are still unclear about the function of sleep, we are learning how various structures in the brain turn it off and on, and how our body dances not only to a daily rhythm but to another that repeats itself 16 times a day and controls our fluctuations in alertness, daydreaming, and night dreaming.

Consciousness is also giving up its secrets as researchers bring modern technologies to bear on awareness, attention, and memory. In other words, what was once a taboo topic is becoming accessible to the research strategies of science, and is providing a whole new arena of opportunities to observe the brain at work.

In this final chapter we have explored a unique field of research. The study of sleep has demonstrated neuroscience's ability to unravel mysteries and dispel superstition. The investigation of consciousness has been more daring, taking scientists where none had gone before. That is the job of science, to push back darkness whether by finding a treatment for depression or explaining humanity's most unique capabilities. But we have traveled a road filled with questions and uncertain facts, and the words of the schizophrenia researcher that "almost everything remains to be done" still seem appropriate. If all this ambiguity has left you with a vaguely unsatisfied feeling, that is good; you may have the makings of a scientist. And we have left the most exciting discoveries for you.

In Perspective Summary

Sleep and Dreaming

- Circadian rhythms are rhythms that repeat on a daily basis, affecting the timing of sleep and several bodily processes. The suprachiasmatic nucleus is the most important control center, but not the only one. The rhythm is primarily entrained to light.

- Several ultradian rhythms occur within the day. One involves alternating periods of arousal during waking and stages that vary in arousal during sleep.

- REM sleep is when most dreaming occurs, but it has also been implicated in neural development and nondeclarative learning.

- Slow wave sleep may restore cerebral and cognitive functioning.

- Sleep and waking are controlled by separate networks of brain structures, each with a center in the basal forebrain area.

- Sleep is an active period, a state of consciousness that is neither entirely conscious nor unconscious.

The Neural Bases of Consciousness

- Any very specific definition of consciousness is premature, but normal consciousness includes awareness, attention, and a sense of self.

- How awareness comes about is unclear, but the thalamus apparently is involved, possibly as the coordinator of synchronous firing of neurons in involved areas, which is hypothesized to produce binding.
- Attention allocates the brain's resources, actually shifting neural activity among neurons or brain locations.

The Sense of Self

- The body image is an important part of the sense of self, illustrated most dramatically in people who have lost limbs or lost sensation from the body.

- Memory provides the past that a sense of identity is built upon; loss of memory is particularly disabling for that reason.
- Split-brain surgery provides an interesting research opportunity into consciousness which has prompted debates about each hemisphere's contribution to consciousness and to the self.
- Dissociative identity disorder involves what appear to be distinct personalities or selves. Reports indicate that the different states include different physical and physiological characteristics.

➤ For Further Thought

- Animals cycle on a 24-hour schedule, either sleeping at night and being active during the day or vice versa. An alternative would be to sleep when fatigue overtakes the body, regardless of the time. What advantages does a regular schedule have?
- Machines and, probably, some simpler animals function just fine without awareness.

Our best guess at this point is that awareness places a heavy demand on neural resources. What adaptive benefits do you see?
- Do you think we will be able to understand consciousness at the neural level? Why or why not?

➤ Testing Your Understanding

1. Discuss the functions of sleep, including the REM and slow wave stages of sleep.

2. Discuss attention as a neural phenomenon.

3. Discuss the function of confabulation in dreaming and in the behavior of split-brain patients and Korsakoff's patients.

Select the one best answer:

1. The most important function of sleep is:

   a. restoration of the body.
   b. restoration of the brain.
   c. safety.
   d. all of these.
   e. uncertain.

2. The body's own rhythm, when the person is isolated from light, is:

   a. approximately 24 hours long.
   b. approximately 25 hours long.

   c. approximately 28 hours long.
   d. unclear because of conflicting studies.

3. Jim is totally blind, but he follows a 24-hour day-night cycle like the rest of us, and seems comfortably adapted to it. He probably relies on:

   a. a built-in rhythm in his SCN.
   b. nonvisual receptors in his eyes
   c. clocks and social activity
   d. a and b.
   e. b and c.

4. According to the activation-synthesis hypothesis, dreams are the result of a combination of random neural activity and:

   a. external stimuli.
   b. wishes.
   c. concerns from the day.
   d. memories.

continued

5. Evidence that REM sleep specifically enhances consolidation is that:

   a. REM increases after learning.
   b. REM deprivation interferes with learning.
   c. performance improves following REM sleep.
   d. a and b.
   e. a, b, and c.

6. If there is an "excecutive" sleep and waking center in the brain, it would appear to be the:

   a. basal forebrain area.   b. POAH.
   c. locus coeruleus.   d. raphe nuclei.

7. The magnocellular nucleus is responsible for:

   a. initiating sleep.
   b. waking the individual.
   c. switching between REM and NREM sleep.
   d. producing atonia during REM.

8. Cataplexy is:

   a. sleep without a REM component.
   b. a waking experience of atonia.
   c. a more severe form of narcolepsy.
   d. clinically significant insomnia.

9. The binding problem arises because:

   a. there is no clear dividing line between consciousness and unconsciousness.

   b. we are unsure what the function of sleep is.
   c. there is no single place where all the components of an experience are integrated.
   d. we lack agreement on what consciousness is.

10. An EEG at 40 Hz is associated with:

    a. binding.   b. dreaming.
    c. consolidation.   d. attention.

11. The part of the brain that shifts attention among stimuli may be the:

    a. basal forebrain area.   b. magnocellular nucleus.
    c. pulvinar.   d. raphe nuclei.

12. An explanation offered for confabulation links it to damage to the:

    a. locus coeruleus.   b. temporal lobes.
    c. pulvinar.   d. frontal areas.

13. The credibility of dissociative identity disorder is increased by:

    a. the high frequency of its diagnosis.
    b. different patterns of physiological measures.
    c. patients' lack of incentive to fake the symptoms.
    d. location of damage in a particular brain area.

Answers: 1. **e** 2. **d** 3. **b** 4. **d** 5. **e** 6. **a** 7. **d** 8. **b** 9. **c** 10. **a** 11. **c** 12. **d** 13. **b**

 On the Web

1. **The National Sleep Foundation** has information on sleep disorders, links to sites of sleep research and support organizations, and results of polls on topics such as Sleep in America and Sleep Since 9/11 at

   http://www.sleepfoundation.org/

   Sleepnet.com has information on sleep disorders, a sleep test, and links to sleep clinicians at

   http://www.sleepnet.com/

The Sleep Well is the website of William Dement, noted sleep researcher. It covers a variety of topics, including sleep disorders, sleep tests, and links to other sleep sites, at

   http://www.stanford.edu/~dement/

2. **Exploring the Consciousness Problem** is Bryn Mawr's contribution to the topic, in the form of a reading list, discussions, and extensive links to online papers at

   http://serendip.brynmawr.edu/bb/ consciousness/

The American Association for the Scientific Study of Consciousness has full-text contents of conferences and seminars on consciousness at

http://assc.caltech.edu/

 • For additional information about the topics covered in this chapter, please look at InfoTrac College Edition, at

http://www.infotrac-college.com/wadsworth

Try search terms you think up yourself, or use these: *consciousness; dissociative identity disorders; melatonin; narcolepsy.*

 On the CD-ROM: Exploring Biological Psychology

Video: Sleep Cycle
Stages of Sleep on an EEG
Simulation: EEG
Animation: Awake
Animation: Stage 1

Animation: Stage 2
Animation: Stage 3
Animation: Stage 4
Animation: REM

 For Further Reading

The Sleepwatchers, by William Dement (1992, Stanford Alumni Association), is an entertaining description of sleep research by the most widely known expert.

The Feeling of What Happens, by Antonio Damasio (1999, Harcourt), discusses the contributions of the body and emotions to consciousness and the self. It is highly praised by professionals and very readable as well.

The Split Brain Revisited, by Michael Gazzaniga (2002, *Scientific American*,

Special Edition, "The Hidden Mind," pp. 27–31), is a good summary of what we have learned from split-brain patients.

The Scientific American Book of the Brain (1999, Lyons Press) includes three very interesting articles on consciousness by experts in the field: *The Puzzle of Conscious Experience*, by David Chalmers, *Can Science Explain Consciousness?*, by John Horgan, and *The Problem of Consciousness*, by Francis Crick and Christof Koch.

 Key Terms

activation-synthesis hypothesis *405*

attention *413*

basal forebrain area *407*

binding problem *412*

brain interpreter *418*

cataplexy *408*

dissociative identity disorder (DID) *419*

melatonin *401*

narcolepsy *408*

non-REM (NREM) sleep *404*

PGO waves *408*

pulvinar *415*

rapid eye movement (REM) sleep *404*

slow wave sleep (SWS) *403*

suprachiasmatic nucleus (SCN) *399*

ultradian rhythm *402*

Methods of Nervous System Research

The brain does not give up its secrets easily. If we remove the case from a clock and observe the gears turn and the spring expand, we can get a pretty good idea how a clock measures time; but if we open the skull, how the brain works remains just as much a mystery as before. For that reason, understanding the nervous system has depended as much on the development of new research techniques as it has on the insight of researchers. Your understanding of the information that fills the rest of this book—and of the limitations of that information—will require some knowledge of how the researchers came by their conclusions. The following review of a few major research methods is an abbreviated list, but it will help you navigate your way through the rest of the book and we will add other methods as we go along.

STAINING AND LABELING NEURONS

It didn't take long to exhaust the possibilities for viewing the nervous system with the naked eye, but the invention of the microscope took researchers many steps beyond what the pioneers in gross anatomy could do. The capability of the light microscope is limited, however, not due to the skills of the lens maker but to the nature of light itself; increases in magnification beyond about 1,500 times yield little additional information. The electron microscope, on the other hand, can distinguish features as small as a few hundred millionths of a centimeter; with that resolution we can, for example, examine the fine details of the structure of nerve cells. The electron microscope works by passing a beam of electrons through a thin slice of tissue onto a photographic film; because the different parts of the tissue absorb electrons to different degrees, an image is formed on the film.

Unfortunately, nerve cells, or *neurons*, are greatly intertwined and are difficult to distinguish from each other, even when magnified. The information the microscope provided was dramatically increased around 1875 when the Italian anatomist Camillo Golgi discovered the staining procedure that bears his name. **The *Golgi stain* method randomly stains about 5% of neurons, placing them in relief against the background of seeming neural chaos.** An example of Golgi-stained neurons appears in Figure A.1. Golgi's Spanish contemporary, Santiago Ramón y Cajal, used the technique to learn a great deal about the structure of the nervous system, including the previously unknown fact that neurons are separate cells. Golgi and Cajal jointly received the 1906 Nobel Prize in physiology and medicine for their contributions.

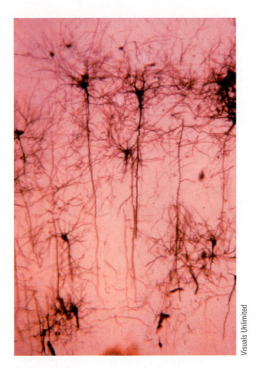

Figure A.1
Golgi stain
Golgi stains emphasize individual neurons.

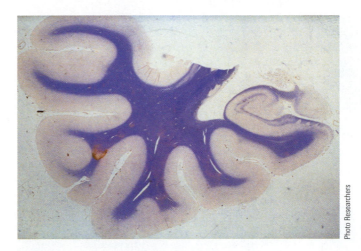

Figure A.2
Myelin staining of a human brain
Notice how the middle areas are stained dark; myelin stains emphasize neural pathways.

Myelin stains **are taken up by the fatty myelin that wraps and insulates the part of neurons that carry messages to other locations; the stain thus identifies neural pathways.** In Figure A.2 the brain is heavily stained in the inner areas where many pathways converge, and stained lightly or not at all in the perimeter. *Nissl stains* **do the opposite; they identify the other main part of a nerve cell, the cell body, which is where neural processing occurs.** In the rat brain shown in Figure A.3, each dot is a cell body.

Staining does not tell us anything about function. *Autoradiography* **makes neurons stand out visibly just as staining does, but it also reveals which neurons are active, and this information can be correlated with the behavior the animal was engaged in.** The animal is injected with a substance that has been made radioactive, such as a type of sugar called 2-deoxyglucose (2-DG). Then the researcher usually stimulates the animal, for instance, by presenting a visual pattern or requiring the subject to learn a task. Active nerve cells take up more glucose; because 2-DG is similar to glucose, the neurons involved in the activity become radioactively "labeled." The animal is sacrificed and the part of the brain being studied is cut into thin slices which are placed on X-ray film; the radioactivity produces an image of the active cells on the

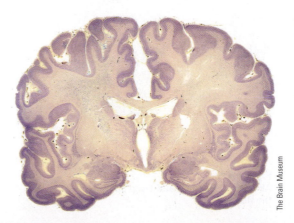

Figure A.3
Nissl stain of rat brain
Nissl stains emphasize cell bodies of nerve cells, where the processing of the nervous system occurs.

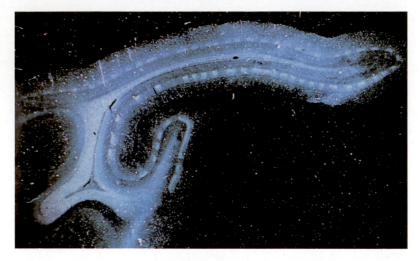

Figure A.4
Autoradiograph of part of the visual cortex
Radioactively labeled amino acid was injected into the right eye of an anesthetized animal. The dark bands indicate that the light-receptive cells of each eye project to alternating columns of cells in the cortex.
Source: Hubel & Wiesel, 1979.

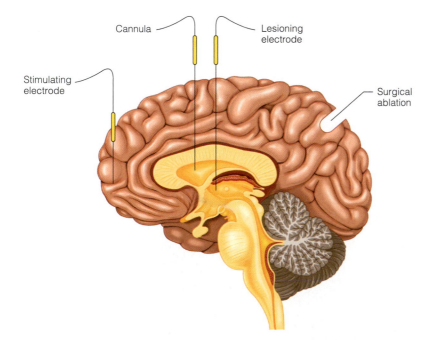

Figure A.5
Ablation, Lesioning, and Deep Stimulation of the Brain

film (Figure A.4). In a variation of this method, a radioactive amino acid (the building block that proteins are made of) is injected into an area where there are cell bodies, such as the light-sensitive back of the eye. The amino acid is taken up and transported through the neuron to its end in the brain. This modification is very useful in determining exactly how parts of the brain are connected.

ABLATION AND STEREOTAXIC TECHNIQUES

One of the ways to find out what function a part of the brain has is to destroy the tissue in question, then observe the behavior of the animal to see what changes occur. This is not a foolproof method; the structure destroyed may be only a part of a complex system, or the behavioral change may be caused by damage to tracts passing through, rather than by damage to the structure itself. Assuming that the structure is responsible for the change in behavior is like turning off your computer's monitor, then concluding that it is the monitor that does the computing. The results of studies that destroy neural tissue must be compared with findings from other kinds of research.

Removal of brain tissue is called *ablation* (see Figure A.5). Ablation can be done with a scalpel, but *aspiration* is a more precise technique, and it allows access to deeper structures. The skull is opened and a fine-tipped glass micropipette connected to a vacuum pump is used to suck out neural tissue. **Lesions, or damage to neural tissue**, can be produced with knife cuts, chemical injection, heat, cold, or electrical current.

For lesioning of small structures, the location must be determined very precisely. With humans this is done individually by doing a brain scan beforehand, but with nonhuman animals researchers use a map of the brain called a *stereotaxic atlas*. An atlas for the rat brain is developed by removing the brains of rats and slicing them into extremely thin cross sections. A drawing is made of each slice and the structures are outlined on the drawings, based on averages from a large number of rats (Figure A.6). A number on each drawing indicates how far the particular slice is from a landmark suture on the skull (where two plates of the skull meet). The scales on the side and the bottom of the drawing tell the researcher how deep and how far from the midline the electrode should be located.

A *stereotaxic instrument* **is a device used for the precise positioning in the brain of an electrode or other device** (Figure A.7). The rat is anesthetized and placed in the instrument; its head is fixed in place with clamps and the scalp is opened. The researcher uses the knobs on the instrument to adjust the electrode carrier to the desired horizontal location, marks the location on the skull, then drills a hole in the skull with a small drill. Then, the instrument is used to lower an electrode, which is insulated except for its tip, to the proper depth in the brain. Because the measurements used were averages, the researcher must sacrifice the animals at the end of the study and examine each brain to make sure the electrode was in the right place before the behavioral data from that animal can be used.

Using the same technique, the researcher can also insert an electrode for stimulating the brain. A low-voltage electrical stimulus will cause neurons near the electrode tip to fire. The researcher can monitor responses in other parts of the brain or in the body while the still-anesthetized animal's brain is stimulated; or the wound can be closed and, after a few days of recovery, the rat's behavior can be studied during stimulation. Alternatively, an implanted electrode can be used to record neural activity while the researcher subjects the animal to a learning task, presents visual or auditory stimuli, or introduces a member of the other sex. An additional possibility is to insert a cannula (a small tube) for delivering a drug to a precise location or for extracting fluids for analysis.

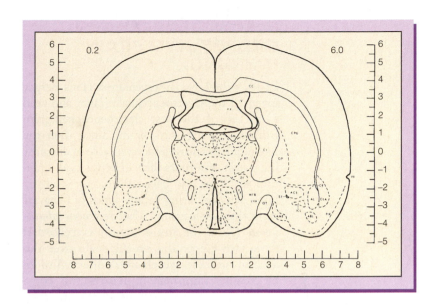

Figure A.6
A plate from a stereotaxic atlas
From L. J. Pellegrino, A. S. Pellegrino, and A. J. Cushman, "A stereotaxic atlas of the rat brain," 2nd Edition, Kluwer Academic/Plenum Publishers. Copyright 1979, Plenum Publishers. Reprinted with permission.

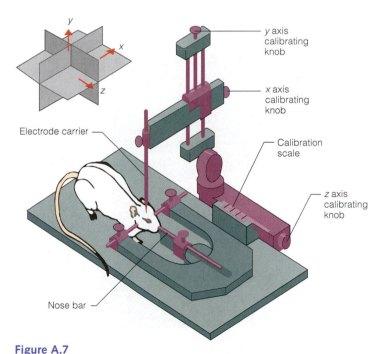

Figure A.7
A stereotaxic instrument
This device allows the researcher to precisely locate an electrode or cannula at the right horizontal position and depth in the animal's brain.

ELECTROENCEPHALO-GRAPHY AND BRAIN IMAGING

In 1929 the German psychiatrist Hans Berger invented the electroencephalograph, and used it to record the first electroencephalogram from his young son's brain. Since then the technique has proved indispensable in diagnosing brain disorders like epilepsy and brain tumors; it has also been valuable for studying brain activity during various kinds of behavior from sleep to learning. **The *electroencephalogram* (*EEG, or brain waves*) is recorded from two electrodes on the scalp over the area of interest, which are connected to an electronic amplifier; it detects the combined electrical activity of all the neurons between the two electrodes** (see Figure A.8). (The abbreviation EEG is also used to refer to the method, electroencephalography.) The temporal (time) resolution of EEG is good; it can distinguish events only 1 millisecond (msec) apart in time, so it can track the brain's

Table A.1 Resolution of EEG and Imaging Techniques		
Technique	**Temporal Resolution**	**Spatial Resolution**
EEG	1 msec	10–15 mm
PET	45 sec	4 mm
MRI	3–5 sec	1–1.5 mm
Source: Volkow, Rosen, & Farde, 1997.		

responses to rapidly changing events. However, its spatial resolution, or ability to detect precisely where in the brain the signal is coming from, is poor (Table A.1 compares EEG with two of the imaging techniques to be discussed later). An offsetting feature is that it is inexpensive, an important factor when the cost of the imaging techniques is considered.

EEG is not good at detecting the response to a brief stimulus because the "noise" of the brain's other ongoing activity drowns it out. Combining electroencephalography with the computer enables researchers to measure *evoked potentials*. A stimulus is repeated

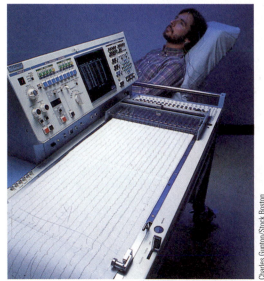
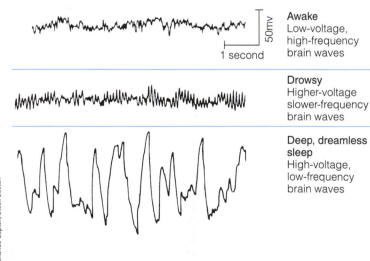

Charles Gupton/Stock Boston

Awake
Low-voltage, high-frequency brain waves

50mv
1 second

Drowsy
Higher-voltage slower-frequency brain waves

Deep, dreamless sleep
High-voltage, low-frequency brain waves

Figure A.8
An electroencephalograph and a sample EEG
The machine on the left is used to record the electrical activity of the brain using electrodes on the scalp. The EEG tracings on the right show how the pattern of activity changes as a person goes from waking to sleeping.
Source: (Right) From *Current Concepts: The Sleep Disorders* by P. Hauri, 1982. The Upjohn Company, Kalamazoo, MI.

many times and the digitized record of the EEG from each of these presentations is averaged. The noise of ordinary brain activity cancels itself out because the electrical signal goes positive as often as it goes negative. The response that is unique to the stimulus, however, has nothing to cancel it out and so it remains. A researcher can use the technique to determine that spoken words produce a greater response in the left hemisphere than in the right, or to detect the increase in attention when a novel stimulus occurs among familiar ones.

The first modern medical imaging technique came into use in the early 1970s. *Computed tomography (CT) produces a series of X rays taken from different angles; these are combined by a computer, and the researcher or diagnostician can later scan through the "slices" to obtain a three-dimensional view of the brain or other part of the body* (Figure A.9). The CT added

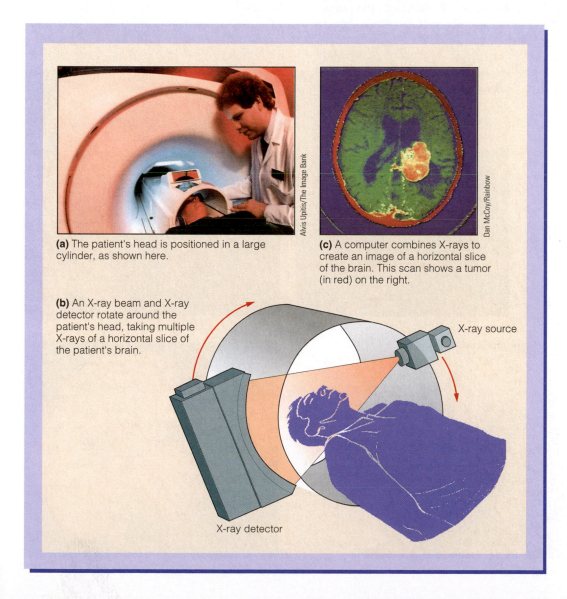

(a) The patient's head is positioned in a large cylinder, as shown here.

(c) A computer combines X-rays to create an image of a horizontal slice of the brain. This scan shows a tumor (in red) on the right.

(b) An X-ray beam and X-ray detector rotate around the patient's head, taking multiple X-rays of a horizontal slice of the patient's brain.

X-ray source

X-ray detector

Figure A.9
Computed tomography scanning procedure
The scan in (c) reveals a tumor on the right side of the brain.

considerable capability for detecting tumors and correlating brain damage with behavioral symptoms, but its slowness limits its value for researchers who want to study function.

Magnetic resonance imaging (MRI) involves measuring the radio-frequency waves emitted by hydrogen atoms when they are subjected to a strong magnetic field. Because different structures have different concentrations of hydrogen atoms, the waves can be used to form a detailed image of the brain (Figure A.10). Although the temporal resolution of the MRI is respectable, its strength is that it can detect activity in very small structures or areas. However, it also tells us only about structure, not function.

Positron emission tomography (PET) involves injecting a radioactive substance into the bloodstream, which is taken up by parts of the brain according to how active they are. The scanner makes an image that is color coded to show the relative amounts of activity (see Figure A.11). Radioactive 2-DG is often the substance that is injected because more active nerve cells take up more of it, so it provides a measure of metabolic

Figure A.10
Magnetic resonance imaging
The individual is slid into the device (left). On the right is a sample scan, which has detected a tumor (red arrow).

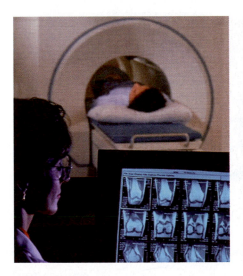

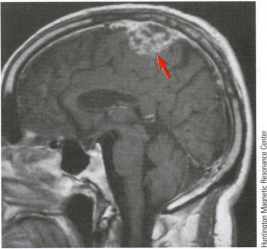

Huntington Magnetic Resonance Center

Figure A.11
Positron emission tomography
The apparatus on the left detects concentrations of radioactivity where activity is high; the computer produces a color-coded image like the one on the right. The individual was working on a verbal task, so areas involved in language processing were activated.

Burt Glinn/Magnum

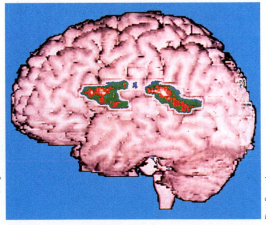

Photo Researchers

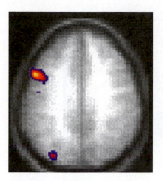 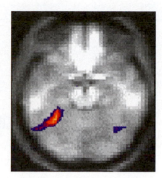

Figure A.12
A fMRI scan
The colored areas were more active when research participants were processing words that were later remembered than when they processed words that were not remembered.
Reprinted with permission from Wagner et al., "Building memories: Remembering and forgetting of verbal experiences as predicted by brain activity." *Science, 281,* 1188–1191. Copyright 1998 American Association for the Advancement of Science.

activity. Other radioactive substances can be used to monitor blood flow, oxygen uptake, or the activity of receptors on nerve cells as they are stimulated by a particular chemical messenger. PET has better spatial resolution than CT, and has the added benefit that it reveals function by showing activity level. Its slowness is a major limitation in psychological studies, because it cannot detect brain changes during behaviors that are briefer than 45 seconds. PET does not image the brain tissue itself, so the results are often displayed overlaid on a brain image produced by another means, such as MRI. The equipment is expensive and requires a sophisticated staff; the facility must also be near a cyclotron, and there are very few of those in the country.

A recent modification of MRI takes advantage of the fact that oxygenated blood has different magnetic properties from blood that has given up its oxygen to cells; *functional magnetic resonance imaging (fMRI) measures brain activation by detecting the increase in oxygen levels in active neural structures* (Figure A.12). Functional MRI has the advantage over PET and CT that it involves no radiation, so it is safe to use in studies that require repeated measurements. In addition, fMRI measures activity like PET, and produces an image of the brain with good spatial resolution like MRI. Researchers have been able to see activity in 1-mm-wide groups of neurons in the visual cortex (Barinaga,

1997). The fMRI machines are pricey, though, with current machines running in the $5–7 million range.

The fact that four people have won Nobel Prizes for the development of the CT scan and for the procedure that was the forerunner of the MRI indicates the importance of the imaging techniques (Raichle, 1994). Current research is focused on combining the procedures—to marry the sharpness of detail of fMRI and PET with the time resolution of EEG (Barinaga, 1997). You can be sure that many important future developments in neuroscience will depend on these imaging techniques, just as they have in the past 20 years.

BEHAVIORAL METHODS

The preceding methods involve rather direct manipulation or observation of neural functioning; behavioral techniques look at the *product* of the neural functioning in the form of an individual's behavior. A particularly valuable class of techniques includes psychological tests that measure emotional, cognitive, or intellectual function; these are often administered to brain-damaged patients by a specialist called a *neuropsychologist.*

Neuroscientists have also come up with a variety of tasks—some of them ingenious—for eliciting behaviors that will indicate what is going on in the brain. These may be used to

Figure A.13
**Apparatus for present-
ing visual information
to one hemisphere**
Source: Gazzaniga, 1967.

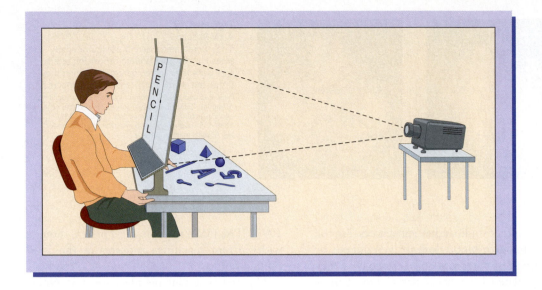

learn how the brain participates in the performance of a particular task, or to assess
changes resulting from drug ingestion, brain
stimulation, brain damage, and so on. The
technique used in studies of patients with a
severed corpus callosum, described in
Chapters 3 and 14, is a good example.

Figure A.13 shows the apparatus used to
present visual information to these patients. A
projector presents information on the right or
left side of the screen while the individual fixates on a spot in the middle of the screen;
because of the way the eyes are connected to
the two sides of the brain (hemispheres), **visual
information appearing on the left or the
right of the midpoint of the field of view
goes to the hemisphere on the opposite
side. For this reason, the technique is
known as *hemifield presentation*.** In patients
whose hemispheres have been surgically disconnected to prevent severe epileptic seizures
from traveling across to the other side of the
brain, this information is not shared with the
other hemisphere, so the researcher can study
how well each hemisphere performs various
kinds of tasks. The technique can be used with
intact individuals as well; if the stimulus is presented briefly, say for 1/10 second, the information does not cross the corpus callosum very
effectively. Most people can read words presented in the right visual field (to the left hemisphere) but do poorly when the words fall to
the left of the midline and go to the right
hemisphere.

A similar method for studying the two hemispheres' processing of auditory information
is the ***dichotic listening* technique, which
involves presenting stimuli to one ear at a
time with stereo headphones.** While the
information goes *primarily* to the opposite
hemisphere, each ear also sends weaker signals
to the hemisphere on the same side as the stimulated ear. So the researcher occupies that
hemisphere by simultaneously presenting
another word or random noise in the other
headphone. These studies show that the left
hemisphere is better at processing verbal information in most people, and the right is better
at other tasks, like recognizing melodies.
A modification of the technique has allowed
researchers to show that even mice process
vocalizations of other mice in their left
hemisphere.

Key Terms

Glossary

Numbers in parentheses indicate figures in which the item is illustrated.

2-deoxyglucose (2-DG) A type of sugar similar to glucose that can be made radioactive. Active neurons in experimental animals take up the glucose substitute and become radioactively labeled.

5-hydroxyindoleacetic acid (5-HIAA) A product of serotonin metabolism; used in research as an indicator of serotonin activity.

ablation Removal of brain tissue. (Figure A.5)

absolute refractory period A brief period during the action potential in which the neuron cannot be fired again because the sodium channels are closed.

absorptive phase The period of a few hours following a meal during which the body relies on the nutrients arriving from the digestive system. (Figure 5.6)

ACC See *anterior cingulate cortex.*

ACTH See *adrenocorticotropic hormone.*

action potential An abrupt depolarization of the membrane that allows the neuron to communicate over long distances. (Figure 2.6)

activating effects Hormonal effects on sexual development that can occur at any time in an individual's life; their duration depends on the presence of the hormone.

activation-synthesis hypothesis The hypothesis that during REM sleep the forebrain integrates neural activity generated by the brain stem with information stored in memory; an attempt to explain dreaming.

acute Referring to symptoms that develop suddenly and are usually more responsive to treatment.

AD See *Alzheimer's disease.*

addiction A preoccupation with obtaining a drug, compulsive use of the drug, and a high tendency to relapse after quitting.

adequate stimulus The energy form for which a receptor is specialized.

adipose tissue Tissue in which fat is stored; fat cells.

adoption study In heredity research, a study that compares a characteristic in individuals reared in an adoptive home and in individuals reared by their biological parents to determine whether the characteristic might be inherited.

adrenocorticotropic hormone (ACTH) Hormone that stimulates the adrenal glands to release the stress hormones epinephrine, norepinephrine, and cortisol.

agonist Any substance that mimics or enhances the effect of a neurotransmitter.

agonist treatment Addiction treatment that replaces the addicting drug with another drug that has a similar effect.

agraphia The inability to write due to brain damage.

alcohol Ethanol, a drug fermented from fruits, grains, and other plant products, which acts at many brain sites to produce euphoria, anxiety reduction, motor incoordination, and cognitive impairment.

aldehyde dehydrogenase (ALDH) An enzyme that metabolizes the alcohol byproduct acetaldehyde into acetate. A genetic deficiency in ALDH, or inhibition of ALDH by the anti-alcohol drug Antabuse, makes the drinker ill.

alexia The inability to read due to brain damage.

allele An alternate form of a gene.

all-or-none law The principle that an action potential occurs at full strength or it does not occur at all.

ALTD See *associative long-term depression.*

ALTP See *associative long-term potentiation.*

Alzheimer's disease (AD) A disorder characterized by progressive brain deterioration and impaired memory and mental abilities; the most common cause of dementia. (Figures 11.12–11.14)

amino acids The building blocks of peptides, which in turn make up proteins. In digestion, the result of the breakdown of proteins.

amphetamine One of a group of synthetic drugs that produce euphoria and increase confidence and concentration.

amplitude The physical energy in a sound; the sound's intensity.

amygdala Structure in each temporal lobe that receives input from all the sense modalities and produces fear and anxiety by targeting a variety of brain structures that produce emotional responses. (Figure 7.6)

analgesic Pain relieving.

anandamide An endogenous ligand for the cannabinoid receptor.

androgen insensitivity syndrome (AI) A form of male pseudohermaphroditism, involving decreased sensitivity of androgen receptors. The person has male sex chromosomes and male internal sex organs, and external sex organs that are female or ambiguous. It is caused by a mutation of the gene responsible for producing androgen receptors. (Figure 6.11)

androgens A class of hormones responsible for a number of male characteristics and functions.

angiotensin II A hormone that signals lowered blood volume and, thus, volemic thirst to the brain. (Figure 5.3)

angular gyrus A gyrus at the border of the parietal and occipital lobes containing pathways that connect the visual area with auditory, visual, and somatosensory association areas in the temporal and parietal lobes. Damage results in alexia and agraphia. (Figures 8.18, 8.22)

anorexia nervosa An eating disorder in which the person restricts food intake to maintain weight at a level so low that it is threatening to health.

ANS See *autonomic nervous system.*

Antabuse The trade name for disulfiram, used as an aversive treatment for alcohol addiction; it inhibits the ability of ALDH to break down the alcohol by-product acetaldehyde, making the drinker ill.

antagonist Any substance that reduces the effect of a neurotransmitter.

antagonist treatment A form of treatment for drug addiction using drugs that block the effects of the addicting drug.

antagonistic muscles Muscles that produce opposite movements at a joint. (Figure 10.14)

anterior Toward the front. (Figure 3.8)

anterior cingulate cortex (ACC) A part of the limbic system that has connections to many other limbic structures and is active during the emotion of pain. (Figure 7.6)

anterior commissure One of the cerebral commissures; according to some research, it is larger in gay men and heterosexual women than in heterosexual men. (Figures 3.5, 5.2)

anterograde amnesia An impairment in forming new memories.

antidrug vaccine A form of anti-addiction treatment using synthetic molecules that resemble the drug but that have been modified to stimulate the animal's immune system to make antibodies that will break down the drug.

antisense RNA A technology that temporarily disables a targeted gene or reduces its effectiveness.

antisocial personality disorder (APD) A condition in which people behave recklessly, violate social norms, commit antisocial acts like fighting, stealing, using drugs, and engaging in sexual promiscuity, and show little or no remorse for their behavior.

anxiolytic Anxiety reducing.

APD See *antisocial personality disorder.*

aphasia Language impairment caused by damage to the brain.

area postrema A part of the brain lacking protection from the blood-brain barrier; bloodborne toxins entering here induce vomiting.

arousal theory The theory that people behave in ways that keep them at their preferred level of arousal.

artificial neural network A group of simulated neurons that carry out cognitive-like functions. (Figure 2.16)

association cortex Brain areas that carry out further processing beyond what the primary projection area does, often combining information from other senses.

associative long-term depression (ALTD) Weakening of a synapse when two presynaptic neurons fire at different times.

associative long-term potentiation (ALTP) Strengthening of a weakly stimulated synapse as well as a strongly stimulated synapse on the same postsynaptic neuron when both synapses are stimulated at the same time.

attention The brain's means of allocating its limited resources by focusing on some neural inputs to the exclusion of others.

auditory cortex The area of cortex on the superior temporal gyrus, which is the primary projection area for auditory information. (Figures 3.7, 8.22)

auditory object The association of a sound with its source.

autism A disorder that typically includes compulsive, ritualistic behavior, impaired sociability, and mental retardation.

autistic savant An autistic individual with an isolated exceptional capability.

autoimmune disorder A disorder in which the immune system attacks the body's own cells.

autonomic nervous system (ANS) One of the two branches of the peripheral nervous system; includes the sympathetic and parasympathetic nervous systems. (Figures 3.19, 3.21)

autoradiography A technique for identifying brain structures involved in an activity; it involves injecting a radioactive substance (such as 2-DG) that will be absorbed most by the more active neurons, which then will show up on x-ray film. (Figure A.4)

autoreceptor A receptor on a neuron terminal that senses the amount of transmitter in the synaptic cleft and reduces the presynaptic neuron's output when the level is excessive. (Figure 2.14)

aversive treatment A form of addiction treatment that causes a negative reaction when the person takes the drug.

axon An extension from a neuron's cell body that carries information to other locations. (Figures 2.1, 2.2)

B cell A type of immune cell that fights intruders by producing antibodies that attack a particular intruder. (Table 7.1)

barbiturate A class of drugs that act selectively on higher cortical centers, especially those involved in inhibiting behavior, so they produce talkativeness and increased social interaction. In higher doses they act as hypnotics. Used to treat anxiety, aid sleep, and prevent epileptic convulsions.

basal forebrain area An area just anterior to the hypothalamus that contains both sleep-related and waking-related neurons.

basal ganglia The caudate nucleus, putamen, and globus pallidus, located subcortically in the frontal lobes; they participate in motor activity by smoothing movements using information from the primary and secondary motor areas and the somatosensory cortex. (Figure 10.20)

basal metabolism The amount of energy required to fuel the brain and other organs and to maintain body temperature.

basilar membrane The membrane in the cochlea that separates the cochlear canal from the tympanic canal, and on which the organ of Corti is located. (Figure 8.5c)

benzodiazepine A class of drugs that have effects similar to barbiturates in releasing inhibition and producing talkativeness and increased social interaction, but are safer because they do not open the chloride channel. Used to treat anxiety, aid sleep, and prevent epileptic convulsions.

binaural Involving the use of both ears.

binding problem The question of how the brain combines all the information about an object into a unitary whole.

biopsychology The branch of psychology that studies the relationships between behavior and the body, particularly the brain.

bipolar disorder Depression and mania that occur together in alternation.

birth complications Difficulties in birth, including premature or late birth, prolonged labor, umbilical cord around the neck, use of forceps during delivery, and so on.

bisexual An individual who is not entirely heterosexual or homosexual.

blood-brain barrier The brain's protection from toxic substances and neurotransmitters in the bloodstream; the small openings in the capillary walls prevent large molecules from passing through unless they are fat soluble or carried through by special transporters. (Figure 3.18)

body mass index (BMI) The person's weight in kilograms divided by the squared height in meters; an indication of the person's deviation from the ideal weight for the person's height. (Figure 5.11)

brain interpreter A hypothetical mechanism that integrates all the cognitive processes going on simultaneously in other modules of the brain.

Broca's aphasia Language impairment caused by damage to Broca's area and surrounding cortical and subcortical areas.

Broca's area The area anterior to the precentral gyrus (motor cortex) that sends output to the facial motor area to produce speech, and also provides grammatical structure to language. (Figures 3.7, 8.18)

BSTc See *central bed nucleus of the stria terminalis.*

bulimia nervosa An eating disorder involving bingeing on food, followed by purging by vomiting or using laxatives.

caffeine A drug that produces arousal, increased alertness, and decreased sleepiness; the active ingredient in coffee.

CAH See *congenital adrenal hyperplasia.*

cardiac muscles The muscles that make up the heart.

castration Removal of the gonads (testes or ovaries).

cataplexy A disorder in which a person has a sudden experience of atonia similar to that seen in REM sleep and falls to the floor, but remains awake.

CCK See *cholecystokinin.*

central bed nucleus of the stria terminalis (BSTc) A structure in the pathway between the amygdala and the preoptic area; in some research its size has been related to transsexualism, but not homosexuality. (Figure 6.17)

central nervous system The part of the nervous system made up of the brain and spinal cord. (Figure 3.19)

central pattern generator (CPG) A neuronal network that produces a rhythmic pattern of motor activity, such as those involved in walking, swimming, flying, and breathing.

central sulcus The groove between the precentral gyrus and the postcentral gyrus that separates the frontal lobe from the parietal lobe in each hemisphere. (Figure 3.7)

cerebellum Structure in the hindbrain that helps maintain balance and refines movements initiated by the motor cortex by controlling their speed, intensity, and direction. It is also necessary for learning motor skills and contributes to cognitive activities. (Figures 3.2, 3.12)

cerebral commissures Large bundles of neurons that carry information between the two cerebral hemispheres; include the corpus callosum and the anterior and posterior commissures. (Figures 3.5, 3.12)

cerebral hemispheres The large, wrinkled structures that are the dorsal or superior part of the brain and that are covered by the cortex. (Figures 3.2, 3.3. 3.4, 3.6, 3.7)

cerebrospinal fluid Fluid in the ventricles and spinal canal that carries material from the blood vessels to the central nervous system, and transports waste materials in the other direction. It also helps cushion the brain and spinal cord.

cholecystokinin (CCK) A hormone released as food passes into the duodenum. CCK acts as a signal to the brain that reduces meal size.

chronic Referring to symptoms that develop gradually and persist for a long time with poor response to treatment.

circadian rhythm A rhythm that is a day in length, such as the wake-sleep cycle.

circuit formation The third stage of nervous system development, in which the developing neurons send processes to their target cells and form functional connections.

circuit pruning The fourth stage of nervous system development, in which neurons that are unsuccessful in finding a place on the appropriate target cell, or that arrive late, die.

cocaine A drug extracted from the South American coca plant, which produces euphoria, decreased appetite, increased alertness, and relief from fatigue.

cochlea The snail-shaped structure where the ear's sound-analyzing structures are located. (Figure 8.5)

cochlear canal The middle canal in the cochlea; contains the organ of Corti. (Figure 8.5b)

cocktail party effect The ability to sort out meaningful auditory messages from a complex background of sounds.

cognitive theory Theory of emotion which states that a person relies on a cognitive assessment of the stimulus situation to identify which emotion is being experienced. (Figure 7.3)

coincidence detectors Neurons that fire most when they receive input from both ears at the same time; involved in sound localization. (Figure 8.17)

color agnosia Loss of the ability to perceive colors due to brain damage.

color constancy The ability to recognize the natural color of an object in spite of the illuminating wavelength.

compensation A response to nervous system injury, in which surviving presynaptic neurons sprout new terminals, postsynaptic neurons add more receptors, or surrounding tissue takes over functions.

complementary colors Colors that cancel each other out to produce a neutral gray or white. (Figure 9.7)

complex cell A type of cell in the visual cortex that continues to respond (unlike simple cells) when a line or edge moves to a different location. (Figure 9.21)

complex sound A sound composed of more than one pure tone. (Figure 8.3e, f)

computed tomography An imaging technique that produces a series of x rays taken from different angles; these are combined by a computer, and the researcher or diagnostician can later scan through the "slices" to obtain a three-dimensional view of the brain or other part of the body. (Figure A.9)

concentration gradient Difference in concentration of ions between the inside and outside of a neuron membrane, which causes ions to move to the side of less concentration. (Figure 2.5)

concordance rate The frequency that relatives are alike in a characteristic.

confabulation Fabrication of stories and facts, which are then accepted by the individual, to make up for those missing from memory.

confounded Mingled or confused, for example, when hereditary effects cannot be distinguished from environmental effects in research.

congenital adrenal hyperplasia (CAH) A form of female pseudohermaphroditism, characterized by XX chromosomes, female internal sex organs, and ambiguous external sex organs. It is caused by excess production of androgens during prenatal development.

congenital insensitivity to pain A condition present at birth in which the person is insensitive to pain.

consolidation Process in which the brain forms a permanent representation of a memory.

Coolidge effect An increase in sexual activity when the variety of sexual partners increases. (Figure 6.5)

corpus callosum The largest of the cerebral commissures. (Figures 3.5, 3.12)

correlation A statistical measure that varies between the values of 0.0 and ±1.0, and indicates the degree to which two variables are related, such as the IQs of parents with the IQs of their offspring.

correlational study A study in which the researcher does not control an independent variable, but determines whether two variables are related to each other. (Figure 1.6)

cortex The grayish 1.5- to 4-mm-thick surface of the hemispheres, composed mostly of cell bodies, where the highest level processing occurs in the brain.

cortisol A hormone released by the adrenal glands that increases energy levels by converting proteins to glucose, increasing fat availability, and increasing metabolism. The increase is more sustained than that produced by epinephrine and norepinephrine. (Figure 7.9)

CPG See *central pattern generator*.

cranial nerves The 12 pairs of nerves that enter and leave the underside of the brain; part of the peripheral nervous system. (Figure 3.20)

Dale's principle The idea that a neuron is able to release only one neurotransmitter.

db See *diabetes gene*.

deception In research, failing to tell the participants the exact purpose of the research or what will happen during the study, or actively misinforming them.

declarative memory The memory process that records memories of facts, people, and events, which the person can verbalize, or *declare*.

defensive aggression Aggression that occurs in response to threat and is motivated by fear.

delirium tremens A reaction in some cases of withdrawal from alcohol, including hallucinations, delusions, confusion, and, in extreme cases, seizures and possible death.

dendrites Extensions that branch out from the neuron cell body and receive information from other neurons.

dendritic spines Outgrowths from the dendrites that partially bridge the synaptic cleft and make the synapse more sensitive. (Figure 11.11)

deoxyribonucleic acid (DNA) A double-stranded chain of chemical molecules that looks like a ladder that has been twisted around itself; genes are composed of DNA. (Figure 1.8)

dependent variable (DV) In an experiment, the variable used to measure the effect of the independent variable. (Figure 1.6)

depressant A drug that reduces central nervous system activity.

depression An intense feeling of sadness.

dermatome A segment of the body served by a spinal nerve. (Figure 10.3)

diabetes gene (db) A gene on chromosome 4 that produces diabetes and obesity; mice with the gene are insensitive to leptin.

dichotic listening A technique for assessing differences in processing in the two hemispheres by presenting auditory stimuli to one ear at a time with stereo headphones.

DID See *dissociative identity disorder*.

diethylstilbestrol (DES) A synthetic female hormone once given to pregnant women to prevent miscarriage that, unlike others, did not masculinize the genitals of female offspring but appears in some research to have partially masculinized the brains and behavior of some of them.

difference in intensity A binaural cue to the location of a sound coming from one side, which results from the sound shadow created by the head; most effective above 2000–3000 Hz. (Figure 8.16)

difference in time of arrival A binaural cue to the location of a sound coming from one side, due to the time the sound requires to travel the distance between the ears. (Figure 8.16)

dihydrotestosterone A derivative of testosterone that masculinizes the genitals of males.

dissociative identity disorder (DID) The disorder previously known as multiple personality, which involves shifts in consciousness and behavior that appear to be distinct personalities or selves.

distributed The term for any brain function that occurs across a relatively wide area of the brain.

dizygotic (DZ) Referring to two separately fertilized eggs, which result in *fraternal* twins.

dominant The term referring to a gene that will produce its effect regardless of which gene it is paired with in the fertilized egg.

dopamine hypothesis The hypothesis that schizophrenia involves excess dopamine activity in the brain.

dorsal Toward the back side of the body. (Figure 3.8)

dorsal root The branch of a spinal nerve through which neurons enter the spinal cord. (Figure 3.17)

dorsal stream The visual processing pathway that extends into the parietal lobes; it is especially concerned with the location of objects in space. (Figure 9.24)

Down syndrome Mental retardation characterized by IQs in the 40 to 55 range, caused by the presence of an extra 21st chromosome.

drive An aroused condition resulting from a departure from homeostasis, such as depletion of nutrients (hunger) or a drop in temperature.

drive theory Theory based on the assumption that the body maintains a condition of homeostasis.

drug Any substance that on entering the body changes the body or its functioning.

dualism The idea that the mind and the brain are separate.

duodenum The initial 25 cm of the small intestine, where most digestion occurs. (Figures 5.6, 5.8)

DV See *dependent variable*.

dyslexia An impairment of reading, which can be developmental or acquired through brain damage.

early-onset alcoholism Cloninger's Type 2 alcoholism, which involves early onset, frequent drinking without guilt, and characteristics of antisocial personality behavior.

ECT See *electroconvulsive therapy*.

EEG See **electroencephalogram**.

efferent Referring to neural activity flowing from the brain to the periphery.

electrical gradient A difference in electrical charge between the inside and outside of a neuron, which forces ions to move to the side that has a charge opposite their own. (Figure 2.5)

electrical stimulation of the brain (ESB) A procedure in which animals (or humans) learn to press a lever or perform some other action to deliver mild electrical stimulation to certain parts of their brain.

electroconvulsive therapy (ECT) The application of 70–130 volts of electricity to the head of a lightly anesthetized patient, which produces a grand mal seizure; a treatment for major depression. (Figure 13.12)

electroencephalogram (EEG) A measure of brain activity recorded from two electrodes on the scalp over the area of interest, which are connected to an electronic amplifier; it detects the combined electrical activity of all the neurons between the two electrodes. (Figure A.8)

embryo An organism in the early prenatal period, for humans, during the first eight weeks.

empiricism The procedure of obtaining information through observation.

endogenous Generated within the body; usually used to refer to natural ligands for neurotransmitter receptors.

endorphins Substances produced in the body that function both as neurotransmitters and as hormones, and act on opiate receptors in many parts of the nervous system.

EPSP See *excitatory postsynaptic potential*.

equipotentiality The idea that the brain functions as an undifferentiated whole.

estrogen A class of hormones responsible for a number of female characteristics and functions, produced by the ovaries in women and, to a lesser extent, by the adrenal glands in males and females.

estrus A period when a nonhuman female animal is ovulating and sex hormone levels are high.

euphoria A sense of happiness or ecstasy; many abused drugs produce euphoria.

evoked potential An EEG technique for measuring the brain's responses to brief stimulation; it involves presenting a stimulus repeatedly and averaging the EEG over all the presentations to cancel out random activity, leaving the electrical activity associated with the stimulus. (Figure 4.15)

excitatory postsynaptic potential (EPSP) A hypopolarization of the dendrites and cell body, which makes the neuron more likely to fire.

experiment A study in which the researcher manipulates an independent variable and observes its effect on one or more dependent variables. (Figure 1.6)

fabrication In research, the faking of data or results.

familial Term referring to a characteristic that occurs more frequently among relatives of a person with the characteristic than it does in the population.

family study A study of the degree of relationship of a characteristic among relatives.

FAS See *fetal alcohol syndrome.*

fasting phase The period following the absorptive phase, when the glucose level in the blood drops and the body must rely on its energy stores. (Figure 5.6)

fatty acids Breakdown product of fat, which supplies the muscles and organs of the body (except for the brain).

fetal alcohol syndrome A condition caused by the mother's use of alcohol during the third trimester of pregnancy; neurons fail to migrate properly, often resulting in retardation. The leading cause of mental retardation in the Western world. (Figures 3.26, 4.5)

fetus An organism after the initial prenatal period; in humans, after the first eight weeks.

fissure A groove between gyri of the cerebral hemispheres that is larger and deeper than a sulcus. (Figures 3.4, 3.7)

fMRI See *functional magnetic resonance imaging.*

form vision The detection of an object's boundaries and features, such as texture.

fovea A 1.5-mm-wide area in the middle of the retina in which cones are most concentrated, and visual acuity and color discrimination are greatest. (Figure 9.2)

fraternal twins Twins produced from two separately fertilized eggs.

frequency A characteristic of sound; the number of cycles or waves of alternating compression and decompression of the vibrating medium that occur in a second.

frequency theory Any one of a number of theories of auditory frequency analysis which state that the frequency of a sound is represented in the firing rate of each neuron or a group of neurons.

frequency-place theory The theory that frequency following accounts for the discrimination of frequencies up to about 200 Hz and higher frequencies are represented by the place of greatest activity on the basilar membrane.

frontal lobe The area of each cerebral hemisphere anterior to the central sulcus and superior to the lateral fissure. (Figure 3.7)

functional magnetic resonance imaging (fMRI) A brain imaging procedure that measures brain activation by detecting the increase in oxygen levels in active neural structures. (Figure A.12)

ganglion A group of cell bodies in the peripheral nervous system.

gate control theory The idea that pressure signals arriving in the brain trigger an inhibitory message that travels back down the spinal cord, where it closes a neural "gate" in the pain pathway.

gay The term used to refer to homosexual men.

gender identity The sex a person identifies as being.

gender nonconformity A tendency to engage in activities usually preferred by the other sex, and an atypical preference for other-sex playmates and companions while growing up.

gender role A set of behaviors society considers appropriate for members of the same sex.

genetic engineering Manipulation of an organism's genes or their functioning.

genotype The combination of genes an individual has.

glial cell Type of cells that make up 90% of the cells in the brain, and that produce myelin and provide other support functions for neurons. (Figure 2.7)

glucagon A hormone released by the pancreas that stimulates the liver to transform stored glycogen back into glucose during the fasting phase.

glucose One of the sugars; the body's main source of energy, reserved for the nervous system during the fasting phase; a major signal for hunger and satiation. (Figures 5.6, 5.7)

glutamate theory The theory that reduced glutamate activity is involved in schizophrenia.

glycerol A breakdown product of fats, which is converted to glucose for the brain during the fasting period. (Figure 5.6)

glycogen Form in which glucose is stored in the liver and muscles during the absorptive phase; converted back to glucose for the brain during the fasting phase. (Figure 5.6)

Golgi stain A staining method that randomly stains about 5% of neurons, which makes them stand out individually. (Figure A.1)

Golgi tendon organs Receptors that detect tension in a muscle.

gonads The primary reproductive organs, the testes in the male or the ovaries in the female.

growth cone A formation at the tip of a migrating neuron that samples the environment for directional cues. (Figure 3.24)

gyrus A ridge in the cerebral cortex; the area between two sulci. (Figure 3.5)

hashish The dried resin of the marijuana plant, which is particularly high in the major psychoactive ingredient THC.

hemifield presentation A technique for assessing differences in processing in the two hemispheres. A projector presents information on the right or left side of the screen while the individual fixates on a spot in the middle of the screen, and the image is registered in the hemisphere on the opposite side. (Figure A.13)

hepatic portal vein Blood vessel through which nutrients are transported from the intestinal wall to the liver. (Figures 5.5, 5.7)

heritability The percentage of the variation among individuals in a characteristic that can be attributed to heredity.

heroin A major drug of addiction synthesized from morphine.

heterozygous Having a pair of genes for a specific characteristic that are different from each other.

hierarchical processing A type of processing in which lower levels of the nervous system analyze their information and pass the results on to the next higher level for further analysis.

homeostasis Condition in which any particular body system is in balance or equilibrium.

homozygous Having a pair of genes for a specific characteristic that are identical with each other.

HPA See *hypothalamus-pituitary-adrenal cortex axis*.

Human Genome Project An international project with the goal of mapping the location of all the genes on the human chromosomes and determining the base sequences of the genes.

huntingtin A protein with unknown function that is produced by the *huntingtin* gene.

Huntington's disease (HD) A degenerative disorder of the motor system, with critical cell loss in the striatum.

Hurvich-Jameson theory A color vision theory which states that there are three types of color receptors—red-, green-, and blue-sensitive—which are interconnected in an opponent-process fashion at the ganglion cells, accounting for complementary colors and the experience of yellow. (Figure 9.10)

hydrocephalus A disorder in which cerebrospinal fluid fails to circulate and builds up in the cerebral ventricles, crowding out neural tissue and usually causing retardation. (Figure 12.10)

hyperpolarization An increase in the polarization of a neuron membrane, which is inhibitory and makes an action potential less likely to occur.

hypnotic Sleep inducing.

hypopolarization A decrease in the polarization of a neuron membrane, which is excitatory and makes an action potential more likely to occur.

hypothalamus A subcortical structure in the forebrain just below the thalamus, which plays a major role in controlling the internal environment and in motivated behaviors and emotion. (Figures 3.12, 5.2)

hypothalamus-pituitary-adrenal cortex axis (HPA) A group of structures that helps the body cope with stress. (Figure 7.9)

hypothesis A statement about the expected relationship between two or more variables.

hypovolemic thirst A fluid deficit that occurs when the blood volume drops due to a loss of extracellular water.

identical twins Twins who result from a single egg that splits and develops into two individuals.

immune system The cells and cell products that kill infected and malignant cells and protect the body against foreign substances, including bacteria and viruses. (Table 7.1)

INAH 3 See *third interstitial nucleus of the anterior hypothalamus*.

incentive theory A theory which recognizes that people are motivated by external stimuli (incentives), not just internal needs.

independent variable (IV) In an experiment, a condition that is manipulated by the experimenter and is expected to affect the research participant's behavior. (Figure 1.6)

inferior Below another structure. (Figure 3.8)

inferior colliculi Part of the tectum in the brain stem that is involved in auditory functions such as locating the direction of sounds. (Figures 3.12, 3.15)

inferior temporal cortex Area in the lower part of the temporal lobe that plays a major role in the visual identification of objects. (Figures 3.7, 9.24)

informed consent Voluntary participation after receiving full information about any risks, discomfort, or other adverse effects that might occur.

inhibitory postsynaptic potential (IPSP) A hyperpolarization of the dendrites and cell body, which makes a neuron less likely to fire.

inner hair cells A single row of about 3,400 hair cells located on the basilar membrane toward the inside of the cochlea's coil; they play the major role in auditory frequency analysis, compared to the outer hair cells. (Figure 8.5c)

instinct A complex behavior that is automatic and unlearned, and occurs in all the members of a species.

insulin A hormone secreted by the pancreas that enables entry of glucose into cells (not including the nervous system) during the absorptive phase, and facilitates storage of excess nutrients.

intelligence The capacity for learning, reasoning, and understanding.

intelligence quotient (IQ) The measure typically used for intelligence.

intensity The physical energy in a sound; the sound's amplitude.

interneuron A neuron that has a short axon or no axon at all and connects one neuron to another in the same part of the central nervous system. (Figure 2.2)

iodopsin The photopigment in cones.

ion An atom that is charged because it has lost or gained one or more electrons. (Figure 2.5)

IPSP See *inhibitory postsynaptic potential*.

IQ See *intelligence quotient*.

IV See *independent variable*.

James-Lange theory The idea that physiological arousal is not the result of an emotional experience, but precedes and *causes* feelings of emotion. (Figure 7.3)

knockout mice Mice in which a gene with a nonfunctioning mutation was inserted during the embryonic stage.

Korsakoff's syndrome A form of dementia in which brain deterioration is almost always caused by chronic alcoholism.

language acquisition device A part of the brain hypothesized to be dedicated to learning and controlling language.

late-onset alcoholism Cloninger's Type 1 alcoholism, involving late onset, long periods of abstinence with binges, guilt over drinking, and cautious and emotionally dependent personality.

lateral Toward the side. (Figure 3.8)

lateral fissure The fissure that separates the temporal lobe from the frontal and parietal lobes. (Figure 3.7)

lateral inhibition A method of enhancing neural information in which each neuron's activity inhibits the activity of its neighbors, and in turn its activity is inhibited by them. (Figure 9.16)

***L*-dopa** See *levodopa*.

learned taste aversion Learned avoidance of a food (based on its taste) eaten prior to becoming ill.

learned taste preference Preference for a food containing a needed nutrient (identified by the food's taste), learned, presumably, because the nutrient makes the individual feel better.

leptin Hormone secreted by fat cells, which is proportional to the percentage of body fat, and which signals fat level to the brain.

lesbian The term for a homosexual woman.

lesion Damage to neural tissue. This can be brought about surgically for research or therapeutic reasons, or it can result from trauma, disease, or developmental error. (Figure A.5)

leukocytes White blood cells, which include macrophages, T cells, and B cells; part of the immune system. (Figure 7.10, Table 7.1)

levodopa (*L*-dopa) The precursor for dopamine; used to treat Parkinson's disease.

Lewy bodies Abnormal clumps of protein that form within neurons, found in some patients with Parkinson's disease, and in patients with a form of Alzheimer's disease. (Figure 10.21)

ligand Any substance that binds to a receptor.

limbic system A group of forebrain structures arranged around the upper brain stem, which have roles in emotion, motivated behavior, and learning. (Figures 3.13, 7.6)

lithium A metal administered in the form of lithium carbonate, the medication of choice for bipolar illness.

lobotomy A surgical procedure that disconnects the prefrontal areas from the rest of the brain; it reduces emotionality and pain, but leaves the person emotionally blunted, distractible, and childlike in behavior. (Figure 3.10)

localization The idea that specific parts of the brain carry out specific functions.

longitudinal fissure The large fissure that runs the length of the brain, separating the two cerebral hemispheres. (Figures 3.4, 3.5)

long-term depression (LTD) Weakening of a synapse when the presynaptic neuron is not firing while the postsynaptic neuron is firing (due to stimulation by other neurons).

long-term potentiation (LTP) An increase in synaptic strength following repeated stimulation.

loudness The term for our *experience* of sound intensity.

LTD See *long-term depression.*

LTP See *long-term potentiation.*

macrophage A type of leukocyte that ingests intruders. (Figure 7.10, Table 7.1)

magnetic resonance imaging (MRI) An imaging technique that involves measuring the radio-frequency waves emitted by hydrogen atoms when they are subjected to a strong magnetic field. Because different structures have different concentrations of hydrogen atoms, the waves can be used to form a detailed image of the brain. (Figure A.10)

magnocellular hypothesis The hypothesis that some symptoms of dyslexia result from developmental errors in the magnocellular visual pathway, which is concerned with rapidly moving stimuli and detects eye movements.

magnocellular system A division of the visual system, extending from the retina through the visual association areas, that is specialized for brightness contrast and movement.

major depression A disorder involving feelings of sadness to the point of hopelessness for weeks at a time, along with slowness of thought, sleep disturbance, and loss of energy and appetite and the ability to enjoy life; in some cases the person is also agitated or restless.

major histocompatibility complex (MHC) A group of genes that contribute to the functioning of the immune system.

mania A disorder involving excess energy and confidence that often leads to grandiose schemes; decreased need for sleep, increased sexual drive and, often, abuse of drugs.

marijuana The dried and crushed leaves and flowers of the Indian hemp plant *cannabis sativa.*

materialistic monism The view that the body and the mind and everything else are physical.

medial Toward the middle. (Figure 3.8)

medial amygdala Part of the amygdala that apparently responds to sexually exciting stimuli. In both male and female rats, it is active during copulation and it causes the release of dopamine in the MPOA.

medial forebrain bundle (MFB) A part of the mesolimbic dopamine system and a potent reward area. (Figure 4.10)

medial preoptic area (MPOA) A part of the preoptic area of the hypothalamus (see Figure 5.2) that appears to be important for sexual performance, but not sexual motivation in male and female rats.

medulla The lower part of the hindbrain; its nuclei are involved with control of essential life processes such as cardiovascular activity and respiration. (Figures 3.12, 3.15)

melatonin A hormone secreted by the pineal gland that induces sleepiness.

meninges A three-layered membrane that encloses and protects the brain.

mesolimbic dopamine system A pathway including the ventral tegmental area, medial forebrain bundle, nucleus accumbens, and projections into prefrontal areas. The pathway is important in reward effects from drugs, ESB, and activities like eating and sex. (Figure 4.10)

methadone A synthetic opiate used as an agonist treatment for opiate addiction.

MFB See *medial forebrain bundle.*

MG See *myasthenia gravis.*

midbrain The middle part of the brain, consisting of the tectum *(roof)* on the dorsal side and the tegmentum on the ventral side. (Figures 3.12, 3.15)

migrate In brain development, movement of newly formed neurons from the ventricular zone to their final destination. (Figure 3.23)

mind-brain problem The issue of the nature of the mind and its relationship to the brain.

model A proposed mechanism for how something works.

modular processing The segregation of the various components of processing in the brain into separate locations.

monism The idea that the mind and the body consist of the same substance.

monoamine hypothesis The hypothesis that depression involves reduced activity at norepinephrine and serotonin synapses.

monozygotic (MZ) Referring to a single fertilized egg that results in *identical* twins.

motivation The set of factors that initiate, sustain, and direct behavior.

motor cortex The area in the frontal lobes that controls voluntary (nonreflexive) body movements; the primary motor cortex is on the precentral gyrus. (Figures 3.7, 10.17)

motor neuron A neuron that carries commands to the muscles and organs. (Figure 2.1)

movement agnosia The inability to perceive movement.

MPOA See *medial preoptic area.*

MRI See *magnetic resonance imaging.*

MS See *multiple sclerosis.*

Müllerian ducts Early structures that in the female develop into the uterus, fallopian tubes, and inner vagina. (Figure 6.8)

Müllerian inhibiting hormone A hormone released in the male that causes the Müllerian ducts to degenerate.

multiple sclerosis (MS) A disorder resulting from the deterioration of the myelin sheaths *(demyelination)* in the central nervous system.

muscle spindles Receptors that detect stretching in muscles.

myasthenia gravis (MG) A disorder of muscular weakness caused by reduced numbers or sensitivity of acetylcholine receptors. (Figure 10.24)

myelin A fatty tissue that wraps around an axon to insulate it from the surrounding fluid and from other neurons. (Figure 2.7)

myelin stain A staining method that stains myelin, thus identifying neural pathways. (Figure A.2)

MZ twins See *monozygotic.*

NAcc See *nucleus accumbens.*

naltrexone A drug that occupies opiate receptors, blocking the effects of endorphins and opiate drugs. It is used as an antagonist treatment for opiate and alcohol addiction and, in research, to help determine whether an analgesic effect involves endorphins.

narcolepsy A disorder in which individuals fall asleep suddenly during the daytime and go directly into REM sleep.

natural killer cell A type of immune cell that attacks and destroys certain kinds of cancer cells and cells infected with viruses. (Table 7.1)

natural selection The principle that those whose genes endow them with greater speed, intelligence, or health are more likely to survive and transmit their genes to more offspring.

nature versus nurture The issue of the relative importance of heredity and environment.

negative color aftereffect The experience of a color's complement following stimulation by the color. (Figure 9.8)

negative symptoms Symptoms of schizophrenia characterized by the absence or insufficiency of normal behaviors, including lack of affect (emotion), inability to experience pleasure, lack of motivation, poverty of speech, and impaired attention. (Table 13.1)

neglect A disorder in which the person ignores objects, people, and activity on the side opposite the brain damage.

nerve A bundle of axons running together in the peripheral nervous system.

neurofibrillary tangles Abnormal webs of filaments that develop inside the neurons and are associated with the death of brain cells in people with Alzheimer's disease and Down syndrome. (Figure 11.12)

neurogenesis The birth of new neurons.

neuromuscular junction The synapse between a neuron and a muscle cell. (Figure 10.13)

neuron A specialized cell that conveys sensory information into the brain, carries out the operations involved in thought and feeling and action, or transmits commands out into the body to control muscles and organs; a single nerve cell, in contrast to a *nerve.*

neuropeptide Y (NPY) A transmitter released in the PVN that is a powerful stimulant for eating and conserves energy. (Figure 5.7)

neuroscience The multidisciplinary study of the nervous system and its role in behavior.

neurotoxin A neuron poison; substance that impairs the functioning of a neuron.

neurotransmitter A chemical substance that a neuron releases to carry a message across the synapse to the next neuron or to a muscle or organ. (Figures 2.9, 2.14, 2.15; Table 2.1)

neurotrophins Chemicals that enhance development and survival in neurons.

nicotine The primary psychoactive and addictive ingredient in tobacco.

Nissl stain A staining method that stains cell bodies. (Figure A.3)

node of Ranvier A gap in the myelin sheath covering an axon.

nondeclarative memory Nonstatable memories, which result from procedural or skills learning, emotional learning, and simple conditioning.

non-REM sleep (NREM) The periods of sleep that are not rapid eye movement sleep.

NPY See *neuropeptide Y.*

NREM See *non-REM sleep.*

NST See *nucleus of the solitary tract.*

nucleus (1) The part of every cell that contains the chromosomes and governs activity in the cell. (2) A group of neuron cell bodies in the central nervous system.

nucleus accumbens (NAcc) A forebrain structure that is part of the mesolimbic dopamine system and a potent center for reward. (Figure 4.10)

nucleus of the solitary tract (NST) A part of the medulla that monitors several signals involved in the regulation of eating. (Figure 5.7)

ob See *obesity gene.*

obesity gene (ob) A gene on chromosome 6 that causes obesity; in mice it results in an inability to produce leptin.

object agnosia Impairment of the ability to recognize objects visually.

objective Referring to the characteristic of observational studies that two observers will reach the same conclusion about what is being observed.

obsessive-compulsive disorder (OCD) A disorder consisting of obsessions (recurring thoughts) and compulsions (repetitive, ritualistic acts the person feels compelled to perform). (Figure 13.19)

occipital lobe The most posterior part of each cerebral hemisphere, and the location of the visual cortex. (Figure 3.7)

OCD See *obsessive-compulsive disorder.*

offensive aggression An unprovoked attack on another person or animal.

opiate Any drug derived from the opium poppy. The term is also used to refer to effects at opiate receptors, including those by endorphins.

opponent process theory A color vision theory that attempts to explain color vision in terms of opposing neural processes. (Figure 9.10)

organ of Corti The sound-analyzing structure on the basilar membrane of the cochlea; it consists of four rows of hair cells, their supporting cells, and the tectorial membrane. (Figure 8.5)

organizing effects Hormonal effects of sexual development that occur during the prenatal period and shortly after birth, and are permanent.

organum vasculosum lamina terminalis (OVLT) A structure bordering the third ventricle that monitors fluid content in the cells and contributes to the control of osmotic thirst. (Figure 5.3)

osmotic thirst Thirst that occurs when the fluid content is low inside the body's cells.

ossicles Tiny bones that transfer vibration from the tympanic membrane to the cochlea; they operate in a lever fashion and produce a slight amplification of the sound. (Figures 8.4, 8.5)

outer hair cells Three rows of about 12,000 cells located on the basilar membrane toward the outside of the cochlea's coil; their function may be to influence inner hair cell sensitivity by adjusting the tension of the tectorial membrane. (Figures 8.5c, 8.6)

oval window A thin, flexible membrane on the face of the vestibular canal, which the ossicles strike in transmitting vibration into the cochlea. (Figure 8.5a)

ovaries The female gonads, where the ova develop. (Figure 6.8)

OVLT See *organum vasculosum lamina terminalis.*

oxytocin A neuropeptide hormone and neurotransmitter, dubbed the "sociability molecule" because it affects social behavior and bonding in lower animals.

PAG See *periaqueductal gray.*

parasympathetic nervous system The branch of the autonomic nervous system that slows the activity of most organs to conserve energy and activates digestion to renew energy. (Figures 3.19, 3.21, 7.2)

paraventricular nucleus (PVN) A structure in the hypothalamus that monitors several signals involved in the regulation of eating, including input from the NST. (Figure 5.7)

parietal lobe The part of each cerebral hemisphere located above the lateral fissure and between the central sulcus and the occipital lobe; it contains the somatosensory cortex and visual association areas. (Figure 3.7)

Parkinson's disease (PD) A movement disorder characterized by motor tremors, rigidity, loss of balance and coordination, and difficulty in moving, especially in initiating movements; it is caused by deterioration of the substantia nigra. (Figures 10.21, 10.22)

parvocellular system A division of the visual system, extending from the retina through the visual association areas, that is specialized for fine detail and color.

PD See *Parkinson's disease.*

perception The interpretation of sensory information.

periaqueductal gray (PAG) A brain-stem structure with a large number of endorphin synapses; stimulation reduces pain transmission at the spinal cord level. The PAG also produces symptoms of drug withdrawal. (Figure 10.9; Chapter 10 Application box)

peripheral nervous system (PNS) The part of the nervous system made up of the cranial nerves and spinal nerves.

PET See *positron emission tomography.*

PGO waves Waves of excitation that flow from the pons through the lateral geniculate nucleus of the thalamus to the occipital area and appear to initiate the EEG desynchrony of REM sleep. (Figure 14.10)

phantom pain Pain that seems to be in a missing limb.

phase difference A binaural cue to the location of a sound coming from one side; at frequencies below 1,500 Hz, the sound will be in a different phase of the wave at each ear. (Figure 8.15)

phenotype In heredity, the characteristic of the individual.

phenylketonuria An inherited form of mental retardation in which the body fails to metabolize the amino acid phenylalanine, which interferes with myelination during development.

pheromones Airborne chemicals released by an animal that have physiological or behavioral effects on another animal of the same species.

photopigment A light-sensitive chemical in the visual receptors that initiates the neural response.

phototherapy A treatment for winter depression involving the use of high-intensity lights for a period of time each day. (Figure 13.13)

phrenology The theory in the early 1900s that "faculties" of emotion and intellect were located in precise areas of the brain and could be assessed by feeling bumps on the skull. (Figure 3.16)

pineal gland A gland located just posterior to the thalamus, which secretes sleep-inducing melatonin; it controls seasonal cycles in nonhuman animals and participates with other structures in controlling daily rhythms in humans. (Figures 3.12, 3.15)

pinna The ear flap on each side of the head; the outer ear. (Figure 8.4)

pioneer neuron In nervous system development, neurons that develop early and lead the way for other neurons during migration.

pitch The *experience* of the frequency of a sound.

pituitary gland A gland located just below the hypothalamus; under the control of the hypothalamus, it influences much of the endocrine gland system. (Figures 3.12, 3.20)

place theory Theory which states that the frequency of a sound is identified by the location of maximal vibration on the basilar membrane, and which neurons are firing most.

plagiarism The theft of another's work or ideas.

planum temporale The area in each temporal lobe which is the location in the left hemisphere of Wernicke's area, and which is larger on the left in most people.

plaques Clumps of amyloid, a type of protein, that cluster among axon terminals and interfere with neural transmission in the brains of people with Alzheimer's disease and Down syndrome. (Figure 11.12)

plasticity The ability to be modified, a characteristic of the nervous system.

PM See *premotor cortex.*

PMS See *premenstrual syndrome.*

PNS See *peripheral nervous system.*

polarization A difference in electrical charge between the inside and outside of a neuron.

polygenic Determined by several genes rather than a single gene.

polygraph A device for recording several physiological measures at the same time.

pons A part of the brain stem that contains centers related to sleep and arousal. (Figures 3.12, 3.15)

positive symptoms Symptoms of schizophrenia that involve the presence or exaggeration of behaviors, such as delusions, hallucinations, thought disorder, and bizarre behavior. (Table 13.1)

positron emission tomography (PET) An imaging technique that reveals function. It involves injecting a radioactive substance into the bloodstream, which is taken up by parts of the brain according to how active they are; the scanner makes an image that is color coded to show the relative amounts of activity. (Figure A.11)

posterior Toward the rear. (Figure 3.8)

posterior parietal cortex (PPC) An association area that brings together the body senses, vision, and audition. It determines the body's orientation in space, the location of the limbs, and the location in space of objects detected by touch, sight, and sound. (Figures 10.4, 10.17)

postsynaptic Term referring to a neuron that receives transmission from another neuron.

potential A difference in electrical charge between two points.

PPC See *posterior parietal cortex.*

precentral gyrus The gyrus anterior to, and extending the length of, the central sulcus; it is the location of the primary motor cortex.

predatory aggression Aggression in which an animal attacks and kills its prey.

prefrontal cortex The most anterior cortex of the frontal lobes; it is involved in working memory, planning and organization of behavior, and regulation of behavior in response to its consequences. It also integrates information about the body with information from the world, to initiate motor planning. (Figures 3.7, 10.17)

premenstrual syndrome (PMS) Mood disruption and, occasionally, increased aggressiveness just before the menstrual period.

premotor cortex (PM) Area anterior to the primary motor cortex that combines information from the prefrontal cortex and the posterior parietal cortex and begins the programming of a movement. (Figure 10.17)

preoptic area Structure in the hypothalamus that contains warmth-sensitive cells and cold-sensitive cells and participates in the control of body temperature. See *medial preoptic area* regarding regulation of sexual behavior. (Figure 5.2)

presynaptic Term referring to a neuron that transmits to another neuron.

presynaptic excitation Increased release of neurotransmitter from a neuron's terminal as the result of another neuron's release of neurotransmitter onto the terminal (an axoaxonic synapse). (Figure 2.14)

presynaptic inhibition Decreased release of neurotransmitter from a neuron's terminal as the result of another neuron's release of neurotransmitter onto the terminal (an axoaxonic synapse). (Figure 2.14)

primary motor cortex The area on the precentral gyrus responsible for the execution of voluntary movements. (Figure 10.17)

primary somatosensory cortex (S-I) The first stage in the cortical level processing of body sensory information, which is processed through S-I's four subareas, then passed on to S-II. (Figure 10.17)

projection neuron A neuron similar to an interneuron, but which has a longer axon and communicates over somewhat longer distances within the central nervous system.

proliferation The first stage of nervous system development in which cells that will become neurons multiply at the rate of 250,000 new cells every minute.

proprioception The sense that informs us about the position and movement of our limbs and body.

prosopagnosia The inability to visually recognize familiar faces.

pseudohermaphrodite Individuals who have ambiguous internal and external sexual organs, but whose gonads are consistent with their chromosomes. (Figures 6.11, 6.12)

psychedelic drug Any compound that causes perceptual distortions in the user.

psychoactive drug Any drug that has psychological effects, such as anxiety relief or hallucinations.

psychosurgery The use of surgical intervention to treat cognitive and emotional disorders.

pulvinar A cluster of nuclei in the thalamus that research suggests shifts attention among stimuli.

pure tone A sound consisting of a single frequency. (Figure 8.3 a–d)

PVN See *paraventricular nucleus.*

radial glial cells Specialized glial cells that provide a scaffold for migrating neurons to climb to their destination. (Figure 3.23)

rapid eye movement (REM) sleep The stage of sleep during which most dreaming occurs; research indicates it is also a time of memory consolidation during which neural activity from the day is replayed.

rate law Principle that intensity of a stimulus is represented in an axon by the frequency of action potentials.

reactive depression Feelings of sadness over events or circumstances such as disappointing grades, a bad relationship, or loss of a loved one.

receptive field In vision, the area of the retina from which a cell in the visual system receives its input.

receptor A cell, often a specialized neuron, that is suited by its structure and function to respond to a particular form of energy, such as sound.

recessive The term referring to a gene that will have an influence only when it is paired with the same recessive gene on the other chromosome.

reflex A simple, automatic movement in response to a sensory stimulus. (Figures 3.17, 10.15)

regeneration The growth of severed axons; in mammals it is limited to the peripheral nervous system.

relative refractory period Period during which a neuron can be fired again following an action potential, but only by an above-threshold stimulus.

REM See *rapid eye movement sleep.*

reorganization A shift in neural connections that changes the function of an area of the brain.

resting potential The difference in charge between the inside and outside of the membrane of a neuron at rest.

reticular formation A collection of many nuclei running through the middle of the hindbrain and the midbrain, with a role in sleep and arousal.

retina The structure at the rear of the eye, which is made up of light-sensitive receptor cells and the neural cells that are connected to them. (Figure 9.2)

retinal disparity A discrepancy in the location of an object's image on the two retinas; a cue to the distance of a focused object. (Figure 9.5)

retinotopic map A map of the retina in the visual cortex, which results from adjacent receptors in the retina activating adjacent cells in the visual cortex. (Figure 9.14)

retrieval The process of accessing stored memories.

retrograde amnesia The inability to remember events prior to impairment.

reuptake Process by which a neurotransmitter is taken back into the presynaptic terminals.

reward The positive effect on a user from a drug, ESB, sex, food, and so on.

rhodopsin The photopigment in rods.

ribonucleic acid (RNA) A copy that deoxyribonucleic acid makes of one of its strands; RNA directs protein construction. (Figure 1.11)

RNA See *ribonucleic acid.*

round window A flexible membrane at the base end of the tympanic canal, which bulges outward during sound stimulation; this increases the amount of sound energy that can flow through the cochlea.

SAD See *seasonal affective disorder.*

saltatory conduction Conduction in the axon in which action potentials jump from one node of Ranvier to the next.

schizophrenia A disabling disorder characterized by perceptual, emotional, and intellectual deficits, loss of contact with reality, and inability to function in life.

SCN See *suprachiasmatic nucleus.*

SCR See *skin conductance response.*

SDN See *sexually dimorphic nucleus.*

seasonal affective disorder (SAD) Depression that is seasonal, being more pronounced in the summer in some people and in the winter in others.

secondary somatosensory cortex (S-II) The part of the somatosensory cortex that receives information from S-I, from both sides of the body. (Figure 10.17)

sedative A calming effect of a drug.

sensation The acquisition of sensory information.

sensory neuron A neuron that carries information from the body and from the outside world into the central nervous system. (Figure 2.2)

sensory-specific satiety Decreased attractiveness of a food as the person or animal eats more of it.

set point A value in a control system that serves as the system's point of homeostasis; departures from this value initiate actions to restore the set-point condition; as particularly applied to weight regulation.

sex The term for the biological characteristics that divide humans and other animals into the categories of male and female.

sexually dimorphic nucleus (SDN) A part of the MPOA important to male sexual behavior. It is larger in male rats and their level of sexual activity depends on SDN size. (Figure 6.4)

S-I See *primary somatosensory cortex.*

S-II See *secondary somatosensory cortex.*

simple cell A cell in the visual cortex that responds to a line or an edge that is at a *specific orientation* and at a *specific place* on the retina. (Figures 9.19, 9.20)

skeletal muscles The muscles that move the body and limbs.

skin conductance response (SCR) A measure of sweat gland activation and thus sympathetic nervous system activity.

skin senses Touch, warmth, cold, and pain; the senses that arise from receptors in the skin.

slow wave sleep (SWS) Stages 3 and 4 of sleep, characterized by delta EEG and increased body activity; it appears to be a period of brain recuperation and may play a role in consolidation of declarative memory.

SMA See *supplementary motor area.*

smooth muscles Muscles that control the internal organs other than the heart.

sodium-potassium pump Large protein molecules that move sodium ions through the neuron membrane to the outside and potassium ions back inside, helping to maintain the resting potential. (Figure 2.5)

soma The cell body of a neuron, which contains the cell's nucleus, most of the cytoplasm, and structures that convert nutrients into energy and eliminate waste materials.

somatic nervous system The division of the peripheral nervous system that carries sensory information into the central nervous system and motor commands from the CNS to the skeletal muscles. (Figure 3.19)

somatosensory cortex The area in the parietal lobes that processes the body senses (the skin senses and the senses that inform us about body position and movement, or proprioception); the primary somatosensory cortex is on the postcentral gyrus. (Figures 3.7, 3.9, 10.4)

SP See *substance P.*

spatial frequency theory The theory that visual cortical cells do a Fourier frequency analysis of the luminosity variations in a scene. (Figure 9.22)

spatial summation The process of combining potentials that occur simultaneously at different locations on the dendrites and cell body. (Figure 2.12)

spectrum disorder Milder symptoms of a disorder that do not qualify for a diagnosis.

spinal cord A part of the central nervous system; the spinal nerves, which commu-

nicate with the body below the head, enter and leave the spinal cord. (Figures 3.17, 3.21)

spinal nerves The peripheral nerves that enter and leave the spinal cord at each vertebra and communicate with the body below the head.

stem cells Undifferentiated cells that have the potential of becoming any type of cell in the body. (Figure 1.17)

stereotaxic instrument A device used for the precise positioning in the brain of an electrode or other device, such as a cannula. (Figure A.7)

stimulant A drug that activates the nervous system to produce arousal, increased alertness, and elevated mood.

stress A condition in the environment that makes unusual demands on the organism, such as threat, failure, or bereavement; the individual's negative response to a stressful situation.

striatum The caudate nucleus and putamen of the basal ganglia.

subfornical organ (SFO) One of the structures bordering the third ventricle that increases drinking when stimulated by angiotensin. (Figure 5.3)

substance P (SP) A neuropeptide involved in pain signaling.

substantia nigra The nucleus that sends dopamine-releasing neurons to the striatum, and which deteriorates in Parkinson's disease.

sudden cardiac death Death occurring when stress causes excessive sympathetic activity that sends the heart into fibrillation, contracting so rapidly that little or no blood is pumped.

sulcus The groove or space between two gyri. (Figure 3.5)

superior Above another structure. (Figure 3.8)

superior colliculi Part of the tectum in the brain stem that is involved in visual functions such as guiding eye movements and fixation of gaze. (Figures 3.12, 3.15)

supplementary motor area (SMA) The prefrontal area that assembles sequences of movements, such as those involved in eating or playing the piano, prior to execution by the primary motor cortex. (Figure 10.17)

suprachiasmatic nucleus (SCN) A structure in the hypothalamus that (1) was found to be larger in gay men than in heterosexual men, (2) regulates the reproductive cycle in female rats, and (3) is the main biologi-

cal clock, controlling several activities of the circadian rhythm. (Figure 14.2)

SWS See *slow wave sleep.*

sympathetic ganglion chain The structure running along each side of the spine through which most sympathetic neurons pass (and many synapse) on their way to and from the body's organs. (Figure 3.21)

sympathetic nervous system The branch of the autonomic nervous system that activates the body in ways that help it cope with demands, such as emotional stress and physical emergencies. (Figures 3.19, 3.21, 7.2)

synapse The connection between two neurons. (Figures 2.9, 2.11, 2.14, 2.15)

synaptic cleft The small gap between a presynaptic neuron and a postsynaptic neuron.

T cell A type of leukocyte that attacks specific invaders. (Table 7.1)

tardive dyskinesia Tremors and involuntary movements caused by blocking of dopamine receptors in the basal ganglia due to prolonged use of neuroleptics.

tectorial membrane A shelflike membrane overlying the hair cells and the basilar membrane in the cochlea. (Figure 8.5c)

telephone theory A theory of auditory frequency analysis which stated that the auditory neurons transmit the actual sound frequencies to the cortex.

temporal lobe The part of each cerebral hemisphere ventral to the lateral fissure; it contains the auditory cortex, visual and auditory association areas, and Wernicke's area.

temporal summation The process of combining potentials that arrive a short time apart on a neuron's dendrites and cell body. (Figure 2.12)

terminal A swelling on the branches at the end of a neuron which contains neurotransmitters; also called an end bulb. (Figures 2.1, 2.9, 2.11, 2.14, 2.15)

testes The male gonads, which produce sperm.

testosterone The major sex hormone in males, a member of the class androgens.

thalamus A forebrain structure lying just below the lateral ventricles, which receives information from all sensory systems except olfaction and relays it to the respective cortical projection areas. It has additional roles in movement, memory, and consciousness. (Figures 3.12, 3.13, 3.15, 10.20)

theory A system of statements that integrate and interpret diverse observations in an attempt to explain some phenomenon.

theory of mind The ability to impute mental states to oneself and to others.

third interstitial nucleus of the anterior hypothalamus (INAH 3) A nucleus found to be half as large in gay men and heterosexual women as in heterosexual men. (Figure 6.15)

tolerance After repeated drug use, a requirement for increasing amounts of a drug to produce the same results.

tonotopic map The form of topographic organization in the auditory cortex, such that each successive area responds to successively higher frequencies. (Figures 8.9, 8.11)

topographical organization Neurons from adjacent receptor locations project to adjacent cells in the cortex. (Figures 8.9, 8.11, 9.14, 10.5)

Tourette's syndrome A disorder characterized by motor and phonic (sound) tics.

tract A bundle of axons in the central nervous system.

transducer A device that converts energy from one form to another. A sensory receptor is a form of transducer.

transgenic mice Mice in which a foreign gene was inserted during the embryonic stage.

transsexual An individual who dresses and lives as the other sex and often seeks surgery to change the sexual appearance.

trichromatic theory The theory that three color processes account for all the colors we are able to distinguish.

twin study In heredity research, a study that compares a characteristic in twins to separate the effects of heredity and environment and determine their relative contributions.

tympanic membrane The eardrum, a very thin membrane stretched across the end of the auditory canal; its vibration transmits sound energy to the ossicles. (Figure 8.5a)

ultradian rhythm A rhythm with a length of less than a day, including the sleep stages and the basic rest and activity cycle during the day.

unipolar depression Depression without mania.

ventral Toward the stomach side. (Figure 3.8)

ventral horns Enlarged areas of the white matter in the spinal cord, which contain most of the cell bodies of the motor neurons exiting the cord. (Figure 3.17)

ventral root The branch of each spinal nerve through which the motor neurons exit. (Figure 3.17)

ventral stream The visual processing pathway that extends into the temporal lobes; it is especially concerned with the identification of objects. (Figure 9.24)

ventral tegmental area (VTA) A part of the mesolimbic dopamine system, which sends neurons to the nucleus accumbens and is a potent reward area. (Figure 4.10)

ventricles Cavities in the brain filled with cerebrospinal fluid. (Figures 3.12, 3.14)

ventromedial nucleus A nucleus in the hypothalamus important for sexual behavior in female rats; activity increases there during copulation and destruction reduces the female's responsiveness to a male's advances. It is also involved in eating behavior. Destruction in rats increases parasympathetic activity in the vagus nerve, producing a persistent absorptive phase and extreme obesity. (Figure 5.2)

vesicle A membrane-enclosed container that stores neurotransmitter in the neuron terminal. (Figures 2.9, 2.14)

vestibular sense The sense that helps us maintain balance, and that provides information about head position and movement; the receptors are located in the vestibular organs. (Figure 10.1)

visual acuity Ability to distinguish visual details.

visual cortex The cortex in each occipital lobe where visual information is processed. (Figures 3.7, 9.4, 9.24)

visual field The part of the environment that is being registered on the retina.

VNO See *vomeronasal organ.*

volley theory Theory of auditory frequency analysis which states that groups of neurons follow the frequency of a sound when the frequency exceeds the firing rate capability of a single neuron. (Figure 8.8)

vomeronasal organ (VNO) A cluster of receptors in the nasal cavity that detect pheromones. (Figure 6.6)

VTA See *ventral tegmental area.*

vulnerability The idea that there is some threshold of causes that must be exceeded in order for illness to occur, and that environmental challenges may combine with a person's biological susceptibility to exceed that threshold.

vulnerability model The idea that environmental challenges combine with a person's genetic vulnerability for a disease to exceed the threshold for the disease.

Wernicke's aphasia Language impairment resulting from damage to Wernicke's area; the person has difficulty understanding and producing spoken and written language.

Wernicke's area The area just posterior to the auditory cortex (in the left hemisphere in most people) which interprets spoken and written language input and generates spoken and written language. (Figures 3.7, 8.18, 8.22)

winter birth effect The tendency for more schizophrenics to be born during the winter and spring months than any other time of the year. (Figure 13.11)

Wisconsin Card Sorting Test A test of prefrontal functioning that requires the individual to sort cards using one criterion and then change to another criterion.

withdrawal A negative reaction that occurs when drug use is stopped.

Wolffian ducts The early structures that in the male develop into the seminal vesicles and the vas deferens. (Figure 6.8)

working memory A memory function that provides a temporary "register" for information while it is being used.

X-linked In heredity, a condition in which a gene on the X chromosome is not paired with a gene on the shorter Y chromosome, so that a single recessive gene is adequate to produce a characteristic.

zygote A fertilized egg.

References

The end numbers in parentheses are the chapters in which the citations to these references appear.

Abe, K., Kroning, J., Greer, M. A., & Critchlow, V. (1979). Effects of destruction of the suprachiasmatic nuclei on the circadian rhythms in plasma corticosterone, body temperature, feeding and plasma thyrotropin. *Neuroendocrinology, 29,* 119–131. (14)

Abel, E. L., & Sokol, R. J. (1986). Fetal alcohol syndrome is now leading cause of mental retardation. *Lancet, 2,* 1222. (4)

Aboody, K. S., Brown, A., Rainov, N. G., Bower, K. A., Liu, S., Yang, W., Small, J. E., Herrlinger, U., Ourednik, V., Black, P. McL., Breakefield, X. O., & Snyder, E. Y. (2000). Neural stem cells display extensive tropism for pathology in adult brain: Evidence from intracranial gliomas. *Proceedings of the National Academy of Sciences, USA, 97,* 12846–12851. (1)

A brighter day for Edward Taub. (1997). *Science, 276,* 1503. (1)

Acland, G. M., Aguirre, G. D., Ray, J., Zhang, Q., Aleman, T. S., Cideciyan, A. V., Pearce-Kelling, S. E., Anand, V., Zeng, Y., Maguire, A. M., Jacobson, S. G., Hauswirth, W. W., & Bennett, J. (2001). Gene therapy restores vision in a canine model of childhood blindness. *Nature Genetics, 28,* 92–95. (9)

Adams, D. B., Gold, A. R., & Burt, A. D. (1978). Rise in female-initiated sexual activity at ovulation and its suppression by oral contraceptives. *New England Journal of Medicine, 299,* 1145–1150. (6)

Adolphs, R., Damasio, H., Tranel, D., & Damasio, A. R. (1996). Cortical systems for the recognition of emotion in facial expressions. *Journal of Neuroscience, 16,* 7678–7687. (7)

Adolphs, R., Tranel, D., & Damasio, A. R. (1998). The human amygdala in social judgment. *Nature, 393,* 470–474. (7)

Adolphs, R., Tranel, D., Damasio, H., & Damasio, A. (1995). Fear and the human amygdala. *Journal of Neuroscience, 15,* 5879–5891. (7)

Agnew, B. (2000). Financial conflicts get more scrutiny in clinical trials. *Science, 289,* 1266–1267. (1)

Ahissar, E., Vaadia, E., Ahissar, M., Bergman, H., Arieli, A., & Abeles, M. (1992). Dependence of cortical plasticity on correlated activity of single neurons and on behavioral context. *Science, 257,* 1412–1415. (11)

Akbarian, S., Bunney, W. E., Potkin, S. G., Wigal, S. B., Hagman, J. O., Sandman, C. A., & Jones, E. G. (1993). Altered distribution of nicotinamide-adenine dinucleotide phosphate-diaphorase cells in frontal lobe of schizophrenics implies disturbances of cortical development. *Archives of General Psychiatry, 50,* 169–177. (13)

Akbarian, S., Viñuela, A., Kim, J. J., Potkin, S. G., Bunney, W. E., & Jones, E. G. (1993). Distorted distribution of nicotinamide-adenine dinucleotide phosphate-diaphorase neurons in temporal lobe of schizophrenics implies anomalous cortical development. *Archives of General Psychiatry, 50,* 178–187. (13)

Alam, N., Szymusiak, R., & McGinty, D. (1995). Local preoptic/anterior hypothalamic warming alters spontaneous and evoked neuronal activity in the magnocellular basal forebrain. *Brain Research, 696,* 221–230. (14)

Albert, D. J., Walsh, M. L., & Jonik, R. H. (1993). Aggression in humans: What is its biological foundation? *Neuroscience and Biobehavioral Reviews, 17,* 405–425. (7)

Albert, M. S., Diamond, A. D., Fitch, R. H., Neville, H. J., Rapp, P. R., & Tallal, P. A. (1999). Cognitive development. In M. J. Zigmond, F. E. Bloom, S. C. Landis, J. L., Roberts, & L. R. Squire (Eds.), *Fundamental neuroscience.* New York: Academic Press. (11)

Albrecht, D. G., De Valois, R. L., & Thorell, L. G. (1980). Visual cortical neurons: Are bars or gratings the optimal stimuli? *Science, 207,* 88–90. (9)

Albuquerque, E. X., Daly, J. W., & Warnick, J. E. (1988). Macromolecular sites for specific neurotoxins and drugs on chemosensitive synapses and electrical excitation in biological membranes. *Ion Channels, 1,* 95–162. (2)

Aldhous, P. (2000). Stem cells: Panacea, or Pandora's box? *Nature, 408,* 897–898. (1)

Alexander, C. N., Langer, E. J., Newman, R. I., Chandler, H. M., & Davies, J. L. (1989). Transcendental meditation, mindfulness, and longevity: An experimental study with the elderly. *Journal of Personality and Social Psychology, 57,* 950–964. (7)

Alexander, G. E., & Crutcher, M. D. (1990). Preparation for movement: Neural representations of intended direction in three motor areas of the monkey. *Journal of Neurophysiology, 64,* 133–150. (10)

Alkire, M. T., Haier, R. J., Fallon, J. H., & Cahill, L. (1998). Hippocampal, but not amygdala, activity at encoding correlates with long-term free recall of nonemotional information. *Proceedings of the National Academy of Sciences, USA, 95,* 14506–14510. (11)

Allegretta, M., Nicklas, J. A., Sriram, S., & Albertini, R. J. (1990). T cells responsive to myelin basic protein in patients with multiple sclerosis. *Science, 247,* 718–721. (10)

Allen, L. S., & Gorski, R. A. (1992). Sexual orientation and the size of the anterior commissure in the human brain. *Proceedings of the National Academy of Sciences, USA, 89,* 7199–7202. (6)

Allison, T., & Cicchetti, D. V. (1976). Sleep in mammals: Ecological and constitutional correlates. *Science, 194,* 732–734. (14)

Alzheimer's Association. (2000, March 21). Race against time: Alzheimer's epidemic hits as America ages. Available: http://www.alz.org/Media/newsreleases/archived/032100PPA.htm. (11)

American Association for the Advancement of Science. (2000). Human inheritable genetic modifications: Findings and recommendations (Online). Available: http://www.aaas.org/spp/dspp/sfrl/germline/main.htm. (1)

American Medical Association. (1992). *Use of animals in biomedical research: The challenge and response.* Chicago: Author. (1)

American Psychiatric Association. (1994). *Diagnostic and statistical manual of mental disorders* (4th ed.). Washington, DC: Author. (12, 14)

American Psychological Association. (1992). Ethical principles of psychologists and code of conduct. *American Psychologist, 47,* 1597–1611. (1)

American Psychological Association. (2001, February 8). Guidelines for ethical conduct in the care and use of animals (Online). Available: http://www.apa.org/science/anguide.html. (1)

Anderson, A. E., & Holman, J. E. (1997). Males with eating disorders: Challenges for treatment and research. *Psychopharmacology Bulletin, 33,* 391–397. (5)

Anderson, A. K., & Phelps, E. A. (2001). Lesions of the human amygdala impair enhanced perception of emotionally salient events. *Nature, 411,* 305–309. (7)

Anderson, B., & Harvey, T. (1996). Alterations in cortical thickness and neuronal density in the frontal cortex of Albert Einstein. *Neuroscience Letters, 210,* 161–164. (12)

Anderson, R. H., Fleming, D. E., Rhees, R. W., & Kinghorn, E. (1986). Relationships between sexual activity, plasma testosterone, and the volume of the sexually dimorphic nucleus of the preoptic area in prenatally stressed and non-stressed rats. *Brain Research, 370,* 1–10. (6)

Anderson, S. W., Bechara, A., Damasio, H., Tranel, D., & Damasio, A. R. (1999). Impairment of social and moral behavior related to early damage in human prefrontal cortex. *Nature Neuroscience, 2,* 1032–1037. (3, 7)

Ando, J., Ono, Y., & Wright, M. J. (2001). Genetic structure of spatial and verbal working memory. *Behavior Genetics, 31,* 615–624. (12)

Andrade, J. (1995). Learning during anaesthesia: A review. *British Journal of Psychology, 86,* 479–506. (14)

Andreasen, N. C. (1984). *The broken brain.* New York: Harper & Row. (13)

Andreasen, N. C., Flaum, M., Swayze, V. W., II, Tyrrell, G., & Arndt, S. (1990). Positive and negative symptoms in schizophrenia: A critical reappraisal. *Archives of General Psychiatry, 47,* 615–621. (13)

Andreasen, N. C., Rezai, K., Alliger, R., Swayzee, V. W., II, Flaum, M., Kirchner, P., Cohen, G., & O'Leary, D. S. (1992). Hypofrontality in neuroleptic-naive patients and in patients with chronic schizophrenia: Assessment with xenon 133 single-photon emission computed tomography and the Tower of London. *Archives of General Psychiatry, 49,* 943–958. (3, 13)

Ankney, C. D. (1992). Sex differences in relative brain size: The mismeasure of woman, too? *Intelligence, 16,* 329–336. (12)

Anonymous. (1970). Effects of sexual activity on beard growth in man. *Nature, 226,* 869–870. (6)

Archer, J. (1991). The influence of testosterone on human aggression. *British Journal of Psychology, 82,* 1–28. (6, 7)

Arendt, J., Skene, D. J., Middleton, B., Lockley, S. W., & Deacon, S. (1997). Efficacy of melatonin treatment in jet lag, shift work, and blindness. *Journal of Biological Rhythms, 12,* 604–617. (14)

Arendt, T., Allen, Y., Sinden, J., Schugens, M. M., Marchbanks, R. M., Lantos, P. L., & Gray, J. A. (1988). Cholinergic-rich brain transplants reverse alcohol-induced memory deficits. *Nature, 332,* 448–450. (3)

Aroniadou, V. A., & Teyler, T. J. (1991). The role of NMDA receptors in long-term potentiation (LTP) and depression (LTD) in rat visual cortex. *Brain Research, 562,* 136–143. (11)

Aschoff, J. (1969). Desynchronization and resynchronization of human circadian rhythms. *Aerospace Medicine, 40,* 844–849. (14)

Aschoff, J. (1984). Circadian timing. *Annals of the New York Academy of Sciences, 423,* 442–468. (14)

ASCI White Lawrence Livermore Lab. (2001). (Online). Available: http://www.glendhu.com/ai/supercomputers/asciwhite.html. (2)

Ashour, M. H., Jain, S. K., Kattan, K. M., al-Daeef, A. Q., Abdal-Jabbar, M. S., al-Tahan, A. R., & al-Moallami, M. (1995). Maximal thymectomy for myasthenia gravis. *European Journal of Cardio-thoracic Surgery, 9,* 461–464. (10)

Aston-Jones, G., & Bloom, F. E. (1981). Activity of norepinephrine-containing locus coeruleus neurons in behaving rats anticipates fluctuations in the sleep-waking cycle. *Journal of Neuroscience, 1,* 876–886. (14)

Avery, D., & Winokur, G. (1978). Suicide, attempted suicide, and relapse rates in depression: Recurrence after ECT and antidepressant therapy. *Archives of General Psychiatry, 35,* 749–753. (13)

Ax, A. (1953). The physiological differentiation between fear and anger in humans. *Psychosomatic Medicine, 15,* 433–442. (1, 7)

Axel, R. (Oct., 1995). The molecular logic of smell. *Scientific American, 273,* 154–159. (6)

Bach-y-Rita, P. (1990). Brain plasticity as a basis for recovery of function in humans. *Neuropsychologia, 28,* 547–554. (3)

Bailey, A., Le Couteur, A., Gottesman, I., Bolton, P., Simonoff, E., Yuzda, E., & Rutter, M. (1995). Autism as a strongly genetic disorder: Evidence from a British twin study. *Psychological Medicine, 25,* 63–77. (12)

Bailey, C. H., Bartsch, D., & Kandel, E. R. (1996). Toward a molecular definition of long-term memory storage. *Proceedings of the National Academy of Sciences, USA, 93,* 13445–13452. (1, 11)

Bailey, J. M., & Bell, A. P. (1993). Familiality of female and male homosexuality. *Behavior Genetics, 23,* 313–322. (6)

Bailey, J. M., & Benishay, D. S. (1993). Familial aggregation of female sexual orientation. *American Journal of Psychiatry, 150,* 272–277. (6)

Bailey, J. M., & Pillard, R. C. (1991). A genetic study of male sexual orientation. *Archives of General Psychiatry, 48,* 1089–1096. (1, 6)

Bailey, J. M., Pillard, R. C., Neale, M. C., & Agyei, Y. (1993). Heritable factors influence sexual orientation in women. *Archives of General Psychiatry, 50,* 217–223. (1, 6)

Baizer, J. S., Ungerleider, L. G., & Desimone, R. (1991). Organization of visual inputs to the inferior temporal and posterior parietal cortex in macaques. *Journal of Neuroscience, 11,* 168–190. (9)

Balzac, H. de (1996). The pleasures and pains of coffee (Robert Onopa, Trans.). *Michigan Quarterly Review, 35,* 273–277. (Original work published 1839). (4)

Bandmann, O., Vaughan, J., Holmans, P., Marsden, C. D., & Wood, N. W. (1997). Association of slow acetylator genotype for N-acetyltransferase 2 with familial Parkinson's disease. *Lancet, 350,* 1136–1139. (10)

Bannon, A. W., Decker, M. W., Holladay, M. W., Curzon, P., Donnelly-Roberts, D., Puttfarcken, P. S., Bitner, R. S., Diaz, A., Dickenson, A. H., Porsolt, R. D., Williams, M., & Arneric, S. P. (1998). Broad-spectrum, non-opioid analgesic activity by selective modulation of neuronal nicotinic acetylcholine receptors. *Science, 279,* 77–81. (10)

Barbaro, N. M. (1988). Studies of PAG/PVG stimulation for pain relief in humans. *Progress in Brain Research, 77,* 165–173. (10)

Barbeau, H., McCrea, D. A., O'Donovan, M. J., Rossignol, S., Grill, W. M., & Lemay, M. A. (1999). Tapping into spinal circuits to restore motor function. *Brain Research Reviews, 30,* 27–51. (10)

Barinaga, M. (1996). Guiding neurons to the cortex. *Science, 274,* 1100–1101. (3)

Barinaga, M. (1997). New imaging methods provide a better view into the brain. *Science, 276,* 1974–1981. (App.)

Barinaga, M. (1999). Learning visualized, on the double. *Science, 286,* 1661. (11)

Barinaga, M. (2000). Fetal neuron grafts pave the way for stem cell therapies. *Science, 287,* 1421–1422. (1)

Barnes, C. A., & McNaughton, B. L. (1985). An age comparison of the rates of acquisition and forgetting of spatial information in relation to long-term enhancement of hippocampal synapses. *Behavioral Neuroscience, 99,* 1040–1048. (11)

Bartlett, D. L., & Steele, J. B. (1979). *Empire: The life, legend, and madness of Howard Hughes*. New York: Norton. (13)

Basbaum, A. I., & Fields, H. L. (1984). Endogenous pain control systems: Brainstem spinal pathways and endorphin circuitry. *Annual Review of Neuroscience, 7,* 309–338. (10)

Basbaum, A. I., & Jessell, T. M. (2000). The perception of pain. In E. R. Kandel, J. H. Schwartz, & T. M. Jessell (Eds.), *Principles of neural science* (4th ed., pp. 472–491). New York: McGraw-Hill. (10)

Batista, A. P., Buneo, C. A., Snyder, L. H., & Andersen, R. A. (1999). Reach plans in eye-centered coordinates. *Science, 285,* 257–260. (10)

Bauer, R. M. (1984). Autonomic recognition of names and faces in prosopagnosia: A neuropsychological application of the guilty knowledge test. *Neuropsychologia, 22,* 457–469. (9)

Baulac, S., Huberfeld, G., Gourinkel-An, I., Mitropoulou, G., Beranger, A., Prud'homme, J.-F., Baulac, M., Brice, A., Bruzone, R., & LeGuern, E. (2001). First genetic evidence of GABA^A receptor dysfunction in epilepsy: A mutation in the γ2-subunit gene. *Nature Genetics, 28,* 46–48. (2)

Baum, A., Gatchel, R. J., & Schaeffer, M. A. (1983). Emotional, behavioral, and physiological effects of chronic stress at Three Mile Island. *Journal of Consulting and Clinical Psychology, 51,* 565–572. (7)

Baxter, L. R., Phelps, M. E., Mazziotta, J. C., Guze, B. H., Schwartz, J. M., & Selin, C. E. (1987). Local cerebral glucose metabolic rates in obsessive-compulsive disorder. *Archives of General Psychiatry, 44,* 211–218. (13)

Baxter, L. R., Phelps, M. E., Mazziotta, J. C., Schwartz, J. M., Gerner, R. H., Selin, C. E., & Sumida, R. M. (1985). Cerebral metabolic rates for glucose in mood disorders: Studies with positron emission tomography and fluorodeoxyglucose F 18. *Archives of General Psychiatry, 42,* 441–447. (13)

Baxter, L. R., Schwartz, J. M., Phelps, M. E., Mazziotta, J. C., Guze, B. H., Selin, C. E., Gerner, R. H., & Sumida, R. M. (1989). Reduction of prefrontal cortex glucose metabolism common to three types of depression. *Archives of General Psychiatry, 46,* 243–249. (13)

Bayley, H. (1997, September). Building doors into cells. *Scientific American,* 62–67. (2)

Bechara, A., Damasio, H., Damasio, A. R., & Lee, G. P. (1999). Different contributions of the human amygdala and ventromedial prefrontal cortex to decision-making. *Journal of Neuroscience, 19,* 5473–5481. (7)

Bechara, A., Damasio, H., Tranel, D., & Damasio, A. R. (1997). Deciding advantageously before knowing the advantageous strategy. *Science, 275,* 1293–1295. (3)

Bechara, A., Tranel, D., Damasio, H., Adolphs, R., Rockland, C., & Damasio, A. R. (1995). Double dissociation of conditioning and declarative knowledge relative to the amygdala and hippocampus in humans. *Science, 269,* 1115–1118. (11)

Beck, A. T., & Galef, B. G. (1989). Social influences on the selection of a protein-sufficient diet by Norway rats (*Rattus norvegicus*). *Journal of Comparative Psychology, 103,* 132–139. (5)

Becker, A. E., Burwell, R. A., Gilman, S. E., Herzog, D. B., & Hamburg, P. Eating behaviours and attitudes following prolonged exposure to television among ethnic Fijian adolescent girls. *British Journal of Psychiatry, 180,* 509–514. (5)

Beecher, D. K. (1956). Relationship of significance of wound to pain experienced. *Journal of the American Medical Association, 161,* 1609–1613. (7)

Begley, S., & Biddle, N. A. (1996, February 26). For the obsesssed, the mind can fix the brain. *Newsweek, 60.* (13)

Békésy, G. von. (1951). The mechanical properties of the ear. In Stevens, S. S. (Ed.), *The handbook of experimental psychology* (pp. 1075–1115). New York: Wiley. (8)

Békésy, G. von. (1956). Current status of theories of hearing. *Science, 123,* 779–783. (8)

Bell, A. P., Weinberg, M. S., & Hammersmith, S. K. (1981). *Sexual preference*. Bloomington: Indiana University Press. (6)

Bellis, D. J. (1981). *Heroin and politicians: The failure of public policy to control addiction in America*. Westport, CT: Greenwood Press. (4)

Bengzon, J., Kokaia, Z., Elmér, E., Nanobashvili, A., Kokaia, M., & Lindvall, O. (1997). Apoptosis and proliferation of dentate gyrus neurons after single and intermittent limbic seizures. *Proceedings of the National Academy of Sciences, USA, 94,* 10432–10437. (3)

Beninger, R. J., & Hahn, B. L. (1983). Pimozide blocks establishment but not expression of amphetamine-produced environment-specific conditioning. *Science, 220,* 1304–1306. (4)

Benoit, E., & Dubois, J. M. (1986). Toxin I from the snake *Dendroaspis polylepsis polylepsis*: A highly specific blocker of one type of potassium channel in myelinated nerve fiber. *Brain Research, 377,* 374–377. (2)

Benson, D. F., Djenderedjian, A., Miller, B. L., Pachana, N. A., Chang, L., Itti, L., & Mena, I. (1996). Neural basis of confabulation. *Neurology, 46,* 1239–1243. (11, 14)

Benton, A. L. (1980). The neuropsychology of facial recognition. *American Psychologist, 35,* 176–186. (9)

Berenbaum, S. A., & Hines, M. (1992). Early androgens are related to childhood sex-typed toy preferences. *Psychological Science, 3,* 203–206. (6)

Berkow, I. (1995, January 5). The sweetest sound of all. *New York Times,* p. B8. (8)

Bernard, L. L. (1924). *Instinct*. New York: Holt, Rinehart & Winston. (5)

Bernhardt, P. C., Dabbs, J. M., Jr., Fielden, J. A., & Lutter, C. D. (1998). Testosterone changes during vicarious experiences of winning and losing among fans at sporting events. *Physiological Behavior, 65,* 59–62. (7)

Bernstein, I. L. (1978). Learned taste aversions in children receiving chemotherapy. *Science, 200,* 1302–1303. (5)

Bernstein, L. J., & Robertson, L. C. (1998). Illusory conjunctions of color and motion with shape following bilateral parietal lesions. *Psychological Science, 9,* 167–175. (14)

Berridge, V., & Edwards, G. (1981). *Opium and the people: Opiate use in nineteenth-century England*. New York: St. Martin's Press. (4)

Berson, D. M., Dunn, F. A., & Takao, M. (2002). Phototransduction by retinal ganglion cells that set the circadian clock. *Science, 295,* 1070–1073. (14)

Betarbet, R., Sherer, T. B., MacKenzie, G., Garcia-Osuna, M., Panov, A. V., & Greenamyre, J. T. (2000). Chronic systemic pesticide exposure reproduces features of Parkinson's disease. *Nature Neuroscience, 3,* 1301–1306. (10)

Bezzi, P., Carmignoto, G., Pasti, L., Vesce, S., Rossi, D., Rizzini, B. L., Pozzan, T., & Volterra, A. (1998). Prostaglandins stimulate calcium-dependent glutamate release in astrocytes. *Nature, 391,* 281–285. (2)

Billington, C. J., & Levine, A. S. (1992). Hypothalamic neuropeptide Y regulation of feeding and energy metabolism. *Current Opinion in Neurobiology, 2,* 847–851. (5)

Billy, J. O. G., Tanfer, K., Grady, W. R., & Klepinger, D. H. (1993). The sexual behavior of men in the United States. *Family Planning Perspectives, 25*(2), 52–60. (6)

Blake, P. Y., Pincus, J. H., Buckner, C. (1995). Neurologic abnormalities in murderers. *Neurology, 45,* 1641–1647. (7)

Blanchard, D. C., & Blanchard, R. J. (1972). Innate and conditioned reactions to threat in rats with amygdaloid lesions. *Journal of Comparative and Physiological Psychology, 81,* 281–290. (7)

Blehar, M. C., & Rosenthal, N. E. (1989). Seasonal affective disorders and phototherapy. *Archives of General Psychiatry, 46,* 469–474. (13)

Bliss, E. L. (1980). Multiple personalities: A report of 14 cases with implications for schizophrenia and hysteria. *Archives of General Psychiatry, 37,* 1388–1397. (14)

Bliss, T. V. P., & Lømo, T. (1973). Long-lasting potentiation of synaptic transmission in the dentate area of the anaesthetized rabbit following stimulation of the perforant path. *Journal of Physiology, 232*, 331–356. (11)

Bloch, G. J., Butler, P. C., and Kohlert, J. G. (1996). Galanin microinjected into the medial preoptic nucleus facilitates female- and male-typical sexual behaviors in the female rat. *Physiology and Behavior, 59*, 1147–1154. (6)

Bloch, G. J., Butler, P. C., Kohlert, J. G., & Bloch, D. A. (1993). Microinjection of galanin into the medial preoptic nucleus facilitates copulatory behavior in the male rat. *Physiology and Behavior, 54*, 615–624. (6)

Blonder, L. X., Bowers, D., & Heilman, K. M. (1991). The role of the right hemisphere in emotional communication. *Brain, 114*, 1115–1127. (7)

Blum, D. (1994). *The monkey wars*. New York: Oxford. (1)

Bock, D. R., & Kolakowski, D. (1973). Further evidence of sex-linked major-gene influence on human spatial visualizing ability. *American Journal of Human Genetics, 25*, 1–14. (6)

Boecker, H., Dagher, A., Ceballos-Baumann, A. O., Passingham, R. E., Samuel, M., Friston, K. J., Poline, J., Dettmers, C., Conrad, B., & Brooks, D. J. (1998). Role of the human rostral supplementary motor area and the basal ganglia in motor sequence control: Investigations with H_2 150 PET. *Journal of Neurophysiology, 79*, 1070–1080. (10)

Bogardus, C., Lillioja, S., Ravussin, E., Abbott, W., Zawadzki, J. K., Young, A., Knowler, W. C., Jacobowitz, R., & Moll, P. P. (1986). Familial dependence of the resting metabolic rate. *New England Journal of Medicine, 315*, 96–100. (5)

Bogerts, B., Meertz, E., & Schönfeldt-Bausch, R. (1985). Basal ganglia and limbic system pathology in schizophrenia: A morphometric study of brain volume and shrinkage. *Archives of General Psychiatry, 42*, 784–791. (13)

Bohman, M. (1978). Some genetic aspects of alcoholism and criminality: A population of adoptees. *Archives of General Psychiatry, 35*, 269–276. (4)

Boivin, D. B., Duffy, J. F., Kronauer, R. E., & Czeisler, C. A. (1996). Dose-response relationships for resetting of human circadian clock by light. *Nature, 379*, 540–542. (14)

Bolles, R. C. (1975). *Theory of motivation*. New York: Harper & Row. (5)

Bonda, E., Petrides, M., Frey, S., & Evans, A. (1995). Neural correlates of mental transformations of the body-in-space. *Proceedings of the National Academy of Sciences, USA, 92*, 11180–11184. (10)

Bonebakker, A. E., Bonke, B., Klein, J., Wolters, G., Stijnene, T., Passchier, J., & Merikle, P. M. (1996). Information processing during general anesthesia: Evidence for unconscious memory. *Memory and Cognition, 24*, 766–776. (14)

Bonnet, M. H., & Arand, D. L. (1996). Metabolic rate and the restorative function of sleep. *Physiology and Behavior, 59*, 777–782. (14)

Bonora, E., Bacchelli, E., Levy, E. R., Blasi, F., Marlow, A., Monaco, A. P., & Maestrini, E. (2002). Mutation screening and imprinting analysis of four candidate genes for autism in the 7q32 region. *Molecular Psychiatry, 7*, 289–301. (12)

Bontempi, B., Laurent-Demir, C., Destrade, C., & Jaffard, R. (1999). Time-dependent reorganization of brain circuitry underlying long-term memory storage. *Nature, 400*, 671–675. (11)

Bouchard, C. (1989). Genetic factors in obesity. *Medical Clinics of North America, 73*, 67–81. (5)

Bouchard, C., Tremblay, A., Després, J.-P., Nadeau, A., Lupien, P. J., Thériault, G., Dussault, J., Moorjani, S., Pinalult, S., & Fournier, G. (1990). The response to long-term overfeeding in identical twins. *New England Journal of Medicine, 322*, 1477–1482. (5)

Bouchard, T. J. (1994). Genes, environment, and personality. *Science, 264*, 1700–1701. (1)

Bouchard, T. J., Jr., & McGue, M. (1981). Familial studies of intelligence: A review. *Science, 212*, 1055–1059. (1, 12)

Bouchard, T. J., & Segal, N. L. (1985). Environment and IQ. In B. B. Wolman (Ed.), *Handbook of intelligence: Theories, measurements, and applications* (pp. 391–464). New York: Wiley. (12)

Boulant, J. A. (1981). Hypothalamic mechanisms in thermoregulation. *Federation Proceedings, 40*, 2843–2850. (5)

Bourgeois, J.-P., & Rakic, P. (1993). Changes of synaptic density in the primary visual cortex of the macaque monkey from fetal to adult stage. *Journal of Neuroscience, 13*, 2801–2820. (3)

Bower, B. (1994). Temporary emotional states act like multiple personalities. In R. M. Klein & B. K. Doane (Eds.), *Psychological concepts and dissociative disorders*. Hillsdale, NJ: Erlbaum. (14)

Bowmaker, J. K., & Dartnall, H. J. A. (1980). Visual pigments of rods and cones in a human retina. *Journal of Physiology (London), 298*, 501–511.

Boyce, N. (2000). Is anyone in there? *New Scientist, 167*, 36–37. (14)

Bozarth, M. A., & Wise, R. A. (1984). Anatomically distinct opiate receptor fields mediate reward and physical dependence. *Science, 224*, 516–517. (4)

Bozarth, M. A., & Wise, R. A. (1985). Toxicity associated with long-term intravenous heroin and cocaine self-administration in the rat. *Journal of the American Medical Association, 254*, 81–83. (4)

Bracha, H. S., Torrey, E. F., Gottesman, I. I., Bigelow, L. B., & Cunniff, C. (1992). Second-trimester markers of fetal size in schizophrenia: A study of monozygotic twins. *American Journal of Psychiatry, 149*, 1355–1361. (13)

Bradbury, T. N., & Miller, G. A. (1985). Season of birth in schizophrenia: A review of evidence, methodology, and etiology. *Psychological Bulletin, 98*, 569–594. (13)

Bradley, S. J., Oliver, G. D., Chernick, A. B., & Zucker, K. J. (1998). Experiment of nature: Ablatio penis at 2 months, sex reassignment at 7 months, and a psychosexual follow-up in young adulthood (Online). Available: http://www.pediatrics.org/cgi/content/full/102/1/e9. (6)

Brain shrinks, yet thinks. (1983). *Science Digest, 10*, 71. (3)

Brannon, E. M., & Terrace, H. S. (1998). Ordering of the numerosities 1 to 9 by monkeys. *Science, 282*, 746–749. (12)

Braude, S., Tang-Martinez, Z., & Taylor, G. T. (1999). Stress, testosterone, and the immunoredistribution hypothesis. *Behavioral Ecology, 10*, 345. (7)

Braun, B. G. (1985). *Treatment of multiple personality disorder*. Washington, DC: American Psychiatric Press. (14)

Bray, G. A. (1992). Drug treatment of obesity. *American Journal of Clinical Nutrition, 55*, 538S–544S. (5)

Brecher, E. M. (1972). *Licit and illicit drugs*. Boston: Little, Brown. (4)

Breier, A., Buchanan, R. W., Elkashef, A., Munson, R. C., Kirkpatrick, B., & Gellad, F. (1992). Brain morphology and schizophrenia: A magnetic resonance imaging study of limbic, prefrontal cortex, and caudate structures. *Archives of General Psychiatry, 49*, 921–926. (13)

Breitner, J. C., Folstein, M. E., & Murphy, E. A. (1986). Familial aggregation in Alzheimer dementia-1. A model for the age-dependent expression of an autosomal dominant gene. *Journal of Psychiatric Research, 20*, 31–43. (1)

Bremer, J. (1959). *Asexualization: A follow-up study of 244 cases*. New York: Macmillan. (6)

Bremner, J. D., Randall, P., Scott, T. M., Bronen, R. A., Seibyl, J. P., Southwick, S. M., Delaney, R. C., McCarthy, G., Charney, D. S., & Innis, R. B. (1995). MRI-based measurement of hippocampal volume in patients with combat related posttraumatic stress disorder. *American Journal of Psychiatry, 152*, 973–981. (7)

Bremner, J. D., Randall, P., Vermetten, E., Staib, L., Bronen, R. A., Mazure, C., Capelli, S., McCarthy, G., Innis, R. B., & Charney, D. S. (1997). Magnetic resonance imaging-based measurement of hippocampal volume in posttraumatic stress disorder related to childhood physical and sexual abuse—a preliminary report. *Biological Psychiatry, 41*, 23–32. (7)

Brennan, P. A., Grekin, E. R., & Mednick, S. A. (1999). Maternal smoking during pregnancy and adult male criminal outcomes. *Archives of General Psychiatry, 56*, 215–219. (4, 7)

Brinkman, C. (1984). Supplementary motor area of the monkey's cerebral cortex: Short- and long-term deficits after unilateral ablation and the effects of subsequent callosal section. *Journal of Neuroscience, 4*, 918–929. (10)

Brinkman, R. R., Mezei, M. M., Theilmann, J., Almqvist, E., & Hayden, M. R. (1997). The likelihood of being affected with Huntington disease by a particular age, for a specific CAG size. *American Journal of Human Genetics, 60*, 1202–1210. (10)

Broca, P. (1861). Remarques sur le siège de la faculté du langage articulé, suivies d'une observation d'aphemie (perte de la parole). *Bulletin de la Société Anatomique (Paris), 36*, 330–357. (1, 8)

Broughton, R. (1975). Biorhythmic variations in consciousness and psychological functions. *Canadian Psychological Review, 16*, 217–239. (14)

Broughton, R., Billings, R., Cartwright, R., Doucette, D., Edmeads, J., Edward, H. M., Ervin, F., Orchard, B., Hill, R., & Turrell, G. (1994). Homicidal somnambulism: A case report. *Sleep, 17*, 253–264. (14)

Brown, C. M., & Nuttal, A. L. (1984). Efferent control of cochlear inner hair cell responses in the guinea-pig. *Journal of Physiology, 354*, 625–646. (8)

Brown, K., & Wald, G. (1964). Visual pigments in single rods and cones of the human retina. *Science, 143*, 45–52. (9)

Brown, M. A., & Sharp, P. E. (1995). Simulation of spatial learning in the Morris water maze by a neural network model of the hippocampal formation and nucleus accumbens. *Hippocampus, 5*, 171–188. (2)

Brown, T. H., Chapman, P. F., Kairiss, E. W., & Keenan, C. L. (1988). Long-term synaptic potentiation. *Science, 242*, 724–727. (11)

Brownell, W. E., Bader, C. R., Bertrand, D., & de Ribaupierre, Y. (1985). Evoked mechanical responses of isolated cochlear outer hair cells. *Science, 227*, 194–196. (8)

Buchsbaum, M. S., Hollander, E., Haznedar, M. M., Tang, C., Spiegel-Cohen, J., Wei, T. C., Solimando, A., Buchsbaum, B. R., Robins, D., Bienstock, C., Cartwright, C., & Mosovich, S. (2001). Effect of fluoxetine on regional cerebral metabolism in autistic spectrum disorders: A pilot study. *International Journal of Neuropsychopharmacology, 4*, 119–125. (12)

Buckner, R. L., & Koutstaal, W. (1998). Functional neuroimaging studies of encoding, priming, and explicit memory retrieval. *Proceedings of the National Academy of Sciences, USA, 95*, 891–898. (11)

Buell, S. J., & Coleman, P. D. (1979). Dendritic growth in the aged human brain and failure of growth in senile dementia. *Science, 206*, 854–856. (3, 11)

Bunney, W. E., Jr., Murphy, D. L., Goodwin, F. K., & Borge, G. F. (1972). The "switch process" in manic-depressive illness: I. A systematic study of sequential behavioral changes. *Archives of General Psychiatry, 27*, 295–302. (13)

Bünning, E. (1973). *The physiological clock: Circadian rhythms and biological chronometry* (3rd ed). New York: Springer-Verlag. (14)

Bureau of the Census. (2000, January 13). Projections of the total resident population by 5-year age groups, and sex with special age categories. Available at: http://www.census.gov/population/www/projections/natproj.html. (11)

Bushman, B. J., & Cooper, H. M. (1990). Effects of alcohol on human aggression: An integrative research review. *Psychological Bulletin, 107*, 341–354. (7)

Bushnell, M. C., Duncan, G. H., Hofbauer, R. K., Ha, B., Chen, J.-I., & Carrier, B. (1999). Pain perception: Is there a role for primary somatosensory cortex? *Proceedings of the National Academy of Sciences, USA, 96*, 7705–7709. (10)

Butterworth, B. (1999). A head for figures. *Science, 284*, 928–929. (12)

Buxbaum, J. D., Silverman, J. M., Smith, C. J., Kilifarski, M., Richert, J., Hollander, E., Lawlor, B. A., Fitzgerald, M., Greenberg, D. A., & Davis, K. L. (2001). Evidence for a susceptibility gene for autism on chromosome 2 and for genetic heterogeneity. *American Journal of Human Genetics, 68*, 1514–1520. (12)

Buydens-Branchey, L., Branchey, M. H., Noumair, D., & Lieber, C. S. (1989). Age of alcoholism onset. II. Relationship to susceptibility to serotonin precursor availability. *Archives of General Psychiatry, 46*, 231–236. (7)

Cadoret, R. J., Troughton, E., O'Gorman, T. W., & Heywood, E. (1986). An adoption study of genetic and environmental factors in drug abuse. *Archives of General Psychiatry, 43*, 1131–1136. (4)

Caffeine prevents post-op headaches. (1996). *United Press International, MSNBC* (Online). Available: http://www.msnbc.com/news/36911.asp (4)

Caggiula, A. R. (1970). Analysis of the copulation-reward properties of posterior hypothalamic stimulation in male rats. *Journal of Comparative and Physiological Psychology, 70*, 399–412. (4)

Cahill, L., Haier, R. J., Fallon, J., Alkire, M. T., Tang, C., Keator, D., Wu, J., & McGaugh, J. L. (1996). Amygdala activity at encoding correlated with long-term, free recall of emotional information. *Proceedings of the National Academy of Sciences, USA, 93*, 8016–8021. (11)

Calles-Escandón, J., & Horton, E. S. (1992). The thermogenic role of exercise in the treatment of morbid obesity: A critical evaluation. *American Journal of Clinical Nutrition, 55*, 533S–537S. (5)

Campfield, L. A., Smith, F. J., & Burn, P. (1998). Strategies and potential molecular targets for obesity treatment. *Science, 280*, 1383–1387. (5)

Campione, J. C., Brown, A. L., & Ferrara, R. A. (1982). Mental retardation and intelligence. In R. J. Sternberg (Ed.), *Handbook of human intelligence* (pp. 391–490). Cambridge: Cambridge University Press. (12)

Canavan, A. G. M., Sprengelmeyer, R., Diener, H.-C., & Hömberg, V. (1994). Conditional associative learning is impaired in cerebellar disease in humans. *Behavioral Neuroscience, 108*, 475–485. (10)

Cannon, W. B. (1927). The James-Lange theory of emotions: A critical examination and an alternative. *American Journal of Psychology, 39*, 106–124. (7)

Cannon, W. B. (1942). "Voodoo" death. *American Anthropologist, 44*, 169–181. (7)

Cao, Y. Q., Mantyh, P. W., Carlson, E. J., Gillespie, A. M., Epstein, C. J., & Basbaum, A. I. (1998). Primary afferent tachykinins are required to experience moderate-to-intense pain. *Nature, 392*, 390–394. (10)

Carlezon, W. A., & Wise, R. A. (1996). Rewarding actions of phencyclidine and related drugs in nucleus accumbens shell and frontal cortex. *Journal of Neuroscience, 16*, 3112–3122. (4)

Carlson, A. (1991, March). When is a woman not a woman? *Women's Sports and Fitness, 13*, 24–29. (6)

Carlson, M. (1981). Characteristics of sensory deficits following lesions of Brodmann's areas 1 and 2 in the postcentral gyrus of Macaca mulatta. *Brain Research, 204*, 424–430. (10)

Carr, C. E., & Konishi, M. (1990). A circuit for detection of interaural time differences in the brain stem of the barn owl. *Journal of Neuroscience, 10*, 3227–3246. (8)

Carraher, T. N., Carraher, D. W., & Schliemman, A. D. (1985). Mathematics in the streets and in schools. *British Journal of Developmental Psychology, 3*, 21–29. (12)

Carrera, M. R., Ashley, J. A., Parsons, L. H., Wirsching, P., Koob, G. F., & Janda, K. D. (1995). Suppresssion of psychoactive effects of cocaine by active immunization. *Nature, 378*, 727–730. (4)

Carroll, J. B. (1993). *Human cognitive abilities: A survey of factor-analytic studies*. Cambridge, England: University of Cambridge Press. (12)

Catterall, W. A. (1984). The molecular basis of neuronal excitability. *Science, 223*, 653–661. (2)

Cavazzana-Calvo, M., Hacein-Bey, S., de Saint Basile, G., Gross, F., Yvon, E., Nusbaum, P., Selz, F., Hue, C., Certain, S., Casanova, J.-L., Bousso, P., Le Deist, F., & Fischer, A. (2000). Gene therapy of human severe combined immunodeficiency (SCID)-X1 disease. *Science, 288*, 669–671. (1)

Ceci, S. J., & Liker, J. (1986). A day at the races: A study of IQ, expertise, and cognitive complexity. *Journal of Experimental Psychology: General, 115*, 255–266. (12)

Chagnon, Y. C., Pérusse, L., Weisnagel, S. J., Rankinen, T., & Bouchard, C. (1999). The human obesity gene map: The 1999 update. *Obesity Research, 8*, 89–117. (5)

Chapman, P. F., White, G. L., Jones, M. W., Cooper-Blacketer, D., Marshall, V. J., Irizarry, M., Younkin, L., Good, M. A., Bliss, T. V. P., Hyman, B. T., Younkin, S. G., & Hsiao, K. K. (1999). Impaired synaptic plasticity and learning in aged amyloid precursor protein transgenic mice. *Nature Neuroscience, 2*, 271–276. (11)

Charney, D. S., Woods, S. W., Krystal, J. H., & Heninger, G. R. (1990). Serotonin function and human anxiety disorders. In P. M. Whitaker-Azmitia & S. J. Peroutka (Eds.), *Annals of the New York Academy of Sciences. Special Issue: The Neuropharmacology of Serotonin, 600*, 558–573. (13)

Chase, V. D. (1999, May/June). Seeing is believing. *Techreview* (Online). Available: http://www.techreview.com/magazine/may99/chase.asp. (9)

Chawla, D., Rees, G., & Friston, K. J. (1999). The physiological basis of atentional modulation in extrastriate visual areas. *Nature Neuroscience, 2*, 671–675. (14)

Chemelli, R. M., Willie, J. T., Sinton, C. M., Elmquist, J. K., Scammell, T., Lee, C., Richardson, J. A., Williams, S. C., Xiong, Y., Kisanuki, Y., Fitch, T. E., Nakazato, M., Hammer, R. E., Saper, C. B., & Yanagisawa, M. (1999). Narcolepsy in orexin knockout mice: Molecular genetics of sleep regulation. *Cell, 98*, 437–451. (14)

Chen, D. F., Schneider, G. E., Martinou, J.-C., & Tonegawa, S. (1997). Bcl-2 promotes regeneration of severed axons in mammalian CNS. *Nature, 385*, 434–438. (3)

Chen, J., Paredes, W., Li, J., Smith, D., Lowinson, J., & Gardner, E. L. (1990). Delta⁹-tetrahydrocannabinol produces naloxone-blockable enhancement of presynaptic basal dopamine efflux in nucleus accumbens of conscious, freely-moving rats as measured by intracerebral microdialysis. *Psychopharmacology, 102*, 156–162. (4)

Chen, J.-F., Xu, K., Petzer, J. P., Staal, R., Xu, Y.-H., Beilstein, M., Sonsalla, P. K., Castagnoli, K., Catagnoli, N., Jr., & Schwarzschild, M. A. (2001). Neuroprotection by caffeine and A₂ₐ adenosine receptor inactivation in a model of Parkinson's disease. *Journal of Neuroscience, 21*, 1–6. (10)

Chen, W. R., Lee, S., Kato, K., Spencer, D. D., Shepherd, G. M., & Wiliamson, A. (1996). Long-term modifications of synaptic efficacy in the human inferior and middle temporal cortex. *Proceedings of the National Academy of Sciences, USA, 93*, 8011–8015. (11)

Cherney, N. I. (1996). Opioid analgesics: Comparative features and prescribing guidelines. *Drugs, 51*, 713–737. (4)

Chicurel, M. (2000). The sandman's secrets. *Nature, 407*, 554–556. (14)

Cho, A. K. (1990). Ice: A new dosage form of an old drug. *Science, 249*, 631–634. (4)

Chomsky, N. (1980). *Rules and representations.* New York: Columbia University Press. (8)

Chorney, M. J., Chorney, J., Seese, N., Owen, M. J., Daniels, J., McGuffin, P., Thompson, L. A., Detterman, D. K., Benbow, C., Lubinski, D., Eley, T., & Plomin, R. (1998). A quantitative trait locus associated with cognitive ability in children. *Psychological Science, 9*, 159–165. (12)

Chuang, R. S.-I., Jaffe, H., Cribbs, L., Perez-Reyes, E., & Swartz, K. J. (1998). Inhibition of T-type voltage-gated calcium channels by a new scorpion toxin. *Nature Neuroscience, 1*, 668–674. (2)

Chwalisz, K., Diener, E., & Gallagher, D. (1988). Autonomic arousal feedback and emotional experience: Evidence from the spinal cord injured. *Journal of Personality and Social Psychology, 54*, 820–828. (7)

Ciaranello, A. L., & Ciaranello, R. D. (1995). The neurobiology of infantile autism. *Annual Reviews of Neuroscience, 18*, 101–128. (12)

Cibelli, J. B., Grant, K. A., Chapman, K. B., Cunniff, K., Worst, T., Green, H. L., Walker, S. J., Gutlin, P. H., Vilner, L., Tabar, V., Dominko, T., Kane, J., Wettsein, P. J., Lanza, R. P., Studer, L., Vrana, K. E., & West, M. D. (2002). Parthenogenetic stem cells in nonhuman primates. *Science, 295*, 819. (1)

Ciompi, L. (1980). Catamnestic long-term study on the course of life and aging of schizophrenics. *Schizophrenia Bulletin, 6*, 607–618. (13)

Clark, J. T., Kalra, P. S., & Kalra, S. P. (1985). Neuropeptide Y stimulates feeding but inhibits sexual behavior in rats. *Endocrinology, 117*, 2435–2442. (5)

Clark, R. E., & Squire, L. R. (1998). Classical conditioning and brain systems: The role of awareness. *Science, 280*, 77–81. (14)

Clarren, S. K., Alvord, E. C., Sumi, S. M., Streissguth, A. P., & Smith, D. W. (1978). Brain malformations related to prenatal exposure to alcohol. *Journal of Pediatrics, 92*, 64–67. (3)

Clayton, J. D., Kyriacou, C. P., & Reppert, S. M. (2001). Keeping time with the human genome. *Nature, 409*, 829–831. (14)

Cloninger, C. R. (1987). Neurogenetic adaptive mechanisms in alcoholism. *Science, 236*, 410–416. (4)

Cloninger, C. R. (1991). D₂ dopamine receptor gene is associated but not linked with alcoholism. *Journal of the American Medical Association, 266*, 1833–1834. (4)

Coccaro, E. F., & Kavoussi, R. J. (1997). Fluoxetine and impulsive aggressive behavior in personality-disordered subjects. *Archives of General Psychiatry, 54*, 1081–1088. (7)

Cohen, J. D., & Tong, F. (2001). The face of controversy. *Science, 293*, 2405–2407. (9)

Cohen, L. G., Celnik, P., Pascual-Leone, A., Corwell, B., Faiz, L., Dambrosia, J., Honda, M., Sadato, N., Gerloff, C., Catalá, M. D., & Hallett, M. (1997). Functional relevance of cross-modal plasticity in blind humans. *Nature, 389*, 180. (3)

Cohen, N. J., Eichenbaum, H., Deacedo, B. S ., & Corkin, S. (1985). Different memory systems underlying acquisition of procedural and declarative knowledge. *Annals of the New York Academy of Sciences, 444*, 54–71. (11)

Cohen, S., Frank, E., Doyle, W. J., Skoner, D. P., Rabin, B. S., & Gwaltney, J. M., Jr. (1998). Types of stressors that increase susceptibility to the common cold in healthy adults. *Health Psychology, 17*, 214–223. (7)

Cohen, S., Tyrrell, D. A., & Smith, A. P. (1991). Psychological stress and susceptibility to the common cold. *New England Journal of Medicine, 325*, 606–612. (7)

Colby, C. L., & Goldberg, M. E. (1999). Space and attention in parietal cortex. *Annual Review of Neuroscience, 22*, 319–349. (10)

Coleman, D. L. (1973). Effects of parabiosis of obese with diabetes and normal mice. *Diabetologia, 9*, 294–298. (5)

Collaer, M. L., & Hines, M. (1995). Human behavioral sex differences: A role for gonadal hormones during early development? *Psychological Bulletin, 118*, 55–107. (6)

Colt, E. W. D., Wardlaw, S. L., & Frantz, A. G. (1981). The effect of running on plasma β-endorphin. *Life Sciences, 28*, 1637–1640. (10)

Comuzzie, A. G., & Allison, D. B. (1998). The search for human obesity genes. *Science, 280*, 1374–1377. (5)

Conner, J. M., Darracq, M. A., Roberts, J., & Tuszynski, M. H. (2001). Nontropic actions of neurotrophins: Subcortical nerve growth factor gene delivery reverses age-related degeneration of primate cortical cholinergic innervation. *Proceedings of the National Academy of Sciences, USA, 98,* 1941–1946. (11)

Considine, R. V., Sinha, M. K., Heiman, M. L., Kriauciunas, A., Stephens, T. W., Nyce, M. R., Ohannesian, J. P., Marco, C. C., McKee, L. J., Bauer, T. L., & Caro, J. F. (1996). Serum immunoreactive-leptin concentrations in normal-weight and obese humans. *New England Journal of Medicine, 334,* 292–295. (5)

Constantinidis, C., & Steinmetz, M. A. (1996). Neuronal activity in posterior parietal area 7a during the delay periods of a spatial memory task. *Journal of Neurophysiology, 76,* 1352–1355. (11)

Cook, E. H., Courchesne, R., Lord, C., Cox, N. J., Yan, S., Lincoln, A., Haas, R., Courchesne, E., & Leventhal, B. L. (1997). Evidence of linkage between the serotonin transporter and autistic disorder. *Molecular Psychiatry, 2,* 247–250. (12)

Corbett, D., & Wise, R. A. (1980). Intracranial self-stimulation in relation to the ascending dopaminergic systems of the midbrain: A moveable electrode mapping study. *Brain Research, 185,* 1–15. (4)

Corbetta, M., Miezin, F. M., Dobmeyer, S., Shulman, G. L., & Petersen, S. E. (1990). Attentional modulation of neural processing of shape, color, and velocity in humans. *Science, 248,* 1556–1559. (14)

Corkin, S. (1984). Lasting consequences of bilateral medial temporal lobectomy: Clinical course and experimental findings in H. M. *Seminars in Neurology, 4,* 249–259. (11)

Corkin, S., Amaral, D. G., González, R. G., Johnson, K. A., & Hyman, B. T. (1997). HM's medial temporal lobe lesion: Findings from magnetic resonance imaging. *Journal of Neuroscience, 17,* 3964–3979. (11)

Cosgrove, G. R., & Eskandar, E. (1998). Thalamotomy and pallidotomy. Available at: http://neurosurgery.mgh.harvard.edu/pallidt.htm. (10)

Costall, B., & Naylor, R. J. (1992). Anxiolytic potential of 5-HT3 receptor antagonists. *Pharmacology and Toxicology, 70,* 157–162. (13)

Cotton, J. L. (1981). A review of research on Schachter's theory of emotion and the misattribution of arousal. *European Journal of Social Psychology, 11,* 365–397. (7)

Courtney, S. M., Ungerleider, L. G., Keil, K., & Haxby, J. V. (1997). Transient and sustained activity in a distributed neural system for human working memory. *Nature, 386,* 608–611. (9)

Cox, D. J., Merkel, R. L., Kovatchev, B., & Seward, R. (2000). Effect of stimulant medication on driving performance of young adults with attention-deficit hyperactivity disorder: A preliminary double-blind placebo controlled trial. *Journal of Nervous and Mental Disease, 188,* 230–234. (2)

Crane, G. E. (1957). Iproniazid (Marsilid®) phosphate, a therapeutic agent for mental disorders and debilitating diseases. *Psychiatry Research Reports, 8,* 142–152. (13)

Crick, F. (1994). *The astonishing hypothesis: The scientific search for the soul.* New York: Scribner. (9, 14)

Crick, F., & Koch, C. (1992, September). The problem of consciousness. *Scientific American, 267,* 153–159. (9)

Crick, F., & Mitchison, G. (1995). REM sleep and neural nets. *Behavioral Brain Research, 69,* 147–155. (14)

Crow, T. J. (1985). The two-syndrome concept: Origins and current status. *Schizophrenia Bulletin, 11,* 471–486. (13)

Culp, R. E., Cook, A. S., & Housley, P. C. (1983). A comparison of observed and reported adult-infant interactions: Effects of perceived sex. *Sex Roles, 9,* 475–479. (6)

Cutler, W. B., Friedmann, E., & McCoy, N. L. (1998). Pheromonal influences on sociosexual behavior in men. *Archives of Sexual Behavior, 27,* 1–13. (6)

Cutler, W. B., Preti, G., Krieger, A., Huggins, G. R., Garcia, C. R., & Lawley, H. J. (1986). Human axillary secretions influence women's menstrual cycles: The role of donor extract from men. *Hormones and Behavior, 20,* 463–473. (6)

Czeisler, C. A., Duffy, J. F., Shanahan, T. L., Brown, E. N., Mitchell, J. F., Rimmer, D. W., Ronda, J. M., Silva, E. J., Allan, J. S., Emens, J. S., Dijk, D.-J., & Kronauer, R. E. (1999). Stability, precision, and near-24-hour period of the human circadian pacemaker. *Science, 284,* 2177–2181. (14)

Czeisler, C. A., Johnson, M. P., Duffy, J. F., Brown, E. N., Ronda, J. M., & Kronauer, R. E. (1990). Exposure to bright light and darkness to treat physiologic maladaptation to night work. *New England Journal of Medicine, 322,* 1253–1259. (14)

Czeisler, C. A., Moore-Ede, M. C., & Coleman, R. M. (1982). Rotating shift work schedules that disrupt sleep are improved by applying circadian principles. *Science, 217,* 460–463. (14)

Czeisler, C. A., Richardson, G. S., Coleman, R. M., Zimmerman, J. C., Moore-Ede, M. C., Dement, W. C., & Weitzman, E. D. (1981). Chronotherapy: Resetting the circadian clocks of patients with delayed sleep phase insomnia. *Sleep, 4,* 1–21. (14)

Czeisler, C. A., Shanahan, T. L., Klerman, E. B., Martens, H., Brotman, D. J., Emens, J. S., Klein, T., & Rizzo, J. F., III. (1995). Suppression of melatonin secretion in some blind patients by exposure to bright light. *New England Journal of Medicine, 332,* 6–11. (14)

d'Alfonso, A. A., Aleman, A., Kessels, R. P., Schouten, E. A., Postma, A., van Der Linden, J. A., Cahn, W., Greene, Y., de Haan, E. H., & Kahn, R. S. (2002). Transcranial magnetic stimulation of left auditory cortex in patients with schizophrenia: Effects on hallucinations and neurocognition. *Journal of Neuropsychiatry and Clinical Neurosciences, 14,* 77–79. (13)

D'Esposito, M., & Postle, B. R. (1999). The dependence of span and delayed response performance on prefrontal cortex. *Neuropsychologia, 37,* 1303–1315. (11)

Dabbs, J. J., Jr., Frady, R. L., Carr, T. S., & Besch, N. F. (1987). Saliva testosterone and criminal violence in young adult prison inmates. *Psychosomatic Medicine, 49,* 174–182. (7)

Dabbs, J. J., Jr., & Hargrove, M. F. (1997). Age, testosterone, and behavior among female prison inmates. *Psychosomatic Medicine, 59,* 477–480. (7)

Dabbs, J. M., Jr., Carr, T. S., Frady, R. L., & Riad, J. K. (1995). Testosterone, crime, and misbehavior among 692 male prison inmates. *Personality and Individual Differences, 18,* 627–633. (7)

Dabbs, J. M., Jr., & Mohammed, S. (1992). Male and female salivary testosterone concentrations before and after sexual activity. *Physiology and Behavior, 52,* 195–197. (6)

Dallos, P., & Cheatham, M. A. (1976). Production of cochlear potentials by inner and outer hair cells. *Journal of the Acoustical Society of America, 60,* 510–512. (8)

Dalton, R. (2000). NIH cash tied to compulsory training in good behavior. *Nature, 408,* 629. (1)

Daly, M., & Wilson, M. (1988). *Homicide.* New York: Aldine de Gruyter. (6)

Damasio, A. (1994). *Descartes' error: Emotion, reason, and the human brain.* New York: Putnam. (7)

Damasio, A. R. (1985). Prosopagnosia. *Trends in Neurosciences, 8,* 132–135. (9)

Damasio, A. R., Grabowski, T. J., Bechara, A., Damasio, H., Ponto, L. L. B., Parvizi, J., & Hichwa, R. D. (2000). Subcortical and cortical brain activity during the feeling of self-generated emotions. *Nature Neuroscience, 3,* 1049–1056. (7)

Damasio, H., Grabowski, T. J., Tranel, D., Hichwa, R. D., & Damasio, A. R. (1996). A neural basis for lexical retrieval. *Nature, 380,* 499–505. (8)

Damasio, H., Grabowski, T., Frank, R., Galaburda, A. M., & Damasio, A. R. (1994). The return of Phineas Gage: Clues about the brain from the skull of a famous patient. *Science, 264,* 1102–1105. (1, 3)

Damsma, G., Pfaus, J. G., Wenkstern, D., & Phillips, A. G. (1992). Sexual behavior increases dopamine transmission in the nucleus accumbens and striatum of male rats: Comparison with novelty and locomotion. *Behavioral Neuroscience, 106*, 181–191. (4)

Dancey, C. P. (1990). Sexual orientation in women: An investigation of hormonal and personality variables. *Biological Psychology, 30*, 251–264. (6)

Daniel, D., Weinberger, D. R., Jones, D. W., Zigun, J. R., Coppola, R., Handel, S., Bigelow, L. B., Goldberg, T. E., Berman, K. F., & Kleinman, J. E. (1991). The effect of amphetamine on regional cerebral blood flow during cognitive activation in schizophrenia. *Journal of Neuroscience, 11*, 1907–1917. (13)

Dartnall, H. J. A., Bowmaker, J. K., & Mollon, J. D. (1983). Human visual pigments: Microspectrophotometric results from the eyes of seven persons. *Proceedings of the Royal Society of London, B, 220*, 115–130. (9)

Darwin, C. (1859). *On the origin of species.* London: Murray. (1)

Darwin, C. (1872/1965). *The expression of emotions in man and animals.* New York: University of Chicago Press. (7)

Das, A., & Gilbert, C. D. (1995). Long-range horizontal connections and their role in cortical reorganization revealed by optical recording of cat primary visual cortex. *Nature, 375*, 780–784. (3)

Davidson, M., Harvey, P. D., Bergman, R. L., Powchik, P., Kaminsky, R., Losonczy, M. F., & Davis, K. L. (1990). Effects of the D1 agonist SKF-38393 combined with haloperidol in schizophrenic patients. *Archives of General Psychiatry, 47*, 190–191. (13)

Davis, C. M. (1928). Self selection of diet in newly weaned infants: An experimental study. *American Journal of Diseases of Children, 36*, 651–679. (5)

Davis, K. L., Kahn, R. S., Ko, G., & Davidson, M. (1991). Dopamine in schizophrenia: A review and reconceptualization. *American Journal of Psychiatry, 148*, 1474–1486. (13)

Davis, M. (1992). The role of the amygdala in fear and anxiety. *Annual Review of Neuroscience, 15*, 353–375. (7)

De Biasi, S., & Rustioni, A. (1988). Glutamate and substance P coexist in primary afferent terminals in the superficial laminae of spinal cord. *Proceedings of the National Academy of Sciences, USA, 85*, 7820–7824. (10)

de Castro, J. M. (1993). Genetic influences on daily intake and meal patterns of humans. *Physiology and Behavior, 53*, 777–782. (5)

De Felipe, C., Herrero, J. F., O'Brien, J. A., Palmer, J. A., Doyle, C. A., Smith, A. J. H., Laird, J. M. A., Belmonte, C., Cervero, F., & Hunt, S. P. (1998). Altered nociception, analgesia and aggression in mice lacking the receptor for substance P. *Nature, 392*, 394–397. (10)

de Fockert, J. W., Rees, G., Frith, C. D., & Lavie, N. (2001). The role of working memory in visual selective attention. *Science, 291*, 1803–1806. (14)

de Jonge, F. H., Louwerse, A. L., Ooms, M. P., Evers, P., Endert, E., & Van de Poll, N. E. (1989). Lesions of the SDN-POA inhibit sexual behavior of male Wistar rats. *Brain Research Bulletin, 23*, 483–492. (6)

de Jonge, F. H., Oldenburger, W. P., Louwerse, A. L., & Van de Poll, N. E. (1992). Changes in male copulatory behavior after sexual exciting stimuli: Effects of medial amygdala lesions. *Physiology and Behavior, 52*, 327–332. (6)

de la Fuente-Fernández, R., Ruth, T. J., Sossi, V., Schulzer, M., Calne, D. B., & Stoessl, A. J. (2001). Expectation and dopamine release: Mechanism of the placebo effect in Parkinson's disease. *Science, 293*, 1164–1166. (10)

de Lacoste, M. C., Holloway, R. L., & Woodward, D. J. (1986). Sex differences in the fetal human corpus callosum. *Human Neurobiology, 5*, 93–96. (6)

de Lacoste-Utamsing, C., & Holloway, R. L. (1982). Sexual dimorphism in the human corpus callosum. *Science, 216*, 1431–1432. (6)

De Leon, J. (1996). Smoking and vulnerability for schizophrenia. *Schizophrenia Bulletin, 22*, 405–409. (13)

de Leon, M. J., Convit, A., Wolf, O. T., Tarshish, C. Y., DeSanti, S., Rusinek, H., Tsui, W., Kandil, E., Scherer, A. J., Roche, A., Imossi, A., Thorn, E., Bobinski, M., Caraos, C., Lesbre, P., Schyler, D., Poirier, J., Reisberg, B., & Fowler, J. (2001). Prediction of cognitive decline in normal elderly subjects with 2-[^{18}F]fluoro-2-deoxy-D-glucose/positron-emission tomography (FDG/PET). *Proceedings of the National Academy of Sciences, USA, 98*, 10966–10971. (11)

De Valois, R. L. (1960). Color vision mechanisms in the monkey. *Journal of General Physiology, 43*, 115–128. (9)

De Valois, R. L., Abramov, I., & Jacobs, G. H. (1966). Analysis of response patterns of LGN cells. *Journal of the Optical Society of America, 56*, 966–977. (9)

De Valois, R. L., Thorell, L. G., & Albrecht, D. G. (1985). Periodicity of striate-cortex-cell receptive fields. *Journal of the Optical Society of America, 2*, 1115–1123. (9)

Deacon, T. W. (1990). Rethinking mammalian brain evolution. *American Zoologist, 30*, 629–705. (3)

DeArmond, S. J., Fusco, M. M., & Dewey, M. M. (1989). *Structure of the human brain: A photographic atlas.* Oxford University Press: New York. (3)

Deep-Brain Stimulation for Parkinson's Disease Study Group. (2001). Deep-brain stimulation of the subthalamic nucleus or the pars interna of the globus pallidus in Parkinson's disease. *New England Journal of Medicine, 345*, 956–963. (10)

Degreef, G., Ashtari, M., Bogerts, B., Bilder, R. M., Jody, D. N., Alvir, J., Ma, J., & Lieberman, J. A. (1992). Volumes of ventricular system subdivisions measured from magnetic resonance images in first-episode schizophrenic patients. *Archives of General Psychiatry, 49*, 531–537. (13)

Dehaene, S. (1997). *The number sense: How the mind creates mathematics.* New York: Oxford University Press. (12)

Dehaene, S., & Cohen, L. (1997). Cerebral pathways for calculation: Double dissociation between rote verbal and quantitative knowledge of arithmetic. *Cortex, 33*, 219–250. (12)

Dehaene, S., Spelke, E., Pinel, P., Stanescu, R., & Tsivkin, S. (1999). Sources of mathematical thinking: Behavioral and brain-imaging evidence. *Science, 284*, 970–974. (12)

DeLong, M. R. (2000). The basal ganglia. In E. R. Kandel, J. H. Schwartz, & T. M. Jessell (Eds.), *Principles of neural science* (4th ed., pp. 853–867). New York: McGraw-Hill. (10)

Dement, W. (1960). The effect of dream deprivation. *Science, 131*, 1705–1707. (14)

Denissenko, M. F., Pao, A., Tang, M., & Pfeifer, G. P. (1996). Preferential formation of Benzo[*a*]pyrene adducts at lung cancer mutational hotspots in *P53. Science, 274*, 430–432. (4)

Deol, M. S., & Gluecksohn-Waelsch, S. (1979). The role of inner hair cells in hearing. *Nature, 278*, 250–252. (8)

DePue, R. A., & Iacono, W. G. (1989). Neurobehavioral aspects of affective disorders. *Annual Review of Psychology, 40*, 457–492. (13)

Derogatis, L. R., Abeloff, M. D., & Melisaratos, N. (1979). Psychological coping mechanisms and survival time in metastatic breast cancer. *Journal of the American Medical Association, 242*, 1504–1508. (7)

Descartes, René. (1984). *Treatise on man.* In J. Cottingham, R. Stoothoff, and D. Murdoch (Trans.). *The philosophical writings of Descartes.* New York: Cambridge University Press. (Original work published about 1662). (1)

Desimone, R., Albright, T. D., Gross, C. G., & Bruce, C. (1984). Stimulus-selective properties of inferior temporal neurons in the macaque. *Journal of Neuroscience, 4*, 2051–2062. (9)

D'Esposito, M., & Postle, B. R. (1999). The dependence of span and delayed response performance on prefrontal cortex. *Neuropsychologia, 37*, 1303–1315. (11)

Devane, W. A., Hanus, L., Breuer, A., Pertwee, R. G., Stevenson, L. A., Griffin, G., Gibson, D., Mandelbaum, A., Etinger, A., & Mechoulam, R. (1992). Isolation and structure of a brain constituent that binds to the cannabinoid receptor. *Science, 258,* 1946–1949. (4)

Dew, M. A., Reynolds, C. F., 3rd., Buysse, D. J., Houck, P. R., Hoch, C. C., Monk, T. H., & Kupfer, D. J. (1996). Electroencephalographic sleep profiles during depression. Effects of episode duration and other clinical and psychosocial factors in older adults. *Archives of General Psychiatry, 53,* 148–156. (13)

Dewey, S. L., Brodie, J. D., Gerasimov, M., Horan, B., Gardner, E. L., & Ashby, C. R., Jr. (1999). A pharmacologic strategy for the treatment of nicotine addiction. *Synapse, 31,* 76–86. (4)

Dewey, S. L., Morgan, A. E., Ashby, C. R., Jr., Horan, B., Kushner, S. A., Logan, J., Volkow, N. D., Fowler, J. S., Gardner, E. L., & Brodie, J. D. (1998). A novel strategy for the treatment of cocaine addiction. *Synapse, 30,* 119–129. (4)

Di Chiara, G., & Imperato, A. (1987). Preferential stimulation of dopamine release in the nucleus accumbens by opiates, alcohol, and barbiturates: Studies with transcerebral dialysis in freely moving rats. *Annals of the New York Academy of Sciences, 473,* 367–381. (4)

Di Pellegrino, G., & Wise, S. P. (1993). Effects of attention on visuomotor activity in the premotor and prefrontal cortex of a primate. *Somatosensory and Motor Research, 10,* 245–262. (11)

Diamond, J. (1992, June). Turning a man. *Discover, 13,* 71–77. (6)

Diamond, M. (1965). A critical evaluation of the ontogeny of human sexual behavior. *Quarterly Review of Biology, 40,* 147–175. (6)

Diamond, M. C., Scheibel, A. B., Murphy, G. M., Jr., & Harvey, T. (1985). On the brain of a scientist: Albert Einstein. *Experimental Neurology, 88,* 198–204. (12)

Diamond, M., & Sigmundson, H. K. (1997). Sex reassignment at birth: Long-term review and clinical implications. *Archives of Pediatric and Adolescent Medicine, 151,* 298–304. (6)

DiFiglia, M., Sapp, E., Chase, K. O., Davies, S. W., Bates, G. P., Vonsattel, J. P., & Aronin, N. (1997). Aggregation of huntingtin in neuronal intranuclear inclusions and dystrophic neurites in brain. *Science, 277,* 1990–1993. (10)

DiLalla, L. F., & Gottesman, I. I. (1991). Biological and genetic contributors to violence—Widom's untold tale. *Psychological Bulletin, 109,* 125–129. (7)

Dimitrijevic, M. R., Gerasimenko, Y., & Pinter, M. M. (1998). Evidence for a spinal central pattern generator in humans. *Annals of the New York Academy of Sciences, 860,* 360–376. (10)

Dobelle, W. H. (2000). Artificial vision for the blind by connecting a television camera to the visual cortex. *American Society for Artificial Internal Organs Journal, 46,* 3–9. (9)

Dollfus, S., Everitt, B., Ribeyre, J. M., Assouly-Besse, F., Sharp, C., & Petit, M. (1996). Identifying subtypes of schizophrenia by cluster analysis. *Schizophrenia Bulletin, 22,* 545–555. (13)

Dominguez, J. M., & Hull, E. M. (2001). Stimulation of the medial amygdala enhances medial preoptic dopamine release: Implications for male rat sexual behavior. *Brain Research, 917,* 225–229. (6)

Doria, J. J. (1995). Gene variability and vulnerability to alcoholism. *Alcohol Health and Research World, 19,* 245–248. (4)

Dörner, G. (1974). Sex-hormone-dependent brain differentiation and sexual functions. In G. Dörner (Ed.), *Endocrinology of sex* (pp. 30–37). Leipzig: J. A. Barth. (6)

Dörner, G. (1988). Neuroendocrine response to estrogen and brain differentiation in heterosexuals, homosexuals, and transsexuals. *Archives of Sexual Behavior, 17,* 57–75. (6)

Dowling, J. E., & Boycott, B. B. (1966). Organization of the primate retina. *Proceedings of the Royal Society of London, B, 166,* 80–111. (9)

Dracheva, S., Marras, S. A. E., Elhakem, S. L., Kramer, F. R., Davis, K. L., & Haroutunian, V. (2001). N-methyl-D-aspartic acid receptor expression in the dorsolateral prefrontal cortex of elderly patients with schizophrenia. *American Journal of Psychiatry, 158,* 1400–1410. (13)

Dreifus, C. (1996, February 4). And then there was Frank. *New York Times Magazine,* 23–25. (6)

Drevets, W. C., Price, J. L., Simpson, J. R., Todd, R. D., Reich, T., Vannier, M., & Raichle, M. E. (1997). Subgenual prefrontal cortex abnormalities in mood disorders. *Nature, 386,* 824–827. (13)

Drevets, W. C., & Raichle, M. E. (1995). Positron emission tomographic imaging studies of human emotional disorders. In Gazzaniga, M. S. (Ed.), *The cognitive neurosciences.* Cambridge, MA: MIT Press. (13)

Drevets, W. C., Videen, T. O., Price, J. L., Preskorn, S. H., Carmichael, S. T., & Raichle, M. E. (1992). A functional anatomical study of unipolar depression. *Journal of Neuroscience, 12,* 3628–3641. (13)

Driver, J., & Mattingley, J. B. (1998). Parietal neglect and visual awareness. *Nature Neuroscience, 1,* 17–22. (9)

Dronkers, N. F., Pinker, S., & Damasio, A. (2000). Language and the aphasias. In E. R. Kandel, J. H. Schwartz, & T. M. Jessell (Eds.), *Principles of neural science* (4th ed.) (pp. 1169–1187). New York: McGraw-Hill. (8)

Dryden, S., Wang, O., Frankish, H. M., Pickavance, L., & Williams, G. (1995). The serotonin (5-HT) antagonist methysergide increases neuropeptide Y (NPY) synthesis and secretion in the hypothalamus of the rat. *Brain Research, 699,* 12–18. (5)

Duarte, C. B., Santos, P. F., & Carvalho, A. P. (1999). Corelease of two functionally opposite neurotransmitters by retinal amacrine cells: Experimental evidence and functional significance. *Journal of Neuroscience Research, 58,* 475–479. (2)

Duffy, A., & Milin, R. (1996). Case study: Withdrawal syndrome in adolescent chronic cannabis users. *Journal of the American Academy of Child and Adolescent Psychiatry, 35,* 1618–1621. (4)

Dujardin, K., Guerrien, A., & Leconte, P. (1990). Sleep, brain activation and cognition. *Physiology and Behavior, 47,* 1271–1278. (14)

Duncan, J., Seitz, R. J., Kolodny, J., Bor, D., Herzog, H., Ahmed, A., Newell, F. N., & Emslie, H. (2000). A neural basis for general intelligence. *Science, 289,* 457–460. (12)

Dutton, D. G., & Aron, A. P. (1974). Some evidence for heightened sexual attraction under conditions of high anxiety. *Journal of Personality and Social Psychology, 30,* 510–517. (7)

Eagly, A. H. (1995). The science and politics of comparing women and men. *American Psychologist, 50,* 145–158. (6)

Earnest, D. J., Liang, F.-Q., Ratcliff, M., & Cassone, V. M. (1999). Immortal time: Circadian clock properties of rat suprachiasmatic cell lines. *Science, 283,* 693–695. (14)

Egan, V., Chiswick, A., Santosh, C., & Naidu, K. (1994). Size isn't everything: A study of brain volume, intelligence and auditory evoked potentials. *Personality and Individual Differences, 17,* 357. (12)

Ehrhardt, A. A., Meyer-Bahlburg, H. F. L., Rosen, L. R., Feldman, J. F., Veridiana, N. P., Zimmerman, I., & McEwen, B. S. (1985). Sexual orientation after prenatal exposure to exogenous estrogen. *Archives of Sexual Behavior, 14,* 57–75. (6)

Ekman, P., & Friesen, W. V. (1971). Constants across cultures in the face and emotion. *Journal of Personality and Social Psychology, 17,* 124–129. (7)

Eksioglu, Y. Z., Scheffer, I. E., Cardenas, P., Knoll, J., DiMario, F., Ramsby, G., Berg, M., Kamuro, K., Berkovic, S. F., Duyk, G. M., Parisi, J., Huttenlocher, P. R., & Walsh, C. A. (1996). Periventricular heterotopia: An x-linked dominant epilepsy locus causing aberrant cerebral cortical development. *Neuron, 16,* 77–87. (3)

Elbert, T., Pantev, C., Wienbruch, C., Rockstroh, B., & Taub, E. (1995). Increased cortical representation of the fingers of the left hand in string players. *Science, 270,* 305–307. (3)

Ellis, L., & Ames, M. A. (1987). Neurohormonal functioning and sexual orientation: A theory of homosexuality-heterosexuality. *Psychological Bulletin, 101,* 233–258. (6)

Emmen, A. (2002, April 20). Japanese "computenik" earth simulator shatters US supercomputer hegemony (Online). Available: http://www.hoise.com/primeur/02/articles/weekly/AE-PR-05-02-59.html. (2)

Enard, W., Khaitovich, P., Klose, J., Zöllner, S., Heissig, F., Giavalisco, P., Nieselt-Struwe, K., Muchmore, E., Varki, A., Ravid, R., Doxiadis, G. M., Bontrop, R. E., & Paabo, S. (2002). Intra- and interspecific variation in primate gene expression patterns. *Science, 296,* 340–343. (1)

Engel, A. K., König, P., Kreiter, A. K., & Singer, W. (1991). Interhemispheric synchronization of oscillatory neuronal responses in cat visual cortex. *Science, 252,* 1177–1179. (14)

Engel, A. K., Kreiter, A. K., König, P., & Singer, W. (1991). Synchronization of oscillatory neuronal responses between striate and extrastriate visual cortical areas of the cat. *Proceedings of the National Academy of Sciences, USA, 88,* 6048–6052. (14)

Engert, F., & Bonhoeffer, T. (1999). Dendritic spine changes associated with hippocampal long-term synaptic plasticity. *Nature, 399,* 66–70. (11)

Ernulf, K. E., Innala, S. M., & Whitam, F. L. (1989). Biological explanation, psychological explanation, and tolerance of homosexuals: A cross-national analysis of beliefs and attitudes. *Psychological Reports, 65,* 1003–1010. (6)

España, R. A., Baldo, B. A., Kelley, A. E., & Berridge, C. W. (2001). Wake-promoting and sleep-suppressing actions of hypocretin (orexin): Basal forebrain sites of action. *Neuroscience, 106,* 699–715. (14)

Evans, D. A., Funkenstein, H. H., Albert, M. S., Scherr, P. A., Cook, N. R., Chown, M. J., Hebert, L. E., Hennekens, C. H., Taylor, J. O. (1989). Prevalence of Alzheimer's disease in a community population of older persons. Higher than previously reported. *Journal of the American Medical Association, 262,* 2551–2556. (11)

Evarts, E. V. (1979, March). Brain mechanisms of movement. *Scientific American, 241,* 164–179. (10)

Everitt, B. J., & Robbins, T. W. (1997). Central cholinergic systems and cognition. *Annual Review of Psychology, 48,* 649–684. (11)

Faedda, G. L., Tondo, L., Teicher, M. H., Baldessarini, R. J., Gelbard, H. A., & Floris, G. F. (1993). Seasonal mood disorders: Patterns of seasonal recurrence in mania and depression. *Archives of General Psychiatry, 50,* 17–23. (13)

Fagot, B. I. (1978). The influence of sex of child on parental reactions to toddler children. *Child Development, 49,* 459–465. (6)

Fahle, M., & Daum, I. (1997). Visual learning and memory as functions of age. *Neuropsychologia, 35,* 1583–1589. (11)

Faigel, H. C., Szuajderman, S., Tishby, O., Turel, M., & Pinus, U. (1995). Attention deficit disorder during adolescence: A review. *Journal of Adolescent Health, 16,* 174–184. (2)

Falk, D., Froese, N., Sade, D. S., & Dudek, B. C. (1999). Sex differences in brain/body relationships of Rhesus monkeys and humans. *Journal of Human Evolution, 36,* 233–238. (12)

Falzi, G., Perrone, P., & Vignolo, L. A. (1982). Right-left asymmetry in anterior speech region. *Archives of Neurology, 39,* 239–240. (8)

Fambrough, D. M., Drachman, D. B., & Satyamurti, S. (1973). Neuromuscular junction in myasthenia gravis: Decreased acetylcholine receptors. *Science, 182,* 293–295. (10)

Fancher, R. E. (1979). *Pioneers of psychology.* New York: W. W. Norton. (1)

Farooqi, I. S., Jebb, S. A., Langmack, G., Lawrence, E., Cheetham, C. H., Prentice, A. M., Hughes, I. A., McCamish, M. A., & O'Rahilly, S. (1999). Effects of recombinant leptin therapy in a child with congenital leptin deficiency. *New England Journal of Medicine, 341,* 879–884. (5)

Farrer, C., & Frith, C. D. (2002). Experiencing oneself vs another person as being the cause of an action: The neural correlates of the experience of agency. *NeuroImage, 15,* 596–603. (14)

Fatemi, S. H., Earle, J. A., & McMenomy, T. (2000). Reduction in Reelin immunoreactivity in hippocampus of subjects with schizophrenia, bipolar disorder and major depression. *Molecular Psychiatry, 5,* 654–663. (13)

Fausto-Sterling, A. (1993, March/April). The five sexes: Why male and female are not enough. *The Sciences,* 20–25. (6)

Fawzy, F. I., Fawzy, N. W., Hyun, C. S., Elashoff, R., Guthrie, D., Fahey, J. L., & Morton, D. L. (1993). Malignant melanoma. Effects of an early structured psychiatric intervention, coping, and affective state on recurrence and survival 6 years later. *Archives of General Psychiatry, 50,* 681–689. (7)

Feinsod, M., Kreinin, B., Chistyakov, A., & Klein, E. (1998). Preliminary evidence for a beneficial effect of low-frequency, repetitive transcranial magnetic stimulation in patients with major depression and schizophrenia. *Depression and Anxiety, 7,* 65–68. (13)

Ferguson-Smith, M. A., & Ferris, E. A. (1991). Gender verification in sport: The need for change? *British Journal of Sports Medicine, 25,* 17–20. (6)

Fergusson, D. M., Woodward, L. J., & Horwood, L. J. (1998). Maternal smoking during pregnancy and psychiatric adjustment in late adolescence. *Archives of General Psychiatry, 55,* 721–727. (4)

Fernández, G., Effern, A., Grunwald, T., Pezer, N., Lehnertz, K., Dümpelmann, M., Roost, D. V., & Elger, C. E. (1999). Real-time tracking of memory formation in the human rhinal cortex and the hippocampus. *Science, 285,* 1582–1585. (11)

Fertuck, H. C., & Salpeter, M. M. (1974). Localization of acetylcholine receptor by 125I-labeled alpha-bungarotoxin binding at mouse motor endplates. *Proceedings of the National Academy of Sciences, USA, 71,* 1376–1378. (2)

Feuerstein, T. J., & Jackisch, R. (1986). Why do some antidepressants promote suicide? *Psychopharmacology, 90,* 422. (13)

Fibiger, H. C., LePiane, F. G., Jakubovic, A., & Phillips, A. G. (1987). The role of dopamine in intracranial self-stimulation of the ventral tegmental area. *Journal of Neuroscience, 7,* 3888–3896. (4)

Fiez, J. (1996). Cerebellar contributions to cognition. *Neuron, 16,* 13–15. (3)

Fike, M. L. (1990). Clinical manifestations in persons with multiple personality disorder. *American Journal of Occupational Therapy, 44,* 984–990. (14)

Fink, M. (1977). Myths of "shock therapy." *American Journal of Psychiatry, 134,* 991–996. (13)

Fink, M. (1978). Efficacy and safety of induced seizures (EST) in man. *Comprehensive Psychiatry, 19,* 1–18. (13)

Fink, M. (1984). Meduna and the origins of convulsive therapy. *American Journal of Psychiatry, 141,* 1034–1041. (13)

Fiorino, D. F., Coury, A., & Phillips, A. G. (1997). Dynamic changes in nucleus accumbens dopamine efflux during the Coolidge effect in male rats. *Journal of Neuroscience, 17,* 4849–4855. (6)

Fiske, D. W., & Maddi, S. R. (1961). *A conceptual framework.* In D. W. Fiske & S. R. Maddi (Eds.), *Functions of varied experience.* Homewood, IL: Dorsey Press. (5)

Fitzsimons, J. T., & Moore-Gillon, M. J. (1980). Drinking and antidiuresis in response to reductions in venous return in the dog: Neural and endocrine mechanisms. *Journal of Physiology, 308,* 403–416. (5)

Flam, F. (2002, March 3). Genetic screening of fetuses raises questions about ethics. *San Luis Obispo Tribune,* A18. (11)

Fleming, R., Baum, A., Gisriel, M. M., & Gatchel, R J. (1982). Mediating influences of social support on stress at Three Mile Island. *Journal of Human Stress, 8*, 14–22. (7)

Flood, J. F., & Morley, J. E. (1991). Increased food intake by neuropeptide Y is due to an increased motivation to eat. *Peptides, 12*, 1329–1332. (5)

Flor, H., Elbert, T., Knecht, S., Wienbruch, C., Pantev, C., Birbaumer, N., Larbig, W., & Taub, E. (1995). Phantom-limb pain as a perceptual correlate of cortical reorganization following arm amputation. *Nature, 375*, 482–484. (3, 10)

Flynn, J. R. (1987). Massive IQ gains in 14 nations: What IQ tests really measure. *Psychological Bulletin, 101*, 171–191. (12)

Folstein, S. E., & Piven, J. (1991, June). Etiology of autism: Genetic influences. *Pediatrics, 87*, 767–773. (12)

Fouriezos, G., Hansson, P., & Wise, R. A. (1978). Neuroleptic-induced attenuation of brain stimulation reward in rats. *Journal of Comparative and Physiological Psychology, 92*, 661–671. (4)

Fouts, R. S., Fouts, D. S., & Schoenfeld, D. (1984). Sign language conversational interactions between chimpanzees. *Sign Language Studies, 42*, 1–12. (8)

Fowler, J. S., Volkow, N. D., Wang, G.-J., Pappas, N., Logan, J., MacGregor, R., Alexoff, D., Shea, C., Schlyer, D., Wolf, A. P., Warner, D., Zezulkova, I., & Cilento, R. (1996). Inhibition of monoamine oxidase B in the brains of smokers. *Nature, 379*, 733–736. (13)

Fowler, R. (1986, May). Howard Hughes: A psychological autopsy. *Psychology Today*, 22–33. (13)

Fowles, D. C. (1992). Schizophrenia: Diathesis-stress revisited. *Annual Review of Psychology, 43*, 303–336. (13)

Fox, N. C., Crum, W. R., Scahill, R. I., Stevens, J. M., Janssen, J. C., & Rossor, M. N. (2001). Imaging of onset and progression of Alzheimer's disease with voxel-compression mapping of serial magnetic resonance images. *Lancet, 358*, 201–205. (11)

Francis, H. W., Koch, M. E., Wyatt, J. R., & Niparko, J. K. (1999). Trends in educational placement and cost-benefit considerations in children with cochlear implants. *Archives of Otolaryngology—Head and Neck Surgery, 125*, 499–505. (8)

Frankland, P. W., O'Brien, C., Ohno, M., Kirkwood, A., & Silva, A. J. (2001). α-CaMKII-dependent plasticity in the cortex is required for permanent memory. *Nature, 411*, 309–313. (11)

Fratiglioni, L., & Wang, H. X. (2000). Smoking and Parkinson's and Alzheimer's disease: Review of the epidemiological studies. *Behavioral Brain Research, 113*, 117–120. (10)

Freed, C. R., Greene, P. E., Breeze, R. E., Tsai, W.-Y., DuMouchel, W., Kao, R., Dillon, S., Winfield, H., Culver, S., Trojanowski, J. Q., Eidelberg, D., & Fahn, S. (2001). Transplantation of embryonic dopamine neurons for severe Parkinson's disease. *New England Journal of Medicine, 344*, 710–719. (10)

Freed, W. J., de Medinaceli, L., & Wyatt, R. J. (1985). Promoting functional plasticity in the damaged nervous system. *Science, 227*, 1544–1552. (3)

Freedman, D. J., Riesenhuber, M., Poggio, T., & Miller, E. K. (2001). Categorical representation of visual stimuli in the primate prefrontal cortex. *Science, 291*, 312–316. (9)

Freedman, M. S., Lucas, R. J., Soni, B., von Schantz, M., Muñoz, M., David-Gray, Z., & Foster, R. (1999). Regulation of mammalian circadian behavior by non-rod, non-cone ocular photoreceptors. *Science, 284*, 502–504. (14)

Freeman, T. B., Cicchetti, F., Hauser, R. A., Deacon, T. W., Li, X.-J., Hersch, S. M., Nauert, G. M., Sanberg, P. R., Kordower, J. H., Saporta, S., & Isacson, O. (2000). Transplanted fetal striatum in Huntington's disease: Phenotypic development and lack of pathology. *Proceedings of the National Academy of Sciences, USA, 97*, 13877–13882. (10)

French roast. (1996). *Harper's Magazine, 293*, 28–30. (4)

French, E. D. (1994). Phencyclidine and the midbrain dopamine system: Electrophysiology and behavior. *Neurotoxicology and Teratology, 16*, 355–362. (4)

Freud, S. (1900). *The interpretation of dreams.* London: Hogarth. (14)

Fried, P. A. (1995). The Ottawa Prenatal Prospective Study (OPPS): Methodological issues and findings—it's easy to throw the baby out with the bath water. *Life Sciences, 56*, 23–24. (4)

Fries, P., Reynolds, J. H., Rorie, A. E., & Desimone, R. (2001). Modulation of oscillatory neuronal synchronization by selective visual attention. *Science, 291*, 1560–1563. (14)

Frisch, H. L. (1977). Sex stereotypes in adult-infant play. *Child Development, 48*, 1671–1675. (6)

Frith, C., & Dolan, R. (1996). The role of the prefrontal cortex in higher cognitive functions. *Cognitive Brain Research, 5*, 175–181. (13)

Frith, U. (1993, June). Autism. *Scientific American, 268*, 108–114. (12)

Frith, U., Morton, J., & Leslie, A. M. (1991). The cognitive basis of a biological disorder: Autism. *Trends in Neuroscience, 14*, 433–438. (12)

Fritsch, G., & Hitzig, E. (1870). Über die elektrische Erregbarkeit des Grosshirns [Concerning the electrical stimulability of the cerebrum]. *Archiv für Anatomie Physiologie und Wissenschaftliche Medicin*, 300–332. (1)

Fritschy, J.-M., & Grzanna, R. (1992). Degeneration of rat locus coeruleus neurons is not accompanied by an irreversible loss of ascending projections. *Annals of the New York Academy of Sciences, 648*, 275–278. (3)

From neurons to thoughts: Exploring the new frontier. (1998). *Nature Neuroscience, 1*, 1–2. (1)

Fukuda, M., Mentis, M. J., Ma, Y., Dhawan, V., Antonini, A., Lang, A. E., Lozano, A. M., Hammerstad, J., Lyons, K., Koller, W. C., Moeller, J. R., & Eidelberg, D. (2001). Networks mediating the clinical effects of pallidal brain stimulation for Parkinson's disease. *Brain, 124*, 1601–1609. (10)

Fuster, J. M. (1989). *The prefrontal cortex: Anatomy, physiology, and neuropsychology of the frontal lobe*, 2nd ed. Raven: New York. (3)

Fuster, J., & Jervey, J. P. (1981). Inferotemporal neurons distinguish and retain behaviorally relevant features of visual stimuli. *Science, 212*, 952–955. (11)

Gabrieli, J. D. E. (1998). Cognitive neuroscience of human memory. *Annual Review of Psychology, 49*, 87–115. (11)

Gabrielli, W. F., Jr., & Mednick, S. A. (1982). Electroencephalograms in children of alcoholic fathers. *Psychophysiology, 19*, 404–407. (4)

Gackenbach, J., & Bosveld, J. (1989). *Control your dreams.* New York: Harper & Row. (14)

Gage, F. H. (2000). Mammalian neural stem cells. *Science, 287*, 1433–1438. (1, 3)

Gainotti, G., Caltagirone, C., & Zoccolotti, P. (1993). Left/right and cortical/subcortical dichotomies in the neuropsychological study of human emotions. *Cognition and Emotion, 7*, 71–94. (7)

Galaburda, A. M. (1993). Neurology of developmental dyslexia. *Current Opinion in Neurobiology, 3*, 237–242. (8)

Gallo, V., & Chittajallu, R. (2001). Unwrapping glial cells from the synapse: What lies inside? *Science, 292*, 872–873. (2)

Gallup, G. G. (1983). Toward a comparative psychology of mind. In R. L. Mellgren (Ed.), *Animal cognition and behavior.* New York: North-Holland. (14)

Gallup, G., Jr., & Povinelli, D. J. (1998, Winter). Can animals empathize? *Scientific American Presents*, 66–75. (14)

Gangestad, S. W., & Thornhill, R. (1998). Menstrual cycle variation in women's preferences for the scent of symmetrical men. *Proceedings of the Royal Society of London, B, 265*, 927–933. (6)

Gannon, P. J., Holloway, R. L., Broadfield, D. C., & Braun, A. R. (1998). Asymmetry of chimpanzee planum temporale: Humanlike pattern of Wernicke's brain language area homolog. *Science, 279,* 220–222. (8)

Gao, X.-M., Sakai, K., Roberts, R. C., Conley, R. R., Dean, B., & Tamminga, C. A. (2000). Ionotropic glutamate receptors and expression of *N*-methyl-D-aspartate receptor subunits in subregions of human hippocampus: Effects of schizophrenia. *American Journal of Psychiatry, 157,* 1141–1149. (13)

Garavan, H., Pankiewicz, J., Bloom, A., Cho, J.-K., Sperry, L., Ross, T. J., Salmeron, B. J., Risinger, R., Kelley, D., & Stein, E. A. (2000). Cue-induced cocaine craving: Neuroanatomical specificity for drug users and drug stimuli. *American Journal of Psychiatry, 157,* 1789–1798. (4)

Garb, J. L., & Stunkard, A. J. (1974). Taste aversions in man. *American Journal of Psychiatry, 131,* 1204–1207. (5)

Garbutt, J. C., West, S. L., Carey, T. S., Lohr, K. N., & Crews, F. T. (1999). Pharmacological treatment of alcohol dependence: A review of the evidence. *Journal of the American Medical Association, 281,* 1318–1325. (4)

Garcia-Velasco, J., & Mondragon, M. (1991). The incidence of the vomeronasal organ in 1000 human subjects and its possible clinical significance. *Journal of Steroid Biochemistry and Molecular Biology, 39,* 561–563. (6)

Gardner, B. T., & Gardner, R. A. (1975). Evidence for sentence constituents in the early utterances of child and chimpanzee. *Journal of Experimental Psychology: General, 104,* 244–267. (8)

Gardner, E. P., & Kandel, E. R. (2000). Touch. In E. R. Kandel, J. H. Schwartz, & T. M. Jessell (Eds.), *Principles of neural science* (4th ed., pp. 451–471). New York: McGraw-Hill. (10)

Gardner, E. P., Martin, J. H., & Jessell, T. M. (2000). The bodily senses. In E. R. Kandel, J. H. Schwartz, & T. M. Jessell (Eds.), *Principles of neural science* (4th ed., pp. 430–450). New York: McGraw-Hill. (10)

Gardner, G., & Halweil, B. (2000). *Overfed and underfed: The global epidemic of malnutrition.* Washington, DC: Worldwatch Institute. (5)

Gardner, H. (1975). *The shattered mind.* New York: Alfred A. Knopf. (8)

Gardner, R. A., & Gardner, B. T. (1969). Teaching sign language to a chimpanzee. *Science, 165,* 664–672. (8)

Garris, P. A., Kilpatrick, M., Bunin, M. A., Michael, D., Walker, Q. D., & Wightman, R. M. (1999). Dissociation of dopamine release in the nucleus accumbens from intracranial self-stimulation. *Nature, 398,* 67–69. (4)

Gartrell, N. K. (1982). Hormones and homosexuality. In W. Paul, J. D. Weinrich, J. C. Gonsiorek & M. E. Hotvedt (Eds.), *Homosexuality: Social, psychological, and biological issues.* Beverly Hills, CA: Sage Publications. (6)

Gatchel, R. J. (1996). Psychological disorders and chronic pain: Cause-and-effect relationships. In R. J. Gatchel & D. C. Turk (Eds.), *Psychological approaches to pain management: A practitioner's handbook* (pp. 33–52). New York: Guilford Press. (7)

Gauthier, I., Skudlarski, P., Gore, J. C., & Anderson, A. W. (2000). Expertise for cars and birds recruits brain areas involved in face recognition. *Nature Neuroscience, 3,* 191–197. (9)

Gauthier, I., Tarr, M. J., Anderson, A. W., Skudlarski, P., & Gore, J. C. (1999). Activation of the middle fusiform 'face area' increases with expertise in recognizing novel objects. *Nature Neuroscience, 2,* 568–573. (9)

Gawin, F. H. (1991). Cocaine addiction: Psychology and neurophysiology. *Science, 251,* 1580–1586. (4)

Gazzaley, A. H., Siegel, S. J., Kordower, J. H., Mufson, E. J., & Morrison, J. H. (1996). Circuit-specific alterations of *N*-methyl-D-aspartate receptor subunit 1 in the dentate gyrus of aged monkeys. *Proceedings of the National Academy of Sciences, USA, 93,* 3121–3125. (11)

Gazzaniga, M. S. (1967). The split brain in man. *Scientific American, 217,* 24–29. (3, App.)

Gazzaniga, M. S. (1970). *The bisected brain.* New York: Appleton-Century-Crofts. (14)

Gazzaniga, M. S. (2002). The split brain revisited. *Scientific American, 12(1),* 27–31. (14)

Gazzaniga, M. S., Ivry, R. B., & Mangun, G. R. (1998). *Cognitive neuroscience: The biology of the mind.* New York: Norton. (14)

Gebhardt, C. A., Naeser, M. A., & Butters, N. (1984). Computerized measures of CT scans of alcoholics: Thalamic region related to memory. *Alcohol, 1,* 133–140. (11)

Geinisman, Y., de Toledo-Morrell, L., Morrell, F., Persina, I. S., & Rossi, M. (1992). Age-related loss of axospinous synapses formed by two afferent systems in the rat dentate gyrus as revealed by the unbiased stereological dissector technique. *Hippocampus, 2,* 437–444. (11)

George, M. S., Wassermann, E. M., Williams, W. A., Callahan, A., Ketter, T. A., Basser, P., Hallett, M., & Post, R. M. (1995). Daily repetitive transcranial magnetic stimulation (rTMS) improves mood in depression. *Neuroreport, 6,* 1853–1856. (13)

Georgopoulos, A. P., Taira, M., & Lukashin, A. (1993). Cognitive neurophysiology of the motor cortex. *Science, 260,* 47–52. (10)

Gershon, E. S., Bunney, W. E., Leckman, J. F., Van Eerdewegh, M., & DeBauche, B. A. (1976). The inheritance of affective disorders: A review of data and of hypotheses. *Behavior Genetics, 6,* 227–261. (13)

Gershon, S., & Soares, J. C. (1997). Current therapeutic profile of lithium. *Archives of General Psychiatry, 54,* 16–19. (13)

Geschwind, N. (1970). The organization of language and the brain. *Science, 170,* 940–944. (8)

Geschwind, N. (1972). Language and the brain. *Scientific American, 226 (4),* 76–83. (8)

Geschwind, N. (1979, September). Specializations of the human brain. *Scientific American, 241,* 180–199. (8)

Geschwind, N., & Levitsky, W. (1968). Human brain: Left-right asymmetries in temporal speech region. *Science, 161,* 186–187. (8)

Ghez, C., & Krakauer, J. (2000). The organization of movement. In E. R. Kandel, J. H. Schwartz, & T. M. Jessell (Eds.), *Principles of neural science* (4th ed., pp. 653–673). New York: McGraw-Hill. (10)

Ghez, C., & Thach, W. T. (2000). The cerebellum. In E. R. Kandel, J. H. Schwartz, & T. M. Jessell (Eds.), *Principles of neural science* (4th ed., pp. 832–852). New York: McGraw-Hill. (10)

Gilbert, C. D. (1993). Rapid dynamic changes in adult cerebral cortex. *Current Opinion in Neurobiology, 3,* 100–103. (3)

Giles, D. E., Biggs, M. M., Rush, A. J., & Roffwarg, H. P. (1988). Risk factors in families of unipolar depression: I. Psychiatric illness and reduced REM latency. *Journal of Affective Disorders, 14,* 51–59. (13)

Gitlin, M. J., & Altshuler, L. L. (1997). Unanswered questions, unknown future for one of our oldest medications. *Archives of General Psychiatry, 54,* 21–23. (13)

Givens, B. S., & Olton, D. S. (1990). Cholinergic and GABAergic modulation of medial septal area: Effect on working memory. *Behavioral Neuroscience, 104,* 849–855. (11)

Giza, B. K., Scott, T. R., & Vanderweele, D. A. (1992). Administration of satiety factors and gustatory responsiveness in the nucleus tractus solitarius of the rat. *Brain Research Bulletin, 28,* 637–639. (5)

Glaser, R., Rice, J., Sheridan, J., Fertel, R., Stout, J., Speicher, C., Pinsky, D., Kotur, M., Post, A., Beck, M., & Kiecolt-Glaser, J. (1987). Stress-related immune suppression: Health implications. *Brain, Behavior, and Immunity, 1,* 7–20. (7)

Glasson, B. I., Duda, J. E., Murray, I. V. J., Chen, Q., Souza, J. M., Hurtig, H. I., Ischiropoulos, H., Trojanowski, J. Q., & Lee, V. M.-Y. (2000). Oxidative damage linked to neurodegeneration by selective α-synuclein nitration in synucleinopathy lesions. *Science, 290,* 985–989. (10)

Glees, P. (1980). Functional cerebral reorganization following hemispherectomy in man and after small experimental lesions in primates. In Bach-y-Rita, P. (Ed.). *Recovery of function: Theoretical considerations for brain injury rehabilitation.* Bern, Switzerland: Hans Huber. (3)

Gloor, P., Olivier, A., Quesney, L. F., Andermann, F., & Horowitz, S. (1982). The role of the limbic system in experiential phenomena of temporal lobe epilepsy. *Annals of Neurology, 12,* 129–144. (7)

Goate, A., Chartier-Harlin, M. C., Mullan, M., Brown, J., Crawford, F., Fidani, L., Giuffra, L., Haynes, A., Irving, N., James, L., Mant, R., Newton, P., Rooke, K., Roques, P., Talbot, C., Paticak-Vance, M., Roses, A., Williamson, R., Rossor, M., Owen, M., & Hardy, J. (1991). Segregation of a missense mutation in the amyloid precursor protein gene with familial Alzheimer's disease. *Nature, 349,* 704–706. (11, 12)

Goffen, B. S. (1984). ECT seizure monitoring. *Archives of General Psychiatry, 41,* 106. (13)

Gold, M. S. (1997). Cocaine (and crack): Clinical aspects. In J. H. Lowinson, P. Ruiz, R. B. Millman, & J. G. Langrod (Eds.), *Substance abuse: A comprehensive textbook* (pp. 181–199). Baltimore: Williams & Wilkins. (4)

Gold, P. W., Goodwin, F. K., & Chrousos, G. P. (1988). Clinical and biochemical manifestations of depression: Relation to the neurobiology of stress. *New England Journal of Medicine, 319,* 348–353. (13)

Goldberg, M. E., & Hudspeth, A. J. (2000). *The vestibular system.* In E. R. Kandel, J. H. Schwartz, & T. M. Jessell (Eds.), *Principles of neural science* (4th ed., pp. 801–815). New York: McGraw-Hill. (10)

Goldberg, M., & Rosenberg, H. (1987). New muscle relaxants in outpatient anesthesiology. *Dental Clinics of North America, 31,* 117–129. (2)

Goldman-Rakic, P. S., & Selemon, L. D. (1997). Functional and anatomical aspects of prefrontal pathology in schizophrenia. *Schizophrenia Bulletin, 23,* 437–458. (13)

Goldman-Rakic, P. S., Bates, J. F., & Chafee, M. V. (1992). The prefrontal cortex and internally generated motor acts. *Current Opinion in Neurobiology, 2,* 830–835. (10)

Goldstein, E. B. (1999). *Sensation and perception* (5th ed.). Pacific Grove, CA: Brooks-Cole. (9)

Gomez-Tortosa, E., Martin, E. M., Gaviria, M., Charbel, F., & Auman, J. I. (1995). Selective deficit of one language in a bilingual patient following surgery in the left perisylvian area. *Brain and Language, 48,* 320–325. (8)

Gongwer, M. A., Murphy, J. M., McBride, W. J., Lumeng, L., & Li, T.-K. (1989). *Alcohol, 6,* 317–320. (4)

Goodman, D. C., Bogdasarian, R. S., & Horel, J. A. (1973). Axonal sprouting of ipsilateral optic tract following opposite eye removal. *Brain, Behavior, and Evolution, 8,* 27–50. (3)

Goodwin, D. W. (1986). Heredity and alcoholism. *Annals of Behavioral Medicine, 8,* 3–6. (1)

Gorelick, P. B., & Ross, E. D. (1987). The aprosodias: Further functional-anatomical evidence for the organisation of affective language in the right hemisphere. *Journal of Neurology, Neurosurgery, and Psychiatry, 50,* 553–560. (7)

Gorski, R. A. (1974). The neuroendocrine regulation of sexual behavior. In G. Newton & A. H. Riesen (Eds.), *Advances in psychobiology* (Vol. 2). New York: Wiley. (6)

Gorski, R. A., Gordon, J. H., Shryne, J. E., & Southam, A. M. (1978). Evidence for a morphological sex difference within the medial preoptic area of the rat brain. *Brain Research, 148,* 333–346. (6)

Gottesman, I. I. (1991). *Schizophrenia genesis: The origins of madness.* New York: Freeman. (1)

Gottesman, I. I., & Bertelsen, A. (1989). Confirming unexpressed genotypes for schizophrenia. *Archives of General Psychiatry, 46,* 867–872. (13)

Gottesman, I. I., McGuffin, P., & Farmer, A. E. (1987). Clinical genetics as clues to the "real genetics" of schizophrenia (A decade of modest gains while playing for time). *Schizophrenia Bulletin, 13,* 12–47. (13)

Gouras, P. (1968). Identification of cone mechanisms in monkey ganglion cells. *Journal of Physiology, 199,* 533–547. (9)

Govoni, S., Petkov, V. V., Montefusco, O., Missale, C., Battaini, F., Spano, P. F., & Trabuchi, M. (1984). Differential effects of caffeine on dihydroxyphenylacetic acid concentrations in various rat brain dopaminergic structures. *Journal of Pharmaceutical Pharmacology, 36,* 458–460. (4)

Grace, A. A. (1991) Phasic versus tonic dopamine release and the modulation of dopamine system responsivity: A hypothesis for the etiology of schizophrenia. *Neuroscience, 41,* 1–24. (13)

Grady, D. (June, 1992). Sex test of champions. *Discover,* 79–82. (6)

Grant, K. A. (1995). The role of 5-HT$_3$ receptors in drug dependence. *Drug and Alcohol Dependence, 38,* 155–171. (4)

Grant, S., London, E. D., Newlin, D. B., Villemagne, V. L., Liu, X., Contoreggi, C., Phillips, R. L., Kimes, A. S., & Margolin, A. (1996). Activation of memory circuits during cue-elicited cocaine craving. *Proceedings of the National Academy of Sciences, USA, 93,* 12040–12045. (4)

Gray, J. (1992). *Men are from Mars, women are from Venus: A practical guide for improving communication and getting what you want in your relationships.* New York: HarperCollins. (6)

Graybiel, A. M. (1998). The basal ganglia and chunking of action repertoires. *Neurobiology of Learning and Memory, 70,* 119–136. (10)

Graziano, M. S. A., Cooke, D. F., & Taylor, C. S. R. (2000). Coding the location of the arm by sight. *Science, 290,* 1782–1786. (10)

Graziano, M. S. A., Yap, G. S., & Gross, C. G. (1994). Coding of visual space by premotor neurons. *Science, 266,* 1054–1057. (10)

Greenough, W. T. (1975). Experiential modification of the developing brain. *American Scientist, 63,* 37–46. (3)

Greer, S. (1991). Psychological response to cancer and survival. *Psychological Medicine, 21,* 43–49. (7)

Gressens, P., Lammens, M., Picard, J. J., & Evrard, P. (1992). Ethanol-induced disturbances of gliogenesis and neurogenesis in the developing murine brain: An *in vitro* and an *in vivo* immunohistochemical and ultrastructural study. *Alcohol and Alcoholism, 27,* 219–226. (3, 4)

Griffith, J. D., Cavanaugh, J., Held, J., & Oates, J. A. (1972). Dextroamphetamine: Evaluation of psychomimetic properties in man. *Archives of General Psychiatry, 26,* 97–100. (4)

Grigorenko, E. L. (2001). Developmental dyslexia: An update on genes, brains, and environments. (8)

Grillner, S. (1985). Neurobiological bases of rhythmic motor acts in vertebrates. *Science, 228,* 143–149. (10)

Grilo, C. M., & Pogue-Geile, M. F. (1991). The nature of environmental influences on weight and obesity: A behavior genetic anlaysis. *Psychological Bulletin, 110,* 520–537. (5)

Grindlinger, H. M., & Ramsay, E. (1991). Compulsive feather-picking in birds. *Archives of General Psychiatry, 48,* 857. (13)

Gross, C. G., Rocha-Miranda, C. E., & Bender, D. B. (1972). Visual properties of neurons in inferotemporal cortex of the macaque. *Journal of Neurophysiology, 35,* 96–111. (9)

Guerreiro, M., Castro-Caldas, A., & Martins, I. P. (1995). Aphasia following right hemisphere lesion in a woman with left hemisphere injury in childhood. *Brain and Language, 49,* 280–288. (3, 8)

Guidotti, A., Auta, J., Davis, J. M., Gerevini, V. D., Dwivedi, Y., Grayson, D. R., Impagnatiello, F., Pandey, G., Pesold, C., Sharma, R., Uzunov, D., & Costa, E. (2000). Decrease in Reelin and glutamic acid decarboxylase67 (GAD67) expression in schizophrenia and bipolar disorder. *Archives of General Psychiatry, 57,* 1061–1069. (13)

Guillamon, A., & Segovia, S. (1997). Sex differences in the vomeronasal system. *Brain Research Bulletin, 44,* 377–382. (6)

Gunne, L. M., Änggård, E., & Jönsson, L. E. (1972). Clinical trials with amphetamine-blocking drugs. *Psychiatria, Neurologia, Neurochirurgia, 73,* 225–226. (4)

Gur, R. C., Turetsky, B. I., Matsui, M., Yan, M., Bilker, W., Hughett, P., & Gur, R. E. (1999). Sex differences in brain gray and white matter in healthy young adults: Correlations with cognitive performance. *Journal of Neuroscience, 19,* 4065–4072. (12)

Gurd, J. M., & Marshall, J. C. (1992). Drawing upon the mind's eye. *Nature, 359,* 590–591. (9)

Gustavson, C. R., Garcia, J., Hankins, W. G., & Rusiniak, K. W. (1974). Coyote predation control by aversive conditioning. *Science, 184,* 581–583. (5)

Gustavson, C. R., Kelly, D. J., Sweeney, M., & Garcia, J. (1976). Prey lithium aversions I: Coyotes and wolves. *Behavioral Biology, 17,* 61–72. (5)

Haier, R. J., Chueh, D., Touchette, P., Lott, I., Buchsbaum, M. S., MacMillan, D., Sandman, C., LaCasse, L., & Sosa, E. (1995). Brain size and cerebral glucose metabolic rate in nonspecific mental retardation and Down syndrome. *Intelligence, 20,* 191–210. (12)

Haier, R. J., Siegel, B., Tang, C., Abel, L, & Buchsbaum, M. S. (1992). Intelligence and changes in regional cerebral glucose metabolic rate following learning. *Intelligence, 16,* 415–426. (12)

Halaas, J. L., Gajiwala, K. S., Maffei, M., Cohen, S. L., Chait, B. T., Rabinowitz, D., Lallone, R. L., Burley, S. K., & Friedman, J. M. (1995). Weight reducing effects of the plasma protein encoded by the *obese* gene. *Science, 269,* 543–546. (5)

Hall, N. R. S., O'Grady, M., & Calandra, D. (1994). Transformation of personality and the immune system. *Advances: The Journal of Mind-Body Health, 10,* 7–15. (14)

Hall, S. M., Reus, V. I., Muñoz, R. F., Sees, D. O., Humfleet, G., Hartz, D. T., Frederick, S., & Triffleman, E. (1998). Nortriptyline and cognitive-behavioral therapy in the treatment of cigarette smoking. *Archives of General Psychiatry, 55,* 683–690. (4)

Hallett, M. (2000). Transcranial magnetic stimulation and the human brain. *Nature, 406,* 147–150. (13)

Hallmayer, J., Hebert, J. M., Spiker, D., Lotspeich, L., McMahon, W. M., Petersen, P. B., Nicholas, P., Pingree, C., Lin, A. A., Cavalli-Sforza, L. L., Risch, N., & Ciaranello, R. D. (1996). Autism and the X chromosome. Multipoint sib-pair analysis. *Archives of General Psychiatry, 53,* 985–989. (12)

Hallmayer, J., Spiker, D., Lotspeich, L., McMahon, W. M., Petersen, P. B., Nicholas, P., Pingree, C., & Ciaranello, R. D. (1994). Male-to-male transmission in extended pedigrees with multiple cases of autism. *American Journal of Medical Genetics, 67,* 13–18. (12)

Halmi, K. A., Eckert, E., LaDu, T. J., & Cohen, J. (1986). Anorexia nervosa: Treatment efficacy of cyproheptadine and amitriptyline. *Archives of General Psychiatry, 43,* 177–181. (5)

Hamann, S. B., Ely, T. D., Grafton, S. T., & Kilts, C. D. (1999). Amygdala activity related to enhanced memory for pleasant and aversive stimuli. *Nature Neuroscience, 2,* 289–293. (11)

Hamer, D. H. (1999). Genetics and male sexual orientation. *Science, 285,* 803a. (6)

Hamer, D. H., Hu, S., Magnuson, V. L., Hu, N., & Pattatucci, A. M. L. (1993). A linkage between DNA markers on the X chromosome and male sexual orientation. *Science, 261,* 321–327. (6)

Han, Z.-S., Zhang, E.-T., & Craig, A. D. (1998). Nociceptive and thermoreceptive lamina I neurons are anatomically distinct. *Nature Neuroscience, 1,* 218–225. (10)

Haney, M., Ward, A. S., Comer, S. D., Foltin, R. W., & Fischman, M. W. (1999). Abstinence symptoms following smoked marijuana in humans. *Psychopharmacology, 141,* 395–404. (4)

Hannibal, J., Hindersson, P., Knudsen, S. M., Georg, B., & Fahrenkrug, J. (2002). The photopigment melanopsin is exclusively present in pituitary adenylate cyclase-activating polypeptide-containing retinal ganglion cells of the retinohypothalamic tract. *Journal of Neuroscience, 22:*RC191, 1–7. (14)

Hanson, R. A. (1975). Consistency and stability of home environmental measures related to IQ. *Child Development, 46,* 470–480. (12)

Happé, F., & Frith, U. (1996). The neuropsychology of autism. *Brain, 119,* 1377–1400. (12)

Haqq, C. M., King, C.-Y., Ukiyama, E., Falsafi, S., Haqq, T. N., Donahoe, P. K., & Weiss, M. A. (1994). Molecular basis of mammalian sexual determination: Activation of Müllerian inhibiting substance gene expression by SRY. *Science, 266,* 1494–1500. (6)

Harada, S., Agarwal, D. P., Goedde, H. W., Tagaki, S., & Ishikawa, B. (1982). Possible protective role against alcoholism for aldehyde dehydrogenase isozyme deficiency in Japan. *Lancet, 2,* 827. (4)

Harmon, L. D., & Julesz, B. (1973). Masking in visual recognition: Effects of two-dimensional filtered noise. *Science, 180,* 1194–1197. (9)

Hartman, L. (1995). Cats as possible obsessive-compulsive disorder and medication models. *American Journal of Psychiatry, 152,* 1236. (13)

Harvey, S. M. (1987). Female sexual behavior: Fluctuations during the menstrual cycle. *Journal of Psychosomatic Research, 31,* 101–110. (6)

Hattar, S., Liao, H.-W., Takao, M., Berson, D. M., & Yau, K.-W. (2002). Melanopsin-containing retinal ganglion cells: Architecture, projections, and intrinsic photosensitivity. *Science, 295,* 1065–1070. (14)

Hauser, M. D., MacNeilage, P, & Ware, M. (1996). Numerical representations in primates. *Proceedings of the National Academy of Sciences, USA, 93,* 1514–1517. (12)

Haxby, J. V., Gobbini, M. I., Furey, M. L., Ishai, A., Schouten, J. L., & Pietrini, P. (2001). Distributed and overlapping representations of faces and objects in ventral temporal cortex. *Science, 293,* 2425–2430. (9)

Hayes, K. J., & Hayes, C. (1953). Picture perception in a home-raised chimpanzee. *Journal of Comparative and Physiological Psychology, 46,* 470–474. (8)

Heath, R. G. (1964). *The role of pleasure in behavior.* New York: Harper & Row. (7)

Hécaen, H., & Angelergues, R. (1964). Localization of symptoms in aphasia. In A. V. S. de Reuck & M. O'Connor (Eds.), *Ciba Foundation symposium: Disorders of language* (pp. 223–260). Boston: Little, Brown. (8)

Hedges, L. V., & Nowell, A. (1995). Sex differences in mental test scores, variability, and numbers of high-scoring individuals. *Science, 269,* 41–45. (6)

Heilman, K. M., Watson, R. T., & Bowers, D. (1983). Affective disorders associated with hemispheric disease. In K. M. Heilman & P. Satz (Eds.), *Neuropsychology of human emotion* (pp. 45–64). New York: Guilford Press. (7)

Heim, N. (1981). Sexual behavior of castrated sex offenders. *Archives of Sexual Behavior, 10,* 11–19. (6)

Helmholtz, H. von. (1852). On the theory of compound colors. *Philosophical Magazine, 4,* 519–534. (9)

Helmholtz, H. von. (1948). On the sensations of tone as a physiological basis for the theory of music (A. J. Ellis, Trans.). New York: P. Smith. (Original work published 1863). (8)

Helmuth, L. (2001). Boosting brain activity from the outside in. *Science, 292,* 1284–1286. (13)

Helmuth, L. (2002). A generation gap in brain activity. *Science, 296,* 2131–2132. (12)

Hendry, S. H. C., & Reid, R. C. (2000). The koniocellular pathway in primate vision. *Annual Review of Neuroscience, 23,* 127–153. (9)

Henke, K., Weber, B., Kneifel, S., Wieser, H. G., & Buck, A. (1999). Human hippocampus associates information in memory. *Proceedings of the National Academy of Sciences, USA, 96,* 5884–5889. (11)

Hennevin, E., Hars, B., Maho, C., & Bloch, V. (1995). Processing of learned information in paradoxical sleep: Relevance for memory. *Behavioral Brain Research, 69,* 125–135. (14)

Herbert, T. B., & Cohen, S. (1993). Depression and immunity: A meta analytic review. *Psychological Bulletin, 113,* 472–486. (7)

Herbert, T. B., Cohen, S., Marsland, A. L., Bachen, E. A., Rabin, B. S., Muldoon, M. F., & Manuck, S. B. (1994). Cardiovascular reactivity and the course of immune response to an acute psychological stressor. *Psychosomatic Medicine, 56,* 337–344. (7)

Hering, E. (1878). *Zur lehre vom lichtsinne.* Vienna: Gerold. (9)

Heritch, A. J. (1990). Evidence for reduced and dysregulated turnover of dopamine in schizophrenia. *Schizophrenia Bulletin, 16,* 605–615. (13)

Herkenham, M. (1992). Cannabinoid receptor localization in brain: Relationship to motor and reward systems. *Annals of the New York Academy of Sciences, 654,* 19–32. (4)

Hernán, M. A., Zhang, S. M., Lipworth, L., Olek, M. J., & Ascherio, A. (2001). Multiple sclerosis and age at infection with common viruses. *Epidemiology, 12,* 306–306. (10)

Herrnstein, R. J., & Murray, C. (1994). *The bell curve: Intelligence and class structure in American life.* New York: The Free Press. (12)

Hervey, G. R. (1952). The effects of lesions in the hypothalamus in parabiotic rats. *Journal of Physiology, 145,* 336–352. (5)

Herzog, D. B., Dorer, D. J., Keel, P. K., Selwyn, S. E., Ekeblad, E. R., Flores, A. T., Greenwood, D. N., Burwell, R. A., & Keller, M. B. (1999). Recovery and relapse in anorexia and bulimia nervosa: A 7.5-year follow-up study. *Journal of the American Academy of Child and Adolescent Psychiatry, 38,* 829–837. (5)

Herzog, H. A. (1998). Understanding animal activism. In L. A. Hart (Ed.), *Responsible conduct with animals in research.* New York: Oxford University Press. (1)

Heston, L. L. (1970). The genetics of schizophrenic and schizoid disease. *Science, 167,* 249–256. (13)

Hickok, G., Bellugi, U., & Klima, E. S. (1996). The neurobiology of sign language and its implications for the neural basis of language. *Nature, 381,* 699–702. (8)

Hier, D. B., & Crowley, W. F., Jr. (1982). Spatial ability in androgen-deficient men. *New England Journal of Medicine, 306,* 1202–1205. (6)

Higley, J. D., Mehlman, P. T., Poland, R. E., Taub, D. M., Vickers, J., Suomi, S. J., & Linnoila, M. (1996). CSF testosterone and 5-HIAA correlate with different types of aggressive behaviors. *Biological Psychiatry, 40,* 1067–1082. (7)

Higuchi, S., Usui, A., Murasaki, M., Matsushita, S., Nishioka, N., Yoshino, A., Matsui, T., Muraoka, H., Ishizuka, Y., Kanba, S., & Sakurai, T. Plasma orexin-A is lower in patients with narcolepsy. *Neuroscience Letters, 318,* 61–64. (14)

Hill, J. O., & Peters, J. C. (1998). Environmental contributions to the obesity epidemic. *Science, 280,* 1371–1374. (5)

Hill, J. O., Schlundt, D. G., Sbrocco, T., Sharp, T., Pope-Cordle, J., Stetson, B., Kaler, M., & Heim, C. (1989). Evaluation of an alternating-calorie diet with and without exercise in the treatment of obesity. *American Journal of Nutrition, 50,* 248–254. (5)

Hill, S. Y., Muka, D., Steinhauer, S., and Locke, J. (1995). P300 amplitude decrements in children from families of alcoholic female probands. *Biological Psychiatry, 38,* 622–632. (4)

Hines, M. (1982). Prenatal gonadal hormones and sex differences in human behavior. *Psychological Bulletin, 92,* 56–80. (6)

Hines, M., & Green, R. (1991). Human hormonal and neural correlates of sex-typed behaviors. *Review of Psychiatry, 10,* 536–555. (6)

Hines, M., Sloan, K., Lawrence, J., Lipcamon, J., and Chiu, L. (1988). The size of the human corpus callosum relates to language lateralization and to verbal ability. *Abstracts of the Society for Neuroscience, 14,* 1137. (6)

Hines, P. J. (1997). Noto bene: Unconscious odors. *Science, 278,* 79. (6)

Hines, T. (1998). Further on Einstein's brain. *Experimental Neurology, 150,* 343–344. (12)

Hinton, G. E. (1993, March). How neural networks learn from experience. *Scientific American,* 145–151. (2)

Hobson, J. A., & McCarley, R. W. (1977). The brain as a dream state generator: An activation-synthesis hypothesis of the dream process. *American Journal of Psychiatry, 134,* 1335–1348. (14)

Hodgins, S., Kratzer, L., & McNeil, T. F. (2001). Obstetric complications, parenting, and risk of criminal behavior. *Archives of General Psychiatry, 58,* 746–752. (7)

Hoebel, B. G., Monaco, A., Hernandes, L., Aulisi, E., Stanley, B. G., & Lenard, L. (1983). Self injection of amphetamine directly into the brain. *Psychopharmacology, 81,* 158–163. (4)

Hoffman, P. L., & Tabakoff, B. (1993). Ethanol, sedative hypnotics and glutamate receptor function in brain and cultured cells. *Alcohol and Alcoholism Supplement, 2,* 345–351. (4)

Hohmann, G. W. (1966). Some effects of spinal cord lesions on experienced emotional feelings. *Psychophysiology, 3,* 143–156. (7)

Hökfelt, T., Johansson, O., & Goldstein, M. (1984). Chemical anatomy of the brain. *Science, 225,* 1326–1334. (2)

Hölscher, C., Anwyl, R., & Rowan, M. J. (1997). Stimulation on the positive phase of hippocampal theta rhythm induces long-term potentiation that can be depotentiated by stimulation on the negative phase in area CA1 *in vivo. Journal of Neuroscience, 17,* 6470–6477. (11)

Hopfield, J. J., Feinstein, D. I., & Palmer, R. G. (1983). Unlearning has a stabilizing effect in collective memories. *Nature, 304,* 158–159. (14)

Hopkins, W. D., & Morris, R. D. (1993). Hemispheric priming as a technique in the study of lateralized cognitive processes in chimpanzees: Some recent findings. In H. L. Roitblat, L. M. Herman, & P. E. Nachtigall (Eds.), *Language and communication: Comparative perspectives* (pp. 293–309). Hillsdale, NJ: Lawrence Ehrlbaum. (8)

Hopson, J. S. (1979). *Scent signals: The silent language of sex.* New York: Morrow. (6)

Horgan, J. (1999). *The undiscovered mind.* New York: Free Press. (1)

Horne, J. (1988). *Why we sleep: The functions of sleep in humans and other mammals.* New York: Oxford University Press. (14)

Horne, J. (1992). Human slow wave sleep: A review and appraisal of recent findings, with implications for sleep functions, and psychiatric illness. *Experientia, 48,* 941–954. (14)

Horne, J. A., & Harley, L. J. (1989). Human SWS following selective head heating during wakefulness. In J. Horne (Ed.), *Sleep '88.* New York: Gustav Fischer Verlag. (14)

Horne, J. A., & Minard, A. (1985). Sleep and sleepiness following a behaviourally 'active' day. *Ergonomics, 28,* 567–575. (14)

Horne, J. A., & Moore, V. J. (1985). Sleep EEG effects of exercise with and without additional body cooling. *Electroencephalography and Clinical Neurophysiology, 60,* 33–38. (14)

Horner, P. J., & Gage, F. H. (2000). Regenerating the damaged central nervous system. *Nature, 407,* 963–970. (3)

Hoshi, E., Shima, K., & Tanji, J. (2000). Neuronal activity in the primate prefrontal cortex in the process of motor selection based on two behavioral rules. *Journal of Neurophysiology, 83*, 2355–2373. (10)

Hoshi, E., & Tanji, J. (2000). Integration of target and body-part information in the premotor cortex when planning action. *Nature, 408*, 466–470. (10)

House, J. S., Landis, K. R., & Umberson, D. (1988). Social relationships and health. *Science, 241*, 540–545. (7)

Howlett, A. C., Bidaut-Russell, M., Devane, W. A., Melvin, L. S., Johnson, M. R., & Herkenham, M. (1990). The cannabinoid receptor: Biochemical, anatomical and behavioral characterization. *Trends in Neurosciences, 13*, 420–423. (4)

Hser, Y.-I., Hoffman, V., Grella, C. E., & Anglin, M. D. (2001). A 33-year follow-up of narcotics addicts. *Archives of General Psychiatry, 58*, 503–508. (4)

Hsiao, S. S., O'Shaughnessy, D. M., & Johnson, K. O. (1993). Effects of selective attention on spatial form processing in monkey primary and secondary somatosensory cortex. *Journal of Neurophysiology, 70*, 444–447. (10)

Hu, S., Pattatucci, A. M. L., Patterson, C., Li, L., Fulker, D. W., Cherny, S. S., Kruglyak L., & Hamer, D. H. (1995). Linkage between sexual orientation and chromosome Xq28 in males but not in females. *Nature Genetics, 11*, 248–256. (6)

Hubel, D. H. (1979). The Brain. In *The Brain*. San Francisco: W. H. Freeman. (3)

Hubel, D. H. (1982). Exploration of the primary visual cortex, 1955–78. *Nature, 299*, 515–524. (9)

Hubel, D. H., & Wiesel, T. N. (1959). Receptive fields of single neurons in the cat's striate cortex. *Journal of Physiology, 148*, 574–591. (9)

Hubel, D. H., & Wiesel, T. N. (1979, March). Brain mechanisms of vision. *Scientific American*, 150–163. (App.)

Huber, G., Gross, G., Schüttler, R., & Linz, M. (1980). Longitudinal studies of schizophrenic patients. *Schizophrenia Bulletin, 6*, 593–605. (13)

Hudspeth, A. J. (1983). Mechanoelectrical transduction by hair cells in the acousticolateralis sensory system. *Annual Review of Neuroscience, 6*, 187–215. (8)

Hudspeth, A. J. (1989). How the ear's works work. *Nature, 341*, 397–404. (8)

Hudspeth, A. J. (2000). Hearing. In E. R. Kandel, J. H. Schwartz, & T. M. Jessell (Eds.), *Principles of neural science* (4th ed., pp. 590–613). New York: McGraw-Hill. (8)

Hull, C. L. (1951). *Essentials of behavior*. New Haven, CT: Yale University Press. (5)

Humphreys, P., Kaufman, W. E., & Galaburda, A. M. (1990). Developmental dyslexia in women: Neuropathological findings in three patients. *Annals of Neurology, 28*, 727–738. (8)

Hunt, G. L., & Hunt, M. W. (1977). Female-female pairing in western gulls (*Larus occidentalis*) in southern California. *Science, 196*, 1466–1467. (6)

Hunt, G. L., Jr., Newman, A. L., Warner, M. H., Wingfield, J. C., & Kaiwi, J. (1984). Comparative behavior of male-female and female-female pairs among western gulls prior to egg laying. *The Condor, 86*, 157–162. (6)

Huntington's Disease Collaborative Research Group. (1993). A novel gene containing a trinucleotide repeat that is expanded and unstable on Huntington's disease chromosomes. *Cell, 72*, 971–983. (1, 10)

Hurvich, L, M, & Jameson, D. (1957). An opponent-process theory of color vision. *Psychological Review, 64*, 384–404. (9)

Hyde, J. S. (1986). Gender differences in aggression. In J. S. Hyde & M. C. Linn (Eds.), *The psychology of gender: Advances through meta-analysis*. Baltimore: Johns Hopkins University Press. (6)

Hyde, J. S. (1996). Where are the gender differences? Where are the gender similarities? In D. M. Buss & N. M. Malamuth (Eds.), *Sex, power, conflict: Evolutionary and feminist perspectives*. New York: Oxford University Press. (6)

Hyman, B. T., Van Horsen, G. W., Damasio, A. R., & Barnes, C. L. (1984). Alzheimer's disease: Cell-specific pathology isolates the hippocampal formation. *Science, 225*, 1168–1170. (11)

Hynd, G. W., & Semrud-Clikeman, M. (1989). Dyslexia and brain morphology. *Psychological Bulletin, 106*, 447–482. (8)

Hyvärinen, J. (1981). Regional distribution of functions in parietal association area 7 of the monkey. *Brain Research, 206*, 287–303. (10)

Hyvärinen, J., & Poranen, A. (1978). Movement-sensitive cutaneous receptive fields in the hand area of the post-central gyrus in monkeys. *Journal of Physiology, 283*, 523–537. (10)

Imperato, A., & Di Chiara, G. (1986). Preferential stimulation of dopamine release in the nucleus accumbens of freely moving rats by ethanol. *Journal of Pharmacology and Experimental Therapeutics, 239*, 219–228. (4)

Imperato-McGinley, J., Peterson, R. E., Gautier, T., & Sturla, E. (1979). Androgen and the evolution of male-gender identity among male pseudohermaphrodites with 5α-reductase deficiency. *New England Journal of Medicine, 300*, 1233–1237. (6)

Imperato-McGinley, J., Peterson, R. E., Stoller, R., & Goodwin, W. E. (1979). Male pseudohermaphroditism secondary to 17β-hydroxysteroid dehydrogenase deficiency: Gender role change with puberty. *Journal of Clinical Endocrinology and Metabolism, 49*, 391–395. (6)

Imperato-McGinley, J., Pichardo, M., Gautier, T., Voyer, D., & Bryden, M. P. (1991). Cognitive abilities in androgen-insensitive subjects: Comparison with control males and females from the same kindred. *Clinical Endocrinology, 34*, 341–347. (6)

Ingelfinger, F. J. (1944). The late effects of total and subtotal gastrectomy. *New England Journal of Medicine, 231*, 321–327. (5)

Inouye, S.-I. T., & Kawamura, H. (1979). Persistence of circadian rhythmicity in a mammalian hypothalamic "island" containing the suprachiasmatic nucleus. *Proceedings of the National Academy of Sciences, USA, 76*, 5962–5966. (14)

Insel, T. R. (1992). Toward a neuroanatomy of obsessive-compulsive disorder. *Archives of General Psychiatry, 49*, 739–744. (13)

Insel, T. R., O'Brien, D. J., & Leckman, J. F. (1999). Oxytocin, vasopressin, and autism: Is there a connection? *Biological Psychiatry, 45*, 145–157. (12)

Insel, T. R., Zohar, J., Benkelfat, C., & Murphy, D. L. (1990). Serotonin in obsessions, compulsions, and the control of aggressive impulses. In P. M. Whitaker-Azmitia & S. J. Peroutka (Eds.), *Annals of the New York Academy of Sciences. Special Issue: The Neuropharmacology of Serotonin, 600*, 574–586. (13)

International Human Genome Sequencing Consortium. (2001). Initial sequencing and analysis of the human genome. *Nature, 409*, 860–921. (1)

International Molecular Genetic Study of Autism Consortium (2001). A genomewide screen for autism: Strong evidence for linkage to chromosomes 2q, 7q, and 16p. *American Journal of Human Genetics, 69*, 570–581. (12)

Iqbal, N., & van Praag, H. M. (1995). The role of serotonin in schizophrenia. *European Neuropsychopharmacology Supplement*, 11–23. (13)

Iriki, A., Pavlides, C., Keller, A., & Asanuma, H. (1989). Long-term potentiation in the motor cortex. *Science, 245*, 1385–1387. (11)

Irwin, M., Daniels, M., Risch, S. C., Bloom, E., & Weiner, H. (1988). Plasma cortisol and natural killer cell activity during bereavement. *Biological Psychiatry, 24*, 173–178. (7)

Iurato, S. (1967). *Submicroscopic structure of the inner ear*. Oxford, England: Pergamon Press. (10)

Iversen, S., Kupfermann, I., & Kandel, E. R. (2000). Emotional states and feelings. In E. R. Kandel, J. H. Schwartz, & T. M. Jessell (Eds.), *Principles of neural science* (4th ed., pp. 982–997). New York: McGraw-Hill. (7)

Iwamura, Y., Iriki, A., & Tanaka, M. (1994). Bilateral hand representation in the postcentral somatosensory cortex. *Nature, 369*, 554–556. (10)

Izard, C. E. (1971). *The face of emotion*. New York: Appleton-Century Crofts. (7)

Jacobs, B. L. (1987). How hallucinogenic drugs work. *American Scientist, 75*, 386–392. (4)

James, W. (1893). *Psychology*. New York: Henry Holt. (3, 7)

Janowsky, J. S., Oviatt, S. K., & Orwoll, E. S. (1994). Testosterone influences spatial cognition in older men. *Behavioral Neuroscience, 108*, 325–332. (6)

Janus, C., Pearson, J., McLaurin, J., Mathews, P. M., Jiang, Y., Schmidt, S. D., Chishti, M. A., Horne, P., Heslin, D., French, J., Mount, H. T. J., Nixon, R. A., Mercken, M., Bergeron C., Fraser, P. E., St. George-Hyslop, P., & Westaway, D. (2000). Aß peptide immunization reduces behavioural impairment and plaques in a model of Alzheimer's disease. *Nature, 408*, 979–982. (11)

Jaretzki, A., 3rd., Penn, A. S., Younger, D. S., Wolff, M., Olarte, M. R., Lovelace, R. E. , & Rowland, L. P. (1988). "Maximal" thymectomy for myasthenia gravis. Results. *Journal of Thoracic and Cardiovascular Surgery, 95*, 747–757. (10)

Javitt, D. C., Zylberman, I., Zukin, S. R., Heresco-Levy, U., & Lindenmayer, J. P. (1994). Amelioration of negative symptoms in schizophrenia by glycine. *American Journal of Psychiatry, 151*, 1234–1236. (13)

Jeffords, J. M., & Daschle, T. (2001). Political issues in the genome era. *Science, 291*, 1249–1251. (1)

Jensen, A. R. (1969). How much can we boost IQ and scholastic achievement? *Harvard Educational Review, 39*, 1–123. (12)

Jensen, A. R. (1981). Raising the IQ: The Ramey and Haskins study. *Intelligence, 5*, 29–40. (12)

Jensen, A. R. (1998). *The g factor*. Westport, CT: Praeger. (11, 12)

Jensen, T. S., Genefke, I. K., Hyldebrandt, N., Pedersen, H., Petersen, H. D., & Weile, B. (1982). Cerebral atrophy in young torture victims. *New England Journal of Medicine, 307*, 1341. (7)

Jentsch, J. D., & Roth, R. H. (1999). The neuropsychopharmacology of phencyclidine: From NMDA receptor hypofunction to the dopamine hypothesis of schizophrenia. *Neuropsychopharmacology, 20*, 201–225. (4)

Jo, Y.-H., & Schlichter, R. (1999). Synaptic corelease of ATP and GABA in cultured spinal neurons. *Nature Neuroscience, 2*, 241–245. (2)

Johnson, B. A., & Cowen, P. J. (1993). Alcohol-induced reinforcement: Dopamine and 5-HT$_3$ receptor interactions in animals and humans. *Drug Development Research, 30*, 153–169. (4)

Jones, E. G., & Mendell, L. M. (1999). Assessing the decade of the brain. *Science, 284*, 739. (1)

Jones, F. W., & Holmes, D. S. (1976). Alcoholism, alpha production, and biofeedback. *Journal of Consulting and Clinical Psychology, 44*, 224–228. (4)

Jones, L. B., Stanwood, G. D., Reinoso, B. S., Washington, R. A., Wang, H.-Y., Friedman, E., & Levitt, P. (2000). *In utero* cocaine-induced dysfunction of dopamine D$_1$ receptor signaling and abnormal differentiation of cerebral cortical neurons. *Journal of Neuroscience, 20*, 4606–4614. (4)

Jönsson, L., Änggård, E., & Gunne, L. (1971). Blockade of intravenous amphetamine euphoria in man. *Clinical Pharmacology and Therapy, 12*, 889–896. (4)

Joseph, J. A., Shukitt-Hale, B., Denisova, N. A., Bielinski, D., Martin, A., McEwen, J. J., & Bickford, P. C. (1999). Reversals of age-related declines in neuronal signal transduction, cognitive, and motor behavioral deficits with blueberry, spinach, or strawberry dietary supplementation. *Journal of Neuroscience, 19*, 8114–8121. (11)

Julien, R. M. (2001). *A primer of drug action* (9th ed.). New York: Freeman. (4)

Jung, R. (1974). Neuropsychologie und der Neurophysiologie des Kontur- und Formsehens in Zeichnung und Malerei. In H. H. Wieck (Ed.), *Psychopathologie musicher Gestaltungen* (pp. 29–88). Stuttgart: Schattauer. (9)

Jütte, A., & Grammer, K. (1998, December). Female attractiveness and copulins. Paper presented at the meeting of the British Psychological Society, London. (6)

Kalil, R. E. (1989, December). Synapse formation in the developing brain. *Scientific American*, 76–85. (3)

Kanbayashi, T., Inoue, Y., Chiba, S., Aizawa, R., Saito, Y., Tsukamoto, H., Fujii, Y., Nishino, S., & Shimizu, T. (2002). CSF hypocretin-1 (orexin-A) concentrations in narcolepsy with and without cataplexy and idiopathic hypersomnia. *Journal of Sleep Research, 11*, 91–93. (14)

Kandel, E. R., & O'Dell, T. J. (1992). Are adult learning mechanisms also used for development? *Science, 258*, 243–245. (3)

Kandel, E. R., & Siegelbaum, S. A. (2000a). Overview of synaptic transmission. In E. R. Kandel, J. H. Schwartz, & T. M. Jessell (Eds.), *Principles of neural science* (4th ed.) (pp. 175–186). New York: McGraw-Hill. (2)

Kandel, E. R., & Siegelbaum, S. A. (2000b). Signaling at the nerve-muscle synapse: Directly gated transmission. In E. R. Kandel, J. H. Schwartz, & T. M. Jessell (Eds.), *Principles of neural science* (4th ed.) (pp. 187–206). New York: McGraw-Hill. (2)

Kandel, E. R., & Siegelbaum, S. A. (2000c). Synaptic integration. In E. R. Kandel, J. H. Schwartz, & T. M. Jessell (Eds.), *Principles of neural science* (4th ed.) (pp. 207–228). New York: McGraw-Hill. (2)

Kang, J., Jiang, L., Goldman, S. A., & Nedergaard, M. (1998). Astrocyte-mediated potentiation of inhibitory synaptic transmission. *Nature Neuroscience, 1*, 683–692. (2)

Kanigel, R. (1988, October/November). Nicotine becomes addictive. *Science Illustrated*, 12–14, 19–21. (4)

Kapur, S., Zipursky, R. B., and Remington, G. (1999). Clinical and theoretical implications of 5-HT2 and D2 receptor occupancy of clozapine, risperidone, and olanzapine in schizophrenia. *American Journal of Psychiatry, 156*, 286–293. (13)

Karni, A., Tanne, D., Rubenstein, B. S., Askenasy, J. J. M., & Sagi, D. (1994). Dependence on REM sleep of overnight improvement of a perceptual skill. *Science, 265*, 679–682. (14)

Karno, M., Golding, J. M., Sorenson, S. B., & Burnam, M. A. (1988). The epidemiology of obsessive-compulsive disorder in five US communities. *Archives of General Psychiatry, 45*, 1094–1099. (13)

Kast, B. (2001). Decisions, decisions . . . *Nature, 411*, 126–128. (3)

Kastner, S., & Ungerleider, L. G. (2000). Mechanisms of visual attention in the human cortex. *Annual Review of Neuroscience, 23*, 315–341. (14)

Katz, L. C., & Shatz, L. C. (1996). Synaptic activity and the construction of cortical circuits. *Nature, 274*, 1133–1138. (3)

Kausler, D. H. (1985). Episodic memory: Memorizing performance. In N. Charness (Ed.), *Aging and human performance* (pp. 101–139). New York: Wiley. (12)

Kawai, N., & Matsuzawa, T. (2000). Numerical memory span in a chimpanzee. *Nature, 403*, 39–40. (12)

Kaye, V., & Brandstater, M. E. (2002). Transcutaneous electrical nerve stimulation. *eMedicine*, [On-line]. Available: http://www.emedicine.com/pmr/topic206.htm. (10)

Kaye, W. H. (1997). Anorexia nervosa, obsessional behavior, and serotonin. *Psychopharmacology Bulletin, 33*, 335–341. (5)

Kaye, W. H., Ebert, M. H., Gwirtsman, H. E., & Weiss, S. R. (1984). Differences in brain serotonergic metabolism between nonbulimic and bulimic patients with anorexia nervosa. *American Journal of Psychiatry, 141*, 1598–1601. (5)

Kayman, S., Bruvold, W., & Stern, J. S. (1990). Maintenance and relapse after weight loss in women: Behavioral aspects. *American Journal of Clinical Nutrition, 52*, 800–807. (5)

Keele, S. W., & Ivry, R. (1990). Does the cerebellum provide a common computation for diverse tasks? A timing hypothesis. *Annals of the New York Academy of Sciences, 608,* 179–207. (10)

Keesey, R. E., & Powley, T. L. (1986). The regulation of body weight. *Annual Reviews of Psychology, 37,* 109–133. (5)

Kellogg, W. N. (1968). Communication and language in the home-raised chimpanzee. *Science, 162,* 423–427. (8)

Kelsey, J. E., Carlezon, W. A., Jr., & Falls, W. A. (1989). Lesions of the nucleus accumbens in rats reduce opiate reward but do not alter context-specific opiate tolerance. *Behavioral Neuroscience, 103,* 1327–1334. (4)

Kelso, S. R., & Brown, T. H. (1986). Differential conditioning of associative synaptic enhancement in hippocampal brain slices. *Science, 232,* 85–86. (11)

Kemper, T. L. (1984). Asymmetrical lesions in dyslexia. In N. Geschwind & A. M. Galaburda (Eds.), *Cerebral dominance: The biological foundations* (pp. 75–89). Cambridge, MA: Harvard University Press. (8)

Kendler, K. S., Heath, A. C., Neale, M. C., Kessler, R. C., & Eaves, L. J. (1992). A population based twin study of alcoholism in women. *Journal of the American Medical Association, 268,* 1877–1882. (4)

Kendler, K. S., MacLean, C., Neale, M., Kessler, R., Heath, A., & Eaves, L. (1991). The genetic epidemiology of bulimia nervosa. *American Journal of Psychiatry, 148,* 1627–1637. (5)

Kendler, K. S., Neale, M. C., Kessler, R. C., Heath, A. C., & Eaves, L. J. (1992). Major depression and generalized anxiety disorder: Same genes, (partly) different environments? *Archives of General Psychiatry, 49,* 716–722. (13)

Kendler, K. S., Prescott, C. A., Neale, M. C., & Pedersen, N. L. (1997). Temperance board registration for alcohol abuse in a national sample of Swedish male twins, born 1902 to 1949. *Archives of General Psychiatry, 54,* 178–184. (4)

Kendler, K. S., & Robinette, C. D. (1983). Schizophrenia in the National Academy of Sciences-National Research Council twin registry: A 16-year update. *American Journal of Psychiatry, 140,* 1551–1563. (13)

Kendler, K. S., Walters, E. E., Neale, M. C., Kessler, R. C., Heath, A. C., & Eaves, L. J. (1995). The structure of the genetic and environmental risk factors for six major psychiatric disorders in women: Phobia, generalized anxiety disorder, panic disorder, bulimia, major depression, and alcoholism. *Archives of General Psychiatry, 52,* 374–383. (13)

Kennaway, D. J., & van Dorp, C. F. (1991). Free-running rhythms of melatonin, cortisol, electrolytes, and sleep in humans in Antarctica. *American Journal of Physiology, 260,* R1137–R1144. (14)

Kessler, R. C., McGonagle, K. A., Zhao, S., Nelson, C. B., Hughes, M., Eshleman, S., Wittchen, H-U., and Kendler, K. S. (1994). Lifetime and 12-month prevalence of DSM-III-R psychiatric disorders in the United States. *Archives of General Psychiatry, 51,* 8–19. (13)

Khachaturian, Z. S. (1997, July/August). Plundered memories. *The Sciences,* 20–25. (11)

Kiang, N. Y.-S. (1965). *Discharge patterns of single fibers in the cat's auditory nerve.* Cambridge, MA: MIT Press. (8)

Kigar, D. L., Witelson, S. F., Glezer, I. I., & Harvey, T. (1997). Estimates of cell number in temporal neorcortex in the brain of Albert Einstein. *Society for Neuroscience Abstracts, 23,* 213. (12)

Kim, K. H. S., Relkin, N. R., Lee, K.-M., & Hirsch, J. (1997). Distinct cortical areas associated with native and second languages. *Nature, 388,* 171–174. (8)

King, F. A., Yarbrough, C. J., Anderson, D. C., Gordon, T. P., & Gould, K. G. (1988). Primates. *Science, 240,* 1475–1482. (1)

King, J. A., Davila-Garcia, M., Azmitia, E. C., & Strand, F. L. (1991). Differential effects of prenatal and postnatal ACTH or nicotine exposure on 5-HT high affinity uptake in the neonatal rat brain. *Journal of Developmental Neuroscience, 9,* 281–286. (7)

King, M.-C., & Wilson, A. C. (1975). Evolution at two levels in humans and chimpanzees. *Science, 188,* 107–116. (8)

Kinney, H. C., Korein, J., Panigrahy, A., Dikkes, P., & Goode, R. (1994). Neuropathological findings in the brain of Karen Ann Quinlan: The role of the thalamus in the persistent vegetative state. *New England Journal of Medicine, 330,* 1469–1475. (14)

Kinsey, A. C., Pomeroy, W. B., Martin, C. E., & Gebhard, P. H. (1953). *Sexual behavior in the human female.* Philadelphia: Saunders. (6)

Kipman, A., Gorwood, P., Mouren-Simeoni, M. C., & Ad'es, J. (1999). Genetic factors in anorexia nervosa. *European Psychiatry, 14,* 189–198. (5)

Kitada, T., Asakawa, S., Hattori, N., Matsumine, H., Yamamura, Y., Minoshima, S., Yokochi, M., Mizuno, Y., & Shimizu, N. (1998). Mutations in the parkin gene cause autosomal juvenile parkinsonism. *Nature, 392,* 605–608. (10)

Klein, E., Kreinin, I., Chistyakov, A., Koren, D., Mecz, L., Marmur, S., Ben-Shachar, D., & Feinsod, M. (1999). Therapeutic efficacy of right prefrontal slow repetitive transcranial magnetic stimulation in major depression. *Archives of General Psychiatry, 56,* 315–320. (13)

Kline, P. (1991). *Intelligence: The psychometric view.* New York: Routledge, Chapman, & Hall. (12)

Klose, M., & Bentley, D. (1989). Transient pioneer neurons are essential for formation of an embryonic peripheral nerve. *Science, 245,* 982–983. (3)

Knowlton, B. J., Mangels, J. A., & Squire, L. R. (1996). A neostriatal habit learning system in humans. *Science, 273,* 1399–1402. (10)

Knutson, B., Wolkowitz, O. M., Cole, S. W., Chan, T., Moore, E. A., Johnson, R. C., Terpstra, J., Turner, R. A., & Reus, V. I. (1998). Selective alteration of personality and social behavior by serotonergic intervention. *American Journal of Psychiatry, 155,* 373–379. (7)

Kobatake, E., Tanaka, K., & Tamori, Y. (1992). Long-term learning changes the stimulus selectivity of cells in the inferotemporal cortex of adult monkeys. *Neuroscience Research, S17,* S237. (9)

Koenig, R. (1999). European researchers grapple with animal rights. *Science, 284,* 1604–1606. (1)

Koester, J., & Siegelbaum, S. A. (2000). Local signaling: Passive electrical properties of the neuron. In E. R. Kandel, J. H. Schwartz, & T. M. Jessell (Eds.), *Principles of neural science* (4th ed.) (pp. 140–149). New York: McGraw-Hill. (2)

Komisaruk, B. R., & Steinman, J. L. (1987). Genital stimulation as a trigger for neuroendocrine and behavioral control of reproduction. *Annals of the New York Academy of Sciences, 474,* 64–75. (10)

Koob, G. F., & Bloom, F. E. (1988). Cellular and molecular mechanisms of drug dependence. *Science, 242,* 715–723. (4)

Koob, G. F., Sanna, P. P., & Bloom, F. E. (1998). Neuroscience of addiction. *Neuron, 21,* 467–476. (4)

Kopelman, M. D. (1995). The Korsakoff syndrome. *British Journal of Psychiatry, 166,* 154–173. (11)

Kosambi, D. D. (1967, February). Living prehistory in India. *Scientific American, 216,* 105–114. (7)

Koulack, D., & Goodenough, D. R. (1976). Dream recall and dream recall failure: An arousal-retrieval model. *Psychological Bulletin, 83,* 975–984. (14)

Kozlowski, S., & Drzewiecki, K. (1973). The role of osmoreception in portal circulation in control of wafer intake in dogs. *Acta Physiologica Polonica, 24,* 325–330. (5)

Kraemer, H. C., Becker, H. B., Brodie, H. K. H., Doering, C. H., Moos, R. H., & Hamburg, D. A. (1976). Orgasmic frequency and plasma testosterone levels in normal human males. *Archives of Sexual Behavior, 5,* 125–132. (6)

Krakauer, J., & Ghez, C. (2000). Voluntary movement. In E. R. Kandel, J. H. Schwartz, & T. M. Jessell (Eds.), *Principles of neural science* (4th ed., pp. 756–781). New York: McGraw-Hill. (10)

Krall, W. J., Sramek, J. J., & Cutler, N. R. (1999). Cholinesterase inhibitors: A therapeutic strategy for Alzheimer disease. *Annals of Pharmacotherapy, 33,* 441–450. (11)

Kreiman, G., Koch, C., & Fried, I. (2000). Category-specific visual responses of single neurons in the human medial temporal lobe. *Nature Neuroscience, 3,* 946–953. (9)

Kripke, D. F., & Sonnenschein, D. (1973). A 90 minute daydream cycle [Abstract]. *Sleep Research, 70,* 187. (14)

Krüger, R., Kuhn, W., Müller, T., Woitalla, D., Graeber, M., Kösel, S., Przuntek, H., Epplen, J. T., Schöls, L., & Riess, O. (1998). Ala30Pro mutation in the gene encoding alpha-synuclein in Parkinson's disease. *Nature Genetics, 18,* 106–108. (10)

Kruijver, F. P., Zhou, J. N., Pool, C. W., Hofman, M. A., Gooren, L. J., & Swaab, D. F. (2000). Male-to-female transsexuals have female neuron numbers in a limbic nucleus. *Journal of Clinical Endocrinology and Metabolism, 85,* 2034–2041. (6)

Kuffler, S. W. (1953). Discharge patterns and functional organization of mammalian retina. *Journal of Neurophysiology, 16,* 37–68. (9)

Kupfer, D. J. (1976). REM latency: A psychobiologic marker for primary depressive disease. *Biological Psychiatry, 11,* 159–174. (13)

Kupferman, I., Kandel, E. R., & Iversen, S. (2000). Motivational and addictive states. In E. R. Kandel, J. H. Schwartz, & T. M. Jessell (Eds.), *Principles of neural science* (4th ed.) (pp. 998–1013). New York: McGraw-Hill. (5)

Kurihara, K., & Kashiwayanagi, M. (1998). Introductory remarks on umami taste. *Annals of the New York Academy of Sciences, 855,* 393–397. (5)

Kuwada, J. Y. (1986). Cell recognition by neuronal growth cones in a simple vertebrate embryo. *Science, 233,* 740–746. (3)

Lai, C. S. L., Fisher, S. E., Hurst, J. A., Vargha-Khadem, F., & Monaco, A. P. (2001). A forkhead-domain gene is mutated in a severe speech and language disorder. *Nature, 413,* 519–523. (8)

LaMantia, A. S., & Rakic, P. (1990). Axon overproduction and elimination in the corpus callosum of the developing rhesus monkey. *Journal of Neuroscience, 10,* 2156–2175. (3)

Lamb, T., & Yang, J. E. (2000). Could different directions of infant stepping be controlled by the same locomotor central pattern generator? *Journal of Neurophysiology, 83,* 2814–2824. (10)

Lancaster, E. (1958). *The final face of Eve.* New York: McGraw-Hill. (14)

Landry, D. W. (1997, February). Immunotherapy for cocaine addiction. *Scientific American,* 42–45. (4)

Lane, R. D., Reiman, E. M., Ahern, G. L., Schwartz, G. E., & Davidson, R. J. (1997). Neuroanatomical correlates of happiness, sadness, and disgust. *American Journal of Psychiatry, 154,* 926–933. (7)

Laplane, D., Talairach, J., Meininger, V., Bancaud, J., & Orgogozo, J. M. (1977). Clinical consequences of corticectomies involving the supplementary motor area in man. *Journal of the Neurological Sciences, 34,* 301–314. (10)

Larson, G. (1995). *The Far Side gallery 5.* Kansas City: Andrews and McMeel. (10)

Lawrence, J. (1993). *Introduction to neural networks: Design, theory, and applications.* Nevada City, CA.: California Scientific Software. (2)

Lee, D. S., Lee, J. S., Oh, S. H., Kim, S.-K., Kim, J.-W., Chung, J.-K., Lee, M. C., & Kim, C. S. (2001). Cross-modal plasticity and cochlear implants. *Nature, 409,* 149–150. (8)

Lehky, S. R., & Sejnowski, T. J. (1990). Neural network model of visual cortex for determining surface curvature from images of shaded surfaces. *Proceedings of the Royal Society of London, B, 240,* 251–278. (2, 9)

Lehrman, S. (1999). Virus treatment questioned after gene therapy death. *Nature, 401,* 517–518. (1)

Leibel, R. L., Rosenbaum, M., & Hirsch, J. (1995). Changes in energy expenditure resulting from altered body weight. *New England Journal of Medicine, 332,* 621–628. (5)

Leibowitz, S. F., & Alexander, J. T. (1998). Hypothalamic serotonin in control of eating behavior, meal size, and body weight. *Biological Psychiatry, 44,* 851–864. (5)

Leland, J., & Miller, M. (1998, August 17). Can gays convert? *Newsweek,* 47–53. (6)

Lenneberg, E. H. (1969). On explaining language. *Science, 164,* 635–643. (8)

Lenzenweger, M. F., & Gottesman, I. I. (1994). Schizophrenia. In V. S. Ramachandran (Ed.), *Encyclopedia of human behavior.* San Diego, CA: Academic Press. (13)

Leonard, H. L., Lenane, M. C., Swedo, S. E., Rettew, D. C., & Rapoport, J. L. (1991). A double-blind comparison of clomipramine and desipramine treatment of severe onychophagia (nail-biting). *Archives of General Psychiatry, 48,* 821–826. (13)

Leonard, H. L., Lenane, M. C., Swedo, S. E., Rettew, D. C., Gershon, E. S., & Rapoport, J. L. (1992). Tics and Tourette's disorder: A 2- to 7-year follow-up of 54 obsessive-compulsive children. *American Journal of Psychiatry, 149,* 1244–1251. (13)

Leonard, S., Adams, C., Breese, C. R., Adler, L. E., Bickford, P., Byerley, W., Coon, H., Griffith, J. M., Miller, C., Myles-Worsley, M., Nagamoto, H. T., Rollins, Y., Stevens, K. E., Waldo, M., & Freedman, R. (1996). Nicotinic receptor function in schizophrenia. *Schizophrenia Bulletin, 22,* 431–445. (13)

Leopold, D. A., & Logothetis, N. K. (1996). Activity changes in early visual cortex reflect monkeys' percepts during binocular rivalry. *Nature, 379,* 549–553. (14)

Leor, J., Poole, W. K., & Kloner, R. A. (1996). Sudden cardiac death triggered by an earthquake. *New England Journal of Medicine, 334,* 413–419. (7)

Leroy, E., Boyer, R., Auburger, G., Leube, B., Ulm, G., Mezy, E., Harta, G., Brownstein, M. J., Jonnalagada, S., Chernova, T., Dehejia, A., Lavedan, C., Gasser, T., Steinbach, P. J., Wilkinson, K. D., & Polymeropoulos, M. H. (1998). The ubiquitin pathway in Parkinson's disease. *Nature, 395,* 451–452. (10)

Leshner, A. I. (1997). Addiction is a brain disease, and it matters. *Science, 278,* 45–47. (4)

LeVay, S. (1991). A difference in hypothalamic structure between heterosexual and homosexual men. *Science, 253,* 1034–1037. (6)

LeVay, S. (1996). *Queer science: The use and abuse of research into homosexuality.* Cambridge, MA: MIT Press. (6)

Levenson, R. W. (1992). Autonomic nervous system differences among emotions. *Psychological Science, 3,* 23–27. (7)

Levenson, R. W., Ekman, P., & Friesen, W. V. (1990). Voluntary facial action generates emotion-specific autonomic nervous system activity. *Psychophysiology, 27,* 363–384. (7)

Levin, H. S., Culhane, K. A., Hartmann, J., Evankovich, K., Mattson, A. J., Harward, H., Ringholz, G., Ewing-Cobbs, L., & Fletcher, J. M. (1991). Developmental changes in performance on tests of purported frontal lobe functioning. *Developmental Neuropsychology, 7,* 377–395. (3)

Levin, N., Nelson, C., Gurney, A., Vandlen, R., & de Sauvage, F. (1996). Decreased food intake does not completely account for adiposity reduction after ob protein infusion. *Proceedings of the National Academy of Sciences, USA, 93,* 1726–1730. (5)

Levine, J. A., Eberhardt, N. L., & Jensen, M. D. (1999). Role of nonexercise activity thermogenesis in resistance to fat gain in humans. *Science, 283,* 212–214. (5)

Levine, J. D., Fields, H. L., & Basbaum, A. I. (1993). Peptides and the primary afferent nociceptor. *Journal of Neuroscience, 13,* 2273–2286. (10)

Levy, B. (1996). Improving memory in old age through implicit self-stereotyping. *Journal of Personality and Social Psychology, 71,* 1092–1107. (12)

Levy, J. (1969). Possible basis for the evolution of lateral specialization of the human brain. *Nature, 224,* 614–615. (6)

Lewicki, P., Hill, T., & Czyzewska, M. (1992). Nonconscious acquisition of information. *American Psychologist, 47,* 796–801. (14)

Lewin, R. (1980). Is your brain really necessary? *Science, 210,* 1232–1234. (3, 12)

Lewis, E. R., Everhart, T. E., & Zeevi, Y. Y. (1969). Studying neural organization in *Aplysia* with the scanning electron microscope. *Science, 165,* 1140–1143. (2)

Lewis, H. B., Goodenough, D. R., Shapiro, A., & Sleser, I. (1966). Individual differences in dream recall. *Journal of Abnormal Psychology, 71,* 52–59. (14)

Lewis, M., & Brooks-Gunn, J. (1979). *Social cognition and the acquisition of self.* New York: Plenum Press. (14)

Lewis, P. D. (1985). Neuropathological effects of alcohol on the developing nervous system. *Alcohol and Alcoholism, 20,* 195–200. (3)

Lewy, A. J., Sack, R. L, Miller, L. S., & Hoban, T. M. (1987). Antidepressant and circadian phase-shifting effects of light. *Science, 235,* 352–354. (13)

Lichtman, S. W., Pisarska, K., Berman, E. R., Pestone, M., Dowling, H., Offenbacher, E., Weisel, H., Heshka, S., Matthews, D. E., & Heymsfield, S. B. (1992). Discrepancy between self-reported and actual caloric intake and exercise in obese subjects. *New England Journal of Medicine, 327,* 1893–1898. (5)

Lieberman, H. R., Wurtman, J. J., & Chew, B. (1986). Changes in mood after carbohydrate consumption among obese individuals. *American Journal of Clinical Nutrition, 44,* 772–778. (5)

Liechti, M. E., & Vollenweider, F. X. (2000). Acute psychological and physiological effects of MDMA ("ecstasy") after haloperidol pretreatment in healthy humans. *European Neuropsychopharmacology, 10,* 289–295. (4)

Lilenfeld, L. R., Kaye, W. H., Greeno, C. G., Merikangas, K. R., Plotnicov, K., Pollice, C., Rao, R., Strober, M., Bulik, C. M., & Nagy, L. (1998). A controlled family study of anorexia nervosa and bulimia nervosa: Psychiatric disorders in first degree relatives and effects of proband comorbidity. *Archives of General Psychiatry, 55,* 603–610. (5)

Lim, K. O., Tew, W., Kushner, M., Chow, K., Matsumoto, B., & DeLisi, L. E. (1996). Cortical gray matter volume deficit in patients with first-episode schizophrenia. *American Journal of Psychiatry, 153,* 1548–1553. (13)

Lindvall, O., Brundin, P., Widner, H., Rehncrona, S., Gustavii, B., Frackowiak, R., Leenders, K. L., Sawle, G., Rothwell, J. C., Marsden, C. D., & Bjorklund, A. (1990). Grafts of fetal dopamine neurons survive and improve motor fuction in Parkinson's disease. *Science, 247,* 574–577. (1)

Linnoila, M., Virkkunen, M., Scheinin, M., Nuutila, A., Rimon, R., & Goodwin, F. K. (1983). Low cerebrospinal fluid 5-hydroxyindoleacetic acid concentration differentiates impulsive from nonimpulsive violent behavior. *Life Sciences, 33,* 2609–2614. (7)

Lipska, B. K., Jaskiw, G. E., & Weinberger, D. R. (1993). Postpubertal emergence of hyperresponsiveness to stress and to amphetamine after neonatal excitotoxic hippocampal damage: A potential animal model of schizophrenia. *Neuropsychopharmacology, 9,* 67–75. (13)

Lisman, J., & Morris, R. B. M. (2001). Why is the cortex a slow learner? *Nature, 411,* 248–249. (11)

Liu, J., Solway, K., Messing, R. O., & Sharp, F. R. (1998). Increased neurogenesis in the dentate gyrus after transient global ischemia in gerbils. *Journal of Neuroscience, 18,* 7768–7778. (3)

Livingstone, D. (1858/1971). *Missionary travels.* New York: Harper & Brothers. (10)

Livingstone, M., & Hubel, D. (1988). Segregation of form, color, movement, and depth: Anatomy, physiology, and perception. *Science, 240,* 740–749. (9)

Livingstone, M. S., Rosen, G. D., Drislane, F. W., & Galaburda, A. M. (1991). Physiological and anatomical evidence for a magnocellular defect in developmental dyslexia. *Proceedings of the National Academy of Sciences, USA, 88,* 7943–7947. (8)

Locurto, C. (1990). The malleability of IQ as judged from adoption studies. *Intelligence, 14,* 275–292. (12)

Loehlin, J. C., & Nichols, R. C. (1976). *Heredity, environment and personality: A study of 850 twins.* Austin: University of Texas Press. (12)

Loewi, O. (1953). *From the workshop of discoveries.* Lawrence, KS: University of Kansas Press. (2)

Loftus, E. F. (1997, September). Creating false memories. *Scientific American,* 70–75. (11)

Loftus, T. M., Jaworsky, D. E., Frehywot, G. L., Townsend, C. A., Ronnett, G. V., Lane, M. D., & Kuhajda, F. P. (2000). Reduced food intake and body weight in mice treated with fatty acid synthase inhibitors. *Science, 288,* 2379–2381. (5)

Logothetis, N. K., Pauls, J., & Poggio, T. (1995). Shape representation in the inferior temporal cortex of monkeys. *Current Biology, 5,* 552–563. (9)

London, E. D., Cascella, N. G., Wong, D. F., Phillips, R. L., Dannals, R. F., Links, J. M., Herning, R., Grayson, R., Jaffe, J. H., & Wagner, H. N., Jr. (1990). Cocaine-induced reduction of glucose utilization in human brain. *Archives of General Psychiatry, 47,* 567–574. (4)

Loring, D. W., Meador, K. J., Lee, G. P., Murro, A. M., Smith, J. R., Flanigin, H. F., Gallagher, B. B., & King, D. W. (1990). Cerebral language lateralization: Evidence from intracarotid amobarbital testing. *Neuropsychologia, 28,* 831–838. (8)

Loring, J. F., Wen, X., Lee, J. M., Seilhamer, J., & Somogyi, R. (2001). A gene expression profile of Alzheimer's disease. *DNA and Cell Biology, 20,* 683–695. (11)

Lott, I. T. (1982). Down's syndrome, aging, and Alzheimer's disease: A clinical review. *Annals of the New York Academy of Sciences, 396,* 15–27. (11)

Louie, K., & Wilson, M. A. (2001). Temporally structured replay of awake hippocampal ensemble activity during rapid eye movement sleep. *Neuron, 29,* 145–156. (11)

Lowenstein, R. J., & Putnam, F. W. (1990). The clinical phenomenology of males with MPD: A report of 21 cases. *Dissociation, 3,* 135–143. (14)

Lowing, P. A., Mirsky, A. F., & Pereira, R. (1983). The inheritance of schizophrenia spectrum disorders: A reanalysis of the Danish adoptee study data. *American Journal of Psychiatry, 140,* 1167–1171. (13)

Lubinski, D., & Humphreys, L. G. (1992). Some bodily and medical correlates of mathematical giftedness and commensurate levels of socioeconomic status. *Intelligence, 16,* 99–115. (12)

Lucas, R. J., Freedman, M. S., Muñoz, M., Garcia-Fernández, J.-M., & Foster, R. G. (1999). Regulation of the mammalian pineal by non-rod, non-cone, ocular photoreceptors. *Science, 284,* 505–507. (14)

Luciano, M., Wright, M., Smith, G. A., Geffen, G. M., Geffen, L. B., & Martin, N. G. (2001). Genetic covariance among measures of information processing speed, working memory, and IQ. *Behavior Genetics, 31,* 581–592. (12)

Lupien, S. J., de Leon, M., de Santi, S., Convit, A., Tarshish, C., Thakur, M., McEwen, B. S., Hauger, R. L, & Meaney, M. J. (1998). Cortisol levels during human aging predict hippocampal atrophy and memory deficits. *Nature Neuroscience, 1,* 69–73. (7)

Ly, D. H., Lockhart, D. J., Lerner, R. A., & Schultz, P. G. (2000). Mitotic misregulation and human aging. *Science, 287,* 2486–2492. (1)

Lyons, S. (2001, May 20). A will to eat, a fight for life. *San Luis Obispo Tribune,* A1. (5)

Maas, L. C., Lukas, S. E., Kaufman, M. J., Weiss, R. D., Daniels, S. L., Rogers, V. W., Kukes, T. J., & Renshaw, P. F. (1998). Functional magnetic resonance imaging of human brain activation during cue-induced cocaine craving. *American Journal of Psychiatry, 155,* 124–126. (4)

Maccoby, E. E., & Jacklin, C. N. (1974). *The psychology of sex differences.* Stanford, CA: Stanford University Press. (6)

Maccoby, E. E., & Jacklin, C. N. (1980). Sex differences in aggression: A rejoinder and reprise. *Child Development, 51,* 964–980. (6)

Macilwain, C. (2000). Self-policing backed for research on humans. *Nature, 406,* 7. (1)

Macrae, J. R., Scoles, M. T., & Siegel, S. (1987). The contribution of Pavlovian conditioning to drug tolerance and dependence. *British Journal of Addiction, 82,* 371–380. (4)

Maddison, D., & Viola, A. (1968). The health of widows in the year following bereavement. *Journal of Psychosomatic Research, 12,* 297–306. (7)

Magavi, S. S., Leavitt, B. R., & Macklis, J. D. (2000). Induction of neurogenesis in the neocortex of adult mice. *Nature, 405,* 951–955. (3)

Maguire, E. A., Gadian, D. G., Johnsrude, I. S., Good, C. D., Ashburner, J., Frackowiak, R. S. J., & Frith, C. D. (2000). Navigation-related structural change in the hippocampi of taxi drivers. *Proceedings of the National Academy of Sciences, USA, 97,* 4398–4403. (11)

Maier, M. A., Bennett, K. M., Hepp-Reymond, M. C., & Lemon, R. N. (1993). Contribution of the monkey corticomotoneuronal system to the control of force in precision grip. *Journal of Neurophysiology, 69,* 772–785. (10)

Maier, S. F., Drugan, R. C., & Grau, J. W. (1982). Controllability, coping behavior, and stress-induced analgesia in the rat. *Pain, 12,* 47–56. (10)

Malakoff, D. (2000). Texas scientist admits falsifying results. *Science, 290,* 245–246. (1)

Maldonado, R., Salardi, A., Valverde, O., Samad, T. A., Roques, B. P., & Borrelli, E. (1997). Absence of opiate rewarding effects in mice lacking dopamine D₂ receptors. *Nature, 388,* 586–589. (4)

Maletic-Savatic, M., Malinow, R., & Svoboda, K. (1999). Rapid dendritic morphogenesis in CA1 hippocampal dendrites induced by synaptic activity. *Science, 283,* 1923–1927. (11)

Malison, R. T., McDougle, C. J., van Dyck, C. H., Scahill, L., Baldwin, R. M., Seibyl, J. P., Price, L. H., Leckman, J. F., & Innis, R. B. (1995). [¹²³I]β-CIT SPECT imaging of striatal dopamine transporter binding in Tourette's disorder. *American Journal of Psychiatry, 152,* 1359–1361. (13)

Mann, J. J., Arango, V., & Underwood, M. D. (1990). Serotonin and suicidal behavior. In P. M. Whitaker-Azmitia & S. J. Peroutka (Eds.), *Annals of the New York Academy of Sciences. Special Issue: The Neuropharmacology of Serotonin, 600,* 476–485. (13)

Mansari, M., Sakai, K., & Jouvet, M. (1989). Unitary characteristics of presumptive cholinergic tegmental neurons during the sleep-waking cycle in freely moving cats. *Experimental Brain Research, 76,* 519–529. (14)

Mapes, G. (1990, April 10). Beating the clock: Was it an accident Chernobyl exploded at 1:23 in the morning? *Wall Street Journal,* A-1. (14)

Marczynski, T. J., & Urbancic, M. (1988). Animal models of chronic anxiety and "fearlessness." *Brain Research Bulletin, 21,* 483–490. (13)

Marks, W. B., Dobelle, W. H., & MacNichol, E. F., Jr. (1964). Visual pigments of single primate cones. *Science, 143,* 1181–1183. (9)

Marshall, E. (1998). Medline searches turn up cases of suspected plagiarism. *Science, 279,* 473–474. (1)

Marshall, E. (2000a). Antiabortion groups target neuroscience study at Nebraska. *Science, 287,* 202–203. (1)

Marshall, E. (2000b). Gene therapy on trial. *Science, 288,* 951–957. (1)

Marshall, E. (2000c). How prevalent is fraud? That's a million-dollar question. *Science, 290,* 1662–1663. (1)

Marshall, E. (2000d). Moratorium urged on germ line gene therapy. *Science, 289,* 2023. (1)

Martin, A., Haxby, J. V., Lalonde, F. M., Wiggs, C. L., & Ungerleider, L. G. (1995). Discrete cortical regions associated with knowledge of color and knowledge of actions. *Science, 270,* 102–105. (11)

Martin, A., Wiggs, C. L., & Weisberg, J. (1997). Modulation of human medial temporal lobe activity by form, meaning, and experience. *Hippocampus, 7,* 587–593. (11)

Martin, A., Wiggs, C. L., Ungerleider, L. G., & Haxby, J. V. (1996). Neural correlates of category-specific knowledge. *Nature, 379,* 649–652. (8, 11)

Martin, J. B. (1987). Molecular genetics: Applications to the clinical neurosciences. *Science, 238,* 765–772. (10)

Martinez, J. L., & Derrick, B. E. (1996). Long-term potentiation and learning. *Annual Review of Psychology, 47,* 173–203. (11)

Martini, F. (1988). *Fundamentals of anatomy and physiology* (4th ed.). Upper Saddle River, NJ: Prentice Hall. (10)

Martins, I. P., & Ferro, J. M. (1992). Recovery of acquired aphasia in children. *Aphasiology, 6,* 431–438. (8)

Marx, J. (1998). New gene tied to common form of Alzheimer's. *Science, 281,* 507–509. (11)

Mas, M., Fumero, B., & González-Mora, J. L. (1995). Voltammetric and microdialysis monitoring of brain monoamine neurotransmitter release during sociosexual interactions. *Behavioural Brain Research, 71,* 69–79. (6)

Masica, D. N., Money, J., Ehrhardt, A. A., & Lewis, V. G. (1969). IQ, fetal sex hormones and cognitive patterns: Studies in the testicular feminizing syndrome of androgen insensitivity. *Johns Hopkins Medical Journal, 124,* 34–43. (6)

Mâsse, L. C., & Tremblay, R. E. (1997). Behavior of boys in kindergarten and the onset of substance use during adolescence. *Archives of General Psychiatry, 54,* 62–68. (4)

Masters, W., & Johnson, V. (1966). *The human sexual response.* Boston: Little, Brown. (6)

Mateer, C. A., & Cameron, P. A. (1989). Electrophysiological correlates of language: Stimulation mapping and evoked potential studies. In F. Boller & J. Grafman, J. (Eds.), *Handbook of neuropsychology* (Vol. 2, pp. 91–116). New York: Elsevier. (8)

Matsuda, L. A., Lolait, S. J., Brownstein, M. J., Young, A. C., & Bonner, T. I. (1990). Structure of a cannabinoid receptor and functional expression of the cloned cDNA. *Nature, 346,* 561–564. (4)

Mattay, V. S., Berman, K. F., Ostrem, J. L., Esposito, G., Van Horn, J. D., Bigelow, L. B., & Weinberger, D. R. (1996). Dextroamphetamine enhances "neural network-specific" physiological signals: A positron-emission tomography rCBF study. *Journal of Neuroscience, 16,* 4816–4822. (2)

Matuszewich, L., Lorrain, D. S., & Hull, E. M. (2000). Dopamine release in the medial preoptic area of female rats in response to hormonal manipulation and sexual activity. *Behavioral Neuroscience, 114,* 772–782. (6)

Mazur, A., & Lamb, T. A. (1980). Testosterone, status, and mood in human males. *Hormones and Behavior, 14,* 236–246. (7)

Mazzocchi, F., & Vignolo, L. A. (1979). Localisation of lesions in aphasia: Clinical-CT scan correlations in stroke patients. *Cortex, 15,* 627–653. (8)

McCann, U. D., Lowe, K. A., & Ricaurte, G. A. (1997). Long-lasting effects of recreational drugs of abuse on the central nervous system. *The Neuroscientist, 3,* 399–411. (4)

McClearn, G. E., Johansson, B., Berg, S., Pedersen, N. L., Ahern, F., Petrill, S. A., & Plomin, R. (1997). Substantial genetic influence on cognitive abilities in twins 80 or more years old. *Science, 276,* 1560–1563. (12)

McClelland, J. L., McNaughton, B. L., & O'Reilly, R. C. (1995). Why there are complementary learning systems in the hippocampus and neocortex: Insights from the successes and failures of connectionist models of learning and memory. *Psychological Review, 102,* 419–457. (11)

McClintock, M. K. (1971). Menstrual synchrony and suppression. *Nature, 229,* 244–245. (6)

McConnell, S. K., Ghosh, A., & Shatz, C. J. (1989). Subplate neurons pioneer the first axon pathway from the cerebral cortex. *Science, 245,* 978–981. (3)

McCormick, C. M., & Witelson, S. F. (1991). A cognitive profile of homosexual men compared to heterosexual men and women. *Psychoneuroendocrinology, 16,* 459–473. (6)

McCormick, D. A., & Thompson, R. F. (1984). Cerebellum: Essential involvement in the classically conditioned eyelid response. *Science, 223,* 296–299. (10)

McCoy, N. L., & Davidson, J. M. (1985). A longitudinal study of the effects of menopause on sexuality. *Maturitas, 7,* 203–210. (6)

McDonald, J. W., Becker, D., Sadowsky, C. L., Jane, J. A., Conturo, T. E., & Schultz, L. M. (2002). Late recovery following spinal cord injury: Case report and review of the literature. *Journal of Neurosurgery: Spine, 97,* 252–265. (3)

McDonald, J. W., Liu, X.-Z., Qu, Y., Liu, S., Mickey, S. K., Turetsky, D., Gottlieb, D. I., & Choi, D. W. (1999). Transplanted embryonic stem cells survive, differentiate and promote recovery in injured rat spinal cord. *Nature Medicine, 5,* 1410–1412. (1)

McDonald, R. J., & White, N. M. (1993). A triple dissociation of memory systems: Hippocampus, amygdala, and dorsal striatum. *Behavioral Neuroscience, 107,* 3–22. (11)

McDougall, W. (1908). *An introduction to social psychology.* London: Methuen. (5)

McDougle, C. J., Holmes, J. P., Carlson, D. C., Pelton, G. H., Cohen, D. J., & Price, L. H. (1998). A double-blind, placebo-controlled study of Risperidone in adults with autistic disorder and other pervasive developmental disorders. *Archives of General Psychiatry, 55,* 633–641. (12)

McFadden, D., & Pasanen, E. G. (1998). Comparison of the auditory systems of heterosexuals and homosexuals: Click-evoked otoacoustic emissions. *Proceedings of the National Academy of Sciences, USA, 95,* 2709–2713. (6)

McGarry-Roberts, P. A., Stelmack, R. M., & Campbell, K. B. (1992). Intelligence, reaction time, and event-related potentials. *Intelligence, 16,* 289–313. (12)

McGaugh, J. L. (2000). Memory—A century of consolidation. *Science, 287,* 248–251. (11)

McGaugh, J. L., Cahill, L., & Roozendaal, B. (1996). Involvement of the amygdala in memory storage: Interaction with other brain systems. *Proceedings of the National Academy of Sciences, USA, 93,* 13508–13514. (11)

McGue, M., & Bouchard, T. J. (1998). Genetic and environmental influences on human behavioral differences. *Annual Review of Neuroscience, 21,* 1–24. (1)

McGuire, P. K., Shah, G. M. S., & Murray, R. M. (1993). Increased blood flow in Broca's area during auditory hallucinations in schizophrenia. *Lancet, 342,* 703–706. (13)

McGuire, P. K., Silbersweig, D. A., Wright, I., Murray, R. M., David, A. S., Frackowiak, R. S. J., & Frith, C. D. (1995). Abnormal monitoring of inner speech: A physiological basis for auditory hallucinations. *Lancet, 346,* 596–600. (13)

McIntosh, A. R., Rajah, M. N., & Lobaugh, N. J. (1999). Interactions of prefrontal cortex in relation to awareness in sensory learning. *Science, 284,* 1531–1533. (14)

McKeon, J., McGuffin, P., & Robinson, P. (1984). Obsessive-compulsive neurosis following head injury: A report of 4 cases. *British Journal of Psychiatry, 144,* 190–192. (13)

McKinnon, W., Weisse, C. S., Reynolds, C. P., Bowles, C. A., & Baum, A. (1989). Chronic stress, leukocyte subpopulations, and humoral response to latent viruses. *Health Psychology, 8,* 389–402. (7)

Meberg, P. J., Barnes, C. A., McNaughton, B. L., & Routtenberg, A. (1993). Protein kinase C and F1/GAP-43 gene expression in hippocampus inversely related to synaptic enhancement lasting 3 days. *Proceedings of the National Academy of Sciences, USA, 90,* 12050–12054. (11)

Meister, M., Wong, R. O. L., Baylor, D. A., & Shatz, C. J. (1991). Synchronous bursts of action potentials in ganglion cells of the developing mammalian retina. *Science, 252,* 939–943. (3)

Melichar, J. K., Daglish, M. R. C., & Nutt, D. J. (2001). Addiction and withdrawal-current views. *Current Opinion in Pharmacology, 1,* 84–90. (4)

Meltzer, H. Y. (1990). Role of serotonin in depression. In P. M. Whitaker-Azmitia & S. J. Peroutka (Eds.), *Annals of the New York Academy of Sciences. Special Issue: The Neuropharmacology of Serotonin, 600,* 486–500. (13)

Melzack, R. (1973). *The puzzle of pain.* New York: Basic Books. (7)

Melzack, R. (1992, April). Phantom limbs. *Scientific American, 266,* 120–126. (10, 14)

Melzack, R., & Wall, P. D. (1965). Pain mechanisms: A new theory. *Science, 150,* 971–979. (10)

Menon, D. K., Owen, A. M., Williams, E. J., Minhas, P. S., Allen, C. M. C., Boniface, S. J., Pickard, J. D., & the Wolfson Brain Imaging Centre Team. (1998). Cortical processing in persistent vegetative state. *Lancet, 352,* 200. (14)

Merzenich, M. M., Knight, P. L., & Roth, G. L. (1975). Representation of cochlea within primary auditory cortex in the cat. *Journal of Neurophysiology, 61,* 231–249. (8)

Meston, C. M., & Frohlich, P. F. (2000). The neurobiology of sexual function. *Archives of General Psychiatry, 57,* 1012–1030. (6)

Mesulam, M.-M. (1986). Frontal cortex and behavior. *Annals of Neurology, 19,* 320–325. (3)

Meyer-Bahlburg, H. F. L. (1984). Psychoendocrine research on sexual orientation. Current status and future options. *Progress in Brain Research, 61,* 375–398. (6)

Michael, R., Gagnon, J., Laumann, E., & Kolata, G. (1994). *Sex in America.* Boston: Little, Brown. (6)

Miles, C., Green, R., Sanders, G., & Hines, M. (1998). Estrogen and memory in a transsexual population. *Hormones and Behavior, 34,* 199–208. (6)

Miles, D. R., & Carey, G. (1997). Genetic and environmental architecture of human aggression. *Journal of Personal and Social Psychology, 72,* 207–217. (7)

Miles, L. E. M., Raynal, D. M., & Wilson, M. A. (1977). Blind man living in normal society has circadian rhythms of 24.9 hours. *Science, 198,* 421–423. (14)

Miller, A. (1967). The lobotomy patient—a decade later: A follow-up study of a research project started in 1948. *Canadian Medical Association Journal, 96,* 1095–1103. (3)

Miller, B. L., Boone, K., Cummings, J. L., Read, S. L., & Mishkin, F. (2000). Functional correlates of musical and visual ability in frontotemporal dementia. *British Journal of Psychiatry, 176,* 458–463. (12)

Miller, D. S., & Parsonage, S. (1975). Resistance to slimming: Adaptation or illusion? *Lancet, 1,* 773–775. (5)

Miller, E. K., Erickson, C. A., & Desimone, R. (1996). Neural mechanisms of visual working memory in prefrontal cortex of the Macaque. *Journal of Neuroscience, 16,* 5151–5167. (11)

Miller, G. E., Cohen, S., Rabin, B. S., Skoner, D. P., & Doyle, W. J. (1999). Personality and tonic cardiovascular, neuroendocrine, and immune parameters. *Brain, Behavior, and Immunity, 13*, 109–123. (7)

Miller, L. T., & Vernon, P. A. (1992). The general factor in short-term memory, intelligence, and reaction time. *Intelligence, 16*, 5–29. (12)

Miller, N. F. (1985). The value of behavioral research on animals. *American Psychologist, 40*, 423–440. (1)

Miller, S. D., & Triggiano, P. J. (1992). The psychophysiological investigation of multiple personality disorder: Review and update. *American Journal of Clinical Hypnosis, 35*, 47–61. (14)

Miller, T. Q., Smith, T. W., Turner, C. W., Guijarro, M. L., & Hallet, A. J. (1996). A meta-analytic review of research on hostility and physical health. *Psychological Bulletin, 119*, 322–348. (7)

Milner, B. (1970). Memory and the temporal regions of the brain. In K. H. Pribram & D. E. Broadbent, *Biology and memory*. New York: Academic Press. (11)

Milner, B. (1974). Hemispheric specialization: Scope and limits. In F. O. Schmitt & F. G. Worden (Eds.), *The neurosciences: Third study program* (pp. 75–89). Cambridge, MA: MIT Press. (8)

Milner, B., Corkin, S., & Teuber, H.-L. (1968). Further analysis of the hippocampal amnesic syndrome: 14-year follow-up study of HM. *Neuropsychologia, 6*, 215–234. (11)

Milner, T. (1977). How much distraction can you hear? *Stereo Review*.

Miltner, W. H. R., Braun, C., Arnold, M., Witte, H., & Taub, E. (1999). Coherence of gamma-band EEG activity as a basis for associative learning. *Nature, 397*, 434–436. (14)

Mitchell, S. W. (1866, July). The case of George Dedlow. *Atlantic Monthly, 18*, 1–11. (14)

Mitler, M. M., Carskadon, M. A., Czeisler, C. A., Dement, W. C., Dinges, D. F., & Graeber, R. C. (1988). Catastrophes, sleep, and public policy: Consensus report. *Sleep, 11*, 100–109. (14)

Miyashita, Y. (1993). Inferior temporal cortex: Where visual perception meets memory. *Annual Review of Neuroscience, 16*, 245–263. (9)

Miyashita, Y., & Chang, H. S. (1988). Neuronal correlate of pictorial short-term memory in the primate temporal cortex. *Nature, 331*, 68–70. (11)

Modahl, C., Green, L., Fein, D., Morris, M., Waterhouse, L., Feinstein, C., & Levin, H. (1998). Plasma oxytocin levels in autistic children. *Biological Psychiatry, 43*, 270–277. (12)

Moeller, F. G., Dougherty, D. M., Swann, A. C., Collins, D., Davis, C. M., & Cherek, D. R. (1996). Tryptophan depletion and aggressive responding in healthy males. *Psychopharmacology, 126*, 97–103. (7)

Mogilner, A., Grossman, J. A. I., Ribary, U., Jolikot, M., Volkmann, J., Rapaport, D., Beasley, R. W., & Llinas, R. R. (1993). Somatosensory cortical plasticity in adult humans revealed by magnetoencephalography. *Proceedings of the National Academy of Sciences, USA, 90*, 3593–3597. (3)

Moldin, S. O., Reich, T., & Rice, J. P. (1991). Current perspectives on the genetics of unipolar depression. *Behavior Genetics, 21*, 211–242. (13)

Molfese, D. L., Freeman, R. B., Jr., & Palermo, D. S. (1975). The ontogeny of brain lateralization for speech and nonspeech stimuli. *Brain and Language, 2*, 356–368. (8)

Mombaerts, P. (1999). Seven-transmembrane proteins as odorant and chemosensory receptors. *Science, 286*, 707–711. (6)

Money, J. (1968). *Sex errors of the body and related syndromes: A guide to counseling children, adolescents, and their families*. Baltimore: Paul H. Brookes. (6)

Money, J., & Ehrhardt, A. A. (1972). *Man & woman, boy & girl*. Baltimore: Johns Hopkins University Press. (6)

Money, J., Devore, H., & Norman, B. F. (1986). Gender identity and gender tansposition: Longitudinal outcome study of 32 male hermaphrodites assigned as girls. *Journal of Sex and Marital Therapy, 12*, 165–181. (6)

Money, J., Schwartz, M., & Lewis, V. G. (1984). Adult erotosexual status and fetal hormonal masculinization and demasculinization: 46, XX congenital virilizing adrenal hyperplasia and 46, XY androgen-insensitivity syndrome compared. *Psychoneuroendocrinology, 9*, 405–414. (6)

Montague, C. T., Farooqi, I. S., Whitehead, J. P., Soos, M. A., Rau, H., Wareham, N. J., Sewter, C. P., Digby, J. E., Mohammed, S. N., Hurst, J. A., Cheetham, C. H., Earley, A. R., Barnett, A. H., Prins, J. B., & O'Rahilly, S. (1997). Congenital leptin deficiency is associated with severe early-onset obesity in humans. *Nature, 387*, 903–908. (5)

Monte, A. P., Waldman, S. R., Marcona-Lewicka, D., Wainscott, D. B., Nelson, D. L., Sanders-Bush, E., & Nichols, D. E. (1997). Dihydrobenzofuran analogues of hallucinogens. 4. Mescaline derivatives. *Journal of Medicinal Chemistry, 40*, 2997–3008. (4)

Monti-Bloch, L., Jennings-White, C., Dolberg, D. S., & Berliner, D. L. (1994). The human vomeronasal system. *Psychoneuroendocrinology, 19*, 673–686. (6)

Morgan, D., Diamond, D. M., Gottschall, P. E., Ugen, K. E., Dickey, C., Hardy, J., Duff, K., Jantzen, P., DiCarlo, G., Wilcock, D., Conner, K., Hatcher, J., Hope, C., Gordon, M., & Arendash, G. W. (2000). Aß peptide vaccination prevents memory loss in an animal model of Alzheimer's disease. *Nature, 408*, 982–985. (11)

Morley, K. I., & Montgomery, G. W. (2001). The genetics of cognitive processes: Candidate genes in humans and animals. *Behavior Genetics, 31*, 511–531. (12)

Morrel-Samuels, P., & Herman, L. M. (1993). Cognitive factors affecting comprehension of gesture language signs: A brief comparison of dolphins and humans. In H. L. Roitblat, L. M. Herman, & P. E. Nachtigall, (Eds.), *Language and communicaton: Comparative perspectives* (pp. 311–327). Hillsdale, NJ: Lawrence Ehrlbaum. (8)

Morris, J. McL. (1953). The syndrome of testicular feminization in male pseudohermaphrodites. *American Journal of Obstetrics and Gynecology, 65*, 1192–1211. (6)

Morris, J. S., Frith, C. D., Perrett, D. I., Rowland, D., Young, A. W., Calder, A. J., & Dolan, R. J. (1996). A differential neural response in the human amygdala to fearful and happy facial expressions. *Nature, 383*, 812–815. (7)

Morris, N. M., Udry, J. R., Khan-Dawood, F., & Dawood, M. Y. (1987). Marital sex frequency and midcycle female testosterone. *Archives of Sexual Behavior, 16*, 27–37. (6)

Moscovitch, M., & Winocur, G. (1995). Frontal lobes, memory, and aging. *Annals of the New York Academy of Sciences, 769*, 119–150. (11)

Mountcastle, V. B., & Powell, T. P. S. (1959). Neural mechanisms subserving cutaneous sensibility, with special reference to the role of afferent inhibition in sensory perception and discrimination. *Bulletin of the Johns Hopkins Hospital, 105*, 201–232. (10)

Murdoch, D., Pihl, R. O., & Ross, D. (1990). Alcohol and crimes of violence: Present issues. *International Journal of Addiction, 25*, 1065–1081. (7)

Murphy, G. (1949). *Historical introduction to modern psychology*. New York: Harcourt, Brace & World. (1)

Murphy, J. M., McBride, W. J., Lumeng, L., & Li, T.-K. (1987). Contents of monoamines in forebrain regions of alcohol-preferring (p) and -nonpreferring (np) lines of rats. *Pharmacology Biochemistry & Behavior, 26*, 389–392. (4)

Murphy, M. R., Checkley, S. A., Seckl, J. R., & Lightman, S. L. (1990). Naloxone inhibits oxytocin release at orgasm in man. *Journal of Clinical Endocrinology and Metabolism, 71*, 1056–1058. (6)

Murrell, J., Farlow, M., Ghetti, B., & Benson, M. D. (1991). A mutation in the amyloid precusor protein associated with hereditary Alzheimer's disease. *Science, 254*, 97–99. (12)

Nader, K., Schafe, G. E., & Le Doux, J. E. (2000). Fear memories require protein synthesis in the amygdala for reconsolidation after retrieval. *Nature, 406*, 722–726. (11)

Naeser, M. A., Alexander, M. P., Helm-Estabrooks, N., Levine, H. L., Laughlin, S. A., & Geschwind, N. (1982). Aphasia with predominantly subcortical lesion sites. *Archives of Neurology, 39,* 2–14. (8)

Nakahara, D., Ozaki, N., Miura, Y., Miura, H., & Nagatsu, T. (1989). Increased dopamine and serotonin metabolism in rat nucleus accumbens produced by intracranial self-stimulation of medial forebrain bundle as measured by in vivo microdialysis. *Brain Research, 495,* 178–181. (4)

Nakashima, T., Pierau, F. K., Simon, E., & Hori, T. (1987). Comparison between hypothalamic thermoresponsive neurons from duck and rat slices. *Pflugers Archive: European Journal of Physiology, 409,* 236–243. (5)

Naranjo, C. A., Poulos, C. X., Bremner, K. E., & Lanctot, K. L. (1994). Fluoxetine attenuates alcohol intake and desire to drink. *International Clinical Psychopharmacology, 9,* 163–172. (7)

National Foundation for Brain Research. (1992). *The cost of disorders of the brain.* Washington, DC: Author. (3)

National Institute of Mental Health. (1986). *Schizophrenia: Questions and answers.* (DHHS Publication No. ADM 86–1457). Washington, DC: U.S. Government Printing Office. (13)

National Institutes of Health. (1995). Cochlear implants in adults and children: NIH consensus development panel on cochlear implants in adults and children. *Journal of the American Medical Association, 274,* 1955–1961. (8)

Nauta, W. J. H., & Feirtag, M. (1979, March). The organization of the brain. *Scientific American,* 88–111. (App.)

Neave, N., Menaged, M., & Weightman, D. R. (1999). Sex differences in cognition: The role of testosterone and sexual orientation. *Brain and Cognition, 41,* 245–262. (6)

Nebes, R. D. (1974). Hemispheric specialization in commissurotomized man. *Psychological Bulletin, 81,* 1–14. (3)

Neisser, U., Boodoo, G., Bouchard, T. J., Jr., Boykin, A. W., Brody, N., Ceci, S. J., Halpern, D. F., Loehlin, J. C., Perloff, R., Sternberg, R. J., & Urbina, S. (1996). Intelligence: Knowns and unknowns. *American Psychologist, 51,* 77–101. (12)

Netter, F. H. (1983). *CIBA collection of medical illustrations: Vol. 1. Nervous system.* New York: CIBA. (6)

Neville, H. J., Bavelier, D., Corina, D., Rauschecker, J., Karni, A., Lalwani, A., Braun, A., Clark V., Jezzard. P., & Turner, R. (1998). Cerebral organization for language in deaf and hearing subjects: Biological constraints and effects of experience. *Proceedings of the National Academy of Sciences, USA, 95,* 922–929. (8)

Newhouse, P. A., Potter, A., Corwin, J., & Lenox, R. (1992). Acute nicotinic blockade produces cognitive impairment in normal humans. *Psycho–pharmacology, 108,* 480–484. (11)

Nicoll, R. A., & Madison, D. V. (1982). General anesthetics hyperpolarize neurons in the vertebrate central nervous system. *Science, 217,* 1055–1057. (2)

Nieuwenhuys, R., Voogd, J., & vanHuijzen, C. (1988). *The human central nervous system* (3rd rev. ed.). Berlin: Springer-Verlag. (5)

Noble, E. P. (1993). The D_2 dopamine receptor gene: A review of association studies in alcoholism. *Behavior Genetics, 23,* 119–129. (4)

Noble, E. P., Berman, S. M., Ozkaragoz, T. Z., & Ritchie, T. (1994). Prolonged P300 latency in children with the D_2 dopamine receptor A1 allele. *American Journal of Human Genetics, 54,* 658–668. (4)

Noble, E. P., Blum, K., Ritchie, T., Montgomery, A., & Sheridan, P. J. (1991). Allelic association of the D_2 dopamine receptor gene with receptor-binding characteristics in alcoholism. *Archives of General Psychiatry, 48,* 648–654. (4)

Normann, R. A., Maynard, E. M., Rousche, P. J., & Warren, D. J. (1999). A neural interface for a cortical vision prosthesis. *Vision Research, 39,* 2577–2587. (9)

Nottebohm, F. (1977). Asymmetries in neural control of vocalization in the canary. In S. Harnad, R. W. Doty, L. Goldstein, J. Jaynes, & G. Krauthamer, G. (Eds.). *Lateralization in the nervous system.* New York: Academic Press. (8)

Novin, D., VanderWeele, D. A., & Rezek, M. (1973). Infusion of 2-deoxy D-glucose into the hepatic portal system causes eating: Evidence for peripheral glucoreceptors. *Science, 181,* 858–860. (5)

Nulman, I., Rovet, J., Greenbaum, R., Loebstein, M., Wolpin, J., Pace-Asciak, P., & Koren, G. (2001). Neurodevelopment of adopted children exposed in utero to cocaine: The Toronto adoption study. *Clinical and Investigative Medicine, 24,* 129–137. (4)

O'Brien, C. P. (1997). A range of research-based pharmacotherapies for addiction. *Science, 278,* 66–70. (4)

O'Dell, T. J., Hawkins, R. D., Kandel, E. R., & Arancio, O. (1991). Tests of the roles of two diffusible substances in long-term potentiation: Evidence for nitric oxide as a possible early retrograde messenger. *Proceedings of the National Academy of Sciences, USA, 88,* 11285–11289. (11)

Ogden, J. (1989). Visuospatial and other "right-hemispheric" functions after long recovery periods in left-hemispherectomized subjects. *Neuropsychologia, 27,* 765–776. (3)

Ojemann, G. A. (1983). Brain organization for language from the perspective of electrical stimulation mapping. *Behavioral and Brain Sciences, 2,* 189–230. (8)

Oken, B. S., Storzbach, D. M., & Kaye, J. A. (1998). The efficacy of Ginkgo biloba on cognitive function in Alzheimer disease. *Archives of Neurology, 55,* 1409–1415. (11)

Okubo, Y., Suhara, T., Suzuki, K., Kobayashi, K., Inoue, O., Terasaki, O., Someya, Y., Sassa, T., Sudo, Y., Matsushima, E., Iyo, M., Tateno, Y., & Toru, M. (1997). Decreased prefrontal dopamine D1 receptors in schizophrenia revealed by PET. *Nature, 634,* 634. (13)

Olanow, C. W., & Tatton, W. G. (1999). Etiology and pathogenesis of Parkinson's disease. *Annual Review of Neuroscience, 22,* 123–144. (10)

Oliet, S. H. R., Piet, R., & Poulain, D. A. (2001). Control of glutamate clearance and synaptic efficacy by glial coverage of neurons. *Science, 292,* 923–925. (2)

Olson, B. R., Freilino, M., Hoffman, G. E., Stricker, E. M., Sved, A. F., & Verbalis, J. G. (1993). C-fos expression in rat brain and brainstem nuclei in response to treatments that alter food intake and gastric motility. *Molecular and Cellular Neuroscience, 4,* 93–106. (5)

Ong, W. Y., & Mackie, K. (1999). A light and electron microscopic study of the CB1 cannabinoid receptor in primate brain. *Neuroscience, 92,* 1177–1191. (4)

Orlans, F. B. (1993). *In the name of science.* New York: Oxford University Press. (1)

O'Rourke, D., Wurtman, J. J., Wurtman, R. J., Chebli, R., & Gleason, R. (1989). Treatment of seasonal depression with d-fenfluramine. *Journal of Clinical Psychiatry, 50,* 343–347. (13)

Paean to Nepenthe. (1961, November 24). *Time,* 68. (4)

Palmer, A. R. (1987). Physiology of the cochlear nerve and cochlear nucleus. In M. P. Haggard and E. F. Evans (Eds.), *Hearing* (pp. 838–855). Edinburgh: Churchill Livingstone. (8)

Pappone, P. A., & Cahalan, M. D. (1987). *Pandinus imperator* scorpion venom blocks voltage-gated potassium channels in nerve fibers. *Journal of Neuroscience, 7,* 3300–3305. (2)

Parent, J. M., Yu, T. W., Leibowitz, R. T., Geschwind, D. H., Sloviter, R. S., & Lowenstein, D. H. (1997). Dentate granule cell neurogenesis is increased by seizures and contributes to aberrant network reorganization in the adult rat hippocampus. *Journal of Neuroscience, 17,* 3727–3738. (3)

Parks, R. W., Becker, R. E., Rippey, R. F., Gilbert, D. G., Matthews, J. R., Kabatay, E., Young, C. S., Vohs, C., Danz, V., Keim, P., Collins, G. T., Zigler, S. S., & Urycki, P. G. (1996). Increased regional cerebral glucose metabolism and semantic memory performance in Alzheimer's disease: A pilot double blind transdermal nicotine positron emission tomography study. *Neuropsychology Review, 6*, 61–79. (11)

Parpura, V., & Haydon, P. G. (2000). Physiological astrocytic calcium levels stimulate glutamate release to modulate adjacent neurons. *Proceedings of the National Academy of Sciences, USA, 97*, 8629–8634. (2)

Pascual-Leone, A., & Torres, F. (1993). Plasticity of the sensorimotor cortex representation of the reading finger in Braille readers. *Brain, 116*, 39–52. (3)

Pascual-Leone, A., & Walsh, V. (2001). Fast backprojections from the motion to the primary visual area necessary for visual awareness. *Science, 292*, 510–512. (14)

Pasti, L., Volterra, A., Pozzan, T., & Carmignoto, G. (1997). Intracellular calcium oscillations in astrocytes: A highly plastic, bidirectional form of communication between neurons and astrocytes *in situ*. *Journal of Neuroscience, 17*, 7817–7830. (2)

Patel, A. M., Honoré, E., Lesage, F., Fink, M., Romey, G., & Lazdunski, M. (1999). Inhalational anesthetics activate two-pore-domain background K+ channels. *Nature Neuroscience, 2*, 422–426. (2)

Pauls, D. L., Towbin, K. E., Leckman, J. F., Zahner, G. E. P., & Cohen, D. J. (1986). Gilles de la Tourette's syndrome and obsessive-compulsive behavior: Evidence supporting a genetic relationship. *Archives of General Psychiatry, 43*, 1180–1182. (13)

Pavlidis, I., Eberhardt, N. L., & Levine, J. A. (2002). Seeing through the face of deception. *Nature, 415*, 35. (7)

Pearlson, G. D., Kim, W. S., Kubos, K. L., Moberg, P. J., Jayaram, G., Bascom, M. J., Chase, G. A., Goldfinger, A. D., & Tune, L. E. (1989). Ventricle-brain ratio, computed tomographic density, & brain area in 50 schizophrenics. *Archives of General Psychiatry, 46*, 690–697. (13)

Pellegrino, L. J., Pellegrino, A. S., & Cushman, A. J. (1979). *A stereotaxic atlas of the rat brain* (2nd ed.). New York: Plenum. (App.)

Penfield, W. (1955). The permanent record of the stream of consciousness. *Acta Psychologica, 11*, 47–69. (3)

Penfield, W. (1958). *The excitable cortex in conscious man.* Springfield, IL: Charles C. Thomas. (3)

Penfield, W., & Rasmussen, T. (1950). *The cerebral cortex of man.* New York: Macmillan. (3, 10)

Pennington, B. (2001). Genetics of learning disabilities. In E. A. Zillmer & M. V. Spiers, *Principles of neuropsychology*, pp. 262–263. Belmont, CA: Wadsworth/Thomson Learning. (8)

Pentel, P. R., Malin, D. H., Ennifar, S., Hieda, Y., Keyler, D. E., Lake, J. R., Milstein, J. R., Basham, L. E., Coy, R. T., Moon, J. W., Naso, R., & Fattom, A. (2000). A nicotine conjugate vaccine reduces nicotine distribution to brain and attenuates its behavioral and cardiovascular effects in rats. *Pharmacology, Biochemistry, and Behavior, 65*, 191–198. (4)

Pepperberg, I. M. (1993). Cognition and communication in an African Grey parrot (*Psittacus erithacus*): Studies on a nonhuman, nonprimate, nonmammalian subject. In H. L. Roitblat, L. M. Herman, & P. E. Nachtigall (Eds.), *Language and communication: Comparative perspectives* (pp. 221–248). Hillsdale, NJ: Lawrence Erlbaum. (8)

Perkins, A., & Fitzgerald, J. A. (1992). Luteinizing hormone, testosterone, and behavioral response of male-oriented rams to estrous ewes and rams. *Journal of Animal Science, 70*, 1787–1794. (6)

Perry, D. (2000). Patients' voices: The powerful sound in the stem cell debate. *Science, 287*, 1423. (1)

Pert, C. B., & Snyder, S. H. (1973). Opiate receptor: Demonstration in nervous tissue. *Science, 179*, 1011–1014. (4, 10)

Peters, M. L., Uyterlinde, S. A., Consemulder, J., & van der Hart, O. (1998). Apparent amnesia on experimental memory tests in dissociative identity disorder: An exploratory study. *Consciousness and Cognition, 7*, 27–41. (14)

Petersen, M. R., Beecher, M. D., Zoloth, S. R., Moody, D. B., & Stebbins, W. C. (1978). Neural lateralization of species-specific vocalizations by Japanese Macaques (*Macaca fuscata*). *Science, 202*, 324–326. (8)

Petersen, S. E., Fox, P. T., Snyder, A. Z., & Raichle, M. E. (1990). Activation of extrastriate and frontal cortical areas by visual words and word-like stimuli. *Science, 249*, 1041–1044. (8)

Petitto, L. A., Holowka, S., Sergio, L. E., & Ostry, D. (2001). Language rhythms in baby hand movements. *Nature, 413*, 35–36. (8)

Petitto, L. A., & Marentette, P. F. (1991). Babbling in the manual mode: Evidence for the ontogeny of language. *Science, 251*, 1493–1496. (8)

Pettinati, H. M., Volpicelli, J. R., Kranzler, H. R., Luck, G., Rukstalis, M. R., & Cnaan, A. (2000). Sertraline treatment for alcohol dependence: Interactive effects of medication and alcoholic subtype. *Alcoholism, Clinical, and Experimental Research, 24*, 1041–1049. (4)

Pfaff, D. W., & Sakuma, Y. (1979). Deficit in the lordosis reflex of female rats caused by lesions in the ventromedial nucleus of the hypothalamus. *Journal of Physiology, 288*, 203–210. (6)

Pfaus, J. G., Kleopoulos, S. P., Mobbs, C. V., Gibbs, R. B., & Pfaff, D. W. (1993). Sexual stimulation activates c-fos within estrogen-concentrating regions of the female rat forebrain. *Brain Research, 624*, 253–267. (6)

Phillips, R. J., & Powley, T. L. (1996). Gastric volume rather than nutrient content inhibits food intake. *American Journal of Physiology, 271*, R766–R779. (5)

Pianezza, M. L., Sellers, E. M., & Tyndale, R. F. (1998). Nicotine metabolism defect reduces smoking. *Nature, 393*, 750. (4)

Pihl, R. O., & Peterson, J. B. (1993). Alcohol, serotonin, and aggression. *Alcohol Health and Research World, 17*, 113–116. (4, 7)

Pihl, R. O., Peterson, J. B., & Lau, M. A. (1993). A biosocial model of the alcohol-aggression relationship. *Journal of Studies of Alcohol Supplement, 11*, 128–139. (7)

Pillard, R. C., & Bailey, J. M. (1998). Human sexual orientation has a heritable component. *Human Biology, 70*, 347–365. (6)

Pinker, S. (1994). *The language instinct.* New York: Morrow. (8, 12)

Pinker, S. (2001). Talk of genetics and vice versa. *Nature, 413*, 465–466. (8)

Pi-Sunyer, X., Kissileff, H. R., Thornton, J., & Smith, G. P. (1982). C terminal octapeptide of cholecystokinin decreases food intake in obese men. *Physiology and Behavior, 29*, 627–630. (5)

Plihal, W., & Born, J. (1997). Effects of early and late nocturnal sleep on declarative and procedural memory. *Journal of Cognitive Neuroscience, 9*, 534–547. (14)

Plomin, R. (1989). Environment and genes: Determinants of behavior. *American Psychologist, 44*, 105–111. (12)

Plomin, R. (1990). The role of inheritance in behavior. *Science, 248*, 183–188. (1, 12)

Plomin, R., & McClearn, G. E. (Eds.) (1993). *Nature, nurture, and psychology.* Washington, D.C.: American Psychological Association. (1)

Plomin, R., Owen, M. J., & McGuffin, P. (1994). The genetic basis of complex human behaviors. *Science, 264*, 1733–1739. (1)

Poggio, G. F., & Poggio, T. (1984). The analysis of stereopsis. *Annual Review of Neuroscience, 7*, 379–412. (9)

Polymeropoulos, M. H., Lavedan, C., Leroy, E., Ide, S. E., Dehejia, A., Dutra, A., Pike, B., Root, H., Rubenstein, J., Boyer, R., Stenroos, E. S., Chandrasekharappa, S., Athanassiadou, A., Papapetropoulos, T., Johnson, W. G., Lazzarini, A. M., Duvoisin, R. C., Di Iorio, G., Golbe, L. I., & Nussbaum, R. L. (1997). Mutation in the α-synuclein gene identified in families with Parkinson's disease. *Science, 276*, 2045–2047. (10)

Pontieri, F. E., Tanda, G., & Di Chiara, G. (1995). Intravenous cocaine, morphine, and amphetamine preferentially increase extracellular dopamine in the "shell" as compared with the "core" of the rat nucleus accumbens. *Proceedings of the National Academy of Sciences, USA, 92,* 12304–12308. (4)

Porter, R. H., & Moore, J. D. (1981). Human kin recognition by olfactory cues. *Physiology and Behavior, 27,* 493–495. (6)

Posey, D. J., & McDougle, C. J. (2001). Pharmacotherapeutic management of autism. *Expert Opinion on Pharmacotherapy, 2,* 587–600. (12)

Posthuma, D., de Geus, E. J., & Boomsma, D. I. (2001). Perceptual speed and IQ are associated through common genetic factors. *Behavior Genetics, 31,* 593–602. (12)

Preti, G., Cutler, W. B., Garcia, C. R., Huggins, G. R., & Lawley, H. J. (1986). Human axillary secretions influence women's menstrual cycles: The role of donor extract of females. *Hormones and Behavior, 20,* 474–482. (6)

Price, D. D. (2000). Psychological and neural mechanisms of the affective dimension of pain. *Science, 288,* 1769–1772. (7)

Price, J. (1968). The genetics of depressive behavior. *British Journal of Psychiatry,* Special Publication No. 2, 37–45. (13)

Price, R. A., Kidd, K. K., Cohen, D. J., Pauls, D. L., & Leckman, J. F. (1985). A twin study of Tourette syndrome. *Archives of General Psychiatry, 42,* 815–820. (13)

Proof? The joke was on Bischoff, but too late. (1942). *Scientific American, 166* (3), 145. (3)

Provencio, I., Rollag, M. D., & Castrucci, A. M. (2002). Photoreceptive net in the mammalian retina. *Nature, 415,* 493. (14)

Public Health Service. (1986). Policy on humane care and use of laboratory animals (Online). Available: http://grants.nih.gov/grants/olaw/references/phspol.htm. (1)

Putnam, F. W. (1991). Recent research on multiple personality disorder. *Psychiatric Clinics of North America, 14,* 489–502. (14)

Putnam, F. W., Zahn, T. P., & Post, R. M. (1990). Differential autonomic nervous system activity in multiple personality disorder. *Psychiatry Research, 31,* 251–260. (14)

Qin, Y.-L., McNaughton, B. L., Skaggs, W. E., & Barnes, C. A. (1997). Memory reprocessing in corticocortical and hippocampocortical neuronal ensembles. *Philosophical Transactions of the Royal Society of London, B, 352,* 1525–1533. (11)

Raboch, J., & Stárka, L. (1973). Reported coital activity of men and levels of plasma testosterone. *Archives of Sexual Behavior, 2,* 309–315. (6)

Ragsdale, D. S., McPhee, J. C., Scheuer, T., & Catterall, W. A. (1994). Molecular determinants of state-dependent block of Na$^+$ channels by local anesthetics. *Science, 265,* 1724–1728. (2)

Raichle, M. E. (1994, April). Visualizing the mind. *Scientific American,* 58–64. (App.)

Raine, A., Lencz, T., Bihrle, S., LaCasse, L., & Colletti, P. (2000). Reduced prefrontal gray matter volume and reduced autonomic activity in antisocial personality disorder. *Archives of General Psychiatry, 57,* 119–127. (7)

Raine, A., Meloy, J. R., Bihrle, S., Stoddard, J., LaCasse, L., & Buchsbaum, M. S. (1998). Reduced prefrontal and increased subcortical brain functioning assessed using positron emission tomography in predatory and affective murderers. *Behavioral Science and Law, 16,* 319–332. (7)

Raine, A., Stoddard, J., Bihrle, S., & Buchsbaum, M. (1998). Prefrontal glucose deficits in murderers lacking psychosocial deprivation. *Neuropsychiatry, Neuropsychology, and Behavioral Neurology, 11,* 1–7. (7)

Rainer, G. S., Rao, C., & Miller, E. K. (1999). Prospective coding for objects in primate prefrontal cortex. *Journal of Neuroscience, 19,* 5493–5505. (10)

Rainnie, D. G., Grunze, H. C., McCarley, R. W., & Greene, R. W. (1994). Adenosine inhibition of mesopontine cholinergic neurons: Implications for EEG arousal. *Science, 263,* 689–692. (14)

Rainville, P., Duncan, G. H., Price, D. D., Carrier, B., & Bushnell, M. C. (1997). Pain affect encoded in human anterior cingulate but not somatosensory cortex. *Science, 227,* 968–971. (7)

Ramachandran, V. S., & Blakeslee, S. (1998). *Phantoms in the brain.* New York: Morrow. (12)

Ramamurthi, B. (1988). Stereotactic operation in behaviour disorders. Amygdalotomy and hypothalamotomy. *Acta Neurochirurgica, Supplement, 44,* 152–157. (7)

Ramey, C. T., Campbell, F. A., Burchinal, M., Skinner, M. L., Gardner, D. M., & Ramey, S. L. (2000). Persistent effects of early childhood education on high-risk children and their mothers. *Applied Developmental Science, 4,* 2–14. (12)

Ramon y Cajal, S. (1928). *Degeneration and regeneration of the nervous system.* New York: Hafner. (3)

Ramón y Cajal, S. (1989). *Recollections of my life* (E. H. Craigie & J. Cano, Trans.). Cambridge, MA: MIT Press. (Original work published 1937) (2)

Rao, S. C., Rainer, G., & Miller, E. K. (1997). Integration of what and where in the primate prefrontal cortex. *Science, 276,* 821–824. (11)

Rapoport, J. L. (1991). Recent advances in obsessive-compulsive disorder. *Neuropsychopharmacology, 5,* 1–10. (13)

Räsänen, P., Hakko, H., Isohanni, M., Hodgins, S., & Järvelin, M.-R. (1999). Maternal smoking during pregnancy and risk of criminal behavior among adult male offspring in the northern Finland 1966 birth cohort. *American Journal of Psychiatry, 156,* 857–862. (7)

Rasmussen, T., & Milner, B. (1977). The role of early left-brain injury in determining lateralization of cerebral speech functions. *Annals of the New York Academy of Sciences, 299,* 355–369. (8)

Ratliff, F., & Hartline, H. K. (1959). The responses of Limulus optic nerve fibers to patterns of illumination on the receptor mosaic. *Journal of General Physiology, 42,* 1241–1255. (9)

Recht, L. D., Lew, R. A., & Schwartz, W. J. (1995). Baseball teams beaten by jet lag. *Nature, 377,* 583. (14)

Redelmeier, D. A., & Tibshirani, R. J. (1997). Association between cellular-telephone calls and motor vehicle collisions. *New England Journal of Medicine, 336,* 453–458. (14)

Reed, J. J., & Squire, L. R. (1998). Retrograde amnesia for facts and events: Findings from four new cases. *Journal of Neuroscience, 18,* 3943–3954. (11)

Reed, T. E. (1985). Ethnic differences in alcohol use, abuse, and sensitivity: A review with genetic interpretations: *Social Biology, 32,* 195–209. (4)

Reed, T. E., & Jensen, A. R. (1992). Conduction velocity in a brain nerve pathway of normal adults correlates with intelligence level. *Intelligence, 16,* 259–272. (12)

Reiman, E. M., Raichle, M. E., Robins, E., Butler, F. K., Herscovitch, P., Fox, P., & Perlmutter, J. (1986). The application of positron emission tomography to the study of panic disorder. *American Journal of Psychiatry, 143,* 469–477. (13)

Reinisch, J. M. (1981). Prenatal exposure to synthetic progestins increases potential for aggression in humans. *Science, 211,* 1171–1173. (6)

Reiss, A. L., & Freund, L. (1992). Behavioral phenotype of fragile X syndrome: DSM-III-R autistic behavior in male children. *American Journal of Medical Genetics, 43,* 35–46. (12)

Reiss, D., & Marino, L. (2001). Mirror self-recognition in the bottlenose dolphin: A case of cognitive convergence. *Proceedings of the National Academy of Sciences, USA, 98,* 5937–5942. (14)

Rekling, J. C., Funk, G. D., Bayliss, D. A., Dong, X.-W., & Feldman, J. L. (2000). Synaptic control of motoneuronal excitability. *Physiological Reviews, 80,* 767–852. (2)

Rempel-Clower, N. L. , Zola, S. M., Squire, L. R., & Amaral, D. G. (1996). Three cases of enduring memory impairment after bilateral damage limited to the hippocampal formation. *Journal of Neuroscience, 16,* 5233–5255. (11)

Ren, J., Tate, B. A., Sietsma, D., Marciniak, A., Snyder, E. Y., & Finklestein, S. P. (2000, November). Co-administration of neural stem cells and BFGF enhances functional recovery following focal cerebral infarction in rat. Poster session presented at the annual meeting of the Society for Neuroscience, New Orleans. (1)

Renault, B., Signoret, J.-L., Debruille, B., Breton, F., & Bolger, F. (1989). Brain potentials reveal covert facial recognition in prosopagnosia. *Neuropsychologia, 27,* 905–912. (9)

Resnick, S. M., Berenbaum, S. A., Gottesman, I. I., & Bouchard, T. J. (1986). Early hormonal influences on cognitive functioning in congenital adrenal hyperplasia. *Developmental Psychology, 22,* 191–198. (6)

Rice, G., Anderson, C., Risch, N., & Ebers, G. (1999). Male homosexuality: Absence of linkage to microsatellite markers at Xq28. *Science, 284,* 665–667. (6)

Riedel, G., Micheau, J., Lam, A. G. M., Roloff, E. v. L., Martin, S. J., Bridge, H., de Hoz, L., Poeschel, B., McCulloch, J., & Morris, R. G. M. (1999). Reversible neural inactivation reveals hippocampal participation in several memory processes. *Nature Neuroscience, 2,* 898–905. (11)

Riehle, A., & Requin, J. (1989). Monkey primary motor and premotor cortex: Single-cell activity related to prior information about direction and extent of an intended movement. *Journal of Neurophysiology, 61,* 534–549. (10)

Rikowski, A. & Grammar, K. (1999). Human body odour, symmetry, and attractiveness. *Proceedings of the Royal Society of London, B, 266,* 869–874. (6)

Rinaman, L., Hoffman G. E., Dohanics, J., Le, W. W., Stricker, E. M., & Verbalis, J. G. (1995). Cholecystokinin activates catecholaminergic neurons in the caudal medulla that innervate the paraventricular nucleus of the hypothalamus in rats. *Jounal of Comparative Neurology, 360,* 246–256. (5)

Risky Alzheimer's surgery could hold promise. (2002, January 25). CNN.com./HEALTH. (online) Available: http://www.cnn.com/2002/HEALTH/conditons/01/25/alzheimers.surgery/index.html. (11)

Ritter, R. C., Slusser, P. G., & Stone, S. (1981). Glucoreceptors controlling feeding and blood glucose: Location in the hindbrain. *Science, 213,* 451–453. (5)

Ritter, S., & Taylor, J. S. (1990). Vagal sensory neurons are required for lipoprivic but not glucoprivic feeding in rats. *American Journal of Physiology, 258,* R1395–R1401. (5)

Roberts, G. W. (1990). Schizophrenia: The cellular biology of a functional psychosis. *Trends in the Neurosciences, 13,* 207–211. (13)

Robins, L. N., Helzer, J. E., Weissman, M. M., Orvaschel, H., Gruenberg, E., Burke, J. D., & Regier, D. A. (1984). Lifetime prevalence of specific psychiatric disorders in three sites. *Archives of General Psychiatry, 41,* 949–958. (13)

Robinson, D. L., & Petersen, S. E. (1992). The pulvinar and visual salience. *Trends in Neuroscience, 15,* 127–132. (14)

Rodier, P. M., Ingram, J. L., Tisdale, B., Nelson, S., & Romano, J. (1996). Embryological origin for autism: Developmental anomalies of the cranial nerve motor nuclei. *Journal of Comparative Neurology, 370,* 247–261. (12)

Rodin, J., Schank, D., & Striegel-Moore, R. (1989). Psychological features of obesity. *Medical Clinics of North America, 73,* 47–66. (5)

Rodriguez, E., George, N., Lachaux, J.-P., Martinerie, J., Renault, B., & Varela, F. J. (1999). Perception's shadow: Long-distance synchronization of human brain activity. *Nature, 397,* 430–433. (14)

Roffwarg, H. P., Muzio, J. N., & Dement, W. C. (1966). Ontogenetic development of the human sleep-dream cycle. *Science, 152,* 604–619. (14)

Rogan, M. T., Stäubli, U. V., & LeDoux, J. E. (1997). AMPA receptor facilitation accelerates fear learning without altering the level of conditoned fear acquired. *Journal of Neuroscience, 17,* 5928–5935. (11)

Rogers, J., & Morrison, J. H. (1985). Quantitative morphology and regional and laminar distributions of senile plaques in Alzheimer's disease. *Journal of Neuroscience, 5,* 2801–2808. (11)

Rolls, B. J., Rolls, E. T., Rowe, E. A., & Sweeney, K. (1981). Sensory specific satiety in man. *Physiology and Behavior, 27,* 137–142. (5)

Rolls, B. J., Rowe, E. A., & Turner, R. C. (1980). Persistent obesity in rats following a period of consumption of a mixed, high energy diet. *Journal of Physiology, 298,* 415–427. (5)

Rolls, B. J., Wood, R. J., & Rolls, R. M. (1980). Thirst: The initiation, maintenance, and termination of drinking. In J. M. Sprague & A. N. Epstein (Eds.), *Progress in psychology and physiological psychology.* New York: Academic Press. (5)

Rose, J. E., Brugge, J. F., Anderson, D. J., & Hind, J. E. (1967). Phase-locked response to low-frequency tones in single auditory nerve fibers of the squirrel monkey. *Journal of Neurophysiology, 30,* 769–793. (8)

Rose, R. J. (1995). Genes and human behavior. *Annual Review of Psychology, 46,* 625–654. (1)

Rosenthal, N. E., Sack, D. A., Carpenter, C. J., Parry, B. L., Mendelson, W. B., & Wehr, T. A. (1985). Antidepressant effects of light in seasonal affective disorder. *American Journal of Psychiatry, 142,* 163–170. (13)

Rösler, A., & Witztum, E. (1998). Treatment of men with paraphilia with a long-acting analogue of gonadotropin-releasing hormone. *New England Journal of Medicine, 338,* 416–422. (6)

Ross, C. A., Miller, S. C., Reagor, P., Bjornson, L., Fraser, G. A., & Anderson, G. (1990). Structured interview data on 102 cases of multiple personality disorder from four centers. *American Journal of Psychiatry, 147,* 596–601. (14)

Ross, G. W., Abbott, R. D., Petrivotch, H., Morens, D. M., Grandinetti, A., Tung, K.-H., Tanner, C. M., Masaki, K. H., Blanchette, P. L., Curb, J. D., Popper, J. S., & White, L. R. (2000). Association of coffee and caffeine intake with the risk of Parkinson disease. *Journal of the American Medical Association, 283,* 2674–2679. (10)

Ross-Kossack, P., & Turkewitz, G. (1984). Relationship between changes in hemispheric advantage during familiarization to faces and proficiency in facial recognition. *Neuropsychologia, 22,* 471–477. (9)

Rowland, L. P. (2000a). Diseases of chemical transmission at the nerve-muscle synapse: Myasthenia gravis. In E. R. Kandel, J. H. Schwartz, & T. M. Jessell (Eds.), *Principles of neural science* (4th ed., pp. 298–309). New York: McGraw-Hill. (10)

Rowland, L. P. (2000b). Diseases of the motor unit. In E. R. Kandel, J. H. Schwartz, & T. M. Jessell (Eds.), *Principles of neural science* (4th ed., pp. 695–712). New York: McGraw-Hill. (10)

Rowland, L. P., Hoefer, P. F. A., & Aranow, H., Jr. (1960). Myasthenic syndromes. *Research Publications-Association for Research in Nervous and Mental Disease, 38,* 547–560. (10)

Roy, A., DeJong, J., & Linnoila, M. (1989). Cerebrospinal fluid monoamine metabolites and suicidal behavior in depressed patients: A 5-year follow-up study. *Archives of General Psychiatry, 46,* 609–612. (13)

Royce, J. M., Darlington, R. B., & Murray, H. W. (1983). Pooled analyses: Findings across studies. In Consortium for Longitudinal Studies. *As the twig is bent . . . Lasting effects of preschool programs.* Hillsdale, NJ: Erlbaum. (12)

Rozin, P. (1967). Specific aversions as a component of specific hungers. *Journal of Comparative and Physiological Psychology, 64,* 237–242. (5)

Rozin, P. (1969). Adaptive food sampling patterns in vitamin deficient rats. *Journal of Comparative and Physiological Psychology, 69,* 126–132. (5)

Rozin, P. (1976). The selection of foods by rats, humans, and other animals. *Advances in the Study of Behavior, 6,* 21–76. (5)

Rubens, A. B. (1977). Anatomical asymmetries of human cerebral cortex. In S. Harnad, R. W. Doty, L. Goldstein, J. Jaynes, & G. Krauthamer (Eds.), *Lateralization in the nervous system.* New York: Academic Press. (8)

Rumbaugh, D. M. (1990). Comparative psychology and the great apes: Their competence in learning, language, and numbers. *Psychological Record, 40,* 15–39. (8)

Rushton, J. P., Fulker, D. W., Nealle, M. C., Nias, D. K. B., & Eysenck, H. J. (1986). Altruism and aggression: The heritability of individual differences. *Journal of Personality and Social Psychology, 50,* 1192–1198. (6)

Rutter, M. (1983). Cognitive deficits in the pathogenesis of autism. *Journal of Child Psychology and Psychiatry, 24,* 513–531. (12)

Sack, D. A., Nurnberger, J., Rosenthal, N. E., Ashburn, E., & Wehr, T. A. (1985). Potentiation of antidepressant medications by phase advance of the sleep-wake cycle. *American Journal of Psychiatry, 142,* 606–608. (13)

Sackeim, H. A., Luber, B., Katzman, G. P., Moeller, J. R., Prudic, J., Devanand, D. P., & Nobler, M. S. (1996). The effects of electroconvulsive therapy on quantitative electroencephalograms: Relationship to clinical outcome. *Archives of General Psychiatry, 53,* 814–823. (13)

Sackeim, H. A., Prohovnik, I., Moeller, J. R., Brown, R. P., Apter, S., Prudic, J., Devanand, D. P., & Mukherjee, S. (1990). Regional cerebral blood flow in mood disorders: I. Comparison of major depressives and normal controls at rest. *Archives of General Psychiatry, 47,* 60–70. (13)

Sacks, O. & Wasserman, R. (1987, November 19). The case of the colorblind painter. *New York Review of Books,* 25–34. (9)

Sacks, O. (1990). *The man who mistook his wife for a hat and other clinical tales.* New York: HarperPerennial. (3, 9, 10, 12, 13, 14)

Sacks, O. (1995). *An anthropologist on Mars.* New York: Vintage Books. (12)

Sakata, H., Takaoka, Y., Kawarasaki, A., & Shibutani, H. (1973). Somatosensory properties of neurons in the superior parietal cortex (area 5) of the rhesus monkey. *Brain Research, 64,* 85–102. (10)

Sakimura, K., Kutsuwada, T., Ito, I., Manaabe, T., Takayama, C., Kushiya, E., Yagi, T., Aizawa, S., Inoue, Y., Sugiyama, H., et al. (1995). Reduced hippocampal LTP and spatial learning in mice lacking NMDA receptor epsilon 1 subunit. *Nature, 373,* 151–155. (10)

Salamy, J. (1970). Instrumental responding to internal cues associated with REM sleep. *Psychonomic Science, 18,* 342–343. (14)

Salib, E., & Hillier, V. (1997). A case-control study of smoking and Alzheimer's disease. *International Journal of Geriatric Psychiatry, 12,* 295–300. (11)

Salthouse, T. A., & Babcock, R. L. (1991). Decomposing adult age differences in working memory. *Developmental Psychology, 27,* 763–776. (12)

Saper, C. B., Chou, T. C., & Scammell, T. E. (2001). The sleep switch: Hypothalamic control of sleep and wakefulness. *Trends in Neurosciences, 24,* 726–731. (14)

Saper, C. B., Iverson, S., & Frackowiak, R. (2000). Integration of sensory and motor function, In E. R. Kandel, J. H. Schwartz, & T. M. Jessell (Eds.), *Principles of neural science* (4th ed., pp. 349–380). New York: McGraw-Hill. (10)

Sapolsky, R. M., Uno, H., Rebert, C. S., & Finch, C. E. (1990). Hippocampal damage associated with prolonged glucocorticoid exposure in primates. *Journal of Neuroscience, 10,* 2897–2902. (7)

Sáry, G., Vogels, R., & Orban, G. A. (1993). Cue-invariant shape selectivity of macaque inferior temporal neurons. *Science, 260,* 995–997. (9)

Sasaki, M., Honmou, O., Akiyama, Y., Uede, T., Hashi, K., & Kocsis, J. D. (2000, November). Neuronal differentiation and functional synapse formation of adult human neural stem cell *in vitro.* Poster session presented at the annual meeting of the Society for Neuroscience, New Orleans. (1)

Sato, M. (1986). Acute exacerbation of methamphetamine psychosis and lasting dopaminergic supersensitivity-A clinical survey. *Psychopharmacology Bulletin, 22,* 751–756. (4)

Savage-Rumbaugh, E. S., Murphy, J., Sevcik, R. A., Brakke, K. E., Williams, S. L., & Rumbaugh, D. M. (1993). Language comprehension in ape and child. *Monographs of the Society for Research in Child Development, 58,* 1–222. (8)

Savage-Rumbaugh, S. (1987). A new look at ape language: Comprehension of vocal speech and syntax. *Nebraska Symposium on Motivation, 35,* 201–255. (8)

Savage-Rumbaugh, S., McDonald, K., Sevcik, R. A., Hopkins, W. D., & Rubert, E. (1986). Spontaneous symbol acquisition and communicative use by pygmy chimpanzees *(Pan paniscus). Journal of Experimental Psychology: General, 115,* 211–235. (8)

Savin-Williams, R. C. (1996). Self-labeling and disclosure among gay, lesbian, and bisexual youths. In J. Laird and R.-J. Green (Eds.), *Lesbians and gays in couples and families: A handbook for therapists.* San Francisco: Jossey-Bass. (6)

Sawa, A., & Snyder, S. H. (2002). Schizophrenia: Diverse approaches to a complex disease. *Science, 296,* 692–695. (13)

Scarr, S., & Carter-Saltzman, L. (1982). Genetics and intelligence. In R. J. Sternberg (Ed.), *Handbook of human intelligence* (pp. 792–896). New York: Cambridge University Press. (12)

Scarr, S., Pakstis, A. J., Katz, S. H., & Barker, W. B. (1977). Absence of a relationship between degree of white ancestry and intellectual skills within a black population. *Human Genetics, 39,* 69–86. (12)

Scarr, S., & Weinberg, R. A. (1976). IQ test performance of black children adopted by white families. *American Psychologist, 31,* 726–739. (12)

Schaal, B., & Porter, R. H. (1991). "Microsmatic humans" revisited: The generation and perception of chemical signals. *Advances in the Study of Behavior, 20,* 135–199. (6)

Schachter, S., & Singer, J. E. (1962). Cognitive, social, and physiological determinants of emotional state. *Psychological Review, 69,* 379–399. (7)

Schacter, D. L., Alpert, N. M., Savage, C. R., Rauch, S. L., & Albert, M. S. (1996). Conscious recollection and the human hippocampal formation: Evidence from positron emission tomography. *Proceedings of the National Academy of Sciences, USA, 93,* 321–325. (11)

Schacter, D. L., Norman, K. A., & Koutstaal, W. (1998). The cognitive neuroscience of constructive memory. *Annual Review of Psychology, 49,* 289–318. (11)

Schacter, D. L., & Wagner, A. D. (1999). Remembrance of things past. *Science, 285,* 1503–1504. (11)

Schaie, K. W. (1994). The course of adult intellectual development. *American Psychologist, 49,* 304–311. (11, 12)

Scheich, H., & Zuschratter, W. (1995). Mapping of stimulus features and meaning in gerbil auditory cortex with 2-deoxyglucose and c-fos antibodies. *Behavioural Brain Research, 66,* 195–205. (8)

Schein, S. J., & Desimone, R. (1990). Spectral properties of V4 neurons in the macaque. *Journal of Neuroscience, 10,* 3369–3389. (9)

Schelling, T. C. (1992). Addictive drugs: The cigarette experience. *Science, 255,* 430–433. (4)

Schenck, C. H., Milner, D. M., Hurwitz, T. D., Bundlie, S. R., & Mahowald, M. W. (1989). A polysomnographic and clinical report on sleep-related injury in 100 adult patients. *American Journal of Psychiatry, 146,* 1166–1173. (14)

Schiemeier, Q. (1998). Animal rights activists turn the screw. *Nature, 396,* 505. (1)

Schildkraut, J. J. (1965). The catecholamine hypothesis of affective disorders: A review of supporting evidence. *American Journal of Psychiatry, 122,* 509–522. (13)

Schiller, P. H., & Logothetis, N. K. (1990). The color-opponent and broadband channels of the primate visual system. *Trends in Neurosciences, 13,* 392–398. (9)

Schmalz, J. (1993, March 5). Poll finds an even split on homosexuality's cause. *New York Times,* A-14. (6)

Schmidt, P. J., Nieman, L. K., Danaceau, M. A., Adams, L. F., & Rubinow, D. R. (1998). Differential behavioral effects of gonadal steroids in women with and in those without premenstrual syndrome. *New England Journal of Medicine, 338,* 209–216. (7)

Schnider, A., & Ptak, R. (1999). Spontaneous confabulators fail to suppress currently irrelevant memory traces. *Nature Neuroscience, 2*, 677–681. (11, 14)

Schou, M. (1959). Lithium in psychiatric therapy: Stock-taking after ten years. *Psychopharmacologia, 1*, 65–78. (13)

Schuckit, M. A. (1994). Low level of response to alcohol as a predictor of future alcoholism. *American Journal of Psychiatry, 151*, 184–189. (4)

Schull, W. J., Norton, S., & Jensh, R. P. (1990). Ionizing radiation and the developing brain. *Neurotoxicology and Teratology, 12*, 249–260. (3)

Schulsinger, F., Parnas, J., Petersen, E. T., Schulsinger, H., Teasdale, T. W., Mednick S. A., Møller, L., & Silverton, L. (1984). Cerebral ventricular size in the offspring of schizophrenic mothers. *Archives of General Psychiatry, 41*, 602–606. (13)

Schulz, S. C., Koller, M. M., Kishore, P. R., Hamer, R. M., Gehl, J. J., & Friedel, R. O. (1983). Ventricular enlargement in teenage patients with schizophrenia spectrum disorder. *American Journal of Psychiatry, 140*, 1592–1595. (13)

Schuman, E. M., & Madison, D. V. (1991). A requirement for the intercellular messenger nitric oxide in long-term potentiation. *Science, 254*, 1503–1506. (11)

Schwartz, A. S., & Marchok, P. L. (1974). Depression of morphine-seeking behaviour by dopamine inhibition. *Nature, 246*, 257–258. (4)

Schwartz, J. M., Stoessel, P. W., Baxter, L. R., Martin, K. M., & Phelps, M. E. (1996). Systematic changes in cerebral glucose metabolic rate after successful behavior modification treatment of obsessive-compulsive disorder. *Archives of General Psychiatry, 53*, 109–113. (13)

Schwartz, M. S. (1994). Ictal language shift in a polyglot. *Journal of Neurology, Neurosurgery, and Psychiatry, 57*, 121. (8)

Schwartz, M. W., & Seeley, R. J. (1997). The new biology of body weight regulation. *Journal of the American Dietetic Association, 97*, 54–58. (5)

Schwartz, W. J., & Gainer, H. D. (1977). Suprachiasmatic nucleus: Use of ¹⁴C-labeled deoxyglucose uptake as a functional marker. *Science, 197*, 1089–1091. (14)

Scott, E. M., & Verney, E. L. (1947). Self selection of diet. VI. The nature of appetites for B vitamins. *Journal of Nutrition, 34*, 471–480. (5)

Scott, K. G., & Carran, D. T. (1987). The epidemiology and prevention of mental retardation. *American Psychologist, 42*, 801–804. (12)

Scott, L., Kruse, M. S., Forssberg, H., Brismar, H., Greengard, P., & Aperia, A. (2002). Selective up-regulation of dopamine D1 receptors in dendritic spines by NMDA receptor activation. *Proceedings of the National Academy of Sciences, USA, 99*, 1661–1664. (13)

Sedaris, D. (1998). *Naked*. Boston: Little, Brown. (13)

Seeman, P., Lee, T., Chau-Wong, M., & Wong, K. (1976). Antipsychotic drug doses and neuroleptic/dopamine receptors. *Nature, 261*, 717–719. (13)

Sejnowski, T. J. (1977). Statistical constraints on synaptic plasticity. *Journal of Theoretical Biology, 69*, 385–389. (11)

Sejnowski, T. J., & Rosenberg, C. R. (1987). Parallel networks that learn to pronounce English text. *Complex Systems, 1*, 145–168. (2)

Selfe, L. (1977). *Nadia: A case of extraordinary drawing ability in children*. London: Academic Press. (12)

Selkoe, D. J. (1997). Alzheimer's disease: Genotypes, phenotype, and treatments. *Science, 275*, 630–631. (11)

Shaffery, J. P., Roffwarg, H. P., Speciale, S. G., & Marks, G. A. (1999). Ponto-geniculo-occipital-wave suppression amplifies lateral geniculate nucleus cell-size changes in monocularly deprived kittens. *Brain Research. Developmental Brain Research, 114*, 109–119. (14)

Shah, A., & Lisak, R. P. (1993). Immunopharmacologic therapy in myasthenia gravis. *Clinical Neuropharmacology, 16*, 97–103. (10)

Shallice, T. (1999). The origin of confabulations. *Nature Neuroscience, 2*, 588–590. (14)

Sham, P. C., O'Callaghan, E. , Takei, N., Murray, G. K., Hare, E. H., & Murray, R. M. (1992). Schizophrenia following pre-natal exposure to influenza epidemics between 1939 and 1960. *British Journal of Psychiatry, 160*, 461–466. (13)

Shapiro, C. M., Bortz, R., Mitchell, D., Bartel, P., & Jooste, P. (1981). Slow-wave sleep: A recovery period after exercise. *Science, 214*, 1253–1254. (14)

Shaywitz, S. E., Shaywitz, B. A., Pugh, K. R., Fulbright, R. K., Constable, R. T., Mencl, W. E., Shankweiler, D. P., Liberman, A. M., Skudlarski, P., Fletcher, J. M., Katz, L., Marchione, K. E., Lacadie, C., Gatenby, C., & Gore, J. C. (1998). Functional disruption in the organization of the brain for reading in dyslexia. *Proceedings of the National Academy of Sciences, USA, 95*, 2636–2641. (8)

Shearman, L. P., Sriram, S., Weaver, D. R., Maywood, E. S., Chaves, I., Zheng, B., Kume, K., Lee, C. C., van der Horst, G. T. J., Hastings, M. H., & Reppert, S. M. (2000). Interacting molecular loops in the mammalian circadian clock. *Science, 288*, 1013–1019. (14)

Sherin, J. E., Shiromani, P. J., McCarley, R. W., & Saper, C. B. (1996). Activation of ventrolateral preoptic neurons during sleep. *Science, 271*, 216–219. (14)

Sherwin, B. B., & Gelfand, M. M. (1987). The role of androgen in the maintenance of sexual functioning in oophorectomized women. *Psychosomatic Medicine, 49*, 397–409. (6)

Shi, S.-H., Hayashi, Y., Petralia, R. S., Zaman, S. H., Wenthold, R. J., Svoboda, K., & Malinow, R. (1999). Rapid spine delivery and redistribution of AMPA receptors after synaptic NMDA receptor activation. *Science, 284*, 1811–1816. (11)

Shifren, J. L., Braunstein, G. D., Simon, J. A., Casson, P. R., Buster, J. E., Redmond, G. P., Burki, R. E., Ginsburg, E. S., Rosen, R. C., Leiblum, S. R., Caramelli, K. E., & Mazer, N. A. (2000). Transdermal testosterone treatment in women with impaired sexual function after oophorectomy. *New England Journal of Medicine, 343*, 682–688. (6)

Shima, K., & Tanji, J. (2000). Neuronal activity in the supplementary and presupplementary motor areas for temporal organization of multiple movements. *Journal of Neurophysiology, 84*, 2148–2160. (10)

Shimamura, A., Berry, J. M., Mangels, J. A., Rusting, C. L., & Jurica, P. J. (1995). Memory and cognitive abilities in university professors: Evidence for successful aging. *Psychological Science, 6*, 271. (11)

Shimura, H., Schlossmacher, M. G., Hattori, N., Frosch, M. P., Trockenbacher, A., Schneider, R., Mizuno, Y., Kosik, K. S., & Selkoe, D. J. (2001). Ubiquitination of a new form of α-synuclein by parkin from human brain: Implications for Parkinson's disease. *Science, 293*, 263–269. (10)

Shimura, T., & Shimokochi, M. (1990). Involvement of the lateral mesencephalic tegmentum in copulatory behavior of male rats: Neuron activity in freely moving animals. *Neuroscience Research, 9*, 173–183. (6)

Shouse, M. N., & Siegel, J. M. (1992). Pontine regulation of REM sleep components in cats: Integrity of the pedunculopontine tegmentum (PPT) is important for phasic events but unnnecessary for atonia during REM sleep. *Brain Research, 571*, 50–63. (14)

Shreeve, J. (1993, June). Touching the phantom. *Discover*, 35–42. (14)

Siegel, A., Roeling, T. A., Gregg, T. R., & Kruk, M. R. (1999). Neuropharmacology of brain-stimulation-evoked aggression. *Neuroscience and Biobehavior Review, 23*, 359–389. (7)

Siegel, J. M. (2001). The REM sleep-memory consolidation hypothesis. *Science, 294*, 1058–1063. (14)

Siegel, S. (1984). Pavlovian conditioning and heroin overdose: Reports by overdose victims. *Bulletin of the Psychonomic Society, 22*, 428–430. (4)

Siegel, S., Hinson, R. E., Krank, M. D., & McCully, J. (1982). Heroin "overdose" death: Contribution of drug-associated environmental cues. *Science, 216,* 436–437. (4)

Siever, L. J., Kahn, R. S., Lawlor, B. A., Trestman, R. L., Lawrence, T. L., & Coccaro, E. F. (1991). II. Critical issues in defining the role of serotonin in psychiatric disorders. *Pharmacological Reviews, 43,* 509–525. (13)

Silbersweig, D. A., Stern, E., Frith, C., Cahill, C., Homes, A., Grootoonk, S., Seawrd, J., McKenna, P., Chua, S. E., Schnorr, L., Jones, T., & Frackowiak, R. S. J. (1995). A functional neuroanatomy of hallucinations in schizophrenia. *Nature, 378,* 176–179. (13)

Silicon chips implanted into the eyes of three patients to treat blindness. (2001, July 30). (Online). Available: http://www.optobionics.com/010730pressrelease.htm. (9)

Silinsky, E. M. (1989). Adenosine derivatives and neuronal function. *Seminars in the Neurosciences, 1,* 155–165. (4)

Simpson, J. B., Epstein, A. N., & Camardo, J. S., Jr. (1978). Localization of receptors for the dipsogenic action of angiotensin II in the subfornical organ of rat. *Journal of Comparative and Physiological Psychology, 92,* 581–601. (5)

Sinclair, D. (1981). *Mechanisms of cutaneous sensation.* Oxford, England: Oxford University Press. (10)

Singer, W. (1995). Development and plasticity of cortical processing architectures. *Science, 270,* 758–764. (3)

Singh, M., Meyer, E. M., Millard, W. J., & Simpkins, J. W. (1994). Ovarian steroid deprivation results in a reversible learning impairment and compromised cholinergic function in female Sprague-Dawley rats. *Brain Research, 644,* 305–312. (11)

Singh, V. K., Lin, S. X., & Yang, V. C. (1998). Serological association of measles virus and human herpesvirus-6 with brain autoantibodies in autism. *Clinical Immunology and Immunopathology, 89,* 105–108. (12)

Sirevaag, A. M., & Greenough, W. T. (1987). Differential rearing effects on rat visual cortex synapses. III. Neuronal and glial nuclei, boutons, dendrites, and capillaries. *Brain Research, 424,* 320–332. (11)

Sizemore, C. C. (1989). *A mind of my own.* New York: William Morrow. (14)

Skaggs, W. E., & McNaughton, B. L. (1996). Replay of neuronal firing sequences in rat hippocampus during sleep following spatial experience. *Science, 271,* 1870–1873. (11, 14)

Skilling, S. R., Smullin, D. H., Beitz, A. J., & Larson, A. A. (1988). Extracellular amino acid concentrations in the dorsal spinal cord of freely moving rats following veratridine and nociceptive stimulation. *Journal of Neurochemistry, 51,* 127–132. (10)

Slimp, J. C., Hart, B. L., & Goy, R. W. (1978). Heterosexual, autosexual and social behavior of adult male rhesus monkeys with medial preoptic-anterior hypothalamic lesions. *Brain Research, 142,* 105–122. (6)

Slooter, A. J., Bronzova, J., Witteman, J. C., Van Broeckhoven, C., Hofman, A., & van Duijn, C. M. (1999). Estrogen use and early onset Alzheimer's disease: A population-based study. *Journal of Neurological and Neurosurgical Psychiatry, 67,* 779–781. (11)

Smaglik, P. (2000). Clinical trials end at gene-therapy institute. *Science, 405,* 497. (1)

Small, S. A., Stern, Y., Tang, M., & Mayeux, R. (1999). Selective decline in memory function among healthy elderly. *Neurology, 52,* 1392–1396. (11)

Smith, C. (1995). Sleep states and memory processes. *Behavioural Brain Research, 69,* 137–145. (14)

Smith, C. (1996). Sleep states, memory processes and synaptic plasticity. *Behavioural Brain Research, 78,* 49–56. (14)

Smith, C., & Lloyd, B. (1978). Maternal behavior and perceived sex of infant: Revisited. *Child Development, 49,* 1263–1265. (6)

Smith, C. A. D., Gough, A. C., Leigh, P. N., Summers, B. A., Harding, A. E., Maranganore, D. M., Sturman, S. G., Schapira, A. H. V., Williams, A. C., Spurr, N. K., & Wolf, C. R. (1992). Debrisoquine hydroxylase gene polymorphism and susceptibility to Parkinson's disease. *Lancet, 339,* 1375–1377. (10)

Smith, D. E., Roberts, J., Gage, F. H., & Tuszynski, M. H. (1999). Age-associated neuronal atrophy occurs in the primate brain and is reversible by growth factor gene therapy. *Proceedings of the National Academy of Sciences, USA, 96,* 10893–10898. (11)

Smith, G. P., Jerome, C., & Norgren, R. (1985). Afferent axons in abdominal vagus mediate satiety effect of cholecystokinin in rats. *American Journal of Physiology, 249,* R638–R641. (5)

Smith, G. S., Dewey, S. L., Brodie, J. D., Logan, J., Vitkun, S. A., Simkowitz, P., Schloesser, R., Alexoff, D. A., Hurley, A., Cooper, T., & Volkow, N. D. (1997). Serotonergic modulation of dopamine measured with [11C]raclopride and PET in normal human subjects. *American Journal of Psychiatry, 154,* 490–496. (13)

Smith, M. A., Brandt, J., & Shadmehr, R. (2000). Motor disorder in Huntington's disease begins as a dysfunction in error feedback control. *Nature, 403,* 544–549. (10)

Smith, S. S., O'Hara, B. F., Persico, A. M., Gorelick, D. A., Newlin, D. B., Vlahov, D., Solomon, L., Pickens, R., & Uhl, G. R. (1992). Genetic vulnerability to drug abuse: The D_2 dopamine receptor *Taq* I B1 restriction fragment length polymorphism appears more frequently in polysubstance abusers. *Archives of General Psychiatry, 49,* 723–727. (4)

Smythies, J. (1997). The functional neuroanatomy of awareness: With a focus on the role of various anatomical systems in the control of intermodal attention. *Consciousness and Cognition, 6,* 455–481. (14)

Snyder, A. W., & Mitchell, D. J. (1999). Is integer arithmetic fundamental to mental processing? The mind's secret arithmetic. *Proceedings of the Royal Society of London B, 266,* 587–592. (12)

Snyder, S. H. (1972). Catecholamines in the brain as mediators of amphetamine psychosis. *Archives of General Psychiatry, 27,* 169–179. (4)

Snyder, S. H. (1984). Drug and neurotransmitter receptors in the brain. *Science, 224,* 22–31. (2)

Snyder, S. H. (1997). Knockouts anxious for new therapy. *Nature, 388,* 624. (4)

Snyder, S. H., Banerjee, S. P., Yamamura, H. I., & Greenberg, D. (1974). Drugs, neurotransmitters, and schizophrenia. *Science, 184,* 1243–1253. (13)

Society for Neuroscience. (1998). Responsible conduct regarding scientific communication (Online). Available: http://www.sfn.org/guidelines. (1)

Soto-Otero, R., Méndez-Alvarez, E., Sánchez-Sellero, J., Cruz-Landeira, A., & López-Rivadulla, L. M. (2001). Reduction of rat brain levels of the endogenous dopaminergic proneurotoxins 1,2,3,4-tetrahydroisoquinoline and 1,2,3,4-tetrahydro-beta-carboline by cigarette smoke. *Neuroscience Letters, 298,* 187–190. (10)

Sowell, E. R., Thompson, P. M., Holmes, C. J., Jernigan, T. L., & Toga, A. W. (1999). *In vivo* evidence for post-adolescent brain maturation in frontal and striatal regions. *Nature Neuroscience, 2,* 859–861. (3)

Spanos, N. P. (1994). Multiple identity enactments and multiple personality disorder: A sociocognitive perspective. *Psychological Bulletin, 116,* 143–165. (14)

Spence, S., Shapiro, D., & Zaidel, E. (1996). The role of the right hemisphere in the physiological and cognitive components of emotional processing. *Psychophysiology, 33,* 112–122. (7)

Sperry, R. W. (1943). Effect of 180 degrees rotation of the retinal field on visuomotor coordination. *Journal of Experimental Zoology, 92,* 263–279. (3)

Sperry, R. W. (1945). Restoration of vision after crossing of optic nerves and after contralateral transplantation of eye. *Journal of Neurophysiology, 8,* 15–28. (3)

Spiegel, D. (1996). Cancer and depression. *British Journal of Psychiatry, 168,* 109–116. (7)

Spiegel, D., Sephton, S. E., Terr, A. I., & Stites, D. P. (1998). Effects of psychosocial treatment in prolonging cancer survival may be mediated by neuroimmune pathways. *Annals of the New York Academy of Sciences, 840,* 674–683. (7)

Spillantini, M. G., Schmidt, M. L., Lee, V. M.-Y., Trojanowski, J. Q., Jakes, R., & Goedert, M. (1997). α-Synuclein in Lewy bodies. *Nature, 388,* 839–840. (10)

Spoont, M. (1992). Modulatory role of serotonin in neural information processing: Implications for human psychopathology. *Psychological Bulletin, 112,* 330–350. (7)

Springer, S. P., and Deutsch, G. (1998). *Left brain, right brain.* New York: Freeman. (9)

Spurzheim, J. G. (1908). *Phrenology* (rev. ed.). Philadelphia: Lippincott. (3)

Squire, L. R., Amaral, D. G., & Press, G. A. (1990). Magnetic resonance imaging of the hippocampal formation and mammillary nuclei distinguish medial temporal lobe and diencephalic amnesia. *Journal of Neuroscience, 10,* 3106–3117. (11)

Squire, L. R., Amaral, D. G., Zola-Morgan, S., Kritchevsky, M., & Press, G. (1989). Description of brain injury in the amnesic patient N.A. based on magnetic resonance imaging. *Experimental Neurology, 105,* 23–35. (11)

Squire, L. R., Ojemann, J. G., Miezin, F. M., Petersen, S. E., Videen, T. O., & Raichle, M. E. (1992). Activation of the hippocampus in normal humans: A functional anatomical study of memory. *Proceedings of the National Academy of Sciences, USA, 89,* 1837–1841. (11)

Stanley, B. G., Kyrkouli, S. E., Lampert, S., & Leibowitz, S. F. (1986). Neuropeptide Y chronically injected into the hypothalamus: A powerful neurochemical inducer of hyperphagia and obesity. *Peptides, 7,* 1189–1192. (5)

Stanley, M., Stanley, B., Traskman-Bendz, L, Mann, J. J., & Meyendorff, E. (1986). Neurochemical findings in suicide completers and suicide attempters. *Suicide and Life-Threatening Behavior, 16,* 286–299. (13)

Stein, E., & Tessier-Levigne, M. (2001). Hierarchical organization of guidance receptors: Silencing of netrin attraction by slit through a robo/DCC receptor complex. *Science, 291,* 1928–1938. (3)

Stein, J. (2001). The magnocellular theory of developmental dyslexia. *Dyslexia, 7,* 12–36. (8)

Stellar, J. R., & Stellar, E. (1985). *The neurobiology of motivation and reward.* New York: Springer-Verlag. (5)

Stephan, F. K., & Nunez, A. A. (1977). Elimination of circadian rhythms in drinking, activity, sleep, and temperature by isolation of the suprachiasmatic nuclei. *Behavioral Biology, 20,* 1–16. (14)

Steriade, M., Paré, D., Bouhassira, D., Deschênes, M., & Oakson, G. (1989). Phasic activation of lateral geniculate and perigeniculate thalamic neurons during sleep with ponto-geniculo-occipital waves. *Journal of Neuroscience, 9,* 2215–2229. (14)

Stern, K., & McClintock, M. K. (1998). Regulation of ovulation by human pheromones. *Nature, 392,* 177–179. (6)

Sternbach, R. A. (1968). *Pain: A psychophysiological analysis.* New York: Academic Press. (7)

Sternberg, R. J. (1988). *The triarchic mind: A new theory of human intelligence.* New York: Viking. (12)

Sternberg, R. J. (2000). The holey grail of general intelligence. *Science, 289,* 399–401. (12)

Stickgold, R., Hobson, J. A., Fosse, R., & Fosse, M. (2001). Sleep, learning, and dreams: Off-line memory reprocessing. *Science, 294,* 1052–1057. (11, 14)

Stickgold, R., James, L., & Hobson, J. A. (2000). Visual discrimination learning requires sleep after training. *Nature Neuroscience, 3,* 1237–1238. (11)

Stickgold, R., Whidbee, D., Schirmer, B., Patel, V., & Hobson, J. A. (2000). Visual discrimination task improvement: A multi-step process occurring during sleep. *Journal of Cognitive Neuroscience, 12,* 246–254. (14)

Strack, F., Martin, L. L., & Stepper, S. (1988). Inhibiting and facilitating conditions of the human smile: A nonobtrusive test of the facial feedback hypothesis. *Journal of Personality and Social Psychology, 54,* 768–777. (7)

Streissguth, A. P., Barr, H. M., Bookstein, F. L., Sampson, P. D., & Olson, H. C. (1999). The long-term neurocognitive consequences of prenatal alcohol exposure: A 14-year study. *Psychological Science, 10,* 186–190. (4)

Stricanne, B., Andersen, R. A., & Mazzoni, P. (1996). Eye-centered, head-centered, and intermediate coding of remembered sound locations in area LIP. *Journal of Neurophysiology, 76,* 2071–2076. (10)

Strömland, K., Nordin, V., Miller, M., Åkerström, B., & Gillberg, C. (1994). Autism in thalidomide embryopathy: A population study. *Developmental Medicine and Child Neurology, 36,* 351–356. (12)

Suddath, R. L., Casanova, M. F., Goldberg, T. E., Daniel, D. G., Kelsoe, J. R., & Weinberger, D. R. (1989). Temporal lobe pathology in schizophrenia: A quantitative magnetic resonance imaging study. *American Journal of Psychiatry, 146,* 464–472. (13)

Suddath, R. L., Christison, G. W., Torrey, E. F., Casanova, M. F., & Weinberger, D. R. (1990). Anatomical abnormalities in the brains of monozygotic twins discordant for schizophrenia. *New England Journal of Medicine, 322,* 789–794. (13)

Sullivan, P. F. (1995). Mortality in anorexia nervosa. *American Journal of Psychiatry, 152,* 1073–1074. (5)

Sulser, F., & Sanders-Bush, E. (1989). From neurochemical to molecular pharmacology of antidepressants. In E. Costa (Ed.), *Neurochemical pharmacology—A tribute to B. B. Brodie.* New York: Raven Press. (13)

Sulzer, D., & Rayport, S. (2000). Dale's principle and glutamate corelease from ventral midbrain dopamine neurons. *Amino Acids, 19,* 45–52. (2)

Suzdak, P. D., Glowa, J. R., Crawley, J. N., Schwartz, R. D., Skolnick, P., & Paul, S. M. (1986). A selective imidazobenzodiazepine antagonist of ethanol in the rat. *Science, 234,* 1243–1247. (4)

Svensson, T. H., Grenhoff, J., & Aston-Jones, G. (1986). Midbrain dopamine neurons: Nicotinic control of firing pattern. *Society for Neuroscience Abstracts, 12,* 1154. (4)

Swaab, D. F. (1996). Desirable biology. *Science, 382,* 682–683. (6)

Swaab, D. F., & Fliers, E. (1985). A sexually dimorphic nucleus in the human brain. *Science, 228,* 1112–1115. (6)

Swaab, D. F., & Hofman, M. A. (1990). An enlarged suprachiasmatic nucleus in homosexual men. *Brain Research, 537,* 141–148. (6)

Swaab, D. F., Slob, A. K., Houtsmuller, E. J., Brand, T., & Zhou, J. N. (1995). Increased number of vasopressin neurons in the suprachiasmatic nucleus (SCN) of 'bisexual' adult male rats following perinatal treatment with the aromatase blocker ATD. *Developmental Brain Research, 85,* 273–279. (6)

Swedo, S. E., Rapoport, J. L., Leonard, H. L., Lenane, M., & Cheslow, D. (1989). Obsessive-compulsive disorder in children and adolescents: Clinical phenomenology of 70 consecutive cases. *Archives of General Psychiatry, 46,* 335–341. (13)

Swedo, S. E., Rapoport, J. L., Leonard, H. L., Schapiro, M. B., Rapoport, S. I., & Grady, C. L. (1991). Regional cerebral glucose metabolism of women with trichotillomania. *Archives of General Psychiatry, 48,* 828–833. (13)

Swedo, S. E., Schapiro, M. B., Grady, C. L., Cheslow, D. L., Leonard, H. L., Kumar, A., Friedland, R., Rapoport, S. I., & Rapoport, J. L. (1989). Cerebral glucose metabolism in childhood-onset obsessive-compulsive disorder. *Archives of General Psychiatry, 46,* 518–523. (13)

Szalavitz, M. (2000). Drugs to fight drugs. HMS Beagle (Online). Available: http://news.bmn.com/hmsbeagle/91/notes/feature1 (4)

Szymusiak, R. (1995). Magnocellular nuclei of the basal forebrain: Substrates of sleep and arousal regulation. *Sleep, 18,* 478–500. (14)

Tabrizi, S. J., Cleeter, M. W., Xuereb, J., Taanman, J. W., Cooper, J. M., & Schapira, A. H. (1999). Biochemical abnormalities and excitotoxicity in Huntington's disease brain. *Annals of Neurology, 45,* 25–32. (10)

Talbot, J. D., Marrett, S., Evans, A. C., Meyer, E., Bushnell, M. C., & Duncan, G. H. (1991). Multiple representations of pain in human cerebral cortex. *Science, 251,* 1355–1358. (7)

Tanaka, K. (1996). Inferotemporal cortex and object vision. *Annual Review of Neuroscience, 19,* 109–139. (9)

Tanda, G., Munzar, P., & Goldberg, S. R. (2000). Self-administration behavior is maintained by the psychoactive ingredient of marijuana in squirrel monkeys. *Nature Neuroscience, 3,* 1073–1074. (4)

Tanda, G., Pontieri, F. E., & Di Chiara, G. (1997). Cannabinoid and heroin activation of mesolimbic dopamine transmission by a common μ_1 opioid receptor mechanism. *Science, 276,* 2048–2050. (4)

Tanji, J., & Shima, K. (1994). Role for supplementary motor area cells in planning several movements ahead. *Nature, 371,* 413–416. (10)

Tanner, C. M., Ottman, R., Goldman, S. M., Ellenberg, J., Chan, P., Mayeux, R., & Langston, J. W. (1999). Parkinson disease in twins: An etiologic study. *Journal of the American Medical Association, 281,* 341–346. (10)

Taubes, G. (1998). As obesity rates rise, experts struggle to explain why. *Science, 280,* 1367–1368. (5)

Taylor, D. N. (1995). Effects of a behavioral stress-management program on anxiety, mood, self-esteem, and T-cell count in HIV-positive men. *Psychological Reports, 76,* 451–457. (7)

Tellegen, A., Lykken, D. T., Bouchard, T. J., Wilcox, K. J., Segal, N. L., & Rich, S. (1988). Personality similarity in twins reared apart and together. *Journal of Personality and Social Psychology, 54,* 1031–1039. (6)

Temoshok, L. (1987). Personality, coping style, emotion and cancer: Towards an integrative model. *Cancer Survivor, 6,* 545–567. (7)

Temple, E., & Posner, M. I. (1998). Brain mechanisms of quantity are similar in 5-year-old children and adults. *Proceedings of the National Academy of Sciences, USA, 95,* 7836–7841. (12)

Tepas, D. I., & Carvalhais, A. B. (1990). Sleep patterns of shiftworkers. *Occupational Medicine, 5,* 199–208. (14)

Terman, L. M. & Oden, M. H. (1959). *Genetic studies of genius: Vol. 5. The gifted group at mid-life.* Stanford, CA: Stanford University Press. (12)

Terrace, H. S., Petitto, L. A., Sanders, R. J., & Bever, T. G. (1979). Can an ape create a sentence? *Science, 206,* 891–901. (8)

Tessier-Lavigne, M., & Goodman, C. S. (1996). The molecular biology of axon guidance. *Science, 274,* 1123–1132. (3)

Thallmair, M., Metz, G. A. S., Z'Graggen, W. J., Raineteau, O., Kartje, G. L, & Schwab, M. E. (1998). Neurite growth inhibitors restrict plasticity and functional recovery following corticospinal tract lesions. (3)

Thanos, P., K., Volkow, N. D., Freimuth, P., Umegaki, H., Ikari, H., Roth, G., Ingram, D. K., & Hitzemann, R. (2001). Overexpression of dopamine D2 receptors reduces alcohol self-administration. *Journal of Neurochemistry, 78,* 1094–1103. (4)

Thibaut, F., Cordier, B., & Kuhn, J.-M. (1996). Gonadotrophin hormone releasing hormone agonist in cases of severe paraphilia: A lifetime treatment? *Psychoneuroendocrinology, 21,* 411–419. (6)

Thigpen, C. H., & Cleckley, H. M. (1957). *The three faces of Eve.* London: Secker & Warburg. (14)

Thomson, J. A., Itskovitz-Eldor, J., Shapiro, S. S., Waknitz, M. A., Swiergiel, J. J., Marshall, V. S., & Jones, J. M. (1998). Embryonic stem cell lines derived from human blastocysts. *Science, 282,* 1145–1147. (1)

Thornhill, R., & Gangestad, S. W. (1994). Human fluctuating asymmetry and sexual behavior. *Psychological Science, 5,* 297–302. (6)

Thrasher, T. N., & Keil, L. C. (1987). Regulation of drinking and vasopressin secretion: Role of organum vasculosum laminae terminalis. *American Journal of Physiology, 253,* R108–R120. (5)

Ticho, S. R., & Radulovacki, M. (1991). Role of adenosine in sleep and temperature regulation in the preoptic area of rats. *Pharmacology and Biochemistry of Behavior, 40,* 33–40. (14)

Toh, K. L., Jones, C. R., He, Y., Eide, E. J., Hinz, W. A., Virshup, D. M., Ptácek, L. J., & Fu, Y.-H. (2001). An h*Per2* phosphorylation site mutation in familial advanced sleep phase syndrome. *Science, 291,* 1040–1043. (14)

Tomaso, E. di, Beltramo, M., & Piomelli, D. (1996). Brain cannabinoids in chocolate. *Nature, 382,* 677–678. (4)

Toni, N., Buchs, P.-A., Nikonenko, I., Bron, C. R., & Muller, D. (1999). LTP promotes formation of multiple spine synapses between a single axon terminal and a dendrite. *Nature, 402,* 421–425. (11)

Tononi, G., & Edelman, G. M. (1998). Consciousness and complexity. *Science, 282,* 1846–1851. (14)

Tootell, R. B. H., Silverman, M. S., Switkes, E., & De Valois, R. L. (1982). Deoxyglucose analysis of retinotopic organization in primate striate cortex. *Science, 218,* 902–904. (9)

Tordjman, S., Gutknecht, L, Carlier, M., Spitz, E., Antoine, C., Slama, F., Carsalade, V., Cohen, D. J., Ferrari, P., Roubertoux, P. L., & Anderson, G. M. (2001). Role of the serotonin transporter gene in the behavioral expression of autism. *Molecular Psychiatry, 6,* 434–439. (12)

Tordoff, M. G., & Friedman, M. I. (1988). Hepatic control of feeding: Effect of glucose, fructose, and mannitol infusion. *American Journal of Physiology, 254,* R969–R976. (5)

Torgersen, S. (1983). Genetic factors in anxiety disorders. *Archives of General Psychiatry, 40,* 1085. (13)

Townsend, J., Courchesne, E., Covington, J., Westerfield, M., Harris, N. S., Lyden, P., Lowry, T. P., & Press, G. A. (1999). Spatial attention deficits in patients with acquired or developmental cerebellar abnormality. *Journal of Neuroscience, 19,* 5632–5643. (10)

Tranel, D., & Damasio, A. R. (1985). Knowledge without awareness: An autonomic index of facial recognition by prosopagnosics. *Science, 228,* 1453–1454. (9)

Tranel, D., Damasio, A. R., & Damasio, H. (1988). Intact recognition of facial expression, gender, and age in patients with impaired recognition of face identity. *Neurology, 38,* 690–696. (9)

Tranel, D., & Denburg, N. (1999). Evidence of prefrontal brain damage in normal elderly subjects. Manuscript in preparation. (11)

Träskman, L., Åsberg, M., Bertilsson, L., & Sjöstrand, L. (1981). Monoamine metabolites in CSF and suicidal behavior. *Archives of General Psychiatry, 38,* 631–635. (13)

Trautmann, A. (1983). Tubocurarine, a partial agonist for cholinergic receptors. *Journal of Neural Transmission. Supplementum, 18,* 353–361. (2)

Treffert, D. A., & Wallace, G. L. (2002, June). Islands of genius. *Scientific American,* 76–85. (12)

Treisman, A. M., & Gelade, G. (1980). A feature-integration theory of attention. *Cognitive Psychology, 12,* 97–136. (14)

Triandis, H. C. (1994). *Culture and social behavior.* New York: McGraw-Hill. (6)

Triggs, W. J., McCoy, K. J., Greer, R., Rossi, F., Bowers, D., Kortenkamp, S., Nadeau, S. E., Heilman, K. M., & Goodman, W. K. (1999). Effects of left frontal transcranial magnetic stimulation on depressed mood, cognition, and corticomotor threshold. *Biological Psychiatry, 45,* 1440–1446. (13)

Trulson, M. E., Crisp, T., & Trulson, V. M. (1984). Activity of serotonin-containing nucleus centralis superior (raphe medianus) neurons in freely moving cats. *Experimental Brain Research, 54,* 33–44. (14)

Tsai, G. E., Condie, D., Wu, M. T., & Chang, I.-W. (1999). Functional magnetic resonance imaging of personality switches in a woman with dissociative identity disorder. *Harvard Review of Psychiatry*, 7, 119–122. (14)

Tsai, G., Gastfriend, D. R., & Coyle, J. T. (1995). The glutamatergic basis of human alcoholism. *American Journal of Psychiatry*, 152, 332–340. (4)

Tsuang, M. T., Gilbertson, M. W., & Faraone, S. V. (1991). The genetics of schizophrenia: Current knowledge and future directions. *Schizophrenia Research*, 4, 157–171. (1, 13)

Tuiten, A., Van Honk, J., Koppeschaar, H., Bernaards, C., Thijssen, J., & Verbaten, R. (2000). Time course of effects of testotsterone administration on sexual arousal in women. *Archives of General Psychiatry*, 57, 149–153. (6)

Turkheimer, E. (1991). Individual and group differences in adoption studies of IQ. *Psychological Bulletin*, 110, 392–405. (12)

UCSD team performs first surgery in gene therapy protocol for Alzheimer's disease. (2001, April 10). UCSD School of Medicine News (Online). Available: http://health.ucsd.edu/news/2001/04_09_Tusz.html. (11)

Uhl, G., Blum, K., Noble, E., & Smith, S. (1993). Substance abuse vulnerability and D2 receptor genes. *Trends in Neurosciences*, 16, 83–87. (4)

Ullian, E. M., Sapperstein, S. K., Christopherson, K. S., & Barres, B. A. (2001). Control of synapse number by glia. *Science*, 291, 657–660. (2)

Ungerleider, L. G., & Haxby, J. V. (1994). "What" and "where" in the human brain. *Current Opinion in Neurobiology*, 4, 157–165. (9)

U.S. Congress Office of Technology Assessment. (1986). *Alternatives to animal research in testing and education.* Washington, DC: Government Printing Office. (1)

US government shuts down Pennsylvania gene therapy trials. (2000). *Nature*, 403, 354–355. (1)

Valenstein, E. S. (1986). *Great and desperate cures.* New York: Basic Books. (3)

Valzeli, L. (1980). *An approach to neuroanatomical and neurochemical psychophysiology.* Torino, Italy: C. G. Edizioni Medico Scientifiche. (4)

Van Essen, D. C., Anderson, C. H., & Felleman, D. J. (1992). Information processing in the primate visual system: An integrated systems perspective. *Science*, 255, 419–423. (9)

Vanitallie, T. B. (1979). Obesity: Adverse effects on health and longevity. *American Journal of Clinical Nutrition*, 32, 2727. (5)

Van Wyk, P. H., & Geist, C. S. (1984). Psychosocial development of heterosexual, bisexual, and homosexual behavior. *Archives of Sexual Behavior*, 13, 505–544. (6)

Veld, B. A., Ruitenberg, A., Hofman, A., Launer, L. J., Duijn, C. M. van, Stijnen, T., Breteler, M. M. B., & Stricker, B. H. C. (2001). Nonsteroidal anti-inflammatory drugs and the risk of Alzheimer's disease. *New England Journal of Medicine*, 345, 1515–1521. (11)

Venter, J. C. [and 273 others]. (2001). The sequence of the human genome. *Science*, 291, 1304–1351. (1)

Vergnes, M., Depaulis, A., Boehrer, A., & Kempf, E. (1988). Selective increase of offensive behavior in the rat following intrahypothalamic 5, 7-DHT induced serotonin depletion. *Behavioral Brain Research*, 29, 85–91. (7)

Verkes, R. J., Van der Mast, R. C., Hengeveld, M. W., Tuyl, J. P., Zwinderman, A. H., & Van Kempen, G. M. J. (1998). Reduction by paroxetine of suicidal behavior in patients with repeated suicide attempts but not major depression. *American Journal of Psychiatry*, 155, 543–547. (13)

Verlinsky, Y., Rechitsky, S., Verlinsky, O., Masciangelo, C., Lederer, K., & Kulieve, A. (2002). Preimplantation diagnosis for early-onset Alzheimer disease caused by V717L mutation. *Journal of the American Medical Association*, 287, 1018–1021. (11)

Vernon, P. A. (1987). New developments in reaction time research. In P. A. Vernon (Ed.), *Speed of information processing and intelligence* (pp. 1–20). Norwood, NJ: Ablex. (12)

Vernon, P. A., & Mori, M. (1992). Intelligence, reaction times, and peripheral nerve conduction velocity. *Intelligence*, 16, 273–288. (12)

Vink, T., Hinney, A., van Elburg, A. A., van Goozen, S. H. M., Sandkuijl, L. A., Sinke, R. J., Herpertz-Dahlmann, B.-M., Hebebrand, J., Remschmidt, H., van Engeland, H., & Adan, R. A. H. (2001). Association between anagouti-related protein gene polymorphism and anorexia nervosa. *Molecular Psychiatry*, 6, 325–328. (5)

Virkkunen, M., Goldman, D., & Linnoila, M. (1996). Serotonin in alcoholic violent offenders. *Genetics of criminal and antisocial behaviour. Ciba Foundation Symposium 194.* Chichester, England: Wiley. (7)

Virkkunen, M., & Linnoila, M. (1990). Serotonin in early onset, male alcoholics with violent behaviour. *Annals of Medicine*, 22, 327–331. (7)

Virkkunen, M., & Linnoila, M. (1993). Brain serotonin, Type II alcoholism and impulsive violence. *Journal of Studies of Alcohol Supplement*, 11, 163–169. (7)

Virkkunen, M., & Linnoila, M. (1997). Serotonin in early-onset alcoholism. *Recent Developments in Alcohol*, 13, 173–189. (7)

Vogel, G. (1997). From science fiction to ethics quandary. *Science*, 277, 1753–1754. (1)

Vogel, G. (1998). Penetrating insight into the brain. *Science*, 282, 39. (3)

Vogel, G. (2000a). Can old cells learn new tricks? *Science*, 287, 1418–1419. (1)

Vogel, G. (2000b). Researchers get green light for work on stem cells. *Science*, 289, 1442–1443. (1)

Vogel, G. (2001). Bush squeezes between the lines on stem cells. *Science*, 293, 1242–1245. (1)

Vogel, G. W., Buffenstein, A., Minter, K., & Hennessey, A. (1990). Drug effects on REM sleep and on endogenous depression. *Neuroscience and Biobehavioral Review*, 14, 49–63. (13)

Vogels, R. (1999). Categorization of complex visual images by rhesus monkeys. Part 2: Single-cell study. *European Journal of Neuroscience*, 11, 1239–1255. (9)

Volavka, J., Czobor, P., Goodwin, D. W., Gabrielli, W. F., Jr., Penick, E. C., Mednick, S. A., Jensen, P., & Knop, J. (1996). The electroencephalogram after alcohol administration in high-risk men and the development of alcohol use disorders 10 years later. *Archives of General Psychiatry*, 53, 258–263. (4)

Volkow, N. D., Rosen, B., & Farde, L. (1997). Imaging the living human brain: Magnetic resonance imaging and positron emission tomography. *Proceedings of the National Academy of Sciences, USA*, 94, 2787–2788. (App.)

Volkow, N. D., Wang, G.-J., Fischman, M. W., Foltin, R. W., Fowler, J. S., Abumrad, N. N., Vitkun, S., Logan, J., Gatley, S. J., Pappas, N., Hitzemann, R., & Shea, C. E. (1997). Relationship between subjective effects of cocaine and dopamine transporter occupancy. *Nature*, 386, 827–830. (4)

Volpe, B. T., Ledoux, J. E., & Gazzaniga, M. S. (1979). Information processing of visual stimuli in an 'extinguished' field. *Nature*, 282, 722–724. (9)

von der Heydt, R., Peterhans, E., & Dürsteler, M. R.. (1992). Periodic-pattern-selective cells in monkey visual cortex. *Journal of Neuroscience*, 12, 1416–1434. (9)

Vorel, S. R., Liu, X., Hayes, R. J., Spector, J. A., & Gardner, E. L. (2001). Relapse to cocaine-seeking after hippocampal theta burst stimulation. *Science*, 292, 1175–1178. (4)

Voyer, D., Voyer, S., & Bryden, M. P. (1995). Magnitude of sex differences in spatial abilities: A meta-analysis and consideration of critical variables. *Psychological Bulletin*, 117, 250–270. (6)

Wada, J. A., Clarke, R., & Hamm, A. (1975). Cerebral hemispheric asymmetry in humans: Cortical speech zones in 100 adult and 100 infant brains. *Archives of Neurology*, 32, 239–246. (8)

Waeiti, P., Dickinson, A., & Schultz, W. (2001). Dopamine responses comply with basic assumptions of formal learning theory. *Nature, 412*, 43–48. (4)

Wagner, A. D., Schacter, D. L., Rotte, M., Koutstaal, W., Maril, A., Dale, A. M., Rosen, B. R., & Buckner, R. L. (1998). Building memories: Remembering and forgetting of verbal experiences as predicted by brain activity. *Science, 281*, 1188–1191. (App.)

Wagner, H. J., Hennig, H., Jabs, W. J., Sickhaus, A., Wessel, K., & Wandinger, K. P. (2000). Altered prevalence and reactivity of anti-Epstein-Barr virus antibodies in patients with multiple sclerosis. *Viral Immunology, 13*, 497–502. (10)

Wall, T. L., & Ehlers, C. L. (1995). Genetic influences affecting alcohol use among Asians. *Alcohol Health and Research World, 19*, 184–189. (4)

Walsh, B. T., & Devlin, M. J. (1998). Eating disorders: Progress and problems. *Science, 280*, 1387–1390. (5)

Wan, F.-J., Berton, F., Madamba, S. G., Francesconi, W., & Siggins, G. R. (1996). Low ethanol concentrations enhance GABAergic inhibitory postsynaptic potentials in hippocampal pyramidal neurons only after block of GABAB receptors. *Proceedings of the National Academy of Sciences, USA, 93*, 5049–5054. (4)

Warner, R. K., Thompson, J. T., Markowski, V. P., Loucks, J. A., Bazzett, T. J., Eaton, R. C., & Hull, E. M. (1991). Microinjection of the dopamine antagonist cis-flupenthixol into the MPOA impairs copulation, penile reflexes and sexual motivation in male rats. *Brain Research, 540*, 177–182. (6)

Warren, R. P., & Singh, V. K. (1996). Elevated serotonin levels in autism: Association with the major histocompatibility complex. *Biological Psychiatry, 34*, 72–75. (12)

Warren, S., Hämäläinen, H. A., & Gardner, E. P. (1986). Objective classification of motion- and direction-sensitive neurons in primary somatosensory cortex of awake monkeys. *Journal of Neurophysiology, 56*, 598–622. (10)

Waters, A. J., Jarvis, M. J., & Sutton, S. R. (1998). Nicotine withdrawal and accident rates. *Nature, 394*, 137. (4)

Watkins, L. R., & Mayer, D. J. (1982). Organization of endogenous opiate and nonopiate pain control systems. *Science, 216*, 1185–1192. (10)

Watson, C. G., Kucala, T., Tilleskjor, C., & Jacobs, L. (1984). Schizophrenic birth seasonality in relation to the incidence of infectious diseases and temperature extremes. *Archives of General Psychiatry, 41*, 85–90. (13)

Watson, J. D., & Crick, F. H. C. (1953). Genetical implications of the structure of deoxyribonucleic acid. *Nature, 171*, 964–967. (1)

Waxman, S. G., & Ritchie, J. M. (1985). Organization of ion channels in the myelinated nerve fiber. *Science, 228*, 1502–1507. (2)

Waynforth, D. (1998). Fluctuating asymmetry and human male life-history traits in rural Belize. *Proceedings of the Royal Society of London, B, 265*, 1497–1501. (6)

Webb, W. B. (1974). Sleep as an adaptive response. *Perceptual and Motor Skills, 38*, 1023–1027. (14)

Webb, W. B., & Cartwright, R. D. (1978). Sleep and dreams. *Annual Review of Psychology, 29*, 223–252. (14)

Wedekind, C., Seebeck, T., Bettens, F., & Paepke, A. J. (1995). MHC-dependent mate preferences in humans. *Proceedings of the Royal Society of London, B, 260*, 245–249. (6)

Wegesin, D. J. (1998). A neuropsychologic profile of homosexual and heterosexual men and women. *Archives of Sexual Behavior, 27*, 91–108. (6)

Wehr, T. A., Jacobsen, F. M., Sack, D. A., Arendt, J., Tamarkin, L., & Rosenthal, N. E. (1986). Phototherapy of seasonal affective disorder: Time of day and suppression of melatonin are not critical for antidepressant effects. *Archives of General Psychiatry, 43*, 870–875. (13)

Weinberg, R. A. (1989). Intelligence and IQ: Landmark issues and great debates. *American Psychologist, 44*, 98–104. (12)

Weinberg, R. A., Scarr, S., & Waldman, I. D. (1992). The Minnesota transracial adoption study: A follow-up of IQ test performance at adolescence. *Intelligence, 16*, 117–135. (12)

Weinberger, D. R. (1987). Implications of normal brain development for the pathogenesis of schizophrenia. *Archives of General Psychiatry, 44*, 660–669. (13)

Weinberger, D. R., Berman, K. F., Suddath, R., & Torrey, E. F. (1992). Evidence of dysfunction of a prefrontal-limbic network in schizophrenia: A magnetic resonance imaging and regional cerebral blood flow study of discordant monozygotic twins. *American Journal of Psychiatry, 149*, 890–897. (13)

Weinberger, D. R., Berman, K. F., & Zec, R. F. (1986). Physiologic dysfunction of dorsolateral prefrontal cortex in schizophrenia: I. Regional cerebral blood flow evidence. *Archives of General Psychiatry, 43*, 114–124. (13)

Weinberger, D. R., & Lipska, B. K. (1995). Cortical maldevelopment, antipsychotic drugs, and schizophrenia: A search for common ground. *Schizophrenia Research, 16*, 87–110. (13)

Weinberger, D. R., Torrey, E. F., Neophytides, A. N., & Wyatt, R. J. (1979a). Lateral cerebral ventricular enlargement in chronic schizophrenia. *Archives of General Psychiatry, 36*, 735–739. (13)

Weinberger, D. R., Torrey, E. F., Neophytides, A. N., & Wyatt, R. J. (1979b). Structural abnormalities in the cerebral cortex of chronic schizophrenic patients. *Archives of General Psychiatry, 36*, 935–939. (13)

Weinberger, D. R., & Wyatt, R. J. (1983). Enlarged cerebral ventricles in schizophrenia. *Psychiatric Annals, 13*, 412–418. (13)

Weinberger, N. M., Javid, R., & Lepan, B. (1995). Heterosynaptic long-term facilitation of sensory-evoked responses in the auditory cortex by stimulation of the magnocellular medial geniculate body in guinea pigs. *Behavioral Neuroscience, 109*, 10–17. (11)

Weingarten, H. P., Chang, P. K., & McDonald, T. J. (1985). Comparison of the metabolic and behavioral disturbances following paraventricular- and ventromedial-hypothalamic lesions. *Brain Research Bulletin, 14*, 551–559. (5)

Weinstein, S. (1968). Intensive and extensive aspects of tactile sensitivity as a function of body part, sex, and laterality. In D. R. Kenshalo (Ed.), *The skin senses* (pp. 195–222). Springfield, IL: Thomas. (10)

Wekerle, H. (1993). Experimental autoimmune encephalomyelitis as a model of immune-mediated CNS disease. *Current Opinion in Neurobiology, 3*, 779–784. (10)

Weltzin, T. E., Fernstrom, M. H., & Kaye, W. H. (1994). Serotonin and bulimia nervosa. *Nutrition Reviews, 52*, 399–408. (5)

Weltzin, T. E., Hsu, L. K., Pollice, C., & Kaye, W. H. (1991). Feeding patterns in bulimia nervosa. *Biological Psychiatry, 30*, 1093–1110. (5)

Wender, P. H., Rosenthal, D., Kety, S. S., Schulsinger, F., & Welner, J. (1974). Crossfostering: A research strategy for clarifying the role of genetic and experiential factors in the etiology of schizophrenia. *Archives of General Psychiatry, 30*, 121–128. (13)

West, D. B., Fey, D., & Woods, S. C. (1984). Cholecystokinin persistently suppresses meal size but not food intake in free-feeding rats. *American Journal of Physiology, 246*, R776–R787. (5)

Wettstein, A. (2000). Cholinesterase inhibitors and Gingko extracts—Are they comparable in the treatment of dementia? Comparison of published placebo-controlled efficacy studies of at least six months' duration. *Phytomedicine, 6*, 393–401. (11)

Wever, E. G. (1949). *Theory of hearing.* New York: Wiley. (8)

Wever, E. G., & Bray, C. W. (1930). The nature of acoustic response: The relation between sound frequency and frequency of impulses in the auditory nerve. *Journal of Experimental Psychology, 13*, 373–387. (8)

Wheeler, M. A., Stuss, D. T., & Tulving, E. (1997). Toward a theory of episodic memory: The frontal lobes and autonoetic consciousness. *Psychological Bulletin, 121,* 331–354. (14)

Whipple, B., & Komisaruk, B. R. (1988). Analgesia produced in women by genital self-stimulation. *Journal of Sex Research, 24,* 130–140. (10)

Whitman, F. L., Diamond, M., & Martin, J. (1993). Homosexual orientation in twins: A report on 61 pairs and three triplet sets. *Archives of Sexual Behavior, 22,* 187–206. (6)

Whitworth, A. B., Fischer, F., Lesch, O. M., Nimmerrichter, A., Oberbuer, H., Platz, T., Potgieter, A., Walter, H., & Fleischhacker, W. W. (1996). Comparison of acamprosate and placebo in long-term treatment of alcohol dependence. *Lancet, 347,* 1438–1442. (4)

Wickelgren, I. (1997). Getting a grasp on working memory. *Science, 275,* 1580–1582. (11)

Wickelgren, I. (1998). Obesity: How big a problem? *Science, 280,* 1364–1367. (5)

Wickelgren, I. (1999). Nurture helps mold able minds. *Science, 283,* 1832–1834. (12)

Wickett, J. C., Vernon, P. A., & Lee, D. H. (1994). In vivo brain size, head perimeter, and intelligence in a sample of healthy adult females. *Personality and Individual Differences, 16,* 831–838. (12)

Widiger, T. A., Cadoret, R., Hare, R., Robins, L., Rutherford, M., Zanarini, M., Alterman, A., Apple, M., Corbitt, E., Forth, A., Hart, S., Kultermann, J., Woody, G., & Frances, A. (1996). DSM-IV antisocial personality disorder field test. *Journal of Abnormal Psychology, 105,* 3–16. (7)

Wiederman, M. W., & Pryor, T. (1996). Substance abuse and impulsive behaviors among adolescents with eating disorders. *Addictive Behaviors, 21,* 269–272. (5)

Wiesel, T. N., & Hubel, D. H. (1966). Spatial and chromatic interactions in the lateral geniculate body of the rhesus monkey. *Journal of Neurophysiology, 29,* 1115–1156. (9)

Willerman, L., Schultz, R., Rutledge, J. N., & Bigler, E. D. (1991). In vivo brain size and intelligence. *Intelligence, 15,* 223–228. (3, 12)

Willerman, L., Schultz, R., Rutledge, J. N., & Bigler, E. D. (1994). Brain structure and cognitive function. In C. R. Reynolds (Ed.), *Cognitive assessment: A multidisciplinary perspective* (pp. 35–55). New York: Plenum Press. (12)

Williams, J., Spurlock, G., McGuffin, P., Mallet, J., Nöthen, M. M., Gill, M., Aschauer, H., Nulander, P. Q., Macciardi, F., & Owen, M. J. (1996). Association between schizophrenia and T102C polymorphism of the 5-hydroxytriptamine type 2a-receptor gene. European Multicentre Association Study of Schizophrenia (EMASS) Group. *Lancet, 347,* 1294–1296. (13)

Williams, R. W., & Herrup, K. (1988). The control of neuron number. *Annual Review of Neuroscience, 11,* 423–453. (2)

Williams, R. W., Ryder, K., & Rakic, P. (1987). Emergence of cytoarchitectonic differences between areas 17 and 18 in the developing rhesus monkey. *Abstracts of the Society for Neuroscience, 13,* 1044. (3)

Williams, T. J., Pepitone, M. E., Christensen, S. E., Cooke, B. M., Huberman, A. D., Breedlove, N. J., Breedlove, T. J., Jordan, C. I., & Breedlove, S. M. (2000). Finger-length ratios and sexual orientation. *Nature, 404,* 455–456. (6)

Wilska, A. (1935). Methode zur Bestimmung der Horschwellenamplituden der Tromenfells bei verscheden Frequenzen. *Skandinavisches Archiv für Physiologie, 72,* 161–165. (8)

Wilson, A. (1998, September 4). Gray matters memory: How much can we remember? And why is it necessary to forget? *Orange County Register,* E-1. (14)

Wilson, F. A. W., Ó Scalaidhe, S. P., & Goldman-Rakic, P. S. (1993). Dissociation of object and spatial procesing domains in primate prefrontal cortex. *Science, 260,* 1955–1958. (9)

Wise, R. A. (1987). The role of reward pathways in the development of drug dependence. *Pharmacological Therapeutics, 35,* 227–263. (4)

Wise, R. A., & Rompre, P.-P. (1989). Brain dopamine and reward. *Annual Review of Psychology, 40,* 191–225. (4)

Witelson, S. F., Glezer, I. I., & Kigar, D. L. (1995). Women have greater density of neurons in posterior temporal cortex. *Journal of Neuroscience, 15,* 3418–3428. (12)

Witelson, S. F., Kigar, D. L., & Harvey, T. (1999). The exceptional brain of Albert Einstein. *Lancet, 353,* 2149–2153. (12)

Witelson, S. F., & Pallie, W. (1973). Left hemisphere specialization for langugage in the newborn: Neuroanatomical evidence of asymmetry. *Brain, 96,* 641–646. (8)

Wolf, A. M., & Colditz, G. A. (1998). Current estimates of the economic cost of obesity in the United States. *Obesity Research, 6,* 97–106. (5)

Wollberg, Z., & Newman, J. D. (1972). Auditory cortex of squirrel monkey: Response patterns of single cells to species-specific vocalizations. *Science, 175,* 212–214. (8)

Wood, D. L., Sheps, S. G., Elveback, L. R., & Schirger, A. (1984). Cold pressor test as a predictor of hypertension. *Hypertension, 6,* 301–306. (7)

Wood, N. W. (1998). Genetic risk factors in Parkinson's disease. *Annals of Neurology, 44,* S58–S62. (10)

Woods, S. C., Schwartz, M. W., Baskin, D. G., & Seeley, R. J. (2000). Food intake and the regulation of body weight. *Annual Reviews of Psychology, 51,* 255–277. (5)

Woods, S. C., & Stricker, E. M. (1999). Food intake and metabolism. In M. J. Zigmond, F. E. Bloom, S. C. Landis, J. L. Roberts, & L. R. Squire (Eds.), *Fundamental neuroscience.* New York: Academic Press. (5)

Woodworth, R. S. (1941). Heredity and environment: A critical survey of recently published material on twins and foster children. a report prepared for the Committee on Social Adjustment. New York: Social Science Research Council. (1)

Woolley, C. S., & McEwen, B. S. (1993). Roles of estradiol and progesterone in regulation of hippocampal dendritic spine density during the estrous cycle in the rat. *Journal of Comparative Neurology, 336,* 293–306. (11)

Worley, P. F., Heller, W. A., Snyder, S. H., & Baraban, J. M. (1988). Lithium blocks a phosphoinositide-mediated cholinergic response in hippocampal slices. *Science, 239,* 1428–1429. (13)

Wu, J. C., & Bunney, W. E. (1990). The biological basis of an antidepressant response to sleep deprivation and relapse: Review and hypothesis. *American Journal of Psychiatry, 147,* 14–21. (13)

Wurtman, J. J., Wurtman, R. J., Reynolds, S., Tsay, R., & Chew, B. (1987). Fenfluramine suppresses snack intake among carbohydrate cravers but not among noncarbohydrate cravers. *International Journal of Eating Disorders, 6,* 687–699. (5)

Wynn, K. (1992). Addition and subtraction by human infants. *Nature, 358,* 749–750. (12)

Wynn, K. (1998). Psychological foundations of number: Numerical competence in human infants. *Trends in Cognitive Sciences, 2,* 296–303. (12)

Xiao, Z., & Suga, N. (2002). Modulation of cochlear hair cells by the auditory cortex in the mustached bat. *Nature Neuroscience, 5,* 57–63. (8)

Yaffe, K., Barrett-Connor, E., Lin, F., & Grady, D. (2002). Serum lipoprotein levels, statin use, and cognitive function in older women. *Archives of Neurology, 59,* 378–384. (11)

Yam, P. (1998, Winter). Intelligence considered. *Scientific American Presents,* 6–11. (12)

Yeni-Komshian, G. H., & Benson, D. A. (1976). Anatomical study of cerebral asymmetry in the temporal lobe of humans, chimpanzees, and rhesus monkeys. *Science, 192*, 387–389. (8)

Yokel, R. A., & Wise, R. A. (1975). Increased lever pressing for amphetamine after pimozide in rats: Implications for a dopamine theory of reward. *Science, 187*, 547–549. (4)

Youdim, M. B. H., & Riederer, P. (1997, January). Understanding Parkinson's disease. *Scientific American, 276*, 52–58. (10)

Young, A. M., Joseph, M. H., & Gray, J. A. (1993). Latent inhibition of conditioned dopamine release in rat nucleus accumbens. *Neuroscience, 54*, 5–9. (4)

Young, M. J., Ray, J., Whiteley, S. J., Klassen, H., & Gage, F. H. (2000). Neuronal differentiation and morphological integration of hippocampal progenitor cells transplanted to the retina of immature and mature dystrophic rats. *Molecular and Cellular Neurosciences, 16*, 197–205. (9)

Young, M. P., & Yamane, S. (1992). Sparse population coding of faces in the inferotemporal cortex. *Science, 256*, 1327–1331. (9)

Zeki, S. (1983). Colour coding in the cerebral cortex: The reaction of cells in monkey visual cortex to wavelengths and colours. *Journal of Neuroscience, 9*, 741–765. (9)

Zeki, S. (1992, September). The visual image in mind and brain. *Scientific American, 267*, 69–76. (9)

Zepelin, H., & Rechtshaffen, A. (1974). Mammalian sleep, longevity, and energy metabolism. *Brain, Behavior and Evolution, 10*, 425–470. (14)

Zhang, S. P., Bandler, R., & Carrive, P. (1990). Flight and immobility evoked by excitatory amino acid microinjection within distinct parts of the subtentorial midbrain periaqueductal gray of the cat. *Brain Research, 520*, 73–82. (7)

Zhang, Y., Proenca, R., Mafei, M., Barone, M. Leopold, L. & Friedman, J. M. (1994). Positional cloning of the mouse *obese* gene and its human homologue. *Nature, 335*, 311–317.

Zhou, J. N., Hofman, M. A., Gooren, L. J., & Swaab, D. F. (1995). A sex difference in the human brain and its relation to transsexuality. *Nature, 378*, 68–70. (6)

Zihl, J., von Cramon, D., & Mai, N. (1983). Selective disturbance of movement vision after bilateral brain damage. *Brain, 106*, 313–340. (9)

Zillmer, E. A., & Spiers, M. V. (2001). *Principles of neuropsychology.* Belmont, CA: Wadsworth. (2)

Zipser, D., & Andersen, R. A. (1988). A back-propagation programmed network that simulates response properties of a subset of posterior parietal neurons. *Nature, 331*, 679–684. (2)

Zola-Morgan, S., Squire, L. R., & Amaral, D. G. (1986). Human amnesia and the medial temporal region: Enduring memory impairment following a bilateral lesion limited to field CA1 of the hippocampus. *Neuroscience, 6*, 2950–2967. (11)

Zubin, J., & Spring, B. (1977). Vulnerability—A new view of schizophrenia. *Journal of Abnormal Psychology, 86*, 103–126. (1, 13)

Zuckerman, M. (1971). Dimensions of sensation seeking. *Journal of Consulting and Clinical Psychology, 36*, 45–52. (5)

Photo Credits

Chapter 1. 1, F. 1.1 © NASA. **3,** F. 1.2 © Archives of the History of American Psychology, University of Akron. **4,** F. 1.3a © National Library of Medicine, Bethesda, MD. **5,** F. 1.4 © Hulton Archive. **6,** F. 1.5 © Hulton Archive. **16,** F. 1.12 © Bettmann/CORBIS. **21,** F. 1.14left © Courtesy of the Foundation of Biomedical Research. **21,** F. 1.14right © Paul Conklin/PhotoEdit. **22,** F. 1.15 C. Macilwain, "Self-policing backed for research on humans," *Nature*, 406, 7. © 2000. Reprinted with permission. **23,** F. 1.17 © Photo Researchers **Chapter 2. 31,** © Laurence Dutton/Getty Images. **36,** F. 2.4right Photo courtesy of Bob Jacobs, Colorado College. **46,** F. 2.11 © Visuals Unlimited **Chapter 3. 59,** F. 3.1 © Chris Walsh. **60,** F. 3.2 © Visuals Unlimited. **62,** F. 3.4 © Photo Researchers. **63,** F. 3.6 © The Brain Museum. **66,** F. 3.10right Photo courtesy of Dr. Dana Copeland. **67,** Photos reprinted with permission from Damasio et al., "The return of Phineas Gage: Clues about the brain of a famous patient." *Science*, 264: 1102–1105, 1994. Department of Neurology and Image Analysis Facility, University of Iowa. **68,** F. 3.11 © From Wilder Penfield, The Excitable Cortex in Conscious Man, 1958. Courtesy of Dennis Coon and Charles C. Thomas, Publisher, Springfield, Illinois. **73,** F. 3.16 © Bettmann/CORBIS. **79,** F. 3.22 Photos by Kathryn Tosney. **81,** F. 3.24 Photos © Steven Rothman, MD. **82,** F. 3.26 Gressens, Lammens, Picard, & Evard, 1992. **84,** F. 3.27 From A. Mogilner, et al. (1993). Somatosensory cortical plasticity in adult humans revealed by magnetoencephalography. Proceedings of the National Academy of Science, 90, 3593–3597. **87,** F. 3.28 © Steve Liss/Liaison Agency **Chapter 4. 95,** F. 4.1 © Hulton Archive. **99,** F. 4.5 © George Steinmetz. **101,** F. 4.6 Illustration courtesy of The National Library of Medicine. **102,** F. 4.7 © London et al., 1990. **105,** F. 4.8 © McCann, Lowe, & Ricaurte, 1997. **111,** F. 4.12 © Grant et al., 1996. **112,** F. 4.13 © Bettmann/CORBIS. **113,** F. 4.14 Photo courtesy of Jules Asher **Chapter 5. 123,** Nancy R. Cohen/Getty Images. **125,** F. 5.1 © Jayson Mellom. **131,** F. 5.4 © SIU/Peter Arnold, Inc. **132,** Photo © Janet Haas/Rainbow. **139,** F. 5.9 © Courtesy of Neal Miller, Yale University. **143,** F. 5.13 © Zhang et al., 1994. Reprinted by permission of *Nature*, © 1994. **145,** F. 5.15 Reprinted with permission from T. M. Loftus, et al., "Reduced food intake and body weight in mice treated with fatty acid synthase." *Science*, 288, 2379–2381. © 2000 American Society for the Advancement of Science. **147,** F. 5.16left © Schiltman/Liaison Agency. **F. 5.16right** © Evon Agostini/Liaison Agency **Chapter 6. 160,** F. 6.4 © Gorski, 1974. **167,** F. 6.10 © Dörner, 1974. **171,** F. 6.11 © Money & Erhardt, 1972. **172,** F. 6.12 © Money & Erhardt, 1972. **179,** F. 6.15 Reprinted with permission from S. LeVay, "A difference in hypothalamic structure between heterosexual and homosexual men." *Science*, 253, 1034–1047. © 1991, American Association for the Advancement of Science. **182,** F. 6.18 © Burk Uzzle. **Chapter 7. 193,** F. 7.4 © eStock Photo. **195,** F. 7.5 © Dan Frances/Mardan Photography. **196,** Pavlidis, Eberhardt, & Levine, 2002. Reprinted by permission of *Nature* © 2002. **198,** F. 7.7 Morris et al., 1996. Reprinted by permission of *Nature* © 1996. **200,** F. 7.8 Bechara, Damasio, Damasio, & Lee, 1999. © 1999 by the Society for Neuroscience. **205,** F. 7.13 © Alain Evrard/Photo Researchers. **206,** Reprinted with permission from Talbot et al., "Multiple representations of pain in human cerebral cortex." *Science*, 251, 1355–1358. © 1991 American Association for the Advancement of Science. **Chapter 8. 215,** © Ryan McVay/Getty Images. **217,** F. 8.1 Chester Higgins Jr., NYT Pictures. **222,** F. 8.6 © Dr. G. Oran Bredberg/SPl/Photo Researchers. **226,** F. 8.11 Photo © Eric and David Hosking/CORBIS. **227,** F. 8.12 © Bob Garrett. **235,** F. 8.19 © Reprinted with permission from Peterson et al., "Activation of extrastriate and frontal cortical areas by visual words and word-like stimuli." *Science*, 249, 1044–1049. © 1990 American Association for the Advancement of Science. **237,** F. 8.21 © A. M. Galaburda, Harvard Medical School. **239,** F. 8.24 © Laura Ann Petitto. **240,** F. 8.25 Reprinted with permission from H. J. Neville, et al., "Cerebral organizations for language in deaf and hearing subjects: Biological constraints and effects of experience." Proceedings of the National Academy of Sciences, USA, 95, 922–929. © National Academy of Sciences, USA. **241,** F. 8.26 © Kim Relkin, Lee & Hirsch, 1997. By permission of *Nature*, © 1997. **243,** F. 8.27left © Susan Kukllin/Photo Researchers. **F. 8.27right** © Enrico Ferorelli **Chapter 9. 259,** F. (c) Optobionics. **264,** F. 9.14 Reprinted with permission from R. B. H. Tootell et al., "Deoxyglucose analysis of retinoptic organization in primate striate cortex." *Science*, 218, 902–904. © 1982. American Association for the Advancement of Science. **265,** F. 9.15 From *Mach Bands: Quantitative Studies on Neural Networks in the Retina*, by F. Ratcliff, 1965. f. 3.25, p. 107. © 1969 Holden-Day Inc. **269,** F. 9.22 Reprinted with permission from L.O. Harmon and B. Julesz, "Masking in visual recognition: Effects of two-dimensional filtered noise." *Science*, 180, 1194–1197. © 1973. American Association for the Advancement of Science. **270,** F. 9.23 Reprinted with permission from M. Livingstone and D. Hubel, "Segregation of form, color, movement, and depth: Anatomy, physiology, and perception." Science, 240, 740–749. © 1988. American Association for the Advancement of Science. **273,** F. 9.25 © Dana Copeland. **274,** F. 9.27 © Gauthier et al., 1999. **275,** F. 9.28 From F. E. Bloom and A. Lazerson, *Brain, mind and behavior*, 2nd Ed., p. 300. © 1988 W. H. Freeman & Co. **276,** F. 9.29 © Anton Raderscheidt. Photos provided by Ken Roth. **Chapter 10. 290,** F. 10.8 © Hulton Archive. **293,** © Barbaro, 1988. **294,** F. 10.11 Reprinted by permission of *Nature*, © 1995. **295,** F. 10.12 © Ed Reschke. F. 10.13 © Ed Reschke. **301,** F. 10.21 Reprinted by permission of *Nature*, © 1997. **302,** F. 10.22 © 2001 Massachusetts Medical Society. 303, F. 10.23 © Courtesy of Robert E. Schmidt, Washington University. **304,** F. 10.24 © Rowland, Hoefer, & Aranow, 1960. **305,** F. 10.25 © Photo Researchers **Chapter 11. 311,** Suza Scalora/Getty Images. **314,** F. 11.1top Corkin, Amaral, Gonzalez, Johnson, & Hyman, 1997. © 1997 by the Society for Neuroscience. **316,** F. 11.3 © Martin, Wiggs, & Weisberg, 1997. **317,** F. 11.5 Reprinted with permission from D. L. Schacter et al., "Conscious recollection and the human hippocampal formation: Evidence from positron emission tomography." Proceedings of the National Academy of Sciences, USA, 93, 321–325. © 1996 National Academy of Sciences, USA. **318,** F. 11.6 Martin, Wiggs, Ungerleider, & Haxby, 1996. Reprinted by permission of *Nature*, © 1996. **319,** F. 11.8 © Hank Morgan/Photo Researchers. **324,** F. 11.11 Reprinted with permission from M. Barinaga, "Learning visualized on the double." Science, 286, 1661. © 1999. American Association for the Advancement of Science. **328,** F. 11.13 Photos courtesy of Dr. Robert D. Terry. **331,** F. 11.15(a), (b), © From J. M. Conner, et al., "Nontropic actions of neurotrophins: Subcortical nerve growth factor gene delivery reverses age-related degeneration of primate cortical cholinergic innervation." Proceedings of the National Academy of Sciences, USA, 98, 1941–1946. © 2001 National Academy of Sciences, USA. **332,** Photos © Kevin Walsh **Chapter 12. 339,** F. 12.1 © Jim Sugar/Corbis. **342,** F. 12.3 © Historical Pictures Services, Chicago/FPG and Sandra F. Witelson. **343,** F. 12.4 Reprinted with permission from J. Duncan, "A neural basis for general intelligence." *Science*, 289, 457–460. © 2000. American Association for the Advancement of Science. **346,** F. 12.7 Reprinted with permission from B. Butterworth, "Ahead for figures." *Science*, 284, 928–929. © 1999. American Association for the Advancement of Science. **352,** F. 12.10 Reprinted with permission from R. Lewin, "Is your brain really necessary?" *Science*, 210, 1232–1234. © 1980. American Association for the Advancement of Science. **353,** F. 12.11 © Abraham Menashe. **354,** F. 12.12 © Ethan Hill. **355,** F. 12.13left Courtesy of B. L. Miller. Right: B. L. Miller et al., "Emergence of artistic talent in frontotemporal dementia," *Neurology*, 51, 978–982. 1998 by the American Academy of Neurology. **358,** F. 12.14 Courtesy of Roberto Cabeza, Duke University. **Chapter 13. 365,** F. 13.1 © David Young-Wolff/PhotoEdit. **373,** F. 13.8b © 1990 Massachusetts Medical Society. All rights reserved. **374,** F. 13.9 © Weinberger, et al., 1986. **375,** F. 13.10 Reprinted by permission of *Nature*, ©1995. **381,** F. 13.12 © James D. Wilson/Woodfin Camp & Associates. **383,** F. 13.13 © Dan McCoy/Rainbow. **384,** F. 13.14(a) Drevets et al., © 1992 by the Society for Neuroscience. F. 13.14(b) © Baxter et al., 1989. **385,** F. 13.15 Drevets et al., © 1992 by the Society for Neuroscience. F. 13.16 © Baxter et al., 1985. F. 13.17 Reprinted by permission of *Nature*, ©1997. **388,** F. 13.19(a) © Baxter et al., 1987. F. 13.19(b) © Schwartz et al., 1996. **389,** F. 13.20 © Corbis. **390,** F. 13.21 © Malison et al., 1995 **Chapter 14. 399,** F. 14.2 © Norbert Wu. **402,** F. 14.4 Hannibel et al., 2002. © 2002 by the Society for Neuroscience. **409,** F. 14.10 © 1989 by the Society for Neuroscience. F. 14.11 Reprinted by permission of *Nature*, © 2001. **412,** F. 14.12 Courtesy of Wolf Singer, Max-Planck-Institut für Hirnforschung. **415,** F. 14.15 Photos courtesy of Cognitive Evolution Group, University of Louisiana at Lafayette. **421,** F. 14.19 © Tsai et al., 1999. **Appendix. 427,** F. A.1 © Visuals Unlimited. F. A.2 © Photo Researchers. F. A.3 © The Brain Museum. **428,** F. A.4 © Hubel & Wiesel, 1979. **430,** F. A.8left © Charles Gupton/Stock Boston. **431,** F. A.9(a) © Alvis Upitis/The Image Bank. F. A.9(b) © Dan McCoy/Rainbow. **432,** F. A.10right © Huntington Magnetic Resonance Center, Pasadena, California. F. A.11left © Burt Glinn/Magnum. F. A.11right © Photo Researchers. **433,** F. A.12 Reprinted with permission from Wagner, et al., "Building memories: Remembering and forgetting of verbal experiences as predicted by brain activity." *Science*, 281, 1188–1191. © 1998. American Association for the Advancement of Science.

Name Index

Subject Index

TO THE OWNER OF THIS BOOK:

We hope that you have found *Brain and Behavior* useful. So that this book can be improved in a future edition, would you take the time to complete this sheet and return it? Thank you.

School and address: _____

Department: _____

Instructor's name: _____

1. What I like most about this book is: _____

_____

_____

2. What I like least about this book is: _____

_____

_____

3. My general reaction to this book is: _____

_____

4. The name of the course in which I used this book is: _____

_____

5. Were all of the chapters of the book assigned for you to read? _____

   If not, which ones weren't? _____

6. In the space below, or on a separate sheet of paper, please write specific suggestions for improving this book and anything else you'd care to share about your experience in using the book.

_____

_____

_____

_____

_____

Optional:

Your name: _____ Date: _____

May Wadsworth quote you, either in promotion for *Brain and Behavior* or in future publishing ventures?

Yes: _____ No: _____

Sincerely,

Bob Garrett

FOLD HERE

FOLD HERE

Explore a Wide Range of Real-World Examples!

Applications

APPLICATION

Agonists and Antagonists in the Real World

Neurotransmitters are not the only substances that affect transmitters. **Many drugs, as well as other compounds, mimic the effect of a neurotransmitter and are called *agonists*. Any substance that reduces the effect of a neurotransmitter is called an *antagonist*.** Practically all of the drugs that have a psychological effect interact with a neurotransmitter system in the brain, and many of them do so by mimicking or blocking the effect of neurotransmitters (Snyder, 1984).

You have already seen that the effect of acetylcholine is duplicated by nicotine and by muscarine at the two kinds of receptors. Opiate drugs like heroin and morphine also act as agonists, stimulating receptors for opiate-like transmitters in the body. Naloxone acts as an antagonist to opiates,

occupying the receptor sites without activating them; consequently, naloxone can be used to counteract an overdose.

The plant toxin curare blocks acetylcholine receptors at the muscle, causing paralysis (Trautmann, 1983). South American Indians in the Amazon River Basin tip their darts with curare to disable their game (see the photo). A synthetic version of curare, *d*-tubocurarine, was used as a muscle relaxant during surgery before safer and more effective drugs were found (Goldberg & Rosenberg, 1987). Ironically, it has even been used in the treatment of tetanus (lockjaw), which is caused by another neurotoxin; a patient receiving this treatment has to be artificially respirated for weeks until recovery occurs, to prevent suffocation.

Amazonian indians tip their darts with the plant neurotoxin curare